Lecture Notes in Computer Science 7850

Commenced Publication in 1973
Founding and Former Series Editors:
Gerhard Goos, Juris Hartmanis, and Jan van Leeuwen

Dave Clarke   James Noble
Tobias Wrigstad (Eds.)

Aliasing in Object-Oriented Programming

Types, Analysis, and Verification

 Springer

Volume Editors

Dave Clarke
Katholieke Universiteit Leuven, Department of Computer Science
Celestijnenlaan 200A, 3001 Heverlee, Belgium
E-mail: dave.clarke@cs.kuleuven.be

James Noble
Victoria University of Wellington, School of Engineering and Computer Science
Cotton Building, Gate 6, Kelburn Parade, Wellington 6140, New Zealand
E-mail: kjx@ecs.vuw.ac.nz

Tobias Wrigstad
Uppsala University, Department of Information Technology
Lägerhyddsvägen 2, 752 37 Uppsala, Sweden
E-mail: tobias.wrigstad@it.uu.se

ISSN 0302-9743   e-ISSN 1611-3349
ISBN 978-3-642-36945-2   e-ISBN 978-3-642-36946-9
DOI 10.1007/978-3-642-36946-9
Springer Heidelberg Dordrecht London New York

Library of Congress Control Number: 2013932225

CR Subject Classification (1998): D.1.5, D.1.3, D.4.2, D.2.4-5, D.2.7, D.3.1-3, A.1, K.2

LNCS Sublibrary: SL 2 – Programming and Software Engineering

Typesetting: Camera-ready by author, data conversion by Scientific Publishing Services, Chennai, India

Printed on acid-free paper

Springer is part of Springer Science+Business Media (www.springer.com)

Preface

Aliasing is one of the key features of object-oriented programming languages, but it is both a blessing and a curse. On one hand it enables the expression of sophisticated designs involving sharing, but on the other hand it makes reasoning about programs difficult for programmers, for tools such as compilers, and for programming verification.

This book presents a survey of the state of the art on techniques for dealing with aliasing in object-oriented programming. It marks the 20th anniversary of the paper "The Geneva Convention on The Treatment of Object Aliasing" by John Hogg, Doug Lea, Alan Wills, Dennis deChampeaux, and Richard Holt, which stressed the need for a systematic study of aliasing in object-oriented programming. Since that paper was published in 1992, several workshops have been devoted to this topic, including the Intercontinental Workshop on Aliasing in Object Oriented Systems (IWAOOS) in 1999 and five instalments of the International Workshop on Aliasing, Confinement and Ownership in object-oriented programming (IWACO) in 2003, 2007, 2008, 2009 and 2011.

The most recent IWACO was dedicated to 20 years of aliasing in object-oriented languages and at that venue it was decided to produce a state-of-the-art LNCS volume dedicated to research in this field. This is the volume you are reading now.Papers were solicited from contributors to IWACO and other experts in the area. The result is a broad collection of papers covering many aspects of aliasing in object-oriented programming. Each paper has been extensively reviewed to ensure the highest quality. We hope that this collection will be a valuable addition to researchers' bookshelves, and that it will be useful to both active researchers and graduate students alike.

January 2013

Dave Clarke
James Noble
Tobias Wrigstad

Table of Contents

Verification

Programming Languages

Visions

Beyond the Geneva Convention
on the Treatment of Object Aliasing

Dave Clarke[1], James Noble[2], and Tobias Wrigstad[3]

[1] iMinds-DistriNet, Dept. Computer Sciences, KU Leuven, Belgium
[2] Victoria University of Wellington, New Zealand
[3] Department of Information Technology, Uppsala University, Sweden

> *Aliasing must be detected when it occurs,*
> *advertised when it is possible,*
> *prevented where it is not wanted,*
> *and controlled where it is needed.*

Hogg, Lea, Wills, deChampeaux, and Holt [13].

1 Introduction

Aliasing occurs when two or more references to an object exist within the object graph of a running program. Although aliasing is essential in object-oriented programming as it allows programmers to implement designs involving sharing, it is problematic because its presence makes it difficult to reason about the object at the end of an alias—via an alias, an object's state can change underfoot.

Around 20 years ago, John Hogg, Doug Lea, Alan Wills, Dennis deChampeaux and Richard Holt drafted a clear account of the problems of aliasing in object-oriented programming. The resulting document, *The Geneva Convention on the Treatment of Object Aliasing* [13,14], identified four ways of managing aliasing to make it easier to reason about:

detection — statically or dynamically detect aliasing,
advertisement — provide declarations to modularise aliasing properties,
prevention — develop statically-checkable means for disallowing aliasing, and
control — offer means to isolate the effects of aliasing.

Although the original document focused on verification, the problems of aliasing are equally applicable whenever a programmer or compiler needs to reason about a program, to understand it, to optimise it, to refactor it, or to check that it has no data races or deadlocks.

Since the writing of the Geneva Convention, a vast amount of research on aliasing in object-oriented programming has been done. Some early techniques such as Islands [12] and Balloons [2] offered new insights into the problem, by suggesting that objects be grouped into their internal, external and boundary components, but it was not until the invention of Flexible Alias Protection [17] and Ownership Types [9] that work in the field really did blossom. The verification community relied heavily on ideas of ownership [15] and separation [18] in

D. Clarke et al. (Eds.): Aliasing in Object-Oriented Programming, LNCS 7850, pp. 1–6, 2013.

order to develop more feasible verification techniques. These alias control mechanisms have found application concurrency control [5], program visualisation and understanding [1], among other areas. All the while, techniques for alias analysis are being developed and improved upon in the compiler-writer community [22], and a cross-fertilisation of ideas is starting to occur.

This book is dedicated to the state-of-the-art on aliasing in object-oriented programming, It consists of fifteen chapters, written by the leading researchers in their respective fields, and six short vision chapters presenting the views of researchers on the future of aliasing in object-oriented programming.

2 The Chapters

The first chapter, *The Geneva Convention On The Treatment of Object Aliasing* by John Hogg and Doug Lea and Alan Wills and Dennis deChampeaux and Richard Holt [14], is a reprint of the original Geneva Convention paper. It discusses problems with the treatment of aliasing in object-oriented languages, and argues that means for handling aliasing available in programming languages at the time (circa 1990) fail to address the complexities introduced by objects. As mentioned above, the paper introduces four classes of solutions to the aliasing problem: detection, advertisement, prevention and control. The paper analyses these four approaches and discusses existing approaches from the literature. The paper concludes with the pithy quote given at the start of this introduction.

Ownership Types were one of the significant contributions that changed the way aliasing was considered in object-oriented languages. Ownership Types provide a way of encapsulating the so-called representation objects of an aggregate object so that aliases to such objects cannot exist outside of the aggregate that owns them. This is all done in a statically checkable fashion. A large number of papers have extended, adapted or applied Ownership Types, or have taken similar ideas as the basis of an alias control mechanism. In the second chapter, *Ownership Types: A Survey* [8], Dave Clarke, Johan Östlund, Ilya Sergey and Tobias Wrigstad survey this body of work.

In their chapter, *Notions of Aliasing and Ownership* [16], Alan Mycroft and Janina Voigt present an alternative survey of aliasing and ownership, which draws from a wide range of work, including linear logic and operating systems, before focusing on some of the core approaches to alias control. After their review and critique of these approaches, the chapter concludes that a more holistic approach to aliasing is required. The chapter hints of a notion of *aliasing contract*, which mediates access to fields and variables—access is allowed only when the contract is satisfied.

Ownership Types are not phrased in terms of traditional type-theoretic machinery. To obtain a better understanding of their nature, Nicholas Cameron, Sophia Drossopoulou, and James Noble explore the underlying types-depend-on-owners property in terms of dependent type theory in *Understanding Ownership Types with Dependent Types* [7] Their encoding also reveals the phantom type nature of Ownership Types. After addressing a vanilla Ownership Types system, several extensions are also considered, though the soundness of the encoding is a conjecture left for future work.

Object Graphs with Ownership Domains: an Empirical Study by Radu Vanciu and Marwan Abi-Antoun [23] presents empirical evaluation of the Ownership Domains type system on a number of larger programs. These programs were annotated and type checked, and then static analysis was used to extract hierarchical Ownership Object Graphs (OOGs). OOGs provide an abstract view of the ownership structure within a program, offerings a better view on a system than a flat object graph. The results include numerous metrics which help understand the ownership relationships present in code.

Robert L. Bocchino Jr. describes alias control techniques for achieving deterministic parallelism in his chapter *Alias Control for Deterministic Parallelism* [4], which concerns programs that produce the same output on every execution for a given input, irrespective of how its threads are scheduled. Such programs are easier to write, understand, debug and maintain. Aliasing is a core hurdle to achieving deterministic parallelism, as it creates the possibility of data races. This chapter surveys program annotation techniques for controlling aliasing in order to support deterministic parallelism.

Alias analysis techniques are used within compilers and other program understanding tools to determine the aliasing structure between objects. Such information is essential for performing various compiler optimisations and for performing program transformations safely. The chapter *Alias Analysis for Object-Oriented Programs* by Manu Sridharan, Satish Chandra, Julian Dolby, Stephen J. Fink, and Eran Yahav [22] presents a survey of alias analysis for object-oriented programs, including points-to analysis, flow sensitive techniques, and whole-program alias analysis and its limitations. The discussion is framed in the context of the authors' experience in developing industrial-strength analyses for Java.

One of the core ways of reducing that the impact of aliasing is by reducing the effect of mutable references. This falls under the alias control categorisation of the Geneva Convention. *Immutability* by Alex Potanin, Johan Östlund, Yoav Zibin, Michael D. Ernst [20] surveys immutability in the context of object-oriented programming languages. The point of departure is `final` fields in Java and `const` references in C++. These are argued to be inadequate, as they offer only shallow notions of immutability. The chapter then surveys a number of recent proposals, including Javari, IGJ, Joe$_3$, and OIGJ, that overcome the weaknesses of `final` and `const`.

Fractional Permissions are a novel idea that allows precise resource tracking in type systems and specification logics. The key idea is that a whole permission allows unique write access to an object, but that this can be split (and later rejoined) into multiple read permissions. *Fractional Permissions* by John Boyland [6] describes the motivation for Fractional Permission and gives a survey of various models of Fractional Permissions, including those supporting nesting.

Object Ownership in Program Verification by Werner Dietl and Peter Müller [10] surveys the key role played by ownership in program verification in two different realisations: Universe Types and Dynamic Ownership, in the context of verification in the Spec# language. Universe Types form a statically checkable Ownership Types system that includes a notion of read-only to limit computational effects. They were tailored specifically for verifying object-oriented languages. Dynamic Ownership is an alternative approach based on the encoding of notions of ownership in specifications, typically involve so-called model fields. The chapter is structured as a collection of problems one encounters when doing verification, along with ownership-based solutions to these problems.

Refactoring of classes can safely be done whenever the data representation is properly encapsulated, without affecting the correctness of client programs and extensions of a class. Features such as heap-based object structures and re-entrant callbacks make encapsulation difficult to achieve. *State Based Encapsulation for Modular Reasoning about Behavior-Preserving Refactorings* by Anindya Banerjee and David A. Naumann [3] describes a discipline using assertions and auxiliary fields to manage the desired invariants and enable transferable ownership, that is, the passing of encapsulated objects between different objects. The main result of the chapter is a rule for proving the equivalence of class implementations.

Separation logic offers a powerful technology for reasoning about low-level programs. Matthew Parkinson and Gavin Bierman's chapter *Separation Logic for Object-Oriented Programming* [19] describes how this logic can be used to reason about core object-oriented features such as encapsulation, subclassing, inheritance and dynamic dispatch. A modular proof system for these features is presented. A core feature of this proof system is abstract predicate families which represent dynamic dispatch in the logic.

VeriFast is a verify for Java based on separation logic. A lot of effort has gone into making the verifier useable and scalable for non-trivial programs. The verifier itself is based on symbolic execution, which allows the tool to generate concrete counterexamples whenever verification fails. *VeriFast for Java: A Tutorial* by Jan Smans, Bart Jacobs, and Frank Piessens [21] is a tutorial introduction to the core elements of VeriFast and its approach to verifying programs. The chapter concludes by discussing of future extensions, including a more precise permissions system, more automation, and the treatment of a larger subset of Java.

The Object Teams programming model aims to improve the development of modular programs based on the notion of teams which serve as containers for nested classes. Nested classes form the basis for notions of family polymorphism and confinement to ensure that instances of classes are not accessible beyond a given boundary. Stephan Hermann's chapter *Confined Roles and Decapsulation in Object Teams — Contradiction or Synergy?* [11] presents a summary of the Object Teams programming model and describes practical experience with the language. The Object Teams approach generally is based on solving pragmatic problems, so, for instance, trade-offs are made between static type safety and practicality, by using run-time checks where required.

Objects reside in different locations in distributed object systems. This means that different mechanisms are needed to communicate with the objects, depending upon whether they are local or remote to where the code is running. Distinguishing such possibilities in a type system enables, among other things, more direct code to be generated and improved reasoning about programs. *Location Types for Safe Programming with Near and Far References* by Yannick Welsch, Jan Schäfer, and Arnd Poetzsch-Heffter [24] presents such a type system for a core Java-like language along with a type inference algorithm, which is proven to be both sound and complete with respect to the original type system. An implementation of their approach for the ABS language is also described.

3   Visions of the Future

In spite of all the progress in the last 20 years, verification remains a challenge, program understanding is still difficult, particularly as programs become larger, and, as multi-core computers become more prevalent and as more parallelism needs to be safely exposed in programs, finding better techniques for treating aliasing remains an important topic for future research. To provide a glimpse into the future, a number of researchers offer short vision statements: *The Future of Aliasing in Parallel Programming* by Robert L. Bocchino Jr., *Aliasing Visions: Ownership and Location* by Alan Mycroft, *Alias Analysis: Beyond the Code* by Manu Sridharan, *How, Then, Should We Program?* by James Noble, *A Retrospective on Aliasing Type Systems: 2012-2022* by Jonathan Aldrich, and *Structured Aliasing* by Tobias Wrigstad.

References

1. Abi-Antoun, M., Aldrich, J.: Static extraction and conformance analysis of hierarchical runtime architectural structure using annotations. In: Arora, S., Leavens, G.T. (eds.) OOPSLA, pp. 321–340. ACM (2009)
2. Almeida, P.S.: Balloon Types: Controlling Sharing of State in Data Types. In: Akşit, M., Matsuoka, S. (eds.) ECOOP 1997. LNCS, vol. 1241, pp. 32–59. Springer, Heidelberg (1997)
3. Banerjee, A., Naumann, D.A.: State Based Encapsulation for Modular Reasoning about Behavior-Preserving Refactorings. In: Clarke, D., Noble, J., Wrigstad, T. (eds.) Aliasing in Object-Oriented Programming. LNCS, vol. 7850, pp. 319–365. Springer, Heidelberg (2013)
4. Bocchino Jr., R.L.: Alias Control for Deterministic Parallelism. In: Clarke, D., Noble, J., Wrigstad, T. (eds.) Aliasing in Object-Oriented Programming. LNCS, vol. 7850, pp. 156–195. Springer, Heidelberg (2013)
5. Boyapati, C., Lee, R., Rinard, M.C.: Ownership types for safe programming: preventing data races and deadlocks. In: OOPSLA, pp. 211–230 (2002)
6. Boyland, J.: Fractional Permissions. In: Clarke, D., Noble, J., Wrigstad, T. (eds.) Aliasing in Object-Oriented Programming. LNCS, vol. 7850, pp. 270–288. Springer, Heidelberg (2013)
7. Cameron, N., Drossopoulou, S., Noble, J.: Understanding Ownership Types with Dependent Types. In: Clarke, D., Noble, J., Wrigstad, T. (eds.) Aliasing in Object-Oriented Programming. LNCS, vol. 7850, pp. 84–108. Springer, Heidelberg (2013)

8. Clarke, D., Östlund, J., Sergey, I., Wrigstad, T.: Ownership Types: A Survey. In: Clarke, D., Noble, J., Wrigstad, T. (eds.) Aliasing in Object-Oriented Programming. LNCS, vol. 7850, pp. 15–58. Springer, Heidelberg (2013)
9. Clarke, D.G., Potter, J., Noble, J.: Ownership types for flexible alias protection. In: OOPSLA, pp. 48–64 (1998)
10. Dietl, W., Müller, P.: Object Ownership in Program Verification. In: Clarke, D., Noble, J., Wrigstad, T. (eds.) Aliasing in Object-Oriented Programming. LNCS, vol. 7850, pp. 289–318. Springer, Heidelberg (2013)
11. Herrmann, S.: Confined Roles and Decapsulation in Object Teams — Contradiction or Synergy? In: Clarke, D., Noble, J., Wrigstad, T. (eds.) Aliasing in Object-Oriented Programming. LNCS, vol. 7850, pp. 443–470. Springer, Heidelberg (2013)
12. Hogg, J.: Islands: Aliasing protection in object-oriented languages. In: Paepcke, A. (ed.) OOPSLA, pp. 271–285. ACM (1991)
13. Hogg, J., Lea, D., Wills, A., de Champeaux, D., Holt, R.C.: The Geneva convention on the treatment of object aliasing. OOPS Messenger 3(2), 11–16 (1992)
14. Hogg, J., Lea, D., Wills, A., de Champeaux, D., Holt, R.: The Geneva Convention on the Treatment of Object Aliasing. In: Clarke, D., Noble, J., Wrigstad, T. (eds.) Aliasing in Object-Oriented Programming. LNCS, vol. 7850, pp. 7–14. Springer, Heidelberg (2013)
15. Müller, P.: Modular Specification and Verification of Object-Oriented Programs. LNCS, vol. 2262. Springer, Heidelberg (2002)
16. Mycroft, A., Voigt, J.: Notions of Aliasing and Ownership. In: Clarke, D., Noble, J., Wrigstad, T. (eds.) Aliasing in Object-Oriented Programming. LNCS, vol. 7850, pp. 59–83. Springer, Heidelberg (2013)
17. Noble, J., Vitek, J., Potter, J.: Flexible Alias Protection. In: Jul, E. (ed.) ECOOP 1998. LNCS, vol. 1445, pp. 158–185. Springer, Heidelberg (1998)
18. O'Hearn, P.W.: Resources, concurrency, and local reasoning. Theor. Comput. Sci. 375(1-3), 271–307 (2007)
19. Parkinson, M., Bierman, G.: Separation Logic for Object-Oriented Programming. In: Clarke, D., Noble, J., Wrigstad, T. (eds.) Aliasing in Object-Oriented Programming. LNCS, vol. 7850, pp. 366–406. Springer, Heidelberg (2013)
20. Potanin, A., Östlund, J., Zibin, Y., Ernst, M.D.: Immutability. In: Clarke, D., Noble, J., Wrigstad, T. (eds.) Aliasing in Object-Oriented Programming. LNCS, vol. 7850, pp. 233–269. Springer, Heidelberg (2013)
21. Smans, J., Jacobs, B., Piessens, F.: VeriFast for Java: A Tutorial. In: Clarke, D., Noble, J., Wrigstad, T. (eds.) Aliasing in Object-Oriented Programming. LNCS, vol. 7850, pp. 407–442. Springer, Heidelberg (2013)
22. Sridharan, M., Chandra, S., Dolby, J., Fink, S.J., Yahav, E.: Alias Analysis for Object-Oriented Programs. In: Clarke, D., Noble, J., Wrigstad, T. (eds.) Aliasing in Object-Oriented Programming. LNCS, vol. 7850, pp. 196–232. Springer, Heidelberg (2013)
23. Vanciu, R., Abi-Antoun, M.: Object Graphs with Ownership Domains: An Empirical Study. In: Clarke, D., Noble, J., Wrigstad, T. (eds.) Aliasing in Object-Oriented Programming. LNCS, vol. 7850, pp. 109–155. Springer, Heidelberg (2013)
24. Welsch, Y., Schäfer, J., Poetzsch-Heffter, A.: Location Types for Safe Programming with Near and Far References. In: Clarke, D., Noble, J., Wrigstad, T. (eds.) Aliasing in Object-Oriented Programming. LNCS, vol. 7850, pp. 471–500. Springer, Heidelberg (2013)

The Geneva Convention
on the Treatment of Object Aliasing[*]

John Hogg[1], Doug Lea[2], Alan Wills[3], Dennis de Champeaux[4],
and Richard Holt[5]

[1] Bell-Northern Research
[2] SUNY Oswego
[3] University of Manchester
[4] Hewlett-Packard
[5] University of Toronto

1 Introduction

Aliasing has been a problem in both formal verification and practical programming for a number of years. To the formalist, it can be annoyingly difficult to prove the simple Hoare formula $\{x = true\}$ y := **false** $\{x = true\}$. If x and y refer to the same boolean variable, i.e., x and y are *aliased*, then the formula will not be valid, and proving that aliasing cannot occur is not always straightforward. To the practicing programmer, aliases can result in mysterious bugs as variables change their values seemingly on their own. A classic example is the matrix multiply routine mult(left, right, result) which puts the product of its first two parameters into the third. This works perfectly well until the day some unsuspecting programmer writes the very reasonable statement mult(a, b, a). If the implementor of the routine did not consider the possibility that an argument may be aliased with the result, disaster is inevitable.

Over the years, solutions or workarounds have been found for aliasing problems in traditional languages, and the matter is seemingly under control. Unfortunately, as described below these solutions tend to be too conservative to be useful in object-oriented programs.

The object paradigm has been sold partly on the basis of the strong encapsulation that it provides. This is a misleading claim. A single object may be encapsulated, but single objects are not interesting. An object must be part of a system to be useful, and a system of objects is not necessarily encapsulated.

However, the picture is not entirely bleak. Some partial solutions to the object-oriented aliasing problem have been put forward. More research is needed to fill in the rest of the puzzle, but the future looks bright if researchers treat the problem from a truly object-oriented perspective.

This Convention defines and explains aliasing in the object-oriented context. Various approaches are described, and proposals are made as to areas for future research.

---

[*] This is a reprint of the authors' original OOPS Messenger publication [6], with permission of the authors.

D. Clarke et al. (Eds.): Aliasing in Object-Oriented Programming, LNCS 7850, pp. 7–14, 2013.
© Springer-Verlag Berlin Heidelberg 2013

2   Definitions

We will start by defining a few terms informally. The model of object-oriented systems used is a very simple one with a Smalltalk flavour, and terms that are not further defined can be assumed to have their Smalltalk meanings. Every object is either *primitive* (such as an integer or boolean) or *constructed*. A constructed object has a set of *instance variables* which hold references to other objects. (Every variable is thus implicitly a pointer variable.) Every object also has a set of *methods* that make use of instance variables, *local variables* and *parameters*. A method is invoked by sending a *message* to an object, and may in turn send other messages and set variables.

The set of (object address) values associated with variables during the execution of a method is a *context*. It is only meaningful to speak of aliasing occurring within some context; if two instance variables refer to a single object, but one of them belongs to an object that cannot be reached from anywhere in the system, then the aliasing is irrelevant.

In accord with Smalltalk, and with Snyder's Abstract Object Model [11], we assume that *all* method argument and result passing is performed in a manner classically described as "by-reference", but perhaps better labelled as "by-identity".

Objects may be accessed "directly" through a bound variable or pseudovariable, or "indirectly" through the instance variables of other objects. More generally an access *path* is a sequence of variable names. The evaluation of the first variable within the current context yields a new context that is an object with a set of instance variable, and the evaluation of each successive variable in the path yields a further object and context. In particular, access paths may include traversals through the objects held in "collections".

Within any method, objects may be accessed through paths rooted at any of:

1. self.
2. An anonymous locally constructed object.
3. A method argument.
4. A result returned by another method.
5. A (global) variable accessible from the method scope.
6. A local method variable bound to any of the above.

An object is *aliased* with respect to some context if two or more such paths to it exist.

From a conceptual, rather than operational stance, aliasing occurs when one object is accessed through more than one if its possible "roles" in a given program (where the different roles are indicated by multiple names or access paths), and aliasing is a problem whenever these roles conflict. Such conflicts can be as simple as trying to simultaneously serve as a source and destination in a matrix multiplication, or as intricate as an account crediting a payment from itself through various side channels in a complex financial system.

Determination that an object referred to in two different roles is actually the same can be just as surprising conceptually as it is difficult analytically; discovering and dealing with alias conditions in a program can be a semantically meaningful challenge, not merely a technical exercise in determining correctness and safety properties. To illustrate with an ancient example, for many centuries astronomers used the distinct terms "evening star" and "morning star" without realizing that both referred to one object, the planet Venus. While this is disanalogous to programming situations in that detection of aliasing is a matter of analysis rather than scientific discovery, in large enough programs the two are difficult to distinguish.

While some aliasing problems may thus result from insufficient problem analysis, leading to situations in which roles accidentally conflict, perhaps they more typically arise out of class and method design and implementation decisions that either ignore the possibility of aliasing or intentionally disallow it without making this fact visible to clients.

In any case, the fact that objects are referred to by variables describing their roles, but are actually manipulated in terms of their identities means aliasing is essentially always present, and aliasing problems are always possible within the object-based ([12]) paradigm, whether or not constructs like inheritance, concurrency and persistence are supported. However, such features do accentuate and complicate problems. Even simple subclass polymorphism can make aliasing opportunities even more difficult to notice and appreciate, especially in statically typed languages. For example, in a C++ function f(A& a, B& b), a and b may indeed be aliased if B is a subclass of A or vice versa.

3   Aliasing and Objects

The aspect of an object-based system that *does* set it apart from traditional procedural languages is the presence of persistent local state. An object encapsulates a set of variables which are not externally visible, yet which retain their values between method invocations. In traditional languages, all aliasing is *dynamic* in the sense that it only exists for the duration of a particular scope entry. (Global variables exist for the duration of a global scope.) Upon scope exit, any aliases that were created within that scope disappear. By contrast, when a method scope is left, only the dynamic aliases involving its parameters and temporary variables go away. Instance variables retain their values, and this *static* aliasing will still be present when the object scope is reentered.

We worry about aliasing because the execution of a method may change the behaviour of a seemingly uninvolved object, and this may happen even without the affected object being accessed. This is because the real state of an object is not fully specified by just its variables, but also upon the states of the objects to which these variables refer. The value of a predicate (in denotational terms) or the result of a method (in operational terms) may depend upon the states of any object that can be reached from its context, and thus the state of an object is the state of the transitive closure of objects that can be reached from it. Therefore, two objects are *effectively aliased* if the transitive closures of the objects reachable from them have a non-empty intersection.

For example, consider a bank object containing a number of Portfolios, among them port1 and port2. Each Portfolio has (among other attributes) a chequingAccount of class Account. An Account instance understands the methods debit: and credit: which decrease and increase its balance respectively. These methods are also understood by a Portfolio, which will apply them in turn to its chequingAccount. A Portfolio instance also understands a method transferTo:amount: which will debit itself and credit its first parameter by the amount of the second parameter. Now, will port1 transferTo: port2 amount: $100.00 really decrease the amount of money in port1?

There are two ways in which this can fail to happen. First, port1 and port2 may be the same portfolio, i.e., port1 and port2 are aliases. This can at least be recognized from within the bank object: we can require that port1 =!= port2, where =!= is an object identity comparator.

Unfortunately, port1 will also have an unaltered final balance if port1 and port2 are different, but they share a common chequingAccount. That is, if the chequing account is aliased with respect to the bank context, then the two portfolios are effectively aliased. This is more difficult to deal with because we cannot even express the idea in a programming language that claims to provide encapsulation. When the transferTo:amount: method of port1 is entered, there is no way to refer to the Account object held by the Portfolio first parameter.

4   The Treatment of Aliasing

While the object aliasing problem has been known for some time [10], few discussions have reached print. We broadly categorize approaches that we are aware of in terms of:

Detection. Static or dynamic (run-time) diagnosis of potential or actual aliasing.
Advertisement. Annotations that help modularize detection by declaring aliasing properties of methods.
Prevention. Constructs that disallow aliasing in a statically checkable fashion.
Control. Methods that isolate the effects of aliasing.

4.1   Alias Detection

Alias detection is a *post hoc* activity. Rather than determining beforehand whether variables could reasonably be expected to alias the same object, it determines those alias patterns potentially or actually present in a given program through static (compile-time) or dynamic (run-time) techniques.

Especially in the absence of *a priori* information, it is useful for compilers, static analysis tools, and programmers to detect aliasing conflicts present in programs. Compilers can then generate more efficient code, static analyzers can assist formalists in discovering cases where aliasing may invalidate predicates, and programmers can specially deal with troublesome conflicts.

Because aliasing is usually a non-local phenomenon, static detection requires NP-hard "interprocedural" analysis ([8]), resulting in information about whether any two variables *never*, *sometimes*, or *always* alias the same object, where *sometimes-aliased* refers to situations in which variables are aliased during some invocations but not others, including paths that are not necessarily taken during actual execution.

The *never-aliased* and *always-aliased* cases can be very useful for optimization purposes. For example, two arrays that are never aliased can be independently manipulated in vector processors, while two variables that are always aliased can be represented by a single pointer.

Unfortunately, given the ubiquity of aliasing opportunities in object-oriented programs, full analyses are likely to be too slow to be practical, and to result in the *sometimes-aliased* case more often than not. However, techniques like message-splitting and customization pioneered in **self** ([2]) show some promise for improving matters. For example, automatically splitting off and specially generating code for aliased versus non-aliased versions of a method may both simplify further analysis and allow further optimizations.

Programmers themselves should write code to detect aliasing conflicts at run-time, and take evasive action. However, this is not always possible: Run-time alias detection via object identity comparison (=!=) is not fully supported in most object oriented languages. While "pointer identity" operations can sometimes be used for such purposes, they may not always work in all cases. Notable examples include C++ variables where the same object is referred to in terms of more than one of its multiply-inherited base classes, and, in languages without full support for object persistence, identity preservation for objects recovered from secondary storage. Also, as described above, access protection may impede a programmer's ability to check identities.

4.2   Alias Advertisement

Because global detection is impractical, it is important to develop methods and constructs that can lead to more modular analysis. Both programmers and formalists could benefit from constructs that enhance the locality of analysis by annotating methods in terms of their resulting aliasing properties.

Without evidence to the contrary, people tend to make optimistic assumptions about the aliasing properties of methods. For example, most programmers would find it very surprising if the or(arg) method of a Boolean object were programmed to return self (if self held True) else arg. Even though this is "correct" behaviour, programmers expect or to return a new object that would not be aliased to either of the operands in later expressions.

Yet, popular object oriented languages have no means of indicating whether methods "capture" objects by creating access paths (instance variables, return variables, globals) that persist beyond their invocation.

Constructs or annotations indicating which object bindings are captured by a method and/or which aliases a method is able to cope with could play a role similar to, but independent of, qualifiers like const in C++ and related constructs that integrate useful subsets of full behavioural specifications. As with annotations describing mutability, "negatively" expressed qualifiers are likely to be more useful.

Thus, in the same way qualifying a parameter with const advertises that the argument is not modified, an uncaptured qualifier could indicate that an object is never bound to a variable that could cause it to be *further* modified via side channels after the method returns.

For example, a typical constructive implementation of *or* may then declare that both self and arg are both const and uncaptured and that the return variable is also uncaptured.

In addition to indicating (as a postcondition of sorts) that aliases not be propagated, a method may similarly be advertised with the restriction (precondition) that actual arguments *never* be aliased, via a construct like noalias. This is the default restriction in Turing ([7]).

The pattern of const, noalias, uncaptured operands and uncaptured results is an object-oriented analog of "pure" functions (as opposed to procedures). As discussed in [5], languages that specially mark such operations in a special category (as in Turing) thereby enhance informal and formal reasoning about program behaviour.

Actual enforcement of qualifiers like uncaptured and noalias leads to the notion of alias prevention.

4.3 Alias Prevention

Alias prevention techniques introduce constructs that promise that aliasing will not occur in particular contexts in ways that guarantee static checkability by compilers and program analyzers.

Static checkability requires conservative definitions of constructs. For example, a checkable version of uncaptured might prohibit *all* bindings of a variable within a method except in calls to other methods with uncaptured attributes. This would prohibit uses that programmers happen to know do not propagate aliases, but cannot be syntactically determined to be safe.

A statically checkable form of noalias would be even more draconian. For example, the rules used for aliasing prevention in Turing [7] assume that any change to a single entity in a collection is assumed to have affected the entire collection. As a result, the strong aliasing protection of Turing cannot be applied to Object Turing without losing the ability to express common object-oriented idioms.

Conservatism is useful in that it ensures validity: the formalist will not be able to prove formulas that could be invalid due to aliasing, and the programmer will not be able to compile code in which aliasing could produce surprises such as in the example above. However, valid formulas may not be provable (i.e., the proof system is not even complete in the sense of [3]), and perfectly safe code may not compile without errors or warnings.

Thus, fine grained alias prevention constructs have limited utility. Higher level constructs are required in order to overcome these problems.

Islands [5] provide a mechanism for isolating a group of closely-related objects. A set of syntactic mechanisms are used to ensure that no static references can exist across the boundary of an island. An atomic assignment operation that sets a previous reference to null allows objects to be passed in and out across this boundary. Within an island, any system of aliasing control can be used, but a nested island is a completely encapsulated unit. This means that the prevention mechanism scales, and the control strategy can therefore be confined to small groups of objects and need not scale.

A more radical approach is that of [4], in which the traditional assignment operator that copies its right side to its left is replaced by a swapping operator that exchanges the bindings of its two sides. By avoiding reference copying, aliasing is also avoided, and its problems disappear. Naturally, the programmer must learn a different paradigm. It is unclear whether this paradigm can mesh well with mainstream object oriented programming techniques.

4.4 Alias Control

Aliasing prevention is not sufficient in itself because aliasing is not avoidable under the conventional object-oriented paradigm. There will remain cases in which the effects of aliasing cannot be determined without taking into account the runtime state of a system. Under these circumstances, aliasing *control* must be applied. The programmer must determine that the system will never reach a state in which there will be unexpected aliasing, even though this is not precluded by an examination of the code components in isolation. The formalist must show that no predicate is affected by being effectively aliased with the left side of any assignment statement. Control is thus based on some analysis of state reachability.

A proof system for an object-oriented language (SPOOL) is given in [1]. This uses aliasing control exclusively; there is no prevention component to the management strategy. The predicate language is an extension to the programming language in which encapsulation is removed. Within some context, variables in other objects can be referred to using variable paths as defined earlier. In the example above, we could assert that port1:chequingAccount =!= port2:chequingAccount from the context of the bank. This approach is impractical in anything but the smallest application, but it forms the foundation for future work.

In [13] an approach to aliasing control based on *demesnes* is proposed. This concept is related to the reaches of [9]. A demesne is a set of objects which participate in the representation of a given value. The programmer defines for each class a demesne-function, which yields a union of the singleton set containing self, and the demesnes of some or all of the instance variables. 'Backward' pointers and cache variables would be amongst those omitted. Several named demesnes may be provided for one class. The functions need not be implemented, but are used to reason about a program. For example, statements can be made about whether the demesnes of two parameters are allowed to intersect. Statements about framing (what objects may be changed by a method) made in terms of demesnes preserve encapsulation, since the detailed definition of the demesnes is made within their own classes.

5 Conclusion

The aliasing problem is attracting an increasing amount of attention. Component reuse requires adequate description of component behaviour, and this can only be given if components are sufficiently encapsulated for their behaviours to be predictable. To ensure this, aliasing must be detected when it occurs, advertised when it is possible, prevented where it is not wanted, and controlled where it is needed.

References

1. America, P., de Boer, F.: A sound and complete proof system for SPOOL. Technical Report Technical Report 505, Philips Research Laboratories (May 1990)
2. Chambers, C., Ungar, D.: Making pure object-oriented languages practical. In: OOPSLA, pp. 1–15. ACM, New York (1991)
3. Cook, S.A.: Soundness and completeness of an axiom system for program verification. SIAM Journal of Computing 7(1), 70–90 (1978)
4. Harms, D.E., Weide, B.W.: Copying and swapping: influences on the design of reusable software components. IEEE Transactions on Software Engineering 17(5), 424–435 (1991)
5. Hogg, J.: Islands: Aliasing protection in object-oriented languages. In: Conference Proceedings on Object-Oriented Programming Systems, Languages, and Applications, OOPSLA 1991, pp. 271–285. ACM, New York (1991)
6. Hogg, J., Lea, D., Wills, A., de Champeaux, D., Holt, R.C.: The Geneva convention on the treatment of object aliasing. OOPS Messenger 3(2), 11–16 (1992)
7. Holt, R.C., Matthews, P.A., Rosselet, J.A., Cordy, J.R.: The Turing programming language: design and definition. Prentice-Hall, Inc., Upper Saddle River (1987)
8. Landi, W., Ryder, B.G.: Pointer-induced aliasing: a problem taxonomy. In: POPL, pp. 93–103. ACM, New York (1991)
9. Lucassen, J.M., Gifford, D.K.: Polymorphic effect systems. In: POPL, pp. 47–57. ACM, New York (1988)
10. Meyer, B.: Object-Oriented Software Construction, 1st edn. Prentice-Hall, Inc., Upper Saddle River (1988)
11. Snyder, A.: Modeling the C++ Object Model. In: America, P. (ed.) ECOOP 1991. LNCS, vol. 512, pp. 1–20. Springer, Heidelberg (1991)
12. Wegner, P.: Dimensions of object-based language design. In: OOPSLA, pp. 168–182. ACM, New York (1987)
13. Wills, A.: Capsules and Types in Fresco. In: America, P. (ed.) ECOOP 1991. LNCS, vol. 512, pp. 59–76. Springer, Heidelberg (1991)

Ownership Types: A Survey[*]

Dave Clarke[1], Johan Östlund[2], Ilya Sergey[1], and Tobias Wrigstad[2]

[1] iMinds-DistriNet, Department of Computer Science, KU Leuven, Belgium
[2] Department of Information Technology, Uppsala University, Sweden

Abstract. Ownership types were devised nearly 15 years ago to provide a stronger notion of protection to object-oriented programming languages. Rather than simply protecting the fields of an object from external access, ownership types protect also the objects stored in the fields, thereby enabling an object to claim (exclusive) ownership of and access to other objects. Furthermore, this notion is statically enforced by now-standard type-checking techniques.

Originating as the formalisation of the core of Flexible Alias Protection, ownership types have since been extended and adapted in many ways, and the notion of protection provided has been refined into topological and encapsulation dimensions. This article surveys the various flavours of ownership types that have been developed over the years, along with the many applications and other developments. The chapter concludes by suggesting some directions for future work.

> *Aliasing is endemic in object-oriented programming.*
>
> Noble, Vitek, Potter [112].

1 Introduction

Object aliasing is one of the key challenges that must be addressed when constructing large software systems using an object-oriented language. Bugs due to unintentional aliases are notoriously difficult to track down and can lead to unexpected side-effects, invalidated invariants, reasoning based on faulty assumptions, a wealth of security bugs, and more. On the other hand, shared mutable state and a stable notion of object identity are considered to be core ingredients of the object-oriented paradigm, and mutable object structures are frequently used to model real-world situations involving sharing. Dealing with aliasing, by either banning it, clearly advertising it or otherwise managing or controlling its effects, therefore has become a key research issue for object oriented-programming [77,78]. Mainstream object-oriented programming languages such as Java, C# and Scala provide no special means to simplifying working with

---

[*] This research is partly funded by the EU project FP7-231620 HATS: Highly Adaptable and Trustworthy Software using Formal Models (http://www.hats-project.eu), KULeuven BOF Project STRT1/09/031: DesignerTypeLab and the Swedish Research Council within the UPMARC Linnaeus centre of Excellence and the project Structured Aliasing.

D. Clarke et al. (Eds.): Aliasing in Object-Oriented Programming, LNCS 7850, pp. 15–58, 2013.

aliases beyond favouring references instead of pointers, and providing automatic garbage collection (although one Scala plugin does offer support for Uniqueness and Borrowing [71], see Section 6).

In 1998, Noble, Vitek and Potter [112] introduced Flexible Alias Protection as a conceptual model of inter-object relationships. Rather than banning aliasing altogether, the key idea was to limit the visibility of changes to objects via aliases. This was done either by limiting where an alias could propagate and by limiting the changes that could be observed though an alias. The ideas put forward in this work could be statically checked based on programmer-supplied type annotations called aliasing modes.

In order to better understand Flexible Alias Protection, Clarke, Potter and Noble [46] formalised its core mechanisms, resulting in Ownership Types. Although originating as the core of Flexible Alias Protection, the Ownership Types system made a few contributions beyond providing a clean formalisation. Firstly, Flexible Alias Protection did not offer enough machinery to provide a type for `this`; Ownership Types corrected this problem, thereby introducing the notion of owner—the owner of `this` (the current object) is `owner` (the owner of the current object). Secondly, Clarke, Potter and Noble provided a formalisation and proof of a topological property on object graphs enforced by the type system, namely the owners-as-dominators invariant. In their work, a program's heap is divided into hierarchically nested regions, originally called ownership contexts.[1] An ownership context is a set of objects. Every object belongs to a single context, and each object defines a context for its protected representation objects. An object A in the representation context defined by object B is said to be owned by B, and B is called the owner of A. Upon creation, each object was placed firmly in a single ownership context, its owning context, for its life-time. The object also receives a set of permissions to reference objects in other ownership contexts (a subset of those visible at the place of instantiation). Information about the owner of an object appears in its type—hence the name Ownership Types—and this is used to govern which parts of an object are accessible to other objects and when an object can be passed to other objects.

The original Ownership Types system was designed for a small language; for instance, it did not state how to deal with inheritance and subtyping, and it did not provide semantics for the remaining constructs of Flexible Alias Protection. Over the years these issues have been explored and different variations have been proposed. These variants impose different policies that are more flexible and less restrictive than owners-as-dominators; they introduce generalisations or other extensions and apply Ownership Types in different application scenarios. The goal of this article is to survey this, now vast, body of work.

Outline. The paper is organised as follows. Section 2 defines some of the basic concepts used in the Ownership Types literature. Section 3 presents a survey of the different kinds of topological restrictions and notions of encapsulation

---

[1] Originally the word context was used, but for uniformity of presentation, we will use ownership context or simply owner.

based on Ownership Types and related systems. Section 4 considers various extensions to the basic model, including generics, computational effects, dynamic ownership, and ownership transfer. Section 5 discusses the important issue of ownership inference, as ownership types typically impose a significant syntactic overhead. Section 6 gives an overview of applications of Ownership Types. Section 7 briefly discusses some of the foundational work done on Ownership Types and its variants. Section 8 explores some of the empirical studies done on ownership in larger code bases. Finally, Section 9 presents a discussion of future directions for research on Ownership Types and concludes the survey.

2   Groundwork

This section define some concepts required to understand Ownership Types and its variants. To be consistent within this survey, we have tried to present uniform terminology rather than reuse the terms given in the original research papers.

Ownership Types systems work in two ways to restrict object graphs underlying the run-time heap of object-oriented programs. The first is by providing *topological restrictions* on the reference structure of the object graph. The second approach is to enforce *encapsulation*, which occurs by limiting operations that can be performed via certain references in the object graph so that the places where mutation of objects can occur are restricted in scope.

The core concept of any Ownership Types system is *object ownership*, namely that objects are owned by other objects or perhaps other entities (global owners, stack-based owners, ...). An *Ownership Types system* is a type system where types are annotated or otherwise associated with information about object ownership.

An *ownership context* is a region of the heap or a collection of objects. More informally, it is a box into which objects are placed [61]. These boxes are generally organised hierarchically: all objects have boxes to store (and protect) the objects they own, and each object is considered to be *inside* the object whose box it is placed in. The hierarchy induces a *nesting* relationship between objects. If the ownership context corresponds to an object, typically this object is referred to as the *owner*. In the literature ownership contexts are also called ownership domains [4], contexts [46], boxes [33], and regions [25].

The objects residing in the ownership context of some object are called the *representation* of the object. From a semantic point of view, the representation of an object consists of the objects that contribute to the implementation of the abstraction that the object represents. Being able to directly access the representation of an object, and thereby violate the invariants of that object, is called *representation exposure*. Some Ownership Types systems prevent access to representation objects (a topological restriction). Other systems allow in addition objects to be logically contained in an object [4], but impose no topological restrictions. Yet other systems allow access to representation objects, but only via references with limited capabilities (thereby enforcing encapsulation).

Objects in the same ownership context are called *siblings* or *peers*.

In the type system, classes may have parameters which will be supplied with different owners when the class is instantiated, thereby allowing *owner polymorphism*. These parameters are called *owner parameters*. The syntactic mechanism underlying ownership parameterisation is analogous to type parameterisation. The owner of an instance is indicated using one such parameter; this parameter is often implicit in the class header and is generally referred to using keyword **owner** within the class body. Parameterisation can occur at the level of methods, resulting in owner polymorphic methods.

Ownership Types systems generally have an ownership context into which *shared objects* are placed. Generally, this ownership context is accessible to all other objects. In various systems this is known as **shared**, **world** and, originally, **norep**. *Manifest ownership* occurs when the owner of all instances of a class is defined to be a particular, typically globally known, owner. Manifest ownership occurs when a class cannot be parameterised.

One extreme way of controlling aliasing is to remove aliasing all together—this is a topological constraint.

A *unique reference* to an object is the only reference to the object in the system. Various weakenings of this notion exist. For instance, an *externally unique* reference is the only reference to an object that is not (transitively) inside the object's representation. Sometimes multiple references to an object exist, but only one of them can be used. At other times, there may be multiple references to an object, but only one reference can be used to mutate the object. When an object is created, it is typically considered to be *free* (sometimes called *virgin*), meaning that there are no references to it in fields. Similarly, when a field uniquely referring to an object releases that object (perhaps via a nullifying destructive read), then the object can again be considered free. A unique reference or a reference to some owned object may be temporarily passed to another object, generally for the duration of a method call, so that when the method is over all temporary references vanish or become unusable. The references are call *borrowed* or *lent* references and the process is known as *borrowing*.

An alternative way of controlling aliasing is to control the effects of aliasing—this imposes encapsulation.

Immutability means that the state cannot change. An *immutable object* or *value object* is one whose fields cannot change. Some objects have immutable slices, meaning that only some of the fields are immutable. Most work on immutability only considers an object to be immutable if all of its fields reference only immutable objects or primitive values, *i.e.*, immutability is transitive, though variants consider references to (external) mutable objects, with restrictions imposed on how the immutable objects can depend on the mutable objects. Another way of putting this is that immutability is only transitive for owned immutable objects. A *pure method* is a method that does not update any fields of any objects. More refined versions of this notion may be allowed to update object fields, so long as these updates are not observable outside of the method. An *impure method* is a method that is not pure. A *read-only reference* is a reference through which only pure methods can be called. One property of read-only references is that they can observe changes to the object state, resulting in what is called *observational exposure*. A stronger variant of read-only reference is possible, namely one through which only immutable state can be read.

3   Models Restricting Topology and Enforcing Encapsulation

This section discusses Ownership Types systems and the kinds of protection enforced by the systems in terms of topological restrictions and encapsulation discipline. Figure 1 demonstrates some of the core constraints imposed by various Ownership Types disciplines. Owners-as-dominators, which imposes a hierarchical structure on the heap, is the strictest discipline, allowing only a single entry point to the internal objects. This is historically the first topological invariant enforced by an Ownership Types system, and will be discussed first. This has been relaxed in various ways, such as by allowing proxy objects to access internal representation objects, thus weakening the topological restrictions, or by allowing references with less capabilities to access internal objects. After introducing owners-as-dominators, we move on to discussing relaxations of this strong property for stack- and heap-based aliases, and then to systems which take a fundamentally different approach to specifying topological/encapsulation policies, such as owners-as-modifiers, ownership domains and multiple ownership. Finally, we present an overview of the confined types approach, which is syntactically much simpler than other systems, at the cost of a less expressive notion of protection.

3.1   Owners-as-Dominators

Owners-as-dominators is the topological invariant enforced by the original Ownership Types system of Clarke et al. [46]. In this ownership system, an object could be given explicit permission to reference the direct representation of any

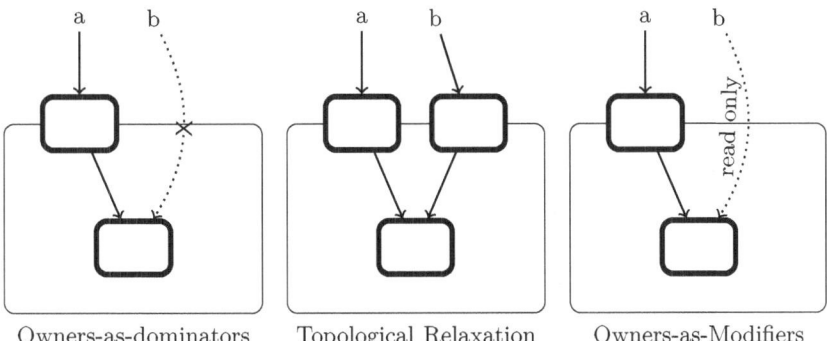

Owners-as-dominators   Topological Relaxation   Owners-as-Modifiers

Fig. 1. Various Ownership Disciplines

enclosing object, in addition to its owner's direct representation, its own representation, and any object at the outermost level of nesting. As a consequence of these constraints, program heaps are tree-structured—a object is inside its owner. The owners-as-dominators invariant provides a strong notion of encapsulation that requires that all external accesses to an object's internals must go via its interface, its owner.

The canonical ownership types example is a list whose links are its representation. In an owners-as-dominators system, the links of the list cannot be aliased outside of the list. This protects any class invariants regarding, for example, the ordering of elements in the list.

```
class List[owner|data] {
  Link[this,data] first;

  Iterator[owner,data] iterator() {
    Iterator i = new Iterator();
    i.current = first; // untypeable
    return i;
  }
}

class Link[owner|data] {
  Link[owner,data] next;
  Object[data] data;
}

class Iterator[owner|data] {
  Link[X,data] current; // not possible -- what is X, this or owner ?
}

List[x,y] myList;
Link[?,y] aLink = myList.first; // not possible -- what is '?' ?
```

The topological restriction of the links is due to the type of first, namely Link[**this**, data]—**this** in the owner (first) position of the type specifies that objects of that type are the representation of the object currently denoted by **this**. The owner **this** is only visible internally to the object, meaning the appropriate type necessary for referencing the List from a variable cannot be formed in some other scope, unless the permission to reference the List's direct representation has been explicitly passed to that scope. The type system prevents such Link objects being passed out of the List object that owns them.

In most Ownership Types systems, types are parameterised by what can be seen as permissions to reference external objects. The first permission parameter doubles as the owner parameter and is always present in a type. Type compatibility within a given scope requires that the corresponding owner parameters of the two types are the same. Passing between scopes, such as when accessing a field of an object or passing an object as a method parameter to another object, requires that the types involved are transformed to test compatibility. This is done by substituting the owner parameters into the type being translated between scopes. As **this** has no meaning to an external object, types with **this** cannot be translated. In classical Ownership Types, preventing types of representation values from being valid externally provides a strong notion of protection.

For concreteness, in systems supporting owners-as-dominators, the rule enforced for an object a to validly reference object b is that either

1. a is the owner of b,

2. a and b are siblings, or

3. b is outside a.[2]

The meaning of outside is the converse of the inside relation. The inside relation is the reflexive, transitive closure of the owned-by relation. That is, a is inside b if $a = b$ or if a is owned by b, transitively. (The reflexive part of the definitions of inside and outside is confusing.)

The strength of the owners-as-dominators property is that it provides a simple, clear and strong guarantee. This can be useful when reasoning about various properties of the code, as we discuss later in the chapter. Unfortunately, the invariant makes programming more difficult, as common idioms involving aliasing cannot be expressed.

3.2   Ownership and Subclassing

Ownership typing interacts with subclassing in a relatively straightforward fashion. To enforce the owners-as-dominators invariant in the presence of subtyping, the nesting relation between owners is lifted into the type system, and the nesting assumptions on the owner parameters of a class need to be satisfied for a type to be well-formed. Otherwise, inherited code might make nesting assumptions on owners that are not satisfied in a derived class. Finally, the owner needs to be preserved. That is, the owner of the superclass needs to be the same as that of the subclass [44], and it can never be eliminated via subtyping, since that would be equivalent to an object losing information about its owner, and owners are used to determine who can access an object.

The example below defines a class Circle and another class ColouredCircle which subclasses the first. Circle has two owner parameters—its mandatory owner and point, which is the owner of a point object that will act as the circle's centre. The subclass ColouredCircle also takes two parameters, **owner** and colour, and instantiates its superclass' point parameter with **owner**—expressing the constraint that in coloured circles, the centre point object must be a sibling of the coloured circle object itself.

---

[2] As pointed out by one of our reviewers, these rules are very similar to Algol's scoping roles for block-structured languages.

```
class Circle[owner|point outside owner] {
  Point[point] centre;
}

class ColouredCircle[owner|colour outside owner]
               extends Circle[owner,owner] {
  Colour[colour] c;
}
```

When calculating a type's supertype, the extends clause in the class declaration establishes a mapping from parameters in the subclass to parameters in the superclass. Based on this, the supertype of ColouredCircle[a,b] is Circle[a,a], which loses information b from the type. In Java-like ownership systems such as Joline [42], Circle has an implicit extends clause **extends Object[owner]**, which is a straightforward adaptation of Java. Consequently, the only possible supertype of Circle[a,a] is Object[a].

In the example above, the following four owners are accessible when forming the supertype in ColouredCircle: **owner** and colour (from the parameter declaration), **this** (denoting the coloured circle's representation) and **world**, which is the outermost owner in which all others are nested. Giving the coloured circle the super type Circle[**world,this**] would not be valid for two reasons. Firstly, the owner parameter must always be the same.[3] Secondly, passing **this** as a parameter is not valid since it is not nested outside **owner**—the condition colour **outside owner** would be invalidated.

Constraints similar to the ones described above are applicable to other Ownership Types systems.

Regarding the List example above, owners-as-dominators excludes many common programmings patterns such as external iterators, since that would require an external object (which is not the list itself) that has a reference to a list's links. To support more programming patterns—and for other reasons—, several systems introduce relaxations of owners-as-dominators: such as temporary, stack-based relaxations (Section 3.3), owners-as-modifiers (Section 3.4) and owners-as-ombudsmen (Section 3.6). Beyond these, Ownership Domains (Section 3.5) avoid imposing a single policy, but instead allow programmers to specify policies for certain data structures or for a whole program. Multiple ownership systems (Section 3.6) do not impose a tree structure on the heap, but it uses an effects system to allow reasoning about the origin or target of a strong update.

3.3   Stack-Based Relaxations of Owners-as-Dominators

Most ownership systems support some kind of relaxation of the topological property for stack-based variables. In Joe$_1$ [44], myList's representation can be typed outside of the list using the myList variable as the external name corresponding to the internal name **this**, provided the variable is not assignable, following

---

[3] The only case where this is not true is when *manifest ownership* [39,119] is used, which occurs when all instances of a class will have the same owner. In this case, the class has no parameters, and the superclass's owner will be some fixed owner.

the so-called 'dot notation' [35]—these are a form of path-dependent type. This mechanism allows both the creation of representation objects external to the intended owning object, as well as returning temporary references to internal objects. Although this mechanism temporarily relaxes the topological restriction, it could be used safely to implement iterators that could access a list's links, without allowing the iterator to escape the dynamic scope in which it is defined. In any case, one can view this as a mechanism vs. policy issue. Such owners provide a mechanism for temporarily violating the protection, but it can only be used if the interface of the class exposes methods/fields with **this** in their type.

Joline [42] and Buckley's thesis [29] take a different approach, and instead support a notion of borrowing implemented through owner-polymorphic methods: a method may be granted permissions to reference any object accessible to its caller for the duration of its execution. (Owner-polymorphic methods were also suggested in Clarke's thesis [39].) This structured principle allows an object to give out temporary permission to reference its representation when calling a method on another object, with the guarantee that when this method returns, all such references will have been invalidated. This does not, however, allow external initialisation of representation, nor returning references to representation, which is possible in Joe_1. Hence, it is not flexible enough to express iterators in any direct fashion.

Joline also introduced the notion of *generational ownership*, which enabled new owners to be introduced for the life-time of a stack frame (called scoped owners). Objects can be created to be owned by these owners, thereby allowing an entire heap whose life-time is tied to a particular stack frame, reminiscent of regions in the region calculus [134]. Objects in such a heap can refer, in principle, to any object in the main heap or any object in the heap associated with a pre-existing stack frame, so long as the appropriate permissions have been passed in. This is depicted in Figure 2.

Boyapati's SafeJava [20,22] relaxes owners-as-dominators for instances of Java inner classes. In Java, an inner class is always instantiated relative to some enclosing instance to which it has privileged access, that is, access to its private members. To preserve owners-as-dominators, instances of inner classes should belong to the enclosing instance's representation, however SafeJava allows instead instances of inner classes to be owned by the owner of the enclosing instances. This allows patterns such as iterators to be expressed. From a programming standpoint, this relaxation is always intentional as the inner class must be provided explicitly and it is internal to the class whose representation is to be exposed. Systems for multiple ownership (see Section 3.6) formalise this style of ownership, but address it in a more structured fashion with a clearer semantics.

3.4   Owners-as-Modifiers

The owners-as-modifiers property, first introduced in the Universes type system [105,54], relaxes owners-as-dominators for *read-only references*. In the context of Universes, a read-only reference is a reference which can only be used to read fields and to call *pure methods*. Pure methods may not modify any

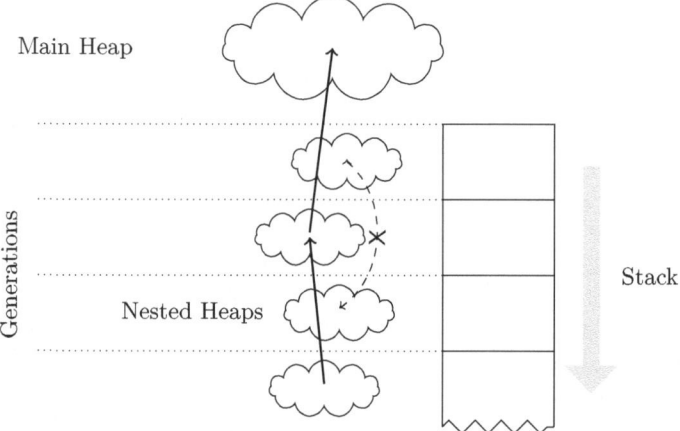

Fig. 2. Generational Ownership. References can refer to earlier generations, but not newer ones.

existing object, including their receiver. The underlying principle is that aliasing is unrestricted, but modifications of an object can only be initiated by its owner. Although the owners-as-modifiers discipline was originally inspired by Flexible Alias Protection, the main driving force behind the design of Universes has been requirements coming from the verification of object-oriented programs. Indeed, Universes have been used extensively to support the verification of object-oriented programs [107,106], and they have been integrated into JML, the Java Modelling Language [56]. Universes have been carefully formalised and proven sound using Isabelle/HOL [85] based on a Featherweight Java-like system extended with field updates.

In systems supporting owners-as-modifiers, the rule enforced for an object a to validly reference object b through a reference r, is that either

1. a is the owner of b,

2. a and b are siblings,

3. b is outside a—permitted in Generic Universe Types [54], but not Universes—, or

4. r is a read-only reference and only pure methods can be called on it.

The following code revisits the List example from owners-as-dominators. Here, the keyword **rep** has the same meaning as **this** above when interpreted as an owner, and **peer** is the same as **owner**. The keyword **any** is new and denotes a read-only reference to an object with unknown owner. The lack of permission parameters requires that the Links of a List store read-only references to their data elements—though this can be fixed using generics. The line marked (∗∗∗) shows that leaking references to representation objects is possible, but only via read-only references.

```
class List {
  rep Link first;

  peer Iterator iterator() {
    peer Iterator i = new Iterator();
    i.current = first;
    return i;
  }
}

class Link {
  peer Link next;
  any Object data;
}

class Iterator {
  any Link current;
}

rep List myList;
any Link aLink = myList.first; // ok, aLink is read-only (***)
```

The owners-as-modifiers discipline increases the flexibility of the reference structures that can be expressed and relieves the programmer of the burden of propagating permissions through the code, at the cost of losing modification rights. Mode **any** expresses that the programmer does not care about ownership information. While this loses topological information associated with owner names, this is a design choice, as **any** references are used not to restrict the topology of a program, but to enforce encapsulation—modifications cannot occur through an **any** reference. Generic Universe Types [54] also include a mode **lost** which refers to indicate that information about ownership has been lost in the type system ('don't know'). References with this mode cannot be updated; the presence of **lost** is like an existential type, with a restriction on the operations permitted on such references.

Later work on Universes adds generic types to the underlying language and further separates the mechanisms to specify encapsulation and to restrict the topology of the object graph [54,60]. This separation of concerns allows for a cleaner formalisation and the better reuse of the two mechanisms. A detailed analysis of this system has been performed, resulting in the following characterisation: no modification to an object can occur unless the object's owner appears as the target of a method call on the stack. Similar characterisation theorems have not been presented for other Ownership Types systems.

3.5 Ownership Domains

In an effort to decouple the underlying topological invariant from the language definition, Aldrich and Chambers proposed the notion of Ownership Domains [4] with the purpose of separating the encapsulation policy from the mechanism expressing policies, thereby allowing different aliasing policies for different circumstances.

Ownership Domains is a flexible system in which programmers specify one or more *ownership domains* (which act as the owners) for each object and then explicitly link these together to control the permitted reference structure of a (part of a) program. Objects in a public domain are accessible to everyone which can access the object enclosing the domain—they are considered part of the object's interface. In contrast, objects in a private domain are encapsulated inside the enclosing object. Public domains express containment, private domains express topological restriction. In addition, the links between two domains specifies that objects in one domain can access objects in the other domain. In Ownership Domains, all domains are explicitly named, as this arguably conveys design intent better than an implicit context can. The resulting system is therefore very flexible, and can express both different kinds of invariants than other ownership systems. In particular, Ownership Domains can express more than one private domain and how different parts of an object interact in terms of aliasing.

The following code example defines a linked list in Ownership Domains with support for an iterator inspired by an example in the original Ownership Domains paper [4][4] A list defines a private domain `cells` for the `Cells` and a public domain `iterators`. Data elements in the `List` are **shared**, the equivalent of **world** above (this is a simplification in this example), and therefore accessible by all. The `Cells`, however, are completely encapsulated in the `List` object, except for references from objects in the public `iterator` domain. This domain will only contain `Iterator` objects, which are only accessible to objects that can refer to the list itself.

```
class List {
  private domain cells;
  public domain iterator;
  link cells -> shared;
  link iterator -> shared;
  link iterator -> cells;

  links Cell first;

  iterator IteratorI iterator() {
    iterator Iterator<cells> i = new Iterator<cells>();
    i.current = first;
    return (iterator IteratorI) i;
  }
}

class Cell {
  shared Object element;
  owner Cell next;
}
```

---

[4] Class Link is renamed Cell to avoid confusion with Ownership Domain's keyword **link**.

```
interface IteratorI { ... }

class Iterator<what> extends IteratorI {
  what Cell current;
}
```

The inherent flexibility of the system shifts the problem of fitting a program to a given aliasing policy to correctly expressing, or proving, that a program conforms to a certain policy. For example, giving objects in a public domain access to objects in a private domain exposes them via proxy objects in a way similar to the inner classes in SafeJava, discussed above, though independently of the class hierarchy. The constraints assumed/imposed by link declaration in Ownership Domains need to be satisfied when building types; furthermore, they are propagated when subclassing. A consequence of this they will be preserved in the presence of subtyping.

One of the potential problems of Ownership Domains comes from its flexibility, which may make it difficult to understand the consequences of a given collection of annotations. One way around this problem is to use tools to help visualise and hence understand the structure imposed by annotations. In this direction, Abi-Antoun et al. [3] propose SCHOLIA, a tool for extracting conservative approximations of runtime object graphs from static ownership domains annotations. Such graphs may also help identifying deviations from the desired encapsulation policy.

To further increase the flexibility of Ownership Domains, Schäfer and Poetzsch-Heffter developed Simple Loose Ownership Domains [124]. This model keeps the public and private domains of the Ownership Domains model, though it hard codes a single private and single public domain per object, whereas Ownership Domains allows multiple public and multiple private domains per object. In addition, Simple Loose Ownership Domains omit link and domain declarations to reduce the syntactic overhead at the cost of a loss of the ability to express fine structure. Each object has a boundary domain which stores objects that are both publicly accessible and can access private objects. In addition, their model supports loose domains which allow one to abstract from the precise domain to which an object belongs, though for soundness reasons field update and method call are prohibited on loose domains. Their system enforces a property referred to as *boundary-as-dominator*, which means that the only access paths to an objects representation are via objects that it advertises as boundary objects, namely, those in boundary domains.

Although not the same as Ownership Domains, Lu and Potter [96] adopt the 'separate mechanism from policy' philosophy and explore a type system that separates the ownership assignment from the restrictions imposed on owners in, for example, the original Ownership Types system. Their model also allows ownership to vary, which can be seen as a form of ownership transfer. The type system specifies not only who owns an object but also who can reference it.

Their system is similar in spirit to ownership domains, but the underlying mechanism is more lightweight in Lu and Potter's system. This is also one of the few type systems that permit owner variance, using lightweight, programmer-specified variance annotations, which increases the expressiveness of the language.

3.6 Multiple Ownership and Owners-as-Ombudsmen

Several researchers have identified problems with the strong topological requirement imposed by ownership types, namely that having single owners for objects requires that the ownership relation embedded in the heap is organised into a tree-shape. But many programs and idioms do not fit into a tree structure, such as the iterator example discussed above.

To express design patterns where multiple objects interact and share ownership of objects, Cameron et al. [33], proposed a system of multiple ownership, called MOJO, wherein the ownership relation instead forms a DAG. MOJO does not impose any particular topology on a program's heap, rather, it relies on an elaborate effect system to statically capture interference using ownership information, thereby imposing an encapsulation discipline in spite of the looser topology. Following up on MOJO, Li, Cameron and Noble proposed the Mojojojo system [91]. Mojojojo simplifies and generalises MOJO; for example, it can express that an object lives in the intersection or the union of two objects' representations, which is useful for expressing sharing constraints while still preserving some locality.

Östlund and Wrigstad's *owners-as-ombudsmen* proposal [113] relaxes the owners-as-dominators property by allowing multiple objects to define a shared *aggregate owner*. An aggregate owner can have one or more *bridge objects* between the representation and the external objects. This allows components to express the topology underlying a restricted common state with multiple entry points to it. With owners-as-ombudsmen, the dominator for an object inside an aggregate is the dominator of the bridge objects defining the aggregate.

In systems supporting owners-as-ombudsmen, the rule enforced for an object a to validly reference object b is that either

1. a is the owner of b,

2. a and b are siblings,

3. b is outside a, or

4. a is owned by the aggregate owner b.

The owners-as-ombudsmen topological invariant can be understood as a simplification of Mojojojo, without requiring the effects system.

Using owners-as-ombudsmen, iterators can be expressed in a way that makes the List's Links part of an aggregate defined by the List and its Iterator objects.

```
class List[owner|data] {
  Link[aggregate,data] first;

  Iterator[bridge,data] iterator() {
    Iterator[bridge,data] i = new Iterator[bridge,data]();
    i.current = first;
    return i;
  }
}

class Link[owner|data] {
  Link[owner,data] next;
  Object[data] data;
}

class Iterator[owner|data] {
  Link[this,data] current;
}

List[x,y] myList;
Iterator[x,y] iter = myList.iterator(); // note bridge -> owner
```

The type Iterator[**bridge**,owner] captures the fact that the i variable points to another bridge object of the shared aggregate. When an external object calls the iterator method, it will see a type that has the same owner as the list itself, since **bridge**, like **this**, is an owner which is not visible externally. As a consequence, the links are writeable by sibling objects.

Another approach that produces the effect of multiple object owners is Tribal Ownership [34]. This was proposed by Cameron, Noble and Wrigstad and relies on earlier work by Clarke et al. on the virtual class calculus Tribe [41]. In Tribal Ownership, ownership nesting is reflected in the nesting of virtual classes and each object has an **out** reference to its enclosing object, equal to being able to name one's owner. Tribal Ownership allows different prescriptive ownership policies to be plugged into the system which gives rise to different levels of protection. Tribal Ownership furthermore allows a novel owners-as-local-dominators policy, which allows owners-as-dominators to be enforced in local subheaps of a program, as opposed to having one single system which imposes owners-as-dominators on the entire heap.

3.7   Confined Types

Confined Types [136,137] are a lightweight approach to enforcing the confinement of objects. Very few annotations are required to express the desired confinement discipline, at the cost of some expressiveness compared to other ownership systems. Confined Types, in their original form, enforce the following informal soundness condition:

An object of confined type is encapsulated within its defining scope [148].

This is enforced using a small set of annotations and a statically checkable set of rules. Firstly, classes may be annotated as **confined** to indicate that their instances are confined types and cannot be accessed outside their defining package. Secondly, methods that can safely be inherited by confined types must be marked as **anonymous**—anonymous methods cannot export the **this** reference. Finally, there are a collection of statically checkable rules such as the following (quoting [148]):

C1. A confined type must not appear in the type of a public (or protected) field or the return type of a public (or protected) method.

C2. A confined type must not be public.

C3. Methods invoked on an expression of confined type must either be defined in a confined class or be anonymous methods.

C4. Subtypes of a confined type must be confined.

C5. Confined types can be widened only to other confined types.

C6. Overriding must preserve anonymity of methods.

A1. The **this** reference is used only to select fields and as the receiver in the invocation of other anonymous methods.

The first six rules ensure that instances of some confined type do not escape the scope by ensuring that it does not appear in the interface of a public class (C1), that the class itself is not public (C2), that confined value do not leak via untrusted methods (C3) or by forgetting that the type is confined (C5). The rules (C4) and (C6) ensure that the property of being confined and being an anonymous method is preserved via subclassing. The last rule (A1) ensures that anonymous methods do not leak the **this** reference. If these rules are observed, the Java compiler does the remainder of the checks, even when compiled against code is not aware of the Confined Types discipline.

In the following code sample, all instances of class Link are confined to the package listpackage:

```
package listpackage;

class List {
  Link first;

  Iterator iterator() {
    Iterator i = new Iterator();
    i.current = first;
    return i;
  }
}

confined class Link {
  Link next;
  Object data;
}
```

```
class Iterator {
  Link current;
}
```

Confined Types are related to ownership types, but they differ in two significant ways. Firstly, confined types attempts to reduce the syntactic overhead imposed by the type system by relying on package- or class-level annotations or defaults, thus avoiding the annotation of types. The second difference is the degree of confinement provided. In earlier systems of Confined Types[136,137], the degree of confinement was at the package level, meaning that confined objects could only be referenced by other objects within the same package. Later systems achieved object level confinement [9,145,133], though without the same degree of flexibility as Ownership Types—types parameterised by the owner of their members cannot be expressed. The original Confined Types system [136,137] was presented as a collection of informal rules. These were latter formalised and proven to be sound [147,148]. An inference tool was also developed for Confined Types to make it easier to apply them with existing code bases [69].

The original motivation of Confined Types was to address some security properties that could not be expressed in Java's type system. This security property was extended further and applied in the context of Enterprise Java Beans to ensure that beans do not escape their defining context without being appropriately wrapped [47]. Applications of Confined Types to memory management [9,145,133] are surveyed in more detail in Section 6.3. Both Reflexes [129] and SteamFlex [130] apply notions of implicit Confined Types in the context of high performance stream processing applications. In all of these systems, the underlying sets of rules differ—each is tailored to the specific application domain.

4   Extensions

Ownership Types systems have been extended in a number of dimensions beyond the kind of policy they enforce. Ownership has been combined with generics and computational effects systems. More dynamic notions of ownership have been explored, including systems supporting a notion of ownership transfer. Ownership has also been explored beyond the mainstream object-oriented paradigm. The remainder of this section explores these topics.

4.1   Ownership and Generics

Modern programming languages support generic classes and bounded parametric-polymorphic type systems. A natural question is how ownership interacts with these mechanisms, especially considering that both mechanisms introduce a kind of parameterisation into classes.

The original Flexible Alias Protection proposal [112] was phrased in terms of a language with generics. Generic parameters served as a vehicle for delivering aliasing modes into a class in the sense that the alias modes annotated generic parameters, and only generic parameters, to avoid too much syntactic overhead. Such an approach does not allow ownership parameterisation isolated from type parameterisation.

In Clarke's PhD thesis [39] Ownership Types are encoded in terms of Abadi and Cardelli's object calculus [1]. Clarke also adapted Abadi and Cardelli's encoding of classes to include ownership in the obvious manner: as genericity is achieved using type parameters, ownership polymorphism is achieved using owner parameters. Both can also be constrained by the appropriate kinds of bounds.

SafeJava [20] offered both type parameters and ownership parameters in independent syntactic categories, but this can lead to significant annotation overhead. The language underlying Ownership Domains also included both type and ownership parameters in a single parameter space [4]. Constraints on the owners of type parameters could optionally be specified to help define the relationship between various ownership domains. Generic Universes [53] also separate type and ownership parameters. Only ownership parameters were, however, included in their formalisation. It is arguable that there are cases when it is useful to have ownership parameters independently of type parameters, and that it would be unnatural to introduce a type parameter just to pass around an ownership parameter.

The idea of piggybacking ownership (and other) information onto generic parameters, instead of treating them as orthogonal, has been explored extensively by Potanin and his coauthors [119,120,150]. With a suitable choice of defaulting mechanisms, the approach reduces the annotation overhead and the conceptual burden, as classes take only one kind of parameter. For example, using piggybacking, the class declaration

```
class List[owner|data outside owner,Data extends Object[data]] { ... }
```

can be replaced by

```
class List[owner|Data extends Object[data]] { ... }
```

Here the owner data is not explicitly declared, but it presence and the constraints on it can be inferred from the context. Similarly, when forming an element of this type, the implicit data parameter need not be specified. The improvement this approach offers is much greater when the class has more parameters. Potanin et al. applied this technique to confinement [119], ownership [120], and ownership and immutability combined [150].

Jo∃ [32,30] adds existential types on top of a generic Ownership Type system. Ownership information is passed as additional type parameters and existential quantification allows owners to vary. The main advantage of existential quantification is to allow more precise reasoning about unknown owners—rather than marking them with a '?', existential types can be used, thereby naming the owners and being more explicit about the relationship between them: compare types C[?|?] with ∃o.C[o|o]: the latter expresses a relationship between the two owner parameters, even though they are unknown. A variant $\text{Jo}\exists_{deep}$ enforces the owners-as-dominators policy.

Dietl, Drosspoloulou and Müller [53,60] extended Universes to include generics. This was the first type system to combine the owners-as-modifiers discipline with type genericity. Their approach also aims for a seamless integration of genericity with the ownership mechanisms and enables the separation of the specification of the topology from the encapsulation constraints, which opens the door for more flexible systems to be expressed [54].

4.2 Ownership and Effects

Computational effects systems, such as those expressing abstractly the possible field reads and writes a method can perform, become more when combined with Ownership Types. Clarke and Drossopoulou [44] demonstrated that combining an Ownership Types system enforcing the owners-as-dominators policy with an effects system offers strong guarantees, not only about the object on which the method is called but on whole chunks of the heap. This system also included a notion of sub-effecting that exploited the hierarchical structure of the ownership tree. Taking a different view on ownership and effects, Yu, Potter and Xue [98] present an alternative to Ownership Types based on effect encapsulation instead of restrictions to the reference topology. References may leak out of their defining scope, but what can be done with those references is limited using an effects system. This system can also be considered as an owners-as-modifiers system, due to the constraints imposed on leaked references.

The combination of ownership and effects is particularly important for reasoning about concurrent systems [82,83,84], and for guaranteeing race and deadlock freedom [21,20,24,51]. See Section 6.1 and Bocchino's chapter [19] for more details. Boyapati et al.'s application of Ownership Types to object upgrades also relies on effects to achieve modularity [23]. Yu and Potter use Ownership Types and effects to reason about object invariants based on the notion of validity effects that capture the objects that may be invalidated by some code block [97]. The multiple ownership type system uses effects to reason about when different owners are guaranteed to be disjoint, even though the ownership relation can be DAG shaped [33]. Finally, Clifton et al.'s MAO combines ownership and effects to reason about aspect-oriented programs [48].

The related notions of readonly references and immutability limit computational effects without requiring the tracking of effects by building permissions (such as whether a field write is permitted) into types. As already mentioned, Universes [105,54] have a notion of readonly reference built in. Östlund et al. [114] present a system combining ownership, uniqueness and immutability to obtain more powerful invariants than would be possible without them. For instance, the system allows the staged initialisation of immutable objects, meaning that an object can be initialised, hence mutated, in multiple places before eventually becoming immutable. Ownership Immutability Generic Java (OIGJ) [150] extends Featherweight Generic Ownership [120] to capture both ownership and immutability within a single type system, leveraging off Generic Java's type system, without introducing new syntactic categories to, capture notions of ownership and immutability. Immutability is considered in more detail in Potanin et al.'s chapter [121].

4.3 Dynamic Ownership

In early Ownership Types systems, checking is performed purely statically. While this provides strong guarantees, it has expressiveness limitations that make exploratory programming difficult. Various degrees of support for dynamic ownership have been explored, including run-time ownership information to support downcasts and Gradual Ownership typing, all the way to fully dynamic ownership where all checking occurs at run-time. The information required at run-time can be simply the owner of each object, but it generally includes the values of all owner parameters and the run-time nesting relationship between objects.

Systems supporting dynamic type casts include SafeJava [20], Generic Universe Types [53], and Gradual Ownership Types [127]. In terms of the amount of checking performed, approaches supporting downcast perform checks only when an explicit downcast is made, whereas Sergey and Clarke's Gradual Ownership typing approach also performs boundary checks when objects are passed between different objects. As an alternative approach to downcasts, Wrigstad and Clarke [142] present a lightweight approach to run-time downcasts which relies on existential types. Downcasting from a well-formed type C[a] to another well-formed type D[a,b] can be compiled as a regular downcast from C to D, ignoring ownership. If the cast succeeds at run-time, the additional owner parameter introduced by the downcast must exist, and its relation to owner a can be inferred from the declaration of the class D. This allows the introduction of the owner b as an existential owner parameter visible on the stack in a branch where the downcast was successful, without any need for run-time owner representation.

Dynamic ownership delays the checking of the properties expected by ownership types systems until run-time. A preliminary experiment of this idea was performed in the context of a prototype-based programming language [111]. This work was adapted to a class-based setting by Gordon and Noble, who introduced the scripting language ConstrainedJava [67]. The ownership structure is represented using an owner pointer in every object. Operations are provided to make use of and change these owner pointers. The semantics of the language relies on a message-passing protocol with a specific kind of monitoring. Messages are classified into several categories based on their relative positions of the message sender and receiver in the ownership tree. "Bad" messages are detected using run-time monitoring.

Leino and Müller [90] make use of dynamic ownership in the context of Spec# to control which parts of the heap class invariants may depend on. In contrast to most other ownership systems, the ownership relations of their system are conditions that need not always hold. Invariants may, for example, be temporarily broken during ownership transfer, as this is not an atomic operation, and involves passing the reference and changing the owner field of the moved object.

4.4   Ownership Transfer

One restriction common to early ownership systems is that the owner of an object must be set upon creation and then fixed for the lifetime of the object. Several attempts at removing this restriction have been presented over the years, thereby allowing the transfer of ownership.

Older systems, AliasJava [5], SafeJava [20] and Flexible Alias Protection [112] provide limited notions of uniqueness, corresponding to a reference that has not been assigned to a field or is stored in just one field (that is, no aliases). While this appears to be a perfectly reasonable notion of uniqueness, it fails to exploit the structure of the heap given by the ownership hierarchy. It also suffers from an abstraction problem, identified by Clarke and Wrigstad [42], namely that changes to the internal implementation of a class modifies the behaviour of code using unique references, for instance, an internal change to a method implementation could steal the unique reference upon which the method is called. Such changes need to be reported in the interface of the class, and this change tends to propagate through to client code.

Clarke and Wrigstad's language Joline offers a novel approach uniqueness called External Uniqueness [42,141], exploiting the nesting information provided by Ownership Types, in such a way that the above mentioned abstraction problem does not arise. Ownership Types can identify aggregate boundaries and safely allow aliasing between objects within those boundaries. The approach to uniqueness taken in External Uniqueness is that an externally unique reference is the only reference to an object from outside that object; the internal aliases to an object are permitted and can be ignored in the definition of uniqueness. Thus unique references refer to aggregates not just individual objects. The property enforced by External Uniqueness is called *owners-as-dominating-edges*, which means that all paths to an object accessible through a unique reference must include that reference. This is illustrated in Figure 3. Uniqueness is preserved using a destructive read operation. To preserve owners-as-dominators, however, transfer may only go inwards in the ownership hierarchy. As owners-as-dominators requires that all owner parameters are outside the owner of an object, allowing transfer of objects outwards in the hierarchy would result in a violation of this invariant.

In his Alias Burying proposal, Boyland [26] showed that destructive reads are not necessary for the preservation of uniqueness. Instead, it is sufficient to ensure that any aliases to a unique value are destroyed, for example, when a method exits, and thus preserve uniqueness. Checking that this is the case requires sophisticated static analysis.

Banerjee and Naumann elaborate on sufficient conditions for confinement and object transfer between owners [14,13]. Their objective was to provide a confinement policy similar to other ownership proposals, but without requiring ownership annotations. In order to support transfer, the system builds on a notion of separation similar to External Uniqueness, but which also requires that an aggregate does not have outwards pointing references into the source's representation when transferred to a new owner. This notion was later also adopted Haller and Odersky [71], described below.

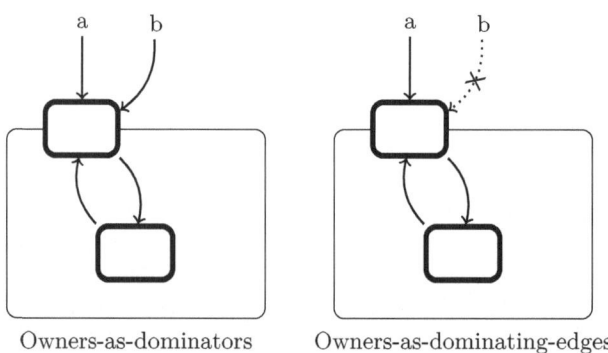

Owners-as-dominators   Owners-as-dominating-edges

Fig. 3. Owners-as-dominators and External Uniqueness

UTT [108] is Universe Types extended with transfer for externally unique aggregates. In Universes the situation is slightly less involved than in Joline, however, because the types carry less ownership information. The any owner modifier can point inwards, but since it does not convey any ownership information, such references are not an issue for preserving the underlying invariants. Further, Universes does not have owner parameters on classes, and so the restriction on inwards-only transfer is not required. An externally unique aggregate belongs to a specific region, or *cluster*, as they are called in UTT. In place of a destructive read operation, UTT instead employs **release** and **capture** statements to perform the move. The **release** statement will make unusable any external references to the aggregate (similar to Boyland's Alias Burying), stripping the type of information of which cluster it belongs to. The released object is simply free. The **capture** statement performs the actual move by assigning a new type specifying the cluster to which the aggregate now belongs.

Haller and Odersky's Capabilities for Uniqueness and Borrowing [71] use a notion similar to that of Banerjee and Naumann, called *separate uniqueness*. Separate uniqueness restricts external uniqueness so that there can be no outgoing pointers from inside a unique aggregate to the outside. This additional restriction helps guarantee race freedom in a concurrent message-passing setting, such as the Scala Actors Framework it is designed to work with. Separate uniqueness employs a capability system instead of ownership as the foundation for keeping track of uniqueness. Interestingly, a swap operator is used to preserve separate uniqueness, much in the spirit of Harms and Weider's 'copy and swap' proposal [72]. Separate uniqueness is maintained by well-formed construction, wherein a separately unique aggregate may be built out of other separately unique objects.

Object Teams also provide a notion of ownership transfer [73]. The mechanism updates all the dynamic information capturing the ownership structure, namely, the roles each object plays, but the mechanism offers no static security.

Anderson et al. [8] apply notions of ownership and ownership transfer in the context of C to describe data structure sharing strategies in multi-threaded programs.

Ownership transfer combines notions of linear (or uniqueness typing) and non-linear typing in the one system. In a non-object-oriented setting, Fahndrich and DeLine's Adoption and Focus approach [63] combines the benefits of linear types with the flexibility of non-linear types in order to enforce software protocols. The model is close to the notions imposed by ownership, as the reference structure considered is hierarchical—linearly typed objects containing within linearly type objects cannot be accessed directly from 'outside'. References start out having linear type, so that the interaction via them can be precisely tracked. However, it is impractical programming with only linear types. To get around this, the adoption operation allows a linear type to be converted to a non-linear type within the scope of another expression. In order to go the other way, the focus construct provides a temporary linear view on an non-linear type, by ensuring that no change made via other aliases. This is achieved by revoking the capability corresponding to the non-linear type. Adoption and Focus was latter generalised as nesting/carving in Boyland's Fractional Permissions [27,28].

4.5   Other Extensions and Variations

A number of alternative extensions and variations of Ownership Types that do not so easily fit into the categorisation above have been developed.

Lu and Potter [95] present a programmer-specified type system for describing reachability constraints in an object graph. The core restriction made by the system is that any cyclic references structures are constrained so that all objects share a common owner.

Ownership Types have been applied to aspect-oriented programming to simplify the task of reasoning about advice [48]. In this setting, Clifton et al. introduce *concern domains* which store objects related to particular concerns (in the sense of separation of concerns). These are used to reason about which parts of data structures are modified by which advice. The underlying type system is based on a shallow ownership-and-effects system.

The interaction-based object-oriented language Classages [94] uses a variant of Ownership Types is used to ensure that certain objects remain encapsulated within components (called classages), whereas other objects can be passed around between components.

Pedigree Types [144] use a relative addressing scheme to traverse the ownership tree, rather than the parameterised approach of Ownership Types. The general form of owner is given by the grammar $\mathbf{parent}^k.\mathbf{child}^z$, where $k \geq 0$ and $z \in 0, 1$. This can capture all owners accessible in the owners-as-dominators model—$\mathbf{parent}$ traverses up the tree, and $\mathbf{child}$ moves, in effect, to a sibling, except for when $\mathbf{child}$ appears alone, which corresponds to selecting the current object's representation.

Ownership Types have been considered in the context of an object-oriented programming language with relationships [92]. The work covers the problems encountered when trying to combine the two systems, but does not present any solutions to these problems.

Although not strictly following the tradition of Ownership Typing, X10 [37] includes a notion of place types which is similar to Ownership Types in that types partition the space of objects. Places are used to express locality and thereby facilitate better distribution of data across the memory hierarchy of a multicore processor.

5   Ownership Inference

Ownership Types systems generally require a significant amount of annotations to express the types, but this can be burdensome for the programmer. What makes matters worse is that library code also needs to be annotated to work effectively with Ownership Types. Addressing this problem leads naturally to the question of Ownership Type inference. Unfortunately, matters are not so simple. Unlike traditional type systems, ownership annotations are mostly design-driven: it is up to the programmer to decide whether some object should be owned by **this** or by **world**. Many Ownership Type systems admit a trivial type assignment, for example, by setting all objects to be owned by **world**. Consequently, even elaborate approaches to type qualifier inference [38,68] are ineffective, as they infer any solution that satisfies the constraints, but cannot give a best solution.

In this section, we provide a survey of approaches for ownership inference. Two approaches are considered: dynamic inference and static inference.

5.1   Dynamic Inference

Dynamic ownership inference uses snapshots of the run-time object graph to determine an approximation of the ownership structure of the system—these snapshots may involve continual monitoring, in effect taking a snapshot every time the heap changes. The idea is that this information can then be used to help determine a valid ownership typing.

The first work on the dynamic inference of Ownership Types is Wren's master's thesis [140]. The essence of his approach is to run programs with a profiler that keeps track of all heap snapshots, collecting full information about the topology of the heap at any moment. All heap snapshots are then merged and the resulting graph is analysed in order to infer dominance relations between objects. The work provides a graph-theoretical foundation for run-time inference, including a description of the most precise program heap topology with respect to the owners-as-dominators invariant. On the negative side, the dynamically-determined ownership information cannot be mapped directly to types. To remedy this, the author formulates the system of equations to assign annotations to particular object allocation sites.

Dietl and Müller present results on runtime Universe Type inference [57]. As Universe Types require a comparatively lower annotation overhead than Ownership Types, mapping dynamic inference results to static annotations is easier than for the system Wren considered. The inference algorithm is, however, quite in the spirit of Wren's: first a combined representation of the object store is built; then its dominator tree is constructed; finally, conflicts between the information obtained by analyzing the inferred dominator tree and the actual constraints of the type system are resolved by flattening the dominance trees via a procedure referred to as harmonization. The resulting annotations deliver a correct typing of the program with respect to the target type system.

5.2   Static Inference

One of the first attempts to provide Ownership Type inference was by Aldrich et al. [5]. In their system, the programmer needed only to provide a small amount of annotations to indicate the intent that some parts of the program be protected, and the rest of alias annotations were inferred. The approach was not entirely satisfactory, because a large number of parameters were inferred in many cases.

Moelius and Souter [104] employ a variation of an escape analysis [18] to infer ownership annotations. Their algorithm allows borrowed references to be returned from methods and assigned to object fields. No assumptions on ownership parameterisation are made, consequently the algorithm can also result in a large number of parameters, the same problem that Aldrich et al.'s [5] inference algorithm suffered from.

For the same inference problem, Milanova and Liu [101] employ an Andersen-style points-to analysis [7] as part of a static algorithm to infer ownership and universe annotations according to two different ownership protocols: owners-as-dominators and owners-as-modifiers. Both analyses are based on a context-insensitive points-to analysis, therefore they do not distinguish between different allocation and call sites. However, thanks to some Java-related heuristics, their technique handles some idiomatic cases, and good precision is thereby obtained.

Later, Milanova and Vitek presented a static inference algorithm for ownership annotations for the owners-as-dominators invariant based on a static dominance inference algorithm [102]. The algorithm computes approximations of the object graphs using an enhanced global context-insensitive points-to analysis. The candidate ownership annotations are computed based on an approximated dominance tree, built using a variation of *must-point-to* information [52,81]. The approach does not provide any guarantee that the inferred annotations comply with the original Ownership Types system. Naturally, as with any global analysis approach, the issue of scalability is a concern. In subsequent work employing the dominance inference algorithm, Huang and Milanova use the original type checker to verify the correctness of the inferred ownership annotations [80].

Based on the boundary-as-dominator model, where access is permitted either via the owner or other boundary objects, Poetzsch-Heffter et al. [117] present an inference technique that requires that the programmer only annotate the interface types of components and the remaining ownership information is automatically inferred using a constraint-based algorithm. Due to the lack of parameters in the underlying model, this approach delivers reasonable results and represents a good compromise to the inference problem.

Some static analysis-based approaches fail to deliver type annotations directly, but instead extract topological properties similar to those ensured by Ownership Type systems. This is problematic because it make it difficult to view the topological properties in terms of code, and thereby are difficult to reason about. For instance, Geilmann and Poetzsch-Heffter [66] developed a modular abstract interpretation-based analysis to check simple (*i.e.*, non-hierarchical) confinement properties in Java-like programs. This work employs a *box model* [117] instead of dominator trees. The approach is targeted to substitute modular type-checking by modular static analysis, requiring a significantly smaller amount of annotations: only class declarations and object allocation sites need to be annotated. The analysis then takes the implementation of a class, considered as an encapsulated box, and executes it together with its most-general client. The most-general client is an abstraction of all possible clients that is used to create all possible traces through the box. If execution succeeds, the box never exposes any confined object, irrespective of the program that uses the box. The approach is based on formulating ownership as a semantic property of the program and the subsequent construction of an abstraction of the abstract semantics in the style of Cousot and Cousot [49,50].

A general variation of a points-to analysis-based algorithm to infer ownership and uniqueness is presented by Ma and Foster [100]. The algorithm combines constraint-based intraprocedural and interprocedural analyses. The collected information about encapsulation properties is not however mapped to a type system.

Another approach is to generate and solve typing constraints and allow the user to tune the solution. Dietl et al. [55] presented such a static analysis to infer Universe Types according to the user-specified intentions declared with annotations. The first part of the technique is responsible for the generation of equations, based on the program semantics and the rules of the original type system. Constraints of the Universe Type system are encoded as a boolean satisfiability problem. After the constraints have been generated and solved, the second part of the approach is to tune the result of the inference: programmers can indicate a preference for certain typings by adjusting the heuristics or by supplying partial annotations for the program. Dietl et al. empirically demonstrate that the NP-completeness of constraint solving does not result in a significant overhead on real-world programs, compared with other static approaches [80,102,104].

The two lines of research towards Ownership Type inference via points-to analysis and via constraint solving were unified in the work of Huang et al. [79]. The resulted framework implements checking and inference for two systems: Universe Types and Ownership Types. As in the prior work [55], the programmer can influence the inference by adding partial annotations to the program. The algorithms work with a programmer-supplied metric specifying the best typing, which the type inference algorithm attempts to maximise. The underlying analysis is implemented as a Kleene iteration of a monotonic transfer function, based on the program's small-step collecting semantics. The user-provided annotations are taken into account, whereas missing ones are initialised with the bottom element of the appropriate lattice.

An incremental type analysis has also been developed for Confined Types and integrated into the Eclipse platform [62]. The fact that it is incremental means that it provides immediate feedback to programmers as they add their annotations.

6 Applications of Ownership

Ownership Types and related systems have seen many applications. This section surveys their application in concurrency control, verification, memory management, security, object upgrading, and software visualisation and understanding.

6.1 Ownership for Concurrency Control

One application domain where ownership has seen a variety of applications is concurrency. We expect that these approaches merely scratch the surface of what is becoming an increasingly important problem area.

Parameterised Race Free Java (PRFJ) [24] is an ownership-based type system for guaranteeing race-freedom in concurrent Java programs. The discipline PRFJ enforces is called *owners-as-locks*, and is in many ways similar to Flanagan and Abadi's Types for Safe Locking [64], with ownership and parameterisation included for greater flexibility. Each object is associated with a lock, and the encapsulation provided by ownership allows protection of an entire aggregate by acquiring a single lock, namely that of the owner of the aggregate. Further, method annotations reveal what locks must be acquired by the callee prior to method invocation. PRFJ also has thread local variables, annotated with the special owner thisThread. This owner may not occur in the type of a field, but only on local variables. Essentially this means that values owned by this-Thread cannot be shared between threads, and are thus thread local. PRFJ was subsequently extended to ensure deadlock-freedom [21]. Based on programmer-supplied annotations, a partial order on locks could be established. The type system then rejects any programs that do not adhere to the partial order when acquiring locks, again in a similar fashion to Flanagan and Abadi [64]. Permandla et al. [116] continue work in this direction, by designing a similar type system for Java bytecode. The type system enforces race- and deadlock freedom of precompiled files at load time.

Cunningham, Drossopoulou and Eisenbach [51] use the Universes ownership model as the basis for a race-free type system. The system shares many similarities with PRFJ, but it uses a simpler type system that aims to be much more user friendly. To cope with some of the reduced expressiveness, the system uses effects to deal with references to domains not identifiable by immutable paths. A number of extensions were presented that can distinguish between read/writes, prevent deadlocks, verify atomicity, and allow locks to be taken at the granularity of single objects. The authors conjecture that adding genericity to the type system will increase expressiveness.

For the purpose of supporting large numbers of concurrent object-oriented actors, Srinivasan's and Mycroft's [131] implement cooperatively-scheduled green threads on the JVM in their Kilim language. To achieve isolation of actors without incurring a huge copying overhead, they require that messages between actors be tree shaped by using only unique references. These can then trivially be passed between actors at a close-to zero, constant-time cost. In contrast, Clarke et al.'s Joelle language [43] employs ownership types to allow zero-overhead confinement of active objects, each with a single thread. By employing ownership, messages can have complicated graph-like or circular structure and not be limited to simple trees. In Joelle, external uniqueness [42] suffices for efficient object transfer, and where external uniqueness cannot be established, ownership information can be used to perform "sheep cloning" [111], which calculates the minimal safe clone statically. Joelle furthermore supports the safe sharing of immutable subgraphs of otherwise mutable data, similar to the **arg** mode of Flexible Alias Protection [112].

The CoBox (concurrent box) [125] concurrency model unifies the active object model with structured heaps in a similar manner to Minimal Ownership [43]. A key difference is that in the CoBox model multiple objects play the role of the active object. This is realised by associating a single lock with each cobox to ensure that at most one of the objects within each cobox has a thread of control at a time. A Java-based implementation of the CoBox model exists [126], and CoBoxes were incorporated into the ABS programming language [40], where they are called *cogs* (concurrent object groups).

Loci [143] is a type system for thread local data based on the notion of *owners-as-threads*. Using a simple ownership system based on a conceptual division of the heap into a shared area and a private area per thread, objects can be determined to belong to either the shared heap or be thread local, thus belonging to one of the threads. The type system ensures that shared and thread local data are never confused, thus preventing accidental sharing. Thread local objects can be accessed without synchronisation. A similar model is found in the older system Guava [10], except that Guava's rules are presented informally, whereas Loci is completely formalised and proven correct. Guava is a Java dialect that guarantees that shared data is accessed only through synchronised methods. In Guava there are no synchronised methods (in the Java sense). Instead, classes are split into two kinds: monitor classes, where all access are fully synchronised, and ordinary classes, whose instances can only be shared within a single thread, and are thus thread local.

As mentioned in Section 4.4, Haller and Odersky [71] present an Ownership Types system for expressing uniqueness and borrowing to be used with Scala's actor model. The type system ensures that objects can be safely passed between actors without leading to race conditions, thereby avoiding the cost of object cloning.

In a series of papers, Bocchino and his coauthors investigate the use of type and effect systems similar to Ownership Types with effects to enforce a notion of Deterministic Parallelism [82,83,84]. As these efforts are surveyed in another chapter in this volume [19], we keep our discussion brief. After introducing the initial system [83], subsequent work [82] presented a type system for writing user code that will operate properly when used with parallel object-oriented frameworks such as Map-Reduce. The approach is similar to Clarke and Drossopoulou's ownership plus effects system [44], albeit tailored to the demands of a particular application domain. A subsequent paper [84] extends the system to permit safe nondeterminism using special blocks declared by programmers, thereby providing mechanisms encapsulating and controlling the nondeterminism.

Task Types [88] are another approach for preserving atomicity in multithreaded programs. The underlying structures are similar to those enforced by Ownership Types, except that the type system helps express explicit sharing in a more explicit fashion.

6.2 Ownership for Verification

Ownership has played a very solid role in verification, helping deal with issues of *framing*, knowing which properties are affected by a given code block, *invariants*, knowing which properties can be relied on, and *locking*, knowing when a lock needs to be obtained to avoid data races. Ownership has been used both via typing or by encoding the desired invariants into specifications. Notions of ownership have been incorporated into specification languages JML [106], and Spec# [90].

Banerjee and Naumann use ownership to show representation independence properties of classes [11,16,15], which enables one implementation of a class to be replaced by another. Ownership is used to indicate which classes are hidden behind the abstraction boundary. Their work has addressed this problem for increasingly sophisticated program models and relaxed restrictions.

Much more could be said here. Instead duplicating other excellent work on the topic, we invite the reader to consult other the chapters of this volume that discuss the role of ownership in verification [17,58].

6.3 Ownership for Memory Management

The fact that Ownership Types could be applied to memory management was identified early on [122]. It took some time before anyone explored the idea, and all work to date has been done in terms of RTSJ or related systems.

Before continuing, we first present a little background. The Real-time Specification for Java (RTSJ) memory model includes various regions of memory: immortal memory, heap memory, and numerous programmer specified scoped memories. Immortal memory is for objects that remain for the entire application. Heap memory is garbage collected. Scoped memories are allocated and deallocated in a stack-like fashion based on the order in which threads 'enter them' to allocate objects within them. Without going into too much detail, objects in one scoped memory can refer to objects in another, if the lifetime of the former exceeds that of the latter, to avoid memory leaks. RTSJ checks dynamically that the scoped memories are used correctly.

Boyapati et al. [25] were first to explore the application of Ownership Types to memory management in any detail. Their work combines Region Types and Ownership Types in a unified framework to statically enforce object encapsulation and region-based memory management. The memory model underlying the type system is compatible with RTSJ's memory model. Additions beyond the basic ownership machinery include subregions within shared regions to allow long-lived threads to share objects without using the heap and without memory leaks, typed portal fields for enabling inter-thread communication, and thread local regions.

ScopeJ [146] is a variant of confined types tailored for the memory management discipline of RTSJ. ScopeJ imposes a naming discipline based on a few annotations and some simple-to-check rules that statically ensure the correct usage of scoped memory, thereby eliminating the need for dynamic checking. Zhao et al. [145] define Implicit Ownership Types for memory management based on ScopeJ's memory model. The key contribution of this approach is that the programmer does not need to specify any type annotations—ownership is implicit, and therefore not a burden to programmers. A complete formal semantics of the approach is also presented. The work of Andreae et al. [9] uses aspects to facilitate a more modular specification of the code dealing with scoped memories. The ScopeJ approach has also been adapted and applied to SCJ (Safety Critical Java Specification) [133].

6.4   Ownership for Security

One of the original motivations for Confined Types was to address security problems found in the Java library, namely, to prevent certain references from escaping their defining scope. More specifically, each instance of Java Class has a list of signers that the security architecture uses to determine the access rights of the class at run-time. A leaking reference to this internal data structure caused a security flaw in JDK1.1 that allowed untrusted applets to gain all access rights. The problem boiled down to the fact that an alias to the array containing the signers was leaked, rather than a copy of the array. (For more details, see [137].)

As mentioned in Section 3.7, Confined Types [136] are a syntactically simple approach to achieving a topological restriction similar to what Ownership Types do, but with a package-level granularity instead of object-level granularity. Confined Types were originally designed to prevent security bugs, such as the Java class signer bug, resulting from leaking references to sensitive objects. One further example application is ensuring that references to cryptographic keys do not leak beyond the crypto module [137].

In a variant of confined types adapted to the setting of Enterprise Java Beans, Clarke, Richmond and Noble [47] address the problem of leaking EJB objects without the appropriate wrappers. Without these wrappers, beans could be accessed directly, thereby circumventing the persistency, distribution, and security functionality that would otherwise be in place. The scheme was based on a specification of which classes corresponded to confined and to boundary elements. Checking was performed at deployment time by inspecting the bytecode. Only classes mentioned in the specification file needed to be checked, as in the original Confined Types, and thus classes were protected against unchecked attackers who did not necessarily conform to the discipline.

Naumann and Banerjee [12] use a simplified form of ownership to achieve pointer confinement (a topological constraint) in a class-based language, and use the resulting language to prove certain noninterference results. Similarly, Skalka and Smith [128] present an system using ownership-related notions for secure capability-based programming. Their core protection model is similar to that of Confined Types [86] and Clarke's finitary version of Ownership Types in the object calculus [45].

In one of the few systems that allows owners to vary (without using ownership transfer), Yu, Potter and Xue [99] introduce the *owners-as-downgraders* policy which increases the flexibility of ownership types systems by allowing an object to downgrade or declassify an object's owner, thereby allowing previously protected objects to be accessible beyond what usually would be allowed. In this setting, downgrading can be considered as a special case of intransitive noninterference.

Using a variant of Universe Types, Dietl, Müller and Poetzsch-Heffter [59] present a type system for applet isolation on JavaCard smart card. Their system statically detects firewall violations, which would otherwise be detected only using dynamic checks.

In a quite different setting, Patrignani, Clarke and Sangiorgi [115] apply Ownership Types to the Join calculus [65] in order to enforce certain security properties. They prove that secrets owned by some process cannot be leaked, even against untyped attackers, that is, processes that are not typed using the Ownership Types system (or any other type system).

6.5   Ownership for Object Upgrades

Boyapati et al. [23] describe a quite unexpected application of Ownership Types in the context of persistent object stores. Their approach uses Ownership Types to ensure, in a modular way, that a persistent object store can be efficiently updated without stopping the application. Modularity allows the programmer to locally reason about the correctness of their upgrades. Ownership Types with effects annotations help to provide the desired modularity condition. The system was implemented in the context of the Thor language [93].

6.6   Software Visualisation and Understanding

Ownership has been used in techniques to provide better understanding of system structure and behaviour. Many of these techniques have a visual component, based either on the static or dynamic structure of a system.

The notion of ownership has also been used to introduce structure into the visualisation of systems, both of the evolving object graph [75,74,76] and of a static abstraction of it (Object Ownership Graphs (OOGs)) [3,135].[5] These approaches exploit the hierarchical nature of ownership to enable the structuring of objects in a visualisation along with the collapsing of parts of the object graph that are not the current focus of whoever is performing the visualisation. Ammar and Abi-Antoun [6] perform further work on the use of OOGs in program comprehension. Using a group of programmers unfamiliar with notions of ownership, they were able to show in a statistically significant fashion that the use of OOGs improve programmers' comprehension compared to programmers who just used class diagrams.

Mitchell uses techniques based on ownership and dominators to summarise memory footprints in order to better understand the memory usage of a program [103]. In his approach, each dominator tree captures unique ownership. Trees are connected by specific edges that describe responsibility, *i.e.,* transfer of ownership. A profiling technique aggregates these structures and uses thresholds to identify important aggregates. The notion of ownership graph summarises responsibility, and the notion of backbone equivalence is used to aggregates patterns within trees, generating concise summaries of heap usage. The ultimate goal of this work is to understand where excessive memory usage occurs in large programs, not to produce a type assignment.

Rayside et al. [123] take an alternative approach to finding and fixing memory leaks which is also based on object ownership. Their techniques involves determining the ownership hierarchy of objects, the size of each object, the time interval that each object is allocated, and the time interval that it is active. This information is reported visually to the programmer. In conjunction with five memory management anti-patterns that are identified based on the authors' experience with object ownership profiling, their tool can help the programmer to identify memory leaks. The authors apply their techniques to fix memory leaks in the Alloy IDE (V3).

7   Foundational Calculi

Although most work on Ownership Types is formalised, only a relatively small amount of work has been done on their foundations.

Very early on, Clarke's thesis [39] formalised Ownership Types in terms of Abadi and Cardelli's object calculus [1]. In this setting ownership contexts are separate from objects. Every object has two ownership contexts, namely, a representation context, or storing its representation, and an owner context, which was its owner. Whether an object had permission to access another object was determined using the representation context of the referrer and the owner context of the referee. Clarke gave constraints on the relationships between ownership contexts that guaranteed that the owners-as-dominators property held. The

---

[5] Interestingly, it was while studying software visualisation that James Noble realised the pressing need for proper alias control, which eventually lead to Flexible Alias Protection.

formalism also supported type parameterisation and existential quantification of owners.

The foundational calculus F_{own} [87] was built on top of system F to provide a foundation for Ownership Domains. To capture the specifics of the system, a special permissions system based on ownership domains and links was added into the calculus. Being based on system F, the calculus also supported parametric polymorphism.

Cameron and Drossopoulou [32,30] study Ownership Types systems that include notions of owner variance and unknown ownership context—we have seen various systems like this above. Their system Jo∃ casts these systems into a uniform setting and removes many of the limitations of the more ad hoc approaches found in the literature. Their calculus supports parameterisation of types and ownership contexts, and allows variant subtyping of ownership contexts using existential types. The explicit use of existential types makes the type-theoretic foundations of owner variance and unknown ownership context more transparent. Building on this work, Cameron, Drossopoulou and Noble's chapter [31] explains Ownership Types in terms of dependent types, elucidating the idea that Ownership Types are actually a kind of phantom type [89], namely, a type that does not contribute to the run-time representation of values.

Using the Fractional Permissions framework [27,28], Zhao and Boyland [149] encode the owners-as-dominators and owners-as-locks models. Fractional Permissions provide a uniform, albeit low-level, view on these two models, and permit the encoding of other models, such as variants of Multiple Ownership, in the same setting.

A similar approach based on encoding into logic is taken by Wang et al. [138] who add a notion of confinement to separation logic. One of the goals of their work is to reason about confinement independently of any particular confinement discipline. In different work, Wang and Qui [139] present a generic model of confinement aimed at breaking the shackles imposed by purely syntactic definitions by providing semantic definitions for encoding various confinement schemes. In some sense their work provides a more complete formal model of ideas proposed by Noble et al. [110].

8   Empirical Studies

A number of empirical studies of Ownership Types and related systems have been performed. These include programming experiments, such as seeing how Ownership Types interact with design patterns or applying Ownership Types to a given code base and determine what changes need to be made; automatic analysis of the run-time object structures of a corpus of programs; and automatic static analysis of a corpus of programs.

The most natural approaches to evaluating Ownership Types are to apply it to an existing code base or to study the interaction between Ownership Types and design patterns.

AliasJava [5], a precursor to Ownership Domains, was evaluated on various library classes and the Aphyds circuit layout application, which consisted of

12.5kLOC. A core 3kLOC was annotated by the Aphyds developer. Most method parameters were annotated with **lent** and many return values could be annotated with **unique**, indicating that either sharing was absent or temporary. Instances of classes related to circuit elements were, in contrast, shared among many other objects.

In his masters thesis, Hächler applies Universes to an industrial application [70]. The application was the software of a ticket reader for print-at-home tickets, consisting of more than 50kLOC. The process of annotating this system revealed a number of shortcomings of ownership, which required restructuring of the application, and replacing pass-by-reference by pass-by-copy. One interesting proposed extension was the idea of local universes (akin to Clarke and Wrigstad's scoped owners [42]), which allow read and write access within the scope of a pure method in such a way that the mutable effects are encapsulated within the pure method.

An evaluation of ownership domains was done on four real world programs, JHotDraw and HillClimber, each of 15kLOC, Aphyds (8kLOC), and CryptoDB (3kLOC) supported by a reimplementation of the type system and an Eclipse plug-in [3,2]. The case studies identified a few patterns of ownership (e.g., "ownership domains expose tight coupling") and some weaknesses of the existing Ownership Domains type system (e.g., public domains are hard to use, annotations are verbose). More details can be found in Abi-Antoun's PhD Thesis [2]. A further case study considers the amount of effort required to refactor a 16kLOC application (HillClimber) to enforce appropriate architectural constraints expressed with the help of Ownership Domains [3,2]. Again a number of lessons are reported, along with perceived limitations of Ownership Domains. The reader is invited to consult these papers for more details.

In an early exploration of using Ownership Types in practice, Cele and Stureborg [36] found that embedding ownership information in programs made them less flexible, especially for reuse and refactoring. In their qualitative study, balancing flexibility and encapsulation emerged as a key aspect of programming with ownership. A frequent pattern in their programming illustrates this; it relies on subsumption to remove owners from types,[6] such as for call-backs and listeners.

In his master's thesis, Nägeli [109] uses design patterns to evaluate three different Ownership Types systems (Universes, Clarke and Drossopoulou's Joe$_1$, and Ownership Domains). His work identifies numerous difficulties in the various disciplines (and the tool support for them). Based on this study, he lists the following requirements for Ownership Type systems: alias control for representation objects, support for read-only references, multiple ownership, ownership transfer, friend contexts (analogous with friends in C++ [132]). These concepts (apart from friend contexts) have appeared in some form in other systems cited in this survey, but no system includes them all.

The evaluation of OIGJ [150] included a demonstration that their system could express the factory and visitor patterns, and be used to type check the standard java.util collections (except for clone methods) without refactoring

---

[6] It was latter dubbed the "Hide Owner Pattern" [141].

and with only a small number of annotations. Sergey and Clarke's Gradual Ownership Types [127] were empirically evaluated by integrating ownership annotations into a non-generic version of Java's collections framework, resulting in the analysis of about 8,200 lines of code. Only on significant refactoring was required to satisfy the type checker.

The second approach to evaluate Ownership Types is to semi-automatically analyse a large code base—state-of-the-art ownership inference is not good enough to do this fully automatically.

The unified ownership inference framework [79], implemented on top of the Checker Framework,[7] was evaluated experimentally on 110 kLOC, including ejc, Eclipse IDE compiler, and javad, the Java class file disassembler. The results indicated that that a large amount of non-trivial ownership annotations could be applied in these production-quality applications.

For the Confined Types discipline, Grothoff et al. [69] analysed a large body of code, consisting of over 46,000 classes. Their tool Kacheck/J uncovered 24% confined classes and interfaces. In a language with generics (such as modern versions of Java), this number would increase to 30%. After inferring tighter access control modifiers, this number went up even further to 45%, meaning that 45% of all package scoped classes were confined.

Vanciu and Abi-Antoun's chapter [135] present a significant experimental evaluation of the use of Ownership Domains in practice based on Ownership Object Graphs (OOGs), which incorporate ownership information into an object graph to provide abstractions based on ownership and types. Their approach is based on annotating several systems using Ownership Domains and using static analysis to extract OOGs. They added annotations to 100 KLOC of real object-oriented code. The chapter presents a vast range of statistics, which we won't repeat here. Their conclusion is that ownership can make a significant contribution to expressing designs more abstractly.

The third approach to evaluating the potential of Ownership Types is to study the object-graph structures of running programs. To this end, Potanin, Noble and Biddle [118] employed a tool to take snapshots of the heaps of running programs and applied it to a large corpus of Java programs. The tool computed various metrics on the collected heaps related to notions of uniqueness, ownership and confinement, to determine how often such concepts appear in actual running programs. Their results indicate that such concepts are often used in practice—12% of objects were not uniquely referenced, ownership hierarchies were on average five layers deep, and around one third of objects were referred to only by classes in the same package.

9   Discussion and Conclusion

This chapter has presented a comprehensive survey of many variations, extensions and applications of Ownership Types. It is time now to take a step back

---

[7] http://types.cs.washington.edu/checker-framework/

and consider what remains to be done in the future. What follows is based on criticism of Ownership Types, both published and otherwise, discussions at various forums, and our own experience.

Designing good context-dependent constraints. Ownership Types systems need to be better tailored to specific problems domains. When doing this, a statement of invariants or desired properties must come first, and the type system needs to be designed around those within some framework that is capable of linking types to guarantees. Systems such as Ownership Domains cater for this to some degree, and various Confined Types variants have been specifically tailored for given problem domains.

A lot of work already been done add to address the inflexibility of systems, as witnessed by mechanisms such Ownership Domains' separation of mechanism from policy, External Uniqueness, owner-polymorphic methods, among others. These should be considered as possible ingredients in future Ownership Types systems, but it needs to be clear precisely what properties each new ingredient enforces or violates, in relation to the properties that need to be enforced.

Better integration with dynamic mechanisms. Ownership Type systems should rely on and integrate better with mechanisms that dynamically provide guarantees about run-time behaviour, such as synchronised methods or locks. Just as ownership can be used to reduce the amount of synchronisation, synchronisation strengthens temporary guarantees about exclusive ownership.

Larger scale analysis of ownership usage in existing code bases. More thorough empirical analysis of ownership in real systems needs to be performed, to capture both common usage patterns of ownership and how the use of ownership evolves across time, but also to determine and characterise common alias patterns and problems.

Deployment in practice. Numerous case studies with various systems have been carried out (Section 8), a lot of experience both positive in terms of usage patterns and negative in terms of weaknesses has been gathered, and this experience has fed back into the design of better systems. Nevertheless, experience with Ownership Types would benefit significantly if it were used to build real systems, ideally in a commercial setting. A proper scientific analysis of the benefits should accompany this activity.

Reduced syntactic overhead. Ownership Types often impose a heavy syntactic burden on programmers. Many developments in tool support, appropriate default annotations (though we've said little about this), type inference and other program analysis techniques, have helped reduce this load, but more sophisticated and more integrated approaches are needed. Such approaches may rely heavily on static analysis techniques such as alias- and shape-analysis.

Address the library code problem. A problem common to any specialised type system (not just Ownership Types systems) is that library code is not checked using the type system. This problem can be tackled from two directions. One is to provide tool support and automatic analysis. The other is by using notions such as gradual typing [127], which allow some of the code to be annotated and checked statically, leaving other checks to run-time.

Exploitation of the ideas to better support concurrent programming.
Due to the petering out of Moore's law, multicore computers have become mainstream, and increasing amounts of concurrent processing resources are available
on the desktop. Programs need to be concurrent to exploit these resources, but
reasoning about such programs, for humans and compilers alike, is hard, and annotations describing aliasing and ownership offer relief. More needs to be done to
make the ownership annotations fully exploitable by compilers, and sufficiently
powerful for programmers when they need them, and unobtrusive when they
don't.

Acknowledgements. Thanks to Marwan Abi-Antoun, Jonathan Aldrich, Peter
Müller, and the anonymous reviewers for their detailed comments.

References

1. Abadi, M., Cardelli, L.: A theory of objects. Springer (1996)
2. Abi-Antoun, M.: Static Extraction and Conformance Analysis of Hierarchical
   Runtime Architectural Structure. PhD thesis, Carnegie Mellon University, Available as Technical Report CMU-ISR-10-114 (2010)
3. Abi-Antoun, M., Aldrich, J.: Static extraction and conformance analysis of hierarchical runtime architectural structure using annotations. In: OOPSLA, pp.
   321–340 (2009)
4. Aldrich, J., Chambers, C.: Ownership Domains: Separating Aliasing Policy from
   Mechanism. In: Odersky, M. (ed.) ECOOP 2004. LNCS, vol. 3086, pp. 1–25.
   Springer, Heidelberg (2004)
5. Aldrich, J., Kostadinov, V., Chambers, C.: Alias annotations for program understanding. In: OOPSLA, pp. 311–330 (2002)
6. Ammar, N., Abi-Antoun, M.: Empirical Evaluation of Global Hierarchical Object
   Graphs for Coding Activities. In: Working Conference on Reverse Engineering,
   WCRE (2012)
7. Andersen, L.O.: Program Analysis and Specialization for the C Programming Language. PhD thesis, DIKU, Computer Science Department, University of Copenhagen, Copenhagen, Denmark (May 1994), DIKU Rapport 94/19
8. Anderson, Z.R., Gay, D., Naik, M.: Lightweight annotations for controlling sharing
   in concurrent data structures. In: PLDI, pp. 98–109 (2009)
9. Andreae, C., Coady, Y., Gibbs, C., Noble, J., Vitek, J., Zhao, T.: Scoped types
   and aspects for real-time Java memory management. Real-Time Systems 37(1),
   1–44 (2007)
10. Bacon, D.F., Strom, R.E., Tarafdar, A.: Guava: a dialect of Java without data
    races. In: OOPSLA, pp. 382–400 (2000)
11. Banerjee, A., Naumann, D.A.: Representation independence, confinement and
    access control (extended abstract). In: POPL, pp. 166–177 (2002)
12. Banerjee, A., Naumann, D.A.: Secure information flow and pointer confinement
    in a Java-like language. In: CSFW, pp. 253–267 (2002)
13. Banerjee, A., Naumann, D.A.: Ownership transfer and abstraction. Technical re-
    port, Computing and Information Sciences, Kansas State University, USA (2003)
14. Banerjee, A., Naumann, D.A.: Ownership: transfer, sharing, and encapsulation. In:
    Proceedings of the 5th Workshop on Formal Techniques for Java-Like Programs,
    FTfJP 2003 (2003)

15. Banerjee, A., Naumann, D.A.: Ownership confinement ensures representation independence for object-oriented programs. J. ACM 52(6), 894–960 (2005)
16. Banerjee, A., Naumann, D.A.: State Based Ownership, Reentrance, and Encapsulation. In: Gao, X.-X. (ed.) ECOOP 2005. LNCS, vol. 3586, pp. 387–411. Springer, Heidelberg (2005)
17. Banerjee, A., Naumann, D.A.: State Based Encapsulation for Modular Reasoning about Behavior-Preserving Refactorings. In: Clarke, D., Noble, J., Wrigstad, T. (eds.) Aliasing in Object-Oriented Programming. LNCS, vol. 7850, pp. 319–365. Springer, Heidelberg (2013)
18. Blanchet, B.: Escape analysis: correctness proof, implementation and experimental results. In: Cardelli, L. (ed.) POPL 1998: Proceedings of the 25th Annual ACM SIGPLAN-SIGACT Symposium on Principles of Programming Languages, San Diego, California, pp. 25–37 (January 1998)
19. Bocchino Jr., R.L.: Alias Control for Deterministic Parallelism. In: Clarke, D., Noble, J., Wrigstad, T. (eds.) Aliasing in Object-Oriented Programming. LNCS, vol. 7850, pp. 156–195. Springer, Heidelberg (2013)
20. Boyapati, C.: SafeJava: A Unified Type System for Safe Programming. Ph.D., MIT (February 2004)
21. Boyapati, C., Lee, R., Rinard, M.C.: Ownership types for safe programming: preventing data races and deadlocks. In: OOPSLA, pp. 211–230 (2002)
22. Boyapati, C., Liskov, B., Shrira, L.: Ownership types for object encapsulation. In: POPL, pp. 213–223 (2003)
23. Boyapati, C., Liskov, B., Shrira, L., Moh, C.-H., Richman, S.: Lazy modular upgrades in persistent object stores. In: OOPSLA, pp. 403–417 (2003)
24. Boyapati, C., Rinard, M.C.: A parameterized type system for race-free Java programs. In: OOPSLA, pp. 56–69 (2001)
25. Boyapati, C., Salcianu, A., Beebee, W.S., Rinard, M.C.: Ownership types for safe region-based memory management in real-time Java. In: PLDI, pp. 324–337 (2003)
26. Boyland, J.: Alias burying: Unique variables without destructive reads. Software—Practice and Experience 31(6), 533–553 (2001)
27. Boyland, J.: Checking Interference with Fractional Permissions. In: Cousot, R. (ed.) SAS 2003. LNCS, vol. 2694, pp. 55–72. Springer, Heidelberg (2003)
28. Boyland, J.: Fractional Permissions. In: Clarke, D., Noble, J., Wrigstad, T. (eds.) Aliasing in Object-Oriented Programming. LNCS, vol. 7850, pp. 270–288. Springer, Heidelberg (2013)
29. Buckley, A.: Ownership types restrict aliasing. Master's thesis, Imperial College London, London, UK (June 2000)
30. Cameron, N.: Existential Types for Subtype Variance - Java Wildcards and Ownership Types. PhD thesis, Imperial College London (April 2009)
31. Cameron, N., Drossopoulou, S., Noble, J.: Understanding Ownership Types with Dependent Types. In: Clarke, D., Noble, J., Wrigstad, T. (eds.) Aliasing in Object-Oriented Programming. LNCS, vol. 7850, pp. 84–108. Springer, Heidelberg (2013)
32. Cameron, N., Drossopoulou, S.: Existential Quantification for Variant Ownership. In: Castagna, G. (ed.) ESOP 2009. LNCS, vol. 5502, pp. 128–142. Springer, Heidelberg (2009)
33. Cameron, N.R., Drossopoulou, S., Noble, J., Smith, M.J.: Multiple ownership. In: OOPSLA, pp. 441–460 (2007)
34. Cameron, N.R., Noble, J., Wrigstad, T.: Tribal ownership. In: OOPSLA, pp. 618–633 (2010)

35. Cardelli, L., Leroy, X.: Abstract types and the dot notation. Technical Report SRC-RR-90-56, Digital Systems Research Center (March 1990)
36. Cele, G., Stureborg, S.: Ownership types in practise. Master's thesis, Department of Computer and Systems Sciences, Stockholm University and Royal Institute of Technology (2005)
37. Charles, P., Grothoff, C., Saraswat, V.A., Donawa, C., Kielstra, A., Ebcioglu, K., von Praun, C., Sarkar, V.: X10: an object-oriented approach to non-uniform cluster computing. In: OOPSLA, pp. 519–538 (2005)
38. Chin, B., Markstrum, S., Millstein, T., Palsberg, J.: Inference of User-Defined Type Qualifiers and Qualifier Rules. In: Sestoft, P. (ed.) ESOP 2006. LNCS, vol. 3924, pp. 264–278. Springer, Heidelberg (2006)
39. Clarke, D.: Object ownership and containment. PhD thesis, School of Computer Science and Engineering, University of New South Wales, Australia (2002)
40. Clarke, D., Diakov, N., Hähnle, R., Johnsen, E.B., Schaefer, I., Schäfer, J., Schlatte, R., Wong, P.Y.H.: Modeling Spatial and Temporal Variability with the HATS Abstract Behavioral Modeling Language. In: Bernardo, M., Issarny, V. (eds.) SFM 2011. LNCS, vol. 6659, pp. 417–457. Springer, Heidelberg (2011)
41. Clarke, D., Drossopoulou, S., Noble, J., Wrigstad, T.: Tribe: a simple virtual class calculus. In: AOSD, pp. 121–134 (2007)
42. Clarke, D., Wrigstad, T.: External Uniqueness is Unique Enough. In: Cardelli, L. (ed.) ECOOP 2003. LNCS, vol. 2743, pp. 176–200. Springer, Heidelberg (2003)
43. Clarke, D., Wrigstad, T., Östlund, J., Johnsen, E.B.: Minimal Ownership for Active Objects. In: Ramalingam, G. (ed.) APLAS 2008. LNCS, vol. 5356, pp. 139–154. Springer, Heidelberg (2008)
44. Clarke, D.G., Drossopoulou, S.: Ownership, encapsulation and the disjointness of type and effect. In: OOPSLA, pp. 292–310 (2002)
45. Clarke, D.G., Noble, J., Potter, J.M.: Simple Ownership Types for Object Containment. In: Lindskov Knudsen, J. (ed.) ECOOP 2001. LNCS, vol. 2072, pp. 53–76. Springer, Heidelberg (2001)
46. Clarke, D.G., Potter, J., Noble, J.: Ownership types for flexible alias protection. In: OOPSLA, pp. 48–64 (1998)
47. Clarke, D.G., Richmond, M., Noble, J.: Saving the world from bad beans: deployment-time confinement checking. In: OOPSLA, pp. 374–387 (2003)
48. Clifton, C., Leavens, G.T., Noble, J.: MAO: Ownership and Effects for More Effective Reasoning About Aspects. In: Ernst, E. (ed.) ECOOP 2007. LNCS, vol. 4609, pp. 451–475. Springer, Heidelberg (2007)
49. Cousot, P., Cousot, R.: Abstract interpretation: a unified lattice model for static analysis of programs by construction or approximation of fixpoints. In: Sethi, R. (ed.) Proceedings of the Fourth Annual ACM Symposium on Principles of Programming Languages, Los Angeles, California, pp. 238–252 (January 1977)
50. Cousot, P., Cousot, R.: Systematic design of program analysis frameworks. In: Rosen, B.K. (ed.) Proceedings of the Sixth Annual ACM Symposium on Principles of Programming Languages, San Antonio, Texas, pp. 269–282 (January 1979)
51. Cunningham, D., Drossopoulou, S., Eisenbach, S.: Universe Types for Race Safety. In: VAMP 2007, pp. 20–51 (September 2007)
52. Deutsch, A.: Interprocedural alias analysis for pointers: Beyond k-limiting. In: Sarkar, V. (ed.) Proceedings of the ACM SIGPLAN 1994 Conference on Programming Languages Design and Implementation, Orlando, Florida, pp. 230–241 (June 1994)
53. Dietl, W., Drossopoulou, S., Müller, P.: Generic Universe Types. In: Ernst, E. (ed.) ECOOP 2007. LNCS, vol. 4609, pp. 28–53. Springer, Heidelberg (2007)

54. Dietl, W., Drossopoulou, S., Müller, P.: Separating ownership topology and encapsulation with generic universe types. ACM Trans. Program. Lang. Syst. 33(6), 20 (2011)
55. Dietl, W., Ernst, M.D., Müller, P.: Tunable Static Inference for Generic Universe Types. In: Mezini, M. (ed.) ECOOP 2011. LNCS, vol. 6813, pp. 333–357. Springer, Heidelberg (2011)
56. Dietl, W., Müller, P.: Universes: Lightweight ownership for JML. Journal of Object Technology 4(8), 5–32 (2005)
57. Dietl, W., Müller, P.: Runtime universe type inference. In: IWACO 2007: International Workshop on Aliasing, Confinement and Ownership in Object-Oriented Programming (2007)
58. Dietl, W., Müller, P.: Object Ownership in Program Verification. In: Clarke, D., Noble, J., Wrigstad, T. (eds.) Aliasing in Object-Oriented Programming. LNCS, vol. 7850, pp. 289–318. Springer, Heidelberg (2013)
59. Dietl, W., Müller, P., Poetzsch-Heffter, A.: A Type System for Checking Applet Isolation in Java Card. In: Barthe, G., Burdy, L., Huisman, M., Lanet, J.-L., Muntean, T. (eds.) CASSIS 2004. LNCS, vol. 3362, pp. 129–150. Springer, Heidelberg (2005)
60. Dietl, W.M.: Universe Types: Topology, Encapsulation, Genericity, and Tools. Ph.D., Department of Computer Science, ETH Zurich (December 2009); Doctoral Thesis ETH No. 18522
61. Drossopoulou, S., Clarke, D., Noble, J.: Types for Hierarchic Shapes (Summary). In: Sestoft, P. (ed.) ESOP 2006. LNCS, vol. 3924, pp. 1–6. Springer, Heidelberg (2006)
62. Eichberg, M., Kanthak, S., Kloppenburg, S., Mezini, M., Schuh, T.: Incremental confined types analysis. Electr. Notes Theor. Comput. Sci. 164(2), 81–96 (2006)
63. Fähndrich, M., DeLine, R.: Adoption and focus: Practical linear types for imperative programming. In: PLDI, pp. 13–24 (2002)
64. Flanagan, C., Abadi, M.: Types for Safe Locking. In: Swierstra, S.D. (ed.) ESOP 1999. LNCS, vol. 1576, pp. 91–108. Springer, Heidelberg (1999)
65. Fournet, C., Gonthier, G.: The Join Calculus: A Language for Distributed Mobile Programming. In: Barthe, G., Dybjer, P., Pinto, L., Saraiva, J. (eds.) APPSEM 2000. LNCS, vol. 2395, pp. 268–332. Springer, Heidelberg (2002)
66. Geilmann, K., Poetzsch-Heffter, A.: Modular Checking of Confinement for Object-Oriented Components using Abstract Interpretation. In: International Workshop on Aliasing, Confinement and Ownership in Object-Oriented Programming, IWACO 2011 (2011)
67. Gordon, D., Noble, J.: Dynamic ownership in a dynamic language. In: Costanza, P., Hirschfeld, R. (eds.) DLS 2007: Proceedings of the 2007 Symposium on Dynamic Languages, Montreal, Quebec, Canada, pp. 41–52 (2007)
68. Greenfieldboyce, D., Foster, J.S.: Type qualifier inference for Java. In: Bacon, D.F., Lopes, C.V., Steele Jr., G.L. (eds.) OOPSLA 2007: Proceedings of the 22nd Annual ACM SIGPLAN Conference on Object-Oriented Programming Systems, Languages and Applications, Montreal, Quebec, Canada, pp. 321–336 (2007)
69. Grothoff, C., Palsberg, J., Vitek, J.: Encapsulating objects with confined types. ACM Trans. Program. Lang. Syst. 29(6) (2007)
70. Hächler, T.: Applying the Universe type system to an industrial application. Master's thesis, ETH Zurich (2005), http://pm.inf.ethz.ch/projects/student_docs/Thomas_Haechler/Thomas_Haechler_MA_paper.pdf
71. Haller, P., Odersky, M.: Capabilities for Uniqueness and Borrowing. In: D'Hondt, T. (ed.) ECOOP 2010. LNCS, vol. 6183, pp. 354–378. Springer, Heidelberg (2010)

72. Harms, D.E., Weide, B.W.: Copying and swapping: influences on the design of reusable software components. IEEE Transactions on Software Engineering 17(5), 424–435 (1991)
73. Herrmann, S.: Confined Roles and Decapsulation in Object Teams — Contradiction or Synergy? In: Clarke, D., Noble, J., Wrigstad, T. (eds.) Aliasing in Object-Oriented Programming. LNCS, vol. 7850, pp. 443–470. Springer, Heidelberg (2013)
74. Hill, T., Noble, J., Potter, J.: Scalable visualisations with ownership trees. In: TOOLS, vol. (37), pp. 202–213 (2000)
75. Hill, T., Noble, J., Potter, J.: Visualizing the structure of object-oriented systems. In: VL, pp. 191–198 (2000)
76. Hill, T., Noble, J., Potter, J.: Scalable visualizations of object-oriented systems with ownership trees. J. Vis. Lang. Comput. 13(3), 319–339 (2002)
77. Hogg, J., Lea, D., Wills, A., de Champeaux, D., Holt, R.C.: The Geneva convention on the treatment of object aliasing. OOPS Messenger 3(2), 11–16 (1992)
78. Hogg, J., Lea, D., Wills, A., de Champeaux, D., Holt, R.C.: The Geneva Convention on the Treatment of Object Aliasing. In: Clarke, D., Noble, J., Wrigstad, T. (eds.) Aliasing in Object-Oriented Programming. LNCS, vol. 7850, pp. 7–14. Springer, Heidelberg (2013)
79. Huang, W., Dietl, W., Milanova, A., Ernst, M.D.: Inference and Checking of Object Ownership. In: Noble, J. (ed.) ECOOP 2012. LNCS, vol. 7313, pp. 181–206. Springer, Heidelberg (2012)
80. Huang, W., Milanova, A.: Towards efective inference and checking of ownership types. In: International Workshop on Aliasing, Confinement and Ownership in Object-Oriented Programming, IWACO 2011 (2011)
81. Jagannathan, S., Thiemann, P., Weeks, S., Wright, A.K.: Single and loving it: Must-alias analysis for higher-order languages. In: Cardelli, L. (ed.) POPL 1998: Proceedings of the 25th Annual ACM SIGPLAN-SIGACT Symposium on Principles of Programming Languages, San Diego, California, pp. 329–341 (January 1998)
82. Bocchino Jr., R.L., Adve, V.S.: Types, Regions, and Effects for Safe Programming with Object-Oriented Parallel Frameworks. In: Mezini, M. (ed.) ECOOP 2011. LNCS, vol. 6813, pp. 306–332. Springer, Heidelberg (2011)
83. Bocchino Jr., R.L., Adve, V.S., Dig, D., Adve, S.V., Heumann, S., Komuravelli, R., Overbey, J., Simmons, P., Sung, H., Vakilian, M.: A type and effect system for deterministic parallel Java. In: OOPSLA, pp. 97–116 (2009)
84. Bocchino Jr., R.L., Heumann, S., Honarmand, N., Adve, S.V., Adve, V.S., Welc, A., Shpeisman, T.: Safe nondeterminism in a deterministic-by-default parallel language. In: POPL, pp. 535–548 (2011)
85. Klebermaß, M.: An Isabelle Formalization of the Universe Type System. Master's thesis, Technische Universität München (April 2007)
86. Lindskov Knudsen, J. (ed.): ECOOP 2001. LNCS, vol. 2072. Springer, Heidelberg (2001)
87. Krishnaswami, N.R., Aldrich, J.: Permission-based ownership: encapsulating state in higher-order typed languages. In: PLDI, pp. 96–106 (2005)
88. Kulkarni, A., Liu, Y.D., Smith, S.F.: Task types for pervasive atomicity. In: OOPSLA, pp. 671–690 (2010)
89. Leijen, D., Meijer, E.: Domain specific embedded compilers. In: DSL, pp. 109–122 (1999)
90. Leino, K.R.M., Müller, P.: Object Invariants in Dynamic Contexts. In: Odersky, M. (ed.) ECOOP 2004. LNCS, vol. 3086, pp. 491–515. Springer, Heidelberg (2004)

91. Li, P., Cameron, N., Noble, J.: Mojojojo - more ownership for multiple owners. In: International Workshop on Foundations of Object-Oriented Languages, FOOL (2010)
92. Li, P., Nelson, S., Potanin, A.: Ownership for relationships. In: International Workshop on Aliasing, Confinement and Ownership in Object-Oriented Programming, IWACO 2009, pp. 1–3. ACM, New York (2009)
93. Liskov, B., Castro, M., Shrira, L., Adya, A.: Providing Persistent Objects in Distributed Systems. In: Guerraoui, R. (ed.) ECOOP 1999. LNCS, vol. 1628, pp. 230–257. Springer, Heidelberg (1999)
94. Liu, Y.D., Smith, S.F.: Interaction-based programming with classages. In: OOPSLA, pp. 191–209 (2005)
95. Lu, Y., Potter, J.: A Type System for Reachability and Acyclicity. In: Gao, X.-X. (ed.) ECOOP 2005. LNCS, vol. 3586, pp. 479–503. Springer, Heidelberg (2005)
96. Lu, Y., Potter, J.: On Ownership and Accessibility. In: Thomas, D. (ed.) ECOOP 2006. LNCS, vol. 4067, pp. 99–123. Springer, Heidelberg (2006)
97. Lu, Y., Potter, J.: Protecting representation with effect encapsulation. In: POPL, pp. 359–371 (2006)
98. Lu, Y., Potter, J., Xue, J.: Validity Invariants and Effects. In: Ernst, E. (ed.) ECOOP 2007. LNCS, vol. 4609, pp. 202–226. Springer, Heidelberg (2007)
99. Lu, Y., Potter, J., Xue, J.: Ownership Downgrading for Ownership Types. In: Hu, Z. (ed.) APLAS 2009. LNCS, vol. 5904, pp. 144–160. Springer, Heidelberg (2009)
100. Ma, K.-K., Foster, J.S.: Inferring aliasing and encapsulation properties for Java. In: Bacon, D.F., Lopes, C.V., Steele Jr., G.L. (eds.) OOPSLA 2007: Proceedings of the 22nd Annual ACM SIGPLAN Conference on Object-Oriented Programming Systems, Languages and Applications, Montreal, Quebec, Canada, pp. 423–440 (2007)
101. Milanova, A., Liu, Y.: Practical static ownership inference. Technical report, Rensselaer Polytechnic Institute, Troy NY 12110, USA (2010)
102. Milanova, A., Vitek, J.: Static Dominance Inference. In: Bishop, J., Vallecillo, A. (eds.) TOOLS 2011. LNCS, vol. 6705, pp. 211–227. Springer, Heidelberg (2011)
103. Mitchell, N.: The Runtime Structure of Object Ownership. In: Thomas, D. (ed.) ECOOP 2006. LNCS, vol. 4067, pp. 74–98. Springer, Heidelberg (2006)
104. Moelius III, S.E., Souter, A.L.: An object ownership inference algorithm and its applications. In: MASPLAS 2004: Mid-Atlantic Student Workshop on Programming Languages and Systems (2004)
105. Müller, P., Poetzsch-Heffter, A.: Universes: a type system for controlling representation exposure. In: Programming Languages and Fundamentals of Programming. Fernuniversität Hagen (1999)
106. Müller, P., Poetzsch-Heffter, A., Leavens, G.T.: Modular invariants for layered object structures. Science of Computer Programming 62, 253–286 (2006)
107. Müller, P.: Modular Specification and Verification of Object-Oriented Programs. LNCS, vol. 2262. Springer, Heidelberg (2002)
108. Müller, P., Rudich, A.: Ownership transfer in universe types. In: Proceedings of the 22nd Annual ACM SIGPLAN Conference on Object-Oriented Programming Systems and Applications, OOPSLA 2007, pp. 461–478. ACM, New York (2007)
109. Nägeli, S.: Ownership in design patterns. Master's thesis, ETH Zurich (2006), http://pm.inf.ethz.ch/projects/student_docs/Stefan_Naegeli/Stefan_Naegeli_MA_paper.pdf
110. Noble, J., Biddle, R., Tempero, E., Potanin, A., Clarke, D.: Towards a model of encapsulation. In: IWACO 2003: International Workshop on Aliasing, Confinement and Ownership in Object-Oriented Programming, Darmstadt, Germany (2003)

111. Noble, J., Clarke, D.G., Potter, J.: Object ownership for dynamic alias protection. In: TOOLS, vol. (32), pp. 176–187 (1999)
112. Noble, J., Vitek, J., Potter, J.: Flexible Alias Protection. In: Jul, E. (ed.) ECOOP 1998. LNCS, vol. 1445, pp. 158–185. Springer, Heidelberg (1998)
113. Östlund, J., Wrigstad, T.: Multiple Aggregate Entry Points for Ownership Types. In: Noble, J. (ed.) ECOOP 2012. LNCS, vol. 7313, pp. 156–180. Springer, Heidelberg (2012)
114. Östlund, J., Wrigstad, T., Clarke, D., Åkerblom, B.: Ownership, uniqueness, and immutability. In: TOOLS, vol. (46), pp. 178–197 (2008)
115. Patrignani, M., Clarke, D., Sangiorgi, D.: Ownership Types for the Join Calculus. In: Bruni, R., Dingel, J. (eds.) FMOODS/FORTE 2011. LNCS, vol. 6722, pp. 289–303. Springer, Heidelberg (2011)
116. Permandla, P., Roberson, M., Boyapati, C.: A type system for preventing data races and deadlocks in the Java virtual machine language. In: LCTES, pp. 1–10 (2007)
117. Poetzsch-Heffter, A., Geilmann, K., Schäfer, J.: Infering Ownership Types for Encapsulated Object-Oriented Program Components. In: Reps, T., Sagiv, M., Bauer, J. (eds.) Wilhelm Festschrift. LNCS, vol. 4444, pp. 120–144. Springer, Heidelberg (2007)
118. Potanin, A., Noble, J., Biddle, R.: Checking ownership and confinement. Concurrency and Computation: Practice and Experience 16(7), 671–687 (2004)
119. Potanin, A., Noble, J., Clarke, D., Biddle, R.: Featherweight generic confinement. J. Funct. Program. 16(6), 793–811 (2006)
120. Potanin, A., Noble, J., Clarke, D., Biddle, R.: Generic ownership for Generic Java. In: OOPSLA, pp. 311–324 (2006)
121. Potanin, A., Östlund, J., Zibin, Y., Ernst, M.D.: Immutability. In: Clarke, D. (ed.) Aliasing in Object-Oriented Programming. LNCS, vol. 7850, pp. 233–269. Springer, Heidelberg (2013)
122. Potter, J., Noble, J., Clarke, D.G.: The ins and outs of objects. In: Australian Software Engineering Conference, pp. 80–89 (1998)
123. Rayside, D., Mendel, L.: Object ownership profiling: a technique for finding and fixing memory leaks. In: ASE, pp. 194–203 (2007)
124. Schaefer, J., Poetzsch-Heffter, A.: A parameterized type system for simple loose ownership domains. Journal of Object Technology 6(5), 71–100 (2007)
125. Schäfer, J., Poetzsch-Heffter, A.: CoBoxes: Unifying Active Objects and Structured Heaps. In: Barthe, G., de Boer, F.S. (eds.) FMOODS 2008. LNCS, vol. 5051, pp. 201–219. Springer, Heidelberg (2008)
126. Schäfer, J., Poetzsch-Heffter, A.: JCoBox: Generalizing Active Objects to Concurrent Components. In: D'Hondt, T. (ed.) ECOOP 2010. LNCS, vol. 6183, pp. 275–299. Springer, Heidelberg (2010)
127. Sergey, I., Clarke, D.: Gradual Ownership Types. In: Seidl, H. (ed.) ESOP 2012. LNCS, vol. 7211, pp. 579–599. Springer, Heidelberg (2012)
128. Skalka, C., Smith, S.F.: Static use-based object confinement. Int. J. Inf. Sec. 4(1-2), 87–104 (2005)
129. Spring, J.H., Pizlo, F., Privat, J., Guerraoui, R., Vitek, J.: Reflexes: Abstractions for integrating highly responsive tasks into Java applications. ACM Trans. Embedded Comput. Syst. 10(1) (2010)
130. Spring, J.H., Privat, J., Guerraoui, R., Vitek, J.: Streamflex: High-throughput stream programming in Java. In: OOPSLA, pp. 211–228 (2007)
131. Srinivasan, S., Mycroft, A.: Kilim: Isolation-Typed Actors for Java. In: Vitek, J. (ed.) ECOOP 2008. LNCS, vol. 5142, pp. 104–128. Springer, Heidelberg (2008)

132. Stroustrup, B.: The C++ Programming Language, 3rd edn. Addison-Wesley Longman Publishing Co., Inc., Boston (2000)
133. Tang, D., Plsek, A., Vitek, J.: Static checking of safety critical Java annotations. In: JTRES, pp. 148–154 (2010)
134. Tofte, M., Talpin, J.-P.: Region-based memory management. Inf. Comput. 132(2), 109–176 (1997)
135. Vanciu, R., Abi-Antoun, M.: Object Graphs with Ownership Domains: An Empirical Study. In: Clarke, D., Noble, J., Wrigstad, T. (eds.) Aliasing in Object-Oriented Programming. LNCS, vol. 7850, pp. 109–155. Springer, Heidelberg (2013)
136. Vitek, J., Bokowski, B.: Confined types. In: OOPSLA, pp. 82–96 (1999)
137. Vitek, J., Bokowski, B.: Confined types in Java. Softw., Pract. Exper. 31(6), 507–532 (2001)
138. Wang, S., Barbosa, L.S., Oliveira, J.N.: A relational model for confined separation logic. In: TASE, pp. 263–270 (2008)
139. Wang, S., Qiu, Z.: A generic model for confinement and its application. In: TASE, pp. 57–64 (2008)
140. Wren, A.: Inferring ownership. Master's thesis, Imperial College London, London, UK (June 2003)
141. Wrigstad, T.: Ownership-Based Alias Management. PhD thesis, Royal Institute of Technology, Kista, Stockholm (May 2006)
142. Wrigstad, T., Clarke, D.: Existential owners for ownership types. Journal of Object Technology 6(4), 141–159 (2007)
143. Wrigstad, T., Pizlo, F., Meawad, F., Zhao, L., Vitek, J.: Loci: Simple Thread-Locality for Java. In: Drossopoulou, S. (ed.) ECOOP 2009. LNCS, vol. 5653, pp. 445–469. Springer, Heidelberg (2009)
144. Smith, S., Liu, Y.D.: Pedigree types. In: IWACO 2008: International Workshop on Aliasing, Confinement and Ownership in Object-Oriented Programming (2008)
145. Zhao, T., Baker, J., Hunt, J., Noble, J., Vitek, J.: Implicit ownership types for memory management. Sci. Comput. Program. 71(3), 213–241 (2008)
146. Zhao, T., Noble, J., Vitek, J.: Scoped types for real-time Java. In: RTSS, pp. 241–251 (2004)
147. Zhao, T., Palsberg, J., Vitek, J.: Lightweight confinement for featherweight Java. In: OOPSLA, pp. 135–148 (2003)
148. Zhao, T., Palsberg, J., Vitek, J.: Type-based confinement. J. Funct. Program. 16(1), 83–128 (2006)
149. Zhao, Y., Boyland, J.: A fundamental permission interpretation for ownership types. In: TASE, pp. 65–72 (2008)
150. Zibin, Y., Potanin, A., Li, P., Ali, M., Ernst, M.D.: Ownership and immutability in Generic Java. In: OOPSLA, pp. 598–617 (2010)

Notions of Aliasing and Ownership

Alan Mycroft and Janina Voigt

Computer Laboratory, University of Cambridge
William Gates Building, JJ Thomson Avenue,
Cambridge CB3 0FD, UK
Firstname.Lastname@cl.cam.ac.uk

Abstract. We survey notions of aliasing and ownership. An extreme but conceptually useful model is that of pure linear languages where each object is constructed once and read, being consumed, once. We see more realistic programming languages as relaxing this to allow multiple references to an object (spatial aliasing) or multiple sequenced operations on a single live reference (temporal aliasing) before the object is deallocated. Concurrency complicates things (concurrent aliasing) because spatial aliasing may only happen under certain scheduling conditions. We argue that this view of aliasing is closely related to that of type tags in low-level implementations of dynamic types.

Similarly, we argue that ownership corresponds to a higher-level structured view of the net of objects and references, analogous to higher-level types in programming languages. In the same way that not all high-level data-structure consistency requirements can be captured by existing practical syntactic type forms, not all aliasing requirements can be captured by existing syntactic forms of aliasing control (uniqueness, owners-as-dominators, owners-as-modifiers and static capabilities), each of which is successful in a limited domain.

We conclude by arguing for a more holistic approach to the topic of aliasing and ownership.

1 Introduction

The benefits of aliasing are well-known and centre on the idea of mutable data structures—updating an object with one hundred references to it can replace one hundred separate updates. However, this is at the same time the largest source of software engineering problems—how do we ensure all these updates were intentional as opposed to corrupting data intended or assumed to be immutable by a separate programmer? Or, to put it more strongly, how do we tame aliasing and mutability to keep their efficiency advantages while allowing software to grow without becoming a victim of alias-based software rust? The central issue is that while mutation operations are clearly manifest in programming languages, aliasing is not.

Even without aliasing, concurrency combined with mutability adds further, similar, problems to those produced by aliasing. Two accesses to the same

D. Clarke et al. (Eds.): Aliasing in Object-Oriented Programming, LNCS 7850, pp. 59–83, 2013.

variable[1] in different threads in general produces race conditions which make programs non-deterministic at best (and more likely to contain subtle hard-to-reproduce bugs).

Of course, when mutability, aliasing and concurrency all may be combined (as in many modern programming languages), it is increasingly possible to construct hard-to-reason-about programs which rapidly attract software rust.

The Hogg et al. "Geneva Convention" [1] deconstructed issues arising from aliasing into four guideline concepts (quoting from the paper):

Detection. Static or dynamic (run-time) diagnosis of potential or actual aliasing.

Advertisement. Annotations that help modularize detection by declaring aliasing properties of methods.

Prevention. Constructs that disallow aliasing in a statically checkable fashion.

Control. Methods that isolate the effects of aliasing.

We would emphasise that aliasing *per se* is not the problem, but the unstructured use of mutation via aliases to produce complex side-effects beyond comfortable reasoning. For example, a dispatcher which serially invokes well-specified operations on a shared mutable data structure may well be unproblematic even though each of these operations have aliases to the data structure.

A particular focus in this work is the dynamic/static interplay of aliasing and its control. For example types may be checked at run-time or at compile-time, but the form of properties which are easy to check differ significantly. (It is difficult to express and to check 'every array element indexed by a prime is a boolean' statically, and difficult to express dynamically 'this reference will never again be used to access a given object' dynamically; vice versa both are reasonable possible.) Similarly an object only having a unique pointer to it or being used only once is naturally checked dynamically, but being of linear type is a static notion. Capabilities also exist in both dynamic forms (e.g. 'check access via *this reference* is valid') and static forms (e.g. 'access via *this variable* at this program point promises no concurrent access').

We structure our discussion as follows: Section 2 considers language forms, the effects of aliasing and the additional concurrent and distributed-memory effects of multi-core processors. Section 3 returns to the theme of temporal and spatial aliasing. Section 4 makes a detailed analysis of aliasing and ownership comparing them with similar phenomena in low-level dynamic types and higher-level types. Section 5 turns to existing examples of how to represent ownership syntactically (uniqueness, owners-as-dominators, owners-as-modifiers and static capabilities) followed by reviewing real-world implementations. Section 6 gives a higher-level comparative view while Section 7 concludes.

---

[1] For a variable to be accessed by two different threads it must be a global (static) variable and such variables can be thought as fields of a single object to which both threads have pointers. So, at a formal level, data races always involve aliasing.

2   Languages, Aliasing and Processors

We start by considering two extremes: core object-oriented programming and pure functional programming. In the former everything is an object, objects have state and hence identity, fields of any object may refer to any other object, and methods update the state (both local and that reachable via references) either explicitly or by calling other methods. The potential for 'mutable spaghetti data' based on unconstrained references leads to many authors citing *encapsulation* (e.g. Pierce [2]) as a principle in object-oriented design. We return to potential syntactic expression of encapsulation later, but note additionally that the core model assumes that object placement in memory is irrelevant—an assumption which no longer holds for non-uniform or distributed memory architectures.

Pure functional programming by contrast disavows any form of side-effect including mutation. Therefore, assuming that data structures are held in some form of memory, there is no semantic difference between two references to a single data structure and references to two copies of that data structure. While the additional reasoning power thereby gained is very useful there is a theoretical loss of efficiency. Given two lists of length bounded by n, their intersection (list of objects occurring as members of both argument lists) can be computed in $O(n)$ time if the objects are mutable but only in $O(n^2)$ time otherwise.[2]

Lazy functional languages add an interesting twist. While the language itself is referentially transparent, implementations need to suspend evaluations and then later to evaluate them only when demanded. This generally implies use of a mutable and often aliased data structure—the *thunk* [3], which either holds an unevaluated expression or its value after evaluation, effectively behaving as a mutable object with identity. This has consequences for their implementation on non-uniform or distributed memory architectures—see later.

Concurrency and parallelism, for example in the guise of modern multi-core processors, further enrich the above landscape. Indeed any object shared between two threads and mutated by at least one of them brings the risk of introducing races and hence non-determinism as opposed to the core deterministic semantics of most modern object-oriented languages. The traditional solution to this is *locking*. However, programming with locks is very error prone in the same way as aliasing: the semantic effects of locking or its absence manifest themselves in source-code places far from the lock itself.

When a single-core processor is replaced by multi-core, then distributed memory effects also come to the fore. For example local caching of a shared global memory requires a memory model to be specified; this is often non-sequentially-consistent (i.e. parallel instruction streams have additional possible behaviours beyond simple interleaving) [4] and the cache possibly even non-coherent (i.e. different processors may see different values for the same memory location) [5]. Locking is much more expensive than on a single CPU and the cache structure means that sharing memory across processors effectively involves repeated message passing.

---

[2] Given a hashing mechanism and sorting lists by their integer hash, or a function implementing some total order on elements, reduces this time to $O(n \log n)$.

Garbage collection adds further issues. Unless we are interested in real-time guarantees such as bounded latency for memory allocation, on a single processor there is little benefit from concurrent garbage collection—switching to the garbage collection task causes cache-flushing effects which serve to slow the overall computation. Multi-core computers potentially provide speed-up by allowing several cores to co-operate during garbage collection ('parallel GC') or allowing one or more cores to garbage collect while the application threads, often known as the mutator threads, continue to compute ('concurrent GC', originated by Dijkstra et al. [6]). Whatever the source language, low-level implementations of concurrent or parallel collectors involve concurrent access to shared mutable state (a garbage collector needs to mark objects as it traverses reachable objects). In general this requires expensive locking operations, but various papers explore partitioning the heap to avoid concurrent access to an object by multiple cores (see Oancea et al. [7] and its citations). Note that if the source language can express limits on aliasing (e.g. that a data structure is tree-like) then the garbage collector can take advantage of this by increasing the granularity of locking. An interesting data point here is the Harris et al. work on implementing Haskell on a shared-memory multiprocessor [8]. This notes that in a pure functional programming language a garbage collector can exploit the fact that a copy of a value is still equal to the value; hence the 'test if marked' and 'mark object' operations do not have to be locked. The reason is that the low-probability race condition merely causes semantically-invisible object duplication—this trades an expensive lock on every path into an infrequent object duplication.

Alternatives to garbage collection include reference counting (really only applicable to acyclic portions of the heap) and region-based storage allocation (which can free non-escaping local allocations on exit from a block, but which require significant program analysis or annotation) [9]. Garbage collectors implicitly identify the set of references to a given object during garbage collection (its potential set of owners) and indeed reference-counting garbage collection can be easily adapted to maintain such a list throughout execution.

2.1 Concurrency

While we briefly mentioned concurrency in respect of multi-core processors and garbage collection above, for much of the period of evolution of object-oriented and functional languages concurrency was a side-issue. Yes, some applications, for example event-driven ones, could be expressed neatly concurrently. However, the concurrency in event-driven programs is more predictable than interrupt-driven thread switching as it typically happens synchronously. Additionally there was no real incentive to program concurrently as on a single processor this gave no speed-up over a single thread; moreover objects and libraries were often not thread-safe.

As discussed above, multi-core processors and distributed systems obliged programmers to be more aware of concurrency and its issues. Mycroft discusses the interaction of object-oriented design and multi-core processors [10].

There is an interesting connection between the problems of software engineering for threaded programs and those of reasoning about concurrent behaviour. When a large sequential software system is very dependent on the precise form and ordering of its statements, we regard it as likely to have software rust. We often use type-like ideas such as *readonly parameters*, or data structures being only *borrowed* by a caller, to document or preferably enforce (e.g. Aldrich et al. [11]) this design requirement constraining the coupling between different components. The idea then is that the program is less rusty because the reduced coupling imposes fewer constraints on the ordering of individual actions. This is very similar to the concurrency expectation that separate threads have their actions performed with few constraints on inter-thread execution ordering, so techniques which address software rust in sequential systems and correct behaviour in concurrent systems (and indeed correct behaviour in multi-core non-sequentially-consistent memory) have many ideas in common.

It is worth observing that, in the absence of concurrency, a method call is effectively a *transaction* which completes before the following transaction. However, two concurrent method calls may interleave their internal effects in any order (or indeed on multi-core processors produce non-sequentially-consistent composite effects other than those obtained by interleaving). Locking of course can address this, choosing how many locks to use and where to take them, is something which needs precise documentation of which ordering of effects are allowed, which in turn requires detailed knowledge of aliasing.

One model of computation which seems particularly suited to modern multi-core processors, or in general to distributed-memory systems, is the Actor model. While Agha's formalisation of Actors [12] only concerned pure values being transmitted by message passing between computational entities, this generalises easily into a set of processes acting on disjoint regions of memory (memory isolation) regardless of whether underlying processors have physically shared memory or not. The Actor model was popularised by Erlang [13], which has no mutable data structures. However note that no concurrency problems arise, either semantically or in mapping to multi-core processors, in having mutability of process-local memory *provided* the memory-isolation property is maintained (when a mutable data structure is transferred between processors then the sender makes no further access to it). Memory isolation further enables per-thread (and hence per-core) garbage collection. In effect we allow concurrency but garbage collection, and aliasing and mutability problems are kept thread-local and sequential—back into a safer pre-concurrency object-oriented world!

3   Linearity, Temporal and Spatial Aliasing

Girard's Linear Logic [14] is a sub-structural logic[3] which refines the operators of conjunction and disjunction into multiplicative and additive variants. The

---

[3] In a conventional logic, we may use an assumption many times or simply discard it. Formally this is achieved by having *structural rules* along with rules like *modus ponens* for reasoning. Sub-structural logics restrict structural rules, which causes assumptions to behave like resources, e.g. to be required to be used exactly once.

introduction rule for multiplicative conjunction ($\otimes$) requires assumptions to be used by exactly one of the left and right conjuncts.

Intuitionistic Propositional Linear Logic (a sublogic of Linear Logic) has an interesting term calculus by the Curry-Howard (programs as proofs, types as formulae) correspondence—this refines the original Curry-Howard correspondence which relates Intuitionistic Propositional Logic to the typed λ-calculus. Various programming constructs [15,16] have been designed which give syntax to the resource notions arising from $\otimes$ in linear logic. The key idea, however, is that in a pure linear type system a value is created and bound to a variable, this variable is then used exactly once[4] dynamically in the ensuing computation (for example in an if-then-else its use in the then and else branches must be identical). An *affine* type system simply requires a variable to be used at most once, but the effect can be also be achieved within a linear system using a primitive which consumes a value and returns no result.

Linearly typed languages have implicit garbage collection—creating a value allocates it and reading consumes it thereby deallocating it

There are two ways we can relax the notion of linearity which, for discussion purposes, we will call *temporal* and *spatial* aliasing. The former allows a value held in a variable to be used several times during its lifetime (of course it is now important that all its uses, except possibly its last use, do not deallocate the memory used to hold the value). Spatial aliasing is the more standard use of the word 'aliasing' and refers to the existence of two or more live references to the same value at a given time.

This separation is interesting to us because it allows various concepts to be brought together. For example the repeated use of a value in temporal aliasing corresponds to Kobayashi's quasi-linear types [17]; this is closely related to the idea of Typestate [18] in which a type system is enriched to capture the allowable operations on an object-like value—for example that a File object only permits a read operation when the file is open.

Another example representing analysis and optimisation based on determining temporal aliasing is Wansbrough and Peyton-Jones' work on *usage analysis* for Haskell [19]; this is closely related to Typestate. We note that a Haskell thunk is first created, on each read it is first checked for having been evaluated, if so its value payload is used directly, otherwise the suspended expression appearing as its payload is evaluated and overwrites the payload marking the thunk as evaluated. Many of these operations are redundant if we know (i) the thunk is only used once (no need to overwrite the thunk payload) or (ii) if we know the thunk has definitely previously been evaluated (no need to test the 'evaluated' flag).

Concurrency adds further complexity: a data structure may have spatial aliasing on some executions and not on others. We refer to this situation as *concurrent*

---

[4] A subtlety concerns non-terminating computation (which does not correspond to a proof in linear logic but we nonetheless wish to model); it is appropriate to regard a program as using a variable linearly if it uses the variable at most once on every execution path, and exactly once on every terminating path.

aliasing. In systems which possess both temporal and concurrent aliasing, a particularly noteworthy idea is that we can regard the number of live references to an object as part of its state. In just the same way that a File only permits a read when it is open, we might wish to avoid data races by only permitting an object to be mutated when it has only one reference or no other concurrent thread can access it.

3.1 Liveness and Aliasing

We often assume that the word 'alias' has a precise meaning. However one often sees qualification with the word 'live' as above (e.g. 'a single live reference'). We now discuss whether some references should not count as aliases; this is important for linking semantic models of execution with (e.g.) aliases being *borrowed* or *unique*—see later.

For many purposes it is natural to consider the state of an object-oriented program as a heap—where each node is an allocated object and each references is an edge—along with a set of variables pointing into the heap. The state evolves with time, perhaps non-deterministically if concurrency is involved. An object is aliased if it has multiple references (or variables pointing) to it. However, this model is inadequate for many aliasing purposes in that it treats the program as a simple black-box automaton. Firstly certain aliases come and go along with the structure of the program and its execution—for example invoking a method often creates aliases for each of its parameters, these aliases are discarded on return. Secondly, a variable (or a reference from an object) which aliases an object but which is semantically dead—in the sense that no future evolution of the program ever uses it—can be treated as no longer being an alias from the point it becomes dead. Similarly, such a variable which is temporarily inaccessible (perhaps a local variable on the stack belonging to a non-current method) can be regarded as not forming an alias during its inaccessibilty.

It is important when discussing aliasing (or its spatial or temporal variants) to review the context as to whether dead or inaccessible variables count as aliases.

4 What Is Ownership?

This section explores how the various issues discussed above can be structured for programming language use. It is important to separate two notions: one is the low-level details of what an operation does (this often concerns efficiency), and the other is the human-level means of structuring such operations (this concerns the ability to reason about code and the amenability of code to modification). In terms of the topic of this book, the low-level concepts are those of aliasing and locking (discussed briefly in previous sections), and the higher-level concept that of *ownership*, which helps programmers make sense of aliasing and assists them in structuring object relationships and aliasing references in their programs. Note that here we understand 'ownership' as an abstract concept comparable with 'set of entities of a particular form' or that of 'a binary tree being balanced', while a particular programming language determines how (and to what extent) such concepts can be expressed syntactically by the user, e.g. as types, and checked by machine.

Ownership introduces the concept of an object's owner (or owners)—objects which enjoy privileged access to a given object. This could, for example, mean that the owners have exclusive write access to the object they own or that they are the only parts of the system allowed to access the object in any way. Ownership need not be constant throughout an object's lifetime, but can generally be transferred. Since ownership is a concept taken directly from the real world, it is easy to understand and intuitive for programmers; however only certain forms of ownership have been neatly incorporated into programming languages.

One advantage of ownership is that it helps programmers structure software in a way that limits and controls aliasing. It gives them a way to reason about which objects should have access to which other objects, forcing them to think about the semantics of object relationships. For each object, programmers have to answer questions like: who is allowed to access this object? Is it shared by many parts of the system or should access be restricted to a small subset? Does the owner of the object change during execution and, if so, under which circumstances?

Syntactic support for ownership in programming languages further documents the structure developed by programmers and can help enforce it either statically or at run-time. The existence, documentation and enforcement of the ownership structure in turn supports program evolution and prevents software rust. Documenting the ownership structure makes the complex net of references easier to understand; enforcing ownership and the associated restrictions on aliasing minimises bugs (and rust leading to future bugs) introduced by small changes to the code.

An apparent disadvantage of existing static ownership systems is that, unlike type systems in statically typed languages, they are effectively optional—programmers can often merely annotate all objects as *world* to avoid the additional mental burden of ownership and the additional hurdle static of ownership in program design evolution [20].

4.1 Digression: Values and Types

Before discussing the nature of ownership in more detail, first briefly consider the analogy of types in programming languages. While very low-level languages, e.g. assembler or BCPL [21], have only one data type (an n-bit bitstring which is interpreted appropriately to its use in an instruction), most languages associate a type with a value. This might be an integer, a string, or some form of compound value such as a record. A *strongly typed* language will only allow operations appropriate to a value to take place and otherwise generate an exception. This is logically achieved by regarding every value as consisting of a tag describing the type of the value (integer, string, record etc.) followed by the value itself. This is exactly the model adopted by *dynamically typed languages* such as Lisp, Prolog, Python, Javascript. Note there is one subtlety which concerns our central topic of mutability and aliasing and for which such languages may differ. It is quite normal for a *variable* first to contain an integer value and later a string value. However, not all languages support the idea of a given *value* (it is more convenient to regard this as an *object* now given that we impute it identity) changing its type. For example, if x and y refer to the same record value, then can an operator update x to replace field f with field g and, if so, then does the value of y also change? Or even more subtly, if the value of y does not reflect this update then might future modifications of field h of x be still reflected in y? Similar issues recur when we discuss parallels in ownership below.

The previous paragraph used the word 'type' as in 'dynamically typed' to refer to the type of a value—this is associated with its tag. Such types are largely machine-oriented. Many programming languages provide high-level types, for example to define Lists, Trees, DAGs and the like. This has two advantages: one is high-level structuring (we can distinguish the pairing operation used to prepend a value to a list from that used to construct a new tree node from two existing trees avoiding problems involving 'dotted pairs' at the end of Lisp lists), the other is machine efficiency—if high-level types can be expressed statically (and the type system is strongly typed) then at each use of a value we already know its dynamic type and hence tags need not be stored as part of objects. Such statically and strongly typed languages are very common (Java, Ada and the like). C is an exception as it is statically typed but not strongly typed (implementations typically do not store type tags, and hence some programs have *undefined behaviour*). There are a couple of issues to note about high-level types: firstly, invariants anticipated by the user are not always expressible in the type system (for example in Java the user can not model the difference between Trees and DAGs in the type system—researchers have adapted models such as separation logic [22] to this end). Secondly, it is possible to have to have high-level types and to check all or part of them dynamically; (software) *contracts* (see Rosenblum et al. [23,24]) exemplify this. Finally, note that our discussion has avoided interpreting 'statically typed' as the opposite of 'dynamically typed'— instead we have focused on the distinction between low-level types (which are close to traditional dynamic typing) and higher-level types (which are naturally statically checked).

4.2   References and Ownership

Inspired by the previous section, we now draw a parallel between *references* and values and between *ownership* and types. The idea is that ownership represents the same flavour of high-level structure as types, and questions about the number of references to an object are analogous to those concerning the low-level type tag of an object. The range of concepts for ownership is potentially as rich and varied as that for type systems. Seeing ownership as potentially being any binary relation which either holds or does not hold for every pair of objects (perhaps even reified as in Bierman and Wren's first-class relationships [25]) gives a huge universe of possible dynamic ownership techniques.

One particular idea discussed in the previous section is that of an operation on an object preserving its identity but changing its type as seen by other referrers. At the lowest level this is exactly what happens in a reference-counting implementation when a further referring alias is added to an object—all aliases seen the new reference count.

However, just as not all possible machine-level type combinations are sensible to adopt as higher-level type systems (e.g. consider a list which contains integers at prime positions and strings at non-prime positions), not all ownership relationships are sensible as higher-level notions. Nonetheless, we should not be over-hasty to rule out an ownership system which appears expensive when seen as a relation (perhaps 'cancel ownership for any other referrer'); there may be other implementations including static checking.

Most ownership designs have been programming-language oriented, for example those to ensure that no live references remain when an object is deallocated, or those to ensure that a `rep` object is properly encapsulated and only used by the interface object.

To obtain another perspective on what ownership might mean let us consider two financial examples: one where I share a bank account with a chequebook and one where I share a credit card. These have evolved differently in that joint bank accounts tend to be symmetric ('either to sign' or 'both to sign') whereas credit cards tend to have a 'cardholder' and one or more 'additional cardholders' with reduced rights. Both-to-sign accounts represent a relatively race-free situation (assuming messages do not overtake each other to avoid a 'close account' action overtaking a final cheque transaction) but one which appears hard to model using existing static techniques. Either-to-sign accounts are of course full of race conditions when one user closes an account concurrently with another writing a cheque.

Credit cards, perhaps representing more modern legal convenience, provide a single owner 'the cardholder' who takes responsibility for all transactions. An additional cardholder is provided with a card which has a separate identity (and indeed PIN) but, at least in the UK, shares the same account number. The separate levels of capability (authorising the cards via chip-and-pin versus authorising accounts) seems to fit more closely with hierarchical ownership: the cardholder owns both the account and the additional cardholder as peers. Both the account and the additional cardholder own cards.

For an existing bank account or credit card, we may also need to transfer ownership, either by adding a new owner or removing an existing owner. For bank accounts, ownership transfer is a transaction adding and/or removing one or more owners. However, for credit cards this is typically treated as account closure and creating a new account.

One exceptional action concerns the death of an owner; national laws identify one or more people or organisations to wind down the account tidily before distributing any net surplus.

The financial examples above illustrate several important issues in the context of ownership. Firstly, it shows that in the real world there are instances of *multiple ownership.* Although in many cases objects are owned by a single person, accounts are one example where sharing of ownership is common and necessary.

In addition, the credit card example demonstrates that there may be multiple owners with different access rights. In software, it is often useful to restrict write access to a particular owner object but allow read access to occur more widely. This is an example of multiple ownership where different owners enjoy different access privileges.

Given the occurrence of multiple ownership in the real world, this is probably something we want our aliasing systems to support, enabling us to model things like shared bank accounts more easily. Multiple ownership is also necessary to implement some common programming idioms such as iterators. When we have a collection of items, we usually want to model the collection as owning the items; if we then want an iterator to have privileged access to the items in the collection, including traversal and modification rights, the iterator also requires ownership of the items (Boyapati et al. [26] gives more details).

The examples also show that ownership is not necessarily constant throughout the lifetime of an object. In fact, in the real world it is common for ownership transfer to occur, for example when adding and removing bank account owners. Again, this is something ownership systems should support to enable us to model ownership transfer in the real world.

Dual to the concept of ownership transfer of an object while retaining its identity is that of moving an object while retaining ownership. If a multi-core processor provides non-uniform memory then in general we wish to process data near to, or cheapest to access from, the processor working with the object. However, only some forms of ownership provide the ability to move an object: certainly unique ownership suffices as it makes call-by-reference and call-by-copy equivalent and hence moving an object preserves its identity (even though its address changes). In addition an object which is immutable (by ownership guarantees) may be cloned to multiple immutable copies; the only proviso is we must pick either the original object or exactly one of the clones, making the others inaccessible, if we wish to recover a single full-permission object for later use.

In passing we note that cloning an object, mutating disjoint components of the original and the copy, and then somehow rejoining the copies into a single coherent result might require 'field-sensitive' notions of ownership (e.g. one task owning fields f_1 and f_2 of object o while a second owns fields g_1 and g_2).

Finally, while the next section discusses locks in more detail, let us note that ownership and need-to-lock are rather orthogonal concepts; the only exception is that a method which holds the only reference to an object need not lock it even in the presence of concurrency—indeed an analysis which guarantees 'no other reference' can be used to optimise away lock operations for performance benefits.

4.3   Ownership Ideas from Operating Systems

In addition to forms of ownership inspired by pointer topology, operating systems encompass various implicit forms of ownership based on access control. Typically these are based on properly controlling concurrent access (e.g. avoiding data races in favour of structured transactions).

For example, virtual memory provides the ability to restrict access to a physical page on a per-process basis. Some processes might be allowed to read and write, others can only read the data and yet others have all access forbidden.

Similarly, even when there are several processes each having read-write access to an area of memory, we may need to control access (i.e. demand exclusive ownership temporarily) by locks or more syntactically structured techniques such as monitors. Typical locking forms allow restricting entry to a critical region by

- just one process (exclusive access);
- one writer process or multiple reader processes;
- one writer process and multiple reader processes (reader processes must accept concurrent writers and be wary about reading inconsistent data during non-atomic updates).

An alternative approach has been to consider whether clever algorithms can enable method calls to support semantically identical transactions to those using locking—but using cheaper and more fine-grained operations. For example lock-free data structures [27] allow multiple concurrent readers and writers to access a single data structure typically using just a 'compare-and-swap' instruction.

Operating systems were also the original source of the notion of *capability* [28]. An *access-control matrix* represents which principals (e.g. users) may access which objects (e.g. files). This is traditionally achieved via access-control lists, but can equally well be implemented by using capabilities (here an unforgeable token of authority which allows access to a file). Capabilities there are seen as *containing* the object reference while in object-oriented systems we often talk of a (reference, capability) pair, treating the capability as the access permission for the reference. One reason for this difference is that the capability component of a reference is typically not a language value—only existing in the semantics—and, even if it were, a type system could stop the value being abused to generate unsuitable access permissions. Such guarantees are not in general possible in the operating-system context, so there capabilities are often signed cryptographically to avoid forgery.

5   Syntactic Representations of Ownership

Previous sections have discussed the fundamental idea of ownership as being a high-level mechanism for thinking about mutable data structures analogous to the abstract view of a data type representing restrictions on possible values. Syntactic representations of ownership and of types also adhere to this analogy— some restrictions are easily expressible syntactically and others less so or not at all. Indeed, as a general principle, the more sophisticated the requirement the larger the syntactic burden.

The sections below review the most familiar concepts: uniqueness, Clarke-style ownership types, universe types, ownership domains and capabilities. One approach we do not discuss (as it is discussed elsewhere in the volume) is that of compile-time forms of separation logic and fractional ownership [22,29]. Suffice it to say here that these approaches enable us to represent both having distinct data types for Tree and DAG and also representing single-writer multiple-reader ownership.

5.1   Linearity and Uniqueness

Given the advantages that can be gained from the absence of aliasing, many authors have proposed *uniqueness types*, which guarantee that there is always at most one reference to an object or piece of memory. This single reference thus has exclusive access to the object, even in the presence of concurrency, allowing it to safely access, modify and move the object. It is common to distinguish between references from local variables (often called *dynamic aliasing*) and those from fields of other heap objects (often called *static aliasing*) since the former are more easily tracked. Indeed uniqueness is often but not always treated as 'no static aliasing'.

One way to maintain uniqueness is to modify the semantics of assignment to nullify the original variable at the end of the assignment operation; this ensures that ownership of an object can be transferred from one variable to another, while maintaining uniqueness. Clearly nullification is unnecessary if the variable being read is known not to be live after the assignment.

Alternatively, the capability to access the variable can be transferred during the assignment process; Haller et al. take this approach in their work on capabilities [30].

In the context of uniqueness types, *borrowing* is used to *temporarily* transfer (some of) the access rights for an object to another part of the program, for example for the duration of a method's execution.

Linear types, based on Girard's linear logic [14], combine uniqueness with the additional requirement that variables must be used exactly once [16]. Linear types are particularly useful when working with inherently linear objects such as input and output streams. They do, however, require a somewhat different programming style [31]. For example, a function with a linear object must use it exactly once and therefore must either pass the variable to another function, explicitly dispose of it or return it. When passing a linear object to another function, the object often needs to be returned to the caller at the end of the function to enable further use of the object.

The difference between uniqueness types and linear types manifests itself in their treatment of temporal aliasing. Both disallow spatial aliasing, ensuring that there is only one reference to an object at any given time. Linear types further prevent temporal aliasing, requiring each object to be used exactly once.

Kobayashi's *quasi-linear types* [17] form a middle-way between linear and uniqueness types. They 'relax the condition of linearity by extending the types with information on an evaluation order and simple dataflow information' [17], allowing a form of statically determined temporal aliasing.

Uniqueness types are supported by some programming languages, including Clean [32], where a function argument can be declared to be unique if there are no other (live) references to it when the function is executed. This means that destructive updates can be performed safely; furthermore, if the unique argument is not used as part of the function's return value, it can be garbage collected as soon as the function returns.

Minsky proposes so-called *u-objects*, an implementation of uniqueness types which can be referenced by only one variable at a time [33]. Minsky's u-objects suffer from two weaknesses which can be used to circumvent uniqueness. Firstly, the objects contained in u-objects may be standard, shareable objects; this means that the internals of u-objects can be shared and exposed to modification [34]. Secondly, although u-objects cannot be shared directly, indirect sharing can be accomplished through the use of intermediate handle objects: a standard object containing a u-object can be shared freely, thus allowing multiple parts of the system to access the u-object.

Uniqueness modes in Mercury [35] support linear typing, allowing developers to specify 'when there is only one reference to a particular value, and when there will be no more references to that value' [35]. This enables the compiler to perform a variety of optimisations; for example, garbage collection code can be inserted automatically by the compiler to deallocate storage once a value has been consumed.

Baker [31] argues for *use-once-variables* in programming languages. He often refers to these as linear, and hints at using linear type systems to check consistency, but there is no direct connection between the dynamic nature of "use once" and static checking. Nonetheless the paper contains much interesting and still-relevant discussion.

Boyland [36] links static and dynamic notions of linearity with the idea of *alias burying*. He introduces a language with *unique* variables which are either null or refer to an unshared object, achieved by nullification. The language is enriched with methods having *borrowed* parameters which create dynamic aliases which can only exist for the duration of the method call. The language is then given variant semantics: when a unique variable is read, all its aliases are made *undefined* (alias burying); reading these halts the program with error. He then shows that a modular static analysis can identify programs which execute without error (i.e. all buried aliases are semantically dead); such programs give the same result as under nullification semantics—thus nullification can be elided. In retrospect the system thus obtained is a static quasi-linear type system the style of Kobayashi above.

5.2   Clarke-Style Ownership Types, Universe Types and Ownership Domains

A number of alias protection schemes are built around an explicit notion of ownership and features to support the definition of an ownership structure; this includes *Clarke-style ownership types* [37,38], *universe types* [39,40] and *ownership domains* [41,42]. In these schemes, the ownership properties can usually be checked and enforced at compile-time and thus have no effect on the program's execution at run-time. To avoid confusion, note that Clarke-style ownership types, universe types and ownership domains are all particular examples of *static* type systems which protect particular *semantic (or dynamically checked) notions of ownership*—the latter being a much broader concept.

Two significantly different approaches to ownership have been highlighted in previous research: *owners-as-dominators* and *owners-as-modifiers*. Dietl et al. [43] summarise the differences between these approaches. In an owners-as-dominators scheme all read and write accesses to an object must go through the owner. Owners-as-modifiers restricts only write accesses but allows read accesses to bypass an object's owner, arguing that they are harmless as they do not modify state [43]. Clarke-style ownership types and universe types use different types systems to describe the same object topology, where each object has an associated owner. However, as originally presented, Clarke-style ownership types enforce an owners-as-dominators discipline, while universe types enforce owners-as-modifiers.

Unlike universe types and Clarke-style ownership types, *ownership domains* do not support just a single aliasing policy; they separate the ownership mechanism (determining which object owns which other objects) from the aliasing policy which determines which part of the system can access a particular object. Objects are collected in ownership domains; an object's domain is specified when it is created. Links and relationships between domains may also be specified, giving one domain access rights to another domain, regardless of the ownership structure. An object o_1 can access another object o_2 if both objects are in the same ownership domain or if the domain containing o_1 has access permissions to the domain of o_2.

Clarke-style ownership types and universe types enforce single ownership; on creation each object has exactly one owner object determined by the syntactic context in which it is declared and values of variables (typically *this*) at creation time. Thus, the graph having a program's objects as nodes and ownership as edges forms a hierarchical tree structure called the *ownership tree* [44], whose shape is consistent with the syntactic ownership structure of the program. This restriction on the ownership structure makes ownership statically checkable. By contrast ownership domains are more flexible; one object may belong to several domains at the same time, thus allowing multiple ownership.

While single ownership is 'easy to understand, easy to model, and (relatively) easy to formalise and enforce' [45], empirical studies have shown that a rigid ownership structure does not suit all programs: a study conducted by Potanin et al. shows that object graphs in object-oriented programs written in a variety of languages are empirically scale-free networks, where every object is only a few steps from every other object [46]; Cameron et al. argue that such a non-hierarchical structure cannot be modelled with hierarchical ownership tree [45]. Another study of heaps found that multiple ownership was required by 75% of object structures [47].

Some work has been done to loosen the single ownership requirement of owner-ship systems. Boyapati et al. propose 'principled violation of encapsulation' [26] for Clarke-style ownership types, giving special access privileges to inner classes so that they can access the representation of the outer class. They argue that in this way iterators can be implemented as inner classes of collections while maintaining strong encapsulation and local reasoning [26]. Although Boyapati et al.'s proposal loosens the encapsulation policy associated with Clarke-style ownership types, it continues to enforce a tree-shaped object graph, where each object has a single owner.

Cameron et al. propose a system which supports multiple ownership [45]: each object can have multiple owners and thus the ownership graph forms a directed acyclic graph rather than a tree as in other ownership systems. The authors implement multiple ownership in the language MOJO, an extension of existing single-ownership languages. Unlike the other ownership schemes described here, this system is descriptive rather than prescriptive: it does not attempt to enforce an owners-as-dominators discipline and provides no encapsulation guarantees.

In addition to the lack of support for multiple ownership, Clarke-style owner-ship types do not support ownership transfer at run-time since it does not fit well with the static ownership system [38]. This is a serious limitation in practice, as it prevents the implementation of common idioms, such as merging of data structures [40].

Clarke et al. propose the concept of *external uniqueness* of aggregate ob-jects [48]: an aggregate object is said to be externally unique if there is a unique external reference to it; any number of internal references between the objects comprising the aggregate are allowed. An externally unique aggregate object can then be easily transferred from one owner to another without disrupting a program's ownership structure.

Müller et al. apply external uniqueness to universe types [40]; they propose UTT, an extension of universe types, which allows a cluster of objects to be transferred from one owner to another, as long as the cluster is externally unique at the time of the transfer. At any other time, external uniqueness is not required and multiple references may point into the cluster, making the system more flexible than systems requiring continued uniqueness of references.

UTT uses a modular intraprocedural static analysis to ensure that references to clusters are externally unique at the time of ownership transfer. The analysis makes any variable that may be affected by the transfer of a cluster unusable until a new value has been assigned to it [40].

Finally, Boyapati et al. [49] invent a variant of owners-as-dominators for which well-typed programs are guaranteed to be race-free. This approach has become known as 'owners-as-locks' [50].

5.3   Capabilities

Capabilities are run-time values or access rights which one must quote to be able to indirect on a given reference—see Section 4.3 for the operating system con-text. Thus to access an object requires a (reference, capability) pair. However, we can also consider a static version of capabilities that instead are associated with program phrases as in Haller and Odersky's work [30] which we consider later in this section This gives a compile-time (type, capability) pair which enables a compiler to statically check run-time capabilities and thus elide them from execution models—analogously to removing run-time type tags in statically typed languages.

The run-time capabilities of Boyland et al. [51] combine each object reference with a set of access rights. Using capabilities, many other aliasing modifiers can be modelled, including immutable, unique, readonly and borrowed. Their model contains seven different access rights. Three primitive access rights provide read access, write access and identity access (for checking the identity of an object). Three corresponding exclusive access rights guarantee exclusive read, write and identity access, if necessary by stripping incompatible access rights of other capabilities. The final access right, ownership, is used to resolve conflicts between incompatible capabilities. The authors refer to capabilities with the ownership right as an *owned* capability as opposed to a *borrowed* capability. When an owned capability asserts an access right, the incompatible rights of all other capabilities are stripped; on the other hand, a borrowed capability cannot strip the access rights of owned capabilities. Thus the ownership access right allows a variable to hold onto its access rights indefinitely.

Their capability system can model ownership transfer, which occurs when a (value, capability) pair with all seven access rights enters or leaves a context such as at method call or return. This action is only safe if no other variables hold conflicting capabilities at the time the transfer occurs.

Capabilities are flexible enough to model multiple ownership: we can give write, read, identity and ownership capabilities for the same object to several 'owners'. This allows us to model, for example, our 'both-to-sign' bank account from Section 4 by giving ownership capabilities as well as write capabilities to both owners of the account.

Multiple ownership can, however, lead to conflicts when several owned capabilities assert incompatible access rights; this occurs, for example, when we have several capabilities, all with exclusive access rights. In this case, the program's behaviour depends on the order in which the incompatible access rights are asserted: the second capability will strip the conflicting access rights of the first. This can cause problems when it is not clear in which order the capabilities will be asserted, particularly in the context of concurrency. Boyland et al. argue that 'it is up to a policy and supporting analyses to ensure that these owners cooperate' [51]. They suggest that this could be done using either static analysis or run-time checks; no implementation is given, rather the paper gives a framework in which static capability systems can be proved free of run-time errors due to having insufficient capability to access an object.

Haller and Odersky provide a static expression of certain run-time capabilities [30]. In their system, capabilities are represented by static names for disjoint regions of the heap; holding a given capability gives access rights to the corresponding heap region. The type-and-capability checking scheme ensures that a program only type-checks if the run-time object is always properly usable at each point; thus, consuming a static capability at a given program point causes all variables guarded by that capability to become unusable. This allows the modelling of both uniqueness and at-most-once consumption of unique references. Capabilities naturally allow ownership transfer as they are produced and consumed throughout a program's execution.

5.4 Some Example Systems

Having discussed the theoretical background of different approaches to aliasing, we now consider some implementations of linear type systems, ownership and capabilities.

Early examples of linearity being used in practical systems were those of Singularity OS [52] and PacLang [53]. These addressed similar problems, albeit arising from opposing ends of the problem domain. Singularity OS proposed the use of linear message passing within an operating system context to produce software isolation between processes. Linear messages can be passed within an address space without copying by simply passing a pointer.

PacLang focused on the related issue of how to exploit, in high-level programming terms, Intel's Network Processors (arguably its first multi-core distributed-memory processor). The hardware was complex and code could not rely on hardware interlocks to guarantee safe execution. This led to a similar model to Singularity whereby linear buffers could be exchanged between processors (either by-copy or by-reference depending on whether the buffer was cheaply accessible by both sender and recipient). The language was formalised in terms of a quasi-linear type system which allowed local aliases (borrowed parameters), but ensured that every object had a single thread (or an inter-processor queue) which referenced it. This had the added advantage for a Network Processor that storage reclamation could be done at compile time without garbage collection. The type system in PacLang was proved correct with respect to a Chemical Abstract Machine model of its concurrent processors. In both PacLang and Singularity OS, the arrays were logically buffers of bytes even if in principle they could contain marshalled objects but we would additionally require absence of external sharing to the marshalled objects to be able to retain identity when unmarshalled.

Kilim [54] extended the unstructured buffers of PacLang to allow externally unique tree-structured objects to be passed between processes in a way which maintained the process memory-isolation property of Singularity and PacLang. Kilim, while being implemented with a single JVM instance, being a form of Actor model would equally port to distributed-memory architectures. Various notions of capability (permission) were identified (e.g. @free, @cuttable, @safe, @readonly) which gave the callee rights (e.g. respectively and decreasingly, to deallocate the structure, to cut a @free substructure from it, to modify the fields but not the pointer structure, or to make no modifications at all). These naturally refine the points on the capability spectrum between the classical 'borrow' and 'full capability to deallocate'.

Haller and Odersky's work on static capabilities [30] discussed above has been implemented as a Scala pluggable type making it easily accessible.

Spec# is an extension of C# which also supports a form of ownership declaration [55]. An object can annotate its fields with the rep keyword, signalling that they are part of the object's representation and thus owned by it. Any modifying accesses to rep fields must pass through the owner, making Spec# an owners-as-modifiers scheme.

Although ownership in Spec# controls aliasing by restricting modifying accesses to owned objects, its primary purpose is to support program verification. Spec# supports the definition of software contracts, including preconditions, postconditions and class invariants, which can be used to prove the correctness of programs using the static verifier Boogie [56]. Spec# uses ownership primarily to avoid the *indirect invariant effect* [57], which occurs when an object's class invariant is violated because of modifications to its components occurring via aliasing. Therefore, in Spec# class invariants may only be defined in terms of owned objects, thus ensuring that the class invariant cannot be violated through modifications from outside aliases.

A big focus of Spec# is maintaining software contracts and class invariants even in the presence of concurrency and threading; it achieves this by further extending the concept of ownership to threads [58]. A thread can only modify an object which it owns (and transitively any other object owned by that object). A thread can acquire ownership of an object which has no current owner, and later release ownership. Since only one thread can own an object at any one time, an object cannot be modified by two threads concurrently.

6   A Comparative View

In the previous section, we presented several different syntactic approaches to alias *advertisement, prevention* and *control* from the 'Geneva Convention' including linear types, uniqueness, owners-as-dominators, owners-as-modifiers and capabilities. These schemes represent slightly different views on aliasing and as such exhibit various differences in their treatment of ownership.

Ownership is a high-level concept that is used to help developers make sense of aliasing and help them structure programs. As the names suggest, owners-as-dominators and owners-as-modifiers explicitly include the concept of ownership and provide syntactic constructs for declaration of ownership. In these schemes, ownership is a statically declared property between identified objects; this property does not change throughout program execution, although the objects involved in the relationship may change.

In current owners-as-dominators and owners-as-modifiers schemes, such as Clarke-style ownership types and universe types respectively, each object has only a single owner which remains constant throughout the object's lifetime. Thus, these schemes support neither multiple ownership nor ownership transfer, although some proposals have been made to remedy this situation. This fairly rigid ownership structure does not really fit with the concept of ownership in the real world, where multiple ownership and ownership transfer are both common.

By contrast, uniqueness and linear types do not support explicit declarations of ownership; instead of being directly declared in the program, the concept of a (single) owner as the holder of the only reference to an object is implied. Assignment of unique references causes ownership transfer from one part of the program to another. Thus, uniqueness and linear types are similar to owners-as-dominators and owners-as-modifiers in supporting only single ownership, but more flexible with their support for ownership transfer.

The run-time capabilities of Boyland et al. [51] offer a more nuanced view of ownership compared to the binary notion of ownership and non-ownership in the other approaches. A full capability with exclusive read, write and identity access expresses conventional, or full, ownership; capabilities with fewer, and perhaps non-exclusive, access rights represent a more flexible, but not necessarily statically checkable, form of ownership. One final point to note is that Boyland's *ownership capability* does not correspond directly to ownership as discussed here—instead it represents the ability to remove capabilities from aliasing references.

In Section 3, we introduced the distinction between temporal and spatial aliasing. In this context, linear types are the most restrictive, and allow neither temporal nor spatial aliasing involving live references. Uniqueness types and owners-as-dominators both loosen this constraint, allowing temporal but restricting spatial aliasing (none at all, or only via dominators).

Owners-as-modifiers schemes further loosen restrictions on spatial aliasing, allowing it to occur as long as all references except the one held by the owner perform only read accesses. Capabilities are more flexible yet and allow an essentially arbitrary level of restriction to be placed on spatial aliasing: it can be fully restricted so that one reference has exclusive access to an object. At the other extreme, spatial aliasing can be completely unconstrained.

Given locking and concurrency, restricting spatial aliasing to forbid concurrent aliasing is attractive since it ensures that an object cannot be accessed by multiple parts of the program concurrently. Thus, in schemes which enforce single ownership, including linear types, uniqueness types and owners-as-dominators, the owner essentially holds a lock for all objects it currently owns. Thus, under the 'owners-as-locks' banner coined by Zhou et al. [50], we can statically identify programs which are guaranteed to be race-free (Boyapati et al. [49] give a variant of owners-as-dominators and Cunningham et al. [59] a variant of universe types to this end).

Current owners-as-dominators schemes lack the ability to transfer ownership so that the owner object holds a lock to objects it owns for the complete duration of the objects' lifetime. By contrast ownership transfer in uniqueness schemes corresponds to transferring a lock: the old owner relinquishes the lock and the new owner acquires it in an atomic operation.

Unlike owners-as-dominators, owners-as-modifiers does not provide an owner with an exclusive lock. Read accesses may bypass the owner, making owners-as-modifiers problematic in the presence of concurrency.

As mentioned above, run-time capabilities are highly flexible and can express a wide range of different aliasing conditions; in this way, they can be used to imitate some of the other aliasing schemes. Uniqueness types and owners-as-dominators, for example, can be imitated by giving exclusive read, write and identity capabilities to a single reference, the owner. Owners-as-modifiers, on the other hand, corresponds to exclusive write capabilities for owners but non-exclusive read and identity capabilities. Multiple ownership can also be modelled by using non-exclusive capabilities.

One issue, however, is how to deal with conflicting capabilities. If two objects assert exclusive rights over the same object, one approach is to strip the first of these two owners of its access rights when the second owner asserts its capabilities. This corresponds to a forced transfer of ownership or, in the presence of concurrency, to a forced transfer of the lock. Clearly, this has the potential to cause problems.

Overall, we can see that there are significant differences between the various approaches to aliasing we have considered here. Despite certain similarities, linear types, uniqueness types, owners-as-dominators, owners-as-modifiers and capabilities clearly represent very different views of aliasing and how it should be controlled.

7   Conclusions

We have surveyed some of the notions of ownership. In doing so we have attempted to separate the high-level semantic notions of ownership both from their low-level representation and from the extant syntactic representation of ownership. We have also brought notions like Typestate and those involving concurrency and locking into a single framework.

We are left with the slightly disappointing conclusion that existing ownership notions are both inexpressive for the range of notions to be addressed, and overlap in terms of expressiveness with each other. A grand unified theory would be most welcome.

We have started to investigate a semantic framework called *alias contracts* which we hope can be a first step towards such a unification. Here contracts (side-effect-free source-language expressions) are placed on variable and field declarations. Access to an object is only allowed when *all* references stored in variables and fields which refer to it satisfy their contacts. This gives a dynamic ownership scheme which appears to be effective at modelling existing static schemes as special cases.

Acknowledgements. The authors thank the Rutherford Foundation of the Royal Society of New Zealand for the scholarship which partly funded this work. We also thank the editors Dave Clarke, James Noble and Tobias Wrigstad for soliciting this chapter, and the anonymous referees for their helpful comments.

References

1. Hogg, J., Lea, D., Wills, A., de Champeaux, D., Holt, R.C.: The Geneva convention on the treatment of object aliasing. OOPS Messenger 3(2), 11–16 (1992)
2. Pierce, B.C.: Types and programming languages. MIT Press, Cambridge (2002)
3. Bloss, A., Hudak, P., Young, J.: Code optimizations for lazy evaluation. In: LISP and Symbolic Computation, pp. 147–164 (1988)
4. Lamport, L.: How to make a multiprocessor computer that correctly executes multiprocess programs. IEEE Trans. Comput. 28(9), 690–691 (1979)
5. Adve, S.V., Gharachorloo, K.: Shared memory consistency models: A tutorial. IEEE Computer 29, 66–76 (1995)
6. Dijkstra, E.W., Lamport, L., Martin, A.J., Scholten, C.S., Steffens, E.F.M.: On-the-fly garbage collection: an exercise in cooperation. Commun. ACM 21(11), 966–975 (1978)
7. Oancea, C.E., Mycroft, A., Watt, S.M.: A new approach to parallelising tracing algorithms. In: Proceedings of the 2009 International Symposium on Memory Management, ISMM 2009, pp. 10–19. ACM, New York (2009)
8. Harris, T., Marlow, S., Jones, S.L.P.: Haskell on a shared-memory multiprocessor. In: Haskell, pp. 49–61 (2005)
9. Tofte, M., Talpin, J.P.: Region-based memory management. Information and Computation 132(2), 109–176 (1997)
10. Mycroft, A.: Isolation Types and Multi-core Architectures. In: Beckert, B., Damiani, F., Gurov, D. (eds.) FoVeOOS 2011. LNCS, vol. 7421, pp. 33–48. Springer, Heidelberg (2012)
11. Aldrich, J., Kostadinov, V., Chambers, C.: Alias annotations for program understanding. In: Proceedings of the 17th ACM SIGPLAN Conference on Object-Oriented Programming, Systems, Languages, and Applications, OOPSLA 2002, pp. 311–330. ACM, New York (2002)
12. Agha, G.: Actors: a model of concurrent computation in distributed systems. MIT Press, Cambridge (1986)
13. Armstrong, J., Virding, R., Wikström, C., Williams, M.: Concurrent programming in Erlang, 2nd edn. Prentice Hall, Hertfordshire (1996)
14. Girard, J.: Linear logic. Theoretical Computer Science 50(1), 1–102 (1987)
15. Abramsky, S.: Computational interpretations of linear logic. Theor. Comput. Sci. 111(1&2), 3–57 (1993)
16. Wadler, P.: Linear types can change the world! In: Broy, M., Jones, C. (eds.) Programming Concepts and Methods. North-Holland (1990)
17. Kobayashi, N.: Quasi-linear types. In: Proceedings of the 26th ACM SIGPLAN-SIGACT Symposium on Principles of Programming Languages, POPL 1999, pp. 29–42. ACM, New York (1999)
18. Strom, R.E., Yemini, S.: Typestate: A programming language concept for enhancing software reliability. IEEE Trans. Software Eng. 12(1), 157–171 (1986)
19. Wansbrough, K., Peyton Jones, S.: Once upon a polymorphic type. In: Proceedings of the 26th ACM SIGPLAN-SIGACT Symposium on Principles of Programming Languages, POPL 1999, pp. 15–28. ACM, New York (1999)
20. Wrigstad, T., Clarke, D.: Is the world ready for ownership types? is ownership types ready for the world? Technical report, Department of Computer Science, KU Leuven (2011)

21. Richards, M.: BCPL: a tool for compiler writing and system programming. In: Proceedings of the Spring Joint Computer Conference, AFIPS 1969, May 14-16, pp. 557–566. ACM, New York (1969)

22. Reynolds, J.C.: Separation logic: A logic for shared mutable data structures. In: LICS, pp. 55–74 (2002)

23. Rosenblum, D.S.: A practical approach to programming with assertions. IEEE Trans. Software Eng. 21(1), 19–31 (1995)

24. Clarke, L.A., Rosenblum, D.S.: A historical perspective on runtime assertion checking in software development. SIGSOFT Softw. Eng. Notes 31(3), 25–37 (2006)

25. Bierman, G., Wren, A.: First-Class Relationships in an Object-Oriented Language. In: Gao, X.-X. (ed.) ECOOP 2005. LNCS, vol. 3586, pp. 262–286. Springer, Heidelberg (2005)

26. Boyapati, C., Liskov, B., Shrira, L.: Ownership types for object encapsulation. In: Proceedings of the 30th ACM SIGPLAN-SIGACT Symposium on Principles of Programming Languages, POPL 2003, pp. 213–223. ACM, New York (2003)

27. Herlihy, M.: Wait-free synchronization. ACM Trans. Program. Lang. Syst. 13(1), 124–149 (1991)

28. Levy, H.M.: Capability-Based Computer Systems. Butterworth-Heinemann, Newton (1984)

29. Boyland, J.: Checking Interference with Fractional Permissions. In: Cousot, R. (ed.) SAS 2003. LNCS, vol. 2694, pp. 55–72. Springer, Heidelberg (2003)

30. Haller, P., Odersky, M.: Capabilities for Uniqueness and Borrowing. In: D'Hondt, T. (ed.) ECOOP 2010. LNCS, vol. 6183, pp. 354–378. Springer, Heidelberg (2010)

31. Baker, H.: 'Use-once' variables and linear objects: storage management, reflection and multi-threading. ACM SIGPLAN Notices 30, 45–52 (1995)

32. Plasmeijer, R., van Eekelen, M., van Groningen, J.: Clean language report version 2.2 (2011), http://clean.cs.ru.nl/download/doc/CleanLangRep.2.2.pdf

33. Minsky, N.H.: Towards Alias-Free Pointers. In: Cointe, P. (ed.) ECOOP 1996. LNCS, vol. 1098, pp. 189–209. Springer, Heidelberg (1996)

34. Almeida, P.: Balloon Types: Controlling Sharing of State in Data Types. In: Akşit, M., Matsuoka, S. (eds.) ECOOP 1997. LNCS, vol. 1241, pp. 32–59. Springer, Heidelberg (1997)

35. Henderson, F., Conway, T., Somogyi, Z., Jeffery, D., Schachte, P., Taylor, S., Speirs, C., Dowd, T., Becket, R., Brown, M., Wang, P.: The Mercury language reference manual version 11.07 (2011), http://www.mercury.csse.unimelb.edu.au/information/doc-release/reference_manual.pdf

36. Boyland, J.: Alias burying: unique variables without destructive reads. Softw. Pract. Exper. 31, 533–553 (2001)

37. Clarke, D., Drossopoulou, S.: Ownership, encapsulation and the disjointness of type and effect. In: Proceedings of the 17th ACM SIGPLAN Conference on Object-Oriented Programming, Systems, Languages, and Applications, OOPSLA 2002, pp. 292–310. ACM, New York (2002)

38. Clarke, D., Potter, J., Noble, J.: Ownership types for flexible alias protection. ACM SIGPLAN Notices 33, 48–64 (1998)

39. Müller, P., Poetzsch-Heffter, A.: Universes: A type system for controlling representation exposure. In: Poetzsch-Heffter, A., Meyer, J. (eds.) Programming Languages and Fundamentals of Programming (1999)

40. Müller, P., Rudich, A.: Ownership transfer in universe types. In: Proceedings of the 22nd Annual ACM SIGPLAN Conference on Object-Oriented Programming Systems and Applications, OOPSLA 2007, pp. 461–478. ACM, New York (2007)
41. Aldrich, J., Chambers, C.: Ownership Domains: Separating Aliasing Policy from Mechanism. In: Odersky, M. (ed.) ECOOP 2004. LNCS, vol. 3086, pp. 1–25. Springer, Heidelberg (2004)
42. Krishnaswami, N., Aldrich, J.: Permission-based ownership: encapsulating state in higher-order typed languages. In: Proceedings of the 2005 ACM SIGPLAN Conference on Programming Language Design and Implementation, PLDI 2005, pp. 96–106. ACM, New York (2005)
43. Dietl, W., Müller, P.: Universes: Lightweight ownership for JML. Journal of Object Technology 4(8), 5–32 (2005)
44. Potter, J., Noble, J., Clarke, D.: The ins and outs of objects. In: Proceedings of the Australian Software Engineering Conference, pp. 80–89. IEEE Computer Society, Washington, DC (1998)
45. Cameron, N., Drossopoulou, S., Noble, J., Smith, M.: Multiple ownership. In: Proceedings of the 22nd Annual ACM SIGPLAN Conference on Object-Oriented Programming Systems and Applications, OOPSLA 2007, pp. 441–460. ACM, New York (2007)
46. Potanin, A., Noble, J., Frean, M., Biddle, R.: Scale-free geometry in OO programs. Commun. ACM 48, 99–103 (2005)
47. Mitchell, N.: The Runtime Structure of Object Ownership. In: Thomas, D. (ed.) ECOOP 2006. LNCS, vol. 4067, pp. 74–98. Springer, Heidelberg (2006)
48. Clarke, D., Wrigstad, T.: External Uniqueness is Unique Enough. In: Cardelli, L. (ed.) ECOOP 2003. LNCS, vol. 2743, pp. 176–200. Springer, Heidelberg (2003)
49. Boyapati, C., Rinard, M.: A parameterized type system for race-free Java programs. In: Proceedings of the 16th ACM SIGPLAN Conference on Object-Oriented Programming, Systems, Languages, and Applications, OOPSLA 2001, pp. 56–69. ACM, New York (2001)
50. Zhao, Y., Boyland, J.: A fundamental permission interpretation for ownership types. In: TASE 2008: Second IEEE/IFIP International Symposium on Theoretical Aspects of Software Engineering, pp. 65–72. IEEE Computer Society, Washington, DC (2008)
51. Boyland, J., Noble, J., Retert, W.: Capabilities for Sharing: A Generalisation of Uniqueness and Read-Only. In: Lindskov Knudsen, J. (ed.) ECOOP 2001. LNCS, vol. 2072, pp. 2–27. Springer, Heidelberg (2001)
52. Fähndrich, M., Aiken, M., Hawblitzel, C., Hodson, O., Hunt, G., Larus, J., Levi, S.: Language support for fast and reliable message-based communication in singularity OS. In: Proceedings of the 1st ACM SIGOPS/EuroSys European Conference on Computer Systems 2006, EuroSys 2006, pp. 177–190. ACM, New York (2006)
53. Ennals, R., Sharp, R., Mycroft, A.: Linear Types for Packet Processing. In: Schmidt, D. (ed.) ESOP 2004. LNCS, vol. 2986, pp. 204–218. Springer, Heidelberg (2004)
54. Srinivasan, S., Mycroft, A.: Kilim: Isolation-Typed Actors for Java. In: Vitek, J. (ed.) ECOOP 2008. LNCS, vol. 5142, pp. 104–128. Springer, Heidelberg (2008)
55. Barnett, M., DeLine, R., Fähndrich, M., Leino, K.R.M., Schulte, W.: Verification of object-oriented programs with invariants. Journal of Object Technology 3, 27–56 (2004)

56. Barnett, M., Chang, B.-Y.E., DeLine, R., Jacobs, B., Leino, K.R.M.: Boogie: A Modular Reusable Verifier for Object-Oriented Programs. In: de Boer, F.S., Bonsangue, M.M., Graf, S., de Roever, W.-P. (eds.) FMCO 2005. LNCS, vol. 4111, pp. 364–387. Springer, Heidelberg (2006)
57. Meyer, B.: Object-Oriented Software Construction, 2nd edn. Prentice Hall (1997)
58. Jacobs, B., Piessens, F., Leino, K.R.M., Schulte, W.: Safe concurrency for aggregate objects with invariants. In: SEFM 2005: Proceedings of the Third IEEE International Conference on Software Engineering and Formal Methods, pp. 137–147. IEEE Computer Society, Washington, DC (2005)
59. Cunningham, D., Drossopoulou, S., Eisenbach, S.: Universe types for race safety. In: VAMP 2007, pp. 20–51 (September 2007)

Understanding Ownership Types
with Dependent Types

Nicholas Cameron[1], Sophia Drossopoulou[2], and James Noble[1]

[1] Victoria University of Wellington
{ncameron,kjx}@ecs.vuw.ac.nz
[2] Imperial College London
scd@doc.ic.ac.uk

Abstract. In this paper we will explore the relationship between Ownership Types and more fundamental type systems. In particular, we show that ownership types (in both simple and embellished flavours) are dependent types by translating object calculi with object ownership to lambda calculi with dependent types. We discuss which ownership features share features in the underlying dependent type system, and which additional features require additional complexity.

1 Introduction

The goal of this chapter is to shed light on the relationship between ownership types (mostly the parametric variety as first proposed by Clarke et al. [1,2], and developed by many others) and more fundamental type systems. By doing so, we hope that ownership types will be better understood, that we will foster interest in ownership types in the wider type systems community, that we will gain insight into the relative complexity of ownership features, and that we might reveal areas for further research.

We will argue that descriptive ownership types are simply dependent types, and show this by encoding a basic ownership types system into a lambda calculus with dependent types based on Simple ML [3]. We will further show that several extensions to the ownership paradigm can be encoded in the same core calculus.

We postulate that some aspects of ownership types systems are well understood by analogy to type polymorphism — parameter passing, bounds on ownership parameters, top and bottom owners, ordering of regions, variance annotations — but that ownership parameters are not type parameters, as demonstrated by the subtly different behaviour of encodings of ownership types as generic types [4] compared with straightforward ownership formalisms [5]. Other features are not understood, at least in terms of standard type theory. In particular, the typing behaviour of the `owner` and `this` owner parameters. By using a dependent types model we more precisely describe parameterisation in ownership types systems[1].

---

[1] And as a side-effect, we make clear the phantom types nature of OGJ.

D. Clarke et al. (Eds.): Aliasing in Object-Oriented Programming, LNCS 7850, pp. 84–108, 2013.

We postpone giving an overview of the system until Sect. 3, after we have introduced dependent types in Sect. 2; then we will describe our ownership calculus and its translation in stages. We start by encoding a simple version of Featherweight Java with assignment, but no inheritance, and no ownership features (Sect. 4). We then add statically declared, nested regions (Sect. 5), and then change to dynamic nested regions tied to object creation, that is, ownership types (Sect. 6). Although we do not give proofs of correctness, we hope that our explorations are thorough. Finally, we consider some extensions to our source calculus and how they might be encoded (Sect. 7). We explore the encoding of dynamic aliases and owner-polymorphic methods, two common-place extensions. We summarise the use of existential types (and thus dependent sum types) to encode several variance-linked extensions, and also summarise the link between our model and that of OGJ. We speculate on the encoding of multiple ownership, ownership domains, and encapsulation policies, but mainly leave these aspects to future work.

In this chapter we will make use of multiple formal systems; our source calculi are: OT_0, a simple object oriented calculus; OT_r, a region calculus; OT, an ownerhip types calculus; OT_+, a more fully featured ownership types calculus. Our target calculi are: λ_0, the lambda calculus with records and an imperative assignment; λ_Π, a dependent types calculus; λ_Σ, a more advanced dependent types calculus.

2   Background — Dependent Types

We will examine the behaviour of ownership type systems by translating into lambda calculi extended with *dependent types*. In a dependent type system [3,6], the syntax of types includes some or all of the syntax of expressions. There have been many different dependent type systems, for example, Dependent ML [7], λLF [3], and Epigram [8]. Different type systems allow different classes of expression in types; the more general the class of allowed expression, the more complex the type system. Many systems run into issues with decidability due to the expressiveness of type expressions.

A dependent type is a type constructor which maps expressions (as opposed to types) to types. For example, list types may be associated with the length of the list, e.g., List<3> for a list of length three. Functions which can operate over many dependent types (e.g., lists of any length) are formalised using *dependent product* types, equivalent to universal types in type-parametric type systems. The syntax of a dependent product type is $\Pi x{:}U.T$, which is the type of a function which takes a parameter x with type U and returns an object with type T; the novelty being that x may appear in T. For example, we may have a factory function for lists which takes an int and return a list with that length, it can be given the type $\Pi x{:}\texttt{int}.\texttt{List<x>}$. Note that non-dependent functions can be given (trivial) dependent product types where the parameter does not appear in the result type.

Just as dependent products correspond to universal quantification of types, *dependent sum* types (denoted $\Sigma x{:}U.T$) correspond to existential quantification.

Dependent sums can be used to express partial knowledge about a dependent type, for example, to type a list of unknown length: $\Sigma x: \texttt{int}.\texttt{List<x>}$.

Often, the full power (and complexity) of dependent types is not required. For this work on ownership types, we use *index-dependent types*, exemplified by *Simple Dependent ML* [3]. In an index-dependent type system, types are parameterised by index expressions, a subset (or distinct set) of the language's expressions. By restricting the syntax of indices and index expressions, much of the complexity (and undecidability issues) of dependent types can be avoided. The examples above using lists and list lengths can be expressed using index-dependent types, where the indices are integers. The index expressions would depend on the expressivity required of the type system; in the simplest case we might only allow constant indices and index variables; if we wanted a more expressive type system, we could allow arithmetic expressions, and in the most complex case we could allow arbitrary expressions.

In this work, we will use index-dependent types, where the indices are regions of the heap. We will use both dependent product and sum types.

3   Overview

In our final target calculus, λ_Σ, the topology of the heap is made explicit, and reference types include the region that their values point to. Owner-parametricity in the source calculus, OT, is translated into dependent product types in our target. The current object (this) is similarly encoded, and then hidden using dependent sum types. For example, consider a simple (slightly contrived) linked list program:

```
class List<o, d> {
  Node<this, d> head;
  Allocator<world> alloc;
}
class Node<on, dn> {
  Object<dn> datum;
  Node<on, dn> next;
}
new List<world, world>();
```

Here, a list object owns the nodes in the list[2]; all data in the list belongs to some other owner (d). We imagine that memory for the list is allocated by an Allocator object which is owned by the top owner, world. We encode these classes as[3]:

---

[2] In this example and throughout the paper we use the convention that the first owner in the parameter list is the owner of objects and is mandatory. We sometimes use the term "owner" for that argumenr, as is done in ownership languages where the owner is not listed in the parameter list.

[3] We elide bounds on arguments where they are trivial.

$\varLambda$ null:$\perp$,world:Ref.
  let List = $\varLambda$ this:$[\![$List<o, d>$]\!]$,
                      o:{x:Ref},
                      d:{x:Ref}
                      .{head=null, alloc=null} in
    let Node = $\varLambda$ this:$[\![$Node<on, dn>$]\!]$,
                        on:{x:Ref},
                        dn:{x:Ref}:
                        .{datum=null, next=null} in
      let this = ref<world> null in
        this := ref<world> <List[this,world,world],this>

where

$[\![$List<o, d>$]\!]$ = Ref<o> $\varSigma$x:{x:Ref | x $\preceq$ o}.
  {head:Ref<x> $\varSigma$x:{}.{datum:Ref<d>...,next:Ref<o>...},
    alloc:Ref<world> $\varSigma$x:{x:Ref | x $\preceq$ world}.{...}}
$[\![$Node<on, dn>$]\!]$ = Ref<on> $\varSigma$x:{x:Ref | x $\preceq$ on}.
  {datum:Ref<dn>..., next:Ref<on>...}

Classes are encoded as lambda expressions (named using let expressions), these functions generate records; likewise, object types are encoded as record types. Significantly, the encoded types are structural types[4], compared with nominal types in the source language.

In our encoded types, ownership parameters are statically substituted throughout. This demonstrates that ownership parameters (other than the owner of an object) are a convenience to allow owners to be named, rather than a fundamental aspect of the language. An object's owner, on the other hand, is stored in its reference type because we must use this information to ensure that an object's type accurately reflects its position in the heap. This is a novel (compared with standard dependent types) aspect of our target calculi.

Our encoding of classes uses dependent product types (introduced with $\varLambda$). Dependent product types reflect the owner-parametricity of classes in ownership types. Notice that classes are parameterised by their owner and the current object. The owner is used to mark the reference to newly instantiated objects in our encoding of new expressions, and also to own objects within the class, e.g., datum in Node. A class must be parameterised by the current object so that this may be used as an owner within the class, e.g., head in List. However, that owner should not be able to be (permanently[5]) named outside the class (this is a fundamental property of ownership type systems). To accomplish this, we hide this during construction of an object using dependent sum types, introduced as an 'opaque package' using angle brackets, e.g., <List[...], this> which denotes the value given by List[...], but with this hidden in its type.

---

[4] Using structural types here means we cannot encode recursive classes, this is a limitation of our encoding, the problem is hidden by ellipses in the example.

[5] Dynamic aliases [9] allow temporary naming of this hidden owner [5].

The let expression which creates an object can be considered operationally: first we create a reference to an unused location in the heap, initialised to null, then we create an object by applying the class function to the new location and other ownership parameters, then the new object is stored at the new location in the heap, finally the reference to that location is provided as the result of construction.

We encode object types (e.g., List<o, d>) as reference types, since objects in the Java-sense are actually references to objects in the heap. Our reference types are annotated with the owner, e.g., Ref<o>. The reference type wraps an existentially quantified record type, with each field and method in the class being encoded into an entry in the record type (head and alloc in this example). The existential quantification is used to hide this when used as an owner in types in the record type; in the above example encoding, we introduce the variable x to hide this, and x is used in our translated types where we used this in the source language. The bound on x comes from the ownership types invarariant that the current object is inside it's owner in the ownership hierarchy.

4   Getting Started — A Class Calculus

In the next three sections, we will show how the descriptive elements of a basic, parametric ownership types system can be encoded into a lambda calculus with dependent types. To show how different elements of the ownership types system affect the encoding, we will build up our encoding one step at a time, starting by encoding objects without ownership, then adding static, hierarchical regions, and finally proper ownership. In this section we encode a simple Java-like calculus into an extended lambda calculus; no dependent types are used.

The fundamental strategies of our encoding include translating objects to records of references and functions (methods; the this reference is bound early) and making references explicit. Encoding objects is a well-studied area with many treatments much more thorough than this one, but this section is necessary groundwork for our encoding of ownership types.

Our encoding is far from perfect and has many limitations; however, we believe it is good enough to demonstrate the concepts of ownership types. Specifically, we do not model inheritance and the associated concepts of subtyping and dynamic dispatch; these are orthogonal to ownership types. Nor do we support recursive use of classes (i.e., a class C cannot have a field or method parameter or method return type of type C, or any class that (transitively) has such a reference to C). This is a serious limitation, but there are known solutions [10] which could be added to our calculi, at the expense of increased complexity.

4.1   OT$_0$

OT$_0$ is our base-line object-oriented language, it is essentially FJ [11] without inheritance, but with assignment. The syntax is given in Fig. 1, the static semantics are given in the accompanying technical report[12]. Both syntax and semantics follow FJ, and OT$_0$ is a syntactic subset of Java.

e	$::=$	$\texttt{null} \mid \texttt{x} \mid \texttt{x.f} \mid \texttt{x.f = } e \mid \texttt{x.m}(\overline{e}) \mid \texttt{new C}$	*expressions*
Q	$::=$	$\texttt{class C } \{\overline{T\,\texttt{f}};\ \overline{M}\}$	*class declarations*
M	$::=$	$T\,\texttt{m}\,(\overline{T\,\texttt{x}})\ \{\texttt{return } e;\}$	*method declarations*

T,U	$::=$	$\texttt{C}<\overline{a}>$	*types*	$\texttt{x, y, this}$	*variables*
Γ	$::=$	$\overline{\texttt{x}:T}$	*variable environments*	$\texttt{C}$	*class names*

Fig. 1. Syntax of OT_0

4.2 λ_0

We translate OT_0 to λ_0, a lambda calculus extended with references, records, and let expressions, all in the usual ways. We support two kinds of assignment: field update $(e.\texttt{f} = e)$ is functional assignment — the operation creates a new copy of the record with an updated field. Variable assignment $(e := e)$ is imperative, it changes a value in the runtime store (which we call the heap). We use these two operations to encode field update in the source calculus. A single operation could be used, but that is not common or necessary in such calculi.

e	$::=$	$\gamma \mid \{\overline{\texttt{f=}e}\} \mid e.\texttt{f} \mid e.\texttt{f = } e \mid \lambda\overline{\texttt{x}:T}.e \mid e\,\overline{e} \mid \texttt{let } \overline{\texttt{x = }e} \texttt{ in } e$	
		$\mid \texttt{ref } e \mid !e \mid e := e$	*expressions*
v	$::=$	$\{\overline{\texttt{f=}v}\} \mid \iota \mid \lambda\overline{\texttt{x}:T}.e$	
			values
$\mathcal{H}$	$::=$	$\overline{\iota \rightarrow \{v\}}$	*heaps*
T	$::=$	$\{\overline{\texttt{f}:T}\} \mid \texttt{Ref } T \mid \overline{T} \rightarrow T \mid \bot$	*types*
A	$::=$	T	*all sorts*
Γ	$::=$	$\overline{\gamma : A}$	*variable environments*
γ	$::=$	$\texttt{x} \mid \iota$	*variables or locations*
$\texttt{x,null}$			*variables*
ι			*locations*

Fig. 2. Syntax of λ_0

The syntax of λ_0 is given in Fig. 2 and the type rules in Fig. 3. We use $\texttt{ref } e$ to create a reference to e, and $!e$ to dereference e. Our heap is a mapping from locations (ι) to values. We have record types, function types, and reference types. We also support a bottom type, it is used only to describe the type of $\texttt{null}$. The non-terminal A is redundant here, but used later. The variable name $\texttt{null}$ is not distinguished. The type rules are standard.

Expression typing $\boxed{\Gamma \vdash e : T}$

$$\frac{\Gamma \vdash e : T' \quad \vdash T' <: T}{\Gamma \vdash e : T} \quad \vdash T \text{ OK}$$
(T-Subs)

$$\frac{\Gamma(\gamma) = T}{\Gamma \vdash \gamma : T}$$
(T-Var)

$$\frac{\vdash \overline{T} \text{ OK}}{\Gamma, \overline{\mathbf{x}:T} \vdash e : T}{\Gamma \vdash \lambda \overline{\mathbf{x}:T}.e : \overline{T} \to T}$$
(T-Abs)

$$\frac{\Gamma \vdash e : \overline{T} \to T \quad \Gamma \vdash \overline{e : T}}{\Gamma \vdash e\,\overline{e} : T}$$
(T-App)

$$\frac{\Gamma \vdash \overline{e : T} \quad \Gamma, \mathbf{x}:\overline{T} \vdash e : T}{\Gamma \vdash \texttt{let } \overline{\mathbf{x} = e} \texttt{ in } e : T}$$
(T-Let)

$$\frac{\Gamma \vdash e_1 : \texttt{Ref } T \quad \Gamma \vdash e_2 : T}{\Gamma \vdash e_1 := e_2 : \texttt{Ref } T}$$
(T-Assign)

$$\frac{\Gamma \vdash \overline{e : T}}{\Gamma \vdash \{\mathtt{f}=e\} : \{\mathtt{f}:\overline{T}\}}$$
(T-Record)

$$\frac{\Gamma \vdash e : \{\mathtt{f}:T\} \quad \Gamma \vdash e' : T_i}{\Gamma \vdash e.\mathtt{f}_i = e' : \{\mathtt{f}:T\}}$$
(T-Update)

$$\frac{\Gamma \vdash e : \{\mathtt{f}:T\}}{\Gamma \vdash e.\mathtt{f}_i : T_i}$$
(T-Field)

$$\frac{\Gamma \vdash e : T}{\Gamma \vdash \texttt{ref } e : \texttt{Ref } T}$$
(T-Ref)

$$\frac{\Gamma \vdash e : \texttt{Ref } T}{\Gamma \vdash {!}e : T}$$
(T-Deref)

Fig. 3. λ_0 type rules

4.3   Translating OT_0 to λ_0

The translation from OT_0 to λ_0 is given in Fig. 4. Nominal class types are translated to structural record types and objects to records of references and functions (which encode methods). Objects carry all their methods with them, there are no separate method suites, and the this reference is hard-coded into the encoding of an object. References are made explicit. $[\![.]\!]$ gives the translation of some part of a program (we only translate complete source meta-expressions, but the output of translation may be a fragment of a meta-expression in the target language). Variable and class names are not translated, so x in the source program will be x in the translation. $[\![T]\!]$ is the translation of the type T; $type(\mathtt{C})$ and $type(\mathtt{M})$ translate elements of a type, the former gives the record type for object values, the latter gives the function type for an unbound method (i.e., a method where the this reference is free).

Classes are encoded as functions from the this reference to a record which encodes an object. These functions are bound to a variable with the name of the class in a let expression. Object instantiation is translated by creating a 'temporary' variable called this using a let expression, initialised as a reference to null. We then use the class function bound to the class's name, passing in the temporary reference for this. The result is the object and it is saved in the heap at the location pointed to by this. The entire 'let' expression will evaluate to just this reference, which after execution, will be a reference to the newly created object.

Encoding $\boxed{[\![\bullet]\!] = e}$

$$[\![\overline{Q};e]\!] \qquad\qquad = \quad \lambda \texttt{null}\!:\!\bot.\,\overline{[\![Q]\!]}\ [\![e]\!]\ \iota_0$$
$$[\![\texttt{class } \texttt{C}\{\overline{T\,\texttt{f}};M\}]\!] \qquad = \quad \texttt{let } \texttt{C} = \lambda\ \texttt{this}\!:\![\![\texttt{C}]\!].\{\overline{\texttt{f=null}},\overline{[\![M]\!]}\}\ \texttt{in}$$
$$[\![T\,\texttt{m}\,(\overline{T\,\texttt{x}})\ \{\texttt{return } e;\}]\!] \quad = \quad \texttt{m=}\lambda\overline{\texttt{x}\!:\![\![T]\!]}.[\![e]\!]$$

$$[\![\texttt{null}]\!] \qquad\qquad = \quad \texttt{null}$$
$$[\![\texttt{x}]\!] \qquad\qquad = \quad \texttt{x}$$
$$[\![\texttt{x.f}]\!] \qquad\qquad = \quad (\texttt{!x}).\texttt{f}$$
$$[\![\texttt{x.f = } e]\!] \qquad\quad = \quad \texttt{x := ((!x).f = } [\![e]\!])$$
$$[\![\texttt{x.m}(\overline{e})]\!] \qquad\qquad = \quad (\texttt{!x}).\texttt{m } [\![\overline{e}]\!]$$
$$[\![\texttt{new } \texttt{C}]\!] \qquad\qquad = \quad \texttt{let this = ref null in this := ref (C this)}$$
$$[\![\texttt{C}]\!] \qquad\qquad\quad = \quad \texttt{Ref } type(\texttt{C})$$

$$\frac{\texttt{class C } \{\overline{T\,\texttt{f}};\ \overline{M}\}}{type(\texttt{C}) = \{\texttt{f}\!:\![\![\overline{T}]\!], type(\overline{M})\}}$$

$$\frac{M = T\,\texttt{m}\,(\overline{T\,\texttt{x}})\ \{\texttt{return } e;\}}{type(M) = \texttt{m}\!:\![\![\overline{T}]\!] \to [\![T]\!]}$$

Fig. 4. Translating OT_0 to λ_0

We do not translate null, instead we introduce a variable at program scope with the name null. We use a distinguished location in the heap (ι_0) to instantiate the null variable. Dereferencing ι_0 would be a runtime error and results in the operational semantics becoming stuck (because it is not in the heap). We assume that we can always give ι_0 the bottom type for runtime typing.

5   Finitary Nested Regions

In the second stage of our development we add some ownership features; to be precise, we add finitary[6] nested regions. In comparison, ownership types have infinitary nested regions tied to objects. Our source language is OT_r. It includes a static declaration of heap regions along with the usual declaration of classes and an initial expression. These regions contain objects, as in ownership, but are not owned by objects.

We will show how OT_r may be encoded using index-dependent types; in particular, we incorporate region labels into references and reference types, and use dependent product, but not dependent sum, types to encode parametricity.

---

[6] To use Clarke's terminology [2]. Finitary regions are declared statically and, therefore, there is a fixed, finite number of regions in each program run. By contrast, infinitary regions are declared dynamically (the language includes an expression which instantiates a region, either directly or as a side-effect), each program run may have a different number of regions and this number may be infinite.

5.1   OT_r

$$e \quad ::= \quad \texttt{null} \mid \texttt{x} \mid \texttt{x.f} \mid \texttt{x.f = } e \mid \texttt{x.m}(\overline{e}) \mid \texttt{new C<}\overline{a}\texttt{>} \qquad expressions$$

R	$::=$	$\texttt{region r} \lhd \texttt{r}$	*region declarations*
Q	$::=$	$\texttt{class C<o}\rightarrow\texttt{[}b_l \ b_u\texttt{]> }\{\overline{T\,\texttt{f}};\ \overline{M}\}$	*class declarations*
M	$::=$	$T\,\texttt{m}(\overline{T\,\texttt{x}})\ \{\texttt{return } e;\}$	*method declarations*

a	$::=$	$\texttt{o} \mid \texttt{world} \mid \texttt{r}$	*actual regions*	$T,U ::=\ \texttt{C<}\overline{a}\texttt{>}$	*types*
b	$::=$	$a \mid \perp$	*bounds*		

			$\texttt{x, y, this}$	*variables*
Δ	$::=$	$\overline{\texttt{o}\rightarrow\texttt{[}b_l \ b_u\texttt{]}}$ *region environments*	$\texttt{o}$	*formal regions*
Γ	$::=$	$\overline{\texttt{x}:T}$ *variable environments*	$\texttt{r}$	*concrete regions*
			$\texttt{C}$	*class names*

Fig. 5. Syntax of OT_r

Expression typing $\boxed{\Delta; \Gamma \vdash e : T}$

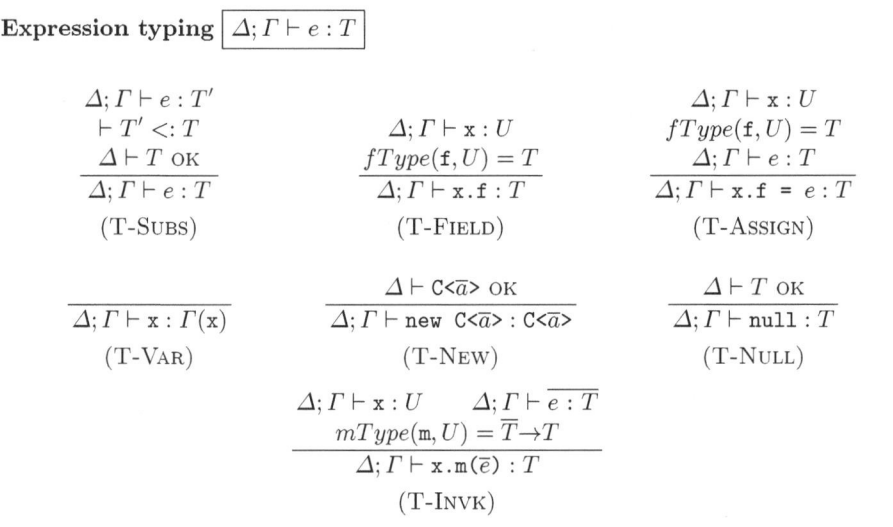

$$\frac{\begin{array}{c}\Delta; \Gamma \vdash e : T' \\ \vdash T' <: T \\ \Delta \vdash T \text{ OK}\end{array}}{\Delta; \Gamma \vdash e : T} \qquad \frac{\begin{array}{c}\Delta; \Gamma \vdash \texttt{x} : U \\ fType(\texttt{f}, U) = T\end{array}}{\Delta; \Gamma \vdash \texttt{x.f} : T} \qquad \frac{\begin{array}{c}\Delta; \Gamma \vdash \texttt{x} : U \\ fType(\texttt{f}, U) = T \\ \Delta; \Gamma \vdash e : T\end{array}}{\Delta; \Gamma \vdash \texttt{x.f = } e : T}$$

$$\text{(T-Subs)} \qquad\qquad \text{(T-Field)} \qquad\qquad \text{(T-Assign)}$$

$$\frac{}{\Delta; \Gamma \vdash \texttt{x} : \Gamma(\texttt{x})} \qquad \frac{\Delta \vdash \texttt{C<}\overline{a}\texttt{>} \text{ OK}}{\Delta; \Gamma \vdash \texttt{new C<}\overline{a}\texttt{>} : \texttt{C<}\overline{a}\texttt{>}} \qquad \frac{\Delta \vdash T \text{ OK}}{\Delta; \Gamma \vdash \texttt{null} : T}$$

$$\text{(T-Var)} \qquad\qquad \text{(T-New)} \qquad\qquad \text{(T-Null)}$$

$$\frac{\begin{array}{cc}\Delta; \Gamma \vdash \texttt{x} : U & \Delta; \Gamma \vdash \overline{e : T} \\ \multicolumn{2}{c}{mType(\texttt{m}, U) = \overline{T}\rightarrow T}\end{array}}{\Delta; \Gamma \vdash \texttt{x.m}(\overline{e}) : T}$$

$$\text{(T-Invk)}$$

Fig. 6. OT_r expression typing rules

The syntax of OT_r is given in Fig. 5. Compared with OT_0, class names are parameterised by region names in types and object instantiations. These regions are declared in a block separate from the rest of the program. Classes are region-parametric; actual region parameters (for types and instantiations) may be formal region parameters, the names of declared regions, or the 'top' region, world; bounds on regions also include the bottom region.

Inside relation $\boxed{\Delta \vdash b \preceq b}$

$$\frac{}{\Delta \vdash b \preceq b}$$
(I-REFLEX)

$$\frac{\Delta \vdash b \preceq b'' \quad \Delta \vdash b'' \preceq b'}{\Delta \vdash b \preceq b'}$$
(I-TRANS)

$$\frac{\Delta \vdash b \text{ OK}}{\Delta \vdash b \preceq \text{world}}$$
(I-WORLD)

$$\frac{\Delta \vdash b \text{ OK}}{\Delta \vdash \bot \preceq b}$$
(I-BOTTOM)

$$\frac{\text{region } r \lhd r'}{\Delta \vdash r \preceq r'}$$
(I-REGION)

$$\frac{\Delta(\mathsf{o}) = [b_l \quad b_u]}{\Delta \vdash \mathsf{o} \preceq b_u} \quad \Delta \vdash b_l \preceq \mathsf{o}$$
(I-BOUND)

Fig. 7. OT_r, the inside relation

The inside relation (Fig. 7) describes the topological relationships between regions. One region is inside another if it is an indirect descendent in the region hierarchy. The inside relation is the reflexive, transitive closure of the topological information provided by the programmer in region declarations and bounds on formal region variables. The inside relation is used to check that actual region variables are within the formal bounds in well-formedness checks. The type rules (Fig. 6) are similar to FJ, the isolation of types by region is accomplished by including region parameters in types and ensuring that subtyping is invariant with respect to region parameters. The remaining semantics are given in the accompanying technical report.

5.2 λ_Π

The target of our translation is λ_Π, which is λ_0 extended with annotated references and dependent product types. The heap is divided into hierarchical regions and values are stored in a specific region, this region is reflected in references and reference types. Reference types are dependent type constructors, although we do not support higher order use. Region parameters on classes and types are encoded as dependent product types.

Types are dependent because regions are concrete entities at runtime, even though they are not first class entities with respect to expressions. In the terminology of Aspinal and Hofmann [3], region names are the indices of λ_Π, region names and region variables are the index terms, and the singleton sort `region` is the concrete index sort.

The syntax of λ_Π is given in Fig. 8, changed and additional type rules (relative to λ_0) are given in Fig. 9, the remaining static semantics are given in the accompanying technical report.

The reference introduction expression now includes the region of the heap in which to store the referenced value; reference types reflect this region; T-REF includes the change. We add expressions to introduce ($\Lambda \overline{\mathsf{o}{:}\mathtt{I}}.e$) and eliminate

$$
\begin{array}{lll}
e & ::= & \gamma \mid \{\overline{\mathtt{f}{=}e}\} \mid e.\mathtt{f} \mid e.\mathtt{f} = e \mid \lambda \mathtt{x}{:}T.e \mid e\ \overline{e} \mid \mathtt{let}\ \overline{\mathtt{x} = e}\ \mathtt{in}\ e \\
& & \mid\ \mathtt{ref}{<}a{>}\ e \mid\ !e \mid e{:}{=}\ e \mid \varLambda \overline{\mathtt{o}{:}I}.e \mid e[\overline{a}] \qquad\qquad\qquad \textit{expressions}
\end{array}
$$

$$
\begin{array}{lll}
v & ::= & \{\overline{\mathtt{f}{=}v}\}\ \mid \iota \mid \lambda \overline{\mathtt{x}{:}T}.e\ \mid \varLambda \overline{\mathtt{o}{:}I}.e \qquad\qquad\qquad\qquad \textit{values} \\
\mathcal{H} & ::= & \mathtt{r} = \iota \rightarrow \{\overline{v}\}; \overline{\mathcal{H}} \qquad\qquad\qquad\qquad\qquad\qquad\qquad \textit{heaps}
\end{array}
$$

$$
\begin{array}{lll}
a & ::= & \mathtt{o} \mid \mathtt{r} \qquad\qquad\qquad\qquad\qquad\qquad\qquad\quad \textit{index terms} \\
b & ::= & a \mid \bot \qquad\qquad\qquad\qquad\qquad\qquad\qquad\qquad\quad \textit{bounds} \\
r & ::= & \mathtt{r} \qquad\qquad\qquad\qquad\qquad\qquad\qquad \textit{runtime index terms}
\end{array}
$$

$$
\begin{array}{lll}
T & ::= & \{\overline{\mathtt{f}{:}T}\}\ \mid\ \mathtt{Ref}{<}a{>}\ T\ \mid \overline{T} \rightarrow T\ \mid \varPi \overline{\mathtt{o}{:}I}.T\ \mid \bot \qquad\qquad \textit{types} \\
I & ::= & \mathtt{region}\ \mid \{\mathtt{o}{:}I \mid\ P\} \qquad\qquad\qquad\qquad\qquad\quad \textit{index sorts} \\
P & ::= & b \prec b\ \mid\ P \wedge P \qquad\qquad\qquad\qquad\qquad\quad \textit{index predicates} \\
A & ::= & T \mid I \qquad\qquad\qquad\qquad\qquad\qquad\qquad\qquad \textit{allsorts}
\end{array}
$$

$$
\begin{array}{lll}
\gamma & ::= & \mathtt{x}\ \mid \iota \qquad\qquad\qquad\qquad\qquad\qquad \textit{variables or locations} \\
\alpha & ::= & \gamma \mid \mathtt{o} \qquad\qquad\qquad\qquad\qquad\qquad\qquad \textit{all variables} \\
\varGamma & ::= & \overline{\alpha{:}A} \qquad\qquad\qquad\qquad\qquad\qquad \textit{variable environments}
\end{array}
$$

$$
\begin{array}{ll}
\mathtt{x,null} & \textit{variables} \\
\mathtt{r,world} & \textit{concrete regions} \\
\mathtt{o} & \textit{formal regions} \\
\iota & \textit{locations}
\end{array}
$$

Fig. 8. Syntax of $\lambda_{\varPi}$

Expression typing $\boxed{\mathcal{H}; \varGamma \vdash e : T}$

$$
\frac{\begin{array}{c} \mathcal{H}; \varGamma \vdash a\ \text{OK} \\ \mathcal{H}; \varGamma \vdash e : T \end{array}}{\mathcal{H}; \varGamma \vdash \mathtt{ref}{<}a{>}\ e : \mathtt{Ref}{<}a{>}\ T}
\qquad
\frac{\begin{array}{c} \mathcal{H}; \varGamma, \overline{\mathtt{o}{:}I} \vdash \overline{I}\ \text{OK} \\ \mathcal{H}; \varGamma, \overline{\mathtt{o}{:}I} \vdash e : T \end{array}}{\mathcal{H}; \varGamma \vdash \varLambda \overline{\mathtt{o}{:}I}.e : \varPi \overline{\mathtt{o}{:}I}.T}
\qquad
\frac{\begin{array}{c} \mathcal{H}; \varGamma \vdash e : \varPi \overline{\mathtt{o}{:}I}.T \\ \mathcal{H}; \varGamma \vdash \overline{a : I} \end{array}}{\mathcal{H}; \varGamma \vdash e[\overline{a}] : [\overline{a/\mathtt{o}}]T}
$$

$$
(\text{T-Ref}) \qquad\qquad\qquad\qquad (\text{T-Abs-Dep}) \qquad\qquad\qquad\qquad (\text{T-App-Dep})
$$

Fig. 9. $\lambda_{\varPi}$ changed type rules

($e[a]$) dependent product types[7], the former are also added to the syntax of values. Within dependent product types and dependent product introduction expressions, regions (indices) are given a sort, the sort must be either region or a *subset sort*, only regions which satisfy the predicate in the subset sort qualify for such a sort. Subset sorts are used to model bounds on regions. We allow $\bot$ as a bound in index predicates to simplify our encoding (we could do without, because of the way index predicates are defined). We add a heap to the

---

[7] In $\lambda_{\varPi}$ we both dependent and non-dependent function introduction and elimination are needed because region variables and expression variables are distinct.

environment under which all type rules are judged. At compile time we use the initial heap (generated from static region declaration, see below).

5.3 Translating OT_r to λ_Π

Encoding $\boxed{[\![\bullet]\!] = e}$

$[\![\overline{R}; \overline{Q}; e]\!]$ $\qquad = \quad \lambda\text{null}{:}\bot.[\![\overline{Q}]\!]\ [\![e]\!]\ \iota_0$

$[\![\text{class C<o} \rightarrow [b_l\ b_u]\text{>}\{\overline{T\ f}; \overline{M}\}]\!] =$

$\qquad$ let C $= \Lambda\text{o}{:}\{x{:}\text{region}\ |\ b_l \prec x \wedge x \prec b_u\ \}.\lambda\text{this}{:}[\![\text{C<}\overline{\text{o}}\text{>}]\!].\{\overline{f\text{=}null}, [\![\overline{M}]\!]\}$ in

$[\![T\ \text{m}\,(\overline{T\ x})\ \{\texttt{return}\ e;\}]\!]$ $\quad = \quad \text{m}{=}\lambda\overline{x}{:}[\![\overline{T}]\!].[\![e]\!]$

$[\![\text{null}]\!]$ $\qquad\qquad\qquad = \quad \text{null}$

$[\![x]\!]$ $\qquad\qquad\qquad\quad = \quad x$

$[\![x.f]\!]$ $\qquad\qquad\qquad\ \ = \quad (!x).f$

$[\![x.f = e]\!]$ $\qquad\qquad\ \ = \quad x := ((!x).f = [\![e]\!])$

$[\![x.\text{m}\,(\overline{e})]\!]$ $\qquad\qquad\ \ = \quad (!x).\text{m}\ [\![\overline{e}]\!]$

$[\![\text{new C<}\overline{a}\text{>}]\!]$ $\qquad\qquad = \quad$ let this $=$ ref<a_0> null in

$\qquad\qquad\qquad\qquad\qquad\qquad$ this := ref<a_0> (C$[\overline{a}]$ this)

$[\![\text{C<}\overline{a}\text{>}]\!]$ $\qquad\qquad\quad = \quad \text{Ref<}a_0\text{>}\ type(\text{C<}\overline{a}\text{>})$

$$\frac{\text{class C<o} \rightarrow [b_l\ b_u]\text{>}\ \{\overline{T\ f};\ \overline{M}\}}{type(\text{C<}\overline{a}\text{>}) = \{\overline{f{:}[\![[\overline{a/o}]T]\!]}, type([\overline{a/o}]M)\}}$$

$$\frac{M = T\ \text{m}\,(\overline{T\ x})\ \{\texttt{return}\ e;\}}{type(M) = \text{m}{:}[\![\overline{T}]\!] \rightarrow [\![T]\!]}$$

Initial heap $\boxed{\vdash \mathcal{H}}$ $\boxed{r \vdash \mathcal{H}}$

$$\frac{\text{world} \vdash \overline{\mathcal{H}}}{\vdash \text{world} = \emptyset; \overline{\mathcal{H}}} \qquad\qquad \frac{\begin{array}{c}\text{region r} \vartriangleleft \text{r}'\\ r \vdash \overline{\mathcal{H}}\end{array}}{r' \vdash r = \emptyset; \overline{\mathcal{H}}}$$

Fig. 10. Translating OT_r to λ_Π

Our translation from OT_r to λ_Π is given in Fig. 10. We extend the translation of OT_0 to handle regions. The region in which an object resides (the first region parameter of an object's type) is added to reference introduction when an object is created and to the reference type of an object. To accommodate region parameters, classes are encoded as dependent product introduction and function definition; object instantiation is dependent product elimination, function elimination, and record introduction. This is necessary because the 'this' reference is an expression variable, not a region variable, and the two kinds of variables are distinct in λ_Π. Bounds on region variables are straightforwardly encoded as subset sorts.

The region to which an object belongs is added to the reference part of an object's type, but the other region parameters do not appear in the translated types. Instead, the actual region parameters are substituted throughout the record type of the object, this fits with the structural approach to types in the Lambda Calculus. Type checking in λ_Π will continue to mirror OT_r, because all relevant region parameters will appear in the type, only deeper.

We illustrate the translation with an example. The following code sketches part of the architecture of a computer game and its initialisation in OT_r (we omit bounds for the sake of brevity):

```
region Game ◁ world;
region Gfx ◁ Game;
region AI ◁ Game;

class Sprite<r> {
  ...
}

Sprite<Gfx> avatar = new Sprite<Gfx>();
```

This is translated to the following in λ_Π (again, we omit bounds, and show only the translation of the class and initial expression):

```
let Sprite = Λ r:{x:region}.λ this:[[Sprite<r>]].{...} in
  let this = ref<Gfx> null in
    this := ref<Gfx> (Sprite[Gfx] this)
```

Where:

$$[[\text{Sprite<r>}]] \;=\; \text{Ref<r> } \{...\}$$

The heap (store) of λ_Π is intrinsically hierarchical (in the syntax, $\overline{\mathcal{H}}$ should be read as part of r), and each region of the heap is labelled. The static region declarations of OT_r are translated into an initial heap which is used to start execution, rather than the more usual empty heap. The rules for this translation are unsurprising: the entire heap is labelled 'world' and declared regions are translated into regions of the heap. Note that since regions in OT_r are finitary, no mechanism for creating heap regions in λ_Π is required or provided.

For our example, the initial heap is:

```
(world = ∅; (Game = ∅; (Gfx = ∅; ∅),(AI = ∅; ∅)))
```

6   Ownership Types

Finally, we get to ownership types proper. Our source calculus is extended to support per-object regions (aka, ownership contexts). Since a new region is created with each new object, regions are now infinitary. Tying region creation to object creation, and the visibility requirements for such regions, require us to extend our target calculus with dependent sum types.

6.1 OT

OT is our ownership type system, it is a stripped down version of the many Featherweight Java [11]-based ownership systems proposed in the last few years [13,14,9]. It elides many features we do not consider essential to the parametric ownership types paradigm. OT is purely descriptive; that is, it does not enforce an encapsulation policy, it only describes the topology of the heap.

OT supports formal and actual context parameters on classes and types, respectively. Formal context parameters have upper and lower bounds. The only supported actual context parameters are the distinguished contexts this and world (the root of the ownership hierarchy), and in-scope formal context parameters. Using world as an upper bound is equivalent to a parameter being unbounded above, likewise for $\perp$ (allowed as a bound, but not an actual context parameter) as a lower bound.

e	$::=$ null $\mid$ x $\mid$ x.f $\mid$ x.f = e $\mid$ x.m($\overline{e}$) $\mid$ new C<$\overline{a}$>		*expressions*

Q	$::=$ class C<$\overline{\text{o} \rightarrow [b_l \ b_u]}$> $\{\overline{T\text{ f}};\ \overline{M}\}$	*class declarations*
M	$::=$ T m($\overline{T\text{ x}}$) $\{$return $e;\}$	*method declarations*

a	$::=$ o $\mid$ world $\mid$ this	*actual owners*	$T,U ::=$ C<$\overline{a}$>		*types*
b	$::=$ $a \mid \perp$	*bounds*			
			x, y, this		*variables*
Δ	$::=$ $\overline{\text{o} \rightarrow [b_l \ b_u]}$	*context environments*	o, owner		*formal owners*
Γ	$::=$ $\overline{\text{x}:T}$	*variable environments*	C		*class names*

Fig. 11. Syntax of OT

The syntax of OT is given in Fig. 11. Similarly to OT_r, class definitions are parameterised by bounded formal context parameters, and types are class names parameterised by actual context parameters. Contexts are generated implicitly by object creation, and we allow this as an owner to signal the context owned by the current object. The nesting of contexts is also implicit, implied by the nesting of the current context inside the current object's owner's context.

$$\frac{\Gamma(\text{this}) = \text{C}<\overline{a}>}{\Delta; \Gamma \vdash \text{this} \preceq a_0}$$

(I-Owner)

$$\frac{\overline{\text{o} \rightarrow [b_l \ b_u]}; \text{this}:\text{C}<\overline{\text{o}}> \vdash \overline{M}, \overline{T} \text{ OK}}{\vdash \text{class C}<\overline{\text{o} \rightarrow [b_l \ b_u]}> \{\overline{T\text{ f}};\ \overline{M}\} \text{ OK}}$$

(T-Class)

Selected static semantics rules are given above, the remaining static semantics are given in the accompanying technical report. I-Owner replaces I-Region of

Expression typing $\boxed{\Delta; \Gamma \vdash e : T}$

$$
\begin{array}{c}
\Delta; \Gamma \vdash e : T' \\
\vdash T' <: T \\
\Delta; \Gamma \vdash T \text{ OK} \\
\hline
\Delta; \Gamma \vdash e : T
\end{array}
\qquad
\begin{array}{c}
\Delta; \Gamma \vdash \mathtt{x} : U \\
fType(\mathtt{f}, U) = T \\
\hline
\Delta; \Gamma \vdash \mathtt{x.f} : [\mathtt{x/this}]T
\end{array}
\qquad
\begin{array}{c}
\Delta; \Gamma \vdash \mathtt{x} : U \\
fType(\mathtt{f}, U) = T \\
\Delta; \Gamma \vdash e : [\mathtt{x/this}]T \\
\hline
\Delta; \Gamma \vdash \mathtt{x.f} = e : [\mathtt{x/this}]T
\end{array}
$$

(T-Subs)   (T-Field)   (T-Assign)

$$
\begin{array}{c}
\\
\hline
\Delta; \Gamma \vdash \mathtt{x} : \Gamma(\mathtt{x})
\end{array}
\qquad
\begin{array}{c}
\Delta; \Gamma \vdash \mathtt{C<}\overline{a}\mathtt{>} \text{ OK} \\
\hline
\Delta; \Gamma \vdash \mathtt{new\ C<}\overline{a}\mathtt{>} : \mathtt{C<}\overline{a}\mathtt{>}
\end{array}
\qquad
\begin{array}{c}
\Delta; \Gamma \vdash T \text{ OK} \\
\hline
\Delta; \Gamma \vdash \mathtt{null} : T
\end{array}
$$

(T-Var)   (T-New)   (T-Null)

$$
\begin{array}{c}
\Delta; \Gamma \vdash \mathtt{x} : U \qquad \Delta; \Gamma \vdash \overline{e} : \overline{[\mathtt{x/this}]T} \\
mType(\mathtt{m}, U) = \overline{T} {\rightarrow} T \\
\hline
\Delta; \Gamma \vdash \mathtt{x.m}(\overline{e}) : [\mathtt{x/this}]T
\end{array}
$$

(T-Invk)

Fig. 12. OT expression typing rules

OT_r, the former extends the inside relation to objects and their owners, rather than the statically declared relationships of the latter rule.

The OT type rules use two environments: context environments (which map formal context parameters to their bounds) and variable environments (which map variables to their types). T-Class shows how environments for type checking are constructed. The expression typing rules (Fig. 12) enforce ownership typing in the same way as OT_r, however, a little extra work must be done substituting the receiver for 'this' in types.

6.2 λ_Σ

Our target calculus is called λ_Σ; it extends λ_Π with dependent sum types and changes the indices from regions of the heap to locations in the heap (since locations are OT's labels for identifying heap regions). The syntactic structure of the heap changes, although its topology does not.

The syntax of λ_Σ is given in Fig. 13, semantics are given in the accompanying technical report; we describe only the changes from λ_Π, changes to the type rules are given in Fig. 14.

Dependent sum types are introduced using the $\langle e, c \rangle$ syntax. This expression creates an opaque package of e, where c is hidden. Dependent sums are eliminated using the open expression (open $\langle \mathtt{x}_1, \mathtt{x}_2 \rangle$ = e_1 in e_2), which has a similar format to unpacking an existential type [15]. e_1 is the expression which is unpacked; within the scope of e_2, the unpacked expression is referred to as $\mathtt{x}_1$, and $\mathtt{x}_2$ allows the hidden context in the type of e_1 to be named.

Since expression variables are index variables, and we will always pass arguments by reference, in λ_Σ, we do not need separate λ and Λ expressions

$$
\begin{array}{lll}
e & ::= & \gamma \mid \{\overline{\texttt{f}=e}\} \mid e.\texttt{f} \mid e.\texttt{f} = e \mid \Lambda\texttt{x}{:}\overline{I}.e \mid e[\overline{c}] \mid \texttt{let } \overline{\texttt{x} = e} \texttt{ in } e \\
& & \mid \texttt{ref<}c\texttt{> } e \mid \texttt{!}e \mid e{:=}\ e \mid \langle e, c\rangle \mid \texttt{open } \langle\texttt{x},\texttt{x}\rangle = e \texttt{ in } e \qquad \textit{expressions}
\end{array}
$$

$$
\begin{array}{lll}
v & ::= & \{\overline{\texttt{f}=v}\} \mid \iota \mid \Lambda\texttt{x}{:}\overline{I}.e \mid \langle v, r\rangle & \textit{values} \\
\mathcal{H} & ::= & \overline{\iota \to \{v; \mathcal{H}\}} & \textit{heaps}
\end{array}
$$

$$
\begin{array}{lll}
c & ::= & \gamma \mid \top & \textit{index terms} \\
b & ::= & c \mid \bot & \textit{bounds} \\
r & ::= & \iota \mid \top & \textit{runtime index terms}
\end{array}
$$

$$
\begin{array}{lll}
T & ::= & \{\overline{\texttt{f}{:}T}\} \mid \texttt{Ref<}c\texttt{> } T \mid \Pi\overline{\texttt{x}{:}\overline{I}}.T \mid \Sigma\texttt{x}{:}I.T \mid \bot & \textit{types} \\
I & ::= & \texttt{Ref} \mid \texttt{Ref<}c\texttt{> } T \mid \{\texttt{x}{:}I \mid P\} & \textit{index sorts} \\
P & ::= & a \prec a \mid P \wedge P & \textit{index predicates} \\
A & ::= & T \mid I & \textit{allsorts}
\end{array}
$$

$$
\begin{array}{lll}
\Gamma & ::= & \overline{\gamma : A} & \textit{variable environments} \\
\gamma & ::= & \texttt{x} \mid \iota & \textit{variables or locations}
\end{array}
$$

$$
\begin{array}{lll}
\texttt{x,null,world} & & \textit{variables} \\
\iota & & \textit{locations}
\end{array}
$$

Fig. 13. Syntax of λ_Σ

Expression typing $\boxed{\Gamma \vdash e : T}$

$$
\frac{\Gamma, \overline{\texttt{x}{:}I} \vdash \overline{I} \text{ OK} \qquad \Gamma, \overline{\texttt{x}{:}I} \vdash e : T}{\Gamma \vdash \Lambda\overline{\texttt{x}{:}\overline{I}}.e : \Pi\overline{\texttt{x}{:}\overline{I}}.T}
$$

(T-Abs-Dep)

$$
\frac{\Gamma \vdash e : \Pi\overline{\texttt{x}{:}\overline{I}}.T \qquad \Gamma \vdash \overline{a} : \overline{I}}{\Gamma \vdash e[\overline{a}] : [\overline{a/\texttt{x}}]T}
$$

(T-App-Dep)

$$
\frac{\Gamma \vdash e_1 : \Sigma\texttt{y}{:}I.U \qquad \Gamma, \texttt{y}{:}I, \texttt{x}{:}U \vdash e_2 : T \qquad \Gamma \vdash T \text{ OK}}{\Gamma \vdash \texttt{open } \langle\texttt{y},\texttt{x}\rangle = e_1 \texttt{ in } e_2 : T}
$$

(T-Open)

$$
\frac{\Gamma \vdash c : I \qquad \Gamma \vdash e : [c/\texttt{x}]T \qquad \Gamma \vdash \Sigma\texttt{x}{:}I.T \text{ OK}}{\Gamma \vdash \langle e, c\rangle : \Sigma\texttt{x}{:}I.T}
$$

(T-Pack)

Fig. 14. λ_Σ changed typing rules

(we use Λ), nor separate expressions for dependent and non-dependent function application.

6.3 Translating OT to λ_Σ

The major change from our previous translations is how we handle the 'this' object as an owner. In particular, new regions are created with object initialisation, rather than explicitly from region declarations. The current object is

Encoding $\boxed{\llbracket \bullet \rrbracket = e}$

$$\llbracket \overline{Q}; e \rrbracket = \Lambda \texttt{null:} \perp ., \texttt{world:Ref} . \llbracket \overline{Q} \rrbracket \; \llbracket e \rrbracket \; \iota_0 \; \iota_0$$

$\llbracket \texttt{class } \texttt{C<o} \rightarrow [b_l \; b_u] \texttt{>} \{\overline{T \, \texttt{f}; M}\} \rrbracket =$

    $\texttt{let } \texttt{C} = \Lambda \texttt{this:} \llbracket \texttt{C<o>} \rrbracket, \texttt{o:} \{\texttt{x:Ref} \mid b_l \prec \texttt{x} \wedge \texttt{x} \prec b_u \;\}.\{\texttt{f=null}, \overline{\llbracket M \rrbracket}\} \text{ in}$

$\llbracket T \, \texttt{m} (\overline{T \, \texttt{x}}) \; \{\texttt{return } e; \} \rrbracket = \texttt{m=} \Lambda \overline{\texttt{x:} \llbracket T \rrbracket} . \llbracket e \rrbracket$

$$\llbracket \texttt{x} \rrbracket = \texttt{x}$$

$\llbracket \texttt{x.f} \rrbracket = \texttt{open } \langle \texttt{this,y} \rangle = !\texttt{x in } \langle \texttt{y.f,this} \rangle$

$\llbracket \texttt{x.f} = e \rrbracket = \texttt{open } \langle \texttt{this,y} \rangle = !\texttt{x in x} := \langle \texttt{y.f} = \llbracket e \rrbracket, \texttt{this} \rangle$

$\llbracket \texttt{x.m}(\overline{e}) \rrbracket = \texttt{open } \langle \texttt{this,y} \rangle = !\texttt{x in let } \overline{\texttt{z}} = \overline{\llbracket e \rrbracket} \text{ in } \langle \texttt{y.m}[\overline{\texttt{z}}], \texttt{this} \rangle$

$\llbracket \texttt{new } \texttt{C<}\overline{a}\texttt{>} \rrbracket =$

    $\texttt{let this} = \texttt{ref<}a_0\texttt{> null in this} := \texttt{ref<}a_0\texttt{> } \langle \texttt{C[this,}\overline{a}\texttt{]}, \texttt{this} \rangle$

$\llbracket \texttt{C<}\overline{a}\texttt{>} \rrbracket = \texttt{Ref<}a_0\texttt{> } \Sigma \texttt{x:} \{\texttt{x:Ref} \mid \texttt{x} \prec a_0\}.[\texttt{x/this}] type(\texttt{C<}\overline{a}\texttt{>})$

$$\frac{\texttt{class } \texttt{C<o} \rightarrow [b_l \; b_u] \texttt{> } \{\overline{T \, \texttt{f}; \; M}\}}{type(\texttt{C<}\overline{a}\texttt{>}) = \{\texttt{f:} \overline{\llbracket [\overline{a/o}] T \rrbracket}, type([\overline{a/o}] M)\}}$$

$$\frac{M = T \, \texttt{m} (\overline{T \, \texttt{x}}) \; \{\texttt{return } e; \}}{type(M) = \texttt{m:} \overline{\llbracket T \rrbracket} \rightarrow \llbracket T \rrbracket}$$

Fig. 15. Translating OT to λ_Σ

treated like another context parameter to a class, but it is always instantiated with the current object. However, since different objects with otherwise identical context parameters and classes should be type-compatible, the 'this' context parameter needs to be hidden in the object's external type. This is achieved using dependent sum types; when an object is created, the 'this' context parameter is hidden using dependent sum introduction, and whenever the object is used, the dependent sum is temporarily eliminated using an 'open' expression. We discuss why this gives the correct behaviour in Sect. 6.5.

Context parameters are encoded in the same way as before, using dependent product types. Since we unify function introduction and dependent product introduction, we need to use `let` expressions in our encoding of method calls to assign the result of evaluating arguments to variables (our 'Λ' expressions are syntactically limited to only taking variables as arguments).

6.4 Properties

We expect both source and target calculi to be type sound in all their flavours (with a suitable operational semantics in the case of source calculi), therefore, we expect the following[8]:

---

[8] We assume that heaps ($\mathcal{H}$) can be used for type checking in place of variable environments (Γ); formalising this is trivial.

Conjecture: subject reduction (λ_Σ)

For all $\mathcal{H}$, $\mathcal{H}'$, e, e', T, if $\mathcal{H}; \emptyset \vdash e : T$ and $e; \mathcal{H} \rightsquigarrow e'; \mathcal{H}'$ then $\mathcal{H}'; \emptyset \vdash e' : T$.

Conjecture: progress (λ_Σ)

For all $\mathcal{H}$, e, T, if $\mathcal{H}; \emptyset \vdash e : T$ then either e is a value or there exists $\mathcal{H}'$ and e' such that $e; \mathcal{H} \rightsquigarrow e'; \mathcal{H}'$.

We hope that translation is also sound, for example:

Conjecture: translation from OT to λ_Σ is sound.

For all Γ, Δ, e, T, if $\Delta; \Gamma \vdash e : T$ then $[\![\Gamma]\!], [\![\Delta]\!] \vdash [\![e]\!] : [\![T]\!]$.

This conjecture as stated is probably too strong because we have omitted the requirement that Δ and Γ are well-formed; we may need additional constraints.

In combination with the type soundness theorems, translation soundness gives type soundness across translation; that is, if an expression type checks under OT we can translate that expression to λ_Σ and execute it, and the result of execution will have the translated type of the original expression. Furthermore, since types in OT completely describe the ownership properties of objects, we will have shown that statically enforcing the ownership hierarchy in OT causes the execution in λ_Σ to respect the ownership hierarchy, even though λ_Σ is not an ownership types system.

6.5 Discussion

We have demonstrated how a simple ownership type system (OT) can be modularly encoded in a lambda calculus with dependent types. In doing so we hope to have shed some light on what makes an ownership system and how such a (relatively) novel system compares to better understood, foundational type systems. Just as encoding objects into the lambda calculus shows a fine-grained view of what constitutes object-orientation (for example, in object construction, the introduction of a record, the introduction of a reference, the relation between an object, its class and super-classes, the typing of 'this'), we hope we have shown the component parts of ownership types — nested regions, context parameters, the 'this' and 'owner' owners, and the relations between objects and contexts.

We have shown that descriptive ownership type systems do nothing more complicated than index-dependent type systems. The correspondence between the two systems is straightforward, and this shows the close relationship between the systems.

We have shown that nested regions can be encoded with only dependent product types. One might wonder if a region calculus without context parameters could be encoded without dependent products, but any parameterisation by indices requires dependent products and we must, at the least, parameterise an object's type by its owner. Moving from finitary to infinitary regions requires a subtle change in our target calculus: regions are directly associated with locations in the heap, note that this is a novel, rather than 'traditional' type system feature; in future work, we hope to encode heaps and regions using monads [16] to further illuminate the relative complexity of finitary v. infinitary regions.

Tying region creation to object creation (object ownership) requires dependent sum types, and so ownership types are quantifiably more complex than infinitary regions. We cannot avoid having the current object as a class's (dependent) type parameter (in our target calculus) because it can be used in the types of fields and in method signatures. The only reasonable alternative is to make this available in a class as an expression variable using non-dependent function abstraction (λ). This fails, however, because this will appear in the structural type of the object (assuming this appears in the type of one or more fields or methods), and cannot be substituted away. this cannot be subsituted because the newly created object cannot be named. In our approach, we get around the problem in object construction by hiding this. Furthermore, even if we could construct objects, we must hide the object in its type so that different objects with the same type in the source calculus are compatible in the target calculus.

In translating from our source to target calculi, we have moved from nominal to structural typing. One consequence of this is that properties of the source calculus will only hold if they are not redundant. More concretely, context parameters of a class in OT will only affect the type of that class in λ_{Σ}, if they are used within that class. This weakness of the encoding should not affect the properties we describe above, but means that two objects which are incompatible in OT may be compatible in λ_{Σ}. If we were to try to prove that our translation was complete (as well as sound), then we would have to assume that all formal context parameters were used somewhere in a class, as well as that all classes have at least one field and that all fields and methods are uniquely named.

Limitations. Our object model is imperfect, the main omission is inheritance, but more subtly we do not support recursive uses of a class; that is, we can't create an object within its class definition. We could support such use by using recursive let (letrec) instead of let in our target calculus.

We have shown how our source calculi can be translated into our target calculi, but we have not shown that each target is the most simple possible. In fact, since all our calculi are Turing Complete, this fact does not hold. We maintain that the translations we have given are the simplest 'straightforward' translations, but cannot rigorously define 'straightforward', so cannot prove this.

7   Extensions to the Basic Ownership Model

In this section, we will discuss some extensions to our baseline ownership types system. We first look in some detail at extending our system with context polymorphic methods and dynamic aliases. We then discuss adding orthogonal generics and using existential quantification of contexts as an intermediate step in encoding a variety of other features. Looking at future work, we briefly discuss ownership domains and multiple ownership, which affect the heap topology, we consider how the Generic Ownership concept relates to our model, and speculate on how two encapsulation policies might be handled.

7.1   OT$_+$

We investigate how to encode context polymorphic methods [17] and dynamic aliases [9] into λ_Σ. The latter allows objects to be owned by local variables and its main use is in relaxing the owners-as-dominators discipline. We call OT with context polymorphic methods and dynamic aliases OT$_+$, and give its syntax in Fig. 16.

e	$::=$ null $\mid$ x $\mid$ x.f $\mid$ x.f $=$ e $\mid$ x.<$\overline{a}$>m($\overline{e}$) $\mid$ new C<$\overline{a}$>		*expressions*

Q	$::=$ class C<$\overline{\text{o}\rightarrow[b_l\ b_u]}$> $\{\overline{T\ \text{f}};\ \overline{M}\}$		*class declarations*
M	$::=$ <$\overline{\text{o}\rightarrow[b_l\ b_u]}$>$T$ m($\overline{T}$ x) $\{$return $e;\}$		*method declarations*

a	$::=$ o $\mid$ world $\mid$ x	*actual owners*	$T,U ::=$ C<$\overline{a}$>	*types*
b	$::=$ $a \mid \perp$	*bounds*		
			x, y, this	*variables*
Δ	$::=$ $\overline{\text{o}\rightarrow[b_l\ b_u]}$	*context environments*	o, owner	*formal owners*
Γ	$::=$ $\overline{\text{x}:T}$	*variable environments*	C	*class names*

Fig. 16. Syntax of OT$_+$

$$\frac{\Delta;\Gamma\vdash\text{x}:U \qquad \Delta;\Gamma\vdash\overline{e:[\text{x/this},\overline{a/\text{o}}]T}}{\begin{array}{c}mType(\text{m},U)=\overline{\text{o}\rightarrow[b_l\ b_u]}.\overline{T}\rightarrow T\\ \Delta;\Gamma\vdash\overline{[\text{x/this},\overline{a/\text{o}}]b_l\preceq a} \qquad \Delta;\Gamma\vdash\overline{a\preceq[\text{x/this},\overline{a/\text{o}}]b_u}\end{array}}{\Delta;\Gamma\vdash\text{x.}<\overline{a}>\text{m}(\overline{e}):[\text{x/this},\overline{a/\text{o}}]T}$$

(T-Invk)

Allowing local variables as owners requires simply relaxing the syntactic category of actual owners to include expression variables (x). Owner-polymorphic methods require a simple syntactic change to method declarations and calls and some extra code in the T-Method and T-Invk rules (shown above). T-Method is extended to add the owner-parameters and their bounds to the environment used to check the body of the method. T-Invk is extended to check that actual owner parameters satisfy the bounds declared on formal parameters and to substitute actual for formal owner parameters throughout the rule. This behaviour is analogous to the treatment of expression variables, which allows us to encode ownership variables in the same way as expression variables.

Encoding $\boxed{[\![\bullet]\!] = e}$

$$[\![\overline{Q}; e]\!] \quad = \quad \lambda \texttt{null}\!:\!\bot. \lambda \texttt{world}\!:\!\top. \overline{[\![Q]\!]}\ [\![e]\!]\ \iota_0\ \iota_0$$

$$[\![\texttt{class C<o} \rightarrow [b_l\ b_u]\texttt{>}\{\overline{T\ \texttt{f}}; \overline{M}\}]\!] \quad = \quad \cdot$$

$$\texttt{let C} = \varLambda \texttt{this}\!:\![\![\texttt{C<}\overline{\texttt{o}}\texttt{>}]\!], \texttt{o}\!:\!\{\texttt{x:Ref} \mid b_l \prec \texttt{x} \wedge \texttt{x} \prec b_u\ \}.\{\overline{\texttt{f=null}}, \overline{[\![M]\!]_{\texttt{C<}\overline{\texttt{o}}\texttt{>}}}\}\ \texttt{in}$$

$$[\![\texttt{<o} \rightarrow [b_l\ b_u]\texttt{>}T\ \texttt{m}\,(\overline{T\ \texttt{x}})\ \{\texttt{return}\ e;\}]\!]_{\texttt{C<}\overline{\texttt{o}}\texttt{>}} \quad = $$

$$\texttt{m=}\varLambda \texttt{o}\!:\!\{\texttt{x:Ref} \mid b_l \prec \texttt{x} \wedge \texttt{x} \prec b_u\ \}, \overline{\texttt{x}}\!:\!\overline{[\![T]\!]}.[\![e]\!]$$

$$[\![\texttt{x}]\!] \quad = \quad \texttt{x}$$

$$[\![\texttt{x.f}]\!] \quad = \quad \texttt{open}\ \langle \texttt{this}, \texttt{y} \rangle\ \texttt{=}\ !\texttt{x in}\ \langle \texttt{y.f}, \texttt{this} \rangle$$

$$[\![\texttt{x.f = }e]\!] \quad = \quad \texttt{open}\ \langle \texttt{this}, \texttt{y} \rangle\ \texttt{=}\ !\texttt{x in x := } \langle \texttt{y.f = }[\![e]\!], \texttt{this} \rangle$$

$$[\![\texttt{x.<}\overline{a}\texttt{>m}(\overline{e})]\!] \quad = \quad \texttt{open}\ \langle \texttt{this}, \texttt{y} \rangle\ \texttt{=}\ !\texttt{x in}$$
$$\texttt{let}\ \overline{\texttt{z=}[\![e]\!]}\ \texttt{in}\ \langle \texttt{y.m}[\overline{a}, \overline{\texttt{z}}], \texttt{this} \rangle$$

$$[\![\texttt{new C<}\overline{a}\texttt{>}]\!] \quad = \quad \texttt{let this = ref<}a_0\texttt{> null in}$$
$$\texttt{this := } \langle \texttt{C}[\texttt{this}, \overline{a}], \texttt{this} \rangle$$

$$[\![\texttt{C<}\overline{a}\texttt{>}]\!] \quad = \quad \texttt{Ref<}a_0\texttt{>}\ \varSigma \texttt{x}\!:\!\{\texttt{x:Ref} \mid \texttt{x} \prec a_0\}.\,[\texttt{x/this}]\mathit{type}(\texttt{C<}\overline{a}\texttt{>})$$

$$\frac{\texttt{class C<o} \rightarrow [b_l\ b_u]\texttt{>}\ \{\overline{T\ \texttt{f}};\ \overline{M}\}}{\mathit{type}(\texttt{C<}\overline{a}\texttt{>}) = \{\overline{\texttt{f}\!:\![\![\,[\overline{a/\texttt{o}}]\,T]\!]}, \mathit{type}([\overline{a/\texttt{o}}]\,M)\}}$$

$$\frac{M = T\,\texttt{m}\,(\overline{T\ \texttt{x}})\ \{\texttt{return}\ e;\}}{\mathit{type}(M) = \texttt{m}\!:\!\overline{[\![T]\!]} \rightarrow [\![T]\!]}$$

Fig. 17. Translating OT_+ to $\lambda_\varSigma$

The translation from OT_+ to $\lambda_\varSigma$ is given in Fig. 17. The translation is mostly similar to the translation from OT, the only addition is that the encoding of a method uses a dependent product introduction, and the dependent product type must be correspondingly eliminated when we call the method. We do not need to take any special measures to deal with dynamic aliases since variable names in expressions and types are not translated anyway, and context and expression variables are unified in $\lambda_\varSigma$.

Since OT_+ is obviously more complex than OT, we might wonder if OT could be encoded into a simpler calculus than $\lambda_\varSigma$. We conjecture that there is no 'straightforward' translation into a simpler dependent types calculus because to encode the additional features in OT_+ we use only dependent product types, which are fundamental to our encoding of OT (and indeed OT_r).

7.2   Orthogonal Generics

'Orthogonal' generics add type parametricity to an ownership types system orthogonally to ownership information. That is, types are parameterised by types in addition to being parameterised by contexts (or reflecting ownership information in some other way). Type variables and context variables cannot be mixed, and type parameters do not affect the ownership properties of an object. Different flavours of orthogonal ownership are found in Generic Universes [13,18],

MOJO [19], and Confined Types [20]. Orthogonal generics improve the expressivity of the type system, but do not affect the ownership properties.

We can add support for orthogonal generics by adding universal types to λ_Σ. The translation is trivial and standard. We do not delve any deeper here since orthogonal generics and ownership types are, well, orthogonal.

7.3 Existential Types

We have previously proposed existential quantification of ownership parameters [21]. Such quantification can trivially be encoded as dependent sums (assuming that the source calculus has explicit introduction and elimination of existential types). Thus the target calculus would remain λ_Σ.

We have previously shown how a number of ownership features (any and readonly in Universe types [22], wildcard owners [19], variant ownership types [14], any/unknown in effective ownership [23], dynamic downcasting [24]) can be encoded using existential quantification [5,25,26,21]. Corresponding encodings could be used to encode these features using dependent sums, we leave the details to future work.

7.4 Extensions to the Topology

The ownership topology may be altered by allowing multiple owners per context (multiple ownership [19]) or multiple contexts per owner (ownership domains [27]). Allowing multiple owners changes the ownership hierarchy (a tree) into a directed acyclic graph, this fundamentally changes the structure of the heap and of types; investigating how these changes must be reflected in translation is planned as future work. Allowing multiple contexts per owner leaves the heap organised into a tree and requires only a single owner per object. We can therefore represent such a model of ownership in λ_Σ.

In fact, Ownership Domains significantly enhance the expressibility of the type system, domains (contexts) can be specified outside of their declaring classes by using paths of the form x.d. We could not find a way to encode such paths in λ_Σ. We believe more powerful dependent types, which allow types to depend on any expression, not just indices, are required. These are found in, for example, Dependent ML [7]. MOJO [19] also supports paths to ownership contexts and these would also require the more powerful type system for encoding.

OT can be extended to support 'local' ownership domains (i.e., multiple, private ownership contexts per object) by representing domains as distinguished fields and hiding these fields in the type in the same way that this is hidden in the translation of OT.

Ownership Domains support their own encapsulation policy, link soundness, we have not yet investigated how it might be incorporated into our translations.

7.5 OGJ and Phantom Types

In the OGJ system [4], ownership types are represented using Java's generic types. The original system used additions to Java's type system to represent the this context. Later work (WOGJ) [5] showed that these extensions could be eliminated by using Java wildcards. Java wildcards are existential types. The Java generics parts of OGJ correspond to dependent products in our target calculus, and the wildcards parts to dependent sums. WOGJ is thus a *Phantom Types* approximation of our calculus. Phantom Types [28] are a technique from functional programming where dependent types are approximated by parametric types, usually only to the extent of universal quantification/dependent products, but here extended to existential quantification/dependent sums. We hope to more deeply describe this relationship in future work.

7.6   Encapsulation Policies

Ownership types systems are often known by their encapsulation policies. These policies use the hierarchical ordering of the heap given by descriptive ownership types to limit how objects may reference or modify other objects. The most well-known polices are owners-as-dominators, which restricts referencing to 'outward' references in the ownership topology, and owners-as-modifiers (associated with Universes systems), which restricts modification to objects transitively owned by the current object.

In WOGJ, owners-as-dominators can be enforced simply by restricting the bounds on wildcards [29,5]. We therefore imagine that the owners-as-dominators policy can easily be simulated in λ_Σ in a similar way. The details are left for future work.

Existential types can be used to restrict writing (e.g., a wildcard list in Java with no lower bound (List<? extends ...>) is 'read-only'[9] with respect to it's contents). By exploiting this effect, it may be possible to simulate the owners-as-modifiers policy in λ_Σ by careful translation — for example, by an extra level of indirection or trickery with parameter passing. However, we have not been able to find such a translation — we can prevent writing to references in the desired way, but it has proved difficult to prevent assignment of null to fields. This corresponds to the wildcards case, where calling a 'set' method on a list with no lower bound is prevented, but calling 'remove' or 'clear' is not.

8   Conclusion

In this chapter, we have shown that ownership types can be encoded in a lambda calculus with dependent types. We have shown that tying heap region creation to object creation (the key feature of object ownership) requires a more complex type system than static heap regions. We have discussed that modelling most ownership extensions does not require any more complex fundamental types. Future work in this area is necessary to prove the conjectures stated in Sect. 6.4, and to further investigate encapsulation polices and extensions to the ownership types paradigm.

---

[9] I.e., we cannot call a 'set' method.

Acknowledgements. We would like to thank the reviewers and editors for their thorough and useful reviews, and patience.

References

1. Clarke, D.G., Potter, J.M., Noble, J.: Ownership Types for Flexible Alias Protection. In: Object-Oriented Programming, Systems, Languages, and Applications, OOPSLA (1998)
2. Clarke, D.G.: Object Ownership and Containment. PhD thesis, School of Computer Science and Engineering, The University of New South Wales, Sydney, Australia (2001)
3. Aspinall, D., Hofmann, M.: Dependent types. In: Pierce, B.C. (ed.) Advanced Topics in Types and Programming Languages, The MIT Press (2004)
4. Potanin, A., Noble, J., Clarke, D., Biddle, R.: Generic Ownership for Generic Java. In: Object-Oriented Programming, Systems, Languages, and Applications, OOPSLA (2006)
5. Cameron, N., Noble, J.: Encoding Ownership Types in Java. In: Vitek, J. (ed.) TOOLS 2010. LNCS, vol. 6141, pp. 271–290. Springer, Heidelberg (2010)
6. McKinna, J.: Why dependent types matter. In: Symposium on Principles of Programming Languages, POPL (2006)
7. Xi, H., Pfenning, F.: Dependent types in practical programming. In: Symposium on Principles of Programming Languages, POPL (1999)
8. McBride, C., McKinna, J.: The view from the left. Journal of Functional Programming 14(1), 69–111 (2004)
9. Clarke, D.G., Drossopoulou, S.: Ownership, Encapsulation and the Disjointness of Type and Effect. In: Object-Oriented Programming, Systems, Languages, and Applications, OOPSLA (2002)
10. Bruce, K.B., Cardelli, L., Pierce, B.C.: Comparing Object Encodings. Information and Computation 155(1-2) (1999)
11. Igarashi, A., Pierce, B.C., Wadler, P.: Featherweight Java: a Minimal Core Calculus For Java and GJ. Transactions on Programming Languages and Systems 23(3), 396–450 (2001); An earlier version of this work appeared at OOPSLA 1999
12. Cameron, N., Drossopoulou, S., Noble, J.: Understanding Ownership Types with Dependent Types. Technical report 23, Vistoria University, School of Engineering and Computer Science (2012)
13. Dietl, W., Drossopoulou, S., Müller, P.: Generic Universe Types. In: Ernst, E. (ed.) ECOOP 2007. LNCS, vol. 4609, pp. 28–53. Springer, Heidelberg (2007)
14. Lu, Y.: On Ownership and Accessibility. In: Thomas, D. (ed.) ECOOP 2006. LNCS, vol. 4067, pp. 99–123. Springer, Heidelberg (2006)
15. Mitchell, J.C., Plotkin, G.D.: Abstract Types have Existential Type. Transactions on Programming Languages and Systems 10(3), 470–502 (1988)
16. Wadler, P.: Comprehending monads. In: Conference on LISP and Functional Programming, LFP (1990)
17. Wrigstad, T.: Ownership-Based Alias Managemant. PhD thesis, KTH, Sweden (2006)
18. Dietl, W., Drossopoulou, S., Müller, P.: Separating ownership topology and encapsulation with Generic Universe Types. Transactions on Programming Languages and Systems (TOPLAS) **33** 20, 20:1–20:62 (2011)

19. Cameron, N., Drossopoulou, S., Noble, J., Smith, M.: Multiple Ownership. In: Object-Oriented Programming, Systems, Languages, and Applications, OOPSLA (2007)
20. Zhao, T., Palsberg, J., Vitek, J.: Type-based Confinement. J. Funct. Program 16(1), 83–128 (2006)
21. Cameron, N., Drossopoulou, S.: Existential Quantification for Variant Ownership. In: Castagna, G. (ed.) ESOP 2009. LNCS, vol. 5502, pp. 128–142. Springer, Heidelberg (2009)
22. Müller, P.: Modular Specification and Verification of Object-Oriented Programs. LNCS, vol. 2262. Springer, Heidelberg (2002)
23. Lu, Y., Potter, J.: Protecting Representation with Effect Encapsulation. In: Principles of Programming Languages, POPL (2006)
24. Wrigstad, T., Clarke, D.G.: Existential Owners for Ownership Types. Journal of Object Technology 6(4) (2007)
25. Cameron, N., Dietl, W.: Comparing Universes and Existential Ownership Types. In: International Workshop on Aliasing, Confinement and Ownership in object-oriented programming, IWACO (2009)
26. Cameron, N.: Existential Types for Variance — Java Wildcards and Ownership Types. PhD thesis, Imperial College London (2009)
27. Aldrich, J., Chambers, C.: Ownership Domains: Separating Aliasing Policy from Mechanism. In: Odersky, M. (ed.) ECOOP 2004. LNCS, vol. 3086, pp. 1–25. Springer, Heidelberg (2004)
28. Hinze, R.: Fun with phantom types. In: The Fun of Programming, pp. 245–262. Palgrave Macmillan (2003)
29. Cameron, N., Noble, J.: OGJ Gone Wild. In: International Workshop on Aliasing, Confinement and Ownership in object-oriented programming, IWACO (2009)

Object Graphs with Ownership Domains: An Empirical Study

Radu Vanciu and Marwan Abi-Antoun

Department of Computer Science
Wayne State University, Detroit, MI 48202 USA
{radu,mabiantoun}@wayne.edu

Abstract. Researchers have proposed many ownership type systems but reported limited experience with most of them on real object-oriented code. Only a few systems have been implemented, and there have been few substantial case studies done with those systems.

In order to better empirically evaluate ownership type systems, we have therefore conducted a number of case studies applying the Ownership Domains type system to programs at a larger scale. To facilitate the study of legacy code, we reimplemented Ownership Domains using available language support for annotations. After annotating and typechecking a range of object-oriented systems, we extracted global, hierarchical, Ownership Object Graphs (OOGs) using static analysis. OOGs provide an abstracted view that is consistent with programmer design intent, compared to flat object graphs that can be extracted without the benefit of the ownership annotations. An OOG also visualizes the system's ownership structure and helps developers refine the annotations they add to better express the system's design.

This paper shares our observations from studying the annotations and the extracted OOGs across several subject systems. We compute metrics on the annotations and on the extracted OOGs, to gain insights into the ownership relationships latent within object-oriented code and to evaluate the effectiveness of the abstraction mechanisms in OOGs.

Keywords: ownership types, object graphs, empirical evaluation.

1 Introduction

Researchers have proposed many ownership type systems [39,21,36,17,9,23,18] but have not reported significant experience with most of them on real object-oriented code. Only a few implementations of the type systems have been reported in the literature [11,9,23,43], and there are few substantial case studies evaluating these systems.

To address this gap, we have conducted a number of case studies applying one ownership type system, Ownership Domains [9], to a broad range of larger-scale object-oriented systems. To facilitate the study of legacy code, we re-implemented Ownership Domains using available language support for annotations. We then annotated several systems and typechecked the annotations.

D. Clarke et al. (Eds.): Aliasing in Object-Oriented Programming, LNCS 7850, pp. 109–155, 2013.

From the annotated systems, we extracted global, hierarchical, Ownership Object Graphs (OOGs) using static analysis [3,2].

The nodes of the OOG represent abstractions of objects and ownership domains. An *ownership domain* is a conceptual group of objects with an explicit name and explicit policies that govern how it can reference objects in other domains [9]. A domain roughly corresponds to an architectural tier, a notion present in most architecture description languages. The nodes of the OOG form a hierarchy: an object can have child objects. A child object can be strictly owned by or conceptually part of the parent object. Instead of making objects direct children of other objects, ownership domains introduce an extra level of indirection. So, in an OOG, an object has domains, which contain other objects to form its substructure, and so on. Edges of the OOG represent reference relations between objects, where the references respect the explicit policies between domains.

Hierarchy is effective to shrink a large, flat graph [47], and enables an OOG to scale, so the size of the top-level diagram does not increase linearly with the size of the program. Hierarchy also provides abstraction since a hierarchical representation enables both high-level understanding and detail, and is commonly used to document software structure.

An OOG provides *abstraction by ownership hierarchy* when it shows architecturally significant objects near the top of the hierarchy and data structures further down. Furthermore, an OOG supports *abstraction by types*, which acts within a domain to collapse objects that share a common supertype into a single representative object. The OOG visualization helps developers refine the annotations they add to better express the system's design. Since there are multiple ways to express design intent, there are multiple ways to annotate a system. The type checker ensures that the annotations are consistent with each other and with the code. Moreover, the OOG is *sound* in two respects. First, each runtime object has exactly one representative in the OOG. Second, the OOG has edges that correspond to all possible runtime points-to relations between those runtime objects.

This paper shares our observations from studying the annotations and the extracted OOGs across several subject systems. To evaluate the subject systems quantitatively, we compute metrics on the annotations and on the extracted OOGs. To show how annotations can be refined over time, we annotated a few systems in stages, gathering metrics at two different milestones along the way.

Goals for Annotation Metrics. We computed metrics on the annotations to:
- understand the ownership relationships latent within legacy code;
- measure the quality of the annotations that we added.

Goals for OOG Metrics. We computed metrics on the OOG to:
- better understand the ownership-based hierarchical structure of legacy code;
- measure the abstraction level of the extracted OOGs: for example, a large number of objects at the top level of the hierarchy indicates that the OOG is too cluttered and not sufficiently abstract.

Outline. The rest of this paper is organized as follows. Section 2 provides background information on the annotations and the OOGs. Section 3 describes our method. Section 4 presents our results for the annotation metrics and the OOG metrics. Section 5 discusses our observations and mentions some limitations and threats to validity. We discuss related work in Section 6 and conclude.

2   Background

This section provides background information on the annotations and the OOGs.

2.1   Review of Ownership Domains

Ownership Domains. An *ownership domain* is a conceptual group of objects with an explicit name and explicit policies that govern how the domain can reference objects in other domains. Each object is assigned to a single domain, which does not change at runtime. A developer indicates the domain of an object by annotating each reference to that object in the program. The annotations define two kinds of object hierarchy, logical containment and strict encapsulation.

1. **Logical Containment (part-of).** A public domain provides *logical containment*, by making an object conceptually *part of* another object. Having access to an object gives access to objects inside all its public domains.
2. **Strict Encapsulation (owned-by).** A private domain provides *strict encapsulation*, by making an object *owned by* its parent object. Then, a `public` method cannot return an alias to an object in a private domain, even though the Java type system allows returning an alias to a field marked with the visibility modifier `private`.

Why Ownership Domains? There are several key features of Ownership Domains that are crucial for expressing design intent in code and extracting OOGs. The first is having explicit "contexts" or domains. Other ownership type systems implicitly treat all objects with the same owner as belonging to an "ownership domain", but one that is implicit [22]. On the other hand, explicit contexts are useful, because developers can define multiple contexts per object to express their design intent as our metrics will show later (Section 4).

Second, Ownership Domains support pushing any object underneath any other object in the ownership hierarchy. A child object may or may not be encapsulated by its parent object, and can still be referenced from outside its owner, if it is part of a public domain of its parent. In addition, an object can grant particular external domains (named by a domain parameter) permission to access objects within one of its private domains, using a domain link specification. These mechanisms for expressing conceptual containment, rather than strict encapsulation, contrast with an *owners-as-dominators* type system [21], which requires any access to a child object to go through its owning object.

Public domains are ideal in an OOG to achieve hierarchy by capturing interesting part-of relationships among objects. Ownership and OOGs are only useful to the extent that a significant hierarchy exist; if most or all objects

$$CL ::= \texttt{class } C<\overline{\alpha},\overline{\beta}> \texttt{ extends } C'<\overline{\alpha}> \texttt{ assumes } \overline{\gamma} \rightarrow \overline{\delta} \; \{ \; \overline{T} \; \overline{f}; \; K \; \overline{D} \; \overline{L} \; \overline{M} \; \}$$

$$K ::= C(\overline{T'} \; \overline{f'}, \overline{T} \; \overline{f}) \; \{ \; \texttt{super}(\overline{f'}); \; \texttt{this}.\overline{f} = \overline{f}; \}$$

$$D ::= [\texttt{public}] \; \texttt{domain } d;$$

$$L ::= \texttt{link } d \rightarrow d';$$

$$M ::= T_R \; m(\overline{T} \; \overline{x}) \; \{ \; \texttt{return } e; \; \}$$

$$e ::= x \mid \texttt{new } C<\overline{p}>(\overline{e}) \mid e.f \mid (T)e \mid e.m(\overline{e}) \mid \ell \mid \ell > e$$

$$n ::= x \mid v$$

$$T ::= C<\overline{p}>$$

$$p ::= \alpha \mid n.d \mid \texttt{shared}$$

$$v, \ell \in locations$$

Fig. 1. Featherweight Domain Java Syntax [9]

are in top-level domains, ownership has not provided any real benefit. But an owners-as-dominators semantics can result in many top-level objects, as completely dominated objects are rare (our metrics will show this). A rule of thumb in software architecture is that each architectural tier should have only five to seven components [33]. Applying this guideline to ownership suggests that OOGs are more readable if top-level domains only contain five to seven abstract objects.

Language. We briefly review the Ownership Domains abstract syntax (Fig. 1) since we present some annotated examples and define the annotation metrics in terms of the abstract syntax. To facilitate the study of legacy code, we re-implemented Ownership Domains using available language support for annotations. For a detailed discussion of the concrete annotation language, see [2, Appendix A].

We discuss the Ownership Domains syntax using an example (Fig. 2). We show the same example using the language extensions (Fig. 2a) and Java annotations (Fig. 2b). The example illustrates how an application would read the contents of an initialization settings ("ini") file (Fig. 3). An "ini" file has multiple paragraphs, with name, value pairs in each paragraph, to persist the various settings, such as the size of the application window when it was last closed.

Domain Declaration. Developers declare a domain before use, using the @Domains annotation (line 1). Domains are declared on a class but are treated like fields, in that fresh domains are created for each instance of that class. For a domain D declared on a class C and two instances o1 and o2 of type C, the domains o1.D and o2.D are distinct, for distinct o1 and o2.

Domain Use. Each object is assigned to a single ownership domain, which does not change at runtime. Developers indicate the domain of an object by annotating each reference to that object in the program. For example, the @Domain annotation declares the reference f of type InputFile in the domain L (line 13).

```
1 public class IniFile<U,L,D> {
2    domain owned;
3    public domain PARAGS;
4    shared String filename;
5
6    owned Hashtable<shared String, PARAGS IniParagraph<U,L,D>> paragraphs;
7    PARAGS IniParagraph<U,L,D> para;
8    ...
9 }
10 public class IniParagraph<U,L,D> {
11   domain owned;
12   L InputFile f;
13   ...
14 }
15 // Root class, used for OOG construction
16 public class System {
17   domain UI, LOGIC, DATA;
18   LOGIC IniFile<UI,LOGIC,DATA> iniFile;
19   ...
20 }
```

(a) Ownership Domains: language extensions.

```
1 @Domains({ "owned", "PARAGS" })
2 @DomainParams({ "U", "L", "D" })
3 public class IniFile {
4    @Domain("shared") String filename;
5    @Domain("owned<shared, PARAGS<U,L,D>>") Hashtable<String,
6                                      IniParagraph> paragraphs;
7    @Domain("PARAGS<U,L,D>") IniParagraph para;
8    ...
9 }
10 @Domains({ "owned" }) // != IniFile's owned
11 @DomainParams({ "U", "L", "D" })
12 public class IniParagraph {
13   @Domain("L") InputFile f;
14   ...
15 }
16 // Root class, used for OOG construction
17 @Domains({"UI","LOGIC","DATA"})
18 public class System {
19   // Outer LOGIC is the domain of the reference
20   // Class IniFile is parameterized with <U,L,D>
21   // We bind the domain parameters as follows:
22   // U := UI, L := LOGIC, D := DATA
23   @Domain("LOGIC<UI,LOGIC,DATA>") IniFile iniFile;
24   ...
25 }
```

(b) Ownership Domains: annotations.

Fig. 2. Ownership Domains: language extensions vs. annotations

```
// Contents of IniFile "sample.ini"
[Appearance]        // IniParagraph1
MainWinXpos = 437 // Name-value pair1
MainWinYpos = 332 // Name-value pair2
...
[Display]           // IniParagraph2
ScaleMethod = 3
...
```

Fig. 3. An "ini" file has multiple paragraphs, with (name, value) pairs in each

This example illustrates the two kinds of object hierarchy, logical containment and strict encapsulation. For example, IniFile declares a public domain, PARAGS, to hold para objects. Strict encapsulation is accomplished using private domains. For example, IniFile stores the Hashtable in a private domain, owned (line 6).

Domain Parameters. Domain parameters on a type allow objects to share state. Developers declare domain parameters using the @DomainParams annotation. For example, the class IniParagraph takes the U, L and D domain parameters, and these are bound to the corresponding domain parameters on IniFile, respectively. This way, both an IniParagraph object and an IniFile object can reference the same InputFile object in the L domain parameter (see the two incoming edges from para and iniFile to f in the OOG).

Special Annotations. There are additional annotations that add expressiveness to the type system [11]: unique indicates an object to which there is only one reference, such as a newly created object, or an object that is passed linearly from one domain to another. One ownership domain can temporarily lend an object to another and ensure that the second domain does not create persistent references to the object by marking it as lent. An object that is shared may be aliased globally but may not alias non-shared references. Unfortunately, the global nature of shared objects makes reasoning difficult, so it is best practice to avoid using shared where possible.

2.2   Review of the Ownership Object Graph (OOG)

While ownership annotations show the relationship between two objects or domains that are currently in scope, OOGs show how these relationships compose to form a global hierarchy. The extraction of an OOG from ownership annotations is subtle, because annotations are expressed in terms of locally visible domain names, which may be type parameters that refer to a domain declared elsewhere. For example, the InputFile object is declared to be in domain L, but L is only a domain parameter (line 13, Fig. 2b). In order to place the InputFile in a hierarchy, we must determine to what declared domain L is bound. In this case, L is bound to the LOGIC domain, (line 23, Fig. 2b) so in our OOG diagram we put the InputFile in the LOGIC domain of the System object (see Fig. 4b).

To start the OOG extraction process, the developer picks a root class as a starting point, the System class in the example (Fig. 2b). The root class is

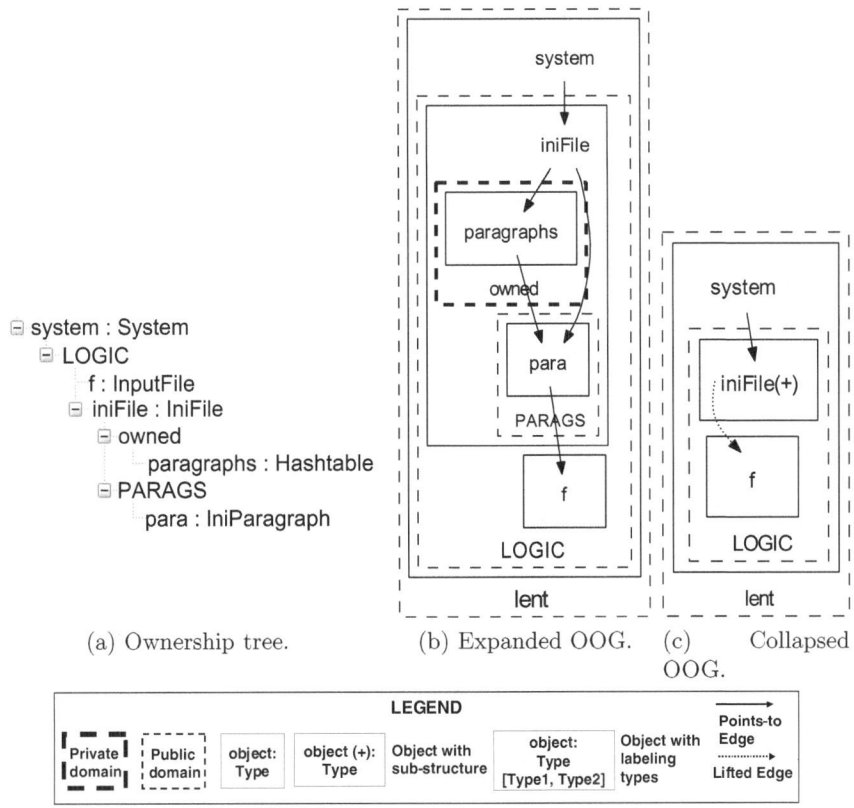

(a) Ownership tree.   (b) Expanded OOG.   (c)   Collapsed
OOG.

Fig. 4. OOG for the earlier example (Fig. 2)

assumed to be instantiated into a root object. The static analysis then uses the
ownership annotations in the code to impose a conceptual ownership hierarchy
on the objects in the system, starting at the root object (Fig. 4a). In the ownership hierarchy, a low-level object such as paragraphs is underneath a more
architecturally interesting object such as iniFile. Fig. 4b and Fig. 4c show the
corresponding OOG of the above example (Fig. 2). Typically, we do not show the
root object, we consider the domains declared on the root class as the top-level
domains, and we call the objects in the top-level domains as top-level objects.

To construct the OOG, the static analysis abstractly interprets the program with the annotations. In particular, it maps formal domain parameters
to the actual domains to which they are bound, which as described above shows
InputFile inside the actual domain LOGIC on the root object. In addition, the
OOG shows points-to edges that correspond to field references.

An OOG is abstract in the sense that one "canonical object" in the OOG corresponds to one or more objects in the system at runtime. Also, an OOG does not
pin things down to individual objects. Instead, it abstracts objects by domains and
types. For example, it merges several objects of the same or similar types that are
in the same domain. If at runtime multiple instances of the IniFile class and of

the IniParagraph class are created, and the latter were all placed into the PARAGS domain on the iniFile object, the OOG would show one para: IniParagraph object in the PARAGS domain. Developers can trace from the canonical object in the OOG to all the lines of code that may create such an object.

Aliasing Invariant. By abstracting objects by domains and types, the OOG also enforces an aliasing invariant: no one runtime object appears as two different canonical objects in the OOG. To enforce this invariant, the analysis relies on the ownership domain annotations, which also give precision about aliasing, without requiring an alias analysis. The type system guarantees that two objects in different domains cannot alias, but two objects in the same domain may alias.

Visualization. The OOG uses box nesting to indicate containment of objects inside domains and domains inside objects (Fig. 4). Dashed-border, white-filled boxes represent domains. Solid-filled boxes represent objects. Solid edges represent field references. An object labeled obj:T indicates an object reference obj of type T, which we then refer to either as "object obj" or as a "T object", meaning "an instance of the T class". A private domain has a thick, dashed border; a public domain, a thin one. Having a hierarchical representation allows expanding or collapsing objects to control the level of visual detail. In Fig. 4b, we fully expanded the OOG. In Fig. 4c, we collapsed the sub-structure of iniFile. The symbol (+) on an object indicates that it has a collapsed sub-structure.

Object Graph. The internal representation of the OOG is the Object Graph (OGraph). An OGraph has two types of nodes, objects and domains. Edges between objects correspond to field reference points-to relations (the thick edges). The root of the graph is the root object, the instance of the developer-specified root class. The metrics we discuss later operate on an OGraph. As a first approximation, the nodes in an OGraph form a hierarchy, where each object node has a unique parent domain, and each domain node a unique parent object (the thin edges illustrate the ownership relations) (Fig. 5a). In fact, the graph is not a strict hierarchy. In order to handle recursive types, the graph can have cycles and have the same domain appear as the child of two objects. For more information about handling recursion, refer to [2, Chap. 3].

Abstraction by Types. An OOG provides architectural abstraction primarily by ownership hierarchy. In addition, an OOG can abstract objects within each domain by their declared types. In many object-oriented systems, many types extend common base classes or implement common interfaces. One heuristic for abstraction by types merges objects in the same domain based on an ordered list of design intent types (DIT) provided by the developer. To decide whether to merge two objects of type C_1 and C_2 in a domain, the analysis finds in DIT a class or interface C, such that $C_1 <: C$ and $C_2 <: C$. If DIT does not include such a type, then abstraction by types does not apply (Fig. 6). Another heuristic merges objects whenever their types share one or more nontrivial types. A developer provides the list of trivial types (TT), which includes interfaces such as Cloneable and Serializable from Java Standard Library. The heuristic does not merge objects that share only trivial types as supertypes.

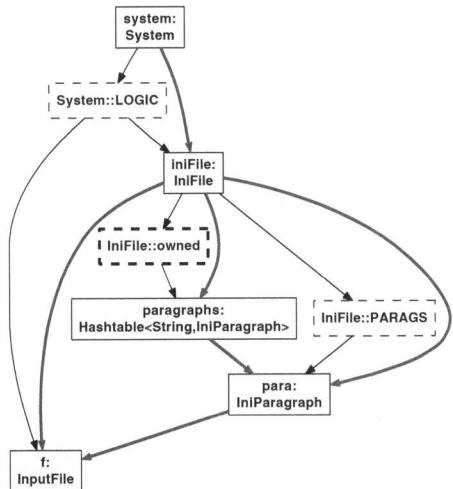

(a) Internal representation of the OOG in Fig. 4 (OGraph).

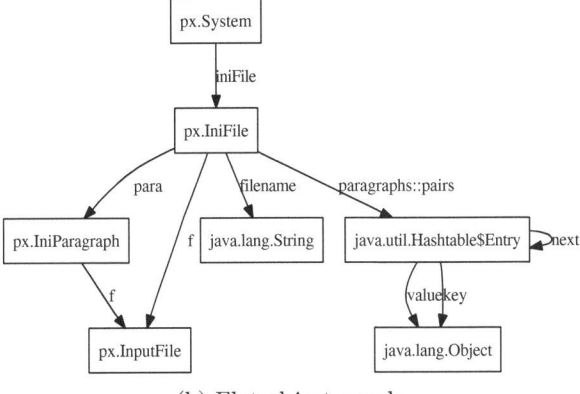

(b) Flat object graph.

Fig. 5. OGraph vs. flat object graph for the earlier example (Fig. 2)

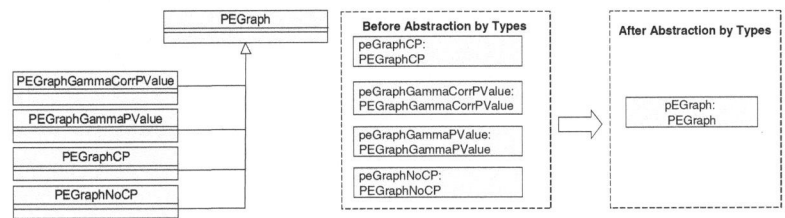

(a) Class inheritance hierarchy.

(b) Abstraction by types on OOG.

Fig. 6. Effect of abstraction by types (example from PX system [29])

Table 1. List of subject systems. The *Version* is stated if it is known. *Abbrev.* is the abbreviated name we use to refer to the system later in this paper.

System	Version	Abbrev.	Open Source?	Domain	Type
JHotDraw	5.3	JHD	Yes	GUI framework	Open Source
DrawLets	2.0	DL	Yes	GUI framework	Commercial
MiniDraw		MD	Yes	Board game framework	Educational
Aphyds		APD	No	Circuit design	Academic
HillClimber		HC	No	Simulation	Academic
PathwayExpress		PX	No	Bioinformatics tool	Academic
ApacheFTPServer	1.0.5	AFS	Yes	FTP server	Open Source
CryptoDB		CDB	Yes	Cryptography database	Educational

Flat object graph. We also extracted a flat object graph (Fig. 5b) using Womble [30] for the same example, ignoring the ownership annotations in place. The flat object graph shows low-level objects (e.g., `para:IniParagraph`) at the same level as the interesting objects (e.g., `iniFile:IniFile`).

3   Method

We first discuss the subject systems we selected (Section 3.1), and the procedure we used to add annotations and extract OOGs from those systems (Section 3.2). We then state our research questions (Section 3.3), and we answer these questions with support from metrics on the annotations (Section 3.4) and on the OOGs (Section 3.5).

3.1   Subject Systems

We selected the subject systems according to the following criteria: large enough to be more interesting than prior case studies but small enough to complete in the time available; having design information available that we could use in order to specify ownership; and covering a diversity of object-oriented applications. The systems selected are discussed below and shown in Table 1. Some aspects of the code structure, including inheritance, interface implementation, and type parametrization, are relevant in the annotation process; these aspects are summarized in Table 2. For brevity, we assign an abbreviated name to each system, and we show it between parentheses in the next paragraphs. In the rest of the paper, we refer to the systems using the abbreviated name.

JHotDraw (JHD). JHotDraw [31] is an open-source, object-oriented framework that is rich with design patterns, uses composition and inheritance heavily and has evolved through several versions. JHotDraw is a significant example in the object-oriented community. The details of the annotation process are discussed elsewhere [2, Chap. 4.6]. The JHD OOG was used to analyze conformance

Table 2. Information about the systems' code structure, obtained using the Eclipse Metrics Plugin [25]. **KLOC** is the size of the system. **#clsss**, **#intrfcs**, **#pckgs** are the number of classes, interfaces and packages. We show the maximum and the mean for the depth of the inheritance tree. **#static mthds** and **flds** are the number of static methods and fields.

Abbr.	KLOC	#clsss	#intrfcs	#pckgs	uses generics?	inh. tree depth		#static	
						max	mean	mthds	flds
JHD	18.0	224	33	8	No	8	2.41	75	121
DL	8.8	94	23	12	No	7	3.66	65	27
MD	1.4	31	17	5	Yes	6	2.00	3	10
APD	8.2	66	0	1	No	6	2.39	6	29
HC	15.6	93	7	2	No	5	3.16	5	131
PX	36	163	9	30	No	7	2.41	153	186
AFS	14.4	159	39	24	Yes	5	1.68	97	109
CDB	2.3	21	1	3	Yes	3	1.57	7	11
Total	104.7	661							

against a reference architecture. It was also shown to three developers during a study exploring the questions that developers ask about object structures [6].

DrawLets (DL). DrawLets [24] is an object-oriented framework implemented in Java for building graphical applications. DrawLets supports a drawing canvas that holds figures and lets users interact with them. The details of adding annotations and extracting OOGs from DrawLets are discussed elsewhere [14, Sec. 4]. The DrawLets OOG was carefully refined by a developer who was implementing code modification tasks, to evaluate if the OOG was useful to understand the system's runtime structure [4].

MiniDraw (MD). MiniDraw [35] is a pedagogical object-oriented framework that is a scaled-down version of JHotDraw. Also, MiniDraw comes with insights into its design, discussed in a textbook [20]. The framework supports the graphical aspects of board games and other applications that let users manipulate two dimensional graphical objects. Some of the sample applications supported by MiniDraw include board games such as BreakThrough. We added annotations to the framework and to the BreakThrough sample application [13]. The MD OOG was carefully refined by a developer while she piloted code modification tasks for a controlled experiment [12, Chap. 3] to evaluate if the OOG helps developers to understand the system's runtime structure during coding activities.

Aphyds (APD). Aphyds [28] is a pedagogical circuit layout application that an electrical engineering professor wrote for one of his classes. Students in the class are given the program with several key algorithms omitted, and are asked to code the algorithms as assignments. Aphyds is interesting because it has available architectural documentation [10]. The APD OOG was used to analyze conformance against a reference architecture. The details of the annotation process are discussed elsewhere [2, Section 7.5].

HillClimber (HC). HillClimber [41] is a Java application developed by undergraduates at the University of British Columbia. HillClimber is part of a collection of Java applications to graphically demonstrate artificial intelligence algorithms, built on the CIspace framework. In particular, HillClimber demonstrates stochastic local search algorithms for constraint satisfaction problems. HillClimber is also interesting because it uses a framework and its architectural structure had degraded over the years. The details of the annotation process are discussed elsewhere [2, Chap. 4.7].

Apache FTP Server (AFS). Apache FTP Server [1] is an open-source implementation of a complete and portable server engine based on the standard File Transfer Protocol (FTP). We added annotations and extracted OOGs guided by the reference architecture available [49].

Pathway-Express (PX). Pathway-Express [29] is an object-oriented, web application implemented in J2EE. PX is part of the Onto-Tools developed in the Intelligent System and Bioinformatics Laboratory at Wayne State University. PX finds, builds, and displays a graphical representation of gene interactions, and has thousands of users spread across several bioinformatics research groups. We studied this system because we had access its maintainers to help us refine the OOGs. After completing the annotations and extracting an initial OOG [8, Sec. 3], we evaluated the PX OOG by showing it to a lead maintainer of the system. We then refined the OOG according to the maintainer's requests [5].

CryptoDB (CDB). CryptoDB [32] is a secure database system designed by a security expert. CryptoDB follows a database architecture that provides cryptographic protections against unauthorized access, and includes a sample implementation in Java. We selected CryptoDB because it has both a Java implementation and an informal architectural description, that guided the process of adding annotations and extracting OOGs [2, Sec. 7.8]. The OOG was then compared against a detailed runtime architecture [7].

3.2 Procedure

We now discuss the procedure for adding and checking the annotations, and extracting and refining the OOGs.

Annotation Goals. When adding annotations, our goals included generating the least number of typechecker warnings. Such warnings indicate that the annotations are inconsistent with the code and with each other. The second goal was making the fewest changes to the code, since we were interested in describing the as-built ownership structure of the legacy systems. Some changes were needed to be able to add annotations. These changes are fairly cosmetic; for example, we extracted local variables in the presence of complex expressions. Finally, the third goal was minimizing the effort involved in adding the annotations. Ideally, we need smart ownership inference tools to generate annotations. Instead, we developed tools for adding boilerplate annotations.

Extraction Goals. When extracting OOGs, our goals included the following: extracting OOGs that are sufficiently abstract, clutter-free, and that convey

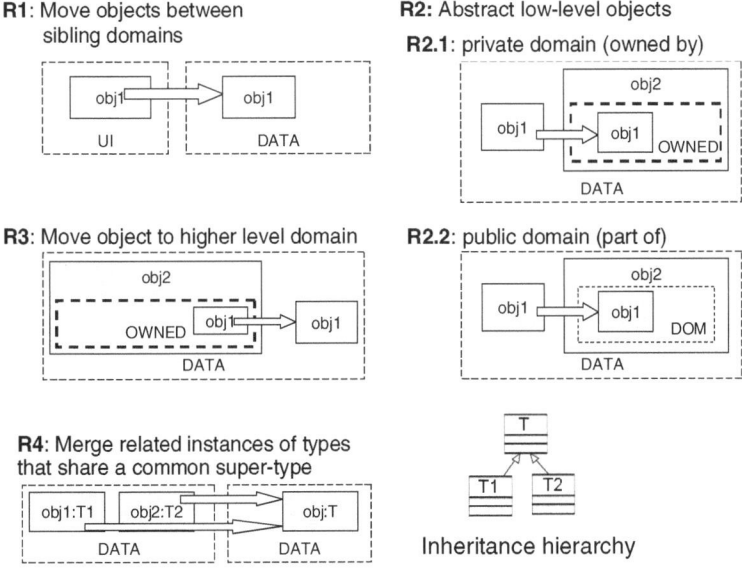

Fig. 7. Possible OOG refinements

design intent; and extracting the as-built OOGs, which may or may not match the maintainers' expectations.

OOG Refinement. Once extracted, one can refine an initial OOG as follows (Fig. 7):

R1 Move an object between sibling domains, e.g., between the top-level domains UI and LOGIC;

R2 Abstract a low-level object from a top-level domain by pushing it underneath a more architecturally relevant object, i.e.:

    R2.1 Make an object conceptually *part of* another object, by pushing it into a public domain of the parent object;

    R2.2 Make an object *owned by* another object, by pushing it into a private domain of the parent object;

R3 Move an object from a lower-level to a higher-level domain;

R4 Collapse related instances of subtypes, using abstraction by types, by adding selected types to DIT or TT list;

R5 Other, such as make an object shared.

To distinguish between architecturally-relevant objects and low-level objects, one can create an application-specific list of low-level types (LLT), and consider all the instances of a type in LLT to be low-level objects. For most applications, LLT contains data structures such as ArrayList, HashMap, or utility classes. A type may be in LLT for one application, but architecturally-relevant for another. For example, an instance of the Rectangle class might be architecturally-relevant for a drawing application, while in a UML editor, an instance of Rectangle might be part of a more complex shape and might be considered low-level.

3.3   Research Questions

Research Question (RQ1). The first research question is about annotations:

> *RQ1: Do Ownership Domains specify, within the code, hints about strict encapsulation, logical containment and architectural tiers?*

We decompose this question, and introduce several metrics that measure the degree to which Ownership Domains are used to capture the relevant design qualities. When applicable, we organize the results of the metrics according to the following scale: *significant* (80% or higher), *large* (80% – 50%), *moderate* (20% – 50%), or *partial* (20% or lower).

RQ1.1   What amount of strict encapsulation do Ownership Domains specify?
We measure the number of references annotated with private domains, and the number of objects in private domains.

RQ1.2   What amount of logical containment do Ownership Domain specify?
We measure the number of object references annotated with public domains, the number of objects in public domains, and the number of incoming edges into public domains.

RQ1.3   Do ownership domains specify architectural tiers?
We measure the number of references annotated with top-level domains, and the number of objects in top-level domains.

Research Question(RQ2). The second research question is about the OOGs:

> *RQ2: Does a global, hierarchical, Ownership Object Graph (OOG) provide more architectural abstraction compared to a flat object graph?*

We decompose this question and measure the degree to which abstraction mechanisms are used and how effective they are. For each of the following research questions, we formulate a corresponding hypothesis.

Abstraction by Ownership Hierarchy. Some research questions are related to abstraction by ownership hierarchy:

RQ2.1   To what extent does an OOG hide low-level objects underneath more architecturally relevant objects?
We hypothesize that the majority of objects that are of a type in LLT are at the lower levels of the OOG. We measure the average depth of low-level objects.

RQ2.2   How many low-level objects does an OOG show in the top-level domains?
We hypothesize that only a few objects of a type in LLT are in the top-level domains. We measure the number of objects that are in top-level domains and are of a type in LLT.

RQ2.3   To what extent does an OOG show architecturally-relevant objects at the top-level, compared to a flat object graph?
We hypothesize that the number of architecturally-relevant objects are one order of magnitude fewer than the number of objects in a flat graph. We measure the number of top-level objects in an OOG divided by the number of objects in a flat graph.

Abstraction by Types. Other research questions are related to abstraction by types:

RQ2.4 To what extent does abstraction by types further merge objects within a domain?

We hypothesize that abstraction by types further reduces the cluttering of the OOG. We compare the OOG metrics before and after using abstraction by types.

RQ2.5 How long are the list of design intent types and list of trivial types?

When using abstraction by types, OOGs uses DIT and TT for customizing the abstraction. It is desirable that these lists are short in order to minimize effort in refining the OOG. We hypothesize that DIT and TT are much smaller, compared to the list of types (classes and interfaces) in the system. We measure the size of the lists for the various systems.

Precision. Some research questions are related to the precision of the OOG:

RQ2.6 How often does an OOG merge objects of the same or similar types that are in the same domain?

An OOG does not pin things down to individual objects. Instead, it merges several objects of the same or similar types that are in the same domain. We hypothesize that by using abstraction by ownership hierarchy and by types an OOG has sufficient precision. We measure the average number of new expressions in the code that correspond to one object in the OOG, and the average number of objects in the OOG that correspond to a new expression.

RQ2.7 How often does an OOG appear as a fully connected graph?

We hypothesize that rarely does an OOG appear as a fully connected graph. We measure the number of points-to edges, and average number of incoming edges into top-level, public, and private domains.

RQ2.8 How often does an OOG collapse all the objects in a domain into a single object?

We hypothesize that rarely does an OOG collapse all the objects in a domain into a single object, in the absence of aliasing information more precise than what ownership annotations provide. We measure the average number of objects per domain.

Overall. Other research questions are related to the combined effects of both abstraction mechanisms on the OOG:

RQ2.9 To what extent does the size of the top-level OOG increase linearly with the size of the program?

The size of the top-level OOG does not increase linearly with the size of the program. We plot the size of the top-level OOG vs. the size of the system[1].

---

[1] For correlation, we measure the value of Pearson's coefficient which is between -1 and +1, inclusively. A value of -1 indicates a perfect negative correlation between the two variables. Correspondingly, a value of +1 indicates a perfect positive correlation between the two variables. If the correlation coefficient is close to 0, then there is no linear relationship between the two variables. We consider a correlation of 0–0.1 trivial, 0.1–0.3 minor, 0.3–0.5 moderate, 0.5–0.7 large, 0.7–0.9 near perfect, and 0.9–1 perfect.

3.4   Annotation Metrics

To describe the defined annotation metrics, we refer to the symbols defined in the FDJ abstract syntax (Fig. 1): $\overline{D}$ for a list of actual domains, $\overline{\alpha}$ and $\overline{\beta}$ for a list of domain parameters, $\overline{L}$ for a list of domain links, and $\overline{\gamma} \rightarrow \overline{\delta}$ for a domain assumption, etc. For $\overline{D}$, we distinguish between private (domain d) and public (public domain d) domains.

Object-Level Metrics. The object-level metrics distinguish between annotations on fields and those on variables. Variables include both local variables and formal method parameters. For each field or variable of a reference type, we record the owning domain, then compute the frequency of the occurrence of a domain, across all fields or variables of a reference type in the program.

For each type of annotation x, we record the frequency $\%x$. The annotation x can be one of the following:
- One of the special annotations: lent shared, or unique. For example, using excessively the shared annotation indicates that we are not reasoning about many objects in the system.
- Domain parameter p_i in scope;
- Special domain parameter, owner;
- A public domain of a final field, $ff.d_i$, where ff is a final field in scope and d_i is a public domain declared on the class of the field;
- Locally declared domain d_i in scope. Further, we distinguish between private domains (domain d_i) and public domains (public domain d_i);
- "other" refers to special cases, i.e., annotations on static methods, inner classes, or an explicit annotation on the receiver (by default, the receiver annotation is either "lent" or "owner").

Some annotations may not occur, so we omit the metrics that are always zero:
- lent annotation cannot occur on fields or method return values;
- unique fields, though valid in AliasJava [11], are not currently supported by the type system and the typechecker.

Class-level Metrics. For each class we measure the size of annotations related to a class. These metrics correspond to the size of the sequence $|\overline{x}|$ averaged over all the classes in the system, where $\overline{x}$ can be one of the following:
- locally declared domains $\overline{D}$;
- domain parameters $\overline{\beta}$;
- domain inherits $\overline{\alpha}$;
- domain links $\overline{L}$;
- domain assumes $\overline{\gamma \rightarrow \delta}$.

3.5   OOG Metrics

We define three categories of object graph metrics to measure the effect of abstraction by ownership hierarchy, abstraction by types, and finally, the differences with flat object graphs. To get better insights, when a metric is an average, we also compute the maximum, minimum, and standard deviation.

Abstraction by Ownership Hierarchy

First, we measure the effect of abstraction by ownership hierarchy.

Graph Size. We count Number of Objects (#O), which is the sum of Number of Top-Level Objects (#TLO), Number of Objects in Public Domains (#OPD), and Number of Objects in Private Domains (#OPrD). We also count Number of Domains (#D), which is the sum of Number of Top-Level Domains (#TLD), Number of Public Domains (#PD), and Number of Private Domains (#PrD). These metrics provide insights on the size of the ownership hierarchy(#O, #D), and give hints about architectural tiers (#TLD), the amount of logical containment(#OPD) and strict encapsulation(#OPrD).

Number of Points-to Edges (#PtE) ranges between 0 and #O(#O-1), the maximum number of possible edges between the objects. The OOG is a directed graph, and there might be two directed edges with different direction between every pair of objects. This metric captures points-to edges that are different from the ownership edges in the internal representation of the OOG, which are covered by other metrics.

Cluttering (COOG) is Number of Points-to Edges (#PtE) divided by #O(#O-1). COOG ranges between 0 and 1, with a value close to 1 indicating a cluttered and imprecise graph. Imprecision occurs due to possible aliasing of references in the same domain. For example, if the type of a field is an interface, the analysis may create points-to edges to all the objects that have a class that implement the interface, and that are in the same domain. Since the analysis uses only the aliasing information provided by domains, and aims to achieve soundness, some of the points-to edges might be false positives [2, Section 2.6.3].

Maximum Depth of Ownership Hierarchy (MXD) is the longest path length in an OGraph counting only ownership edges. We consider the root object to be at level 1. For example, in a path $O_{root} \rightarrow D_1 \rightarrow O_1 \rightarrow D_2 \rightarrow O_2$, the depth is 2. In the presence of cycles, the path is truncated when a cycle is found. For example, in a path $O_{root} \rightarrow D_1 \rightarrow O_1 \rightarrow D_1 \rightarrow O_1$ the depth is 1. MXD ranges between 1 and #O-1. A value of #O-1 indicates that the ownership tree has no branches and one object per domain. A value of 2 indicates that all the objects in the OGraph except the root are in the top-level domains.

Percentage of Top-Level Objects (PTLO) is the number of objects in the top-level domains, divided by the number of objects in the OOG. This metric indicates the effectiveness of abstraction by ownership hierarchy at reducing the number of objects in the top-level domains. The number ranges between 0 and 1, with a value close to 1 indicating that most of the objects are in the top-level domains. A low number indicates that the majority of objects in an application are architecturally irrelevant and abstraction by ownership hierarchy is effective. We measure the effectiveness of ownership hierarchy as 1-PTLO.

Number of Low-Level Objects in Top-Level Domains (#LLOTLD) is the number of low-level objects that are in the top-level domains. A small value (ideally, zero) indicates that the OOG conveys architectural abstraction. Otherwise, the OOG should be further refined.

Since *LLT* varies across applications, for this metric, we consider those types that are common for all the subject systems. To compute #LLOTLD, the list of low-level types include the Java standard library packages java.util, java.awt, or java.lang, and array of primitive types. Examples of low-level types are java.util.List, java.awt.Polygon, java.lang.String, java.lang.Object, java.lang.Boolean, and int[ ][ ].

Depth of Low-Level Objects (LLOD) is the sum of the depth of the low-level objects divided by the total number of low-level objects. It ranges from 0 to maximum depth of the ownership hierarchy, where a high value indicates that an OOG hides low-level objects underneath more architectural ones.

Average Public Domains per Object (PDO) (PrDO, respectively) is the sum of public (private, respectively) domains divided by the total number of objects. PDO and PrDO provide insights about the number of internal nodes in an OOG.

Average In-Degree per Top-Level Domain (IDTLD) is the number of incoming points-to edges for every object in a top-level domain, divided by #TLO. We count only those points-to edges that have as a source a non-sibling object, i.e., an object that has a different parent in the ownership hierarchy (Fig. 8a). IDTLD ranges between 0 and #O-1, with the higher limit indicating a cluttered OOG at the top-level. It indicates how popular the objects in top-level domains are. However, if the number is high, the graph may be too cluttered, and more difficult to understand.

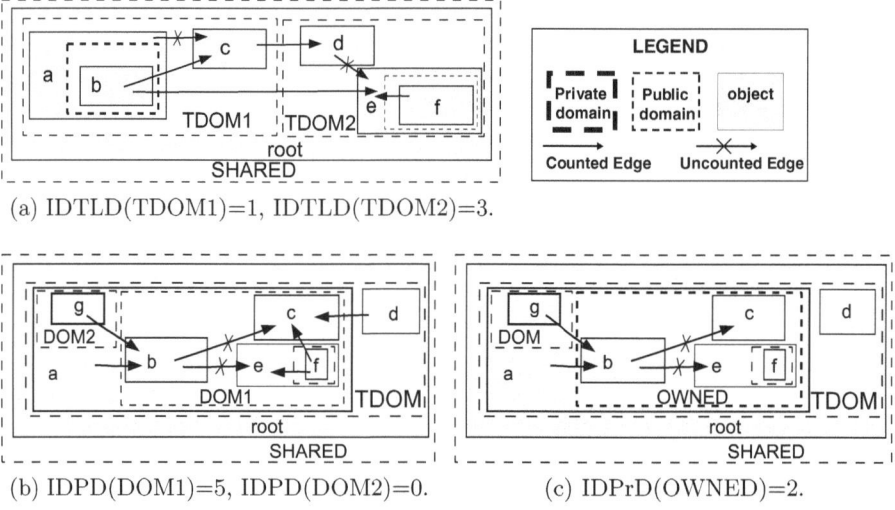

(a) IDTLD(TDOM1)=1, IDTLD(TDOM2)=3.

(b) IDPD(DOM1)=5, IDPD(DOM2)=0.   (c) IDPrD(OWNED)=2.

Fig. 8. Incoming edges from non-sibling objects in top-level, public, and private domains

Average In-Degree per Public Domain (IDPD) is the number of incoming points-to edges for objects in a public domain divided by the total number of objects in a public domain. We count only those points-to edges that have as a source a non-sibling object (Fig. 8b). It ranges between 0 and #O-1, with the higher limit indicating a cluttered OOG. Public domains logically encapsulate objects, without restricting access to these objects from the outside. IDPD gives an indication of how popular the objects in public domains are. A high value justifies the need for public domains.

Average In-Degree per Private Domain (IDPrD) is the number of incoming points-to edges for objects in a private domain divided by the total number of objects in a private domain. Objects in private domains are less accessible given the restrictions imposed by ownership types. They are accessible to the parent object, to other objects in the same domain, or to other objects in sibling domains (Fig. 8c). We intend to use it for comparison with IDPD and IDTLD. A significant difference between IDPrD and the previous two metrics confirms the need of public domains.

Average Objects per Domain (AOD) measures the average number of objects in a domain. The number can be 0 for domains that are only declared without being used. A high value indicates that the graph is precise and does not excessively merge objects. We use this metric to verify the hypothesis that OOGs after abstraction by types provide sufficient precision. We do not include in this metric shared objects, which may be globally aliased because little reasoning can be done about them.

Average Trace to Code per Object (ATCO) is the average number of object allocation expressions in the code that are represented by one object in the OOG. This metric measures the number of traceability links between an object in the OOG and the new expressions in the code. ATCO illustrates how the OOG is summarizing new expressions with an object in the OOG. To distinguish between objects created for two new expressions, a developer can use separate domains, unless the code assigns to each other the references that are in different domains (Fig. 9). A value of ATCO close to 1 supports the hypothesis that rarely such an assignment exists.

```
1  class C{
2    domain DOM1;
3    domain DOM2;
4    A<DOM1> a1 = new A<DOM1>();
5    A<DOM2> a2 = new A<DOM2>();
6    // a1=a2 if such an assignment exists, DOM1 = DOM2
7  }
```

Fig. 9. Placing objects in separate domains

Average Scattering of Objects (ASO) is the average number of object allocation expressions in different files that are merged into one object in the OOG. ASO is similar to ATCO but accounts only for the new expressions that are scattered across different files.

Average Objects of the Same Class (AOSC) is the average number of instances of the same class owned by different domains. A number greater than 1 indicates that the same class is instantiated in different contexts, and the OOG shows separate objects for these instances. AOSC highlights the difference between an OOG and a class diagram, which shows each class as one node. AOSC supports our hypothesis that an OOG has more precision than a class diagram and distinguishes between different instances of the same class.

Abstraction by types

Next, we measure the effect of abstraction by types in combination with abstraction by ownership hierarchy.

Number of Top-Level Objects after Abstraction by Types (ABT-TLO) measures the size of top-level OOG using both abstraction mechanisms. A rule of thumb in architectural documentation is to have 5 to 7 components per tier [33], which in our case translates in having 5 to 7 objects per top-level domain. Ideally, ABTTLO ranges between $5 \times \#TLD$ and $7 \times \#TLD$.

Number of Design Intent Types (DIT) is the number of types in the *DIT* list. A small number indicates that the system has a small number of key interfaces or base classes that many classes implement or extend from.

Number of Trivial Types (NTT) is the number of types in the *TT* list. The list includes by default types such as `java.io.Serializable`, `java.lang.Cloneable`, `java.lang.Iterable`, and `java.lang.Object`. The list of trivial types is typically reusable across systems.

In the following metrics, we take 1 minus the value of the division so that they express the reduction of the abstraction mechanisms.

Abstraction by Types (ABTF) is Average Objects per Domain (AOD) after abstraction by types, divided by AOD before abstraction by types, and indicates the effectiveness of abstraction by types at reducing the cluttering of the OOG by reducing the number of objects at all levels.

Abstraction by Types at Top-Level (ABTTL) is the Number of Top-Level Objects after Abstraction by Types (ABTTLO) divided by the Number of Top-Level Objects (#TLO) before abstraction by types, and indicates the effectiveness of abstraction by types at reducing the cluttering of the OOG at the top level.

Abstraction by Ownership Hierarchy and by Types (ABHBT) is the Number of Top-Level Objects (#TLO) after abstraction by types, divided by the Number of Objects (#O) before abstraction by types and indicates the combined effectiveness of abstraction by ownership hierarchy and abstraction by types at reducing the cluttering of the OOG at the top-level.

Flat object graphs

Finally, we compare the OOG against flat object graphs that we extract from the same programs using Womble [30], by ignoring the ownership annotations in place. A flat object graph has nodes that represent objects with no hierarchical organization. It shows objects representing data structures at the same level as architecturally relevant objects, and may not be suitable to express the system's architecture. By design, Womble graph is unsound with respect to aliasing, i.e., multiple nodes in the flat object graph correspond to the same runtime object.

Percentage of Low-Level Objects in Flat Graph (LFO) is the number of low-level objects divided by the total number of objects in a flat graph. LFO indicates what percentage of the objects in a flat graph are not architecturally relevant. The metric ranges between 0 and 1 with higher values indicating a higher density of data structures.

Hierarchical Reduction (HR) is the number of objects in a flat graph divided by the Number of Top-Level Objects (#TLO) in an OOG with abstraction by types. HR estimates the effectiveness of both abstraction mechanisms compared to a flat object graph. Effective abstraction mechanisms would reduce the number of top-level objects by a number close to an order of magnitude.

4   Empirical Results

We first report the quantitative results[2] of the annotation metrics (Section 4.1) and the OOG metrics (Section 4.2) across all systems. Then, for a few systems, we study how the OOG metrics evolved across two main refinement iterations (Section 4.3).

4.1   Annotation Metrics

We first report the results of the annotation metrics (Tables 3 and 4).

Object-level metrics. We first discuss the metric results regarding object references, namely fields, local variables, method parameters and method return values (Fig. 10). For convenience, we summarize the values of a metric as a boxplot, which shows: minimum, lower quartile, median, upper quartile, and maximum. A boxplot may also indicate outliers (if any).

Regarding fields, there is a high proportion of shared annotations (Fig. 10a). This is understandable, since we used shared for objects such as String, Font and Color, among others. One system in particular, PX, has nearly 70% of its fields annotated as shared (Fig. 11a).

The systems that have a carefully refined OOG have a higher proportion of fields in public domains. In particular MD has about 19% of the fields in public domains (Fig. 11d). On the other hand, most of the subject systems have between 10% and 20% of the fields in private domains. In particular, APD has 55% of the fields in private domains (Fig. 11e). Regarding local variables, a high proportion of them have the lent annotation, which is unsurprising, since lent is used for temporary aliases (Fig. 10b). There is one exception, JHD, which has one third of its local variables annotated as unique (Fig. 11c).

Among method parameters, a large proportion are shared, lent or use domain parameters (Fig. 10c). In particular, in CDB, almost 80% of the method parameter annotations are shared, since most of them are of type String.

---

[2] All the data generated during this study is available at the following location: http://www.cs.wayne.edu/~mabianto/oog_data/

Table 3. Annotation metrics

	JHD		DL		MD		APD		HC		PX		AFS		CDB	
	%	#	%	#	%	#	%	#	%	#	%	#	%	#	%	#
Fields																
shared	40.4	128	36.6	49	29.3	17	7.9	23	64.8	344	69.8	609	60.0	242	63.8	44
private d	22.4	71	18.7	25	12.1	7	55.5	162	9.4	50	16.9	147	9.9	40	8.7	6
public d	1.3	4	0.8	1	19.0	11	7.5	22	1.5	8	0.8	7	13.2	53	11.6	8
p_i	36.0	114	10.4	14	39.7	23	24.3	71	24.3	129	12.5	109	16.9	68	8.7	6
owner	0.0	0	30.6	41	0.0	0	0.3	1	0.0	0	0.0	0	0.0	0	4.3	3
ff.d	0.0	0	0.0	0	0.0	0	0.0	0	0.0	0	0.0	0	0.0	0	2.9	2
other	0.0	0	0.0	0	0.0	0	2.7	8	0.0	0	0.0	0	0.0	0	0.0	0
total	100	317	100	134	100	58	100	292	100	531	100	872	100	403	100	69
Local Variables																
lent	25.6	380	43.8	248	25.6	23	45.9	237	43.0	414	35.5	911	12.3	108	7.7	17
unique	21.9	324	3.9	22	2.2	2	6.8	35	10.4	100	5.3	136	6.5	57	7.2	16
shared	16.3	241	17.1	97	31.1	28	13.2	68	31.1	299	43.6	1120	44.2	388	39.8	88
private d	0.7	10	1.9	11	4.4	4	5.2	27	0.0	0	4.8	122	6.4	56	17.2	38
public d	0.4	6	0.0	0	8.9	8	5.4	28	0.0	0	0.2	4	1.6	14	7.2	16
p_i	25.5	378	7.6	43	27.8	25	16.9	87	15.6	150	10.7	276	26.8	235	12.7	28
owner	0.0	0	25.1	142	0.0	0	0.0	0	0.0	0	0.0	0	0.0	0	1.8	4
ff.d	0.1	2	0.2	1	0.0	0	0.6	3	0.0	0	0.0	0	0.0	0	6.3	14
other	9.5	141	0.3	2	0.0	0	6.0	31	0.0	0	0.0	1	2.2	19	0.0	0
total	100	1482	100	566	100	90	100	516	100	963	100	2570	100	877	100	221
Method Parameters																
lent	41.5	575	51.9	401	16.5	31	51.2	189	47.6	386	24.3	361	18.4	191	4.9	5
unique	0.2	3	0.7	5	0.0	0	1.4	5	0.4	3	1.6	23	0.0	0	0.0	0
shared	15.7	217	12.8	99	45.2	85	13.3	49	29.5	239	60.7	903	33.9	352	78.4	80
private d	0.3	4	0.0	0	0.0	0	1.1	4	0.0	0	0.2	3	0.0	0	0.0	0
public d	0.6	8	0.5	4	0.0	0	4.6	17	0.0	0	0.0	0	0.1	1	4.9	5
p_i	39.6	549	3.5	27	38.3	72	26.6	98	22.5	182	13.3	197	47.6	494	9.8	10
owner	0.0	0	21.0	162	0.0	0	0.3	1	0.0	0	0.0	0	0.0	0	1.0	1
ff.d	0.0	0	0.0	0	0.0	0	0.3	1	0.0	0	0.0	0	0.0	0	0.0	0
other	2.2	31	9.6	74	0.0	0	1.4	5	0.0	0	0.0	0	0.0	0	1.0	1
total	100	1387	100	772	100	188	100	369	100	810	100	1487	100	1038	100	102
Method Return Values																
unique	18.8	126	9.3	31	9.1	5	17.2	25	5.5	13	29.0	204	4.8	24	15.4	10
shared	35.5	238	41.9	139	43.6	24	18.6	27	46.2	109	51.9	365	65.9	329	70.8	46
private d	1.3	9	2.7	9	0.0	0	1.4	2	0.0	0	0.0	0	1.6	8	0.0	0
public d	0.9	6	0.0	0	7.3	4	13.1	19	0.0	0	0.1	1	0.4	2	6.2	4
p_i	42.2	283	2.4	8	40.0	22	47.6	69	48.3	114	19.0	134	27.3	136	3.1	2
owner	0.0	0	32.8	109	0.0	0	0.7	1	0.0	0	0.0	0	0.0	0	3.1	2
ff.d	0.0	0	0.0	0	0.0	0	0.0	0	0.0	0	0.0	0	0.0	0	1.5	1
other	1.3	9	10.8	36	0.0	0	1.4	2	0.0	0	0.0	0	0.0	0	0.0	0
total	100	671	100	332	100	55	100	145	100	236	100	704	100	499	100	65
Class Metrics																
private d	0.52	133	0.98	116	0.58	28	0.88	58	0.59	59	0.94	161	0.79	159	0.5	11
public d	0.04	9	0.04	5	0.23	11	0.29	19	0.13	13	0.03	5	0.07	15	0.36	8
p_i	0.43	111	0.18	21	1.02	49	1.97	130	0.84	84	1.7	293	0.83	168	0.55	12
inherits	1.62	416	0.56	66	1.67	80	0.15	10	0.57	57	0.75	129	1.46	294	0	0
links	0.16	41	0.1	12	0	0	0	0	0	0	0	0	0	0	0.82	18
assumes	3.43	881	0.84	99	0	0	0.03	2	1.1	110	0	0	0	0	0.82	18

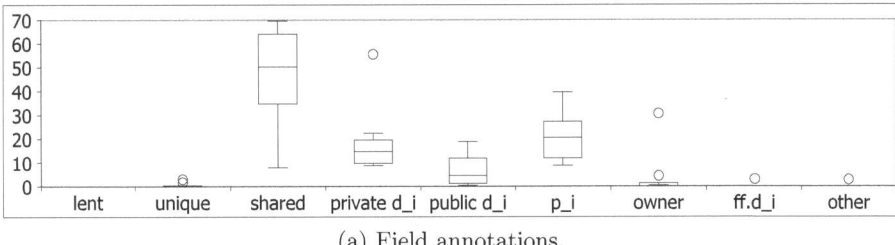

(a) Field annotations.

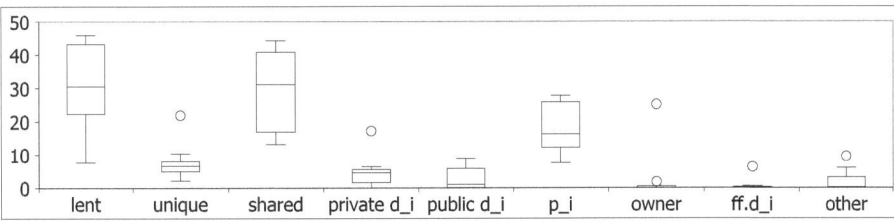

(b) Local variable annotations.

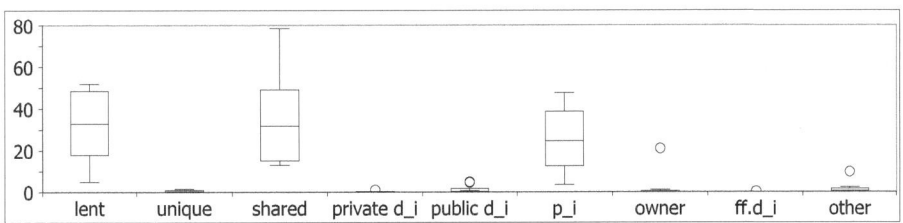

(c) Method parameter annotations.

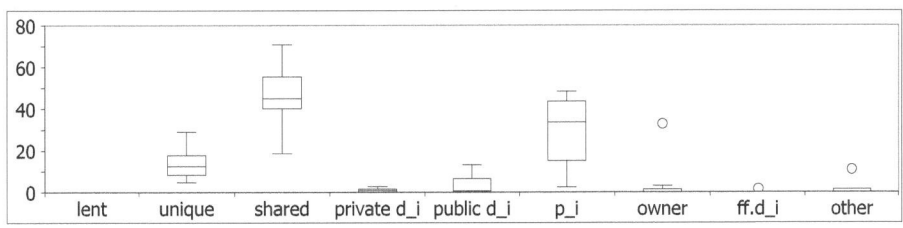

(d) Method return value annotations.

Fig. 10. Distribution of annotations per subject system

Among method return values, a large percentage is `unique`, which indicates that objects are being passed linearly (Fig. 10d). JHD in particular has almost 40% of the return values as `unique` (Fig. 11c).

We observe outliers for "other" annotations. They occur in DL for method domain parameters used for the formal parameters or return value of static methods. In JHD, a high proportion of "other" annotations is for local variables in inner classes, and a small proportion for static methods. APD is the only system that has "other" annotations for the fields in inner classes (Fig. 11f).

Table 4. Global annotation metrics (excluding method return values)

	JHD		DL		MD		APD		HC		PX		AFS		CDB	
	#	%	#	%	#	%	#	%	#	%	#	%	#	%	#	%
lent	955	30.0	649	44.4	54	16.1	426	36.5	800	34.8	1272	25.9	299	12.9	22	5.6
shared	586	18.4	245	16.7	130	38.7	140	12.0	882	38.3	2632	53.6	982	42.4	212	54.1
private d	85	2.7	36	2.5	11	3.3	193	16.5	50	2.2	272	5.5	96	4.1	44	11.2
public d	18	0.6	5	0.3	19	5.7	67	5.7	8	0.3	11	0.2	68	2.9	29	7.4
unique	324	10.2	22	1.5	2	0.6	35	3.0	100	4.3	136	2.8	57	2.5	16	4.1
p_i/owner	1041	32.7	429	29.3	120	35.7	258	22.1	461	20.0	582	11.9	797	34.4	52	13.3
$ff.d_i$	2	0.1	1	0.1	0	0.0	4	0.3	0	0.0	0	0.0	0	0.0	16	4.1
other	172	5.4	76	5.2	0	0.0	44	3.8	0	0.0	1	0.0	19	0.8	1	0.3

Overall, we observe that the percentage of shared annotations is lower for local variables and a higher for method parameters (Fig. 11a). However, for most systems, the percentage of lent is higher than shared for method parameters.

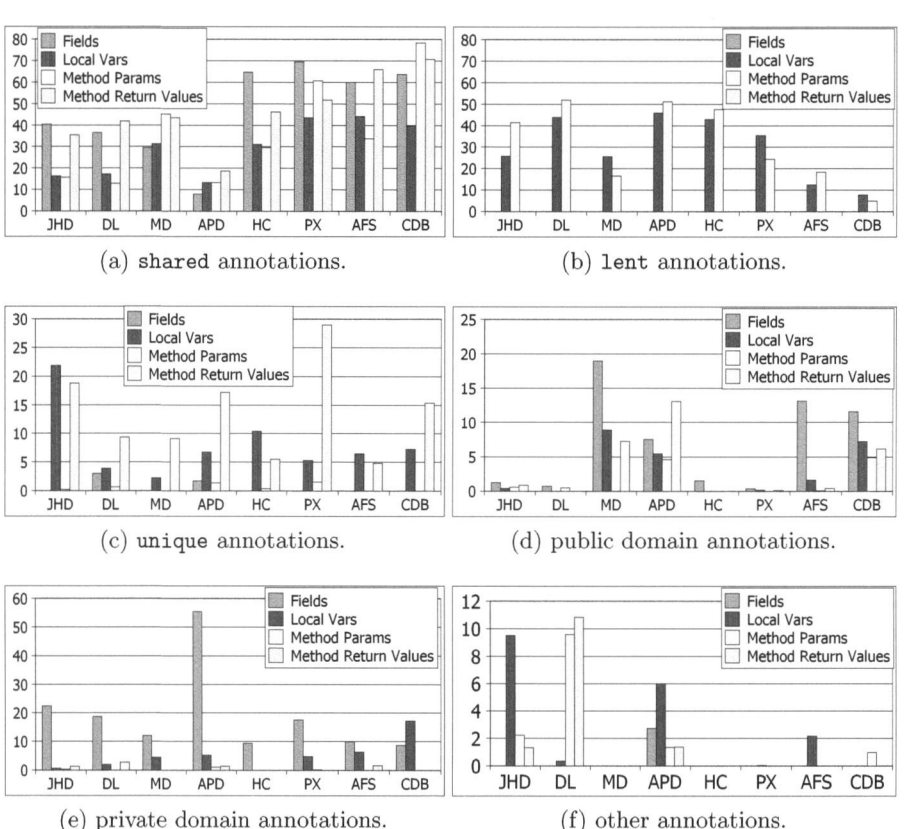

(a) shared annotations.

(b) lent annotations.

(c) unique annotations.

(d) public domain annotations.

(e) private domain annotations.

(f) other annotations.

Fig. 11. Percentage of shared, lent, unique, and public domain annotations

In general domain parameters are heavily used, with all the systems using them. In particular, only in DL `owner` replaces one of the domain parameters.

Class-level metrics. Next, we discuss the metric results for class-level declarations, namely locally declared (private or public) domains, domain parameters, domain inheritance, domain links and domain link assumptions (Fig. 12).

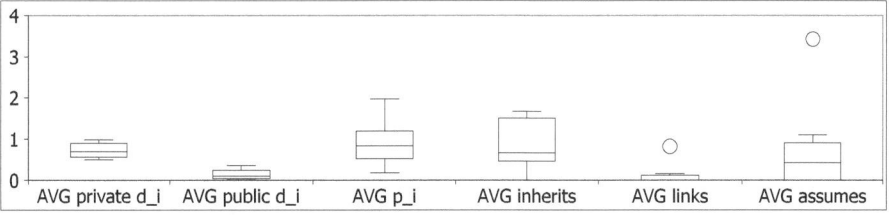

Fig. 12. Class annotations

Regarding locally declared domains, the average number of private domains is almost 1.0 since every class declares an `owned` private domain, except interfaces. Some systems, such as MD, have a much higher proportion of interfaces compared to others, such as PX. The systems that have refined annotations and OOGs, such as MD, have a higher average number of public domains per class to express design intent.

Regarding domain parameters, a class has on average one domain parameter, and inherits 1–2 domain parameters. This is unsurprising since most of the systems are annotated according to a two-tiered (Document-View) or a three-tiered (Model-View-Controller) architecture. DL made use of the `owner` annotation, and saved one domain parameter per class.

Regarding domain inheritance, the number is higher than the number of domain parameters for the systems that have a richer type structure, such as MD and DL, compared to the systems that do not use inheritance, such as PX, HC, and APD. Regarding domain links, not all systems have domain link annotations.

4.2   OOG Metrics (Across All Systems)

We now report the results of the OOG metrics (Table 5). The table has two columns for each system before and after abstraction by types.

Abstraction by Ownership Hierarchy

Graph size. Number of Objects (#O) ranges between 27 and 525, while Number of Top-Level Objects (#TLO) ranges between 8 and 120. For both metrics, the lowest value occur for CDB, and the highest value occurs for JHD. The size of the OOG does not necessarily grow at the same rate as the size of the program. For example, in KLOC, DL is roughly one quarter the size of PX, but the DL OOG has more nodes than the PX OOG.

Table 5. OOG metrics

	JHD	abt	DL	abt	MD	abt	APD	abt	HC	abt	PX	abt	AFS	abt	CDB	abt
#O	525	461	313	284	37	33	133	127	99	60	240	222	163	102	27	25
#TLO	120	18	41	15	14	12	11	11	55	16	59	46	55	45	8	7
#OPD	3	3	1	1	9	7	16	16	16	16	2	2	54	5	5	5
#OPrD	402	440	271	268	14	14	106	100	28	28	179	174	54	52	14	13
#D	173	126	40	14	14	14	38	38	26	14	80	75	35	32	17	16
#TLD	3	3	2	2	3	3	2	2	3	3	3	3	3	3	4	4
PD	3	2	1	1	5	5	10	10	8	1	2	2	5	5	4	4
PrD	167	121	37	11	6	6	26	26	15	10	75	70	27	24	9	8
#PtE	5608	620	334	89	63	53	162	166	350	52	306	234	157	94	29	30
COOG	2.04	0.29	0.34	0.11	4.73	5.02	0.92	1.04	3.61	1.47	0.53	0.48	0.59	0.91	4.13	5.00
MXD	4	5	3	3	4	4	5	5	4	4	5	5	4	4	3	3
AVGD	2.98	3.36	2.86	2.94	2.68	2.70	3.29	3.30	2.47	2.78	3.18	3.24	2.75	2.69	2.67	2.68
PTLO	0.23	0.04	0.13	0.05	0.38	0.36	0.08	0.09	0.56	0.27	0.25	0.21	0.34	0.44	0.30	0.28
LLOTL	0	0	0	0	0	0	0	0	2	2	0	0	0	0	0	0
LLOD	3.32	3.45	3.00	3.00	3.24	3.24	3.65	3.65	3.04	3.04	3.55	3.55	3.32	3.32	3.08	3.08
PDO	0.01	0.01	0.00	0.00	0.14	0.16	0.09	0.08	0.08	0.14	0.01	0.01	0.04	0.05	0.15	0.17
MIN	0	0	0	0	0	0	0	0	0	0	0	0	0	0	0	0
MAX	1	2	1	1	3	3	2	2	1	8	1	1	2	2	1	1
STD	0.08	0.10	0.06	0.06	0.54	0.57	0.31	0.30	0.28	1.04	0.09	0.09	0.22	0.30	0.37	0.38
PrDO	0.35	0.40	0.12	0.13	0.17	0.19	0.20	0.21	0.15	0.25	0.33	0.34	0.17	0.27	0.35	0.38
MIN	0	0	0	0	0	0	0	0	0	0	0	0	0	0	0	0
MAX	1	31	1	9	1	1	1	1	1	5	1	2	1	2	1	2
STD	0.48	1.86	0.32	0.91	0.38	0.40	0.40	0.41	0.36	0.76	0.47	0.52	0.37	0.51	0.49	0.58
IDTLD	23.9	14.9	3.73	1.73	1.86	1.75	1.91	1.91	0.35	0.44	1.05	0.93	0.51	0.36	0.88	0.86
MIN	0	0	0	0	0	0	0	0	0	0	0	0	0	0	0	0
MAX	56	47	7	6	9	8	7	7	3	2	6	5	4	3	2	2
STD	20.1	17.8	2.46	2.09	3.13	2.96	1.81	1.81	0.78	0.73	1.18	0.98	0.98	0.77	0.64	0.69
IDPD	0.67	0.00	0.00	0.00	0.89	0.71	1.19	1.19	1.38	0.19	1.00	1.00	0.98	0.60	1.60	1.60
MIN	0	0	0	0	0	0	0	0	1	0	1	1	0	0	1	1
MAX	1	0	0	0	1	1	8	8	2	1	1	1	1	1	4	4
STD	0.58	0.00	0.00	0.00	0.33	0.49	1.94	1.94	0.50	0.40	0.00	0.00	0.14	0.55	1.34	1.34
IDPrD	0.52	0.31	0.10	0.04	0.43	0.43	0.86	0.85	0.82	0.46	0.66	0.61	0.37	0.38	0.36	0.38
MIN	0	0	0	0	0	0	0	0	0	0	0	0	0	0	0	0
MAX	1	2	1	1	1	1	1	1	1	1	1	1	1	1	1	1
STD	0.50	0.51	0.30	0.20	0.51	0.51	0.35	0.36	0.39	0.51	0.47	0.49	0.49	0.49	0.50	0.51
AOD	3.17	1.82	7.80	5.36	2.57	2.29	3.47	3.32	3.77	2.50	2.99	2.79	4.63	2.94	1.53	1.44
MAX	74	22	34	8	9	7	12	10	23	7	27	23	43	22	5	4
STD	7.03	2.21	4.77	3.10	2.14	1.73	3.06	2.81	5.81	2.07	4.21	3.78	8.89	5.05	1.07	0.81
ATCO	1.28	1.64	1.37	1.49	1.08	1.21	1.68	1.76	1.49	2.35	1.38	1.49	1.23	1.97	1.44	1.56
MAX	13	56	7	12	3	3	12	12	5	21	15	15	12	43	6	6
STD	1.02	3.16	0.76	1.22	0.36	0.6	1.59	1.71	0.85	2.9	1.21	1.34	0.99	4.40	1.09	1.16
ASO	1.03	1.09	1.26	1.32	1.03	1.06	1.00	1.00	1.09	1.40	1.05	1.08	1.12	1.21	1.15	1.16
MAX	3	10	6	10	2	2	1	1	5	12	2	4	3	5	2	2
STD	0.20	0.68	0.69	0.94	0.16	0.24	0.00	0.00	0.45	1.63	0.23	0.33	0.4	0.63	0.36	0.37
AOSC	3.67	8.23	6.39	9.47	1.19	1.18	1.58	1.57	1.43	1.62	1.80	1.87	1.12	1.19	1.13	1.14
MAX	38	57	34	32	3	3	8	8	9	9	26	26	4	4	2	2
STD	7.2	12.3	11.6	13.8	0.48	0.48	1.36	1.34	1.56	1.78	2.76	2.9	0.42	0.52	0.34	0.35

Number of Objects in Public Domains (#OPD) ranges between 1 and 54 and is lower than Number of Objects in Private Domains (#OPrD), which ranges between 14 and 402. Number of Domains (#D) ranges between 14 in MD and 173 in JHD. Number of Top-Level Domains (#TLD) is relatively constant, 2, 3, or 4 and indicates a 2-tier or 3-tier architecture. Number of Public Domains (#PD) ranges between 1 and 10, and indicates a small number of public domains. In contrast, Number of Private Domains (#PrD) ranges between 6 and 167, and indicates that the majority of domains are private domains. Indeed, most of the classes use a private domain (Fig. 13).

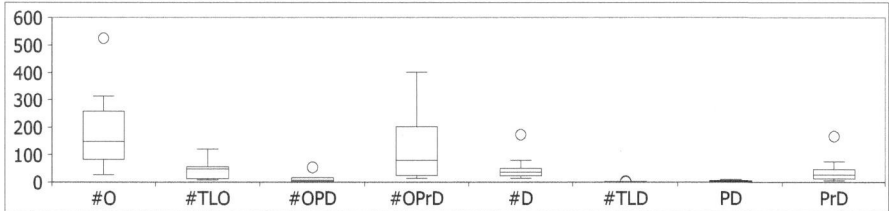

Fig. 13. Object graph size

Number of Points-to Edges (#PtE) ranges between 29 in CDB and 5608 in JHD, and is in general of the same order of magnitude as #O. It indicates a relatively small number of edges, which can highlight interesting reference relations. It also indicates that there are objects with no incoming or outgoing points-to edges. For example, there are 47 such objects in AFS, and 237 objects in DL. In particular, JHD has 10 times more edges than objects and indicates a higher level of cluttering. After applying abstraction by types, the value substantially decreases. However, this metric does not give us sufficient details on the effectiveness of abstraction by types, which we discuss in a later metric.

Cluttering (COOG) ranges between 0.0034 and 0.0473, and indicates a graph with low cluttering. Such a graph can make visually obvious the runtime structure of the program. Since the value is very low, we display the value multiplied by 100.

Maximum Depth of Ownership Hierarchy (MXD) ranges between 3 and 5 and indicates that the depth is relatively constant with respect to the size of the OOGs. The average is relatively constant, and ranges between 2.47 and 3.29. To better understand these values, we also compute the median, which is 2, 3 or 4. For more insight, we computed Pearson's correlation coefficient between MXD and KLOC. The coefficient (0.58) indicates a large positive correlation. Indeed, MXD is relatively constant (Fig. 14) while the size of the system varies. In particular, the median depth for HC is 2, and indicates that in this particular case ownership hierarchy is less effective. The following metric illustrates better the effectiveness of having an ownership hierarchy.

Percentage of Top-Level Objects (PTLO) ranges between 0.08 and 0.56, with the smallest value for APD, and indicates that abstraction by ownership

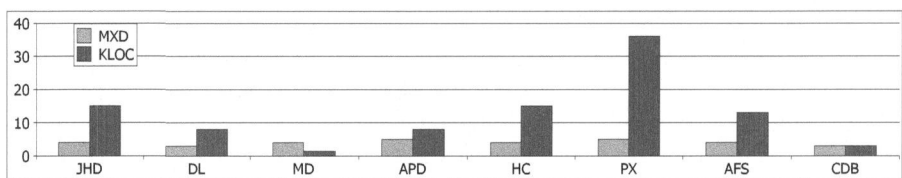

Fig. 14. KLOC vs. OOG depth

hierarchy is effective. Given that the depth of the graph is relatively constant, one can assume that the number of top-level objects increases as the graph grows. However, there is no linear relationship between the percentage of top-level objects is and the size of the program (Pearson's correlation coefficient ≈ 0.02). Using ownership hierarchy, developers can collapse and hide more than half of the objects in most cases. For HC, where the median depth is 2, PTLO is 0.56, and indicates that ownership hierarchy hides 44% of the objects in the top-level domains. In the case of DL, this percentage increases to 87% of the objects. For APD, it increases to 92%. So, in some cases, abstraction by ownership hierarchy reduces the number of objects at the top level by one order of magnitude compared to the entire graph.

Number of Low-Level Objects in Top-Level Domains (#LLOTLD) is zero in most systems, and supports our hypothesis that rarely does an OOG show low-level objects in top-level domains.

Depth of Low-Level Objects (LLOD) ranges between 3 and 3.65, and indicates that the majority of low-level objects are in the lower parts of the ownership trees. It indicates that the low-level objects are pushed underneath more architecturally-relevant ones. One system in particular, DL, has all its low-level objects at level 3, the lowest level of the ownership tree.

Average Public Domains per Object (PDO) ranges between 0 and 0.15, while Average Private Domains per Object (PrDO) ranges between 0.12 and 0.35, and indicates that less than half of the objects are represented as internal nodes of the ownership hierarchy. This is unsurprising given that the depth of the OOG is almost constant and relatively low. At most, an object has 3 public domains and one private domain. Since there are more private domains declared, it is unsurprising that PrDO is higher than PDO.

Average In-Degree per Top-Level Domain (IDTLD) ranges between 0.45 and 23.94. For most systems, IDTLD is low with an outlier for JHD (Fig. 15). Before abstraction by types, the JHD OOG is cluttered, since there are many concrete sub-classes of the interfaces Command, Figure, or Tool. In the code the interface Command has a field of type Figure. The OOG shows points-to edges from all the instances of a class that extends Command in domain CONTROLLER to all the instances of a class that extends Figure in domain MODEL. The high number of edges lead to an almost fully connected graph. After abstraction by types, the values of IDTLD decrease for all systems and range between 0.36 and 14.89. This reduction indicates that abstraction by types can also reduce the edge cluttering in the OOG.

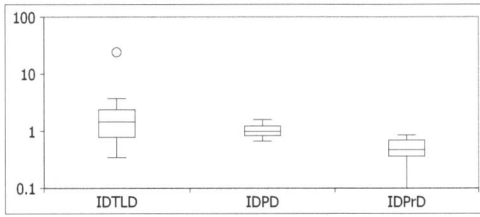

Fig. 15. In degree per top-level, public and private domains

Average In-Degree per Public Domain (IDPD) ranges between 0 and 1.60, and indicates that objects in public domains are accessed by outside objects, other than their siblings or parents. Such a relation would not be possible in the absence of public domains. APD in particular has 8 incoming points-to edges. The low IDPD indicates that public domains do not introduce additional clutter. For example, IDPD is 0.51 for JHD, indicating a lower number of points-to edges for objects in public domains compared to the top-level objects.

For additional insight, we counted the in-degree for objects in public and top-level domains from non-sibling objects, and projected these values against each level of the JHD OOG. The x-axis indicates the level, while the y-axis indicates the in-degree values that occur at that level. We observe that the high in-degree occurs only for top-level objects, while objects at level 3 and 4 have only one incoming edge from a non-sibling object (Fig. 16).

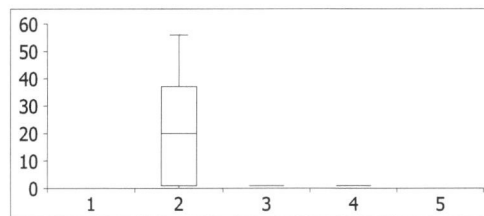

Fig. 16. In-degree from non-siblings objects in JHD

Average In-Degree per Private Domain (IDPrD) ranges between 0.10 and 0.86, and indicates that objects in private domains have at most one incoming points-to edge. This is unsurprising since private domains restrict access to their objects, and few systems use domain links, which can relax this restriction.

Average Objects per Domain (AOD) ranges between 1.53 and 7.80, and indicates a relatively low number of objects per domain. For additional insight, we compute the median and the standard deviation (Fig. 17). For all the systems, the median is less than 10, but given the high number of outliers we cannot draw further conclusions. A closer inspection of the numbers reveals that in most cases, the top-level domains have the highest number of objects, up to 74 for JHD. One system in particular, APD has no outliers. For APD, the highest number of objects occurs for the private domain of a top-level object of type PlaceRouteUI that has 12 objects. After applying abstraction by types, the values decreases and range between 1.44 and 5.36 with a maximum of 23 objects in a top level domain of PX, and 22 objects in the top level domains of JHD. So, abstraction by types can reduce the clutter in the OOG. This metric also indicates that the OOG is precise and does not excessively merge all the objects in the same domain into one object.

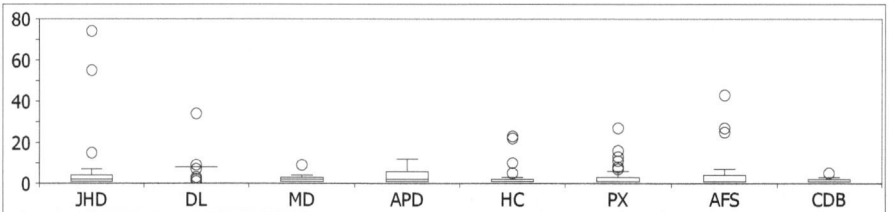

Fig. 17. Average Objects per Domain (AOD)

Average Trace to Code per Object (ATCO) ranges between 1.08 and 1.68 and indicates that there are objects in the OOG that correspond to multiple lines of code, ones that have new expressions. For additional insight, we measured the median and the standard deviation, and we highlighted the outliers (Fig. 18). For example, an object in the PX OOG corresponds to 15 instances of type LinkedList<FunctionBar> in the class BarGraphPanel and each of these objects represents a dataset represented as a block in the bar chart. Similarly, an object in the AFS OOG corresponds to 12 instances of type AtomicInteger in the class DefaultFtpStatistics, to represent various statistics stored by the server such as the number of logins, failed logins, and uploaded files. Overall, the low value of the median of ATCO (1 or 2), and the relatively small number of outliers, indicate that a relatively small number of new expressions correspond to the same object in the OOG.

Average Scattering of Objects (ASO) ranges between 1 and 1.26, while the maximum value ranges between 1 and 6. ASO indicates that an object in the OOG may correspond to multiple lines of code in different files. For example, in DL, there are 7 instances of the class DrawingPoint in 6 different classes, that are all represented by one object in the OOG.

Average Objects of the Same Class (AOSC) ranges between 1.12 and 6.39, while the maximum value ranges between 2 and 38, where JHD, DL, and PX appears to be outliers. For a better insight, we inspected the OOGs for the maximum values. For example, 34 objects of type Vector<Figure> in DL, and 17 objects of type HashTable<String,String> in PX. The values are lower in AFS, and MD. Although one may argue that most of these instances represent collections, we found an interesting example in AFS OOG that shows 4 objects of type FileInputStream. We argue that it is important to reason about different instances since they may play different roles at runtime. Indeed, we traced to code

Table 6. OOG metrics – abstraction by types

	JHD	DL	MD	APD	HC	PX	AFS	CDB
ABTTLO	18	15	12	11	16	46	45	7
DIT	11	4	1	0	0	14	8	1
NTT	48	0	0	0	35	0	0	0
ABTF	0.30	0.26	0.11	0.00	0.29	0.04	0.36	0.02
ABTTL	0.79	0.48	0.14	0.00	0.71	0.16	0.13	0.13
ABHBT	0.97	0.93	0.68	0.92	0.84	0.80	0.72	0.74
LFO	0.21	0.66	0.61	0.20	n/a	0.24	n/a	0.72
HR	3.39	3.93	3.83	19.4	n/a	2.80	n/a	4.50

the objects of type `FileInputStream` in AFS OOG, and found that one object refers to a user configuration file, while another one refers to data transferred from the server to the client.

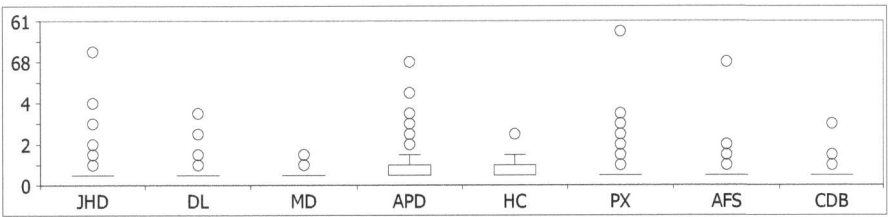

Fig. 18. Average Trace to Code per Object (ATCO)

Abstraction by Types

In systems such as JHD where Average In-Degree per Top-Level Domain (IDTLD) is high, the OOG can be cluttered if there are many related subtypes. The metrics in this section are computed on the display graph, and measure the effectiveness of abstraction by types at reducing the clutter (Table 6).

Number of Top-Level Objects after Abstraction by Types (ABT-TLO) ranges between 7 and 46. For additional insights, we compare these values to an ideal range 5–7 objects per tier (Fig. 19a). The result of the comparison indicates that the JHD, DL, MD, APD, and HC OOGs are more refined than PX and AFS. On the other hand, the CDB OOG might be too abstract with one or two objects in a top-level domain.

We also plot ABTTLO vs. #TLO and vs. the size of the systems (KLOC). The result of the comparison indicates a weak support for our hypothesis that the size of the top-level OOG does not increase linearly with the size of the program (Fig. 19b). There is no perfect correlation between KLOC and ABTTLO, but the value of the Pearson's coefficient is at the low-end of the near perfect range (0.74). In fact, the value of Pearson's coefficient increases after abstraction by types from 0.58 to 0.74.

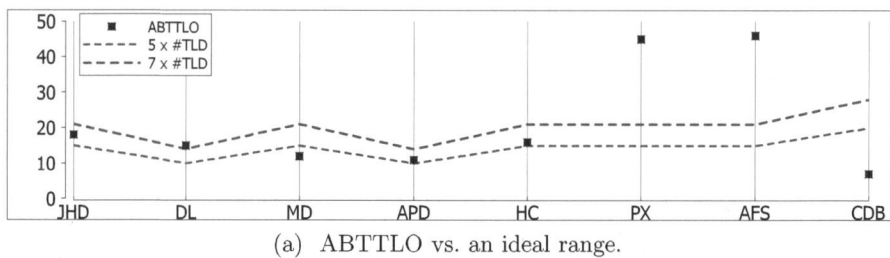

(a) ABTTLO vs. an ideal range.

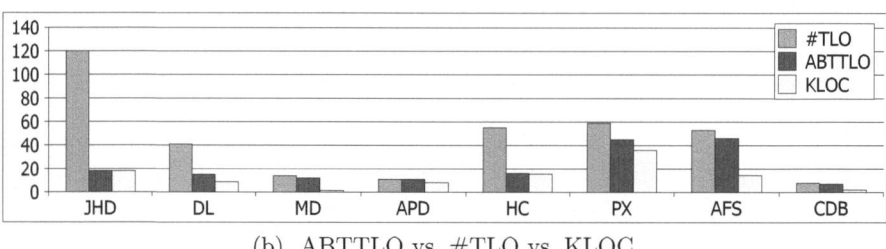

(b) ABTTLO vs. #TLO vs. KLOC

Fig. 19. Number of Top-Level Objects after Abstraction by Types (ABTTLO)

Number of Design Intent Types (DIT) ranges between 0 and 14, which means that the list is not very long. Furthermore, for some systems (JHD, DL) all the types in the DIT list are from a few packages that contain the core framework interfaces. For JHD, the list is much smaller than the total number of types (classes and interfaces) in the system (11 vs. 257).

Number of Trivial Types (NTT), when used, is much larger. The default list includes only four types. For the two systems where it was used (JHD, HC), we had to manually pick 35–50 types. For JHD, abstraction by design intent types is more effective than by trivial types [2, Section 4.6.2].

Abstraction by Types (ABTF) ranges between 0 and 0.36 and indicates a higher effectiveness of abstraction by types for systems with a rich inheritance hierarchy. For JHD, DL, HC and AFS, abstraction by types hides approximately one quarter of all the objects in the OOG. Abstraction by types is less effective for systems that favor composition over inheritance (MD, APD).

Abstraction by Types at Top-Level (ABTTL) ranges between 0 and 0.77, and indicates a higher effectiveness for programs with a rich inheritance hierarchy, when the objects in the top-level domains are of related types. It indicates that abstraction by types merges more than 60% of the objects in the top-level domains for JHD and HC.

Abstraction by Ownership Hierarchy and by Types (ABHBT) ranges between 0.68 and 0.97, and indicates a high effectiveness for all the systems. For three of the systems (JHD, DL, and APD), the combined abstraction mechanisms decrease the number of objects in the top-level domains by one order of magnitude. The higher reduction occurs in JHD, where after abstraction by types, the reduction increases from 0.77 to 0.97 (Fig. 20).

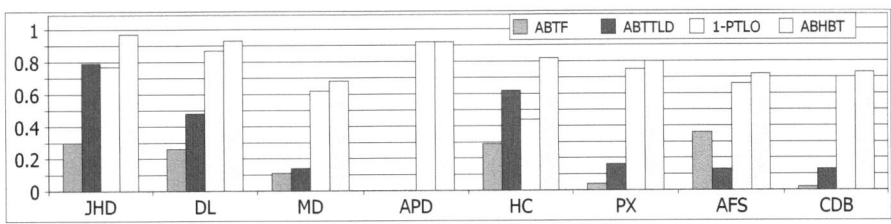

Fig. 20. Abstraction by Ownership Hierarchy and by Types (ABHBT)

In order to capture the reduction more precisely, we count the number of objects at each level of the OOG for each system before and after abstraction by types. We observe that level 3 has the highest number of objects. Similarly to the case of median depth, the exception is HC, for which level 2 has the highest number of objects (Fig. 21a). After using abstraction by types, in most cases, the number of top-level objects (level 2) decreased without a change on the next levels. So abstraction by types is more effective for top-level objects. Abstraction by types changes the trend for HC, so that level 3 has the highest number of objects (Fig. 21b). For the AFS OOG, abstraction by types is more effective on level 3, where the number of objects is reduced by half. Indeed, abstraction by types collapses 43 objects in the public domain COMMAND and 6 objects in the public domain SITE.

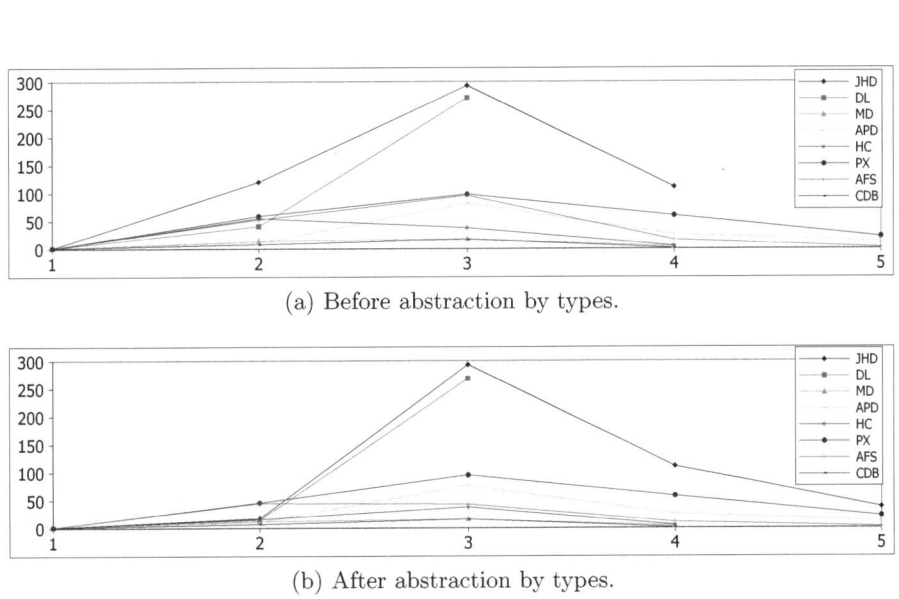

(a) Before abstraction by types.

(b) After abstraction by types.

Fig. 21. Number of objects at each level of the OOG

Flat Object Graphs[3]

Percentage of Low-Level Objects in Flat Graph (LFO) is about 60% for all the systems, indicating a high proportion of low-level objects in flat graphs (Table 6). Since low-level objects are not architecturally-relevant, the numbers confirm that flat object graphs do not convey much architectural abstraction.

Hierarchical Reduction (HR) ranges between 2.80 and 19.45. The numbers support our hypothesis that an OOG has fewer objects at the top level, compared to a flat object graph. The OOG might have more objects than a flat graph (JHD, DL, PX), but the number of architecturally relevant objects (top-level objects) is smaller than the number of objects in a flat graph in all the systems. For example, the DL OOG has 5 times more objects than the DL flat graph. After using abstraction by ownership hierarchy and by types the number of top-level objects is 4 times smaller than the number of objects in the flat graph (Fig. 22). For APD, the number of top-level objects is one order of magnitude smaller than the number of objects in the corresponding flat graph.

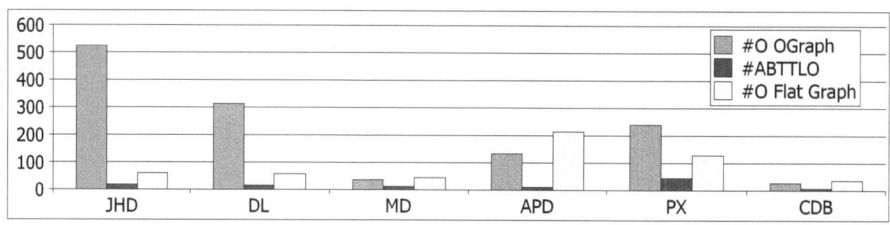

Fig. 22. Number of objects in OOG vs. number of objects in flat graph

4.3   OOG Metrics (within the Same System, Across Refinements)

After analyzing the OOG metrics across all the subject systems, we studied the evolution of the OOG metrics across two main refinement iterations for three of the systems. Between the iterations, the only things that changed are the annotations and possibly the list of design intent types and trivial types. As a result, only the OOGs changed, so we no longer compare against flat graphs.

Procedure. We used our version control history to check-out a snapshot of the code with the annotations in place at the major milestones. We re-extracted OOGs from the earlier versions of the annotated code, and studied how the OOG metrics evolved between the two iterations (Table 7). The OOG extraction tool also stores the list of design intent types and trivial types in separate files that we checked in, so this enabled us to study the evolution of abstraction by types. The refinements involved two actors: the extractor and the maintainer for PX, and the extractor and the developer for DL and MD. For each system, at the first milestone, the extractor finished the first iteration of the annotations, and

---

[3] For a few systems (HC, AFS), the Womble analysis did not converge for unknown reasons, so we reported those numbers as Not Available (n/a).

Table 7. Major milestones for selected systems

System	Milestone	Notes
DrawLets	DL_PRE	Finished annotations; before refinement
DrawLets	DL	After refinements requested during case study [4]
MiniDraw	MD_PRE	Finished annotations; before refinement
MiniDraw	MD	After refinements requested during pilot [12, Chap. 3]
PathwayExpress	PX_PRE	Finished annotations; before meeting with maintainer [8]
PathwayExpress	PX	After incorporating refinements requested by maintainer

Table 8. OOG metrics before and after refinement

	DL_PRE	DL	MD_PRE	MD	PX_PRE	PX
#O	270	313	42	37	222	240
#TLO	40	41	15	14	72	59
#D	37	40	10	14	73	80
#PD	0	1	1	5	2	2
#PrD	35	37	6	6	68	75
#PtE	246	334	62	63	269	306
PTLO	0.15	0.13	0.36	0.38	0.32	0.25
#LLOTLD	2.00	0.00	1.00	0.00	0.00	0.00
IDTLD	1.60	3.73	1.93	1.86	0.22	1.05
MAX	5	7	12	9	2	6
AOD	7.27	7.80	4.10	2.57	3.03	2.99
MAX	32	34	7	9	30	27
ABTTLO	18	15	14	12	68	46
DIT	1	4	1	1	1	8
ABTF	0.12	0.26	0.01	0.11	0.00	0.04
ABTTL	0.40	0.48	0.07	0.14	0.00	0.16
ABHBT	0.93	0.93	0.83	0.68	0.68	0.80

ensured that the annotations at least typechecked, with no major warnings left. Prior to the refinement iteration, however, the extractor used abstraction by types only lightly, e.g., the list of design intent types had only one type compared to the final list, which had 8 types. During refinement, the extractor refined both the annotations and used abstraction by types to make the OOG convey more design intent as the developer or the maintainer requested.

Results. We now show and discuss the evolution of the OOG metrics (Table 8).

Abstraction by Ownership Hierarchy. For all systems, Number of Objects (#O) and Number of Private Domains (#PrD) slightly increased due to a refinement that moved objects from shared to an existing domain, or to a new private domains, as the maintainer requested.

In PX, the Percentage of Top-Level Objects (PTLO) decreased by 7%, while Maximum Depth of Ownership Hierarchy (MXD) slightly increased. Since the maintainer made 40 requests to abstract low-level objects, they were pushed to lower-level domains. Also, no additional objects were moved up to a top-level domain, since the number of objects in the top-level domains was already high [27, Section 4.3]. In DL and MD, Number of Low-Level Objects in Top-Level Domains (#LLOTLD) became 0, and supports our hypothesis that low-level objects need to be pushed to lower levels of the OOG. In MD, since the OOG was too abstract, the extractor reduced abstraction by ownership hierarchy, and PTLO slightly increased.

In MD, the Number of Public Domains (#PD) increased from 1 to 5 in response to a request to push objects that were at the top-level underneath more architecturally-relevant ones. This indicates that public domains are used during the refinement of an OOG.

In all three systems, Number of Points-to Edges (#PtE), Cluttering (COOG), and Average In-Degree per Top-Level Domain (IDTLD) remained relatively low, but slightly increased. One exception in MD, where the maximum IDTLD decreased from 12 to 9 for the objects of type BoardFigure, and BoardDrawing in the top-level domain MODEL. Also, Average Objects per Domain (AOD) slightly increased for DL and decreased for MD and PX with a maximum of 34 for DL.

Abstraction by Types. For PX, the maintainer requested that extractor collapse 20 related objects based on their types [8, Table 2]. The Number of Design Intent Types (DIT) increased from 1 to 8, and allowed the extractor to hide 4% of the objects and 16% of the top-level objects. For DL, in response to a refinement request, the extractor added 3 classes to the list of DIT. Abstraction by Types (ABTF) increased from 12% to 26%, while the Number of Top-Level Objects after Abstraction by Types (ABTTLO) increases from 40% to 48%.

Abstraction by Ownership Hierarchy and by Types (ABHBT) increased for PX, decreased for MD, and remained constant for DL. For MD, the developer suggested that the OOG was too abstract. After the refinement, Number of Objects (#O) decreased from 42 to 37, ABHBT decreased from 0.83 to 0.68, while PTLO increased from 0.36 to 0.38. All these values indicate a less abstract graph. For PX, the maintainer requested additional abstraction. After using abstraction by ownership hierarchy and by types combined, ABHBT increased from 0.68 to 0.80. For DL, where abstraction by ownership hierarchy was more effective in the initial OOG, the extractor relied more on abstraction by types. Since the number of objects in the OOG increased, ABHBT remained constant at 0.93, a value close to the ideal value of five to seven objects per top-level domain. We measured the distances between the ABHBT value and the ideal range before and after refinements. For DL the distance slightly increased from 0.01 to 0.02. For MD and PX the distance decreased from 0.19 to 0.09, and 0.23 to 0.11, respectively. Therefore, for MD and PX, ABHBT got closer to the ideal values (Fig. 23). The extractor consider these ideal values as guidance, rather than rigid targets. There is an ideal level of abstraction targeted while refining the OOG, and this level is difficult to express by simply getting the highest value for one metric. Hypothetically, an OOG with Number of Objects (#O) as 100 and ABHBT as 0.99 would have a single top-level object, and would be too abstract. In fact, for MD, ABHBT decreases from 0.83 to 0.68, while the ideal values range between 0.5 and 0.64. This ideal range becomes very narrow

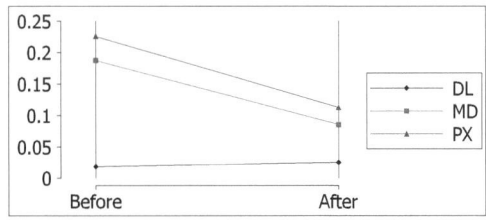

Fig. 23. ABHBT variation after refinement, normalized to an ideal interval

for large systems, and it might be unrealistic to treat it as a rigid value. Getting the ideal value for ABHBT may be insufficient, as indicated by the DL OOG that has ABHBT as 0.93, which is very close to the ideal range of 0.94–0.96. However, the developer requested additional refinements.

Another solution similar to Pareto's Principle (80-20% rule) is to target AB-HBT to be higher than a fixed relative percentage. Based on Pareto's Principle, the extractor may assumes that 20–30% of the objects are architecturally relevant. The solution would apply for PX, where ABHBT increases from 68% to 83% after the meeting with the maintainer. Simply aiming for a fixed percentage might lead to insufficient abstraction for large OOGs. It is the case of JHD OOG where the current ABHBT is 97%. Following this rule, it would also be difficult to justify the decrease of ABHBT for MD from 83% to 68%, and the fact that DL needs additional refinement when ABHBT is 93%.

5   Discussion

We discuss our observations, mention some limitations and threats to validity.

5.1   Observations

Our metrics attached quantitative data to our research questions.

Object Graphs Partially Follow Strict Encapsulation. In practice, we made use of private domains for 2–17% of all fields and variables of a reference type (excluding method return values).

Object Graphs Partially Follow Logical Containment. In practice, we made use of public domains for 0.3–7.4% of all fields and variables of a reference type (excluding method return values). In particular, systems that had carefully refined OOGs used public domains more heavily. During refinement, developers make the OOG reflect their mental model of the system by making an object part of another object.

In fact, for some systems, logical containment (with public domains) was used more often than strict encapsulation (with private domains). For example, in both MD and AFS, there were more fields annotated with a public domain than were annotated with a private domain. Our data suggests that for these

programs, and possibly for others, if we pushed harder to create hierarchical
OOGs, ownership type systems that only provide strict encapsulation will produce hierarchies that are substantially flatter. For expressing design, at least,
logical containment appears to be quite important for some systems.

We observed that the percentage of objects in public domains was in general
greater than the percentage of fields and variables of a reference type in a public domain (Fig. 24). That means, for example, that multiple objects in public
domains correspond to one declaration of a field in a public domain. This observation supports the case that public domains are important for making graphs
more hierarchical. The most interesting cases are MD, AFS, and CDB with 20%
or more objects in public domains.

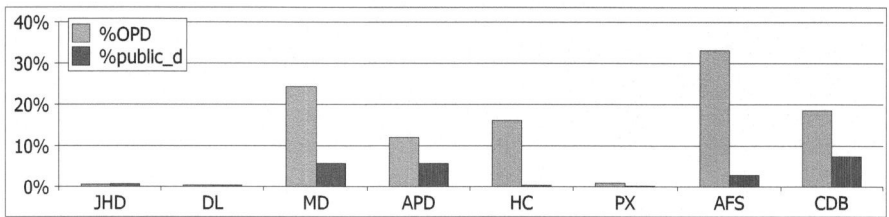

Fig. 24. Percentage of objects in public domains vs. the percentage of variables and
fields in a public domain

Abstraction by Ownership Hierarchy Is Effective in Object Graphs.
Our results show a reduction in the number of objects compared to a flat object
graph, but the reduction was smaller than an order of magnitude. There is a
caveat, however, in that the Womble flat object graphs we compared against were
potentially unsound. Sound flat object graph may actually show more objects
and the reduction would be higher. Further, abstraction by ownership hierarchy
alone is insufficient, in that we still end up with many objects per domain in
some cases.

In principle, abstraction by ownership hierarchy can be applied until the OOG
is clutter-free, but at some point, it will become a less natural expression of design intent. For example, JHD has many sub-classes that are related, such as the
subclasses of Figure, Command and Tool. Ideally, developers want the instances
of these types to be all peers in the ownership hierarchy. It would be less con-
vincing to make an instance of one subclass of Figure (e.g., EllipseFigure) be
part of another instance of another subclass of Figure (e.g., RectangleFigure),
just to reduce the number of objects in a domain.

Abstraction by Types Is Needed in Object Graphs. Our results indicate
that abstraction by types is needed to complement abstraction by ownership
hierarchy. If abstraction by ownership hierarchy produces depth compression in
an object graph, abstraction by types produces width compression, by collapsing
related instances that are in the same domain. Furthermore, the technique was
generally applicable across several systems.

Abstraction by Ownership Hierarchy and by Types Is Effective in Object Graphs. Together, both mechanisms reduce the number of top-level objects in an OOG compared to flat object graphs.

Limits of abstraction by ownership hierarchy and by types. There were a few cases where, despite our efforts, the final OOGs were still too cluttered. For example, for PX, we wanted to use abstraction by types more heavily, but were limited by the system design. For PX, the design issues include the lack of a rich inheritance hierarchy, many loosely typed containers (for many containers, the most precise generic types that can be added are Object or Serializable), and the lack of user-defined types (many fields are Strings) [8, Sections 5.3 and 5.4].

Refining the PX OOG further would have required re-engineering the code, sometimes in simple ways. For example, we could have defined an empty interface, made related classes implement that interface (this is the "marker interface" pattern[4]), then added that interface to the list of design intent types to further control the abstraction by types. Other re-engineering would be more complex.

Other Possible Abstraction Mechanisms. The challenges in achieving an uncluttered graph with PX suggest that additional abstraction mechanisms, beyond ownership hierarchy and types, might be necessary, especially as OOGs are applied to larger and larger systems.

One idea, for example, is to allow "abstraction by name". During the refinement of the PX OOG, the maintainer wanted to merge several objects that have Table in their declared types, like pdTable: PathwayDetailsTable, ipIdGenesTable: InputIdGenesTable and model: PETableModel. Even the maintainer was surprised that the types of these objects do not share a common super-type, other than Object. A similar situation occurred in AFS, where the only super-type shared by the interfaces AuthorizationRequest and FtpRequest is Object. As a result, we could not use abstraction by types to accomplish this merging. If the OOG were to allow "abstraction by name", such a merging would be possible.

More generally, after applying abstraction by ownership hierarchy and types, developers might specify groupings among the remaining objects by their conceptual purpose, even if they are not related by type or by name. This is similar to the manual specification of task-specific abstractions in approaches such as Reflexion Models [37].

The abstraction mechanisms provided by ownership could be quite complementary to the mechanisms provided in Reflexion Models. While task-specific abstractions allow the developer to focus on parts of the system relevant to a particular task, ownership provides a basic form of abstraction that can be customized in a task-specific way. Furthermore, ownership helps developers focus on the important parts of the system quickly, which may facilitate task-specific modeling. Ownership also provides information about logical containment and strict encapsulation that is missing in alternative abstraction mechanisms and also in plain Java code.

---

[4] Item 37: Use marker interfaces to define types [16].

5.2   Limitations

Limitations of Type System. Most of the systems we studied still have a number of annotation warnings. As a result, their OOGs may be unsound.

Limitations of Metrics. Metrics alone do not determine if an OOG is good. Ultimately, a human must decide if the OOG is good enough. One way to evaluate an OOG, like any architectural diagram, is to compare it against a target. This is an approach we followed previously, by abstracting an OOG into a runtime architecture and analyzing conformance [3]. Another way is to give the OOG to developers making code modification tasks, and evaluate if it helps during program comprehension [4].

Unsound Flat Graphs. One big limitation of comparing OOGs to flat graphs is that we used an unsound flat object graph analysis, Womble [30]. Ideally, we should have used a sound one, such as Ajax [40]. To our knowledge, we could have chosen one of the following three candidates: WOMBLE [30], AJAX [40] or PANGAEA [46].

WOMBLE [30] starts with a class diagram and uses heuristics for container classes and multiplicities to refine the object model. The follow-on tool, SUPERWOMBLE [50], uses additional heuristics for merging types but does not attempt to be sound. The unsoundness is an engineering tradeoff that is claimed to produce correct object models in practice, by masking problems due to other weaknesses of the analysis (namely, that it is flow-insensitive). SUPERWOMBLE also uses built-in and user-defined abstraction rules for containers that coalesce a chain of edges in the object model into a single edge [50]. SUPERWOMBLE also analyzes all classes that are transitively referenced (through constructor calls, field references, etc.) from the root set of classes. To avoid analyzing a large number of classes, most of which would not affect the output, a *stop-analysis configuration file* controls what classes or packages the tool analyzes [51].

AJAX[5] [40] uses a sound alias analysis to build a refined object model as a conservative static approximation of the heap graph reachable from a given set of root objects. However, AJAX does not use ownership and produces flat object graphs. AJAX relies heavily on post-processing raw object graphs, such as by eliding all "lumps" with more than seven incoming edges or eliding all subclasses of a given type, e.g., `InputStream` (p. 248). Moreover, the object models that AJAX generates tend to expose internal implementation details (p. 252). OOGs do not typically suffer from this problem since the annotations typically store an object's internal implementation details in private domains. On the other hand, AJAX is able to detect fields that are actually unused. In addition, AJAX can automatically and soundly split classes in the object model, i.e., determine that an object is indeed of type Y and not of type Z—even if Z is a subclass of Y, and

---

[5] AJAX [40] is not publicly available. O'Callahan was kind enough to give us the sources for his tool. But we were unable to run AJAX successfully, even on trivial examples because it requires an obsolete environment (JDK 1.1), and has undocumented dependencies.

without any information other than the code. Finally, AJAX's heavyweight but precise alias analysis does not scale to large programs.

PANGAEA [46] produces a flat object graph without performing an alias analysis and is unsound. For several programs, the PANGAEA output is even more complex than that of WOMBLE. To compare the WOMBLE and PANGAEA flat graphs on JHotDraw, see [2, Figures 4.18 and 4.19].

Another issue when comparing OOGs to flat object graphs is how to deal with library code. In principle, a flat graph can pull in many objects from all the libraries that are in use, and grow arbitrarily large. In an OOG, objects from library code would be considered low-level, and be pushed underneath more architecturally-relevant objects. To avoid an overwhelming number of objects in flat object graphs, we used the Womble feature of a stop-analysis configuration file. Womble used the same configuration for all the systems, and included the packages java.*, com.sun.java.*, as well as packages from system-specific, third-party libraries.

5.3   Threats to Validity

Threats to Internal Validity. Our study may include several threats to internal validity. First, the developers adding ownership annotations had varying experience with object-oriented design and with ownership types. Some of the less experienced developers initially added low-quality annotations. For example, they made too many fields as shared or used heavily the lent annotation, just to quickly reduce the number of annotation warnings. However, in all cases, the typechecker kept the developers on track, by ensuring that the annotations were consistent with each other and with the code. Also, by computing the annotation metrics above, we can better understand their quality.

Second, we refined some of the OOGs more than others. For example, we carefully refined the JHotDraw, DrawLets and MiniDraw OOGs since they were going to be used by other developers during coding tasks. Other OOGs, such as the ones for Aphyds and CryptoDB, were compared against reference architectures. But some of remaining OOGs were not fully evaluated.

Threats to External Validity. Several factors could be affecting the generalization our findings. First, the subject systems we selected may not be representative of all object-oriented code bases. Some of the systems (HC and PX) were developed by students rather than professional programmers. Others (JHD, DL, and MD) were designed by object-oriented experts for illustrative or pedagogical purposes, and as a result, may have been over-engineered to use many of the standard object-oriented design patterns. We mitigated this threat in some of the later subject systems by avoiding extremes, such as systems developed by undergraduates (HC) or by object-oriented experts (JHD). Instead, we picked an open-source application that was developed by professional programmers and that had been evolving (AFS).

Second, the number of subject systems in our study may be lower than is typically seen in empirical studies of the code structure [15] or studies of runtime

heaps using dynamic analysis [42]. Those studies consist of running a fully automated analysis on a large number of systems and comparing the results across
the systems. In our study, we had to manually add annotations to each subject
system before we could analyze it.

The effort to add annotations that typecheck and to extract initial OOGs
is measured to be around 1 hr/KLOC in a carefully timed setting, on the PX
system [8]. Additional, but lesser effort, is required to refine the OOG. For PX,
we spent 3 hours after meeting with the maintainer, compared to the 31 hours
we spent adding annotations and extracting initial OOGs. The meeting with the
maintainer to get the list of refinements lasted a little over 1 hour.

Our subject systems total over 100 KLOC in size, so we estimate the annotation effort to be at least 100 hours, and likely much higher. It is possible
that some of the systems that were annotated earlier while the tools were still
immature took much longer to annotate. It is also possible that some of the
OOGs (JHD, HC, APD, CDB) took more effort to refine because the OOG was
compared against a target architecture, or evaluated by other developers during
code modification tasks (JHD, DL, MD). To minimize outliers, we could have
excluded the systems for which the OOG was not sufficiently refined.

Finally, our subject systems are relatively small- to medium-sized. So, it is
unclear if our results will hold on systems with hundreds of thousands of lines
of code or larger. The scale of the systems we analyzed may pale in comparison
to studies that analyzed the code structure of large systems [15], because our
type-based technique requires developers to manually specify architectural intent
using annotations. Without automated inference of ownership types, analyzing
large systems is prohibitively costly. Since tools for analyzing the runtime structure statically are immature compared to tools for analyzing the code structure,
the scale of the systems we analyzed is not uncommon. For example, related
prior work that used annotations to statically extract object models [34] was
evaluated on one 1700-line system.

6   Related Work

We organize the related work into metrics on the runtime structure and metrics
on the code structure. We also discuss case studies of ownership type systems.

Runtime Structure. Potanin et al. studied aliasing in object-oriented Java-
like programs by analyzing heap snapshots [42]. They measured uniqueness,
ownership and confinement. To calculate the metrics, they analyzed a corpus of
58 heap snapshots from around 35 programs of different sizes.

For each object graph snapshot, they calculated the general metrics, the number of objects in the object graph (NO), the number of unique roots in the Java
heap root set (NUR) and the number of objects accessible by reference traversal (ART) from the root set. For uniqueness, they calculated the percentage of
aliased objects (PAL), where the aliased object is an object with more than one
incoming reference. For object ownership, they calculated the metrics for the
average depth (AD) of an object in the ownership tree and the average depth

after folding (ADF). For confinement, they calculated the number of not confined (NC) objects if there are referrers from a different package, weakly confined (WC) if all referrers are in the same top-level package, strongly confined (SC) if the classes of all the objects which refer to an object of interest are in the same package as that object's class, and the total number of classes (TNC). The study shows that object-oriented programs exhibit evidences of encapsulation in practice, and models of uniqueness, ownership, and confinement can describe the aliasing structures of object-oriented programs.

Our work differs from Potanin et al.'s in that we used only static analysis. Static information is less precise than dynamic information. In particular, our statically extracted and sound OOGs are necessarily more abstract than the runtime heaps that a dynamic analysis can monitor.

Code Structure. Baxter et al. analyzed a number of Java programs to determine whether relationships between different artifacts follow a power law distribution [15]. The paper points out that for small datasets, the results are inconclusive and contradict other studies that indicated that power laws were quite common in software [44,48]. In our work, we have small datasets, and as a result, we did not analyze whether the relationships obey a power law distribution.

Baxter et al. computed metrics on the static code structure, such as number of methods (nM), number of fields (nF) and Return as Client (RC). Our focus is on the runtime structure, but some code structure metrics are related to our annotation metrics. For example, Subclasses as Provider (SP) counts the number of classes extending a given class, and Interfaces as Provider (IP) counts the number of classes implementing a given interface. In Ownership Domains, domain parameters declared on a sub-class must be related to the domain parameters declared on a super-class, and some the annotation metrics reflect that (e.g., "inherits" in Table 3).

We also computed metrics of the code structure such as the Depth of the Inheritance Tree, defined elsewhere [19]. Information about inheritance is relevant since the abstraction by types mechanism in an OOG uses the sub-typing relations in the system.

Case Studies of Ownership Type Systems

Many ownership type systems have been tested only to check if they can express the canonical iterator example [17]. Others have applied ownership types to code that implement one of the standard design patterns in isolation [38]. However, many expressiveness challenges arise in real object-oriented code, and when the same objects are involved in several design patterns at once. In addition, there are multiple ways to implement a standard design pattern in object-oriented code.

Hächler documented a case study in applying the Universes type system [36,23] on an industrial software application and refactoring the code in the process [26]. Although the subject system in the case study was relative large (around 55,000 lines of code), Hächler annotated only a portion of the system, and did not report the exact number of lines of code he annotated. Hächler also manually generated visualizations of the ownership structure. In contrast, during our case studies, we used a tool to extract OOGs and to visualize the ownership structure, then refined the annotations accordingly.

Nägeli evaluated how the Universes and ownership domain type systems express the standard object-oriented design patterns [38]. However, in real world complex object-oriented code, design patterns rarely occur in isolation [45]. Our case studies indicated that it is often these subtle interactions, combined with the type system constraints, that can make adding the annotations difficult in some cases.

Case studies that retro-fit ownership types into legacy code often do not judge the quality of the added ownership types. Even if the ownership types typecheck, they may not be "good" or precise enough. For example, in Ownership Domains, one can annotate every reference as `shared`, which enables little reasoning. In this paper, we extracted OOGs based on the ownership types, and computed metrics which help us measure the quality of the inserted annotations. One could use the metrics to flag a large percentage of `shared` annotations for example.

7   Conclusion

Over the course of several years, we added ownership domain annotations to over 100 KLOC of real object-oriented code from a range of systems, and extracted OOGs. In this paper, we computed metrics on the annotations and on the OOGs. The annotation metrics helped measure the quality of the annotations. The OOG metrics helped explain the shape of object graphs in object-oriented code.

Our results demonstrate that ownership can make substantial contributions to expressing designs more abstractly. The top-level size of extracted ownership diagrams seems to scale sub-linearly with system size, suggesting that ownership will provide increasing benefits as it is applied to larger systems. We found evidence that both strict encapsulation mechanisms and logical containment mechanisms were important in expressing the designs of some programs. We also found evidence that the design characteristics of some programs mean they benefit from ownership but still need additional abstraction mechanisms in order to produce succinct diagrams of the object structures, suggesting there are fruitful directions for continuing work in the area.

Acknowledgements. The authors thank Jonathan Aldrich for detailed and insightful comments on an earlier version of this work. The authors also thank several contributors (Nariman Ammar, Fayez Khazalah, Zeyad Hailat, and Anwar Mohammadi) who, as course projects or for independent study, added annotations to and extracted OOGs from several object-oriented systems (DL, MD, PX, AFS) [14,13,5,49]. Vanciu was supported by Wayne State University. Abi-Antoun was supported by his faculty startup fund at Wayne State University Finally, the authors thank the anonymous reviewers for their helpful feedback.

References

1. Apache FtpServer 1.0.5, http://mina.apache.org/ftpserver/
2. Abi-Antoun, M.: Static Extraction and Conformance Analysis of Hierarchical Runtime Architectural Structure. Ph.D. thesis, Carnegie Mellon University (2010); available as Technical Report CMU-ISR-10-114
3. Abi-Antoun, M., Aldrich, J.: Static Extraction and Conformance Analysis of Hierarchical Runtime Architectural Structure using Annotations. In: OOPSLA (2009)
4. Abi-Antoun, M., Ammar, N.: A Case Study in Evaluating the Usefulness of the Run-time Structure during Coding Tasks. In: Workshop on Human Aspects of Software Engineering, HAoSE (2010)
5. Abi-Antoun, M., Ammar, N., Hailat, Z.: Extraction of ownership object graphs from object-oriented code: an experience report. In: ACM Sigsoft Conference on the Quality of Software Architectures, QoSA (2012)
6. Abi-Antoun, M., Ammar, N., LaToza, T.: Questions about Object Structure during Coding Activities. In: Workshop on Cooperative and Human Aspects of Software Engineering, CHASE (2010)
7. Abi-Antoun, M., Barnes, J.M.: Analyzing Security Architectures. In: ASE, pp. 3–12 (2010)
8. Abi-Antoun, M., Hailat, Z.: A Case Study in Extracting the Runtime Architecture of an Object-Oriented System. Tech. rep., Wayne State University (2011)
9. Aldrich, J., Chambers, C.: Ownership Domains: Separating Aliasing Policy from Mechanism. In: Odersky, M. (ed.) ECOOP 2004. LNCS, vol. 3086, pp. 1–25. Springer, Heidelberg (2004)
10. Aldrich, J., Chambers, C., Notkin, D.: ArchJava: Connecting Software Architecture to Implementation. In: ICSE (2002)
11. Aldrich, J., Kostadinov, V., Chambers, C.: Alias Annotations for Program Understanding. In: OOPSLA (2002)
12. Ammar, N.: Evaluation of the Usefulness of Diagrams of the Run-Time Structure for Coding Activities. Master's thesis, Wayne State University (2011), http://www.cs.wayne.edu/~mabianto/
13. Ammar, N., Abi-Antoun, M.: Adding Ownership Domain Annotations to and Extracting Ownership Object Graphs from MiniDraw. Tech. rep., Wayne State University (2011), http://www.cs.wayne.edu/~mabianto/oog_data/
14. Ammar, N., Khazalah, F., Abi-Antoun, M.: A Case Study in Adding Ownership Domain Annotations. Tech. rep., Wayne State University (2010), http://www.cs.wayne.edu/~mabianto/oog_data/
15. Baxter, G., Frean, M., Noble, J., Rickerby, M., Smith, H., Visser, M., Melton, H., Tempero, E.: Understanding the Shape of Java Software. In: OOPSLA (2006)
16. Bloch, J.: Effective Java. Addison-Wesley (2001)
17. Boyapati, C., Liskov, B., Shrira, L.: Ownership Types for Object Encapsulation. In: POPL (2003)
18. Cameron, N., Drossopoulou, S., Noble, J., Smith, M.: Multiple Ownership. In: OOPSLA (2007)
19. Chidamber, S.R., Kemerer, C.F.: Towards a metrics suite for object oriented design. In: OOPSLA (1991)
20. Christensen, H.B.: Flexible, Reliable Software Using Patterns and Agile Development. Chapman and Hall/CRC (2010)
21. Clarke, D.G., Potter, J.M., Noble, J.: Ownership Types for Flexible Alias Protection. In: OOPSLA (1998)

22. Cunningham, D., Drossopoulou, S., Eisenbach, S.: Universe Types for Race Safety. In: VAMP, pp. 20–51 (2007)
23. Dietl, W., Müller, P.: Universes: Lightweight Ownership for JML. Journal of Object Technology 4(8) (2005)
24. DrawLets, version 2.0 (2002), http://www.rolemodelsoft.com/drawlets/
25. Eclipse Metrics Plugin (2010), http://metrics.sourceforge.net/
26. Hächler, T.: Applying the Universe Type System to an Industrial Application: Case Study. Master's thesis, Department of Computer Science, Federal Institute of Technology Zurich (2005)
27. Hailat, Z., Abi-Antoun, M.: P-X Case Study: Online Appendix (2011), http://www.cs.wayne.edu/%257Emabianto/px/
28. Hauck, S.: Aphyds: The academic physical design skeleton. In: International Conference on Microelectronics Systems Education, pp. 8–9 (2003)
29. Intelligent Systems and Bioinformatics Laboratory, ISBL (2003), http://vortex.cs.wayne.edu/projects.htm/
30. Jackson, D., Waingold, A.: Lightweight Extraction of Object Models from Bytecode. TSE 27(2) (2001)
31. JHotDraw, version 5.3 (1996), http://www.jhotdraw.org
32. Kenan, K.: Cryptography in the Database. Addison-Wesley (2006), accompanying code at http://kevinkenan.blogs.com/downloads/cryptodb_code.zip
33. Koning, H., Dormann, C., van Vliet, H.: Practical Guidelines for the Readability of IT-Architecture Diagrams. In: SIGDOC (2002)
34. Lam, P., Rinard, M.: A Type System and Analysis for the Automatic Extraction and Enforcement of Design Information. In: Cardelli, L. (ed.) ECOOP 2003. LNCS, vol. 2743, Springer, Heidelberg (2003)
35. MiniDraw, http://www.baerbak.com/src/frs-src.zip
36. Müller, P., Poetzsch-Heffter, A.: Universes: a Type System for Controlling Representation Exposure. In: Poetzsch-Heffter, A., Meyer, J. (eds.) Programming Languages and Fundamentals of Programming (1999)
37. Murphy, G., Notkin, D., Sullivan, K.J.: Software Reflexion Models: Bridging the Gap between Design and Implementation. TSE 27(4) (2001)
38. Nägeli, S.: Ownership in Design Patterns. Master's thesis, Department of Computer Science, Federal Institute of Technology Zurich (2006)
39. Noble, J., Vitek, J., Potter, J.: Flexible Alias Protection. In: Jul, E. (ed.) ECOOP 1998. LNCS, vol. 1445, Springer, Heidelberg (1998)
40. O'Callahan, R.W.: Generalized Aliasing as a Basis for Program Analysis Tools. Ph.D. thesis, Carnegie Mellon University (2001)
41. Poole, D., Macworth, A.: CISpace: Tools for learning Computational Intelligence (2001), http://www.cs.ubc.ca/labs/lci/CIspace/
42. Potanin, A., Noble, J., Biddle, R.: Checking Ownership and Confinement. Concurrency and Computation: Practice and Experience 16(7) (April 2004)
43. Potanin, A., Noble, J., Clarke, D., Biddle, R.: Generic Ownership for Generic Java. In: OOPSLA (2006)
44. Potanin, A., Noble, J., Frean, M., Biddle, R.: Scale-Free Geometry in OO Programs. Commun. ACM 48(5) (2005)
45. Riehle, D.: Framework Design: a Role Modeling Approach. Ph.D. thesis, Federal Institute of Technology Zurich (2000)
46. Spiegel, A.: Automatic Distribution of Object-Oriented Programs. Ph.D. thesis, FU Berlin (2002)
47. Storey, M.A.D., Müller, H.A., Wong, K.: Manipulating and Documenting Software Structures. In: Eades, P., Zhang, K. (eds.) Software Visualization (1998)

48. Valverde, S., Ferrer-Cancho, R., Sole, R.V.: Scale-free networks from optimal design. Europhysics Letters 60(4) (2002)
49. Vanciu, R., Abi-Antoun, M.: Adding Ownership Domain Annotations and Extracting OOGs from Apache FTP Server. Tech. rep., Wayne State University (2011), http://www.cs.wayne.edu/~mabianto/oog_data/
50. Waingold, A.: Automatic Extraction of Abstract Object Models. Master's thesis, Department of Electrical Engineering and Computer Science, MIT (2001)
51. Waingold, A., Lee, R.: SuperWomble Manual (2002), http://sdg.lcs.mit.edu/womble/

Alias Control for Deterministic Parallelism

Robert L. Bocchino Jr.[*]

Carnegie Mellon University

Abstract. A parallel program is *deterministic* if it produces the same output on every execution with a given input, regardless of the parallel schedule chosen. Determinism makes parallel programs much easier to write, understand, debug, and maintain. Further, many parallel programs are intended to be deterministic. Therefore a deterministic programming model (i.e., one in which all programs that pass compile-time checking are guaranteed to run deterministically) is attractive. However, aliasing poses difficulties for such a model, because hidden read-write conflicts through shared memory can cause unwanted nondeterminism and even data races. This article surveys the state of the art in program annotations for controlling aliasing in a way that can support a deterministic parallel programming model. It discusses the following techniques: the Deterministic Parallel Java effect system; other effect systems, including systems based on object ownership; permission-based type systems; and annotations based on program logic.

1 Introduction

Single cores have reached the limit of scaling, and multiple cores are now standard on commodity machines, with the number of cores growing according to Moore's law. As a result, programs that used to run sequentially — with each new processor providing faster clock speeds and faster sequential execution "for free" — must be parallelized to take advantage of future hardware improvements. This heralds a big change in the way software is written: parallelism for speedup is no longer limited to specialized domains, such as scientific computing, and is likely to become pervasive.

One cost of this change is that naively introducing parallelism (say with Java threads or pthreads) introduces *nondeterminism*: different parallel tasks can perform conflicting reads and writes; different orders of the reads and writes can produce different answers; and the order can vary from run to run — even with identical input — because it depends on the parallel schedule chosen. This fact makes programs written with threads much harder to reason about, test, debug, and maintain than sequential code.

---

[*] Robert Bocchino is a Postdoctoral Associate at Carnegie Mellon University and is supported by the National Science Foundation under grant #1019343 to the Computing Research Association for the CIFellows Project. His doctoral work at the University of Illinois on Deterministic Parallel Java was supported by the National Science Foundation under grants CCF 07-02724 and CNS 07-20772, and by Intel, Microsoft, and the University of Illinois through UPCRC Illinois.

D. Clarke et al. (Eds.): Aliasing in Object-Oriented Programming, LNCS 7850, pp. 156–195, 2013.

However, a sequential program parallelized for speedup is usually intended to be *deterministic*: it is supposed to produce the same output on every run with a given input. For such programs, it is desirable for the programming model to *guarantee* that the program behaves deterministically. Ideally, a deterministic parallel program should also have a *sequential-equivalent semantics*: i.e., it should be provably equivalent to an "obvious" sequential program (typically the one that results by running all parallel tasks in sequential order). A deterministic programming model with a sequential-equivalent semantics makes life much easier for the parallel programmer, compared to a model with no such guarantee: the programmer can test one output per input again; can reproduce bugs deterministically; can reason about the program more or less sequentially; and can simply forget about notoriously difficult issues such as races, deadlocks, and memory models [1,2]. Less ideal, but still preferable to unrestrained nondeterminism, is a deterministic model with no sequential-equivalent semantics (for instance, one that permits deadlock to occur on some inputs, but guarantees that it will always occur on those inputs).

Guaranteed determinism is available for some styles of programming, such as pure functional programming [3]. However, in languages that support imperative updates to a heap and aliasing of object references — that is, most of the general-purpose languages in widespread use today — providing guaranteed determinism is challenging. For example, suppose task 1 writes field x.f, task 2 writes field y.f, and the writes are unsynchronized. Is it safe to run tasks 1 and 2 in parallel? That depends on whether x and y are aliases. Without special language or runtime support, determining whether two references are aliases is a difficult problem.

The research community has developed many approaches to dealing with this problem. They can be categorized as follows:

1. *Static analysis* or *compiler* approaches take a program "as is" in a traditional language such as C or Java and attempt to prove facts about aliasing with little or no programmer guidance. Traditional compiler analysis such as alias analysis [4] and dependence analysis using ad-hoc methods [5] falls in this category; more formal approaches such as separation logic [6] can also be used. This approach is advantageous when it works because no special annotations or hardware are required, and it works for legacy code. However, static analysis is limited in the kinds of problems it can address successfully.

2. *Runtime* approaches use a hardware or software runtime, or a combination of both, to provide deterministic guarantees. There are many variants of this approach: the runtime may enforce a deterministic order for conflicting accesses to shared memory [7,8]; or it may merge local memories in a deterministic way [9,10]; or it may detect conflicts and roll back [11,12]; or it may detect conflicts and abort [13,14]. The advantage of this approach is that few or no program annotations are required, and the runtime analysis can be very precise; the disadvantage is that the runtime adds overhead (if implemented in software) or requires special hardware. Also, many of the variants do not provide a sequential-equivalent semantics.

3. *Annotation-based* approaches use program annotations, either integrated
   with a type system [15,16] or based on explicit logical assertions [17], to prove
   facts about aliasing and memory conflicts. Such an approach is advantageous
   because it provides a strong guarantee, it can handle cases that programmer-
   unassisted static analysis cannot, and it provides machine-checkable documentation of programmer intent. It also supports modular checking: for
   example, as with standard type systems, uses of a library can be checked
   knowing only the library's interface specification, whereas traditional static
   analysis would typically need the source code for the entire program. The
   disadvantages are the overhead of the annotations and the inherent imprecision of compile-time checking compared to runtime checks.

This is only a rough categorization; in reality these categories overlap, and a
successful solution may borrow from more than one or even all of them.

   This article focuses on category (3), i.e., annotation-based approaches. It surveys the state of the art in program annotations that express or constrain aliasing
properties in such a way that a compile-time analysis can provide a guarantee of
determinism. Section 2 discusses the *effect system* used in the Deterministic Parallel Java (DPJ) language [18]. The effect system describes the way that different
parallel tasks access the heap, so the compiler can ensure there are no conflicting
accesses. Section 3 discusses other effect systems, several of which influenced the
design of DPJ. Section 4 discusses approaches based on *access permissions*, such
as unique variables. Access permissions provide an alternative to effects for controlling aliasing, with different tradeoffs. Section 5 discusses techniques based
on program logic. Logic is very powerful and general (both effects and access
permissions can be thought of as special cases of logic) but also relatively hard
to use and hard to automate. Finally, Section 6 concludes.

2   The DPJ Effect System

Deterministic Parallel Java [18] is a Java-based, explicitly parallel language that
uses annotations called *effects* to provide a compile-time guarantee of determinism. In this system, the programmer writes two kinds of annotations:

1. *Region annotations* that partition the heap into groups of memory locations
   called *regions*.
2. *Method effect summaries* that state the effects of methods in terms of operations on the regions.

The compiler uses a simple type checking-style analysis to check two things:

1. *Correctness of method summaries.* Every method effect summary includes
   all the actual effects of the method it summarizes, as well as the effects of
   any methods overriding that method.
2. *Noninterference.* Any two memory accesses, one from each of two tasks that
   may run in parallel, do not conflict (i.e., either they operate on disjoint
   memory, or they are both reads, or they commute).

The programmer can omit the region and effect annotations for sequential code but must add the annotations to code that is executed in a parallel task.

2.1   Regions and Effects

Figure 1 gives a simple example of regions and effects in DPJ. Line 2 declares region names First and Second. Lines 3 and 4 place instance fields first and second in those regions. To facilitate static analysis, the region names have static scope, e.g., all first fields in any instance of the Pair class reside in the same region Pair.First.[1] DPJ also provides *local regions*, declared within a method scope, for expressing effects on objects that do not escape the method.

```
1   class Pair {
2       region First, Second;
3       int first in First;
4       int second in Second;
5       void setFirst(int first)
6           writes First
7       {
8           this.first = first;
9       }
10      void setSecond(int second)
11          writes Second
12      {
13          this.second = second;
14      }
15      void setBoth(int first, int second) {
16          cobegin {
17              setFirst(first);   /* writes First */
18              setSecond(second); /* writes Second */
19          }
20      }
21  }
```

Fig. 1. Regions and effects in DPJ

Lines 6 and 11 illustrate the use of method effect summaries. The summary writes First in line 6 states that method setFirst writes region First, and similarly for writes Second in line 11. In general, a method effect summary has the form reads *region-list* writes *region-list*. If a method has no effect on the heap, it may be annotated pure. A method effect summary may be omitted entirely (as in line 15); in this case the compiler infers the most conservative

---

[1] DPJ uses *region parameters*, explained in Section 2.2, to assign different regions to different object instances.

effect ("writes the entire heap") for the method. This default is typically used for methods that are never called inside parallel tasks, so it is not important to know their precise effects.

A few simple rules govern the use of method effect summaries. First, all the actual effects of the method must be present in the summary. For example, the only heap effect in the body of setFirst is the write to field first in line 8, so the summary is correct. If the effect in line 6 were pure, the compiler would issue an error.[2] Second, the summary may be conservative, i.e., it may specify more effects than the method actually has. In particular, write effects subsume read effects, so it is permissible but conservative to say writes R in the summary when the method only reads region R. Finally, the effects of an overridden method must include the effects of any overriding method. This rule is similar to how plain Java handles throws clauses; it ensures sound reasoning about effects in the presence of polymorphic method dispatch.

Lines 16–19 show how to write deterministic parallelism. The cobegin block (line 16) says to execute its component statements in parallel. The compiler accumulates the effect of each statement and checks that the effects are pairwise noninterfering. Here, the effect of invoking setFirst in line 17 is writes First (from the definition of method setFirst in line 6); and similarly the effect in line 18 is writes Second. Because First and Second are distinct names, the writes are to disjoint regions, so they are noninterfering. If the effects in lines 17 and 18 were interfering (e.g., they both wrote to the same region), then the compiler would issue a warning. Note that the compiler merely warns of interference, rather than issuing an error; this is so the programmer can incrementally add regions and effects until the warnings go away, but the program will still compile and run.

2.2   Region Parameters

DPJ classes and methods may be written with *region parameters* that become bound to actual regions when the class is instantiated into a type or the method is invoked. Figure 2 illustrates the use of class region parameters. Line 1 declares a class SimpleTree with one region parameter P. Region parameter declarations coexist with Java generic type parameters and use a similar syntax; the keyword region distinguishes region parameters from type parameters. Line 3 places the instance field data in region P. When the class SimpleTree is instantiated with a type, and an object of that type is created with new, the type specifies the actual region of the storage for data, as illustrated in lines 4–5.

The compiler computes effects on fields by using the region specified in the class, after substituting actual regions for formal region parameters. This is illustrated in lines 8–9. The effect of line 8 is writes Left, as shown in the comment,

---

[2] Line 8 also reads the method parameter first. However, method parameters and other local variables in Java cannot have their addresses taken, and different variable names always represent different storage. Therefore, effects on such variables are handled automatically by the compiler and are ignored by the programmer-visible effect system.

```
1    class SimpleTree<region P> {
2       region Left, Right
3       int data in P;
4       SimpleTree<Left> left in Left = new SimpleTree<Left>();
5       SimpleTree<Right> right in Right = new SimpleTree<Right>();
6       void updateChildren(int leftData, int rightData) {
7          cobegin {
8             left.data = leftData;   /* writes Left */
9             right.data = rightData; /* writes Right */
10         }
11      }
12   }
```

Fig. 2. Class region parameters

because the write is to field `left.data`, Line 3 says that `data` is in region P, and line 4 says that the type of `left` has P = Left.[3] Similarly, the effect of line 9 is `writes Right`. Because Left and Right are distinct regions, the `cobegin` statement in lines 7–10 is legal. The DPJ type system ensures that this kind of reasoning is sound: for example, it is a type error to attempt to assign a reference of type `SimpleTree<Left>` to a variable of type `SimpleTree<Right>`.

Region parameters can have *disjointness constraints*. For example, `<region P1, P2 | P1 # P2>` declares two parameters P1 and P2 and constrains them to be disjoint. The compiler uses the constraint to check noninterference in parallel code that uses the parameters. If the disjointness constraint is not satisfied by the actual region arguments at the point where a class is instantiated or a method is invoked, then the compiler issues a warning.

2.3   Region Path Lists (RPLs) and Nested Effects

In deterministic parallel computations, it is often essential to express a *nesting* relationship among regions. For example, to do a parallel update traversal on a binary tree, one must specify effects on "the left subtree" or "the right subtree." A natural way to do this is to put a nesting structure on the regions that mirrors the nesting structure of the tree. DPJ represents this kind of nesting structure using *region path lists*, or RPLs.

An RPL is a colon-separated list of names beginning with Root, such as `Root:Left:Right`. RPLs naturally form a tree, where the RPL specifies the path in the tree from the root to the node that it represents. For example, `Root:Left:Right` is a child of `Root:Left`. In the execution semantics of DPJ, every region is represented as an RPL; a bare region name like Left is equivalent to `Root:Left`. RPLs may be *partially specified* by using * to stand in for any sequence of zero or more names, for example `Root:*:Left` or `Root:Left:*`.

---

[3] There is also a read of field `left` in region Left, but this read is subsumed by the effect `writes Left`.

This is useful in specifying *sets of regions* in types and effects. For example, Root:Left, Root:Left:Left, and Root:Right:Left are all included in the set of regions specified by Root:*:Left.

```
1    class Tree<region P> {
2        region Left, Right;
3        int data in P;
4        Tree<P:Left> left in P:Left;
5        Tree<P:Right> right in P:Right;
6        int increment()
7            writes P:*
8        {
9            ++data; /* writes P */
10           cobegin {
11               /* writes P:Left:* */
12               if (left != null) left.increment();
13               /* writes P:Right:* */
14               if (right != null) right.increment();
15           }
16       }
17   }
```

Fig. 3. A tree class

Figure 3 illustrates the use of RPLs to write a tree that can be traversed in parallel to update its elements. The key feature that makes this work is a *parameterized RPL*: an RPL can begin with a parameter P, as shown in lines 4–5. In the execution semantics, the parameters are erased via left recursive substitution. Figure 4 illustrates this procedure for the root node of a tree, and its two children. Each node of the tree has its data field in a distinct region, the RPL of which reflects the position of the node in the tree. Further, the DPJ type system enforces this structure: for example, it would be illegal to assign the right child to the left field of the root, because the types do not match.

Lines 6–16 show how to write an increment method that traverses the tree recursively in parallel and updates the data fields of the nodes. In line 7, the summary writes P:* says that the method writes P and all regions under P. The effect of line 9 is writes P, because field data is declared in region P (line 3). Line 12 generates two effects: a read of P:Left due to the read of field left, and a write to P:Left:* obtained from the effect summary of the recursively invoked method increment, after substituting P:Left from the type of left for P. Because writes subsume reads, both effects may be summarized as writes P:Left:*, as shown in the comment in line 11. Similarly, the effect of line 14 is writes P:Right:*.

As stated at the outset of this section, the compiler has to check two things: first, that the method summary is correct; and second, that the statements inside

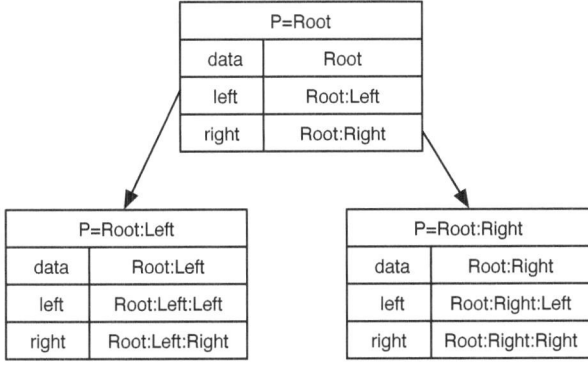

Fig. 4. Runtime representation of the tree

the cobegin (line 10) are noninterfering. The first check succeeds, because all the statement effects are included in the effect writes P:* stated in the summary in line 7. As to the second check, the effects of the two statements in the cobegin are writes P:Left:* and writes P:Right:*. Because of the tree structure of RPLs, these two effects are on disjoint sets of regions for any common binding to P. Therefore the effects are noninterfering, so this check succeeds as well.

2.4   Arrays

In addition to expressing trees, RPLs support two common patterns of parallel computation on arrays that are not well handled by previous type and effect systems: parallel updates of objects through arrays of references and divide-and-conquer updates to arrays.

Parallel Updates of Objects through Arrays of References. DPJ supports this pattern with two features. First, An RPL may include an element [e], where e is an integer expression, representing cell e of an array. This is called an *array RPL element*. Second, the region in the type of an array cell may be parameterized by the index of the cell. This is called an *index-parameterized array*. Together, these features allow the programmer to specify an array of references such that the object pointed to by each reference is instantiated with a distinct region.

Figure 5 shows an example. The class Body has one region parameter P and a field force in region P. The instance method computeForce computes a force and writes it into force. The static method computeForces takes an array of bodies and iterates over it in parallel, calling computeForce on each body. The type of bodies, shown in line 8, is an index-parameterized array type. The notation #i declares an index i in scope over the whole array type. The element type Body< [i] > says that for all natural numbers n, the array element at index n is a reference of type Body<Root: [n] >.

```
1   class Body<region P> {
2       double force in P;
3       void computeForce()
4           reads Root writes P
5       {
6           ...
7       }
8       static void computeForces(Body<[i]>[]#i bodies) {
9           foreach (int i in 0, bodies.length) {
10              /* reads Root writes Root:[i] */
11              bodies[i].computeForce();
12          }
13      }
14  }
```

Fig. 5. Code using an index-parameterized array

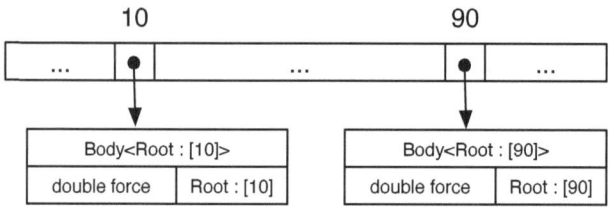

Fig. 6. Runtime representation of the index-parameterized array

Figure 6 shows how the array might look at runtime. The assignment rules in the DPJ type system ensure that the types are correct: for instance bodies[10] must point to an object of type Body<Root:[10]>. Therefore, all the force fields are in distinct regions, and the parallel updates in line 11 of Figure 5 are noninterfering.

Divide-and-Conquer Updates to Arrays. To support this pattern, DPJ allows *dynamic array partitioning*: an array may be divided into two (or more) disjoint parts that are updated in parallel. Figure 7 illustrates how this works for a simple version of quicksort. The quicksort method (line 2) has a region parameter P and takes a DPJArray<P>, which points into a contiguous subset of a Java array. In lines 6–7, the array is split at index p, creating a DPJPartition object holding references to two disjoint subarrays. The cobegin in lines 8–13 calls quicksort recursively on these two subarrays.

Figure 8 shows how this partitioning looks at runtime, for the root of the tree and its children. A DPJPartition object referred to by the final local variable segs points to two DPJArray objects, each of which points into a segment of the original array. The DPJArray objects are instantiated with *owner RPLs*

```
1   static <region P>void quicksort(DPJArray<P> A)
2       writes P:*
3   {
4       /* Ordinary quicksort partition */
5       int p = quicksortPartition(A);
6       /* Split array into two disjoint pieces */
7       final DPJPartition<P> segs = new DPJPartition<P>(A, p);
8       cobegin {
9           quicksort(segs.get(0)); /* writes segs:[0]:* */
10          quicksort(segs.get(1)); /* writes segs:[1]:* */
11      }
12  }
```

Fig. 7. Parallel quicksort

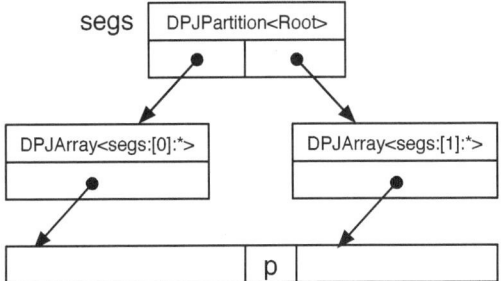

Fig. 8. Runtime representation of the dynamically partitioned array

segs:[0]:* and segs:[1]:* in their types. An owner RPL is like an RPL, except that it begins with a final local reference variable instead of Root.[4] This allows different partitions of the same array to be represented. Again because of the tree structure of DPJ regions, segs:[0]:* and segs:[1]:* are disjoint region sets, and so the effects in lines 9 and 10 are noninterfering. Also, as in ownership type systems, region segs is under the region P bound to the first parameter of its type, so the effect summary writes P:* in line 2 covers the effects of the method body.

The library classes DPJArray and DPJPartition are provided as part of the DPJ distribution. The owner regions in the return type of DPJPartition.get are generated by a type cast inside the implementation of DPJPartition (the single region R of the wrapped DPJArray is split into regions this:[0]:* and this:[1]:*). This type cast is not checked by the DPJ effect system, but it is hidden from the library user.

---

[4] This idea is borrowed from ownership type systems, discussed in Section 3.3.

2.5   Commutativity Annotations

Sometimes a parallel computation is deterministic, even if it does concurrent reads and writes to the same location in a nondeterministic order. For example, consider a set of concurrent operations, each of which does a read-increment-write update on a global counter variable. So long as the read-increment-write operation is atomic (for example, it is guarded by a lock), then n such concurrent operations will always increment the counter by n, regardless of the order in which those operations are scheduled.

```
1   class Counter<region R> {
2       private int value;
3       int getValue() reads R { return value; }
4       commutative synchronized void increment() writes R { ++value; }
5   }
```

Fig. 9. Counter class with commutative annotation

DPJ supports this kind of operation with a commutative annotation on methods (typically API methods for concurrent objects). Figure 9 shows an example. The annotation commutative in line 4 says that invoking any number of increment operations concurrently is equivalent to doing the the operations in sequence (isolation) *and* that all the sequence orders are equivalent (commutativity). This annotation is provided by a library or framework programmer and trusted by the compiler. It is not checked by the DPJ effect system, although recent research has shown how to use verification techniques to check annotations like this for correctness [19].

When the DPJ compiler encounters a method invocation, it generates an *invocation effect* that records both the method that was invoked, and the read-write effects of that method:

```
foreach (int i in 0, n) {
    /* invokes Counter.increment with writes R */
    counter.increment();
}
```

The compiler uses the commutativity annotations to check interference of effect. For example, the effect invokes Counter.increment with writes R is non-interfering with itself (because increment is declared commutative). However, the same effect interferes with invokes Counter.getValue with reads R, so doing those two operations concurrently would produce a warning. Invocation effects may be summarized by just stating their underlying effects at method signatures. For example, a method enclosing the code above could use the summary writes R.

2.6   Other Features of DPJ

DPJ has several other features that support practical parallel programming, which we state briefly below. A full discussion of these features is beyond the scope of this article; the interested reader is referred to the DPJ web site [18], the author's Ph.D. thesis [20], and the papers presented at POPL 2011 [21] and ECOOP 2011 [22].

Determinism by Default. Sometimes pure determinism is too restrictive: for instance, in a branch-and-bound search, we would like to stop when we get to a result that is "good enough" (i.e., meets some predefined criterion of correctness), without requiring that the same result be produced on every run. To support this kind of algorithm, DPJ actually has a *deterministic by default* programming model: nondeterminism is allowed, but it must be explicitly requested and is carefully controlled. Specifically, (1) any nondeterminism must occur in designated constructs foreach_nd or cobegin_nd, where the nd stands for "nondeterministic"; (2) all code is race-free and subject to strong isolation for sections marked atomic; and (3) ordinary foreach and cobegin constructs have a sequential-equivalent semantics, even inside an nd construct. The language provides these guarantees using a software transactional memory (STM) runtime together with *atomic effects* that track which accesses are guarded by transactions. The effect system also lets the compiler boost STM performance by removing unnecessary synchronization on reads and writes that can never interfere.

Object-Oriented Parallel Frameworks. DPJ supports the use of object-oriented parallel frameworks, an important technique in real-world code. For example, a parallel collection class can provide an API that lets the user write a sequential method and apply the method in parallel to each object in the collection. A key challenge in this style of programming is to ensure that the user-defined method does not cause interference (for example, by doing an unsynchronized write to a global variable). DPJ lets the framework writer specify effect constraints in the API, and it checks the user-supplied methods against those constraints. To make the APIs suitably generic, DPJ supports some more features for writing types and effects (a type constructor-like mechanism, and constrained effect variables) beyond those discussed in Sections 2.1 through 2.5.

3   Other Effect Systems

3.1   FX

The first type and effect system was the pioneering work of Lucassen, Gifford, Hammel, and others on FX [23,24,25]. FX added a region-based type and effect system to a language based on Scheme. The system incorporated the following major features:

- As in DPJ, reference types are assigned a *region* (i.e., set of memory locations) describing where the object referred to is allocated on the heap. In FX, a region *R* is either a simple name or a region variable. There is no concept of a region hierarchy.
- Every expression is assigned an *effect*, which may be PURE (no effect) or a read, write, and/or allocation effect on a set of regions. An allocation effect on *R* says that a new object was created in *R*.
- Functions are first-class and have an argument, return type, and effect.
- Functions may be polymorphic in their types, regions, and/or effects.
- The system can *mask* function effects that are invisible to the caller. For example, a function that allocates an object and writes to it but does not store or return a reference to it can have effect PURE.[5]

Here is a simple example (taken from [23]) of an expression in FX:

```
twice = (PLAMBDA (t:TYPE e:EFFECT) (LAMBDA (f:(SUBR (t) e t))
  (LAMBDA (x:t) (f (f x)))))
```

As usual in LISP-derived syntax, there are a lot of parentheses. Reading from the outside in, the expression says that (1) the whole expression is polymorphic in type t and effect e; (2) the expression is a function that takes an argument f to a result expression; (3) the argument f is a function with argument and return type t and effect e; and (4) the result expression is a function that takes an argument x of type t and returns the result of evaluating f (f x).

The authors of FX built a parallelizing compiler [24] that automatically extracted noninterfering parallelism from FX programs. Thus, FX was an *implicitly parallel* language (i.e., the programmer did not explicitly note which sections are to run in parallel, but instead the compiler used the annotations to infer the parallelism). While FX was able to produce some speedup over sequential code (measured by an idealized speedup analysis), it had no region hierarchy or way to associate different regions with different array cells. Therefore it could not handle either disjoint writes to different array cells or divide-and-conquer updates of trees. Later effect systems, such as DPJ and the systems described below, overcame these limitations. However, FX remains not only the seed of all effect systems, but also important and influential early work on effect systems for deterministic parallelism.

3.2   Early Object-Oriented Systems

Starting in the late 1990s, researchers began applying the idea of effect systems to checking object-oriented programs. Leino [26] added "data groups" to Java to assist with program verification. Data groups are essentially regions; in Leino's system a modifies annotation provides the equivalent of write effects. The interesting features of Leino's system are (1) as in DPJ (and unlike FX)

---

[5] DPJ's local regions (Section 2.1) allow masking of effects on objects that do not escape a method context.

regions are declared in classes and fields are placed in regions; (2) regions are hierarchical (however, the hierarchy is statically specified and finite, unlike DPJ and ownership-based systems that can describe arbitrary-depth trees); and (3) a single field can be placed in more than one region.

Greenhouse and Boyland [27] described a system similar to Leino's, but motivated by code-reordering program transformations. Their system has the following salient features. First, regions can be either instance regions (pertaining to a single runtime object) or static regions (pertaining to all objects of a class). In particular, if r is an instance region, then $x.r$ and $y.r$ refer to the same region only if x and y are aliases. A supplemental alias analysis makes this determination. Second, unique fields are supported: if a field f is unique, then effects through f need not be reported to the rest of the program, because no other references can access the object referred to by f. As in Leino's system, regions are nested, but only to finite and statically-specified depth.

Greenhouse and Scherlis [28] extended the system with region parameters and showed how to use it to support annotations describing a *concurrency policy* in threaded programs (for example, that certain pairs of methods should never be called concurrently with each other). However, their system provides a relatively weak guarantee: violations of the concurrency policy must be detected by manual inspection or (unspecified) static analysis.

Finally, Leino has described ad-hoc ways of restricting assignments to support reasoning about effects [29]. In Leino's system, a *pivot field* is a field $o.f$ that points to an object o' that is logically part of the representation of o (for example, an array object that stores data for the parent object). Then *pivot uniqueness* says that a pivot field $x.f$ is never aliased by a local variable y in a scope where it appears, while *owner exclusion* says that a pivot field in region r can be passed as a parameter only to methods that cannot modify r. Leino shows how to enforce these restrictions in a static type system and use them to do sound modular verification.

3.3   Ownership Types

Originally proposed by Clarke et al. as a mechanism for alias control [30], object ownership has grown far beyond this original purpose, and many variant systems have been proposed [31]. Here we confine our discussion to systems that combine ownership with effects.

Object Ownership. All ownership type systems express the concept of *object ownership*, which is based on the following two ideas:

1. Groupings of data on the heap (called regions or data groups in the effect systems discussed above) are associated with runtime object references. In ownership systems, these groupings are often called *contexts*.
2. A notion of *ownership* makes the set of contexts into a tree: If object o owns object o', then o' is a child of o in the tree. The root of the tree is a special context not associated with any object reference called world.

The ownership tree can both describe the structure of the heap and represent effects on nested structures, as in DPJ. In fact, the owner RPL mechanism of DPJ (Section 2.4) is borrowed from ownership type systems.

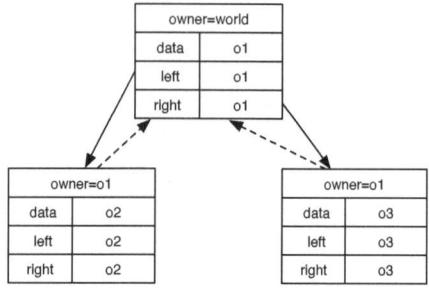

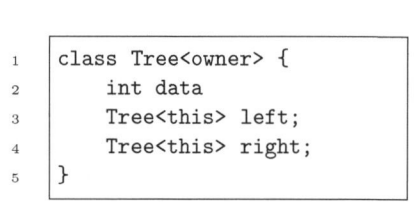

```
1   class Tree<owner> {
2       int data
3       Tree<this> left;
4       Tree<this> right;
5   }
```

Fig. 10. A tree class expressed in an ownership idiom

Fig. 11. Runtime representation of the tree from Figure 10

As an example, Figure 10 shows a tree data structure similar to the DPJ tree in Figure 3, but expressed in an ownership idiom. This example uses the syntax of Java with Ownership and Effects (JOE) [32]. Figure 11 shows a possible runtime configuration of the tree. Solid arrows represent references, while dashed arrows represent the relationship "is owned by."

The following points about this example are salient:

- Classes have *context parameters*, which are similar to region parameters in DPJ. The first parameter is the *owner parameter*, which establishes the owner context for the object. The owner context is the "parent context" for the object.
- In the definition of a class, the context this represents the context of the current object. The this context is a child of the owner context in the context hierarchy.
- All fields of an object implicitly reside in context this.
- Apart from the universal context world (similar to DPJ's Root), contexts are created not by introducing new names, but by creating new objects. At runtime, the object references function as the contexts. For example, in Figure 11, we have labeled the root object o1, so the left child (which is owned by the root) has its owner parameter bound to o1 as shown.

Notice that the two child nodes have different contexts o2 and o3, but they are both owned by the parent context o1, and they both have the same type. Thus, unlike the DPJ code from Figure 3, the type system cannot distinguish the child nodes from each other. However, as discussed below, other styles of ownership (in particular ownership domains [33]) can make this kind of distinction.

Expressing Heap Structure. The original proposal for ownership types [30] grew out of earlier work on flexible alias protection [34]. Two major goals of this work were as follows:

1. To express what objects are part of the representation of another object. For example, an object representing a list data structure can own the link objects that form the backbone of the list.
2. To prevent aliases from crossing the representation boundary. For example, the outside world can be prevented from holding any direct reference to a list backbone object; instead, the outside world refers only to the list, which refers to its own backbone.

In the original paper on ownership types [30], the second property is enforced by requiring that the owner o of an object o' *dominate* o' in the object graph: for any reference path p from an object o'' to o', either o'' is under o in the ownership hierarchy, or p passes through o'. For example, in the tree from Figure 10, the type system would disallow a reference pointing from the root of the tree to a child of a child of the root, because then the root's child would not dominate its child. This structural property of the heap is called the *owner-as-dominator discipline*, and it enforces a very strong notion of encapsulation for the representation of an object. In particular it can be used to establish *external uniqueness* (i.e., that at most one reference from outside a data structure points into the data structure), which is useful for verifying program correctness properties [35]. However, the owner-as-dominator discipline is too restrictive for use in most real-world settings; for example, it prohibits the common pattern of having an external list iterator store a reference into a list backbone.

Because the owner-as-dominator discipline is so restrictive, later variants of ownership usually impose a weaker restriction on the shape of the object graph. One such restriction is the *owner as modifier discipline*. In this variant, while arbitrary references may point to an object, only the owner may modify the object. This variant appears in the Spec# type system [36], Universe Types [37], and Lu and Potter's Effective Ownership [38]. Lu and Potter's system uses effects to enforce the owner-as-modifier discipline, while Universe Types restrict non-owner references to be read-only. The major benefit of the owner as modifier discipline is that since only the owner can update the encapsulated state, invariants on that state can be established just by proving facts about the owner's operations; these proofs need not reason about other aliases in the program.

Another possibility is to place no restriction on the shape of the heap, and simply use the ownership structure to reason about effects or program behavior. MOJO [39] adopts this approach. The DPJ effect system is also in this spirit: it introduces regions and ownership solely to express effects and noninterference, and not to enforce any particular alias discipline.

In fact alias disciplines like owner-as-dominator or owner-as-modifier, while very useful for some verification tasks [40], are not as well suited to enforcing parallel noninterference. The main purpose of these disciplines is to distinguish between the "inside" and the "outside" of a multi-object data structure. But in a parallel traversal over a data structure (like a tree or array) we may need to divide the "inside" into smaller pieces that can be updated in parallel. In this case putting all the "inside" objects into one region doesn't work well. Similarly, while the owner-as-modifier discipline prevents non-owners from updating a data structure, there is nothing to prevent non-owners from reading data in parallel with owners who are updating it. Thus, the owner-as-modifier discipline is not sufficient to prohibit parallel interference.

Expressing Effects. Several ownership type systems incorporate effect annotations for reasoning about noninterference. An important early system in this vein is Java with Ownership and Effects (JOE) [32]. JOE uses syntax like that shown in Figure 10 to express the ownership structure of the heap. It also allows methods to be annotated with read and write effects on *effect shapes*, which are sets of contexts. One kind of effect shape is a simple context, as in `writes v`. This shape represents a write effect on the single context corresponding to the object stored in the local variable v (which must be `final`). Another shape is a *band*, as in `writes v.1`; this represents all contexts that are exactly one position beneath v in the ownership hierarchy. Finally, the shape `under v` refers to all contexts under v in the hierarchy; this allows tree-like effects to be expressed.

JOE was innovative in (1) allowing context variables c to be written with constraints (such as "the context bound to c_1 must be under the context bound to c_2") and (2) allowing `final` local variables to function as contexts. Both of these features influenced the design of DPJ. Further, because JOE was based on ownership and could represent arbitrary-depth trees, it represented an advance over previous work like FX, Greenhouse and Boyland's system, and Leino's system that were limited to either a flat region hierarchy (in the case of FX) or a finite and statically-specified region hierarchy. However, because the type system cannot distinguish the types of the child nodes of a tree node (as shown in Figure 10), the JOE effect system does not support parallel update traversals over trees.

Another important ownership-based effect system is MOJO (Multiple Ownership for Java with Objects) [39]. The main contribution of MOJO is that it supports *multiple ownership* — that is, an object may be placed in more than one context. For example, a `Task` object can belong to a `Worker` object as well as a `Project` object, or a `Task` can belong to multiple workers. Leino's data groups (see Section 3.2) also have this capability, but without arbitrary nesting.

As can be seen, these systems are similar to DPJ in some of their capabilities. Compared to DPJ, the main differences are:

1. These systems do not provide any way to distinguish different array cells or groups of array cells, which is critical for many patterns of deterministic parallelism. DPJ incorporates features like index-parameterized arrays and array partitions for supporting these patterns.
2. These systems do not support putting different fields of the same object in different regions. In practice, this has to be done (for example, to read from a `mass` field and write to a `force` field in an n-body simulation [15]). DPJ supports this kind of field-granularity region mapping, using syntax similar

to that of Greenhouse and Boyland's system (see Section 3.2). DPJ also provides a way to specify "effects on all M fields of objects under R," by writing `writes` $R:*:M$. This is similar to the band capability of JOE, but it provides more flexibility: for example, one may specify that a tree traversal may read the `mass` field of any node and writes the `force` field of a particular node and its children.

3. Because these systems are based on ownership, they couple region creation with object creation. However, there are many cases where a new region is wanted but a new object is not. For example, in Figure 3, it was convenient to be able to associate the names `Left` and `Right` with the left and right children of a tree node, without creating any extra objects. Another example is a method-local region: it is very convenient to be able to say `region r` inside a method scope (or even a statement block scope within a method, such as a loop scope) and then mask effects on `r` outside that scope.

As discussed in Section 2, the DPJ effect system uses explicit region declarations but also incorporates the idea of ownership. Smith's work on effects for *ownership domains* [33], building on work of Aldrich and others [41], represents an alternative way to achieve a similar goal. In Smith's system, one may declare *domains* L and R inside a class definition. Then one can express disjoint traversals over trees by placing the child nodes in distinct contexts `this.L` and `this.R`, similar to `this:L` and `this:R` in DPJ. However, Smith's system does not support field-granularity object partitioning, arrays, or method- and statement-local regions, as DPJ does. Also, as in JOE, effect shapes like $R:*:M$ are not supported.

Wrigstad's *scoped regions* [42] allow a method scope to be treated as an owner, providing some of the capabilities of DPJ's local regions in an ownership setting. Region-based memory management uses a similar technique [43]. However, these systems do not support effect annotations.

Finally, several researchers [44,45,46] have described effect systems for enforcing a locking discipline in nondeterministic programs, to prevent data races and deadlocks. Because they have different goals, these effect systems are very different from the ones discussed in this article, e.g., they cannot express disjoint array updates or nested effects.

4   Permissions

Permissions (also called access permissions or capabilities) are an alternative to effect annotations for reasoning about parallel noninterference. A permission annotates a local variable or field that stores a reference value, and it constrains the ways in which the reference can be used. For example, a `unique` permission states that a variable or field holds the only usable reference to an object on the heap or the stack. If two different heap or stack locations each store a unique permission to an object, then the two locations must point to different objects (i.e., they cannot be aliases), and this fact can be used to reason about noninterference. More generally, unique fields and array cells can represent trees and tree-like data structures, as shown in Figure 12. Similarly, an `immutable` permission states that a variable or field holds a reference that may be used only for reading, but not writing, the object referred to. Again, this fact can be used for reasoning about noninterference, because an access through an immutable reference cannot interfere with a separate access either through a unique reference (which must be disjoint) or through an immutable reference (which may be overlapping, but is read-only).

```
1   class Tree {
2       int data;
3       unique Tree left;
4       unique Tree right;
5   }
```

Fig. 12. A tree class expressed with access permissions

Designing a practical language based on permissions presents several challenges. In the following subsections, we first discuss those challenges and the ways in which they have been addressed in the literature to date. Then we compare permissions with effects as methods of controlling parallel interference. Finally, we discuss the Æminium language project, which aims to develop a robust language for concurrency based on permissions, and Habanero Java, which uses permissions to provide race freedom for parallel programs.

4.1 Technical Challenges

Reading Object Fields. Field access `x.f` is a fundamental feature of object-oriented languages. Yet it poses tricky problems for the permission-based approach.[6] For example, suppose the type of variable x is some class C that has a unique field f, and we assign `x.f` into a variable y. Then in a standard object-oriented language, like Java, y and `x.f` would point to the same object. But if unique means that `x.f` has no aliases, then that can't be right. So what should `y=x.f` mean in a permission-based language? The research literature has developed several answers to this question.

Destructive read. The simplest answer is that assigning `x.f` to a variable y copies the reference from `x.f` into y and *destroys* the original reference in `x.f` (usually by assigning `null` into it). This approach is called *destructive read*. The idea of destructive read appeared as early as Hogg's seminal paper on alias protection in object-oriented languages [47], and later systems have adopted the idea [48]. The main advantage of destructive read is its simplicity: it is easy to

---

[6] Variable access x, where x holds a unique reference, poses analogous issues. However, in a language like Java that does not allow addresses of local variables to be taken or passed around, these issues are easily resolved by standard intra-procedural compiler analysis techniques.

implement, it doesn't require any special typing or analysis mechanisms, and it is intuitive for programmers because it represents permission transfer by physically transferring a reference from one location to another.

However, destructive reads produce an unnatural coding style, particularly when permissions are passed to and returned from methods. For example, in Java we can easily write the code shown in Figure 13. By contrast, in a permission-based language with destructive read, if field f is declared unique, then this code no longer works: the method invocation in line 6 writes null into x.f, and line 7 causes a null pointer exception. Instead m3 must return the reference passed into it through x so it can be assigned back to x.f, as shown in Figure 14.

```
1   class C {
2     C f;
3     void m1() { ... }
4     void m2() { ... }
5     void m3(C x) {
6       x.f.m1();
7       x.f.m2();
8     }
9   }
```

Fig. 13. Calling m1 and then m2 on x.f

```
1   class C {
2     unique C f;
3     C m1() { ... return this; }
4     void m2() { ... }
5     void m3(C x) {
6       x.f=x.f.m1();
7       x.f.m2();
8     }
9   }
```

Fig. 14. Reassigning to x.f to restore its permission

This approach is very awkward, because it requires methods that would ordinarily have void return type (such as m1 in Figure 14) to return non-void values in order to return permissions to their continuations. More fundamentally, these extra assignments can cause problems for parallel programming:

- Both the destructive read itself and the following reassignment produce "phantom effects" that can inhibit parallelism. For example, in Figure 14, the write to x.f in line 6 forces line 7 to be executed after line 6, even if both m1 and m2 have only read effects, and so could otherwise be run in parallel.
- Adding unnecessary writes can hurt cache behavior, particularly in parallel code where several cores simultaneously read the same cache line. In a standard OO language, the line can be present in each core's cache. However, if the cores have to write the line, then in a typical cache coherence protocol, each writer would need exclusive access to the line in turn. The resulting "ping-pong effect" as the line is transferred from writer to writer can destroy parallel performance.

So destructive read, while simple, is not an ideal solution for a deterministic parallel language.

Swap. An alternative approach is to disallow a field read x.f whenever f is a unique field, and instead provide a special *swap* operation that (1) accepts as an argument some other unique reference; (2) stores the argument reference in x.f; and (3) returns the old value of x.f as the value of the operation. Some systems described in the literature use swap for access to unique fields [49,50,51]. Independently of uniqueness typing, Harms and Weide [52] have argued that replacing copy with swap operations can have general software engineering benefits.

By requiring the user to specify a replacement value explicitly, swap may avoid spurious null pointer exceptions. Otherwise, swap is at least as awkward as destructive read. Further, swap doesn't remedy the other defects of destructive read, such as introducing extra writes. So like destructive read, swap is simple and works, but it is not very satisfactory.

Alias types. Yet another approach, first developed by Smith, Walker, Morrisett, and others in the context of a typed assembly language, is called *alias types*[53]. In this approach, the unique permission is associated not with a reference, but with a *key*. Like an ownership context (section 3.3), a key is a compile-time name for a runtime object. Two references associated with the same key are always aliases, while two references associated with different keys are never aliases.

```
1  class Cell<key K> {
2      tracked(K) int[] array;
3  }
```

Fig. 15. A cell class expressed with alias types

Figure 15 illustrates this approach, using syntax like that of Vault [54].[7] Class Cell has a key parameter K and stores an array of integers in a field `array`. The `array` field is annotated `tracked(K)`. That means that the field points to the same object as all other fields and variables annotated `tracked(K)`, and no other fields or variables point to that object.

In this scheme, fields and local variables may be aliases, if they share the same key. For example, we can write the following code:

```
1      // Create new array with fresh key K
2      tracked(K) int[] array = new tracked int[10];
3      // Bind K to parameter of Cell class
4      Cell<K> cell = new Cell<K>();
5      // Assign array into cell
6      cell.array=array;
```

In the last line we have assigned `array` into `cell.array`, creating an alias between the field `cell.array` and the local variable `array`.

Because alias types allow aliasing between fields and local variables, they support non-destructive field access. However, in a practical language design, alias types also have some significant disadvantages:

---

[7] Vault is an extension of C that uses alias types to check protocol usage for device drivers.

- Key parameters support the pattern shown above, i.e., creating a child object, then creating a parent object and assigning the child into it. However, they are less adept at the reverse pattern (creating the parent first), because we need the child's key in order to write the parent's type. For example, in the code above, if we transposed lines 2 and 4, then the code would not type check, because key K would not exist at the point of writing the type Cell<K>. The authors of Vault have devised a technique called *adoption* to deal with this problem [55]: adoption allows an object tracked by a key K to be stored inside another object, without naming K in the type of the parent; while the object is stored in the parent, its aliases are guarded by a fresh key K' created at the point of assignment into the parent. However, adoption is much less simple and intuitive than simply storing into a field, as one would in an ordinary OO language.

- Recursive structures are difficult to represent. Vault's alias types, which require all permissions in the structure to be named in the type of the root, don't support recursion at all [54]. This is a very serious problem for deterministic parallelism, where tree traversal is fundamental. Alias types have been extended to support recursive structures [56], but the resulting system is complex. While this approach has been shown to work well in the context in which alias types were originally developed (i.e., typed assembly language), it is an open question whether it can be made practical for a programming language.

Unpacking. Field access can be supported by *unpacking* unique fields when they are read into variables. The idea of unpacking was first developed to support program verification using class invariants [57]. In that context an invariant (e.g., that two fields point to different objects) may be true most of the time, but may have to be temporarily broken (e.g., while the fields are being swapped with each other). In this case it is useful to be able to distinguish two states of an object: *packed* and *unpacked*. In the packed state, an object conforms to its declared invariants, while in an unpacked state it does not.

Recent work of Naden and others, including the present author, on the Plaid programming language [58] shows how to unpack unique fields in a syntactically simple language, hiding most of the details in the type checker. In that approach, given the tree class shown in Figure 12, one may just pull unique permissions out of the tree, with no special annotations, for example:

```
1    unique Tree tree = new Tree();
2    tree.left = new Tree();
3    tree.right = new Tree();
4    unique Tree left = tree.left;   // tree is unpacked here
5    tree.left = new Tree(); // now tree is packed again
```

The invariant here is that the fields of classes conform to their declared permissions. In line 1, the object pointed to by tree is packed, because both of its fields store null.[8] Assigning new Tree objects into tree.left and tree.right in lines 2 and 3 maintains the invariant, so the object is still packed. In line 4 we create an alias of tree.left and assign it into left. This alias violates the invariant, so we say that tree is unpacked at that point. The type system tracks that fact by assigning permission unique to variable left and noting that tree now has type Tree, *except* that its left field has permission none (i.e., no usable permission). Westbrook et al. [59] describe a similar mechanism called "permission subtraction." In line 5, we assign a new Tree object with unique permission to tree.left. This restores the invariant, so tree becomes packed again.

Here we restored the permission by assignment, but a permission can also be restored from a local variable that goes out of scope or on return from a method; in those cases no reassignment is required. Here is an example:

```
1    unique Tree tree = new Tree();
2    tree.left = new Tree();
3    tree.right = new Tree();
4    {
5      unique Tree left = tree.left;  // tree is unpacked here
6    }
7    // now tree is packed again
```

In line 5 tree is unpacked because of the assignment of tree.left into left; when left goes out of scope in line 7, tree becomes packed again. This pattern of taking a permission out of a field, using it for a while, then putting it back without any reassignment is usually called *borrowing* [60], and it is very useful in permission-based languages. The Plaid type system [58] manages this borrowing automatically; to keep the analysis modular, it uses simple annotations on methods that state the parameter permissions that are required on entry and available on exit.

One challenge for this approach is to keep track of unpacked objects that are passed to methods or stored in the heap. The solution that we have adopted for Plaid is to disallow such passing or storing: in that system, any references passed to methods, returned from methods, or stored in variables or the heap must be packed. This rule keeps the annotations simple; more flexibility could be bought at the price of more complex annotations (for example, introducing structural types that explicitly describe the unpacked state of objects, and annotating method signatures with those types). Another limitation in the Plaid type system is that unpacking x.f is allowed only if x is unique; otherwise the unpack operation could invalidate an invariant seen by an alias of x. Relaxing this limitation is future work.[9]

---

[8] Plaid is actually more rigorous about field initialization and has no null value, but here we stick to the Java style for conformity with the rest of the article.

[9] The *focus* operation of Vault [55] essentially provides a way to temporarily unpack an aliased object in a scope where only one alias is visible. We believe this technique could be adapted for use in Plaid, possibly by adding a runtime check to confirm that no alias of the object is used in the scope where it is treated as unique.

While there is more work to be done, it seems to us that this kind of implicit packing and unpacking is the most promising approach for supporting "normal" OO-style field reads in a language with unique permissions. Like alias types, this approach avoids the serious problems of destructive read and swap; but it is also simpler and more intuitive than techniques such as linear keys and adoption, and it naturally supports recursion.

Borrowing the receiver permission. In a system described by Bierhoff [61], access to a unique field x.f consumes or borrows the permission associated with the receiver variable x. That means at the point of an assignment y=x.f, the permission to x is unavailable unless and until the permission stored in y is returned to x.f (for example, y goes out of scope with all the permission it took from x.f). Compared to Plaid's unpacking of individual fields x.f, this approach is simpler. However, it is also less flexible, because only one unique field can be accessed at a time. In particular, it is not possible to traverse a tree of unique permissions in parallel using this approach.

Ad-hoc analysis. Finally, one may use ad-hoc analysis to determine whether a program respects unique permissions. For example, this is the approach taken in Boyland's seminal paper on borrowing [60]. While this approach is appropriate for an analysis tool, it is less satisfactory for a language design because it is not integrated with the language or type checker and does not provide a clear semantics to the programmer.

Creating Temporary Aliases. Another essential pattern is to exchange a unique permission for several aliases with weaker permission (this is usually called "splitting"), use the weaker permissions for a while, and recreate the unique permission when the weaker permissions go out of scope (this is usually called "joining"). For example, a unique permission to an object could be split into several immutable permissions, the immutable permissions could be used by several tasks to read the object in parallel, and when all the tasks have finished, the immutable permissions could be joined back into a unique permission. The challenge here is to ensure that no aliases are outstanding at the point where the unique permission is regained. The literature describes several ways to do this accounting.

Fractions. Boyland introduced the idea of *fractions* (also called fractional permissions) as a way to account for outstanding aliases of a unique permission [62]. The idea is to treat an immutable permission as a fraction of a unique permission. For example, a single unique permission may be split into two half permissions, each of which may be used for parallel reading; and when the two halves come back, they may be joined into the entire unique permission. On the other hand, if one or both of the halves don't come back (say one of the reading tasks stores its permission in the heap), then the unique permission can't be recreated.

Boyland [63] has shown how to use fractions to check noninterference for a simple fork-join parallel language with reference cells. Terauchi and Aiken [64] have extended Boyland's work to support data-dependent synchronization (such as producer-consumer) and have shown how to infer the permissions in some simple cases. Their language also supports communication over buffered and unbuffered channels. Both languages are presented as core calculi and are fairly far removed from a practical OO language (for example, neither supports field access).

Fractions are a theoretically elegant and powerful way to manage temporary aliases. However, they suffer from several shortcomings in a practical language design:

- To preserve modularity, the input and output fractions of methods can't be hard coded, but must be written using "fraction variables." For example, a reusable method signature must not say "fraction $1/2$ comes in and fraction $1/4$ comes out," but instead "if fraction π comes in, then fraction $\pi/2$ goes out." This makes writing fraction-based method signatures complex.
- Arguably fractions are not the right abstraction to present to programmers: the concept of a "fraction of unique" — while useful for analysis — is not a natural way to think about an immutable reference.

As a result, verification tools like Plural [65], Chalice [66], and VeriFast [67] do not use fractions directly in the abstractions that they present to users, though in some cases they use fractions internally for their analysis.

Alias types. As noted above, the Vault language [55] provides a way to temporarily relinquish a key corresponding to an object and get references to the same object guarded by a different key. Vault uses this technique to store references in data structures, and the authors call it "adoption." In the context of a deterministic parallel language, a similar technique could be used to temporarily exchange a unique key for an immutable key, and get the unique key back when the immutable key goes out of scope.

Permission counting. The approach we used in the Plaid language [58] is to allow a unique permission to be temporarily split into several weaker permissions that are never stored on the heap (we use the annotation `local` to denote these permissions) and have the type system count the number of outstanding permissions. The internal accounting is similar to fractions, but the user-level language is very simple; the user does not have to reason about "fractions of a unique permission" or write down any fraction variables. However, in this system, once a permission is stored in the heap it can never be rejoined to a unique permission. In this respect the system is less powerful than fractions. Bierhoff's idea of *capture and release* [61] may provide a way to extend the Plaid type system to allow temporary storage of local immutable permissions inside heap objects with a scoped lifetime.

4.2   Permissions Versus Effects

Compared to effects based on regions or ownership, unique permissions can provide more flexibility in assignments. For example, consider the DPJ index-parameterized array type `Body<[i]>[]#i` that we described in Section 2.4. That type is very useful for putting several different unique objects into an array and then traversing the array to update them in parallel. However, what happens if we want to rearrange the references in the array? This is a problem, because the array "hard codes" the region in the type of each cell: it says that cell i must point to an object in region i. But that means we can't store a reference from cell j into cell i, if $j \neq i$. Instead, we have to construct a new object in the new region, copying the fields from the old object. That makes it awkward to write some patterns, such as reordering the body array in the Barnes-Hut n-body simulation to improve cache locality [15].

By contrast, some permission-based systems can support this kind of rearrangement. For example, in an array of unique references, all the cells have the same type, unlike in DPJ, where the different cells have different types. Therefore assigning a reference from one cell to another is permissible, so long as the permission accounting is done properly.

However, a unique permission to an object enforces a rather severe restriction: that *no other field or variable in the entire program* may point to that same object. This restriction can be very inconvenient; for example, one cannot write two data structures (say a tree and an array) that share the same data but can each separately traverse the data in parallel. In DPJ one can write such structures, and in fact they are essential to expressing the Barnes-Hut force computation [15]. At CMU we are developing a way to extend unique permissions so they can express this kind of pattern.

Finally, unique permissions and regions (or ownership) can be combined in a pattern known as *ownership transfer*. This pattern provides a way around the problem with index-parameterized arrays stated above. If we know that cell i points to an object with region i in its type, and furthermore that cell i is the only reference to the object, then we can assign the object to cell j by dynamically changing its type. Since no other reference can see the change, this is sound. Several researchers have shown how to support ownership transfer either with unique permissions [48] or with ad-hoc alias restrictions [68].

4.3   Æminium

The Æminium project at CMU and the University of Coimbra, Portugal [16] aims to develop a robust, practical parallel language based on permissions. Æminium is a parallel extension of Plaid [69]. Plaid is a Java-like OO language that uses permissions to reason about object states and transitions. The principal features of Æminium are as follows:

- Æminium uses unique and immutable permissions to reason about deterministic concurrency. Two unique permissions may be sent to different parallel tasks, or a single unique permission may be split into several immutable permissions that are used in different parallel tasks then rejoined to unique. As discussed at the beginning of Section 4, programs written with this technique can be easily checked for noninterference and determinism.
- Æminium supports *shared* permissions that behave like ordinary Java references (i.e., they allow unrestricted aliasing and mutation). Unique permissions may be split into several shared permissions and then rejoined. As in DPJ, atomic blocks synchronize access through shared permissions and prevent data races in nondeterministic code.

– Æminium supports *data groups* for associating permissions with groups of objects.[10] For example, all the nodes of a linked list may be placed in a data group, and the data group given unique permission. This allows more data structures to be expressed: for example, unique reference permissions cannot express a linked list with a tail pointer (because there must be two references to the tail of the list); whereas unique data group permissions can express this pattern.

Like FX (discussed in Section 3.1) and Jade [13], Æminium is an *implicitly parallel language*: instead of directly specifying concurrent tasks, the user writes annotations (permissions and data groups) that the system uses to extract concurrency efficiently on the target platform. The authors of Æminium call this model "concurrency by default." Æminium is the first language to use permissions to support a concurrency by default programming model.

Because it represents dataflow explicitly as permissions, Æminium is also related to dataflow languages such as ID [70] and Sisal [71]. Those languages, developed in the 1980s and 90s, were motivated by *dataflow architectures* that represented programs as graphs of instructions. By contrast, today's processors typically require medium-grain tasks (on the order of thousands of instructions) so that the task-creation overhead does not swamp the concurrency. Therefore, one challenge for the Æminium approach is to automatically partition the computation into efficient-size tasks. Achieving good load balancing and cache locality is also challenging without direct programmer control. However, if these challenges can be solved, then the potential advantages include simplicity (the programmer need not think about low-level details like task granularity, load balancing, and locality) and portability (the programmer need not re-tune the code for different architectures with different requirements).

4.4   Habanero Java

Westbrook et al. [59] have recently extended Habanero Java (HJ), an explicitly parallel dialect of Java, with a type system based on unique and immutable permissions. Their system, called HJp, guarantees race freedom. It includes the following features:

– *Task-private write permissions.* Inside a task, a unique permission may be split into several task-private write permissions. Updates through these permissions are allowed, even though they are aliases. In that sense task-private write permissions provide more flexibility than uniqueness annotations (Section 4.1). Further, they support a common parallel pattern in which objects are created and used inside a parallel task, with their entire lifetime in that one task. However, task-private write permissions do not support parallel update traversals of data structures that persist across tasks (for example,

---

[10] Æminium's data groups are inspired by Leino's data groups. As discussed in Section 3 Leino's data groups are a variant of the regions used in effect systems like DPJ, FX, JOE, etc.

constructing two trees that share data, and then updating one or the other in parallel).

- *Borrowing permissions from fields.* As discussed in Section 4.1 unique permissions stored in fields x.f may be borrowed through an assignment y=x.f by temporarily giving y the permission associated with x.f.
- *Splitting of array permissions.* A unique permission to an array may be split into unique permissions to its subarrays, which are operated on and then rejoined. This technique supports divide-and-conquer updates on arrays in a manner similar to that discussed in Section 2.4
- *Gradual permissions.* The HJp permission system is *gradual*, meaning that at any point where the static type system is unable to prove the existence of a needed permission, it can insert a dynamic acquire operation. If the permission is available when the operation occurs, then execution proceeds; otherwise an exception is thrown.

Because it uses gradual permissions, HJp does not guarantee determinism. For example, if two parallel tasks perform unsynchronized acquires on the same object, then one run on a given input may succeed (if one task happens to acquire and release permission before the other one acquires its permission) while another may fail (if one task attempts to acquire permission while the other one is holding it). However, a successful run has no data races.

The HJp compiler *infers* many of the annotations, and this keeps the programmer-visible syntax lightweight. The authors report that they have coded the DPJ benchmarks from [15] with fewer annotations (measured in source lines of code modified). However, many of the DPJ annotations can be inferred as well [72]. In addition, DPJ provides a stronger guarantee than HJp (determinism vs. race freedom).

5 Program Logic

Program logic is a broad category of formal verification that includes any use of logic for specifying and checking facts about program behavior. Program logic can support a range of verification techniques, including fully automatic analysis [73,6], manual or computer-assisted proofs [74], or automatic checking assisted by programmer annotations [75,76,77]. Here we discuss the leading techniques for using logic to reason about concurrent programs: separation logic, dynamic frames, regional logic, Accord, and Liquid Effects. Finally we briefly compare program logic approaches with the extended type systems described in Sections 2 through 4.

5.1 Separation Logic

Separation logic, first proposed by Reynolds, O'Hearn, and others based on ideas of Burstall [78], is an extension of Hoare logic that provides better facilities for reasoning about programs that manipulate shared memory. Hoare logic is an old idea in formal verification; it goes all the way back to Hoare's seminal 1969 paper [79]. The basic idea of Hoare logic is that we can think of a program as a sequence of statements S, and if we want to specify and check the program's behavior, then we can associate with each statement two logical assertions: a *precondition* and a *postcondition*. The precondition states what is assumed to be true just before executing S, and the postcondition states what we wish to hold after executing S. This idea is formally expressed as a *Hoare triple*

$$\{P\}\ S\ \{Q\},$$

where P is the precondition (for example, true, which makes no assumption about the initial state), S is the statement being checked (for example, x = 5), and Q is the postcondition (for example, the assertion $x = 5$). In this approach, a program is correct (i.e., corresponds to its specification) if, for each statement S in the program, the postcondition can be derived from the precondition. For example,

$$\{\text{true}\}\ \text{x = 5}\ \{x = 5\}$$

is correct, while

$$\{\text{true}\}\ \text{x = 5}\ \{x = 42\}$$

is not.

As originally proposed, Hoare logic was not very good at reasoning about shared heaps, for two reasons. First, it modeled all memory as a fixed set of named variables, which is not realistic for a language like C or Java that dynamically allocates and manipulates shared memory through pointers. Second, it did not provide a way to reason modularly about heap-manipulating programs. For example, consider a function void f() whose precondition is {true} and whose postcondition is $\{x = 5\}$, where x is a global variable. Now suppose we are at a program point where we know $y = 42$ and we see a call to f(). After return from f(), what do we know about y? Well from the specification of f (which doesn't mention y) we know nothing. So we have three choices, none of which is very palatable: (1) look inside the definition of f to see whether it modifies y (which breaks modular verification); or (2) change the specification of f to assert whether it touches y (which breaks the modularity of f's specification); or (3) assume that an arbitrary value is written to y whenever f is called (which is extremely conservative). Once pointers and aliasing are introduced, this problem becomes even worse. For example, even if we assert that calling f does not touch y, what happens if x and y are pointers to the same object? Without complex specifications of aliasing behavior, we would lose all information about the heap whenever we called a function.

Separation logic extends Hoare logic in a way that addresses these problems. First, it models a *store s* consisting of named local variables and a *heap h* consisting of memory cells; both store variables and heap cells may contain values that point to heap cells. Second, separation logic extends the assertion language of Hoare logic (i.e, the formal language used to write assertions P and Q) to express facts such as "x points to a cell containing the value 5" or "x and y point to the same cell." Third, separation logic introduces the *separating conjunction* $P_1 * P_2$, which asserts that the entire heap can be divided into two heaps h_1 and h_2 such that (1) h_1 and h_2 are disjoint (i.e., they have no cells in common); (2) P_1 is true of h_1; and (3) P_2 is true of h_2. Finally, separation logic requires that its specifications be *tight*, in the sense that for any triple $\{P\}\ S\ \{Q\}$, all locations accessed in S must be either mentioned in P or allocated in S. Classical Hoare logic specifications are not tight in this sense; for example, the precondition true did not specify whether f touched variable y.

Together, the separating conjunction and tight specifications allow the introduction of the *frame rule*, which is the key to modular reasoning in separation logic:

$$\frac{\{P\}\ S\ \{Q\}}{\{P * R\}\ S\ \{Q * R\}}$$

This rule says that if we execute a statement S that makes assertions about heap h_1, then any assertions about a disjoint heap h_2 remain true after executing S. For example, if P is "x points to a cell containing 3" and R is "y points to a cell containing 3," then the separating conjunction $P * R$ implies that x and y are not aliases, while the tightness requirement implies that if $\{P\}\ S\ \{Q\}$ holds, then S does not touch any memory not mentioned in P. Since y is not mentioned in P, we can reason that the execution of S y still points to a cell containing 3.

Separation logic provides a natural way to reason about disjoint concurrency (i.e., in which concurrent tasks never touch the same memory). The separating conjunction lets us divide the heap into disjoint pieces which we can pass into concurrent tasks. O'Hearn [74] shows how to do this for quicksort; the annotation style is similar to Accord, which we discuss in Section 5.4.

Separation logic can also handle concurrent accesses to shared state (for example read-only sharing, or sharing protected by locks), but the reasoning here is a bit more awkward. In order to pass disjoint heaps into concurrent tasks, we must rely on a "fiction of disjointness." One way to do this is to use fractions or permission counting [80]. Another way is to use abstraction to define predicates that appear to refer to disjoint state even though the underlying state is shared [81]. Dodds et al. [82] show how to use abstract predicates to support modular verification of fine-grain synchronization constructs for deterministic parallelism.

5.2 Dynamic Frames

Dynamic frames, introduced by Kassios [83], provide an alternative to separation logic for reasoning modularly about shared heaps. In contrast to the low-level approach of separation logic (it starts from basic constructs such as individual heap cells and pointers, which must be composed into structures such as lists and arrays), the dynamic frames approach starts from the high-level assertions of object-oriented verification. As with ownership-based verification (discussed in

Section 3.3), the motivation is the need to assert and prove invariants about objects that are not affected by updating disjoint structures. This is accomplished in the following way:

1. The verification methodology includes the notion of a *frame*. A frame f denotes a set of memory locations on the heap (so it is similar to a region or data group, discussed in Section 3).

2. An invariant may assert that it is *framed by* a frame f. That means that the truth value of the invariant depends only on locations in f, so leaving those location untouched preserves the invariant.

3. To ensure that the frame f does not collide with another frame g, f may be asserted to obey the so-called *swinging pivots requirement*, which means that f does not increase in any way other than the allocation of new memory. (So in particular, f is not augmented to overlap with any other frame g.)

Note that items two and three are similar to the tightness requirement for separation logic specifications.

Compared to separation logic, dynamic frames have the advantage that they naturally support abstract assertions and object-oriented information hiding, whereas in separation logic these constructs must be built up on top of the lower-level logic [81]. Dynamic frames also support read sharing more naturally than separation logic, because they don't require any fractions or fiction of disjointness (see [83] for a discussion of this point in connection with an iterator example). However, because the framing assertions are explicit, specifications based on dynamic frames also tend to be more verbose than corresponding specifications in separation logic. *Implicit dynamic frames* [84] is a later approach that makes the framing implicit (as it is in separation logic) by inferring it from access specifications.

The Chalice language and verification tool [85] uses implicit dynamic frames together with fractional permissions to reason about multithreaded programs. Chalice is an experimental multi-threaded language that supports a subset of standard object-oriented constructs. The verification tool generates conditions using first-order logic which are automatically solved by an off-the-shelf solver such as Z3 [86]. According to [85], Chalice has been used to verify race- and deadlock-freedom, as well as thread compliance with contracts. Presumably the Chalice approach could enforce deterministic parallelism as well.

5.3   Regional Logic

Banerjee et al. [87] have proposed *regional logic* as an alternative to dynamic frames for reasoning modularly about object-oriented verification assertions. The approach is quite similar to dynamic frames, except that instead of frames f the approach uses *regions* (similar to the regions in DPJ and FX) with read and write effect summaries on methods (again similar to DPJ and FX). The regions are used for framing: if two specifications P and Q refer to disjoint regions, then running code with specification P cannot change the truth value of Q. According to [87], the main benefit of using regions instead of implicit dynamic frames is that the specifications rely on a simpler logic (first-order instead of second-order) and so are easier to automate.

Regional logic has been used to carry out verification in conjunction with the Boogie [88] verification tool. Although the examples are sequential (and motivated by the problem of information flow) presumably the approach could support concurrency as well.

5.4   Accord

Karmani et al. [17] have proposed Accord, an annotation language that formally expresses the *coordination strategy* among a set of concurrent threads. A coordination strategy consists of two elements: (1) what memory accesses occur in a read-only or disjoint manner, so they may be accessed without synchronization; and (2) what memory accesses are guarded by locks. As in DPJ, the first element leads to determinism, while the second leads to race-free nondeterminism. Thus the broad goals of Accord are similar to those of DPJ. However, instead of relying on a sound type system, Accord uses a combination of testing and theorem proving. Also, Accord annotations describe only numerical computations on arrays of values; they do not support objects, references, or object-oriented data structures such as lists and trees. However, Accord can check some array-based computations that DPJ currently cannot.

To verify a parallel program using Accord, the programmer carries out the following steps:

1. Write an ordinary parallel program using concurrent tasks.[11]
2. Annotate the tasks with *thread contracts* that formally express the coordination strategy.
3. Test the program to ensure that it conforms to the coordination strategy — that is, that each task's accesses are correctly reported, and all accesses are guarded by the intended locks. The system described in [17] automatically translates the Accord annotations into assertions that support this testing.
4. Use a satisfiability modulo theories (SMT) solver such as Z3 to prove that the coordination strategy guarantees race freedom.

Figure 16 shows how to implement parallel quicksort using Accord contracts. Line 2 bounds the range of the indices accessing array A in function qsort; this is similar to a DPJ effect specification. Line 8 constrains the values that may be attained by p_index, while lines 11 and 16 describe the locations that may be accessed by the parallel tasks created in lines 7 and following. This program would be checked by first testing it to ensure that the annotations correctly describe the memory accesses, and then running the theorem prover to establish that the two parallel tasks write to disjoint segments of array A.

---

[11] Karmani et al. call the tasks "threads," but lightweight tasks such as those provided by Java's ForkJoinTask framework or Intel's Threading Building Blocks could be used.

```
1    void qsort(int* A, int i, int j)
2        writes A[$k] where (i <= $k and $k < j)
3    {
4        if (j-i < 2) return;
5        int pivot = A[i];
6        int p_index = partition(A, pivot, i, j);
7        par
8            requires p_index >= i and p_index < j
9        {
10           thread
11               writes A[$k] where (i <=$k and $k < p_index)
12           {
13               qsort(A, i, p_index);
14           }
15           with thread
16               writes A[$k] where (p_index < $k and $k < j)
17           {
18               qsort(A, p_index + 1, j);
19           }
20       }
21   }
```

Fig. 16. Accord thread contracts

Compare Figure 16 with the DPJ version of quicksort shown in Figure 7. Instead of reasoning directly about array indices, DPJ represents each subarray in the partition as an object and associates a region with each subarray, and it uses the regions to reason about disjointness of effect. The DPJ approach provides a slightly higher level of abstraction and is more in the object-oriented style; however, the Accord approach can express effect shapes on arrays such as "all the odd elements of the array" that DPJ currently cannot. Such shapes are useful, for example, in the technique of *successive over-relaxation*, in which alternate elements of an array or grid are read and written in each phase of the computation. Such computations could be supported in DPJ by extending the array partitioning library to extract (for example) even or odd elements from an array. However, Accord annotations can represent these patterns directly as logical specifications.

Finally, DPJ provides a stronger guarantee than Accord: a well-typed DPJ program is *guaranteed* to be race-free and deterministic by default, whereas an Accord program guarantees correctness only up to the correctness of the annotations, and the annotation correctness is checked by testing, not proof. Also, DPJ supports objects and object-oriented data structures. However, the nondeterministic part of DPJ is currently implemented on top of software transactional memory (STM) [21], whereas Accord supports the use of locks. Therefore, array-based programs that make heavy use of critical sections are likely to perform better in Accord than in DPJ, because of the overhead introduced by the STM.

5.5   Liquid Effects

Kawaguchi et al. [89] have recently described a system called *Liquid Effects* (where "liquid" is derived from "logically qualified") for enforcing determinism in fork-join parallel programs written in C. Like Accord (Section 5.4), the Liquid Effects system uses an SMT solver to check for potential interference between sets of array indices, specified in first-order logic. Unlike Accord, however, the system is fully statically checked: it uses a type system based on linear keys (similar to Vault, discussed in Section 4.1) to track potential aliases between pointers to arrays. The system also includes a commutativity annotation similar to DPJ's (Section 2.5) for marking pairs of otherwise interfering operations that commute.

The Liquid Effects system uses type inference to minimize the number of programmer annotations required. It can infer both function effect summaries and loop invariants. The user provides formulas to guide the inference: the formulas tell the system to look for types and effects of the given form, with wildcards replaced by program variables in scope.

5.6   Logic vs. Type Systems

There is obviously a close connection between the extended type systems discussed in Sections 2 through 4 and program logic. In fact a type system can be thought of as a specialized form of logic, with "easy" deduction rules that admit simple, usually deterministic proofs (i.e., type checking). In some cases, there is direct overlap between the techniques used in the logic and the type system approaches (e.g., the use of FX-like regions and effects in regional logic, or the use of object ownership to support object-oriented verification [36]).

In general program logic is more powerful, general, and flexible than type systems. For example, with sufficiently complex annotations and proofs, logic can support full functional verification, in contrast to the relatively coarse-grained invariants guaranteed by extended type systems. However, extended type systems generally provide more simplicity (both for the user and for the verifier), better usability, and better integration with the underlying language.

In principle, logic should be able to verify determinism for programming patterns that are currently challenging for type systems. For example, as discussed in Section 4.2, if we want to check determinism using state-of-the-art techniques in permissions and effects, then we have to accept some limitations in either our ability to create aliases of mutable objects, or our ability to rearrange structures containing mutable objects. Logic should be able to overcome these limitations, at the cost of additional complexity. The practical challenge is to find the right balance of power, complexity, and automation for a program logic, possibly in combination with a type system.

6   Conclusion

We have surveyed the state of the art in alias control annotations for deterministic parallelism. Building on the extensive prior work in effect systems and object ownership, the DPJ effect system supports fine-grain reasoning about disjoint access to data structures on the heap, including nested data structures such as trees. Access permissions provide an alternate way to reason about heap structure; they purchase flexibility in assignment at the cost of alias restrictions. Program logics such as separation logic, dynamic frames, regional logic, and Accord thread contracts can provide more power than effects or permissions, but they do so at the cost of more complexity in the annotations and/or proofs.

Overall, the techniques discussed in this article are promising: they provide a range of different ways to control aliasing and provide strong guarantees for parallel programs that manipulate shared memory. As future work, it would be interesting to explore the connections between these techniques. At CMU we are currently investigating the connections between effects and permissions on the one hand, and between type systems (including effects and permissions) and logical specifications on the other. In addition to furthering basic understanding, this kind of investigation should lead to new tools and techniques, for example better integration of type checking and logic verification in a single tool or set of tools.

References

1. Lee, E.A.: The problem with threads. IEEE Computer 39, 33–42 (2006)
2. Bocchino, R., Adve, V., Adve, S., Snir, M.: Parallel programming must be deterministic by default. In: HotPar (2009)
3. Loidl, H.W., Rubio, F., Scaife, N., Hammond, K., Horiguchi, S., Klusik, U., Loogen, R., Michaelson, G.J., Pena, R., Priebe, S., Rebón, A.J., Trinder, P.W.: Comparing parallel functional languages: Programming and performance. Higher-Order and Symbolic Computation 16(3), 203–251 (2003)
4. Sridharan, M., Chandra, S., Dolby, J., Fink, S.J., Yahav, E.: Alias Analysis for Object-Oriented Programs. In: Clarke, D., Noble, J., Wrigstad, T. (eds.) Aliasing in Object-Oriented Programming. LNCS, vol. 7850, pp. 196–232. Springer, Heidelberg (2013)
5. Kennedy, K., Allen, J.R.: Optimizing Compilers for Modern Architectures: A Dependence-Based Approach. Morgan Kaufmann Publishers Inc., San Francisco (2002)
6. Raza, M., Calcagno, C., Gardner, P.: Automatic Parallelization with Separation Logic. In: Castagna, G. (ed.) ESOP 2009. LNCS, vol. 5502, pp. 348–362. Springer, Heidelberg (2009)
7. Devietti, J., Lucia, B., Ceze, L., Oskin, M.: DMP: Deterministic shared memory multiprocessing. In: International Conference on Architectural Support for Programming Languages and Operating Systems, ASPLOS (2009)
8. Olszewski, M., Ansel, J., Amarasinghe, S.: Kendo: Efficient deterministic multithreading in software. In: International Conference on Architectural Support for Programming Languages and Operating Systems, ASPLOS (2009)
9. Burckhardt, S., Baldassin, A., Leijen, D.: Concurrent programming with revisions and isolation types. In: ACM Conference on Object-Oriented Programming, Systems, Languages, and Applications, OOPSLA (2010)

10. Aviram, A., Weng, S.C., Hu, S., Ford, B.: Efficient system-enforced deterministic parallelism. In: USENIX Symposium on Operating System Design and Implementation, OSDI (2010)
11. Prabhu, M.K., Olukotun, K.: Using thread-level speculation to simplify manual parallelization. In: ACM Symposium on Principles and Practice of Parallel Programming, PPOPP (2003)
12. Berger, E.D., Yang, T., Liu, T., Novark, G.: Grace: Safe multithreaded programming for C/C++. In: ACM Conference on Object-Oriented Programming, Systems, Languages, and Applications, OOPSLA (2009)
13. Rinard, M.C., Lam, M.S.: The design, implementation, and evaluation of Jade. ACM Transactions on Programming Languages and Systems (TOPLAS) 20(3), 483–545 (1998)
14. Allen, M.D., Sridharan, S., Sohi, G.S.: Serialization sets: A dynamic dependence-based parallel execution model. In: ACM Symposium on Principles and Practice of Parallel Programming, PPOPP (2009)
15. Bocchino, Jr., R.L., Adve, V.S., Dig, D., Adve, S.V., Heumann, S., Komuravelli, R., Overbey, J., Simmons, P., Sung, H., Vakilian, M.: A type and effect system for deterministic parallel Java. In: ACM Conference on Object-Oriented Programming, Systems, Languages, and Applications, OOPSLA (2009)
16. Stork, S., Marques, P., Aldrich, J.: Concurrency by default: Using permissions to express dataflow in stateful programs. In: Onward (2009)
17. Karmani, R.K., Madhusudan, P., Moore, B.M.: Thread contracts for safe parallelism. In: ACM Symposium on Principles and Practice of Parallel Programming, PPOPP (2011)
18. http://dpj.cs.uiuc.edu
19. Kim, D., Rinard, M.C.: Verification of semantic commutativity conditions and inverse operations on linked data structures. In: ACM Conference on Programming Language Design and Implementation, PLDI (2011)
20. Bocchino Jr., R.L.: An effect system and language for deterministic-by-default parallel programming. PhD thesis, University of Illinois at Urbana-Champaign (2010)
21. Bocchino, Jr., R.L., Heumann, S., Honarmand, N., Adve, S.V., Adve, V.S., Welc, A., Shpeisman, T.: Safe nondeterminism in a deterministic-by-default parallel language. In: ACM Symposium on Principles of Programming Languages, POPL (2011)
22. Bocchino Jr., R.L., Adve, V.S.: Types, Regions, and Effects for Safe Programming with Object-Oriented Parallel Frameworks. In: Mezini, M. (ed.) ECOOP 2011. LNCS, vol. 6813, pp. 306–332. Springer, Heidelberg (2011)
23. Lucassen, J.M., Gifford, D.K.: Polymorphic effect systems. In: ACM Symposium on Principles of Programming Languages, POPL (1988)
24. Hammel, R.T., Gifford, D.K.: FX-87 performance measurements: Dataflow implementation. Technical Report MIT/LCS/TR-421 (1988)
25. Gifford, D.K., Jouvelot, P., Sheldon, M.A., O'Toole, J.W.: Report on the FX-91 programming language. Technical Report MIT/LCS/TR-531 (1992)
26. Leino, K.R.M.: Data groups: Specifying the modification of extended state. In: ACM Conference on Object-Oriented Programming, Systems, Languages, and Applications, OOPSLA (1998)
27. Greenhouse, A., Boyland, J.: An Object-Oriented Effects System. In: Guerraoui, R. (ed.) ECOOP 1999. LNCS, vol. 1628, pp. 205–229. Springer, Heidelberg (1999)

28. Greenhouse, A., Scherlis, W.L.: Assuring and evolving concurrent programs: an-
    notations and policy. In: IEEE Computing in Science and Engineering (2002)
29. Leino, K.R.M., Poetzsch-Heffter, A., Zhou, Y.: Using data groups to specify and
    check side effects. In: ACM Conference on Programming Language Design and
    Implementation, PLDI (2002)
30. Clarke, D.G., Potter, J.M., Noble, J.: Ownership types for flexible alias protection.
    In: ACM Conference on Object-Oriented Programming, Systems, Languages, and
    Applications, OOPSLA (1998)
31. Clarke, D., Östlund, J., Sergey, I., Wrigstad, T.: Ownership Types: A Survey. In:
    Clarke, D., Noble, J., Wrigstad, T. (eds.) Aliasing in Object-Oriented Program-
    ming. LNCS, vol. 7850, pp. 15–58. Springer, Heidelberg (2013)
32. Clarke, D., Drossopoulou, S.: Ownership, encapsulation and the disjointness of
    type and effect. In: ACM Conference on Object-Oriented Programming, Systems,
    Languages, and Applications, OOPSLA (2002)
33. Smith, M.: Towards an effects system for ownership domains. In: European Con-
    ference on Object-Oriented Programming, ECOOP (2005)
34. Noble, J., Vitek, J., Potter, J.: Flexible Alias Protection. In: Jul, E. (ed.) ECOOP
    1998. LNCS, vol. 1445, pp. 158–185. Springer, Heidelberg (1998)
35. Clarke, D., Wrigstad, T.: External Uniqueness is Unique Enough. In: Cardelli, L.
    (ed.) ECOOP 2003. LNCS, vol. 2743, pp. 176–201. Springer, Heidelberg (2003)
36. Leino, K.R.M., Müller, P.: Object Invariants in Dynamic Contexts. In: Odersky,
    M. (ed.) ECOOP 2004. LNCS, vol. 3086, pp. 491–515. Springer, Heidelberg (2004)
37. Dietl, W., Müller, P.: Universes: Lightweight ownership for JML. Journal of Object
    Technology (JOT) 4(8), 5–32 (2005)
38. Lu, Y., Potter, J.: Protecting representation with effect encapsulation. In: ACM
    Symposium on Principles of Programming Languages, POPL (2006)
39. Cameron, N.R., Drossopoulou, S., Noble, J., Smith, M.J.: Multiple ownership. In:
    ACM Conference on Object-Oriented Programming, Systems, Languages, and Ap-
    plications, OOPSLA (2007)
40. Dietl, W., Müller, P.: Object Ownership in Program Verification. In: Clarke, D.,
    Noble, J., Wrigstad, T. (eds.) Aliasing in Object-Oriented Programming. LNCS,
    vol. 7850, pp. 289–318. Springer, Heidelberg (2013)
41. Aldrich, J.: Ownership Domains: Separating Aliasing Policy from Mechanism. In:
    Odersky, M. (ed.) ECOOP 2004. LNCS, vol. 3086, pp. 1–25. Springer, Heidelberg
    (2004)
42. Wrigstad, T.: External uniqueness. PhD thesis, Stockholm University/KTH, Stock-
    holm, Sweden (2004)
43. Tofte, M., Talpin, J.P.: Region-based memory management. Information and Com-
    putation 132(2), 109–176 (1997)
44. Boyapati, C., Lee, R., Rinard, M.: Ownership types for safe programming: Pre-
    venting data races and deadlocks. In: ACM Conference on Object-Oriented Pro-
    gramming, Systems, Languages, and Applications, OOPSLA (2002)
45. Abadi, M., Flanagan, C., Freund, S.N.: Types for safe locking: Static race detection
    for Java. ACM Transactions on Programming Languages and Systems (TOPLAS)
    28(2) (2006)
46. Jacobs, B., Piessens, F., Smans, J., Leino, K.R.M., Schulte, W.: A programming
    model for concurrent object-oriented programs. ACM Transactions on Program-
    ming Languages and Systems (TOPLAS) 31(1) (2008)
47. Hogg, J.: Islands: Aliasing protection in object-oriented languages. In: ACM Con-
    ference on Object-Oriented Programming, Systems, Languages, and Applications,
    OOPSLA (1991)

48. Boyapati, C., Rinard, M.: A parameterized type system for race-free Java programs. In: ACM Conference on Object-Oriented Programming, Systems, Languages, and Applications, OOPSLA (2001)
49. Hicks, M., Morrisett, G., Grossman, D., Jim, T.: Experience with safe manual memory-management in Cyclone. In: International Symposium on Memory Management, ISMM (2004)
50. Wolff, R., Garcia, R., Tanter, É., Aldrich, J.: Gradual Typestate. In: Mezini, M. (ed.) ECOOP 2011. LNCS, vol. 6813, pp. 459–483. Springer, Heidelberg (2011)
51. Haller, P., Odersky, M.: Capabilities for Uniqueness and Borrowing. In: D'Hondt, T. (ed.) ECOOP 2010. LNCS, vol. 6183, pp. 354–378. Springer, Heidelberg (2010)
52. Harms, D., Weide, B.: Copying and swapping: Influences on the design of reusable software components. IEEE Transactions on Software Engineering 17, 424–435 (1991)
53. Smith, F., Walker, D., Morrisett, G.: Alias Types. In: Smolka, G. (ed.) ESOP/ETAPS 2000. LNCS, vol. 1782, pp. 366–381. Springer, Heidelberg (2000)
54. DeLine, R., Fähndrich, M.: Enforcing high-level protocols in low-level software. In: ACM Conference on Programming Language Design and Implementation, PLDI (2001)
55. Fähndrich, M., DeLine, R.: Adoption and focus: Practical linear types for imperative programming. In: ACM Conference on Programming Language Design and Implementation, PLDI (2002)
56. Walker, D., Morrisett, G.: Alias Types for Recursive Data Structures. In: Harper, R. (ed.) TIC 2000. LNCS, vol. 2071, pp. 177–206. Springer, Heidelberg (2001)
57. Barnett, M., DeLine, R., Fähndrich, M., Leino, K.R.M., Schulte, W.: Verification of object-oriented programs with invariants. Journal of Object Technology (JOT) 3 (2004)
58. Naden, K., Bocchino, R., Aldrich, J., Bierhoff, K.: A type system for borrowing permissions. In: ACM Symposium on Principles of Programming Languages, POPL (2012)
59. Westbrook, E., Zhao, J., Budimlić, Z., Sarkar, V.: Practical Permissions for Race-Free Parallelism. In: Noble, J. (ed.) ECOOP 2012. LNCS, vol. 7313, pp. 614–639. Springer, Heidelberg (2012)
60. Boyland, J.: Alias burying: Unique variables without destructive reads. Software: Practice and Experience 31(6), 533–553 (2001)
61. Bierhoff, K.: Automated program verification made SYMPLAR: Symbolic permissions for lightweight automated reasoning. In: Onward (2011)
62. Boyland, J.: Fractional Permissions. In: Clarke, D., Noble, J., Wrigstad, T. (eds.) Aliasing in Object-Oriented Programming. LNCS, vol. 7850, pp. 270–288. Springer, Heidelberg (2013)
63. Boyland, J.: Checking Interference with Fractional Permissions. In: Cousot, R. (ed.) SAS 2003. LNCS, vol. 2694, pp. 55–72. Springer, Heidelberg (2003)
64. Terauchi, T., Aiken, A.: A capability calculus for concurrency and determinism. ACM Transactions on Programming Languages and Systems (TOPLAS) 30(5), 1–30 (2008)
65. Bierhoff, K., Aldrich, J.: Modular typestate checking of aliased objects. In: ACM Conference on Object-Oriented Programming, Systems, Languages, and Applications, OOPSLA (2007)
66. Heule, S., Leino, K.R.M., Müller, P., Summers, A.J.: Fractional permissions without the fractions. In: Workshop on Formal Techniques for Java-Like Programs, FTfJP (2011)

67. Smans, J., Jacobs, B., Piessens, F.: VeriFast for Java: A Tutorial. In: Clarke, D., Noble, J., Wrigstad, T. (eds.) Aliasing in Object-Oriented Programming. LNCS, vol. 7850, pp. 407–442. Springer, Heidelberg (2013)
68. Müller, P., Rudich, A.: Ownership transfer in universe types. In: ACM Conference on Object-Oriented Programming, Systems, Languages, and Applications, OOPSLA (2007)
69. http://www.cs.cmu.edu/aldrich/plaid/
70. Nikhil, R.S.: ID version 90.0 reference manual. Technical report, MIT (July 1990)
71. Feo, J.T., Cann, D.C., Oldehoeft, R.R.: A report on the Sisal language project. Journal of Parallel and Distributed Computing 10(4), 349–366 (1990)
72. Vakilian, M., Dig, D., Bocchino, R., Overbey, J., Adve, V., Johnson, R.: Inferring method effect summaries for nested heap regions. In: International Conference on Automated Software Engineering, ASE (2009)
73. Gotsman, A., Berdine, J., Cook, B., Sagiv, M.: Thread-modular shape analysis. In: ACM Conference on Programming Language Design and Implementation, PLDI (2007)
74. O'Hearn, P.W.: Resources, concurrency, and local reasoning. Theoretical Computer Science (2007)
75. Jacobs, B., Smans, J., Philippaerts, P., Vogels, F., Penninckx, W., Piessens, F.: VeriFast: A Powerful, Sound, Predictable, Fast Verifier for C and Java. In: Bobaru, M., Havelund, K., Holzmann, G.J., Joshi, R. (eds.) NFM 2011. LNCS, vol. 6617, pp. 41–55. Springer, Heidelberg (2011)
76. Berdine, J., Calcagno, C., O'Hearn, P.W.: Smallfoot: Modular Automatic Assertion Checking with Separation Logic. In: de Boer, F.S., Bonsangue, M.M., Graf, S., de Roever, W.-P. (eds.) FMCO 2005. LNCS, vol. 4111, pp. 115–137. Springer, Heidelberg (2006)
77. Distefano, D., Parkinson, M.J.: jStar: Towards practical verification for Java. In: ACM Conference on Object-Oriented Programming, Systems, Languages, and Applications, OOPSLA (2008)
78. Reynolds, J.C.: Separation logic: A logic for shared mutable data structures. In: IEEE Symposium on Logic in Computer Science (2002)
79. Hoare, C.A.R.: An axiomatic basis for computer programming. Communications of the ACM 12(10), 576–580 (1969)
80. Bornat, R., Calcagno, C., O'Hearn, P., Parkinson, M.: Permission accounting in separation logic. In: ACM Symposium on Principles of Programming Languages, POPL (2005)
81. Dinsdale-Young, T., Dodds, M., Gardner, P., Parkinson, M.J., Vafeiadis, V.: Concurrent Abstract Predicates. In: D'Hondt, T. (ed.) ECOOP 2010. LNCS, vol. 6183, pp. 504–528. Springer, Heidelberg (2010)
82. Dodds, M., Jagannathan, S., Parkinson, M.J.: Modular reasoning for deterministic parallelism. In: ACM Symposium on Principles of Programming Languages, POPL (2011)
83. Kassios, I.T.: Dynamic Frames: Support for Framing, Dependencies and Sharing Without Restrictions. In: Misra, J., Nipkow, T., Sekerinski, E. (eds.) FM 2006. LNCS, vol. 4085, pp. 268–283. Springer, Heidelberg (2006)
84. Smans, J., Jacobs, B., Piessens, F.: Implicit Dynamic Frames: Combining Dynamic Frames and Separation Logic. In: Drossopoulou, S. (ed.) ECOOP 2009. LNCS, vol. 5653, pp. 148–172. Springer, Heidelberg (2009)
85. Leino, K.R.M., Müller, P.: A Basis for Verifying Multi-threaded Programs. In: Castagna, G. (ed.) ESOP 2009. LNCS, vol. 5502, pp. 378–393. Springer, Heidelberg (2009)

86. de Moura, L., Bjørner, N.S.: Z3: An Efficient SMT Solver. In: Ramakrishnan, C.R., Rehof, J. (eds.) TACAS 2008. LNCS, vol. 4963, pp. 337–340. Springer, Heidelberg (2008)

87. Banerjee, A., Naumann, D.A., Rosenberg, S.: Regional Logic for Local Reasoning about Global Invariants. In: Vitek, J. (ed.) ECOOP 2008. LNCS, vol. 5142, pp. 387–411. Springer, Heidelberg (2008)

88. Banerjee, A., Barnett, M., Naumann, D.A.: Boogie Meets Regions: A Verification Experience Report. In: Shankar, N., Woodcock, J. (eds.) VSTTE 2008. LNCS, vol. 5295, pp. 177–191. Springer, Heidelberg (2008)

89. Kawaguchi, M., Rondon, P., Bakst, A., Jhala, R.: Deterministic parallelism via liquid effects. In: ACM Conference on Programming Language Design and Implementation, PLDI (2012)

Alias Analysis for Object-Oriented Programs

Manu Sridharan[1], Satish Chandra[1], Julian Dolby[1],
Stephen J. Fink[1], and Eran Yahav[2]

[1] IBM T.J. Watson Research Center
[2] Technion
{msridhar,satishchandra,dolby,sjfink}@us.ibm.com,
yahave@cs.technion.ac.il

Abstract. We present a high-level survey of state-of-the-art alias analyses for object-oriented programs, based on a years-long effort developing industrial-strength static analyses for Java. We first present common variants of points-to analysis, including a discussion of key implementation techniques. We then describe flow-sensitive techniques based on tracking of access paths, which can yield greater precision for certain clients. We also discuss how whole-program alias analysis has become less useful for modern Java programs, due to increasing use of reflection in libraries and frameworks. We have found that for real-world programs, an under-approximate alias analysis based on access-path tracking often provides the best results for a variety of practical clients.

1 Introduction

Effective analysis of pointer aliasing plays an essential role in nearly all non-trivial program analyses for object-oriented programs. For example, computing a precise inter-procedural control-flow graph, a necessity for many program analyses, often requires significant pointer reasoning to resolve virtual dispatch. Furthermore, any program analysis attempting to discover non-trivial properties of an object must reason about mutations to that object through pointer aliases.

Building alias analyses that simultaneously scale to realistic object-oriented programs and libraries while providing sufficient precision has been a longstanding challenge for the program analysis community. The twin goals of scalability and precision often conflict with each other, leading to subtle tradeoffs that make choosing the right alias analysis for a task non-obvious. Moreover, as large object-oriented frameworks (e.g., Eclipse[1] for desktop applications or Spring[2] for server-side code) have proliferated, achieving scalability and precision has become increasingly difficult.

In this work, we give a high-level survey of the alias-analysis techniques that we have found most useful during a years-long effort developing industrial-strength analyses for Java programs. We focus on two main techniques:

---

[1] http://www.eclipse.org
[2] http://www.springsource.org

D. Clarke et al. (Eds.): Aliasing in Object-Oriented Programming, LNCS 7850, pp. 196–232, 2013.
© Springer-Verlag Berlin Heidelberg 2013

1. *Points-to analysis*, specifically variants of Andersen's analysis [3] for Java. A points-to analysis result can be used to determine *may-alias* information, i.e., whether it is possible for two pointers to be aliased during program execution.
2. Flow-sensitive tracking of the *access paths* that name an object, where an access path is a variable and a (possibly empty) sequence of field names (see Section 5 for details). Access-path tracking enables determination of *must-alias* information, i.e., whether two pointers must be aliased at some program point.

We also aim to explain particular challenges we have encountered in building analyses that scale to modern Java programs. We have found that as standard libraries and frameworks have grown, difficulties in handling reflection have led us to reduce or eliminate our reliance on traditional points-to analysis. Instead, we have developed an under-approximate approach to alias analysis based on on type-based call graph construction and tracking of access paths. We have found this approach to be more effective for analyzing large Java programs, though traditional points-to analysis remains relevant in other scenarios. Our experiences may shed light on issues in designing analyses for other languages, and in designing future languages to be more analyzable.

This chapter is *not* intended to be an exhaustive survey of alias analysis. Over the past few decades, computer scientists have published hundreds of papers on alias-analysis techniques. The techniques vary widely depending on myriad analysis details, such as policies for flow sensitivity, context sensitivity, demand-driven computation, and optimization tradeoffs. We cannot hope to adequately cover this vast space, and the literature grows each year. Here we focus on alias analyses that we have significant experience implementing and applying to real programs. To the best of our knowledge, the presented alias analyses are the state-of-the-art for our desired analysis clients and target programs. For many of the analyses described here, a corresponding implementation is available as part of the open-source Watson Libraries for Analysis (WALA) [69].

Organization. This chapter is organized as follows. In Section 2, we motivate the alias-analysis problem by showing the importance of precise aliasing information for analysis clients. Then, we discuss points-to analysis for Java-like languages: Section 3 gives formulations of several variants of Andersen's analysis [3], and Section 4 discusses key implementation techniques. Section 5 discusses must-alias analysis based on access-path tracking, which provides greater precision than a typical points-to analysis. In Section 6, we describe challenges in applying points-to analysis to modern Java programs and how under-approximate techniques can be used instead. Finally, Section 7 concludes and suggests directions for future work. Some of the material presented here has appeared in previous work by the authors [62,67,20].

2   Motivating Analyses

Many program analyses for object-oriented languages rely on an effective alias analysis. Here we illustrate a number of alias analysis concerns in the context of an analysis for detecting resource leaks in Java programs, and discuss how these concerns also pertain to other analyses.

2.1   Resource Leaks

```
1 public void test(File file, String enc) throws IOException {
2   PrintWriter out = null;
3   try {
4     try {
5       out = new PrintWriter(
6               new OutputStreamWriter(
7                 new FileOutputStream(file), enc));
8     } catch (UnsupportedEncodingException ue) {
9       out = new PrintWriter(new FileWriter(file));
10    }
11    out.append('c');
12  } catch (IOException e) {
13  } finally {
14    if (out != null) {
15      out.close();
16    }
17  }
18 }
```

Fig. 1. Example of a resource leak

While garbage collection frees the programmer from the responsibility of memory management, it does not help with the management of finite *system resources*, such as sockets or database connections. When a program written in a Java-like language acquires an instance of a finite system resource, it must release that instance by explicitly calling a dispose or close method. Letting the last handle to an unreleased resource go out of scope *leaks* the resource. Leaks can gradually deplete the finite supply of system resources, leading to performance degradation and system crashes. Ensuring that resources are always released, however, is tricky and error-prone.

As an example, consider the Java program in Fig. 1, adapted from code in Apache Ant.[3] The allocation of a FileOutputStream on line 7 acquires a stream, which is a system resource that needs to be released by calling close() on the stream handle. The acquired stream object then passes

---

[3] http://ant.apache.org

into the constructor of `OutputStreamWriter`, which remembers it in a private field. The `OutputStreamWriter` object, in turn, passes into the constructor of `PrintWriter`. In the `finally` block, the programmer calls `close()` on the `PrintWriter` object. This `close()` method calls `close()` on the "nested" `OutputStreamWriter` object, which in turn calls `close()` on the nested `FileOutputStream` object. By using `finally`, it would appear that the program closes the stream, even in the event of an exception.

However, a potential resource leak lurks in this code. The constructor of `OutputStreamWriter` might throw an exception: notice that the programmer anticipates the possibility that an `UnsupportedEncodingException` may occur. If it does, the assignment to the variable `out` on line 5 will not execute, and consequently the stream allocated on line 7 is never closed. A *resource leak analysis* aims to statically detect leaks like this one.

2.2   Role of Alias Analysis

A resource leak analysis should report a potential leak of the stream allocated at line 7 of Fig. 1. But a bug finding client should not *trivially* report all resource acquisitions as potentially leaking, as that would generate too many false positives. Hence, the key challenge of resource leak analysis is in reasoning that a resource in fact does *not* leak, and it is this reasoning that requires effective alias analysis. Here we will consider what it takes to prove that the resource allocated at line 7 does *not* leak along the exception-free path.

Figure 2 shows the relevant parts of the CFG for Fig. 1, along with the CFGs of some of the called methods. We introduced temporary variables `t1` and `t2` when constructing the CFG (a).

Consider the program path 7-6-5-11-14-15 (the exception-free path), starting with the resource allocation on line 7. The constructor on line 6 stores its argument into an instance field `a`; see CFG (b). Likewise, the constructor on line 5 stores its argument into an instance field `b`; see CFG (c). The call `out.close()` on line 15 transitively calls `close()` on expressions `out.b` and `out.b.a` (notice that `this` in CFGs (d) and (e) would be bound appropriately), the last one releasing the tracked resource as it is equal to `t1`. At this point, the (same) resource referred to by the expressions `t1`, `t2.a`, and `out.b.a` is released.

What reasoning is needed for an analysis to prove that the resource allocated on line 7 is definitely released along the path 7-6-5-11-14-15?

1. Data flow must be tracked inter-procedurally, as the call to the `close()` method of the `FileOutputStream` occurs in a callee. For this reason, an accurate *call graph* must be built.
2. The analysis must establish that `this.a` in CFG (e), when encountered along this path *must* refer to the same object assigned to `t1` in CFG (a).

Both cases demand effective alias analysis.

Call Graph Construction. A *call graph* indicates the possibly-invoked methods at each call site in a program. In object-oriented languages, virtual calls

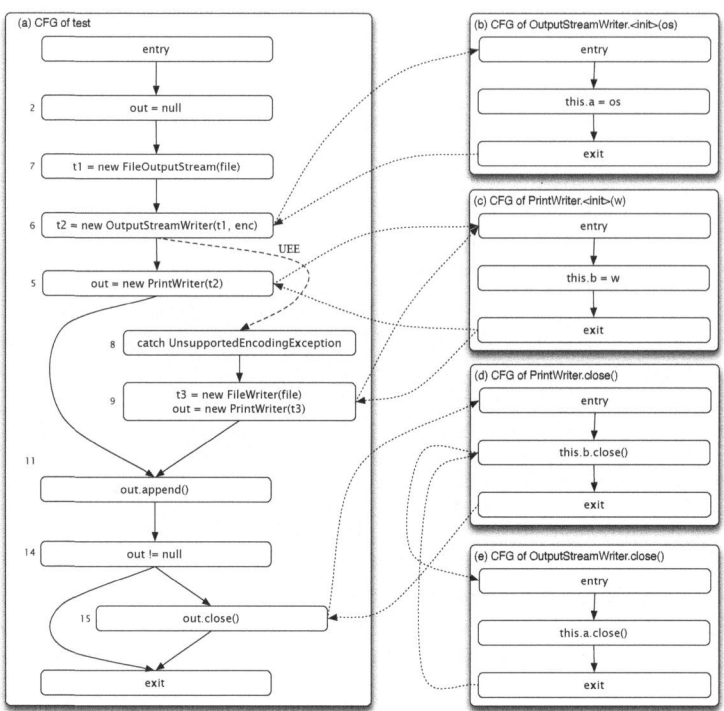

Fig. 2. Control-flow graph of the procedure shown in Fig. 1. Numbers to the left are line numbers. Dotted edges represent inter-procedural control transfers.

make building a call graph non-trivial. Consider CFG (d). Say the field b in class PrintWriter has declared type Writer, which has a number of different subtypes, one of which is OutputStreamWriter. A call graph based solely on the program's class hierarchy (a *class hierarchy analysis* [13]) allows implementations of close() in all possible Writer subtypes to be potential targets of the call this.b.close(). In principle, some subtype of Writer other than OutputStreamWriter could implement close() in a way that does not close the resource, causing a false positive here.[4]

A *points-to analysis* (see Section 3) creates an over-approximation of all the heap values that can possibly flow into each reference by tracing data flow through assignments. In this program, the only heap values that flow into field b of PrintWriter are of type OutputStreamWriter (via the call at line 5) or FileWriter (via line 9). The class FileWriter inherits its close() method from

---

[4] Rapid type analysis (RTA) [4], which only considers allocated types, is generally more accurate than class hierarchy analysis [66], but it would still cause a false positive if the bad Writer subtype were allocated anywhere in the program. We have found that the difference between RTA and class hierarchy analysis tends to vanish in large framework-dependent programs.

OutputStreamWriter. Thus, a call graph based on points-to analysis can correctly narrow down the call target of this.b.close() to the close() method in the class OutputStreamWriter, as shown in edges from CFG (d) to CFG (e), yielding greater precision in the resource leak analysis.

Note that call graph construction and alias analysis are often inter-dependent. In our example, the assignment to the b field of PrintWriter occurs in a callee (the constructor <init>) via the calls at lines 5 and 9. Hence, the points-to analysis must know that this <init> method is in the call graph to properly trace the flow of an OutputStreamWriter into the b field, which in turn implies that OutputStreamWriter.close() can be called from in CFG (d). Multiple approaches exist to address this inter-dependency, to be discussed in Section 3.

Equality. Recall that to prove leak freedom for the path of interest, the analysis needs to show that the object referenced by this.a in CFG (e) refers to the same object pointed by t1 is CFG (a), to ensure that the resource is released. However, this fact cannot be proved using points-to analysis alone, as it only provides *may-alias* information, i.e., it can only state that this.a *may* refer to the same object as t1. Given may-alias information alone, the analysis must consider a case where this.a does not alias t1 on the path, and a false leak will be reported.

To avoid this false report, *must-alias* information is needed, indicating alias relationships that *must* hold at a program point. This reasoning can be accomplished by tracking *must access paths* naming the resource as part of the resource-leak analysis. Much as in the informal reasoning described previously, must access paths are expressions of the form t1, t2.a, and out.b.a, with the property that in the current program state, they must equal the tracked resource. By tracking access paths along the control-flow path of interest, the equality of this.a and t1 in our example can be established, and the false leak report is avoided. As we shall show in Section 5, access-path tracking can provide useful aliasing information for a number of important client analyses.

2.3   Other Analysis Clients

Many client analyses share some or all of the alias analysis needs shown for the resource leak analysis above. Any static analysis performing significant reasoning across procedure boundaries (quite a large set) is likely to benefit from a precise call graph produced via alias analysis, due to the pervasiveness of method calls and virtual dispatch in Java-like languages. Other analyses can be rather directly formulated in terms of possible heap data flow and aliasing, for example, static race detection [43] and taint analysis [68]. Access-path tracking is most often used for analyses that need to track changing properties of objects, like resource leak analysis or typestate verification [12,20], but other analyses may also benefit from the additional precision.

3   Formulating Points-To Analysis

Here we formulate several common variants of Andersen's points-to analysis [3] for Java-like object-oriented languages; implementation techniques will be discussed in Section 4. We begin with a standard formulation of context-insensitive Andersen's analysis that captures its essential points. Then, we extend the formulation with a generic template for context sensitivity, and we present various context-sensitive analyses in the literature as instantiations of the template.

3.1   Context-Insensitive Formulation

A *points-to analysis* computes an over-approximation of the heap locations that each program pointer may point to. Pointers include program variables and also pointers within heap-allocated objects, e.g., instance fields. The result of the analysis is a *points-to relation pt*, with $pt(p)$ representing the *points-to set* of a pointer p. For decidability and scalability, points-to analyses must employ abstraction to finitize the possibly-infinite set of pointers and heap locations arising at runtime. In particular, a *heap abstraction* represents dynamic heap locations with a finite set of *abstract locations*.

Andersen's points-to analysis [3] has the following properties:

- *Flow insensitive*: The analysis assumes statements can execute in any order and any number of times.
- *Subset based*: The analysis models directionality of assignments, i.e., a statement x = y implies $pt(y) \subseteq pt(x)$. In contrast, an equality-based analysis (e.g., that of Steensgaard [65]) would require $pt(y) = pt(x)$ for the same statement, a coarser approximation.

As is typical for Java points-to analyses, we also desire *field sensitivity*, which requires separate reasoning about each instance field of each abstract location. *Field-based* analyses for Java, in which instance field values are merged across abstract locations, may provide sufficient precision for certain clients [32,64]. However, field sensitivity typically adds little expense to a context-insensitive analysis [32], and for context-sensitive analyses (to be discussed in Section 3.2), field sensitivity is essential for precision.

Table 1 gives a standard formulation of context-insensitive, field-sensitive Andersen's analysis for Java, equivalent to those appearing elsewhere in the literature [52,32,72,64].[5] Canonical statements for the analysis are given in the first column. In order, the four statement types enable object allocation, copying pointers, and reading and writing instance fields. More complex memory-access statements (e.g., x.f = y.g.h) are handled through suitable introduction of

---

[5] Points-to analysis has also been formulated as an abstract interpretation [11] (e.g., by Might et al. [41]), yielding a systematic characterization of the analysis result in terms of the target program's concrete semantics. See Might et al. [41] for details of such a formulation and a discussion the relationship of context-sensitive points-to analysis to control-flow analysis for functional languages [56].

Table 1. Canonical statements for context-insensitive Java points-to analysis and the corresponding points-to set constraints

Statement	Constraint
i: x = new T()	$\{o_i\} \subseteq pt(x)$ [NEW]
x = y	$pt(y) \subseteq pt(x)$ [ASSIGN]
x = y.f	$\dfrac{o_i \in pt(y)}{pt(o_i.\text{f}) \subseteq pt(x)}$ [LOAD]
x.f = y	$\dfrac{o_i \in pt(x)}{pt(y) \subseteq pt(o_i.\text{f})}$ [STORE]

temporary variables. Array objects are modeled as having a single field `arr` that may point to any value stored in the array (so, `x[i] = y` is modeled as `x.arr = y`). Section 3.2 discusses handling of method calls.

The inference rules in Table 1 describe how each statement type affects the corresponding points-to sets. Note that since the analysis is field sensitive, points-to sets are maintained both for variables (e.g., $pt(x)$) and for instance fields of abstract locations (e.g., $pt(o_i.\text{f})$). Also note that in the NEW rule, the abstract location o_i is named based on the statement label i, the standard heap abstraction used in Andersen's analysis.

Example Consider the following program (assume type T has a field f):

```
1 a = new T();
2 b = new T();
3 a.f = b;
4 c = a.f;
```

The following is a derivation of of $o_2 \in pt(c)$ according to the rules of Table 1, with rule applications labeled by the corresponding program statement's line number:

$$\dfrac{\dfrac{}{o_2 \in pt(b)}\,\text{L2} \quad \dfrac{\dfrac{}{o_1 \in pt(a)}\,\text{L1}}{pt(b) \subseteq pt(o_1.\text{f})}\,\text{L3}}{o_2 \in pt(o_1.\text{f})} \quad \dfrac{\dfrac{}{o_1 \in pt(a)}\,\text{L1}}{pt(o_1.f) \subseteq pt(c)}\,\text{L4}$$
$$o_2 \in pt(c)$$

3.2 Context Sensitivity

We now extend our points-to analysis formulation to incorporate context-sensitive handling of method calls. We formulate context sensitivity in a generic manner and then show how to instantiate the formulation to derive standard analysis variants.

A *context-sensitive* points-to analysis separately analyzes a method m for each *calling context* that arises at call sites of m. A calling context (or, simply, a *context*) is some abstraction of the program states that may arise at a call site. Separately analyzing a method for each context removes imprecision due to conflation of analysis results across its invocations.

For example, consider the following program:

```
1 id(p) { return p; }
2 x = new Object(); // o1
3 y = new Object(); // o2
4 a = id(x);
5 b = id(y);
```

A context-*insensitive* analysis conflates the effects of all calls to id, in effect assuming that either object o1 or o2 may be passed as the parameter at the calls on lines 4 and 5. This assumption leads to the imprecise conclusions that a may point to o2 and b to o1. Now, consider a context-sensitive points-to analysis that uses a distinct context for each method call site. This analysis will process id separately for its two call sites, thereby precisely concluding that a may only point to o1 and b only to o2.

Formulation. Our generic formulation of context-sensitive points-to analysis appears in Table 2. Compared to Table 1, the two additional statement types respectively allow for invoking and returning from procedures. We assume that a method m has formal parameters m_{this} for the receiver and $m_{p_1}, \ldots, m_{p_n}$ for the remaining parameters, and we use a pseudo-variable m_{ret} to hold its return value.[6]

The analysis formulated in Table 2 maintains a set $contexts(m)$ of the contexts that have arisen at call sites of each method m. For each local pointer variable x, the analysis maintains a separate abstract pointer $\langle x, c \rangle$ to represent x's possible values when its enclosing method is invoked in context c. Abstract locations $\langle o_i, c \rangle$ are similarly parameterized by a context. Finally, note that each constraint in the second column of Table 1 is written under the assumption that the corresponding statement in the first column is from method m.

Our formulation is parameterized by two key functions, which together specify a *context-sensitivity policy*:

- The *selector* function, which determines what context to use for a callee at some call site, and
- The *heapSelector* function, which determines what context c to use in an abstract location $\langle o_i, c \rangle$ at allocation site i.

We first present the inference rules for the analysis without specifying these functions. Then, we show how standard variants of context-sensitive

---

[6] We elide static fields (global variables) and static methods from our formulation, as their handling is straightforward. Since method contexts cannot be applied to global variables, their usage may blunt precision gains from context sensitivity.

Table 2. Inference rules for context-sensitive points-to analysis

Statement in method m	Constraint
i: x = new T()	$$\frac{c \in contexts(m)}{\langle o_i, heapSelector(c)\rangle \in pt(\langle x, c\rangle)} \quad \text{[NEW]}$$
x = y	$$\frac{c \in contexts(m)}{pt(\langle y, c\rangle) \subseteq pt(\langle x, c\rangle)} \quad \text{[ASSIGN]}$$
x = y.f	$$\frac{c \in contexts(m) \qquad \langle o_i, c'\rangle \in pt(\langle y, c\rangle)}{pt(\langle o_i, c'\rangle.\mathtt{f}) \subseteq pt(\langle x, c\rangle)} \quad \text{[LOAD]}$$
x.f = y	$$\frac{c \in contexts(m) \qquad \langle o_i, c'\rangle \in pt(\langle x, c\rangle)}{pt(\langle y, c\rangle) \subseteq pt(\langle o_i, c'\rangle.\mathtt{f})} \quad \text{[STORE]}$$
j: x = r.g(a_1,...,a_n)	$$\frac{\begin{array}{c} c \in contexts(m) \qquad \langle o_i, c'\rangle \in pt(\langle r, c\rangle) \\ m' = dispatch(\langle o_i, c'\rangle, \mathtt{g}) \\ argvals = [\{\langle o_i, c'\rangle\}, pt(\langle a_1, c\rangle), \ldots, pt(\langle a_n, c\rangle)] \\ c'' \in selector(m', c, j, argvals) \end{array}}{\begin{array}{c} c'' \in contexts(m') \\ \langle o_i, c'\rangle \in pt(\langle m'_{this}, c''\rangle) \\ pt(\langle a_k, c\rangle) \subseteq pt(\langle m'_{p_k}, c''\rangle), \ 1 \leq k \leq n \\ pt(\langle m'_{ret}, c''\rangle) \subseteq pt(\langle x, c\rangle) \end{array}} \quad \text{[INVOKE]}$$
return x	$$\frac{c \in contexts(m)}{pt(\langle x, c\rangle) \subseteq pt(\langle m_{ret}, c\rangle)} \quad \text{[RETURN]}$$

points-to analysis can be expressed by instantiating *selector* and *heapSelector* appropriately.

Inference Rules. For the first four statement types, the inference rules in Table 2 are modified from those in Table 1 to include appropriate parameterization with contexts. In each rule, a pre-condition chooses a context c from those that have been created for the enclosing method m, and c is used in the rule's conclusions. The *heapSelector* function from the context-sensitivity policy is used in the NEW rule to obtain contexts for abstract locations. The final RETURN rule in Table 2 models return statements by simulating a copy from the returned variable x to the pseudo-variable m_{ret} for the method. So, $pt(\langle m_{ret}, c\rangle)$ will include all abstract objects possibly returned by m in context c.

By far, the INVOKE rule is the most complex. The first two lines of the rule model reasoning about virtual dispatch. Given a location $\langle o_i, c'\rangle$ that the receiver argument $\langle r, c\rangle$ may point to, a *dispatch* function is invoked to resolve the virtual dispatch of g on $\langle o_i, c'\rangle$ to a target method m'. (For Java, *dispatch* would be implemented based on the type hierarchy and the concrete type of $\langle o_i, c'\rangle$.) This direct reasoning about virtual dispatch implies that the analysis computes its call graph *on-the-fly* [32,52,72], rather than relying on a call graph computed with some less precise analysis (recall the inter-dependence of points-to analysis and call graph construction, discussed in Section 2). The tradeoffs between on-the-fly call graph construction and using a pre-computed call graph have been explored extensively in the literature [21,32]; we have found that on-the-fly call graph construction usually improves both precision *and* performance (see Section 4.4).

Once the target m' of the virtual call is discovered, the analysis uses the *selector* function from the context-sensitivity policy to determine which context(s) to use for this call of m'. *selector* can discriminate contexts for the target method m' based on the caller's context c, the call site id j, and a list of possible parameter values *argvals*. Given a context c'' returned by *selector*, the first conclusion of the INVOKE rule ensures that c'' is in the set of observed contexts for m'. The final three conclusions of the rule model parameter passing and return-value copying for the call.

Entrypoints. Points-to analyses with on-the-fly call graph construction must be provided with a set of *entrypoint* methods E that may be invoked by the environment to begin execution (e.g., a main method for a standard Java program); these methods are assumed to be reachable by the analysis. Given E, the *contexts* sets referenced in Table 1 should be initialized as follows:

- If $m \in E$, then $contexts(m) = \{\texttt{Default}\}$, where Default is a special dummy context value.
- If $m \notin E$, then $contexts(m) = \emptyset$.

With these initial conditions, results will only be computed for methods deemed reachable by the analysis itself, as desired.

Note that an entrypoint method may rely on initialization being performed before it is invoked, e.g., the creation of the String[] array parameter for a main method. In WALA [69], such behavior is modeled in a synthetic "fake root method" that serves as a single root for the call graph and contains invocations of the real entrypoints. The fake root method includes code to pass objects to entrypoint parameters based on customizable heuristics (e.g., passing an object whose concrete type matches the parameter's declared type). In general, precisely modeling how an environment initializes objects before executing an entrypoint can be quite difficult (e.g., for framework-based applications [59]), and this modeling can be critical to getting useful results from a points-to analysis.

Context Sensitivity Variants. In this section, we discuss several standard variants of context-sensitive Andersen's-style points-to analysis, and we show how the analyses can be expressed by instantiating the *selector* and *heapSelector* functions used in Table 2. Note that a context-*insensitive* analysis (with on-the-fly call graph construction) can be expressed using the dummy Default context (we use '_' for an unused argument):

$$selector(\_, \_, \_, \_) = \{\texttt{Default}\}$$
$$heapSelector(\_) = \texttt{Default}$$

Call Strings. A standard technique to distinguish contexts is via *call strings* [55], which abstract the possible call stacks under which a method may be invoked. Call strings are typically represented as a sequence of call site identifiers, corresponding to a (partial) call stack. The following *selector* function gives a call-string-sensitive context for a callee at site j, given the caller context $[j_0, \ldots, j_n]$:

$$selector(\_, [j_0, j_1, \ldots, j_n], j, \_) = \{[j, j_0, j_1, \ldots, j_n,]\} \qquad (1)$$

For full precision, the *heapSelector* function should simply re-use the contexts provided by *selector*, i.e., *heapSelector*$(c) = c$. This choice of *heapSelector* yields a *context-sensitive heap abstraction*.

As a simple example, consider the following program.

```
1 Object f1(T x) { return x.f; }
2 Object f2(T x) { return f1(x); }
3 ...
4 p = f2(q);
5 r = f2(s);
```

Given *selector* as defined above, method f2() will be analyzed in contexts $[s_4]$ and $[s_5]$ (we write s_i for the call site on line i), and f1() will be analyzed in contexts $[s_2, s_4]$ and $[s_2, s_5]$.

Unfortunately, the naïve *selector* function above could cause non-termination in the presence of method recursion, as call strings may grow without bound. Even without recursion, analysis time grows exponentially in the number of methods in the worst case, as the worst-case number of paths in a program's call graph is exponential in the number of methods. In practice, over 10^{14} possible call strings have been observed for a medium-sized program [72], making straightforward use of long call strings intractable.

A standard method for improving scalability of the call-string approach in practice is k-limiting [55], where the maximum call-string length is bounded by a small constant k. This approach has been employed in various previous systems, though the consensus seems to be that bounded object sensitivity (discussed below) provides greater precision for the same or less cost [34]. Instead of using k-limiting in *selector*, Whaley and Lam [72] achieve scalability by using compact BDD data structures (see Section 4) and a context-*insensitive* heap abstraction, i.e., with *heapSelector*$(c) = $ Default. (In essence, k-limiting is performed in the heap selector, with $k = 0$.) While the scalability of their analysis was impressive, later work showed that its precision was lacking for typical clients due to the coarse heap abstraction [34].

For certain classes of program analyses, a result equivalent to using arbitrary-length call strings can be computed efficiently, for example, so-called IFDS problems [51].[7] For this level of precision, the analysis result is typically computed using a summary-based approach [55,51] that is not directly expressible in the formulation of Table 2. However, Reps has shown that full context sensitivity

---

[7] In the literature, an analysis computing such a result is often termed "context-sensitive," but we avoid that usage, as we consider contexts other than call strings.

for a field-sensitive analysis is undecidable [50]. While summary-based points-to analyses have been developed [74,73], we are unaware of any such analysis that scales to large Java programs.

Object Sensitivity. Rather than distinguishing a method's invocations based on call strings, an *object-sensitive* analysis [42][8] uses the (abstract) objects passed as the receiver argument to the method. The intuition behind object sensitivity is that in typical object-oriented design, the state of an object is accessed or mutated via its instance methods (e.g., "setter" and "getter" methods for instance fields). Hence, by using receiver objects to distinguish contexts, an object-sensitive analysis can avoid conflation of operations performed on distinct objects.

In terms of our Table 2 formulation, object-sensitive analysis and more recent variants [58] can be expressed via the following *selector* function:

$$selector(\_, \_, \_, argvals) = \bigcup_{\langle o,c \rangle \in argvals[0]} locToContext(\langle o, c \rangle) \qquad (2)$$

locToContext converts an abstract location (which includes context information) into a context. For standard object sensitivity [42],[9] a context is a list of allocation sites, and *locToContext* simply adds to that list:

$$locToContext(\langle o_i, l \rangle) = cons(o_i, l) \qquad (3)$$

(As in Lisp, $cons(o_i, [o_1, o_2, \ldots]) = [o_i, o_1, o_2, \ldots]$.) As discussed previously, using $heapSelector(c) = c$ yields a context-sensitive heap abstraction.

To illustrate object sensitivity, consider the following example:

```
1 class A { B makeB() { return new B(); } }
2 class B { Object makeObj() { return new Object(); } }
3 ...
4 A a1 = new A();
5 A a2 = new A();
6 B b1 = a1.makeB();
7 B b2 = a2.makeB();
8 Object p1 = b1.makeObj();
9 Object p2 = b2.makeObj();
```

With object-sensitive analysis defined by the *selector* and *heapSelector* function above, makeB() will be analyzed in contexts $[o_4]$ and $[o_5]$ (with abstract objects labeled by allocating line number), and we have $pt(b_1) = \{\langle o_1, [o_4] \rangle\}$ and $pt(b_2) = \{\langle o_1, [o_5] \rangle\}$ due to the context-sensitive heap abstraction. Similarly, makeObj() is analyzed in contexts $[o_1, o_4]$ and $[o_1, o_5]$, $pt(p_1) = \{\langle o_2, [o_1, o_4] \rangle\}$, and $pt(p_2) = \{\langle o_2, [o_1, o_5] \rangle\}$.

---

[8] While Milanova's work [42] introduced the term "object sensitivity," similar ideas were employed in earlier work on object-oriented type inference [45,1].

[9] While alternate object-sensitivity definitions have appeared [35], Smaragdakis et al. [58] showed that Milanova's definition [42] is most effective.

As with call-string sensitivity, k-limiting, either in *selector* or *heapSelector*, is necessary to achieve scalability to realistic programs. The literature contains inconsistent definitions of what exactly it means to limit object-sensitive contexts with a particular value of k; see Smaragdakis et al. [58] for an extended discussion.

In general, the precision of an object-sensitive analysis is incomparable to that of a call-string-sensitive analysis [42]. Object sensitivity can lose precision compared to call-string sensitivity by merging across call sites that pass the same receiver object, but it may gain precision by using multiple contexts at a single call site (when multiple receiver objects are possible). Work by Lhoták and Hendren [34] has shown that for small values of k, object-sensitive analysis yields more precise results for common clients than a call-string-sensitive analysis. In practice, a mix of object- and call-string sensitivity is often used, e.g., with call-string sensitivity being employed only for static methods (which have no receiver argument).

Recently, Smaragdakis et al. [58] have identified *type sensitivity* as a useful technique for obtaining much of the precision of object sensitivity with greater scalability. In one variant of type sensitivity, a context is a list of types rather than allocation sites, and *locToContext* converts the allocation site from the abstract location into a type:

$$locToContext(\langle o_i, l \rangle) = cons(enclosingClass(o_i), l) \qquad (4)$$

Rather than using the concrete type of o_i in the context, the concrete type of the enclosing class for the allocation site is used, yielding greater precision in practice [58]. Another variant of type sensitivity allows for one abstract location to remain in the context:

$$locToContext(\langle o_i, cons(o_j, l) \rangle) = cons(o_i, cons(enclosingClass(o_j), l)) \qquad (5)$$

Again, k-limiting is required for scalability of either of these schemes. Smaragdakis et al. [58] show how k-limited versions of these type-sensitive analyses provide much of the precision of standard object-sensitive analysis with significantly less cost.

Rather than limiting attention to the receiver argument, the *cartesian product algorithm* (CPA) [1] distinguishes contexts based on the objects passed in all argument positions. We can define the *selector* function for CPA as follows:

$$cartProd(argvals) = \prod_{i=0}^{n} argvals[i]$$

$$selector(\_, \_, \_, argvals) = \bigcup_{l \in cartProd(argvals)} locListToContext(l) \qquad (6)$$

The *cartProd* function computes the (generalized) cartesian product of all entries in *argvals*, yielding a set of lists of abstract locations. Each such list l is converted to a context using *locListToContext*, analogous to the use of *locToContext* for object sensitivity. In fact, the object-sensitive analysis variants described above can also be formulated as a special case of CPA, by only using values for the receiver argument in *locListToContext*. The *locToContext* used in Equation 3 for standard object sensitivity can be generalized to handle all argument positions:

$$locListToContext([\langle o_{i_0}, c_0 \rangle, \dots, \langle o_{i_n}, c_n \rangle]) = (cons(o_{i_0}, c_0), \dots, cons(o_{i_n}, c_n)) \quad (7)$$

As formulated above, CPA creates many more contexts per method than the equivalent object-sensitive analysis, a significant scalability barrier. In its original formulation [1], CPA was used for type inference, and the heap abstraction consisted of types rather than allocation sites, making scalability more feasible. While full CPA based on allocation sites may not scale, we believe that contexts based on arguments other than the receiver may still prove useful.

Unification-Based Approaches. Some previous approaches to context-sensitive points-to analysis have employed equality constraints for assignments [16,44,31], which cannot be expressed as a context-sensitivity policy in the formulation of Table 2.[10] In this approach, statement x = y is modeled with constraint $pt(y) = pt(x)$ instead of $pt(y) \subseteq pt(x)$, enabling the use of fast union-find data structures to represent equal points-to sets. While this approach has been shown to scale for C++ programs [31], we are unaware of a scalable implementation for Java-like languages. In particular, the increased use of virtual dispatch in Java negatively affects the scalability of the equality-based approach [44].

4   Implementing Points-To Analysis

Here we present techniques for efficiently implementing the points-to analyses formulated in Section 3. Over the past two decades, advances in implementation techniques (and hardware advances) have shown that some of these variants can scale to relatively large programs (papers reporting analysis of millions of lines of code are now commonplace). We present basic techniques for implementing an Andersen's-style analysis, and then briefly review some of the most prominent advanced techniques which have appeared in the literature.

Unfortunately, the pointer analysis literature contains several different formalisms for describing analyses and implementations. Presentations use various mathematical frameworks, including set constraints [17], context-free-language reachability [49], and Datalog [72]. Each framework elucidates certain issues most clearly, and the choice of framework depends on the best match between the input language, the analysis variant, and the author's taste.

This section discusses implementation techniques based on old-fashioned algorithmic description of imperative code based on fixed-point iteration. A previous paper [62] presented an algorithmic analysis of this algorithm, which sheds some

---

[10] For languages like Java and C#, a context-*insensitive* equality-based approach like Steensgaard's analysis [65] does not work—since all objects are passed as the this parameter to the constructor of the root object type, the analysis would conclude that all points-to sets are equal.

light on the performance issues which arise in practice. We restate some of the key points from that work [62] here. The WALA pointer analysis implementation [69] follows this algorithm directly.

4.1   Algorithm

Here we present an algorithm for Andersen's analysis for Java, as specified in Table 1 in Section 3. The algorithm is most similar to Pearce et al.'s algorithm for C [47] and also resembles existing algorithms for Java (e.g., that of Lhoták and Hendren [32]). We do not give detailed pseudocode for implementing a context-sensitive analysis with on-the-fly call-graph construction, as formulated in Table 2, but we discuss some of the key implementation issues later in the section.

The algorithm constructs a flow graph G representing the pointer flow for a program and computes its (partial) transitive closure, a standard points-to analysis technique (e.g., see [25,17,27]). G has nodes for variables, abstract locations, and fields of abstract locations. At algorithm termination, G has an edge $n \rightarrow n'$ iff one of the following two conditions holds:

1. n is an abstract location o_i representing a statement x = new T(), and n' is x.
2. $pt(n) \subseteq pt(n')$ according to some rule in Table 1.

Given a graph G satisfying these conditions, it is clear that $o_i \in pt(x)$ iff x is reachable from o_i in G. Hence, the transitive closure of G—where only abstract location nodes are considered sources—yields the desired points-to analysis result. Since flow relationships for abstract-location fields depend on the points-to sets of base pointers for the corresponding field field accesses (see the LOAD and STORE rules referencing $pt(o_i.f)$ in Table 1), certain edges in G can only be inserted after some reachability has been determined, yielding a *dynamic transitive closure* (DTC) problem.

Pseudocode for the analysis algorithm appears in Figure 3. The DOANALYSIS routine takes a set of program statements of the forms shown in Table 1 as input. (We assume suitable data structures that, given a variable x, yield all load statements y = x.f and store statements x.f = y in constant time per statement.) The algorithm maintains a flow graph G as just described and computes a points-to set $pt(x)$ for each variable x, representing the transitive closure in G from abstract locations. Note that abstract location nodes are eschewed, and instead the relevant points-to sets are initialized appropriately (line 2).

The algorithm employs *difference propagation* [18,32,47] to reduce the work of propagating reachability facts. For each node n in G, $pt_\Delta(n)$ holds those abstract locations o_i such that (1) the algorithm has discovered that n is reachable from o_i and (2) this reachability information has not yet propagated to n's successors in G. $pt(n)$ holds those abstract locations for which (1) holds and propagation to successors of n is complete. The DIFFPROP routine updates a difference set $pt_\Delta(n)$ with those values from $srcSet$ not already contained in $pt(n)$. After a node n has been removed from the worklist and processed, all current reachability

DoAnalysis()

```
 1  for each statement i: x = new T() do
 2          pt_Δ(x) ← pt_Δ(x) ∪ {o_i}, o_i fresh
 3          add x to worklist
 4  for each statement x = y do
 5          add edge y → x to G
 6  while worklist ≠ ∅ do
 7          remove n from worklist
 8          for each edge n → n' ∈ G do
 9                  DiffProp(pt_Δ(n), n')
10          if n represents a local x
11            then for each statement x.f = y do
12                    for each o_i ∈ pt_Δ(n) do
13                        if y → o_i.f ∉ G
14                          then add edge y → o_i.f to G
15                               DiffProp(pt(y), o_i.f)
16                  for each statement y = x.f do
17                    for each o_i ∈ pt_Δ(n) do
18                        if o_i.f → y ∉ G
19                          then add edge o_i.f → y to G
20                               DiffProp(pt(o_i.f), y)
21          pt(n) ← pt(n) ∪ pt_Δ(n)
22          pt_Δ(n) ← ∅
```

DiffProp(srcSet, n)

```
 1  pt_Δ(n) ← pt_Δ(n) ∪ (srcSet − pt(n))
 2  if pt_Δ(n) changed then add n to worklist
```

Fig. 3. Pseudocode for the points-to analysis algorithm

information has been propagated to n's successors, so $pt_Δ(n)$ is added to $pt(n)$ and emptied (lines 21 and 22).

Theorem 1. DoAnalysis *terminates and computes the points-to analysis result specified in Table 1.*

Proof. (Sketch) DoAnalysis terminates since (1) the constructed graph is finite and (2) a node n is only added to the worklist when $pt_Δ(n)$ changes (line 2 of DiffProp), which can only occur a finite number of times. For the most part, the correspondence of the computed result to the rules of Table 1 is straightforward. One subtlety is the handling of the addition of new graph edges due to field accesses. When an edge $y → o_i.f$ is added to G to handle a putfield statement (line 14), only $pt(y)$ is propagated across the edge, not $pt_Δ(y)$ (line 15). This operation is correct because if $pt_Δ(y) ≠ ∅$, then y must be on the worklist, and hence $pt_Δ(y)$ will be propagated across the edge when y is removed from the worklist. A similar argument holds for the propagation of $pt(o_i.f)$ at line 20. □

4.2   Complexity

A simple algorithmic analysis shows that the algorithm in Figure 3 has worst-case cubic complexity. Note that difference propagation is required to ensure the cubic complexity bound for this worklist-style algorithm [46].

In practice, many papers have reported scaling behavior significantly better than cubic. Two of the authors have published an analysis [62] that explains why this pointer analysis usually runs in quadratic time on strongly-typed languages such as Java. The key insight is that Java's strong type system restricts the structure of the graph G to be relatively sparse for most pointer assignments. By bounding the sparsity of this graph, we can show that the algorithm usually runs in quadratic time. We refer the reader to the previous paper [62] for more details.

The previous work [62] also compares the expected behavior with the observed behavior in the WALA pointer analysis implementation. The paper reports results that show that the WALA implementation scales roughly quadratically with program size on Java programs, as predicted. As a rough characterization of overall scalability, [62] reports that the WALA implementation can usually perform this analysis on programs with a few hundred thousand lines of code in a few minutes. However, this scalability can vary widely, in particular depending on implementation details inside the standard library, to be discussed further in Section 6.

4.3   Optimizations

In practice, an implementation can use several techniques in conjunction with the code in Figure 3 to improve performance by significant constant factors.

Type Filters. In strongly-typed languages, *type filters* provide a simple but highly effective optimization which improves both precision and (usually) performance [21,32].

Consider, for example, the following Java code:

```
Integer i = new Integer(0);
Double d = new Double(0.0);
Object o = new Random().nextBoolean() ? i : d;
Object p = (o instanceof Integer) ? (Integer)o : null;
o.toString();
```

The basic algorithm of Figure 3, which ignores the cast statement, would conclude imprecisely that p may alias d.

Slightly less obviously, consider the alias relation for the receiver (this pointers) in the methods Integer.toString() and Double.toString(). Due to the o.toString() invocation, the basic algorithm would conclude that since o may alias either i or d, then so may the receiver for each toString() method. However, this is imprecise, since the semantics of virtual dispatch ensure that the receiver of Integer.toString() cannot point to an object of type Double.

Type filters provide a simple technique to build these language constraints into the points-to analysis, in order to improve precision. We describe the technique informally as follows. In Figure 3, we add labels to the edges in the graph G. Each label represents a type in the source language – a label T can indicate either a "cone type" (any subtype of T) or a "point type" (only objects of concrete type T).

We modify the algorithm to add labels to the graph based on the source code. For example, for an assignment x = (T) y, we label the edge $y \rightarrow x$ with (cone type) T. We add similar labels for edges that arise from assignments from actual parameters to formal parameters, to capture type constraints imposed by virtual dispatch. Finally, we would modify the DIFFPROP routine to only add appropriately typed objects to points-to sets. This can be accomplished with a bit-vector intersection, updating the bit vector for each each type as allocation sites are discovered.

Cycle Elimination. Consider the following Java code snippet:

```
Object a = ...
Object b = ...
Object c = ...
while (...) {
  if (?) a = b;
  else if (?) b = c;
      else c = b;
}
```

It should be clear that a points-to-analysis will compute the same points-to-set for a, b, and c. This arises from a *cycle* in the flow graph.

Cycles arise relatively frequently in flow graphs for flow-insensitive points-to analysis, especially for weakly-typed languages like C. When a cycle arises in the flow graph, a points-to analysis implementation can collapse the cycle in the flow graph and use a single representative points-to set for all variables in the cycle. This optimization can drastically reduce both space consumption (fewer points-to sets and constraints), and also time (less propagation to a fixed point). A key challenge with cycle elimination is identifying cycles as they arise dynamically (due to flow graph edge additions), and a large body of work studies efficient cycle detection for C points-to analysis [17,27,23].

To our knowledge, the results with cycle elimination for Java points-to analysis have been much less impressive than those for C. We personally experimented with implementing cycle elimination in WALA and found it to provide little benefit. Paradoxically, cycle elimination works best for cases where the points-to analysis is often unable to distinguish between related points-to-sets. Recall that when analyzing Java, we can use type filters to achieve a more precise solution than typical for untyped C programs. Effectively, type filters "break cycles," since a labeled edge breaks the invariant that all variables in a cycle have the same points-to-set. It seems that for analyses with richer abstractions, cycle elimination becomes less effective, since the existence of huge cycles relies on a coarse abstraction that fails to distinguish locations.

Method-Local State. In WALA, if a variable's points-to set is determined entirely by statements in the enclosing method, the points-to set is computed on-demand rather than via the global constraint system. Consider the following example:

```
void m(T x) {
  Object y = new Object();
  Object z = y;
  Object w = x.f;
}
```

For this case, $pt(y)$ and $pt(z)$ would be computed only when required, while the constraint system would be used to compute $pt(w)$ (since it depends on a field of parameter x). Though it complicates the implementation, we have found this optimization to yield significant space savings in practice. Separate handling of local state has been employed in other previous work [73,71].

4.4   Handling Method Calls

On-the-fly call-graph construction (see discussion in Section 3.2) has a significant impact on real-world points-to analysis performance. If constraint generation costs are ignored, on-the-fly call graph reasoning can slow down analysis, as more iterations are required to reach a fixed point [72]. However, if the costs of constraint generation are considered (which we believe is a more realistic model), on-the-fly call graph building improves performance, since constraints need not be generated for unreachable library code. Also, on-the-fly call graph reasoning can make the flow graph for a program more sparse, improving performance.

As discussed in Section 3.2, context-sensitive points-to analysis can often give much more precise results for object-oriented programs than context-insensitive analysis. The most straightforward strategy for implementing context sensitivity is via *cloning*. Recall from Section 3.2 that context-sensitive analysis computes a different solution (points-to set) for local variables that arise in different contexts. With cloning, the implementation simply creates a distinct copy of the relevant program structures for each context distinguished.

For example, consider a context-sensitivity policy employing k-limited call-string contexts with $k = 1$. For this policy, a cloning-based analysis would clone each method for each possible call site, and compute a separate solution for each clone. Intuitively, this can effectively blow up the program size by a quadratic factor — if there are N methods, each might be cloned N times, resulting in N^2 clones.

Data Structures. Cloning for context-sensitivity exacerbates the demand for both time and space. Much work over the last decade has improved techniques to exploit redundancy in the pointer analysis structures to mitigate these factors.

The algorithm of Figure 3 must maintain two data structures, each of which grows super-linearly with program size:

- the set of constraints that represent the flow graph (G), and
- the points-to sets for each program variable.

A straightforward analysis implementation would represent the points-to sets using bit vectors, as commonly presented in textbooks for dataflow analysis [2]. The implementation can map each abstract object (e.g. allocation site) to a natural number, and then use these as identifiers in bit vector indices. At first glance, this seems like a compact representation, since it appears to devote roughly one bit of space to each unique piece of information in the output.

However, better solutions have been developed. Several key advances in pointer analysis implementation have relied on clever data structures to reduce the space costs of constraints and points-to sets by exploiting redundancy. The key insight is that many points-to sets are similar, due to the patterns by which values flow between variables in real programs. So, several works have proposed data structures to exploit these redundancies.

The WALA implementation uses a clever "shared-bit vector" representation presented by Heintze [24]. This implementation exploits the commonalities in bit vector contents, resulting in a bit vector representation that shares large common subsets. Each bit vector is represented as the union of a shared common base and a relatively small delta.

In our experience, the Heintze shared bit vectors can dramatically reduce the space costs of a cloning-based pointer analysis implementation, and allows some limited context sensitivity policies to scale to relatively large programs. However, these techniques cannot suffice for aggressive context-sensitivity policies, such as full call-string context sensitivity for variables [72]. For these policies, the number of clones grows exponentially with program size, to the point where even one bit per clone would demand more memory than there are flip-flops in the universe.

Several groups have presented solutions based on exploiting binary decision diagrams (BDDs), which potentially allow a system to explore an exponential space using a tractable implicit representation. This technique has been used extensively in explicit-state model checking [10], and several papers indicate that similar techniques can work for certain flavors of context-sensitive pointer analysis [6,33,76,72,7]. Compared with shared-bit vectors, BDDs have the advantage of employing the same compact representation for both input constraints and the output points-to relation. Compact constraint representation makes aggressive policies like full call-string sensitivity for variables possible [72]. On the other hand, performance of BDD-based analyses can be fragile with respect to variable orderings [70], and using BDDs requires representing all relevant analysis state in BDD relations, making integration with other systems more difficult (though work has been done to ease this integration [35]).

Employing difference propagation exhaustively as in Figure 3 may double space requirements and hence represent an unattractive space-time tradeoff. A set implementation that enables propagation of abstract locations in parallel, like shared-bit vectors, lessens the need for exhaustive difference propagation in practice. In our experience, the key benefit of difference propagation lies in operations performed for each abstract location in a points-to set, e.g., edge adding (see lines 12 and 17 in Figure 3). To save space, WALA [69] only uses difference propagation for edge adding and for handling virtual call receivers (since with on-the-fly call graph construction, each receiver abstract location may yield a new call target). Also note that the best data structure for the $pt_\Delta(x)$ sets may differ from the $pt(x)$ sets to support smaller sets and iteration efficiently; see [32,46] for further discussion.

4.5 Demand-Driven Analysis

The previous discussion focused on computing an *exhaustive* points-to analysis solution, i.e., computing all points-to sets for a program. However, recall that the primary motivation for pointer analysis is to enable some client, which performs some higher-level analysis such as for program understanding, verification, or optimization. For many such clients, computing the full solution is not required. The client will demand information for only a few program variables, and so it makes sense to compute the information requested *on-demand*.[11]

Heintze and Tardieu presented a highly influential paper describing a demand-driven version of context-insensitive Andersen's analysis, showing performance benefits for a client resolving C function pointers [26]. A demand-driven analysis formulation can also be obtained from a context-free-language reachability formulation of Andersen's analysis [49,64] via the magic-sets transformation [48].[12]

Additional precision benefits can be obtained via *refinement* of the analysis abstraction where relevant to client queries. Guyer and Lin [22] showed the benefits of such an approach for various C points-to analysis clients. Sridharan et al. [64,60] gave a refinement-based points-to analysis that exhibited significant precision and scalability improvements for several Java points-to analysis clients. Finally, recent work by Liang et al. [38,37,36] has shown that precision for clients can be improved with local improvements to the heap abstraction of a points-to analysis.

5 Must-alias Analysis

Heretofore, we have concentrated on flow-insensitive alias analyses. These analyses produce a statically bounded (abstract) representation of the program's runtime heap. The pointer analysis solution indicates which abstract objects each pointer-valued expression in the program may denote.

Unfortunately, these scalable analyses have serious disadvantage when used for verification: they can answer only *may-alias* questions, that is, whether two variable may potentially refer to the same object. They cannot in general answer

---

[11] On-demand computation of purely-local points-to sets was discussed in Section 4.3; here we extend the discussion to on-demand computation of any points-to set.

[12] For C, applying the magic-sets transformation to the Melski-Reps formulation [49] yields an equivalent analysis to that of Heintze and Tardieu [26].

must-alias questions, that is, whether to two variables must always refer to the same object.

May-alias information requires a verifier to model any operation performed through a pointer dereference as an operation that may or may not be performed on the *possible* target abstract objects identified by the pointer analysis – this is popularly known as a "weak update" as opposed to a "strong update" [8].

In this section, we present a flow-sensitive must-alias analysis that is based on dynamic partition of the heap, and show how its greater precision is used to verify typestate properties.

5.1   On the Importance of Strong Updates

```
 1 File makeFile {
 2   return new File(); //   ⟨o₁, init⟩, ⟨o₂, init⟩
 3 }
 4 File f = makeFile(); //   ⟨o₁, init⟩, ⟨o₂, init⟩
 5 File g = makeFile(); //   ⟨o₁, init⟩, ⟨o₂, init⟩
 6 if(?)
 7   f.open(); //   ⟨o₁, open⟩, ⟨o₂, init⟩
 8 else
 9   g.open();
10 f.read(); //   ⟨o₁, open⟩, ⟨o₂, init⟩
11 g.read(); //   ⟨o₁, open⟩, ⟨o₂, err⟩
12 }
```

Fig. 4. Concrete states for a program reading from two `File` objects allocated at the same allocation site. The example shows states for an execution in which the condition evaluates to true.

Consider a `File` type which requires invoking `open()` on a `File` object before invoking `read()`, and consider the simple example program of Fig. 4. The allocation statement in Line 2 allocates two `File` objects in some initial state *init*. In the figure, we write $\langle o, st \rangle$ to denote that an object o is in state st.

In this example, a typical points-to analysis will represent *both* objects allocated at Line 2 by a single abstract object A. The abstract state at Line 2 would therefore be $\langle A, init \rangle$, representing an *arbitrary* number of `File` objects that have been allocated at this point, all of which are in their initial state.

Now, consider the operation `f.open` invoked on the abstract object $\langle A, init \rangle$. What should be the effect of this operation? The abstract object $\langle A, init \rangle$ represents all objects allocated at Line 2. Assuming that the invocation of `f.open` yields the state $\langle A, open \rangle$ is equivalent to assuming that the state of *all* files represented by A has turned to *open*, which is unsound in general. For example, Fig. 5 shows the unsoundness of this scheme for the example from Fig. 4—the possible *err* state at Line 11 is not represented by the abstract states.

```
 1 File makeFile {
 2   return new File(); //   〈A, init〉
 3 }
 4 File f = makeFile(); //   〈A, init〉
 5 File g = makeFile(); //   〈A, init〉
 6 if(?)
 7   f.open(); //   〈A, open〉
 8 else
 9   g.open(); //   〈A, open〉
10 f.read(); //   〈A, open〉
11 g.read(); //   〈A, open〉
12 }
```

Fig. 5. Unsound update of abstract states for the example of Fig. 4

```
 1 File f = new File(); //   〈A, init〉
 2 f.open(); //   〈A, init〉, 〈A, open〉
 3 f.read(); //   〈A, err〉, 〈A, open〉
```

Fig. 6. Simple correct example that cannot be verified directly using weak updates

To guarantee soundness, the effect of f.open() would have to represent the possibility that some concrete objects represented by A remain in their initial state. As a result, the abstract state after f.open() should reflect both possibilities: $\langle A, open \rangle$, where the object is in its open state, and $\langle A, init \rangle$ where the object remains in its initial state. Such an update is referred to as a *weak update*, as it maintains the old state ($\langle A, init \rangle$) as part of the updated state. Using weak updates, however, would fail to verify even a simple program such the one shown in Fig. 6.

Addressing this issue requires knowing *must-alias* information. For Fig. 6, the analysis must prove that at Line 2, f *must* point to the object allocated by Line 1; with this knowledge, the analysis can show that the object can only be in the *open* state after the call, enabling verification. While computing this must-alias information would be straightforward for Fig. 6, in general the problem is much more challenging, due to language features like loops and method calls.

The literature contains many approaches for must-alias analysis, ranging from relatively simple abstractions such as the recency abstraction [5] and random isolation [29], to full-fledged shape analysis [53]. We next review a particular abstraction framework to combine may and must-alias analysis information, developed for typestate verification [20,40,75,57]. The framework is based on maintaining must and must-not points-to information based on *access paths*.

5.2   Access Paths

Abstractions based on allocation sites impose a *fixed* partition on memory locations. We next present an abstraction to allow the name of an abstract object to change *dynamically* based on the program variables (and paths) that point to it. Specifically, we define the notion of an *access path*, a sequence of references that points to a heap allocated object, and name an abstract object by the set of access paths that may/must refer to it.

Concrete Semantics. We assume a standard concrete semantics which defines a program state and evaluation of an expression in a program state. The semantic domains are defined in a standard way as follows:

$$
\begin{aligned}
L^\natural &\in objects^\natural \\
v^\natural &\in Val = objects^\natural \cup \{null\} \\
\rho^\natural &\in Env = VarId \to Val \\
h^\natural &\in Heap = objects^\natural \times FieldId \to Val \\
\sigma^\natural = \langle L^\natural, \rho^\natural, h^\natural \rangle &\in States = 2^{objects^\natural} \times Env \times Heap
\end{aligned}
$$

where $objects^\natural$ is an unbounded set of dynamically allocated objects, $VarId$ is a set of local variable identifiers, and $FieldId$ is a set of field identifiers. We generally use the $\natural$ superscript to denote concrete entities.

A *program state* keeps track of the set of allocated objects ($L^\natural$), an environment mapping local variables to values ($\rho^\natural$), and a mapping from fields of allocated objects to values ($h^\natural$).

We also define the notion of an access path as follows: A *pointer path* $\gamma \in \Gamma = FieldId^*$ is a (possibly empty) sequence of field identifiers. The empty sequence is denoted by ϵ. We use the shorthand f^k where $f \in FieldId$ to mean a sequence of length k of accesses along a field f. An *access path* $p \equiv x.\gamma \in VarId \times \Gamma$ is a pair consisting of a local variable x and a pointer path γ.

We denote by APs all possible access paths in a program. The l-value of access path p, denote by $\sigma^\natural[p]$, is recursively defined using the environment and heap mappings, in the standard manner. Given a concrete object $o^\natural$ in a state $\sigma^\natural$, we denote by $AP^\natural(o^\natural)$ the set of access paths that point to o .

Maintaining Must Points-to Information. To describe our abstraction, we first assume that a preliminary flow-insensitive points-to analysis has run. This analysis generates an abstract points-to graph based on a static set of abstract memory locations. For this discussion, we call each abstract memory location from the preliminary points-to analysis an *instance key*.

The more precise analysis performs a flow-sensitive, context-sensitive interprocedural propagation of abstract states. Each abstract state represents a set of concrete states that may arise during execution, and encodes information regarding certain aliasing relationships which these concrete states share. We represent aliasing relationships with tuples of the form $\langle o, unique, AP_\text{M}, May, AP_\text{MN} \rangle$ where:

- o is an instance key.
- *unique* indicates whether the corresponding allocation site has a single concrete live object.

- AP_M is a set of access paths that must point-to o.
- *May* is a boolean that indicates whether there are access paths (not in the must set) that may point to o.
- AP_{MN} is a set of access paths that do *not* point-to o.

This parameterized abstract representation has four dimensions, for the *length* and *width* of each access path set (must and must-not). The length of an access path set indicates the maximal length of an access path in the set, similar to the parameter k in k-limited context-sensitivity policies. The width of an access path set limits the number of access paths in this set.

An abstract state is a set of tuples. We observe that a conservative representation of the concrete program state must obey the following properties:

1. An instance key can be indicated as unique if it represents a single object for this program state.
2. The access path sets (the must and the must-not) do not need to be complete. This does not compromise the soundness of the abstraction, since other elements in the tuple can indicate the existence of other possible aliases.
3. The must and must-not access path sets can be regarded as another heap partitioning which partitions an instance key into the two sets of access paths: those that a) must alias this abstract object, and b) definitely do not alias this abstract object. If the must-alias set is non-empty, the must-alias partition represents a single concrete object.
4. If $May = false$, the must access path is complete; it contains all access paths to this object.

This can be formally stated as follows:

Definition 1. *A tuple $\langle o, unique, AP_M, May, AP_{MN} \rangle$ is a* sound representation *of object $o^\natural$ at program state $\sigma^\natural$ when the following conditions hold:*
- $o = ik(o^\natural)$
- $unique \Rightarrow \{x^\natural \in live(\sigma^\natural) \mid ik(x^\natural) = o\} = \{o^\natural\}$
- $AP_M \subseteq AP^\natural(o^\natural)$
- $(\neg May \Rightarrow (AP_M = AP^\natural(o^\natural)))$
- $AP_{MN} \cap AP^\natural(o^\natural) = \emptyset$

where ik is an abstraction mapping a concrete object to the instance key that represents it, and $live(\sigma^\natural)$ is defined to be $\{x^\natural \mid AP^\natural(x^\natural) \neq \emptyset\}$.

Definition 2. *An abstract state σ is a* sound representation *of a concrete state $\sigma^\natural = \langle L^\natural, \rho^\natural, h^\natural \rangle$ if for every object $o^\natural \in L^\natural$ there exists a tuple in σ that provides a sound representation of $o^\natural$.*

Abstract Transformers. Table 3 shows how a tuple is transformed by the interpretation of various statements. The effect of a transfer function on a given abstract state is defined by taking the union of applying the tuple transfer functions of Table 3 to each tuple in the abstract state.

The interpretation of an allocation statement "v = new T()" with instance key o will *generate* a tuple $\langle o, true, \{v\}, false, \emptyset \rangle$ representing the newly allocated object. When *May* is false, the AP_{MN} component is redundant and, hence, initialized to be empty.

When a tuple reaches the allocation site that created it, we generate two tuples, one representing the newly created object, and one representing the incoming tuple. We change the uniqueness flag to false for reasons explained earlier. For assignment statements, we update the AP_M and AP_{MN} as appropriate.

Note that since we place a finite bound on access path lengths, there are a finite number of possible abstract states, so fixed-point iteration terminates. The number of possible abstract states is exponential in the access path bound.

To use this aliasing information in a client analysis, we can extend the abstract transformers of Table 3 to also maintain the abstract state of an object being tracked.

For example, consider a simple typestate analysis to verify that only *open* files are *read*. We extend the tuple to track the abstract state of a File object, which can be *init* (just initialized), *open*, or *closed*.

```
1 Collection files = ...
2 while (...) {
3   File f = new File(); // (⟨A, true, {f}, false, ∅⟩, init), (⟨A, false, ∅, true, {f}⟩, open)
4   files.add(f); // (⟨A, true, {f}, true, ∅⟩, init), (⟨A, false, ∅, true, {f}⟩, open)
5   f.open(); // (⟨A, true, {f}, true, ∅⟩, open), (⟨A, false, ∅, true, {f}⟩, open)
6   f.read(); // (⟨A, true, {f}, true, ∅⟩, open), (⟨A, false, ∅, true, {f}⟩, open)
7 }
```

Fig. 7. Illustration of a strong update to the state of a File object using access paths

Consider the example of Fig. 7. In this example, the abstraction is able to capture the fact that at Line 5, f must point to the object allocated by the most recent execution of line 3, and its state can be therefore update to *open*. This means that read() can be safely invoked on the object pointed to by f at Line 6.

When a typestate method is invoked, we can (1) use the AP_{MN} information to avoid changing the typestate of the tuple where possible, (2) use the AP_M information to perform strong updates on the tuple where possible, and (3) use the uniqueness information also to perform strong updates where possible.

There are several more powerful tricks which can use this information to improve precision – notably a *focus* operation which performs a limited form of case splitting to improve abstraction precision. We refer the reader to [20] for further discussion of techniques using these abstractions.

As explained earlier, we enforce limits on the length and the number of access paths allowed in the AP_M and AP_{MN} components to keep the number of tuples generated finite. We designed this abstract domain specifically to discard access-path information soundly, allowing heuristics that trade precision for performance but do not sacrifice soundness. This feature is crucial for scalability;

Table 3. Transfer functions for statements indicating how an incoming tuple $\langle o, unique, AP_M, May, AP_{MN} \rangle$ is transformed, where $pt(e)$ is the set of instance keys pointed-to by e in the flow-insensitive solution, $v \in VarId$. $mayAlias(e_1, e_2)$ iff pointer analysis indicates e_1 and e_2 may point to the same instance key.

Stmt S	Resulting abstract tuples
$v = \textbf{new}\ T()$	$\langle o, false, AP_M \setminus startsWith(v, AP_M), May, AP_{MN} \cup \{v\} \rangle$
where $o = $ Stmt S	$\langle o, true, \{v\}, false, \emptyset \rangle$
$v = \texttt{null}$	$\langle o, unique, AP'_M, May, AP'_{MN} \rangle$
	$AP'_M := AP_M \setminus startsWith(v, AP_M)$
	$AP'_{MN} := AP_{MN} \cup \{v\}$
$v.f = \texttt{null}$	$\langle o, unique, AP'_M, May, AP'_{MN} \rangle$
	$AP'_M := AP_M \setminus \{e'.f.\gamma \mid mayAlias(e', v), \gamma \in \Gamma\}$
	$AP'_{MN} := AP_{MN} \cup \{v.f\}$
$v = e$	$\langle o, unique, AP'_M, May, AP'_{MN} \rangle$
	$AP'_M := AP_M \cup \{v.\gamma \mid e.\gamma \in AP_M\}$
	$AP'_{MN} := AP_{MN} \setminus \{v \mid e \notin AP_{MN}\}$
$v.f = e$	$\langle o, unique, AP'_M, May', AP'_{MN} \rangle$
	$AP'_M := AP_M \cup \{v.f.\gamma \mid e.\gamma \in AP_M\}$
	$May' := May \vee \exists v.f.\gamma \in AP'_M. \exists p \in AP. mayAlias(v, p) \wedge p.f.\gamma \notin AP'_M$
	$AP'_{MN} := AP_{MN} \setminus \{v.f \mid e \notin AP_{MN}\}$
$startsWith(v, P) = \{v.\gamma \mid \gamma \in P\}$	

the analysis would suffer an unreasonable explosion of dataflow facts if it soundly tracked every possible access path, as in much prior work [14,30,9,15].

However, the abstraction just presented still relies on a preliminary sound points-to analysis. The abstraction introduces machinery designed to exploit the points-to analysis, in order to maintain a sound (over-approximate) representation of the set of possible concrete states.

In practice, modern large Java programs introduce substantial barriers to this style of sound verification. As we discuss next, certain features of these programs introduce prohibitive obstacles to running a preliminary, sound points-to analysis. However, we show that access-path tracking in the style described here is still useful in the context of under-approximate analyses, which do not guarantee coverage of all program states.

6   Analyzing Modern Java Programs

In our most recent work, we have found that large libraries and reflection usage in modern Java programs and libraries have made points-to analysis (as described in Sections 3 and 4) a poor basis for alias reasoning. In this section, we describe in more detail why points-to analysis does not work well for modern Java programs and libraries, and how we have worked around this issue with under-approximate techniques based on type-based call graph construction and access-path tracking.

We note that though we have not found points-to analysis to work well for modern desktop and server Java applications, it remains relevant in other domains. Scalability issues with points-to analysis may be less severe in cases where applications tend to have less code and use smaller libraries, e.g., mobile phone applications. Furthermore, for languages where a type-based approach does not yield a reasonable call graph (e.g., JavaScript), points-to analysis remains the most scalable technique for reasoning about indirect function calls [61].

6.1   Points-To Analysis Difficulties

In Java-like languages, *reflection* allows for meta-programming based on string names of program constructs like classes or methods. For example, the following code reflectively allocates an object of the type named by x:

```
class Factory {
  Object make(String x) {
    return Class.forName(x).newInstance();
  }
}
```

Analyzing this code with the assumption that x may name any type yields extremely imprecise results, as is most cases only a few types may be allocated by code like the above. In some cases, tracking string constants flowing into x and only considering those types can help. However, many common idioms make this difficult or ineffective, such as use of string concatenation or reading the string from a configuration file.

Previous work has suggested handling code like the above by exploiting uses of the allocated object [39,7], since the object is often cast to a more specific type before it is used. By tracking data flow of reflectively-created objects to casts and optimistically assuming that the casts succeed, the set of allocated types can often be narrowed significantly. For example, consider the following use of the previously-shown Factory class:

```
Factory f = new Factory();
String widgetClass = properties.get("widgetClassName");
IWidget w = (IWidget) f.make(widgetClass);
```

In this case, the analysis treats the reflective code as allocating any subtype of IWidget.

Unfortunately, techniques like the above cannot save points-to analysis from reflection in general. Sometimes, reflective creations can flow to interfaces like java.io.Serializable, which is implemented by many types. In other cases, reflection is used without any downcasts, e.g., reflective method calls via Java's Method.invoke(). As standard libraries and frameworks have grown, the cost of imprecise reflection handling has increased dramatically, since many more types and methods may be (imprecisely) deemed reachable. In some cases, certain parts of libraries may be manually excluded based on knowledge of the application; e.g., GUI libraries can be excluded when analyzing a program with no graphical interface (this approach is used when running WALA regression tests). However, for cases like server applications that are themselves packaged with many libraries (we have observed more than 75 .jar files in some cases), manual exclusions are not suitable. We are unaware of any automatic technique that is able to handle reflection across large Java applications with sufficient precision, and others have also observed this problem [58, Section 5.1].

6.2   Under-Approximate Techniques

Given the aforementioned difficulties with over-approximate alias analysis, under-approximate techniques present an attractive alternative in cases where sound analysis is not required (e.g., in a bug detection tool). When first exploring this area, we tried to base our approach on a points-to analysis modified to be under-approximate, either via reduced reflection handling or use of a partial result computed in some time bound. However, we found this approach to be unsatisfactory: ignoring reflection often led to missed, important behaviors (particularly in framework-based applications [59]), and time bounds required complex heuristics to ensure that the points-to analysis explored desired parts of the program early. Instead, we have turned to an approach of (i) using a variant of the access-path tracking described in Section 5 to track must-alias information under-approximately, and (ii) employing domain-specific modeling of reflection as needed. We describe these techniques in turn.

Under-Approximation by Using Only Must Information. Section 5 described an access-path analysis based on states of $\langle o, unique, AP_{\mathrm{M}}, May, AP_{\mathrm{MN}} \rangle$ tuples, designed to achieve high precision while relying on a pre-computed points-to analysis for soundness. In the under-approximate setting, we can define a simpler analysis with tuples of the form $\langle o, AP_{\mathrm{M}} \rangle$, carrying only must-alias information. As earlier, each time the transformation of must-access-paths set is computed, we must limit the size of the resulting set. It is necessary to do so for two reasons: (i) in the presence of loops (or recursion), it is possible for access paths to grow without a bound (ii) even loop free code might inflate the sets to needlessly large sizes, compromising efficiency. The transformers over $\langle o, AP_{\mathrm{M}} \rangle$ tuples follow the update for AP_{M} as described in Table 3.

In the following examples, we demonstrate how this abstraction can be used for identifying resource leaks (see Section 2), and consider tuples of the form $\langle o, R, AP_{\mathrm{M}} \rangle$ where R is a resource type. R can be acquired via statement type p = acquire R and released via release R r (where r points to the resource). At a high level, we use the must-alias access-path abstraction to detect resource leaks as follows (see Torlak and Chandra [67] for full details):

- At statement p = acquire R, the analysis generates tuple $\langle p, R, \{p\} \rangle$ (we name resource objects by the variable to which they are first assigned).
- Must aliases are updated as shown in Table 3.
- If statement release R r is reached with tuple $t = \langle p, R, a \rangle$ and $r \in a$, then the analysis kills t.
- If method exit is reached with a tuple $\langle p, R, \{\} \rangle$, then a leak is reported, as no aliases exist to release the resource.

– For additional precision, conditionals performing null checks are interpreted. If a conditional checking $v = null$ is reached with tuple $t = \langle p, R, a \rangle$ and $v \in a$, t is killed on the true branch, as a must-alias for a resource cannot be null. $v \neq null$ is handled similarly.

Example 1. Consider the code fragment shown below. We show the facts accumulated by our analysis after each statement to the right.

`p = acquire R`	$\langle p, R, \{p\} \rangle$
`q.f = p`	$\langle p, R, \{p, q.f\} \rangle$
`r = q.f`	$\langle p, R, \{r, p, q.f\} \rangle$
`branch (r == null) L1`	T: *none*, F: $\langle p, R, \{r, p, q.f\} \rangle$
`release R r`	*none*
`L1:`	*none*

At the `branch` statement, the analysis concludes that only the fall-through successor is feasible: r, being a must-alias to a resource, cannot be a null pointer. At the `release` statement, the analysis uses the AP_M set to establish that r must-alias the resource. Consequently, no fact makes it to L1, and no error is reported.

Had the analysis not interpreted the `branch` statement, fact $\langle p, R, \{r, p, q.f\} \rangle$ would have reached L1. Local variables p, q, and r would then be dropped from the state, giving the fact $\langle p, R, \{\} \rangle$ at the exit. This fact would lead the analysis to conclude that resource p is unreachable at exit, resulting in a false positive.

Example 2. Consider the leaky code fragment shown below. It allocates a resource in a loop, but frees only the last allocated instance. The `branch * L2` has a non-deterministic condition which cannot be interpreted by the analysis.

`p₁ = null`	
`L1`	$\langle p_3, R, \{p_3\} \rangle$, $\langle p_3, R, \{p_2\} \rangle$
`p₂ = φ(p₁,p₃)`	$\langle p_3, R, \{p_2, p_3\} \rangle$, $\langle p_3, R, \{\} \rangle$
`branch * L2`	
`p₃ = acquire R`	$\langle p_3, R, \{p_3\} \rangle$, $\langle p_3, R, \{p_2\} \rangle$
`branch true L1`	
`L2`	$\langle p_3, R, \{p_2, p_3\} \rangle$, $\langle p_3, R, \{\} \rangle$
`release R p₂`	$\langle p_3, R, \{\} \rangle$

This fragment also illustrates the treatment of ϕ nodes. Consider the path taken through the loop two times and then exiting to L2. The analysis generates $\langle p_3, R, \{p_3\} \rangle$ after the `acquire`. The generated fact flows to L1, and the analysis generates $\langle p_3, R, \{p_2, p_3\} \rangle$ after the ϕ, using the effect of $p_2 = p_3$. This, in turn, flows out to L2 via the `branch`, where it is killed by the `release`.

In the next loop iteration, the `acquire` statement overwrites p_3, so the analysis kills the occurrence of p_3 in $\{p_2, p_3\}$, generating the new fact $\langle p_3, R, \{p_2\} \rangle$. After propagation on the back edge, this last fact is transformed by the ϕ statement to $\langle p_3, R, \{\} \rangle$. Finally, when the transformed fact flows out to L2, it cannot be killed by `release` since the must-alias set is empty. The fact reaches method exit, and a leak is reported.

Method Calls. We have not yet addressed how an under-approximate analysis like the resource leak detector reasons about method calls; as discussed in Sections 2 and 3, call graph construction and alias analysis are inter-dependent. We have found that an under-approximate call graph based on the class hierarchy is sufficient for bug-finding tools like the leak detector. In using the class hierarchy, all available code is considered, so certain issues related to insufficient reflection handling are avoided. For call sites with a very large number of possible targets, a subset is chosen heuristically, with the heuristics tunable by the client analysis. For example, in the leak detector [67], the heuristics were tuned to prefer code performing resource allocation.

Domain-Specific Reflection Modeling. In certain cases, key application behaviors are implemented using reflection, necessitating modeling of those reflective behaviors. For example, server-side web applications written in Java are typically built atop Java EE[13] and other frameworks, and the application code is only invoked via reflective calls from the framework. To effectively detect security vulnerabilities in such applications using taint analysis [68], the analysis must have visibility into how these reflective calls invoke application code (e.g., to see how untrusted data is passed). For taint analysis of web applications, recent work describes Framework for Frameworks (F4F) [59], a system that eases modeling the security-relevant behaviors of web-application frameworks. We expect similar modeling to be required in other domains where complex, reflection-heavy frameworks are employed.

7 Conclusions and Future Work

We have presented a high-level overview of state-of-the-art may- and must-alias analyses for object-oriented programs, based on our experiences implementing production-quality static analyses for Java. The sound alias-analysis techniques presented here work well for medium-sized programs, while for large-scale Java programs, an under-approximate alias analysis based on access-path tracking currently yields the most useful results.

We see several potentially fruitful directions for future work, for example:

Reflection. Improved reflection handling could significantly increase the effectiveness of various alias-analysis techniques. Approaches based on analyzing non-code artifacts like configuration files [59] or introducing more analyzable language constructs [28] seem particularly promising.

Dynamically-Typed Languages. As scripting languages like JavaScript gain in popularity, there is an increasing need for effective alias analyses for such languages. Analyzing such languages poses significant challenges, as use of reflective code constructs is even more pervasive than in Java, and optimizations based on the type system (see Section 4.3) may no longer be effective in improving scalability [61].

---

[13] http://www.oracle.com/technetwork/java/javaee/index.html

Developer Tool Integration. Some initial work has been done on developer tools that make significant use of alias analysis [63,54,19], but we believe there is significant further scope for tools to help developers reason about data flow and aliasing in their programs. Better tools for reasoning about aliasing are particularly important since trends indicate increasing usage of dynamically-typed languages and large frameworks, both of which can obscure aliasing relationships in programs.

References

1. Agesen, O.: The Cartesian Product Algorithm: Simple and Precise Type Inference of Parametric Polymorphism. In: Olthoff, W. (ed.) ECOOP 1995. LNCS, vol. 952, pp. 2–26. Springer, Heidelberg (1995)
2. Aho, A.V., Lam, M.S., Sethi, R., Ullman, J.D.: Compilers: Principles, Techniques, & Tools with Gradiance, 2nd edn. Addison-Wesley Publishing Company, USA (2007)
3. Andersen, L.O.: Program Analysis and Specialization for the C Programming Language. PhD thesis, University of Copenhagen, DIKU (1994)
4. Bacon, D., Sweeney, P.: Fast static analysis of C++ virtual function calls. In: Conference on Object-Oriented Programming, Systems, Languages, and Applications (OOPSLA), San Jose, CA (October 1996)
5. Balakrishnan, G., Reps, T.: Recency-Abstraction for Heap-Allocated Storage. In: Yi, K. (ed.) SAS 2006. LNCS, vol. 4134, pp. 221–239. Springer, Heidelberg (2006)
6. Berndl, M., Lhoták, O., Qian, F., Hendren, L., Umanee, N.: Points-to analysis using BDDs. In: Conference on Programming Language Design and Implementation (PLDI) (June 2003)
7. Bravenboer, M., Smaragdakis, Y.: Strictly declarative specification of sophisticated points-to analyses. In: Proceeding of the 24th ACM SIGPLAN Conference on Object Oriented Programming Systems Languages and Applications, OOPSLA 2009, pp. 243–262. ACM, New York (2009)
8. Chase, D.R., Wegman, M., Zadeck, F.: Analysis of pointers and structures. In: Conference on Programming Language Design and Implementation (PLDI), pp. 296–310. ACM Press, New York (1990)
9. Choi, J.-D., Burke, M., Carini, P.: Efficient flow-sensitive interprocedural computation of pointer-induced aliases and side effects. In: POPL, pp. 232–245 (1993)
10. Clarke, E.M.: Model Checking. In: Ramesh, S., Sivakumar, G. (eds.) FST TCS 1997. LNCS, vol. 1346, pp. 54–56. Springer, Heidelberg (1997)
11. Cousot, P., Cousot, R.: Systematic design of program analysis frameworks. In: ACM Symposium on Principles of Programming Languages (POPL), pp. 269–282. ACM Press, New York (1979)
12. Das, M., Lerner, S., Seigle, M.: ESP: path-sensitive program verification in polynomial time. In: Proceedings of the ACM SIGPLAN 2002 Conference on Programming Language Design and Implementation, PLDI 2002, pp. 57–68. ACM, New York (2002)
13. Dean, J., Grove, D., Chambers, C.: Optimization of Object-Oriented Programs Using Static Class Hierarchy Analysis. In: Olthoff, W. (ed.) ECOOP 1995. LNCS, vol. 952, pp. 77–101. Springer, Heidelberg (1995)
14. Dor, N., Adams, S., Das, M., Yang, Z.: Software validation via scalable path-sensitive value flow analysis. In: ISSTA, pp. 12–22 (2004)

15. Emami, M., Ghiya, R., Hendren, L.J.: Context-sensitive interprocedural points-to analysis in the presence of function pointers. In: PLDI 1994: Proceedings of the ACM SIGPLAN 1994 Conference on Programming Language Design and Implementation, pp. 242–256. ACM Press, New York (1994)
16. Fähndrich, M., Rehof, J., Das, M.: Scalable context-sensitive flow analysis using instantiation constraints. In: Conference on Programming Language Design and Implementation (PLDI) (2000)
17. Fändrich, M., Foster, J.S., Su, Z., Aiken, A.: Partial online cycle elimination in inclusion constraint graphs. In: Conference on Programming Language Design and Implementation (PLDI), Montreal, Canada (June 1998)
18. Fecht, C., Seidl, H.: Propagating differences: an efficient new fixpoint algorithm for distributive constraint systems. Nordic J. of Computing 5(4), 304–329 (1998)
19. Feldthaus, A., Millstein, T., Møller, A., Schäfer, M., Tip, F.: Tool-supported refactoring for JavaScript. In: Proceedings of the 2011 ACM International Conference on Object Oriented Programming Systems Languages and Applications, OOPSLA 2011, pp. 119–138. ACM, New York (2011)
20. Fink, S.J., Yahav, E., Dor, N., Ramalingam, G., Geay, E.: Effective typestate verification in the presence of aliasing. ACM Transactions on Software Engineering and Methodology 17(2), 1–34 (2008)
21. Grove, D., Chambers, C.: A framework for call graph construction algorithms. ACM Trans. Program. Lang. Syst. 23(6), 685–746 (2001)
22. Guyer, S.Z., Lin, C.: Client-Driven Pointer Analysis. In: Cousot, R. (ed.) SAS 2003. LNCS, vol. 2694, pp. 214–236. Springer, Heidelberg (2003)
23. Hardekopf, B., Lin, C.: The ant and the grasshopper: fast and accurate pointer analysis for millions of lines of code. In: PLDI, pp. 290–299 (2007)
24. Heintze, N.: Analysis of Large Code Bases: The Compile-Link-Analyze Model (Draft of November 12, 1999)
25. Heintze, N., McAllester, D.: Linear-time subtransitive control flow analysis. SIGPLAN Not. 32(5), 261–272 (1997)
26. Heintze, N., Tardieu, O.: Demand-driven pointer analysis. In: Conference on Programming Language Design and Implementation (PLDI), Snowbird, Utah (June 2001)
27. Heintze, N., Tardieu, O.: Ultra-fast aliasing analysis using CLA: A million lines of C code in a second. In: Conference on Programming Language Design and Implementation (PLDI) (June 2001)
28. Huang, S.S., Smaragdakis, Y.: Morphing: Structurally shaping a class by reflecting on others. ACM Trans. Program. Lang. Syst. 33, 6:1–6:44 (2011)
29. Kidd, N., Reps, T.W., Dolby, J., Vaziri, M.: Finding concurrency-related bugs using random isolation. STTT 13(6), 495–518 (2011)
30. Landi, W., Ryder, B.G.: A safe approximate algorithm for interprocedural aliasing. In: PLDI 1992: Proceedings of the ACM SIGPLAN 1992 Conference on Programming Language Design and Implementation, pp. 235–248. ACM Press, New York (1992)
31. Lattner, C., Lenharth, A., Adve, V.: Making context-sensitive points-to analysis with heap cloning practical for the real world. In: Proceedings of the 2007 ACM SIGPLAN Conference on Programming Language Design and Implementation, PLDI 2007, pp. 278–289. ACM, New York (2007)
32. Lhoták, O., Hendren, L.: Scaling Java points-to analysis using Spark. In: International Conference on Compiler Construction (CC), Warsaw, Poland (April 2003)
33. Lhoták, O., Hendren, L.: Jedd: a BDD-based relational extension of Java. In: Conference on Programming Language Design and Implementation, PLDI (2004)

34. Lhoták, O., Hendren, L.: Evaluating the benefits of context-sensitive points-to analysis using a BDD-based implementation. ACM Trans. Softw. Eng. Methodol. 18, 3:1–3:53 (2008)
35. Lhoták, O., Hendren, L.: Relations as an abstraction for BDD-based program analysis. ACM Trans. Program. Lang. Syst. 19, 19:1–19:63 (2008)
36. Liang, P., Naik, M.: Scaling abstraction refinement via pruning. In: Proceedings of the 32nd ACM SIGPLAN Conference on Programming Language Design and Implementation, PLDI 2011, pp. 590–601. ACM, New York (2011)
37. Liang, P., Tripp, O., Naik, M.: Learning minimal abstractions. In: Proceedings of the 38th Annual ACM SIGPLAN-SIGACT Symposium on Principles of Programming Languages, POPL 2011, pp. 31–42. ACM, New York (2011)
38. Liang, P., Tripp, O., Naik, M., Sagiv, M.: A dynamic evaluation of the precision of static heap abstractions. In: Proceedings of the ACM International Conference on Object Oriented Programming Systems Languages and Applications, OOPSLA 2010, pp. 411–427. ACM, New York (2010)
39. Livshits, B., Whaley, J., Lam, M.S.: Reflection Analysis for Java. In: Yi, K. (ed.) APLAS 2005. LNCS, vol. 3780, pp. 139–160. Springer, Heidelberg (2005)
40. Loginov, A., Yahav, E., Chandra, S., Fink, S., Rinetzky, N., Nanda, M.G.: Verifying dereference safety via expanding-scope analysis. In: ISSTA 2008: International Symposium on Software Testing and Analysis (2008)
41. Might, M., Smaragdakis, Y., Van Horn, D.: Resolving and exploiting the k-CFA paradox: illuminating functional vs. object-oriented program analysis. In: Proceedings of the 2010 ACM SIGPLAN Conference on Programming Language Design and Implementation, PLDI 2010, pp. 305–315. ACM, New York (2010)
42. Milanova, A., Rountev, A., Ryder, B.G.: Parameterized object sensitivity for points-to analysis for Java. ACM Trans. Softw. Eng. Methodol. 14(1), 1–41 (2005)
43. Naik, M., Aiken, A., Whaley, J.: Effective static race detection for Java. In: PLDI, pp. 308–319 (2006)
44. O'Callahan, R.: Generalized Aliasing as a Basis for Program Analysis Tools. PhD thesis, Carnegie Mellon University (November 2000)
45. Palsberg, J., Schwartzbach, M.I.: Object-oriented type inference. In: Conference Proceedings on Object-Oriented Programming Systems, Languages, and Applications, OOPSLA 1991, pp. 146–161. ACM, New York (1991)
46. Pearce, D.J.: Some directed graph algorithms and their application to pointer analysis. PhD thesis, Imperial College of Science, Technology and Medicine, University of London (2005)
47. Pearce, D.J., Kelly, P.H.J., Hankin, C.: Online cycle detection and difference propagation for pointer analysis. In: Proceedings of the Third International IEEE Workshop on Source Code Analysis and Manipulation (2003)
48. Reps, T.: Solving demand versions of interprocedural analysis problems. In: International Conference on Compiler Construction (CC), Edinburgh, Scotland (April 1994)
49. Reps, T.: Program analysis via graph reachability. Information and Software Technology 40(11-12), 701–726 (1998)
50. Reps, T.: Undecidability of context-sensitive data-independence analysis. ACM Trans. Program. Lang. Syst. 22(1), 162–186 (2000)
51. Reps, T., Horwitz, S., Sagiv, M.: Precise interprocedural dataflow analysis via graph reachability. In: ACM Symposium on Principles of Programming Languages (POPL) (1995)

52. Rountev, A., Milanova, A., Ryder, B.G.: Points-to analysis for Java using annotated constraints. In: Conference on Object-Oriented Programming, Systems, Languages, and Applications (OOPSLA), Tampa Bay, Florida (October 2001)
53. Sagiv, M., Reps, T., Wilhelm, R.: Parametric shape analysis via 3-valued logic. ACM Trans. Program. Lang. Syst. 24, 217–298 (2002)
54. Schäfer, M., Sridharan, M., Dolby, J., Tip, F.: Refactoring Java programs for flexible locking. In: Proceeding of the 33rd International Conference on Software Engineering, ICSE 2011, pp. 71–80. ACM, New York (2011)
55. Sharir, M., Pnueli, A.: Two approaches to interprocedural data flow analysis, ch. 7, pp. 189–233. Prentice-Hall (1981)
56. Shivers, O.: Control flow analysis in Scheme. In: Conference on Programming Language Design and Implementation, PLDI (1988)
57. Shoham, S., Yahav, E., Fink, S., Pistoia, M.: Static specification mining using automata-based abstractions. In: Proceedings of the 2007 International Symposium on Software Testing and Analysis, ISSTA 2007, pp. 174–184. ACM, New York (2007)
58. Smaragdakis, Y., Bravenboer, M., Lhoták, O.: Pick your contexts well: understanding object-sensitivity. In: POPL, pp. 17–30 (2011)
59. Sridharan, M., Artzi, S., Pistoia, M., Guarnieri, S., Tripp, O., Berg, R.: F4F: taint analysis of framework-based web applications. In: Proceedings of the 2011 ACM International Conference on Object Oriented Programming Systems Languages and Applications, OOPSLA 2011, pp. 1053–1068. ACM, New York (2011)
60. Sridharan, M., Bodík, R.: Refinement-based context-sensitive points-to analysis for Java. In: Conference on Programming Language Design and Implementation, PLDI (2006)
61. Sridharan, M., Dolby, J., Chandra, S., Schäfer, M., Tip, F.: Correlation Tracking for Points-To Analysis of JavaScript. In: Noble, J. (ed.) ECOOP 2012. LNCS, vol. 7313, pp. 435–458. Springer, Heidelberg (2012)
62. Sridharan, M., Fink, S.J.: The Complexity of Andersen's Analysis in Practice. In: Palsberg, J., Su, Z. (eds.) SAS 2009. LNCS, vol. 5673, pp. 205–221. Springer, Heidelberg (2009)
63. Sridharan, M., Fink, S.J., Bodik, R.: Thin slicing. In: Proceedings of the 2007 ACM SIGPLAN Conference on Programming Language Design and Implementation, PLDI 2007, pp. 112–122. ACM, New York (2007)
64. Sridharan, M., Gopan, D., Shan, L., Bodík, R.: Demand-driven points-to analysis for Java. In: Conference on Object-Oriented Programming, Systems, Languages, and Applications, OOPSLA (2005)
65. Steensgaard, B.: Points-to analysis in almost linear time. In: ACM Symposium on Principles of Programming Languages, POPL (1996)
66. Tip, F., Palsberg, J.: Scalable propagation-based call graph construction algorithms. In: Conference on Object-Oriented Programming, Systems, Languages, and Applications (OOPSLA), Minneapolis, MN (October 2000)
67. Torlak, E., Chandra, S.: Effective interprocedural resource leak detection. In: Proceedings of the 32nd ACM/IEEE International Conference on Software Engineering, ICSE 2010, pp. 535–544. ACM, New York (2010)
68. Tripp, O., Pistoia, M., Fink, S.J., Sridharan, M., Weisman, O.: TAJ: effective taint analysis of web applications. In: PLDI (2009)
69. T.J. Watson Libraries for Analysis (WALA), http://wala.sf.net.
70. Whaley, J., Avots, D., Carbin, M., Lam, M.S.: Using Datalog with Binary Decision Diagrams for Program Analysis. In: Yi, K. (ed.) APLAS 2005. LNCS, vol. 3780, pp. 97–118. Springer, Heidelberg (2005)

71. Whaley, J., Lam, M.S.: An Efficient Inclusion-Based Points-To Analysis for Strictly-Typed Languages. In: Hermenegildo, M.V., Puebla, G. (eds.) SAS 2002. LNCS, vol. 2477, pp. 180–195. Springer, Heidelberg (2002)

72. Whaley, J., Lam, M.S.: Cloning-based context-sensitive pointer alias analysis using binary decision diagrams. In: Conference on Programming Language Design and Implementation (PLDI) (2004)

73. Whaley, J., Rinard, M.: Compositional pointer and escape analysis for Java programs. In: Conference on Object-Oriented Programming, Systems, Languages, and Applications (OOPSLA) (November 1999)

74. Wilson, R.P., Lam, M.S.: Efficient context-sensitive pointer analysis for C programs. In: Conference on Programming Language Design and Implementation, PLDI (1995)

75. Yahav, E., Fink, S.: The SAFE experience. In: Engineering of Software, pp. 17–33. Springer, Heidelberg (2011)

76. Zhu, J., Calman, S.: Symbolic pointer analysis revisited. In: Conference on Programming Language Design and Implementation (PLDI) (2004)

Immutability

Alex Potanin[1], Johan Östlund[2], Yoav Zibin[3], and Michael D. Ernst[4]

[1] School of Engineering and Computer Science, VUW, Wellington, New Zealand
[2] Department of Information Technology, Uppsala University, Uppsala, Sweden
[3] Google New York, NY, USA
[4] Computer Science and Engineering, University of Washington, WA, USA

Abstract. One of the main reasons aliasing has to be controlled, as highlighted in another chapter [1] of this book [2], is the possibility that a variable can unexpectedly change its value without the referrer's knowledge. This book will not be complete without a discussion of the impact of *immutability* on reference-abundant imperative object-oriented languages. In this chapter we briefly survey possible definitions of immutability and present recent work by the authors on adding immutability to object-oriented languages and how it impacts aliasing.

1 Introduction

Traditional imperative object-oriented (OO) programs consist of objects that have *state* and *behaviour*[1]. The behaviour is modelled by the methods. The state is represented by the values of an object's fields — which can either be primitives or references to other objects. *Immutable objects* are those whose state does not change after they are initialised [3–12].

Immutability information is useful in many software engineering tasks, including modeling [13], verification [14], compile- and run-time optimizations [15, 5, 16], program transformations such as refactoring [17], test input generation [18], regression oracle creation [19, 20], invariant detection [21], specification mining [22], and program comprehension [23]. The importance of immutability is highlighted by the documentation of the Map interface in Java that states: "Great care must be exercised if *mutable objects* are used as map keys. The behavior of a map is not specified if the value of an object is changed in a manner that affects equals comparisons while the object is a key in the map."

The notion of immutability is not as straightforward as it might seem, and many different definitions of immutability exist. Immutability may be deep (transitive) or shallow. In deep immutability, every object referred to by an immutable object must itself be immutable; in shallow immutability, the object's fields cannot be reassigned, but their referents may be mutated. Immutability guarantees may hold for every field of an object, or may exclude certain fields such as those used for caching. Immutability may be abstract or concrete. Concrete immutability forbids any change to an object's in-memory representation; abstract immutability permits benevolent side effects that do

---

[1] For example: `http://docs.oracle.com/javase/tutorial/java/concepts/object.html`.

D. Clarke et al. (Eds.): Aliasing in Object-Oriented Programming, LNCS 7850, pp. 233–269, 2013.

not affect the abstraction, such as caching values, rebalancing trees, etc. Immutability guarantees may hold immediately or may be delayed. An immediate guarantee holds as soon as the constructor completes; a delayed guarantee permits initialization of a data structure to continue, effectively modifying an immutable object, which is necessary to allow circular initialisation for immutable data structures. Immutability guarantees can be about objects or references. A read-only reference cannot be used for mutation, but the underlying object can be mutated by an aliasing reference; an immutable object is never changed by any reference to it. This paper discusses these and other issues, and presents language designs that address them.

Outline. Section 2 introduces the rich concept of immutability and its variations. Section 3 outlines the current state of immutability support in object-oriented programming languages. Section 4 provides a number of motivations and describes advantages of proposed ways to support immutability mostly on top of a Java-like language. Section 5 quickly tours through the major recent proposals for adding immutability while extracting common themes and highlighting the differences. Section 6 discusses the immutability concept in more general setting, and Section 7 concludes.

2   What Is Immutability?

An immutable program component remains the same over time. Equivalently, changes to an immutable program component are forbidden.

An immutable object (Section 2.1) never changes. By contrast, a read-only reference (Section 2.2) cannot be used for mutation, but the referred-to object might change via other references. Assignment of fields/variables (Section 2.3) is not a mutation of the referred-to object but is sometimes confused with it.

Currently, there is no support in Java (or any mainstream OO language) to express and check object immutability or read-only references. Rather, programmers must use external tools that add these capabilities, or else resort to manual inspection.

2.1   Immutable Objects

An *immutable object* [11, 12] cannot be modified.

When every object of a given class is immutable, then we say the class is immutable. Examples of immutable classes in Java [24] include String and most subclasses of Number[2] such as Integer and BigDecimal. An immutable class contains no mutating methods that update/modify the receiver; rather, if a different value is required, a client calls a constructor or producer method that returns a new object. In addition to not providing mutating methods, all fields must be hidden from clients (e.g. made private).

Even if a class is not immutable, specific objects of that class may be immutable [11, 12]. For example, some instances of List in a given program may be immutable, whereas others can be modified. Here is example Immutability Generic Java (IGJ) [10] code that instantiates the same class LinkedList as both *mutable* and *immutable* object:

---

[2] java.util.concurrent.AtomicInteger is mutable, though.

```
LinkedList<Mutable> lm = new LinkedList<Mutable>();
LinkedList<Immutable> li = new LinkedList<Immutable>();
```

Object lm can be changed or mutated, for example by adding or removing elements. By contrast, li cannot be changed or mutated, even though it is implemented by the same LinkedList code.

2.2   Read-Only References

A *read-only* reference[3] [3–9] cannot be used to modify its referent. However, there may exist mutable aliases to the object elsewhere in the system. In other words, normal references carry the privilege to mutate the referent, and read-only references do not.

Usually a read-only reference's type is a supertype of a mutable reference's type, so a mutable reference can be used in any context in which a read-only one is legal. For example, continuing the previous list example, this is legal:

```
LinkedList<ReadOnly> lro = lm;
```

Note that lm is a mutable alias that can be used to mutate the list.

Since read-only references do not preclude the existence of mutable aliases, read-only references do not guarantee object immutability, unless read-only references are combined with an alias/escape analysis to guarantee that no mutable aliases to an object exist [25, 3].

A *const* pointer in C++ is a shallow read-only reference.

Read-Only Method Parameters. If a method does not mutate one of its formal parameters, then that formal parameter can be annotated as read-only. Then, it is legal to call the method using a mutable, immutable, or read-only reference as the actual argument. If a method does mutate a formal parameter, then the method can only be called by passing in a mutable object as an argument. The receiver is treated the same as the other formal parameters.

Pure Methods. A *pure* method [26–29] has no externally-visible *side effects*. In other words, calling a pure method is guaranteed to leave every existing object in an unchanged state.[4] This is a stronger guarantee than asserting that every method parameter is (deeply) read-only, since it applies to static variables as well. For example:

```
1 @Pure
2 boolean has(String x) {
3    for (String i : items) {
```

---

[3] "Reference immutability" is another standard term, but we use "read-only reference" to avoid potential confusion if a reader mis-interprets "reference immutability" as stating that the reference itself is immutable. Also see Section 2.3.

[4] Just as there are multiple varieties of immutability, there are multiple varieties of purity. Different definitions forbid all mutations, or permit only mutations of object allocated after the method is entered, or permit benevolent side effects on previously-existing objects.

```
4    if (x == i) { return true; }
5  }
6  return false;
7 }
```

2.3 Non-assignability

Assignment is a property of a variable: it indicates whether the variable is permitted to be reassigned. Assignment of a variable is unrelated to mutation. In particular, no object is mutated in this code:

```
1  Date myVar = ...;  // local variable
2  ...
3  myVar = anotherDate;
```

Assignment of a field is a mutation of the object that contains the field, but is *not* a mutation of either the object that was previously in the field or of the object that is subsequently in the field. For example, in

```
myClass.itsDate = anotherDate;
```

no Date object has been mutated.

The final keyword in Java [24] prohibits assignment but not mutation. In the following example, the variable v is declared final and thus it cannot be reassigned after the declaration, though its value can be mutated:

```
1  final Foo v = new Foo();  // local variable
2  ...
3  v = new Foo();  // compile-time error: assignment is forbidden
4  v.mutate();  // OK: mutation is permitted
```

2.4 Deep vs. Shallow Immutability; Abstract vs. Concrete Immutability

When specifying an immutability property, it is necessary to state whether the property is deep or shallow, and which fields of the object's representation are relevant.

Immutability and read-only references may be deep or shallow, depending on whether transitively-referred to objects are also required to be immutable. In deep immutability, it is forbidden not only to re-assign an object's fields, but also to mutate them. In shallow immutability, it is forbidden to re-assign an object's fields, but permitted to mutate them. Consider the following example:

```
1  class C {
2    D f;
3  }
4  class D {
5    int x;
6  }
7
```

```
8   C<Immutable> myC = ...;
9   ...
10  myC.f = otherD;  // illegal under both deep and shallow immutability
11  myC.f.x++;  // legal under shallow immutability, illegal under deep
```

Most often, a client desires a deep rather than a shallow immutability guarantee. An OO program's representation of some object or concept in the real world often spans multiple objects in the program. As a simple example, a list may be represented by many Link objects connected in a linked list. A client does not know or care about the specific data representation, but wants a guarantee of immutability of the abstract value that the concrete data represents.

An orthogonal axis of immutability is which fields should be considered as protected by the immutability guarantee. A *benevolent side effect* is one that changes an object's representation, but does not change the object's abstract value. A common example is filling in a field that caches a value. Another example is the move-to-front optimization that speeds up looking up elements in a set that is represented as a list. Thus, it is possible that a change to an object's representation is *not* a change to the object's abstract value.

Similarly, just like with ownership-like schemes [30], it might make sense to make only part of an object deeply immutable (e.g. the fields specific to its *representation*) while keeping the other fields mutable. For example, an immutable list might contain mutable elements.

Most often, a client is concerned with the abstract value rather than details of the object's representation such as cached values or the order of objects in a set. However, reasoning about low-level properties such as interactions with the memory system may require a guarantee of *representation immutability* rather than *abstract immutability*.

3   Immutability in the Mainstream Programming Languages

In non-functional object-oriented languages immutability support is extremely limited. The only clear examples are the use of const in C++ and the use of the final keyword in Java, which we shall see are not enough to guarantee immutability of objects. We discuss existing support in popular languages and in the following Section we look into how recent proposals improve the state of affairs.

3.1   C++ const

C [31] and C++ [32] provide a const keyword for specifying immutability. C++'s const keyword is more commonly used as an aid when declaring interfaces, rather than as a way of declaring symbolic constants [32]. Furthermore, there are a number of pitfalls that led Java's designers to omit const.

Because of numerous loopholes, the const notation in C++ does not provide a guarantee of immutability even for accesses through the const reference. First, an unchecked cast can remove const from a variable. Second, C++'s const_cast may also be applied arbitrarily and is not dynamically checked. The const_cast operator was added to C++ to discourage, but not prohibit, use of C-style casts, accidental use of which may convert a read-only pointer or reference to a mutable one. Third, because C++ is not a type safe language, one can (mis)use type system weaknesses such as unions and varargs (unchecked variable-length procedure arguments) to bypass the restrictions on mutability prescribed by const.

Another criticism of C++'s const is that C++ does not permit parameterization of code based on the immutability of a variable. Use of const may lead to code duplication, where several versions of a function are needed depending on const-ness. An example is the two versions of strchr in the C++ standard library.

Finally, declaring a method as const (or read-only) only stops it from modifying the receiver and does not prevent it from modifying any other objects. Thus, a const (read-only) method in C++ is not a *pure* method.

C++'s const is shallow with respect to pointers but deep with respect to fields. C++ permits the contents of a read-only pointer to be modified, and read-only methods protect only the local state of the enclosing object. To guarantee transitive non-mutability, an object's state must be (transitively) held directly in variables/fields rather than accessed by a pointer. However, this precludes sharing, which is a serious disadvantage. Additionally, whereas C++ permits specification of const at each level of pointer dereference, it does not permit doing so at each level of a multi-dimensional array.

Most C++ experts advocate the use of const (for example, Meyers advises using const wherever possible [33]). However, as with many other type systems (including those of C++ and Java), some programmers feel that the need to specify types outweighs the benefits of type checking. At least three studies have found that static type checking reduces development time or errors [34–36]. We are not aware of any empirical (or other) evaluations regarding the costs and benefits of immutability annotations.

A common criticism of const is that transforming a large existing codebase to achieve const correctness is difficult, because const pervades the code: typically, all (or none) of a codebase must be annotated. This propagation effect is unavoidable when types or externally visible representations are changed. Inference of const annotations (such as that implemented by Foster et al. [37]) eliminates such manual effort. Even without a type inference, some [6] found the work of annotation to be greatly eased by fully annotating each part of the code in turn while thinking about its contract or specification, rather than inserting partial annotations and attempting to address type checker errors one at a time. The proper solution, of course, is to write const annotations in the code from the beginning, which takes little or no extra work, as the designer should have already made decisions about mutability.

3.2 Java `final`

Java [24] does not support const. Instead a final keyword was introduced. Java does not have a concept of "const references", and so there is no support for final methods, in the sense that only such methods would be invokable on final receivers. (In Java, final applied to a method means something entirely different: the method cannot be overridden in a subclass.) Similar to C++, marking a member as final only protects the variable, not the object the variable refers to, from being mutated. Thus, immutability in C++ and Java is not *transitive*.

3.3   Immutability in Non-Object-Oriented Languages

Functional languages, such as ML [38], default all variables to being immutable. OCaml [39] combines object-orientation with a `mutable` annotation on fields (for example, references are implemented as a one-compartment mutable record). However, there is little support from type systems to distinguish *mutable* operations from *read-only* operations.

4   How Can We Improve on the State of the Art?

The two major improvements achieved by the immutability proposals of the last decade are: (1) support for *transitive* read-only by supporting the enforcement of not just the reference to an object but also any further references from such object being read-only and (2) support for *object immutability* rather than just read-only references thus guaranteeing that no unexpected *alias* to an immutable object can change its state. Javari [6] supports the former, while Joe_3 [12] and OIGJ [11] support both.

To achieve read-only references, Javari utilizes additional annotations on any variable declaration in Java (e.g. `readonly`) that is then checked by the type system to guarantee that no read-only reference is assigned to or modified. Javari's implementation in Java is available for download[5].

Joe_3 utilizes an ownership-based type system and a very simple effect system which keeps track of which object is modified and prevents any modifications to objects which are *immutable* or *read-only*. A Polyglot-based[6] prototype implementation is available.

OIGJ makes use of Java's generic types to allow the types to state whether the object is *mutable* or *immutable* when creating the object. OIGJ also supports *read-only* types. A Checker-Framework-based[7] prototype implementation is available.

This section presents examples taken from three recent immutability proposals by the authors. Subsection 4.1 presents enforcement of contracts and read-only access to internal data in the Javari system [6] which supports read-only references. Subsection 4.2 presents a larger example similar to `LinkedList` from the Java collections written in the OIGJ [11] system supporting both read-only references and object immutability, among other features. Subsection 4.3 shows how to support flexible lists and context-based read-only in Joe_3 [12], a system supporting object immutability and more. Both OIGJ and Joe_3 make use of *ownership* [40] to be able to properly support deep immutability as discussed later in this chapter. Please refer to Figure 7 for a summary of supported features in the abovementioned systems and several others.

4.1   Cases from Javari

This subsection shows examples of read-only as found in the Javari system.

---

[5] http://types.cs.washington.edu/javari/

[6] http://www.cs.cornell.edu/projects/polyglot/

[7] http://types.cs.washington.edu/checker-framework/

Enforcement of contracts. Consider a voting system containing the following routine:

```
1 ElectionResults tabulate(Ballots votes) { ... }
```

In order to permit verification (e.g. double checking) of the results, it is necessary to safeguard the integrity of the ballots. This requires a machine-checked guarantee that the routine does not modify its input votes. Using Javari, the specification of tabulate could declare that votes is read-only:

```
1 ElectionResults tabulate(readonly Ballots votes) {
2    ... //cannot tamper with the votes
3 }
```

and the compiler ensures that implementers of tabulate do not violate the contract.

Read-only access to internal data. Accessor methods often return data that already exists as part of the representation of the module.

For example, consider the Class.getSigners method, which returns the entities that have digitally signed a particular implementation. In JDK 1.1.1, its implementation is simple and efficient:

```
1   class Class {
2     private Object[] signers;
3     Object[] getSigners() {
4       return signers;
5     }
6   }
```

This is a security hole, because a malicious client can call getSigners and then add elements to the signers array.

Javari permits the following solution:

```
1   class Class {
2     private Object[] signers;
3     readonly Object[] getSigners() {
4       return signers;
5     }
6   }
```

The readonly keyword ensures that the caller of Class.getSigners cannot modify the returned array, thus permitting the simple and efficient implementation of the method to remain in place without exposing the representation to undesired changes.[8]

An alternate solution to the getSigners problem, which was actually implemented in later versions of the JDK, is to return a copy of the array signers [41]. This works,

---

[8] The returned array is aliased by the signers field, so Class code can still change it even if external code cannot. The specification of getSigners does not state the desired semantics in this case, so this is an acceptable implementation. If a different semantics were desired, the method specification could note that the returned reference reflects changes to the signers of the Class; alternately, the method specification, or an external analysis, might require that the result is used before the next modification of signers.

but is expensive. For example, a file system may allow a client read-only access to its contents:

```
1    class FileSystem {
2      private List<Inode> inodes;
3      List<Inode> getInodes() {
4        ··· //Unrealistic to copy
5      }
6    }
```

Javari allows the programmer to avoid the high cost of copying `inodes` by writing the return type of the method as:

```
readonly List<readonly Inode> getInodes()
```

This return type prevents the `List` or any of its contents from being modified by the client. As with all parameterized classes, the client specifies the type argument, including whether it is read-only or not, independently of the parameterized typed.

In this case, the list returned is declared to be read-only and contain read-only elements, and, thus, a client of `getInodes` is unable to modify the list or its elements.

4.2   Cases from OIGJ

Figure 1 shows an implementation of `LinkedList` in OIGJ that follows closely the Sun's implementation but does not contain any additional bounds checking and supporting code that would prevent it from fitting on one page. We explain this example in three stages: (i) we first explain the data-structure, i.e., the fields of a list and its entries (lines 1–6), (ii) then we discuss the *raw* constructors that enable the creation of immutable lists (lines 7–21), and (iii) finally we dive into the complexities of inner classes and iterators (lines 23–47). Note that method guards [42] state that the method is only applicable if the type variable matches the bound stated by the guard (e.g. method `next` inside the `ListItr` can only be called if `ItrI` is a subtype of `Mutable`).

LinkedList data-structure. A linked list has a header field (line 6) pointing to the first entry. Each entry has an `element` and pointers to the `next` and `prev` entries (line 3). We explain first the immutability and then the ownership of each field.

Note that we assume that `O` refers to the current class instance owner and `I` or `ItrI` refer to the appropriate current immutability that is either class instance or method call specific.

An (im)mutable list contains (im)mutable entries, i.e., the entire data-structure is either mutable or immutable as a whole. Hence, all the fields have the same immutability `I`. The underlying generic type system propagates the immutability information without the need for special typing rules.

Next consider the ownership of the fields of `LinkedList` and `Entry`. `This` on line 6 expresses that the reference `header` points to an `Entry` owned by `this`, i.e., the entry is encapsulated and cannot be aliased outside of `this`. `O` on line 3 expresses that the owner of `next` is the same as the owner of the entry, i.e., a linked-list owns *all* its entries. Note how the generics mechanism propagates the owner parameter, e.g., the type of

```
1 class Entry<O,I,E> {
2   E element;
3   Entry<O,I,E> next, prev;
4 }
5 class LinkedList<O,I,E> {
6   Entry<This,I,E> header;
7   <I extends Raw>? LinkedList() {
8     this.header = new Entry<This,I,E>();
9     header.next = header.prev = header;
10  }
11  <I extends Raw>? LinkedList(Collection<?,ReadOnly,E> c) {
12    this(); this.addAll(c);
13  }
14  <I extends Raw>? void addAll(Collection<?,ReadOnly,E> c) {
15    Entry<This,I,E> succ = this.header, pred = succ.prev;
16    for (E e : c) {
17      Entry<This,I,E> en=new Entry<This,I,E>();
18      en.element=e; en.next=succ; en.prev=pred;
19      pred.next = en; pred = en; }
20    succ.prev = pred;
21  }
22  int size() {···}
23  <ItrI extends ReadOnly> Iterator<O,ItrI,I,E> iterator() {
24    return this.new ListItr<ItrI>();
25  }
26  void remove(Entry<This,Mutable,E> e) {
27    e.prev.next = e.next;
28    e.next.prev = e.prev;
29  }
30  class ListItr<ItrI> implements Iterator<O,ItrI,I,E> {
31    Entry<This,I,E> current;
32    <ItrI extends Raw>? ListItr() {
33      this.current = LinkedList.this.header;
34    }
35    <ItrI extends Mutable>? E next() {
36      this.current = this.current.next;
37      return this.current.element;
38    }
39    <I extends Mutable>? void remove() {
40      LinkedList.this.remove(this.current);
41    }
42 } }
43 interface Iterator<O,ItrI,CollectionI,E> {
44   boolean hasNext();
45   <ItrI extends Mutable>? E next();
46   <CollectionI extends Mutable>? void remove();
47 }
```

Fig. 1. LinkedList<O,I,E> in OIGJ

`this.header.next.next` is `Entry<This,I,E>`. Thus, the owner of all entries is the `this` object, i.e., the list. OIGJ provides *deep ownership* or *owners-as-dominators* guarantees as discussed in another chapter [43].

Finally, note that the field `element` has no immutability nor owner parameters, because they will be specified by the client that instantiates the list type, e.g., `LinkedList<This,Mutable,Date<World,ReadOnly>>`

Immutable object creation. A constructor that is making an immutable object must be able to set the fields of the object. It is not acceptable to mark such constructors as `Mutable`, which would permit arbitrary side effects, possibly including making mutable aliases to `this`. OIGJ uses a fourth kind of immutability, *raw*, to permit constructors to perform limited side effects without permitting modification of immutable objects. Phrased differently, `Raw` represents a partially-initialized *raw* object that can still be arbitrarily mutated, but after it is cooked (fully initialized), then the object might become immutable. The constructors on lines 7 and 11 are guarded with `Raw`, and therefore can create both mutable and immutable lists.

Objects must not be captured in their raw state to prevent further mutation after the object is cooked. If a programmer could declare a field, such as `Date<O,Raw>`, then a raw date could be stored there, and later it could be used to mutate a cooked immutable date. Therefore, a programmer can write the `Raw` type only after the `extends` keyword, but *not* in any other way. As a consequence, in a `Raw` constructor, `this` can only escape as `ReadOnly`.

An object becomes *cooked* either when its new expression (construction) finishes executing or when its owner is *cooked*. The entries of the list (line 6) are `this`-owned. Indeed, the entries are mutated after their constructor has finished, but before their owner (list) is cooked, on lines 9, 19, and 20. This shows the power of combining immutability and ownership: we are able to create immutable lists *only* by using the fact that the list owns its entries. If those entries were *not* owned by the list, then this mutation of entries might be visible to the outside world, thus breaking the guarantee that an immutable object never changes. By enforcing ownership, OIGJ ensures that such illegal mutations cannot occur.

OIGJ requires that all access and assignment to a `this`-owned field must be done via `this`. For example, see `header`, on lines 8, 9, 15, and 33. In contrast, fields `next` and `prev` (which are not `this`-owned) do not have such a restriction, as can be seen on lines 27–28. Note that inner classes are treated differently, and are allowed to access the outer object's `this`-owned fields. This arguably gives a more flexible system, which for instance allows the iterator class in the example, but at the cost of less clear containment properties.

Iterator implementation and inner classes. An *iterator* has an underlying *collection*, and the immutability of these two objects might be different. For example, you can have

- a mutable iterator over a mutable collection (the iterator supports both `remove()` and `next()`),
- a mutable iterator over a readonly/immutable collection (the iterator supports `next()` but not `remove()`), or

– a readonly iterator over a mutable collection (the iterator supports `remove()` but not `next()`, which can be useful if you want to pass an iterator to a method that may not advance the iterator but may remove the current element).

Consider the `Iterator<O,ItrI,CollectionI,E>` interface defined on lines 43–47, and used on lines 23 and 30. `ItrI` is the iterator's immutability, whereas `CollectionI` is intended to be the underlying collection's immutability (see on line 30 how the collection's immutability `I` is used in the place of `CollectionI`). Line 45 requires a mutable `ItrI` to call `next()`, and line 46 requires a mutable `CollectionI` to call `remove()`.

Inner class `ListItr` (lines 30–42) is the implementation of `Iterator` for list. Its full name is `LinkedList<O,I,E>.ListItr<ItrI>`, and on line 30 it extends `Iterator<O,ItrI,I,E>`. It reuses the owner parameter `O` from `LinkedList`, but declares a new immutability parameter `ItrI`. An inner class, such as `ListItr<ItrI>`, only declares an immutability parameter because it inherits the owner parameter from its outer class. `ListItr` and `LinkedList` have the same owner `O`, but different immutability parameters (`ItrI` for `ListItr`, and `I` for `LinkedList`). `ListItr` must inherit `LinkedList`'s owner because it directly accesses the (`this`-owned) representation of `LinkedList` (line 33), which would be illegal if their owner was different. For example, consider the types of `this` and `LinkedList.this` on line 33:

```
Iterator<O,ItrI,···> thisIterator = this;
LinkedList<O,I,···> thisList = LinkedList.this;
```

Because line 32 sets the bound of `ItrI` to be `Raw`, `this` can be mutated. By contrast, the bound of `I` is `ReadOnly`, so `LinkedList.this` cannot.

Finally, consider the creation of a new *inner* object on line 24 using `this.new ListItr<ItrI>()`. This expression is type-checked both as a method call (whose receiver is `this`) and as a constructor call. Observe that the bound of `ItrI` is `ReadOnly` (line 23) and the guard on the constructor is `Raw` (line 32), which is legal because a `Raw` constructor can create both mutable and immutable objects.

4.3   Cases from Joe$_3$

This subsection presents a different take on how to specify read-only and immutability, in which the context where an object is used determines its mutability properties.

A short note on effects.   Joe$_3$ employs a very simple effects system to specify what a class or method will mutate. The effects are specified in terms of contexts (or owners) inspired by Joe$_1$ [44]. In Joe$_3$ context parameters are decorated with modes which govern how objects belonging to a particular context may be treated.

Separating Mutability of List and its Contents.   Figure 2 shows part of an implementation of a list class. The class is parameterized over permissions (`data` in this case) which specify that the list has privilege to reference objects in that context. The parameter `data` is decorated with the mode read-only (denoted '-'), indicating that the list will never cause write effects to objects owned by `data`. The owner of the list is called `owner` and is implicitly declared. The method `getFirst()` is annotated with `revoke owner`, which

```
1  class Link<data- strictlyoutside owner> {
2    data:Object obj = null;
3    owner:Link<data> next = null;
4  }
5
6  class List<data- strictlyoutside owner> {
7    this:Link<data> first = null;
8    void addFirst(data:Object obj) {
9      this:Link<data> tmp = new this:Link<data>();
10     tmp.obj = obj;
11     tmp.next = this.first;
12     this.first = tmp;
13   }
14   void filter(data:Object obj) {
15     this:Link<data> tmp = this.first;
16     if (tmp == null) return;
17     while (tmp.next != null)
18       if (tmp.next.obj == obj)
19         tmp.next = tmp.next.next;
20       else
21         tmp = tmp.next;
22     if (this.first != null && this.first.obj == obj)
23       this.first = this.first.next;
24   }
25   data:Object getFirst() revoke owner { return this.first.obj; }
26 }
```

Fig. 2. Fragment of a list class. As the data owner parameter is declared read-only (via '-') in the class header, no method in List may modify an object owned by data. Observe that the syntactic overhead is minimal for an ownership types system.

means that the method will not modify the list or its transitive state. This means the same as if owner- and this- would have appeared in the class header. This allows the method to be called from objects where the list owner is read-only. Finally, strictlyoutside means that the data context must not be the same context as the owner of the list.

This list class can be instantiated in four different ways, depending on the access rights to the owners in the type held by the current context:

- both the list and its data objects are immutable, which only allows getFirst() to be invoked, and its resulting object is immutable;
- both are mutable, which imposes no restrictions;
- the list is mutable but the data objects are not, which imposes no additional restrictions, getFirst() returns a read-only reference; and
- the data objects are mutable, but the list not, which only allows getFirst() to be invoked, and the resulting object is mutable.

The last form is interesting and relies on the fact that it is known, courtesy of ownership types, that the data objects are not part of the representation of the list. Without this distinction one could easily create an example where a mutable alias can be returned from a read-only object.

4.4 Complementing Immutability

In this subsection we explain why blindly adding immutability support to any OO language with aliasing might not be such a good idea and how it can be addressed by careful application of various ownership techniques discussed in the rest of this book.

Boyland [45] criticizes existing proposals for handling read-only references on the following points:

1. Read-only references can be aliased, for example by capturing a method argument;
2. A read-only annotation does not express whether
   (a) the referenced *object* is immutable, so the referent is known to never change;
   (b) a read-only reference is unique and thus effectively immutable;
   (c) mutable aliases of a read-only reference can exist, which makes possible *observational exposure*, which occurs when changes to state are observed through a read-only reference.

Essentially, Boyland is criticizing reference immutability for not being object immutability. In some contexts, object immutability is more useful, and in other contexts, reference immutability is more useful. Furthermore, as we noted earlier, different contexts require other differences (such as representation immutability for reasoning about the memory system, and abstract immutability for reasoning about client code semantics). Boyland's criticisms can be addressed, for those contexts where object immutability is desired, by augmenting reference immutability with object immutability.

For example, Joe$_3$ addresses all of these problems. First, Joe$_3$ supports owner-polymorphic methods, which can express that a method does not capture one or more of its arguments. Second, owners are decorated with modes that govern how the objects owned by that owner will be treated in a particular context. Together with auxiliary constructs inherited from Joline [46], the modes can express immutability both in terms of 2.a) and 2.b), and read-only which permits the existence of mutable aliases (2.c). Moreover, Joe$_3$ supports fractional permissions [47] — converting a mutable unique reference into several immutable references for a certain context. This allows safe representation exposure without the risk for observational exposure.

OIGJ and Joe$_3$ allow both read-only references and immutable objects in the same language. This provides the safety desired by Boyland's second point, but also allows coding patterns which do rely on observing changes in an object. In order to support such flexibility it appears necessary to employ some kind of *alias control* mechanism, which in the cases of OIGJ and Joe$_3$ is ownership.

Ownership and Immutability. Ownership types [40, 48] impose a structure on the references between objects in the program heap. Languages with ownership, such as for instance Joline [46] and OGJ [49], prevent aliasing to the internal state of an object. While preventing exposure of owned objects, ownership does not address exposing immutable parts of an object which cannot break encapsulation, even though the idea was originally sprung out of a proposal supporting that [30].

One possible application of ownership types is the ability to reason about read and write effects [50] which has complimentary goals to object immutability. Universes [9] is a Java language extension combining ownership and read-only references. Most ownership systems enforce that all reference chains to an owned object pass through the owner. Universes relaxes this requirement by enforcing this rule only for mutable references, i.e., read-only references may be shared without restriction.

Universes, OIGJ, and Joe$_3$ provide what we call context-based immutability. Here it is possible to create a writable list with writable elements and pass it to some other context where the elements are read-only. This other context may add elements to the list (or reorder them) but not mutate the elements, while the original creator of the list does not lose the right to mutate the elements.

A read-only reference to an object does not preclude the existence of mutable references to the same object elsewhere in the system. This allows observational exposure [45] — for good and evil. Object immutability imposes all restrictions of a read-only reference, but also guarantees that no aliases with write permission exist in the system. One simple way of creating an immutable object is to move a *unique* reference into a variable with immutable type [51, 12].

5   A Selection of Recent Immutability Proposals

We will now present in more detail the major proposals improving on the status quo in modern popular OO languages, i.e., final in Java and const in C++. Javari [6] was presented in 2004, adding read-only references. In 2007 Immutability Generic Java (IGJ) [10] was proposed, adding immutability and immutability parameterization. Joe$_3$ [12], proposed in 2008, uses ownership, external uniqueness — to support transition from mutable to immutable — and a trivial effects system to support immutability and context-based immutability. OIGJ [11], published in 2010, again employs ownership to achieve immutability, albeit a less strict variant of ownership allowing for more flexibility. OIGJ uses the existing Java generics machinery to encode ownership, which removes the need for an extra parameter clause on classes and methods. While we describe the proposals by the authors of this chapter in great detail, we also provide an overview of the other complementary proposals in the Section 5.5.

5.1   Javari

The Javari [6] programming language extends Java to allow programmers to specify and enforce reference immutability constraints. A read-only reference cannot be used to modify the object, including its transitive state, to which it refers.

Javari's type system differs from previous proposals (for Java, C++, and other languages) in a number of ways. First, it offers reference, not object, immutability. Second, Javari offers guarantees for the entire transitively reachable state of an object — the state of the object and all state reachable by following references through its (non-static) fields. A programmer may use the type system to support reasoning about either the representation state of an object or its abstract state; to support the latter, parts of a class can be marked as not part of its abstract state.

Third, Javari combines static and dynamic checking in a safe and expressive way. Dynamic checking is necessary only for programs that use immutability downcasts, but such downcasts can be convenient for interoperation with legacy code or to express facts that cannot be proved by the type system. Javari also offers parameterization over immutability.

Experience with over 160,000 lines of Javari code, including the Javari compiler itself, indicates that Javari is effective in practice in helping programmers to document their code, reason about it, and prevent and eliminate errors.

The language design issues include the following:

– Should Javari use new keywords (and possibly other syntax) to indicate reference immutability, or should it use Java's annotation mechanism[9]? (Or, should a prototype implementation use annotations, even if Javari itself should eventually use keywords?)
– The immutability downcast adds expressiveness to the Javari language, but it also adds implementation complexity and (potentially pervasive) run-time overhead. Is a language that lacks immutability downcasts practical?
– How can uses of reflection, serialization, and other Java constructs that are outside the scope of the Java type system be handled, particularly without adding run-time overhead?
– The existing Javari template mechanism is unsatisfactory. It is orthogonal to Java generics (even in places where it seems that generics should be a satisfactory solution).

Javari has presented a type system that is capable of expression, compile-time verification, and run-time checking of reference immutability constraints. Read-only references guarantee that the reference cannot be used to perform any modification of a (transitively) referred-to object. The type system should be generally applicable to object-oriented languages, but for concreteness we have presented it in the context of Javari, an extension to the full Java 5 language, including generic types, arrays, reflection, serialization, inner classes, exceptions, and other idiosyncrasies. Immutability polymorphism (templates) for methods are smoothly integrated into the language, reducing code duplication. Tschantz et al. [6] provided a set of formal type rules for a core calculus that models the Javari language and used it to prove type soundness for the Javari type system.

Javari provides a practical and effective combination of language features. For instance, we describe a type system for reference rather than object immutability. Reference immutability is useful in more circumstances, such as specifying interfaces, or objects that are only sometimes immutable. Furthermore, type-based analyses can run after type checking in order to make stronger guarantees (such as object immutability) or to enable verification or transformation. The system is statically type-safe, but optionally permits downcasts that transform compile-time checks into run-time checks for specific references, in the event that a programmer finds the type system too constraining. The language is backward compatible with Java and the Java Virtual Machine, and is interoperable with Java. Together with substantial experience with a prototype for

---

[9] http://java.sun.com/j2se/1.5.0/docs/guide/language/annotations.html

a closely related dialect [3], these design features provide evidence that the language design is effective and useful.

The Javari language presented is an evolutionary improvement of an earlier dialect [3], which we call "Javari2004". In what follows we highlight the main features of the Javari language and justify them in the context of a large user study done using the previous version of the language.

Distinguishing Assignability from Mutability. Javari2004's `mutable` keyword declares that a field is both assignable and mutable: there is no way to declare that a field is only assignable or only mutable. Javari's `assignable` and `mutable` keywords highlight the orthogonality of assignability and mutability, and increase the expressiveness of the language. See appendix of Javari paper for examples of the use of `assignable` and `mutable`.

Generic Types. Javari provides a detailed treatment of generic classes that smoothly integrates read-only references with them. Javari2004 does not supports generic classes, though the OOPSLA 2004 paper speculates about a macro expansion mechanism that is syntactically, but not semantically, similar to the way that Java 5 treats type parameters. Java 5 compiles type parameters via type erasure, but Javari2004 treated the mutability parameters (which appeared in the same list as the type parameters) via code duplication; this distinction complicates implementation, understanding, and use.

Arrays. As with generic classes, Javari permits programmers to independently specify the mutability of each level of an array. By contrast, Javari2004's specification states: "`readonly int[][]` and `readonly (readonly int[])[]` are equivalent," forbidding creation of a read-only array of mutable items.

Within current Javari one may make such as declaration as follows: `readonly Object[]`. One could also declare a mutable array of read-only objects: `/*mutable*/ (readonly Object)[]`.

Method Templates. Javari2004 integrated the syntax for templating a method over mutability with the syntax for Java 5's generic types.

For example, the following method signature is a templated method.

```
public <RO> RO List<RO Invariant> get(RO PptTopLevel ppt) RO;
```

The `<RO>` at the beginning of the signature specifies that `RO` is a type parameter.

Whether a parameter is intended to be a normal type parameter or a mutability type parameter must be inferred from its usage, greatly complicating a compiler (and the prototype Javari2004 implementation required distinct syntax to ease the compiler's task [52, 3]).

Furthermore, Javari2004 allows declaring an arbitrary number of mutability type parameters. Only a single mutability type parameter was deemed sufficient by the Javari designers, so Javari uses a much simpler mechanism (`romaybe`) for indicating a variable mutability. This new approach highlights the orthogonality of the Java 5's generic types and Javari's mutability polymorphism for methods. Furthermore, it does not require any run-time representation of the polymorphism. IGJ [10] and OIGJ [11] have both demonstrated that building on generic types provides a much nicer treatment for immutability parameterization completely removing the need for romaybe.

5.2 IGJ

Immutability Generic Java. (IGJ) is a language that supports class and object immutability and read-only references. Each object is either mutable or immutable, and each reference is Immutable, Mutable, or ReadOnly. Inspired by work that combines ownership and generics [49], the distinctions are expressed without changing Java's syntax by adding one new type parameter (at the beginning of the list of type parameters):

```
 1   //An immutable reference to an immutable date; mutating the
 2   //referent is prohibited, via this or any other reference.
 3   Date<Immutable> immutD = new Date<Immutable>();
 4   //A mutable reference to a mutable date; mutating the referent
 5   //is permitted, via this or any other mutable reference.
 6   Date<Mutable> mutD = new Date<Mutable>();
 7   //A read-only reference to any date; mutating the referent is
 8   //prohibited via this reference, but the referent may be changed
 9   //via an aliasing mutable reference.
10   Date<ReadOnly> roD = ··· ? immutD : mutD;
```

Line 3 shows object immutability in IGJ, and Line 10 shows read-only references.

Java prohibits changes to type arguments, such as in Line 10, to avoid a type loophole. More detailed discussion of the Java language and type system is given by Bracha et al. [53] and Igarashi et al. [54]. Line 10 is legal in IGJ, because IGJ allows covariant changes in the immutability parameter. IGJ even allows covariant changes in other type parameters if mutation is disallowed, e.g., List<ReadOnly,Integer> is a subtype of List<ReadOnly,Number>.

IGJ satisfies the following design principles:

Transitivity. More accurately, IGJ does not require transitivity. Rather, it provides a mechanism by which programmers can specify exactly where transitivity should be applied — and then that transitivity is enforced by the type system.

IGJ provides transitive (deep) immutability that protects the entire abstract state of an object. For example, an immutable graph contains an immutable set of immutable edges.

C++ does not support such transitivity because its const-guarantee does not traverse pointers, i.e., a pointer in a const object can mutate its referent.

IGJ also permits excluding a field from the abstract state. For example, fields used for caching can be mutated even in an immutable object.

Static. IGJ has no runtime representation for immutability, such as an "immutability bit" that is checked before assignments or method calls. IGJ designers believe that testing at runtime whether an object is immutable [4] hampers program understanding.

The IGJ compiler works by type-erasure, without any run-time representation of reference or object immutability, which enables executing the resulting code on any JVM without runtime penalty. A similar approach was taken by Generic Java (GJ) [53] that extended Java 1.4. As with GJ, libraries must either be retrofitted with IGJ types, or fully converted to IGJ, before clients can be compiled. IGJ is backward compatible: every legal Java program is a legal IGJ program.

Polymorphism. IGJ abstracts over immutability without code duplication by using generics and a flexible subtype relation. For instance, all the collection classes in C++'s STL have two overloaded versions of `iterator`, `operator[]`, etc. The underlying problem is the inability to return a reference whose immutability depends on the immutability of `this`:

```
const Foo& getFieldFoo() const;
     Foo& getFieldFoo();
```

Simplicity. IGJ does not change Java's syntax. A small number of additional typing rules make IGJ more restrictive than Java. On the other hand, IGJ's subtyping rules are more relaxed, allowing covariant changes in a type-safe manner.

Phrased differently, IGJ uses rules which fit naturally into Java's design.

Most of the IGJ terminology was borrowed from Javari [6] such as assignable, readonly, mutable, and `this`-mutable. In Javari, `this`-mutable fields are mutable as lvalue and readonly as rvalue. Javari does not support object immutability, and its read-only references are more limited than that of IGJ because Javari has no `this`-mutable parameters, return types, or local variables. Javari's keyword `romaybe` is in essence a template over immutability. IGJ uses generics directly to achieve the same goal.

Javari also supports `this`-assignable fields, which pass the assignability (`final` or `assignable`) of `this` to a field.

Finally, Javari uses `?readonly` which is similar to Java's wildcards. Consider, for instance, the class `Foo` written in Javari's syntax:

```
class Foo { mutable List<Object> list; }
```

Then in a `readonly Foo` the type of `list` is

```
mutable List<? readonly> Object
```

which is syntactic sugar for

```
mutable List<? extends readonly Object
             super mutable Object>
```

Thus, it is possible to insert only mutable elements to `list`, and retrieve only read-only elements. Such complexities, in IGJ designers point of view, make IGJ easier to use than Javari.

5.3 Joe$_3$

This section will present Joe$_3$ in a bit more detail. Joe$_3$ is a Java-like language with deep ownership, owner-polymorphic methods, external uniqueness, an effects (revocation) system and a simple mode system which decorates owners with permissions to indicate how references with the annotated owners may be used. The annotation of owners with modes is the main novelty in Joe$_3$. The modes indicate that a reference may be read or written (+), only read (-), or that the reference is immutable (*). Read and immutable annotations on an owner in the class header represent a promise that the code in the class body will not change objects owned by that owner. The key to preserving and respecting immutability and read-only in Joe$_3$ is a simple effects system, rooted in ownership types, and inspired by Clarke and Drossopoulou's Joe$_1$ [44]. Classes, and hence objects, have rights to read or modify objects belonging to certain owners; only a minor extension to the type system of Clarke and Wrigstad's Joline [55, 56] is required to ensure that these rights are not violated.

Classes are parameterized with owners related to each other by an inside/outside nesting relation. An owner is a permission to reference the representation of another object. Class headers have this form:

```
class List<data- outside owner> { ⋯ }
```

Each class has at least two owner parameters, `this` and `owner`, which represent the representation of the current object and the representation of the owner of the current object, respectively. In the example above, the `List` class has an additional permission to reference objects owned by `data`, which is nested outside `owner`. Types are formed by instantiating the owner parameters, `this:List<owner>`. An object with this type belongs to the representation of the current object and has the right to reference objects owned by `owner`. There are two nesting relations between owners, inside and outside. They exist in two forms each, one reflexive (`inside`/`outside`) and one non-reflexive (`strictly-inside`/`strictly-outside`). Thus, going back to our list example, a type `this:List<this>` denotes a list object belonging to the current representation, holding objects in the current representation.

Apart from ownership types, the key ingredients in Joe$_3$ are the following:

- (externally) unique types (written `unique[p]:Object`), a special *borrowing* construct for temporarily treating a unique type non-uniquely, and *owner casts* for converting unique references permanently into normal references.
- modes on owners — mutable '+', read-only '-', and immutable '*'. These appear on every owner parameter of a class and owner polymorphic methods, though not on types.
- an effects revocation clause on methods which states which owners will not be modified in a method. An object's default set of rights is derived from the modes on the owner parameters in the class declaration.

Annotating owners at the level of classes (that is, for all instances) rather than types (for each reference) is a trade-off. Rather than permitting distinctions to be made using modes on a per reference basis, Joe$_3$ admits only per class granularity. Some potential expressiveness is lost, though the syntax of types does not need to be extended. Nonetheless, the effects revocation clauses regain some expressiveness that per reference modes would give. Another virtue of using per class rather than per reference modes is that some covariance problems found in other proposals are avoided, as what you can do with a reference depends on the context and is not a property of the reference. The covariance problem, similar to Java generics, is essentially that immutability variance in the element parameter of a list makes it possible to mutate read-only elements.

```
1  class ListWriter<o+ outside owner, data- strictlyoutside o> {
2    void mutateList(o:List<data> list) {
3      list.addFirst(new data:Object());
4    }
5  }
6  class ListReader<o- outside owner, data+ strictlyoutside o> {
7    void mutateElements(o:List<data> list) {
8      list.elementAt(0).mutate();
9    }
10 }
11 class Example {
12   void example() {
13     this:List<world> list = new this:List<world>();
14     this:ListWriter<this, world> w = new this:Writer<this, world>();
15     this:ListReader<this, world> r = new this:Reader<this, world>();
16     w.mutateList(list);
17     r.mutateElements(list);
18   }
19 }
```

Fig. 3. Different views of the same list can exist at the same time. r can modify the elements of list but not the list itself, w can modify the list object, but not the list's contents, and instances of Example can modify both the list and its contents.

Context-Based Read-Only. As shown in Figure 3, different clients of the list can have different views of the same list at the same time. The class ListReader does not have permission to mutate the list, but has no restrictions on mutating the list elements. Dually, the ListWriter class can mutate the list but not its elements.

As owner modes only reflect what a class is allowed to do to objects with a certain owner, ListWriter can add data objects to the list that are read-only to itself and the list, but writable by Example and ListReader. This is a powerful and flexible idea. For example, Example can pass the list to ListWriter to filter out certain objects in the list. ListWriter can then consume or change the list, or copy its contents to another list, *but not modify them.* ListWriter can then return the list to Example, without Example losing its right to modify the objects obtained from the returned list. This is similar to the context-based read-only in Universes-based systems [57, 58]. In contrast, however, Joe₃ does not allow representation exposure via read-only references.

Immutable Object Initialization. Immutable objects need to be mutated in their construction phase. Unless caution is taken the constructor might leak a reference to this (by passing this to a method) or mutate other immutable objects of the same class. The standard solution to this problem in related proposals is to limit the construction phase to the constructor [10, 11, 59]. Continuing initialization by calling auxiliary methods *after* the constructor returns is simply not possible. Joe₃, on the other hand, permits *staged construction*, as demonstrated in Figure 4. In this example a client uses a factory to create an immutable list. The factory creates a unique list and populates it. The list is then destructively read and returned to the caller as an immutable. Interestingly enough, if

```
1 class Client<p* outside owner, data+ strictlyoutside p> {
2   void method() {
3     this:Factory<p, data> f = new this:Factory<p, data>();
4     p:List<data> immutable = f.createList();
5   }
6 }
7 class Factory<p* inside world, data+ strictlyoutside p> {
8   p:List<data> createList() {
9     unique[p]:List<data> list = new p:List<data>();
10    borrow list as temp+ l in { // 2nd stage of construct.
11      l.add(new data:Object());
12    }
13    return list--; // unique reference returned
14  }
15 }
```

Fig. 4. Staged construction of an immutable list

an inference mechanism were employed to remove trivial uses of borrowing, such as the one in the figure, then this example could be done without the extra baggage.

Fractional Permissions. Using uniqueness and Joline's borrowing statement, Joe₃ can encode a variant of Boyland's Fractional Permissions [47], where a mutable reference is turned into an immutable reference for a limited time, after which it can be reestablished as a mutable reference with no residual aliasing. This is described in more detail with an example in Section 6.3.

5.4 OIGJ

This section presents the OIGJ language extension that expresses both ownership and immutability information.

OIGJ introduces two new type parameters to each type, called the *owner parameter* and the *immutability parameter*. For simplicity of presentation, we assume that the special type parameters are at the beginning of the list of type parameters. We stress that generics in Java are erased during compilation to bytecode and do not exist at run time, therefore OIGJ does not incur any run-time overhead (nor does it support run-time casts).

In OIGJ, all classes are subtypes of the parameterized root type Object<O, I> that declares an owner and an immutability parameter. In OIGJ, the first parameter is the owner (O), and the second is the immutability (I). All subclasses must invariantly preserve their owner and immutability parameter. The owner and immutability parameters form two separate hierarchies, which are shown in Figure 5. These parameters cannot be extended, and they have no subtype relation with any other types. The subtyping relation is denoted by $\preceq$, e.g., Mutable $\preceq$ ReadOnly. Subtyping is invariant in the owner parameter and covariant in the immutability parameter.

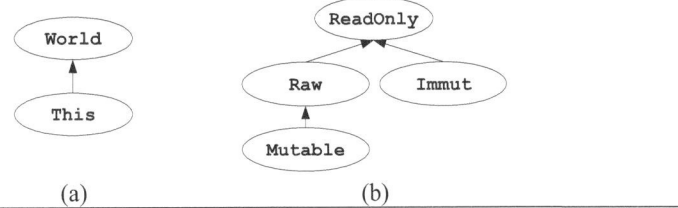

Fig. 5. The type hierarchy of (a) ownership and (b) immutability parameters. World means the entire world can access the object, whereas This means that this owns the object and no one else can access it. A Immut/Mutable reference points to an immutable/mutable object. A ReadOnly reference points to a mutable or immutable object, and therefore cannot be used to mutate the object. Raw represents an object under construction whose fields can be assigned.

Note that the *owner parameter* O is a *type*, whereas the *owner* of an object is an *object*. For example, if the owner parameter is This, then the owner is the object this. Therefore, the owner parameter (which is a type) at compile time corresponds to an owner (which is an object) at run time. (See also paragraph ***Owner vs. Owner-parameter*** below.)

OIGJ syntax borrows from *conditional Java* (cJ) [42], where a programmer can write method *guards*. A guard of the form <X extends Y>? METHOD_DECLARATION has a dual meaning: (i) the method is applicable only if the type argument that substitutes X extends Y, and (ii) the bound of X inside METHOD_DECLARATION changes to Y. The guards are used to express the immutability of this: a method receiver or a constructor result. For example, a method guarded with <I extends Mutable>? means that (i) the method is applicable only if the receiver is mutable and therefore (ii) this can be mutated inside the method.

Class definition example. Figure 6 shows an example of OIGJ syntax. A class definition declares the owner and immutability parameters (line 1); by convention we always denote them by O and I and they always extend World and ReadOnly. If the extends clause is missing from a class declaration, then we assume it extends Object<O, I>.

Immutability example. Lines 3–10 show different kinds of immutability in OIGJ: immutable, mutable, and readonly. A read-only and an immutable reference may seem similar because neither can be used to mutate the referent. However, line 10 shows the difference between the two: a read-only reference may point to a mutable object. Phrased differently, a read-only reference may not mutate its referent, though the referent may be changed via an aliasing mutable reference.

Java's type arguments are invariant (neither covariant nor contravariant), to avoid a type loophole [54], so line 10 is illegal in Java. Line 10 is legal in OIGJ, because OIGJ safely allows covariant changes in the immutability parameter (but not in the owner parameter). OIGJ *restricts* Java by having additional typing rules, while at the same time OIGJ also *relaxes* Java's subtyping relation. Therefore, neither OIGJ nor Java subsumes the other, i.e., a legal OIGJ program may be illegal in Java (and vice versa). However, because generics are erased during compilation, the resulting bytecode can be executed on any JVM.

```
 1  class Foo<O extends World,I extends ReadOnly> {
 2      // An immutable reference to an immutable date.
 3      Date<O,Immut> imD = new Date<O,Immut>();
 4      // A mutable reference to a mutable date.
 5      Date<O,Mutable> mutD = new Date<O,Mutable>();
 6      // A read−only reference to any date.
 7      // Both roD and imD cannot mutate their referent,
 8      // however the referent of roD might be mutated by an alias,
 9      // whereas the referent of imD is immutable.
10      Date<O,ReadOnly> roD = ··· ? imD : mutD;
11      // A date with the same owner and immutability as this.
12      Date<O,I> sameD;
13      // A date owned by this; it cannot leak.
14      Date<This,I> ownedD;
15      // Anyone can access this date.
16      Date<World,I> publicD;
17      // Can be called on any receiver; cannot mutate this.
18      // The method guard "<···>?" is part of cJ's syntax~[42].
19      <I extends ReadOnly>? int readonlyMethod() {···}
20      // Can be called only on mutable receivers; can mutate this.
21      <I extends Mutable>? void mutatingMethod() {···}
22      // Constructor that can create (im)mutable objects.
23      <I extends Raw>? Foo(Date<O,I> d) {
24          this.sameD = d;
25          this.ownedD = new Date<This,I>();
26          // Illegal, because sameD came from the outside.
27          // this.sameD.setTime(···);
28          // OK, because Raw is transitive for owned fields.
29          this.ownedD.setTime(···);
30  } }
```

Fig. 6. An example of OIGJ syntax

The immutability of sameD (line 12) depends on the immutability of this, i.e., sameD is (im)mutable in an (im)mutable Foo object. Similarly, the owner of sameD is the same as the owner of this.

Ownership example. Lines 12–16 show three different owner parameters: O, This, and World. The owner parameter is invariant, i.e., the subtype relation preserves the owner parameter. For instance, the types on lines 12–16 have no subtype relation with each other because they have different owner parameters.

Reference ownedD cannot leak outside of this, whereas references sameD and publicD can potentially be accessed by anyone with access to this. Although sameD and publicD can be accessed by the same objects, they cannot be stored in the same places: publicD can be stored anywhere on the heap (even in a static public variable) whereas sameD can only be stored inside its owner.

We use $O(\ldots)$ to denote the function that takes a type or a reference, and returns its owner parameter; e.g., $O(\texttt{ownedD}) = \texttt{This}$. Similarly, function $I(\ldots)$ returns the immutability parameter; e.g., $I(\texttt{ownedD}) = \texttt{I}$. We say that an object o is *this-owned* (i.e., owned by this) if $O(\texttt{o}) = \texttt{This}$; e.g., ownedD is this-owned, but sameD is not. OIGJ prevents leaking this-owned objects by requiring that this-owned fields (and methods with this-owned arguments or return-type) can only be used via this. For example, this.ownedD is legal, but foo.ownedD is illegal.

Owner vs. owner-parameter. Now we explain the connection between the *owner parameter* $O(o)$, which is a generic type parameter at *compile time*, and the *owner* $\theta(o)$, which is an object at *run time*. This is an owner parameter that represents an owner that is the current this object, and World represents the root of the ownership tree (we treat World both as a type parameter and as an object that is the root of the ownership tree). Formally, if $O(o) = \texttt{This}$ then $\theta(o) = \texttt{this}$, if $O(o) = \texttt{O}$ then $\theta(o) = \theta(\texttt{this})$, and if $O(o) = \texttt{World}$ then $\theta(o) = \texttt{World}$. Two references (in the same class) with the same owner parameter (at compile time) will point to objects with the same owner (at run time), i.e., $O(o_1) = O(o_2)$ implies $\theta(o_1) = \theta(o_2)$.

Finally, OIGJ provides the following *ownership guarantee*: o' can point to o iff $o' \preceq_\theta \theta(o)$. By definition of $\preceq_\theta$, we have that for all o: (i) $o \preceq_\theta o$, (ii) $o \preceq_\theta \theta(o)$, and (iii) $o \preceq_\theta$ World. By part (iii), if $\theta(o) = \texttt{World}$ then anyone can point to o. On lines 12–16, we see that this can point to ownedD, sameD, publicD, whose owner parameters are This, O, World, and whose owners are this, $\theta(\texttt{this})$, World. This conforms with the ownership guarantee according to parts (i), (ii), and (iii), respectively. More complicated pointing patterns can occur by using multiple owner parameters, e.g., an entry in a list can point to an element owned by the list's owner, such as in List<This,I,Date<O,I>>.

There is a similar connection between the immutability type parameter (at compile time) and the object's immutability (at run time). Immutability parameter Mutable or Immut implies the object is mutable or immutable (respectively), ReadOnly implies the referenced object may be either mutable or immutable and thus the object cannot be mutated through the read-only reference. Raw implies the object is still raw and thus can still be mutated, but it might become immutable after it is cooked.

Method guard example. Lines 19 and 21 of Figure 6 show a read-only and a mutating method. These methods are *guarded* with <...>?. Conditional Java (cJ) [42] extends Java with such guards (a.k.a. conditional type expressions). Note that cJ changed Java's syntax by using the question mark in the guard <...>?. OIGJ paper uses cJ for convenience. However, the OIGJ implementation uses type annotations [60] without changing Java's syntax, for conciseness and compatibility with existing tools and code bases.

A guard such as <T extends U>? METHOD_DECLARATION has a dual purpose: (i) the method is included only if T extends U, and (ii) the bound of T is U inside the method. In our example, the guard on line 21 means that (i) this method can only be called on a Mutable receiver, and (ii) inside the method the bound of I changes to Mutable. For instance, (i) only a mutable Foo object can be a receiver of mutatingMethod, and (ii) field sameD is mutable in mutatingMethod. cJ also ensures that the condition of an overriding method is equivalent or weaker than the condition of the overridden method.

IGJ used *declaration annotations* to denote the immutability of this. In this chapter, OIGJ uses cJ to reduce the number of typing rules and handle inner classes more flexibly.[10] OIGJ does not use the full power of cJ: it only uses guards with immutability parameters. Moreover, we modified cJ to treat guards over constructors in a special way.

To summarize, on lines 19–23 we see three guards that change the bound of I to ReadOnly, Mutable, and Raw, respectively. Because the bound of I is already declared on line 1 as ReadOnly, the guard on line 19 can be removed.

Constructor example. The constructor on line 23 is guarded with Raw, and therefore can create both mutable and immutable objects, because all objects start their life cycle as raw. This constructor illustrates the interplay between *ownership* and *immutability*, which makes OIGJ more expressive than previous work on immutability. OIGJ uses ownership information to prolong the *cooking phase* for owned objects: the cooking phase of this-owned fields (ownedD) is longer than that of non-owned fields (sameD). This property is critical to type-check the collection classes.

Consider the following code:

```
1 class Bar<O extends World, I extends ReadOnly> {
2   Date<O, Immut> d = new Date<O, Immut>();
3   Foo<O, Immut> foo = new Foo<O, Immut>(d);
4 }
```

OIGJ provides the following *immutability guarantee*: an immutable object cannot be changed after it is *cooked*. A This-owned object is cooked when its owner is cooked (e.g., foo.ownedD). Any other object is cooked when its constructor finishes (e.g., d and foo). The intuition is that ownedD cannot leak and so the outside world cannot observe this longer cooking phase, whereas d is visible to the world after its constructor finishes and must not be mutated further. The constructor on lines 23–30 shows this difference between the assignments to sameD (line 24) and to ownedD (line 25): sameD can come from the outside world, whereas ownedD must be created inside this. Thus, sameD cannot be further mutated (line 27) whereas ownedD can be mutated (line 29) until its owner is cooked.

An object in a raw method, whose immutability parameter is I, is still considered raw (thus the modified body can still assign to its fields or call other raw methods) iff the object is thisor this-owned. Informally, we say that Raw is *transitive* only for thisor this-owned objects. For example, the receiver of the method call sameD.setTime(...) is not thisnor this-owned, and therefore the call on line 27 is illegal; however, the receiver of ownedD.setTime(...) is this-owned, and therefore the call on line 29 is legal.

5.5   Other Immutability Proposals

JAC Similarly to the proposals in this chapter, JAC [7] has a readonly keyword indicating transitive immutability, an implicit type readonly T for every class and

---

[10] The OIGJ implementation uses *type annotations* to denote immutability of this. A type annotation @Mutable on the receiver is similar to a cJ <I extends Mutable>? construct, but it separates the distinct roles of the receiver and the result in inner class constructors.

interface T defined in the program, and a `mutable` keyword. However, the other aspects of the two languages' syntax and semantics are quite different. For example, JAC provides a number of additional features, such as a larger access right hierarchy (`readnothing` < `readimmutable` < `readonly` < `writeable`) and additional keywords (such as `nontransferrable`) that address other concerns than immutability. The JAC authors propose implementing JAC by source rewriting, creating a new type `readonly` T that has as methods all methods of T that are declared with the keyword `readonly` following the parameter list (and then compiling the result with an ordinary Java compiler). However, the return type of any such method is `readonly`. For example, if class `Person` has a method `public Address getAddress() readonly`, then `readonly Person` has method `public readonly Address getAddress() readonly`. In other words, the return type of a method call depends on the type of the receiver expression and may be a supertype of the declared type, which violates Java's typing rules. Additionally, JAC is either unsound for, or does not address, arrays of `readonly` objects, casts, exceptions, inner classes, and subtyping. JAC `readonly` methods may not change any static field of any class. The JAC paper suggests that `readonly` types can be supplied as type variables for generic classes without change to the GJ proposal, but provides no details. By contrast to JAC, in Javari the return type of a method does not depend on whether it is called through a read-only reference or a non-read-only one. Both IGJ and OIGJ provide a thorough treatment of the generic types and immutability bringing the JAC generics proposal to its logical conclusion.

The above comments also explain why use of read-only interfaces in Java is not satisfactory for enforcing read-only references. A programmer could define, for every class C, an interface RO_C that declares the read-only methods and that achieves transitivity through changing methods that returned (say) B to return RO_B. Use of RO_C could then replace uses of Javari's `readonly` C. This is similar to JAC's approach and shares similar problems. For instance, to permit casting, C would need to implement RO_C, but some method return and argument types are incompatible. Furthermore, this approach does not allow read-only versions of arrays or even `Object`, since RO_Object would need to be implemented by `Object`. It also forces information about a class to be maintained in two separate files, and it does not address run-time checking of potentially unsafe operations or how to handle various other Java constructs. Javari sidesteps these fundamental problems by extending the Java type system rather than attempting to work within it.

Modes for Read-Only. Skoglund and Wrigstad [4] take a different attitude toward immutability than other work: "In our point of [view], a read-only method should only protect its enclosing object's transitive state when invoked on a read reference but not necessarily when invoked on a write reference." A read (read-only) method may behave as a `write` (non-read-only) method when invoked via a `write` reference; a caseModeOf construct permits run-time checking of reference writeability, and arbitrary code may appear on the two branches. This suggests that while it can be proved that read references are never modified, it is not possible to prove whether a method may modify its argument. In addition to read and write references, the system provides context and any references that behave differently depending on whether a method is invoked on a read or write context. Compared to this work and JAC, Javari's, IGJ's and OIGJ's type parameterization gives a less ad hoc and more disciplined way to specify families of declarations.

Immutability Specification. Pechtchanski and Sarkar [5] provide a framework for immutability specification along three dimensions: lifetime, reachability, and context. The lifetime is always the full scope of a reference, which is either the complete dynamic lifetime of an object or, for parameter annotations, the duration of a method call. The reachability is either shallow or deep. The context is whether immutability applies in just one method or in all methods. The authors provide 5 instantiations of the framework, and they show that immutability constraints enable optimizations that can speed up some benchmarks by 5–10%.

Even if all methods of a class are state preserving, the resulting instances might not be immutable, because a mutable `this` object could escape the constructor and its fields can be mutated directly, for instance, if the constructor stores all created objects in a static set. The proposals in this chapter permit both of the lifetimes and supplies deep reachability, which complements the shallow reachability provided by Java's `final` keyword.

Capabilities. Capabilities for sharing [8] are intended to generalize various other proposals for immutability and uniqueness. When a new object is allocated, the initial pointer has 7 access rights: read, write, identity (permitting address comparisons), exclusive read, exclusive write, exclusive identity, and ownership (giving the capability to assert rights). Each (pointer) variable has some subset of the rights. These capabilities give an approximation and simplification of many other annotation-based approaches.

Why not add read-only? Boyland [61] explains "Why we should not add `readonly` to Java (yet)" and concludes that readonly does not address observational exposure, i.e., modifications on one side of an abstraction boundary that are observable on the other side. IGJ's immutable objects address such exposure because their state cannot change, e.g., an immutable address in a person object can be safely shared among many person objects. Sometimes it is impossible to avoid observational exposure, e.g., when a container changes and iterators to the inside of the container exists. Java designed its iterator classes to be *fail-fast*, i.e., the iterator will fail if the collection is mutated (which cannot happen in immutable collections).

Boyland's second criticism was that the *transitivity* principle (see end of Section 3) should be selectively applied by the designer, because, "the elements in the container are not notionally part of the container" [61]. In Joe_3, IGJ, and OIGJ, a programmer can solve this problem by using a different immutability for the container and its elements.

Effects. Effect systems [62–64] specify what state (in terms of regions or of individual variables) can be read and modified by a procedure; they can be viewed as labeling (procedure) types with additional information, which the type rules then manipulate. Type systems for immutability can be viewed as a form of effect system. The proposals in this chapter are finer-grained than typical effect systems, operate over references rather than values, and consider all state reachable from a reference.

Universes. Universe Types [65] were the first ownership type system to provide support for read-only references by introducing "owners as modifiers" discipline. Here, if an object does not have a right to access an object because of ownership restrictions, it is still allowed a read-only reference to such object. This greatly improved the expressiveness of the language albeit weakened the ownership guarantees - as a result both OIGJ and Joe₃ tried to mitigate these issues by providing a more granular interaction between immutability and ownership properties in a language. Finally, the functional methods of Universes [65] are pure methods that are not allowed to modify anything (as opposed to merely not being allowed to modify the receiver object).

Immutable Objects. Immutable Objects for a Java-like Language (**IOJ**) [66] associates with each type its mutability and owner. In contrast to OIGJ, IOJ does not have generics, nor readonly *references*. Moreover, in IOJ, the constructor cannot leak a reference to this. Haack and Poll [66] later added flexible initialization of immutable objects [59], i.e., an immutable object may still be mutated after its constructor returns. They use the annotations RdWr, Rd, Any, and myaccess, which corresponds to our Mutable, Immut, ReadOnly, and I. In addition, they have an inference algorithm that automatically infers the end of object initialization phases. (Their algorithm infers which variables are Fresh(n), which resembles our Raw. However, the programmer cannot write the Fresh annotation explicitly.)

Immutability Inference. Porat et al. [67] provide a type inference that determines (deep) immutability of fields and classes. (Foster et al. [37] provide a type inference for C's (non-transitive) const.) A field is defined to be immutable if its value never changes after initialization and the object it refers to, if any, is immutable. An object is defined to be immutable if all of its fields are immutable. A class is immutable if all its instances are. The analysis is context-insensitive in that if a type is mutable, then all the objects that contain elements of that type are mutable. Libraries are neither annotated nor analyzed: every virtual method invocation (even equals) is assumed to be able to modify any field. The paper discusses only class (static) variables, not member variables. The technique does not apply to method parameters or local variables, and it focuses on object rather than reference immutability, as in Javari. An experiment indicted that 60% of static fields in the Java 2 JDK runtime library are immutable.

Constructing Immutable Objects. Non-null types [68–71] has a similar challenge that IGJ has in constructing immutable objects: a partially-initialized object may escape its constructor. IGJ uses @AssignsFieldsto mark a constructor of immutable objects, and a partially initialized object can escape only as ReadOnly. Non-null types uses a Raw annotation *on references* that might point to a partially-initialized object, and *on methods* to denote that the receiver can be Raw. A non-null field of a Raw object has different lvalue and rvalue: it is possible to assign only non-null values to such field, whereas reading from such field may return null. Similarly to IGJ, non-null types cannot handle cyclic data-structures, express the staged initialization paradigm in which the construction of an object continues after its constructor finishes. OIGJ [11] however addressed most of these IGJ shortcomings.

Frozen Objects. Leino et al. [72] show how ownership can help support immutability by allowing programmers to decide when the object should become immutable. This system takes a verification approach rather than a simple type checker. Frozen Objects show how flexible the initialization stage can potentially be in the presence of ownership and immutability, while, for example, OIGJ shows how much flexibility can be achieved while staying at the type checking level.

Other Proposals. Huang et al. [42] propose an extension of Java (called cJ) that allows methods to be provided only under some static subtyping condition. For instance, a cJ generic class, Date<I>, can define

```
<I extends Mutable>? void setDate(···)
```

which will be provided only when the type provided for parameter Iis a subtype of Mutable. Designing IGJ on top of cJ would make METHOD-INVOCATION RULEredundant, at the cost of replacing IGJ's method annotations with cJ's conditional method syntax. The rest of IGJ's typing rules will remain the same.

Finally, IGJ uses the type system to check immutability statically. Controlling immutability at runtime (for example using assertions or Eiffel-like contractual obligations) falls outside the scope of this chapter.

5.6   Summary of Immutability Work

Figure 7 summarizes several proposals and their supported features. The systems included in the table represent the state of the art of read-only and immutable. Except Joe$_3$, the table includes (in order) SafeJava [51], Universes [57, 73–75], Jimuva [76], Javari [77], IGJ [78], JAC [79], ModeJava [80] and Effective Ownership [81]. We now discuss the different features in the table.

Joe$_3$ and SafeJava support staged construction of immutables.

Boyland suggests that copying rights may lead to observational exposure and proposes that the rights instead be split. Only the one with a complete set of rights may modify an object. SafeJava does not support borrowing to immutables and hence cannot model fractional permissions. It is unclear how allowing borrowing to immutables in SafeJava would affect the system, especially in the presence of back doors that break encapsulation.

To be able to retrieve writable objects from a read-only list, the elements in the list cannot be part of the list's representation. Joe$_3$, Universes, Jimuva and SafeJava can express this through ownership types. Only OIGJ and Joe$_3$ systems, thanks to owner nesting information, allow two non-sibling lists to share mutable data elements. Javari and IGJ allow this through ad-hoc mutable fields which can circumvent read-only if an object stores a reference to itself in a mutable field.

The alias modes proposed by Noble et al. [82]. Here we only describe how the modes have been interpreted for the purpose of Figure 7. The *rep* mode denotes a reference belonging to an object's representation and so should not appear in its interface. A defensive interpretation of *arg* is that all systems that have object or class immutability partially support *arg*, but only OIGJ and Joe$_3$ systems support *parts* of an object being immutable. The *free* mode, interpreted as being equal to uniqueness, is supported by

Feature	OIGJ	Joe₃	SafeJava	Universes	Jimuva	Javari	IGJ	ModeJava	JAC	EO
Expressiveness										
Staged const.	$\times^8$	√	√	×	×	×	×	×	×	×
Fract. perm.	×	√	×	×	×	×	×	×	×	×
Non-rep fields	√	√	$\sqrt{}^1$	$\sqrt{}^1$	$\sqrt{}^1$	$\times^2$	$\times^2$	×	×	×
Flexible Alias Protection Modes										
arg	√	√	$\times^3$	×	$\times^3$	$\times^3$	$\times^3$	$\times^3$	×	×
rep	√	√	√	√	√	×	×	×	×	√
free	×	√	√	√	×	×	×	×	×	×
val [4]	×	×	×	×	×	×	×	×	×	×
var	√	√	√	√	√	√	√	√	√	√
Immutability										
Class	√	√	×	×	√	√	√	$\times^5$	$\times^5$	×
Object	√	√	√	×	√	×	√	×	×	×
Context-based	√	√	×	√	×	$\times^6$	$\times^6$	$\times^6$	×	×
Read-only ref.	√	√	×	√	×	√	√	√	√	√
Shallow Immutability	√	√	×	√	×	√	√	√	√	√
Deep Immutability	√	√	×	×	×	√	√	×	×	×
Abstract Value Immutability	√	√	×	√	×	√	√	√	√	√
Concrete Representation Immutability	√	√	×	√	×	×	×	×	×	×
Confinement and Alias Control										
OT	√	√	√	√	√	×	×	×	×	√
OP meths	√	√	√	√	√	×	×	×	×	×
OAM	×	×	×	√	×	×	×	×	×	√
OAD	$\times^7$	√	$\times^7$	×	×	×	×	×	×	×
Uniqueness	×	√	√	√	×	×	×	×	×	×

Fig. 7. Brief overview of related work. OT=ownership types, OP=owner polymorphic, OAM=owner-as-modifier, OAD=owner-as-dominator, EO=Effective Ownership. [1]) not as powerful as there is no owner nesting; two non sibling lists cannot share *mutable* data elements; [2]) mutable fields can be used to store a reference to this and break read-only; [3]) no modes on owners, and hence no immutable parts of objects; [4]) none of the systems deal with value semantics for complex objects; [5]) if all methods of a class are read-only the class is effectively immutable; [6]) limited notion of contexts via this-mutability; [7]) allows breaking of owners-as-dominators with inner classes. [8]) Raw constructors can construct both mutable and immutable objects, but once the constructor returns immutability is fixed.

Joe₃ and SafeJava. No system handles *val*ue semantics except for primitive types. The *var* aliasing mode expresses non-*rep* references which may be aliased and changed freely as long as they do not interfere with the other modes, for example, in assignments.

6   Discussion

We have shown so far how immutability support can be extended from non-transitive read-only references (e.g. const or final) to transitive read-only references (Javari) and further to object immutability (OIGJ and Joe$_3$) with ownership-like features. A number of interesting observations deserve further discussion, including initialization of immutable objects and covariant subtyping in the presence of immutability information as presented below. We also discuss type states and unique references with fractional permissions as further extensions that can complement immutability.

6.1   Covariant Subtyping

Covariant subtyping allows type arguments to covariantly change in a type-safe manner. Variant parametric types [83] attach a variance annotation to a type argument, e.g., Vector<+Number> (for covariant typing) or Vector<-Number> (for contravariant typing).

Its subtype relation contains this chain:

Vector<Integer> ⪯ Vector<+Integer> ⪯ Vector<+Number> ⪯ Vector<+Object>

The type checker prohibits calling someMethod(X) when the receiver is of type Foo<+X>. For instance, suppose there is a method isIn(X) in class Vector<X>. Then, it is prohibited to call isIn(Number) on a reference of type Vector<+Number>.

Java's wildcards have a similar chain in the subtype relation:

Vector<Integer> ⪯ Vector<? extends Integer>
⪯ Vector<? extends Number> ⪯ Vector<? extends Object>

Java's wildcards and variant parametric types are different in the legality of invoking isIn(? extends Number) on a reference of type Vector<? extends Number>. A variant parametric type system prohibits such an invocation. Java permits such an invocation, but the only value of type ? extends Number is null.

IGJ also contains a similar chain:

Vector<Mutable,Integer> ⪯ Vector<ReadOnly,Integer>
⪯ Vector<ReadOnly,Number> ⪯ Vector<ReadOnly,Object>

The restriction on method calls in IGJ is based on user-chosen *semantics* (whether the method is readonly or not) rather than on *method signature* as in wildcards and variant parametric types. For example, IGJ allows calling isIn(Number) on a reference of type Vector<ReadOnly,Number> iff isIn is readonly. IGJ is still type-safe because of the fact that isIn is readonly and the restriction on method overriding [10].

6.2   Typestates for Objects

In a typestate system, each object is in a certain state, and the set of applicable methods depends on the current state. Verifying typestates statically is challenging due to the existence of aliases, i.e., a state-change in a particular object must affect all its aliases. Typestates for objects [84] describes a system called Fugue that uses linear types to manage aliasing.

Object immutability can be partially expressed using typestates: by using two states (mutable and immutable) and declaring that mutating methods are applicable only in

```
 1 class Client {
 2   <p* inside world> void m1(p:Object obj) {
 3     obj.mutate(); // Error
 4     obj.toString(); // Ok
 5     // assign to field is not possible
 6   }
 7   <p- inside world> void m2(p:Object obj) {
 8     obj.mutate(); // Error
 9     obj.toString(); // Ok
10   }
11 }
12 class Fractional<o+ outside owner> {
13   unique[this]:Object obj = new this:Object();
14   void example(o:Client c) {
15     borrow obj as p*:tmp in {
16       c.m1(tmp);
17       c.m2(tmp);
18     }
19   }
20 }
```

Fig. 8. Fractional permissions using borrowing and unique references

the mutable state. An additional method should mark the transition from a mutable state to an immutable state, and it should be called after the initialization of the object has finished. It remains to be seen if systems such as [84] can handle arbitrary aliases that occur in real programs, e.g., this references that escape the constructor.

6.3 Fractional Permissions

The example in Figure 3 shows that a read-only reference to an object does not preclude the existence of mutable references to the same object elsewhere in the system. This allows observational exposure — for good and evil. The immutability annotation '*' imposes all the restrictions a read-only type has, but it also guarantees that no aliases with write permission exist in the system. Joe$_3$'s simple way of creating an immutable object is to move a *unique* reference into a variable with immutable type, just as in SafeJava [51]. This allows Joe$_3$ to encode fractional permissions using a borrowing construct and do staged construction of immutables. The example in Figure 8 shows an implementation of Fractional Permissions. Joline's borrowing construct [46] is employed to *temporarily* move a mutable unique reference into an immutable variable (line 15), freely alias the reference (while preserving read-only) (lines 16 and 17), and then implicitly move the reference back into the unique variable again and make it mutable. This is essentially Boyland's Fractional Permissions [47]. Both owner-polymorphic methods and borrowing blocks guarantee not to capture the reference. A borrowed reference can be aliased any number of times in any context to which it has been exported, without the need to keep track of "split permissions" [47] as it is guaranteed that all permissions to alias the pointer are invalidated when the borrowing block exits. The price of this convenience is that the conversion from mutable to immutable and back again must be done in the same place.

Interestingly, m1 and m2 are equally safe to call from example. Both methods have revoked their right to cause write effects to objects owned by p, indicated by the * and - annotations on p, respectively. The difference between the two methods is that the first method knows that obj will not change under foot (making it safe to, for example, use obj as a key in a hash table), whereas the second method cannot make such an assumption.

7   Conclusion

In this chapter we have given a flavor of the variety of work on different kinds of immutability proposed for the modern object-oriented languages where aliasing plays an important role. We refer the reader to the respective papers for more information about each system described in this chapter and welcome any feedback.

References

1. Hogg, J., Lea, D., Wills, A., de Champeaux, D., Holt, R.: The Geneva Convention on the Treatment of Object Aliasing. In: Clarke, D., Noble, J., Wrigstad, T. (eds.) Aliasing in Object-Oriented Programming. LNCS, vol. 7850, pp. 7–14. Springer, Heidelberg (2013)
2. Clarke, D., Noble, J., Wrigstad, T. (eds.): Aliasing in Object-Oriented Programming. LNCS, vol. 7850. Springer, Heidelberg (2013)
3. Birka, A., Ernst, M.D.: A practical type system and language for reference immutability. In: OOPSLA, pp. 35–49. ACM Press, New York (2004)
4. Skoglund, M., Wrigstad, T.: A mode system for read-only references in Java. In: FTfJP. Springer, Heidelberg (2001)
5. Pechtchanski, I., Sarkar, V.: Immutability specification and its applications. In: Java Grande, pp. 202–211. ACM Press, Seattle (2002)
6. Tschantz, M.S., Ernst, M.D.: Javari: Adding reference immutability to Java. In: OOPSLA, pp. 211–230. ACM Press, New York (2005)
7. Kniesel, G., Theisen, D.: JAC — access right based encapsulation for Java. Software: Practice and Experience 31(6), 555–576 (2001)
8. Boyland, J., Noble, J., Retert, W.: Capabilities for Sharing: A Generalisation of Uniqueness and Read-Only. In: Lindskov Knudsen, J. (ed.) ECOOP 2001. LNCS, vol. 2072, pp. 2–27. Springer, Heidelberg (2001)
9. Dietl, W., Müller, P.: Universes: Lightweight ownership for JML. Journal of Object Technology (JOT) 4(8), 5–32 (2005)
10. Zibin, Y., Potanin, A., Artzi, S., Kiezun, A., Ernst, M.D.: Object and reference immutability using Java generics. In: Foundations of Software Engineering (2007)
11. Zibin, Y., Potanin, A., Li, P., Ali, M., Ernst, M.D.: Ownership and immutability in generic java. In: OOPSLA, pp. 598–617. ACM Press (2010)
12. Östlund, J., Wrigstad, T., Clarke, D., Åkerblom, B.: Ownership, Uniqueness and Immutability. In: Paige, R.F., Meyer, B. (eds.) TOOLS EUROPE 2008. LNBIP, vol. 11, pp. 178–197. Springer, Heidelberg (2008)
13. Burdy, L., Cheon, Y., Cok, D., Ernst, M.D., Kiniry, J., Leavens, G.T., Leino, K.R.M., Poll, E.: An overview of JML tools and applications. STTT 7(3), 212–232 (2005)

14. Tkachuk, O., Dwyer, M.B.: Adapting side effects analysis for modular program model checking. In: ESEC/FSE, pp. 188–197. ACM Press, New York (2003)
15. Clausen, L.R.: A Java bytecode optimizer using side-effect analysis. Concurrency: Practice and Experience 9(11), 1031–1045 (1997)
16. Sălcianu, A.: Pointer analysis for Java programs: Novel techniques and applications. PhD thesis, MIT Dept. of EECS (September 2006)
17. Fowler, M.: Refactoring: Improving the Design of Existing Code. Addison-Wesley, New York (2000)
18. Artzi, S., Ernst, M.D., Kieżun, A., Pacheco, C., Perkins, J.H.: Finding the needles in the haystack: Generating legal test inputs for object-oriented programs. In: M-TOOS. ACM Press, Portland (2006)
19. Mariani, L., Pezzè, M.: Behavior capture and test: Automated analysis of component integration. In: ICECCS, pp. 292–301. IEEE, Tokyo (2005)
20. Xie, T.: Augmenting Automatically Generated Unit-Test Suites with Regression Oracle Checking. In: Thomas, D. (ed.) ECOOP 2006. LNCS, vol. 4067, pp. 380–403. Springer, Heidelberg (2006)
21. Ernst, M.D., Cockrell, J., Griswold, W.G., Notkin, D.: Dynamically discovering likely program invariants to support program evolution. IEEE TSE 27(2), 99–123 (2001)
22. Dallmeier, V., Lindig, C., Wasylkowski, A., Zeller, A.: Mining object behavior with ADABU. In: WODA, pp. 17–24. ACM Press, New York (2006)
23. Dolado, J.J., Harman, M., Otero, M.C., Hu, L.: An empirical investigation of the influence of a type of side effects on program comprehension. IEEE TSE 29(7), 665–670 (2003)
24. Gosling, J., Joy, B., Steele, G., Bracha, G.: The Java Language Specification, 3rd edn. AW (2005)
25. Boyapati, C.: SafeJava: A Unified Type System for Safe Programming. PhD thesis, MIT Dept. of EECS (February 2004)
26. Sălcianu, A., Rinard, M.: Purity and Side Effect Analysis for Java Programs. In: Cousot, R. (ed.) VMCAI 2005. LNCS, vol. 3385, pp. 199–215. Springer, Heidelberg (2005)
27. Rountev, A.: Precise identification of side-effect-free methods in Java. In: Proceedings of ICSM, pp. 82–91. IEEE Computer Society (2004)
28. Landi, W., Ryder, B.G., Zhang, S.: Interprocedural side effect analysis with pointer aliasing. In: Proceedings of PLDI, pp. 56–67 (1993)
29. Pearce, D.J.: JPure: A Modular Purity System for Java. In: Knoop, J. (ed.) CC 2011. LNCS, vol. 6601, pp. 104–123. Springer, Heidelberg (2011)
30. Noble, J., Vitek, J., Potter, J.: Flexible Alias Protection. In: Jul, E. (ed.) ECOOP 1998. LNCS, vol. 1445, pp. 158–185. Springer, Heidelberg (1998)
31. Kernighan, B.W., Ritchie, D.M.: The C Programming Language, 2nd edn. Software Series. Prentice Hall, Englewood Cliffs (1988)
32. Stroustrup, B.: The C++ Programming Language. Addison-Wesley, Boston (2000)
33. Meyers, S.: Effective C++, 2nd edn. Addison-Wesley (1997)
34. Morris, J.H.: Sniggering type checker experiment. Experiment at Xerox PARC (1978); Personal communication (May 2004)
35. Gannon, J.D.: An experimental evaluation of data type conventions. Communications of the ACM 20(8), 584–595 (1977)
36. Prechelt, L., Tichy, W.F.: A controlled experiment to assess the benefits of procedure argument type checking. IEEE TSE 24(4), 302–312 (1998)
37. Foster, J.S., Fähndrich, M., Aiken, A.: A theory of type qualifiers. In: PLDI, pp. 192–203 (June 1999)
38. Milner, R., Tofte, M., Harper, R.: The Definition of Standard ML. MIT Press (1990)
39. Leroy, X.: The Objective Caml system, release 3.07 (September 29, 2003) with Doligez, D., Garrigue, J., Rémy, D., Vouillon, J.

40. Clarke, D., Potter, J., Noble, J.: Ownership Types for Flexible Alias Protection. In: OOPSLA, pp. 48–64. ACM Press, Vancouver (1998)
41. Bloch, J.: Effective Java Programming Language Guide. Addison Wesley, Boston (2001)
42. Huang, S.S., Zook, D., Smaragdakis, Y.: cJ: Enhancing Java with safe type conditions. In: AOSD, pp. 185–198. ACM Press, New York (2007)
43. Clarke, D., Östlund, J., Sergey, I., Wrigstad, T.: Ownership Types: A Survey. In: Clarke, D., Noble, J., Wrigstad, T. (eds.) Aliasing in Object-Oriented Programming. LNCS, vol. 7850, pp. 15–58. Springer, Heidelberg (2013)
44. Clarke, D., Drossopoulou, S.: Ownership, Encapsulation, and the Disjointness of Type and Effect. In: OOPSLA, pp. 292–310. ACM Press, Seattle (2002)
45. Boyland, J.: Why we should not add readonly to Java (yet). Journal of Object Technology (2006); Special issue: ECOOP 2005 Workshop FTfJP
46. Wrigstad, T.: Ownership-Based Alias Management. PhD thesis, Royal Institute of Technology, Sweden (May 2006)
47. Boyland, J.: Checking Interference with Fractional Permissions. In: Cousot, R. (ed.) SAS 2003. LNCS, vol. 2694, pp. 55–72. Springer, Heidelberg (2003)
48. Clarke, D.: Object Ownership and Containment. PhD thesis, School of Computer Science and Engineering, University of New South Wales, Sydney, Australia (2001)
49. Potanin, A., Noble, J., Clarke, D., Biddle, R.: Generic ownership for generic Java. In: OOPSLA, pp. 311–324. ACM Press, New York (2006)
50. Clarke, D., Drossopoulou, S.: Ownership, encapsulation and the disjointness of type and effect. In: OOPSLA, pp. 292–310. ACM Press, New York (2002)
51. Boyapati, C.: SafeJava: A Unified Type System for Safe Programming. PhD thesis, Electrical Engineering and Computer Science, MIT (February 2004)
52. Birka, A.: Compiler-enforced immutability for the Java language. Technical Report MIT-LCS-TR-908, MIT Lab for Computer Science (June 2003); Revision of Master's thesis
53. Bracha, G., Odersky, M., Stoutamire, D., Wadler, P.: Making the future safe for the past: Adding genericity to the Java programming language. In: OOPSLA, pp. 183–200. ACM Press, New York (1998)
54. Igarashi, A., Pierce, B.C., Wadler, P.: Featherweight Java: a minimal core calculus for Java and GJ. ACM Transactions on Programming Languages and Systems (TOPLAS) 23(3), 396–450 (2001)
55. Clarke, D., Wrigstad, T.: External Uniqueness is Unique Enough. In: Cardelli, L. (ed.) ECOOP 2003. LNCS, vol. 2743, pp. 176–241. Springer, Heidelberg (2003)
56. Wrigstad, T.: Ownership-Based Alias Management. PhD thesis, Royal Institute of Technology, Kista, Stockholm (May 2006)
57. Müller, P., Poetzsch-Heffter, A.: Universes: A type system for controlling representation exposure. Technical report, Fernuniversität Hagen (1999)
58. Müller, P.: Modular Specification and Verification of Object-Oriented Programs. PhD thesis, FernUniversität Hagen (2001)
59. Haack, C., Poll, E.: Type-Based Object Immutability with Flexible Initialization. In: Drossopoulou, S. (ed.) ECOOP 2009. LNCS, vol. 5653, pp. 520–545. Springer, Heidelberg (2009)
60. Ernst, M.D.: Type annotations specification (jsr 308), http://pag.csail.mit.edu/jsr308/ (September 12, 2008)
61. Boyland, J.: Why we should not add readonly to Java (yet). In: FTfJP, Glasgow, Scotland. Springer (July 2005)
62. Lucassen, J.M., Gifford, D.K.: Polymorphic effect systems. In: POPL, pp. 47–57 (January 1988)
63. Talpin, J.P., Jouvelot, P.: The type and effect discipline. In: LICS, pp. 162–173 (June 1992)

64. Nielson, F., Riis Nielson, H.: Type and Effect Systems. In: Olderog, E.-R., Steffen, B. (eds.) Correct System Design. LNCS, vol. 1710, pp. 114–136. Springer, Heidelberg (1999)
65. Müller, P., Poetzsch-Heffter, A.: Universes: A type system for alias and dependency control. Technical Report 279, Fernuniversität Hagen (2001)
66. Haack, C., Poll, E., Schäfer, J., Schubert, A.: Immutable Objects for a Java-Like Language. In: De Nicola, R. (ed.) ESOP 2007. LNCS, vol. 4421, pp. 347–362. Springer, Heidelberg (2007)
67. Porat, S., Biberstein, M., Koved, L., Mendelson, B.: Automatic detection of immutable fields in Java. In: CASCON (November 2000)
68. Fähndrich, M., Leino, K.R.M.: Declaring and checking non-null types in an object-oriented language. In: OOPSLA, pp. 302–312. ACM Press, New York (2003)
69. Fähndrich, M., Xia, S.: Establishing object invariants with delayed types. In: Gabriel, R.P., Bacon, D.F., Lopes, C.V., Steele Jr., G.L. (eds.) OOPSLA, pp. 337–350. ACM Press (2007)
70. Qi, X., Myers, A.C.: Masked types for sound object initialization. In: Shao, Z., Pierce, B.C. (eds.) POPL, pp. 53–65. ACM Press (2009)
71. Summers, A.J., Müller, P.: Freedom before commitment - a lightweight type system for object initialisation. In: OOPSLA. ACM Press (2011)
72. Leino, K.R.M., Müller, P., Wallenburg, A.: Flexible Immutability with Frozen Objects. In: Shankar, N., Woodcock, J. (eds.) VSTTE 2008. LNCS, vol. 5295, pp. 192–208. Springer, Heidelberg (2008)
73. Dietl, W., Müller, P.: Universes: Lightweight Ownership for JML. Journal of Object Technology 4(8), 5–32 (2005)
74. Dietl, W., Drossopoulou, S., Müller, P.: Generic Universe Types. In: Ernst, E. (ed.) ECOOP 2007. LNCS, vol. 4609, pp. 28–53. Springer, Heidelberg (2007)
75. Müller, P., Rudich, A.: Ownership transfer in Universe Types. In: OOPSLA (2007)
76. Haack, C., Poll, E., Schäfer, J., Schubert, A.: Immutable Objects for a Java-Like Language. In: De Nicola, R. (ed.) ESOP 2007. LNCS, vol. 4421, pp. 347–362. Springer, Heidelberg (2007)
77. Tschantz, M.S., Ernst, M.D.: Javari: Adding reference immutability to Java. In: OOPSLA (2005)
78. Zibin, Y., Potanin, A., Artzi, S., Kieżun, A., Ernst, M.D.: Object and reference immutability using Java generics. Technical Report MIT-CSAIL-TR-2007-018, MITCSAIL (2007)
79. Kniesel, G., Theisen, D.: JAC—access right based encapsulation for Java. Software — Practice and Experience (2001)
80. Skoglund, M., Wrigstad, T.: Alias control with read-only references. In: Sixth Conference on Computer Science and Informatics (March 2002)
81. Lu, Y., Potter, J.: Protecting representation with effect encapsulation. In: POPL (2006)
82. Noble, J., Vitek, J., Potter, J.: Flexible Alias Protection. In: Jul, E. (ed.) ECOOP 1998. LNCS, vol. 1445, pp. 158–185. Springer, Heidelberg (1998)
83. Igarashi, A., Viroli, M.: Variant parametric types: A flexible subtyping scheme for generics. ACM Transactions on Programming Languages and Systems (TOPLAS) 28(5), 795–847 (2006)
84. DeLine, R., Fähndrich, M.: Typestates for Objects. In: Odersky, M. (ed.) ECOOP 2004. LNCS, vol. 3086, pp. 465–490. Springer, Heidelberg (2004)

Fractional Permissions*

John Boyland

University of Wisconsin-Milwaukee, USA
boyland@uwm.edu

Abstract. Fractional permissions allow resource tracking type systems to give out multiple read accesses to the same resource without losing the ability to re-form a unique write access later. This paper describes the motivation for fractional permissions, and different fractional models including those for which fractional scaling is required. We describe a particular system of fractional permissions that uses scaling to support the technique of "nesting."

1 Introduction

Fractional permissions were introduced in a paper [1] presented at SAS (Static Analysis Symposium) in 2003. Picked up by Peter O'Hearn and others in the separation logic community [2], they were formalized in Concurrent Separation Logic [3] by Stephen Brookes. Fractions have been used to aid in verification of typestate [4], use of channels [5], use of resources the π-calculus [6], and concurrent programs [7,8,9].

Section 2 explores the motivation behind the introduction of fractions in the first section and then the next section (Sec. 3)) describes various ways in which fractions have been formalized. Section 4 then reviews the definition of fractional permissions with "nesting," followed by a section (Sec. 5) that delves deeper into the motivation of nesting and how it connects and interacts with fractions. After a discussion in Sec. 6, Sec. 7 concludes.

2 Motivation

Fractional permissions were designed as a solution to the "passivity" problem identified by O'Hearn [10]. The linear nature of various heap-logics eventually called "separation logic" enabled analysis of programs to use divide-and-conquer to analyzed composed systems. Before separation logic (and its antecedents), one usually had to maintain a number of complex side-conditions about possible aliasing. Separation logic defines away the problem in that if two parts of a system are separable, they have no shared mutable state and thus cannot interfere. Shared mutable state on the other hand, must be explicitly handled.

---

* Work supported in part by the National Science Foundation (CCF-0702635). The opinions expressed here are not necessarily those of the National Science Foundation or the US Government.

D. Clarke et al. (Eds.): Aliasing in Object-Oriented Programming, LNCS 7850, pp. 270–288, 2013.

An immediate difficulty in applying the idea of separation was the strictness required: what if two separate parts shared read-only or immutable[1] state? In a strict separation logic approach, such parts *interfere* and thus cannot be composed. This response is obviously overly conservative since two reads of the same state do not actually interfere; there is no possible race condition.

For example, consider the following example:

```
a := new; b := new; c = new; d = a;
      *b += *a || *c += *d
        *a += *b + *c ...
```

On the first line, we allocate three cells, and make d an alias of one of them. Then on the second linje, we perform two assignments in parallel. Then after the two parallel actions are complete, more computation happens. The two variables a and d actually refer to the same heap location, and so both forks of the parallel action are reading this location, while writing independent locations. After the parallel section, the main thread has write access to the formerly shared location (*a).

Before fractional permissions, the main approach was to designate some of the state as immutable, and the rest as mutable. Only mutable state required separation [10] State (e.g., the cell pointed to by a) could move from the mutable side to the immutable side dynamically (but not the reverse). It was even possible to treat the state of memory (mutable or immutable) polymorphically [10,11], but in these cases it was not possible to take mutable state, make it temporarily immutable—permitting multiple parts of the program to access it—and then revert the state to being mutable. In other words, we were looking for a way to distribute read permission (e.g., the permission to read the value in |*a|) to multiple recipients and then revoke these permissions later, for example, so that we can recover write permission to *a.

Wadler's let! construct [12] came close to producing this functionality, but imposed strong restrictions on the code that was permitted to locally duplicate a (write) capability as a read capability; lacking the ability to track the (temporarily) immutable references, it simply forbade the body from computing anything (e.g., a function) in which one of these references could "hide."

Linear permissions are lost when one passes them on, making revocation easy, but not allowing multiple recipients. Nonlinear permissions are easy to duplicate but cannot be revoked. *Fractions* permit us to keep a linear flow of permissions, but allows multiple recipients through *splitting*: a single (write) permission can be *split* into multiple pieces, each tracked separately. Any piece of the permission gives one read access, while the original write permission cannot be recovered until we reassemble all the pieces. Splitting permits multiple recipients; linearity preserves revocability.

---

[1] I distinguish *immutable* state, which never changes, *temporarily immutable* state that does not chsnge over the current context, and from *read-only* state which is state that one has read-access to, but which may be written through some other access.

Assuming a and d point to cell 1, b points to cell 2, and c points to cell 3, then the example is handled by giving the left fork full access to the cell 2 and half access to cell 1, while the right fork gets full access to cell 3 and half access to cell 1. After the forks are done, the main thread has full access to all three cells again.

3 Models of Fractions

The original paper on fractional permissions [1] suggested that fractions be real numbers in the range $(0, 1]$ while acknowledging other possibilities. This section discusses various algebraic models of fractions.

3.1 Fraction Addition

Bornat et al. [2], and Brookes [3], Dockins and Hobor [13] and Parkinson [14] propose algebraic models. Here I propose my own model, closely related to the previously cited models: we have a set of values Q with a distinguished top element $\top \in Q$ (representing write access) and a (partial) operation $\oplus : Q \times Q \rightharpoonup Q$ that is

commutative	$x \oplus y = z \implies y \oplus x = z$;
associative	$w \oplus (x \oplus y) = z \implies (w \oplus x) \oplus y = z$;
cancellative	$x \oplus y = x \oplus z \implies y = z$;
without identity	there is no instance of $x \oplus y = y$; and optionally
undefined for $\top$	$\top \oplus x$ is never defined.

Commutativity and associativity[2] make it possible to keep fractional permissions in unordered collections. The ability to cancel means that there aren't spurious differences between functionally equivalent fractions. An identity element (e where $e \oplus x = x$) would be a "zero" fraction that could be endlessly produced without any visible effect thus defeating trackability. Dockins and Hobor [13] include an identity in their model, which causes problems for disjoint unions. Bierhoff and Aldrich's PLAID system [15] uses zero fractions for special purposes but uses additional techniques to avoid the zero fractions from escaping permanently.

To use such an algebraic structure, we start with a write permission $\top$ and then find elements $x, y \in Q$ such that $x \oplus y = \top$, thus splitting the write permission into two read permissions. This process may be repeated yielding successively smaller read permissions. If some $x \in Q$ is reachable in this way, then by commutativity and associativity, we can construct a *complement* $\bar{x}$ such that $x \oplus \bar{x} = \top$. By cancellation, this complement must be unique. If x were not reachable, it would be useless for fractional reasoning. Hence the (optional) requirement that $\top \oplus x$ always be undefined; any result would be useless or else admit a forbidden

---

[2] The formal definitions given here have less usual forms to account for the fact that the operator is partial.

identity: $(\top \oplus x) \oplus y = \top \implies \top \oplus (x \oplus y) = \top$. Of course, not all elements of Q need be *splittable* $(\exists_{y\,z}\, x = y \oplus z)$. Indeed a finite system of permissions must have unsplittable fractions.

The addition operation induces a partial order, where $y < z$ if there exists an x such that $x \oplus y = z$. We have anti-reflexivity since $x < x$ implies the existence of an identity, and anti-symmetricity since $x < y \wedge y < x$ implies $w \oplus x = y \wedge z \oplus y = x$ and hence by associativity, another forbidden identity, $(w \oplus z) \oplus y = y$. We have transitivity since $x < y \wedge y < z$ implies $v \oplus x = y \wedge w \oplus y = z$ and by associativity $(v \oplus w) \oplus x = z$ and hence $x < z$.

Some of the models for addition proposed by Bornat, Brookes, Parkinson, myself and others are the following:

write-only $Q = \{\top\}$ and the $\oplus$ operator is everywhere undefined. This is the vacuous definition with only a write permission. Using this model leaves us in the original separation model.

one-read $Q = \{\top = \mathcal{W}, \mathcal{R}\}$ with $\mathcal{R} \oplus \mathcal{R} = \mathcal{W}$. A write permission can be split into two unsplittable read permissions. This is the smallest model that permits read-read parallelism. This model can be generalized to other finite models:

finite tokens $Q = \{1, 2, \ldots, n = \top\}$ and we use normal integer addition for $\oplus$. We have a fixed and finite number (n) of tokens that can be passed out, with writes permitted only when we have collected all the tokens. An early version of Chalice [9] used this model of fractions where $n = 100$.

Generalizing this to the infinite case leads us to our first infinite model:

infinite tokens $Q = \{1, 2, \ldots\} \cup \{\omega - n \mid n \in \mathbf{N}\}$ where $\top = \omega = \omega - 0$, and

$$m \oplus n = m + n$$
$$(\omega - m) \oplus n = n \oplus (\omega - m) = \omega - (m - n) \quad \text{if } m \geqslant n$$

The fractions $\omega - n$ are infinitely splittable, but only one of the pieces of the split will in turn be infinitely splittable. This model is isomorphic to the following:

reference counting $Q = \mathbf{Z}$, where $\top = 0$ and

$$-m \oplus -n = -(m + n) \quad \text{if } m, n > 0$$
$$m \oplus -n = -n \oplus m = m - n \quad \text{if } m \geqslant n > 0$$

The presence of a zero (0) fraction is safe since the $\oplus$ operation is undefined on zero. The advantage of this model (and the previous isomorphic one) is that the -1 tokens (previously 1) that are split off are indistinguishable from each other which makes it easier to model non-hierarchically nested parallelism, in which each thread is given and returns an identical token.

subsets $Q = \mathcal{P}(\mathbf{Z}) - \{\varnothing\}$ with $\top = \mathbf{Z}$ and $\oplus$ is disjoint set union:

$$q_1 \oplus q_2 = \begin{cases} q_1 \cup q_2 \text{ if } q_1 \cap q_2 = \varnothing \\ \text{undefined otherwise} \end{cases}$$

This construction (due to Parkinson) has the "disjointness" property described in Section 6.1. The set Q however is not countable.

binary fractions $Q = \left\{ \frac{2m+1}{2^n} \mid 2m+1 \leqslant 2^n \right\}$ where $\top = 1 = \frac{1}{1}$ and $\oplus$ is normal rational addition. In this model, every fraction is (infinitely) splittable:

$$\frac{2m+1}{2^n} = \frac{2m+1}{2^{n+1}} \oplus \frac{2m+1}{2^{n+1}}$$

This property makes it easy to model unbounded binary forking, but unlike the referencing counting model, it's not possible to split off an unbounded number of identical tokens. Thus, one can use a composite model:

composite $Q = \{1, 2, \ldots\} \cup \left\{ \frac{2m+1}{2^k} \omega - n \mid 2m+1 \leqslant 2^k \right\}$ where $\top = \omega = \frac{1}{1}\omega - 0$ and

$$m \oplus n = m + n$$
$$(q\omega - m) \oplus n = n \oplus (q\omega - m) = q\omega - (m - n) \quad \text{if } m \geqslant n$$
$$(q\omega - m) \oplus (r\omega - n) = (q + r)\omega - (m + n) \quad \text{if } q + r \leqslant 1$$

Here we have both the ability to split off a unit token:

$$q\omega - n = (q\omega - (n + 1)) \oplus 1$$

and to split any infinite fraction:

$$\frac{2m+1}{2^k}\omega - n = \left(\frac{2m+1}{2^{k+1}}\omega - n \right) \oplus \left(\frac{2m+1}{2^{k+1}}\omega - 0 \right)$$

The use of my infinite tokens model, rather than the reference counting model as the base of this composition makes for a more intuitive addition operator than the isomorphic composite models proposed in previous work [2,3].

iterated composite Let $P = \{1, 2, \ldots\} \cup \left\{ \frac{2m+1}{2^k}\omega - n \mid 2m+1 \leqslant 2^k \right\}$ be the composite model described above, and let $\equiv$ be the reflexive, symmetric and transitive closure of the relation that adds ω to the end of a sequence of values from P, $R = \{(p_1 \ldots p_n, p_1 \ldots p_n \omega) \mid p_i \in P\}$. Then the iterated composite model Q consists of the quotient of sequences of these values by the equivalence relation: $Q = P^* / \equiv$. We define $\top = [\epsilon] = \{\omega^n \mid n \in \mathbf{N}\}$ and addition

$$[p_1 \ldots p_n p] \oplus [p_1 \ldots p_n p'] = [p_1 \ldots p_n (p \oplus p')]$$

using the previous model for the definition of $p \oplus p'$.

This model (inspired by Parkinson) has the advantage that any fraction $[\bar{p}] \ni (\bar{p}\omega)$ can either serve as a source of arbitrarily many identical tokens $[\bar{p}1]$ or be split into two identical tokens: $[\bar{p}\frac{\omega}{2}]$.

3.2   Fraction Multiplication

In the previous section, we define a fraction addition operation; here we define a multiplication operation. A multiplication operation is needed if one wishes to *scale* a permission (and thus in the semantics, to scale a (fractional) heap) by a fraction, for example $q\Pi$ where q is some fractional value.

Scaling of permissions gives a simple way to give read-only access to any predicate by simply scaling it with a fraction less than totality. Furthermore, the counting and infinite split abilities of the fraction model used then carry over to the predicate family directly (assuming the predicates are sufficiently "precise," as explained below). Scaling thus cuts cleanly across abstraction barriers without breaking them.

In the absence of scaling, it is much more difficult to describe a read-only version of a named predicate. The obvious alternative, to use a fraction parameter in an (abstract) named predicate, runs into two problems. Suppose we have a predicate a with parameters, the last one of which represents the fraction. In order for this parameter to really be a fraction, it will be necessary to verify that (say) $a(\overline{X}, q_1) + a(\overline{X}, q_2) = (a\overline{X}, q_1 \oplus q_2)$ for all q_1, q_2 that can be added (which can only be done using the definition of a). But if the abstraction hides any read-only state using a fraction q, then one finds the need to perform multiplication of the parameter with this fraction anyway.

The fraction multiplication operation $\otimes$ is a total (since we wish to apply any fraction to the outside of a formula) binary operator with the following properties:

commutative	$x \otimes y = y \otimes x$;
associative	$w \otimes (x \otimes y) = (w \otimes x) \otimes y$;
cancellative	$x \otimes y = x \otimes z \implies y = z$;
distributive	$w \otimes (x \oplus y) = z \implies (w \otimes x) \oplus (w \otimes y) = z$
factoring	$(w \otimes x) \oplus (w \otimes y) = z \implies w \otimes (x \oplus y) = z$
with identity	$1 \otimes x = x$.

(Here we write 1 for the top element $\top \in Q$ to emphasize that it is the multiplicative identity.) We require commutativity and associativity for simplicity and coherence again. Similarly, cancellation means we don't have equivalent but unequal fractions with regard to multiplication. The distributive property is required so that we can split a compound permission (or fractional heap) into two fractional parts, and factoring to put it back together. We need an identity so that a permission Π is equivalent to the whole permission 1Π.

If we admit fraction multiplication, this has strong implications about addition as well; for instance, if we have any reachable fraction x ($x \oplus \bar{x} = 1$), then by distributivity $y = y \otimes 1 = y \otimes (x \oplus \bar{x}) = (y \otimes x) \oplus (y \otimes \bar{x})$, hence every fraction is splittable. By implication Q must be infinite. Furthermore, abbreviating $x \otimes y$ as xy, we have $1 = x \oplus \bar{x} = x1 \oplus \bar{x} = x(x \oplus \bar{x}) \oplus \bar{x} = xx \oplus x\bar{x} \oplus 1\bar{x} = xx \oplus (x \oplus 1)\bar{x}$, hence $x \oplus 1$ is defined for all reachable x, and thus the (optional) rule disallowing $x \oplus 1$ must be dropped. Using similar arguments we determine that $x \oplus y$ must also defined for all reachable x and y, and so we might as well require $\oplus$ to be total.

As a result only the vacuous model of the above models can admit fractional multiplication. The binary fraction model and supersets such as $Q = (0, 1]$ require addition of fractions greater than 1, although only fractions less than or equal to one will occur in (final) fractional heaps. We have found $\mathbf{Q}^+$, the set of positive rationals, to be a conducive model with which to work.

Expanding an infinite counting model to include multiplication leads to a model with integer polynomials over an infinitesimal ϵ: $a_0 + a_1\epsilon + a_2\epsilon^2 + \ldots + a_n\epsilon^n$ where $a_i \in \mathbf{Z}$ subject to the limitations that $a_n \neq 0$ and the first non-zero a_i must be positive. (Both addition and multiplication are closed over such polynomials). In such a system (written $\mathbf{Z}[\epsilon]^+$), we both have splittability and infinite countability.

3.3   Semantics

Even if multiplication is permitted syntactically, joining of fractions is not necessarily sound: $\frac{1}{2}\Pi + \frac{1}{2}\Pi \equiv \Pi$. The problem is that Π may be "imprecise" [16, page 9], that is, may have different possible meanings in a given heap. For example, suppose Π is the formula that there exists a reference whose f field is null: $\exists o \cdot o.f \to 0$. Then $\frac{1}{2}\Pi$ gives partial access to this field. The object however is not specified, so that two permissions $\frac{1}{2}\Pi$ may refer to two separate fields, and thus cannot be combined into one, Π. Precision has been found important for soundness in other situations, and (major) syntactic restrictions have been found that guarantee precision. In particular, if disjunctions, implications, negation and existentials are omitted from separation logic, formulae are precise. Our approach (outlined in section 4) has been instead to define the semantics of key connectives (such as existentials and implication) so that they are "sufficiently" precise, that is, defined so that fraction joining is sound.

The desire for multiplication leads to literal fractions greater than 1 as explained above. These fractions can appear with scaling, for example:

$$\Pi \equiv \frac{1}{2}\Pi + \frac{1}{2}\Pi \equiv 1(\frac{1}{2}\Pi) + 1(\frac{1}{2}\Pi) \equiv (1+1)(\frac{1}{2}\Pi) \equiv 2(\frac{1}{2})\Pi$$

The existence of fractions over 1 may seem dangerous to the soundness of the system, but is not a problem as long as we require that the final fractional heap (used to represent the semantics of fractional permissions, as seen in section 4) doesn't include fractions over 1.

Furthermore, nesting [17] (or a system of recursive permission equations) allows one to end up with fractions that are the solution of recurrences such as

$$q = 1 + \frac{1}{4}q \quad .$$

The only (numeric) solution is $q = \frac{4}{3}$. Thus, if the model with recursive permissions and multiplication includes the existence of a fraction $\frac{1}{2}$ where $\frac{1}{2} \oplus \frac{1}{2} = 1$, then the model will then include the entire set of positive rational numbers, $\mathbf{Q}^+$.

In summary, with only fraction addition, one has a large variety of models from which to choose, but if scaling is added so that complex predicates can be split arbitarily, the models are all but constrained so that both addition and multiplication are total. Both an infinite fraction model $\mathbf{Q}^+$ and infinite counting model $\mathbf{Z}[\epsilon]^+$ are possible. Furthermore, one must ensure that predicates are sufficiently precise for splitting to be semantically sound. The following section describes one such semantics of permissions.

$$o \in O \quad \text{(object identifiers)}$$
$$q \in Q = \mathbf{Q}^+ \quad \text{(positive rationals)}$$
$$f, p \in F \quad \text{(field identifiers)}$$
$$\rho ::= r \mid o$$
$$\xi ::= z \mid q$$
$$k ::= \rho.f$$
$$\Pi, \Psi ::= v \mid k \to \rho \mid \varnothing \mid \Pi + \Pi \mid \xi\Pi \mid \Gamma \mid \exists r \cdot (k \to r + \Pi) \mid \Gamma ? \Pi : \Pi \mid \Psi \multimap \Pi$$
$$\Gamma ::= \top \mid \neg\Gamma \mid \Gamma \wedge \Gamma \mid \rho = \rho \mid \Psi < k \mid p(\overline{X}) \mid \exists x \cdot \Gamma$$
$$x ::= r \mid z \mid v \quad \text{(variables)}$$
$$X ::= \rho \mid \xi \mid \Pi \quad \text{(variable values)}$$
$$P ::= \left\{ \overline{p(\overline{x}) = \Gamma} \right\}$$
$$\sigma ::= \left[\, \overline{x \mapsto X} \, \right]$$

Fig. 1. Permission Syntax

4 Definitions

The previous section described a problem with precision: the rule $\frac{1}{2}\Pi + \frac{1}{2}\Pi \equiv \Pi$ is not sound if the scaled permissions could refer to incompatible situations that could not be combined. In separation logic, precision can be obtained by removing disjunctions, implications, negation and existentials. In this section, we describe an alternate technique: these connectives are replaced or limited in semantics to achieve sufficient precision. In particular:

- Disjunctions are replaced with conditionals. Equivalently, a disjunction must always be written in the form $(\Gamma \wedge \Pi) \vee (\neg\Gamma \wedge \Pi')$ where Γ is some predicate that doesn't depend on the heap. Here, we use the notation $\Gamma ? \Pi : \Pi'$.
- Implications are limited in semantics. We use an "obligation" semantics for implications; it must be possible to find the antecedent "inside" the consequent. The details are described below in the discussion of Fig. 5.
- Negation is permitted only on heap-independent predicates (a sub-language using the meta-variable Γ).
- Existential permissions are restricted to have the form $\exists r \cdot (k \to r + \Pi)$ where k is a field of some object not dependent on the variable r. This ensures that the witness of existential is available in a known field of the heap. Existential heap-independent predicates are not so restricted.

The figures of this section, with minor (typographical) changes, appeared in previous work [17]. They show the semantics of fractional permissions with nesting, where nesting is used for abstraction purposes, as explained in the following section.

Figure 1 shows the syntax of permissions with scaling ($\xi\Pi$) and nesting ($\Pi < k$). The permission $k \to \rho$ gives write access to the field represented

$$\begin{array}{lll}
\text{Q-IDENTITY} & \text{Q-COMMUTE} & \text{Q-ASSOCIATE} \\
\Pi + \emptyset \Rrightarrow \Pi & \Pi + \Pi' \Rrightarrow \Pi' + \Pi & \Pi + (\Pi' + \Pi'') \Rrightarrow (\Pi + \Pi') + \Pi''
\end{array}$$

$$\text{Q-COMBINE}$$
$$\dfrac{\Pi_1 \Rrightarrow \Pi_1' \quad \Pi_2 \Rrightarrow \Pi_2'}{\Pi_1 + \Pi_2 \Rrightarrow \Pi_1' + \Pi_2'} \qquad
\begin{array}{lll}
\text{Q-ZERO} & \text{Q-ONE} & \text{Q-DISTRIBUTE} \\
q\emptyset \Rrightarrow \emptyset & 1\Pi \Rrightarrow \Pi & q(\Pi + \Pi') \Rrightarrow q\Pi + q\Pi'
\end{array}$$

$$\begin{array}{ll}
\text{Q-MULTIPLY} & \text{Q-ADD} \\
\dfrac{q \otimes q' = q''}{q(q'\Pi) \Rrightarrow q''\Pi} & \dfrac{q \oplus q' = q''}{q\Pi + q'\Pi \Rrightarrow q''\Pi}
\end{array}$$

Fig. 2. Helper Relation for Permission Equivalence: $\Pi \Rrightarrow \Pi$.
The equivalence relation $\equiv$ is the reflexive, symmetric and transitive closure of $\Rrightarrow$.
We define $\Pi_1 \leqslant \Pi_2$ iff $\exists \Pi_0 \cdot \Pi_0 + \Pi_1 \equiv \Pi_2$.

$$N \in O \times F \to \Pi$$
$$h \in O \times F \rightharpoonup Q \times O$$

$$(h_1 \hat{+} h_2)(o, f) \doteq \begin{cases}
h_1(o, f) & \text{if } h_2(o, f) \text{ is undefined} \\
h_2(o, f) & \text{if } h_1(o, f) \text{ is undefined} \\
(q_1 \oplus q_2, o') & \text{where } (q_i, o') = h_i(o, f)
\end{cases}$$

$$(qh)l \doteq (q \otimes q', o) \text{ where } hl = (q', o)$$

Fig. 3. Nesting situation N, and Fractional Heaps h

by k (a heap location of the form $\rho'.f$) known currently to have a reference to object ρ in it. Permissions are collected using "addition" ($+$, similar to separation logic's $\star$ operator), for which the empty permission $\emptyset$ (**emp** in separation logic) is the identity. The formula syntax (Γ) forms a sub-language of non-linear logic of "facts." The existential permission has the restricted form that ensures precision, as explained above. A conditional permission yields one of two permissions depending on the truth value of the condition. The last form of permission ($\Psi \mathbin{-\!\!*} \Pi$) is a linear implication; it can be combined with the permission Ψ to yield Π. It is similar to the "magic wand" ($-\!\!*$) of separation logic.

Equivalence is defined syntactically in Fig. 2. Equivalence works at the level of addition and scaling. Two equivalent permissions are modeled by the same fractional heaps because of the restrictions placed on fraction addition and multiplication. Equivalence will never open up a formula, existential, conditional or implication.

Our formulation of "nesting" generalizes separation logic's resource invariants; every field of every object can be a resource, and accessing a resource is not always connected with acquiring a lock. The "nesting situation" (N in Fig. 3) defines the permissions nested in each field. All but a finite number of fields

B-TRUE
$$A; N \vdash \top \Downarrow \text{true}$$

B-NEG
$$\frac{A; N \vdash \Gamma \Downarrow b}{A; N \vdash \neg\Gamma \Downarrow \neg b}$$

B-ANDFALSE1
$$\frac{A; N \vdash \Gamma_1 \Downarrow \text{false}}{A; N \vdash \Gamma_1 \wedge \Gamma_2 \Downarrow \text{false}}$$

B-ANDFALSE2
$$\frac{A; N \vdash \Gamma_2 \Downarrow \text{false}}{A; N \vdash \Gamma_1 \wedge \Gamma_2 \Downarrow \text{false}}$$

B-ANDTRUE
$$\frac{A; N \vdash \Gamma_1 \Downarrow \text{true} \qquad A; N \vdash \Gamma_2 \Downarrow \text{true}}{A; N \vdash \Gamma_1 \wedge \Gamma_2 \Downarrow \text{true}}$$

B-EQUAL
$$A; N \vdash o{=}o' \Downarrow (o = o')$$

B-NEST
$$\frac{N(o, f) \geqslant \Psi}{A; N \vdash \Psi < o.f \Downarrow \text{true}}$$

B-EXIST
$$\frac{A; N \vdash [x \mapsto X]\Gamma \Downarrow \text{true}}{A; N \vdash \exists x \cdot \Gamma \Downarrow \text{true}}$$

B-AXIOM
$$\frac{\Gamma \in A}{A; N \vdash \Gamma \Downarrow \text{true}}$$

B-PRED
$$\frac{A \cup \{p(\overline{X})\}; N \vdash [\overline{x \to X}]P(p) \Downarrow \text{true}}{A; N \vdash p(\overline{X}) \Downarrow \text{true}}$$

Fig. 4. Evaluation rules for Boolean formulae: $A; N \vdash \Gamma \Downarrow b$

must have the empty permission as their invariant. The nesting situation can "grow" using "monotonically increasing invariants" [17, page 13]: $N \leqslant N'$ iff $\forall_k \cdot Nk \leqslant N'k$.

Figure 3 also defines fractional heaps used to model permissions. A fractional heap is a partial function from field locations to field values along with the fraction that one has to the location. Heaps that agree on field values can be added and can be scaled by fractions.

As mentioned previously, the formula syntax forms a sub-language of permissions. A formula used as a permission gives no access, but must be true. A formula used in a conditional permission must have a defined value to determine which way the condition goes. Evaluation of formulae is defined in Fig. 4. It takes a set of assumptions A, which are predicate calls assumed to return true. Because each predicate call is assumed true when evaluating its expansion, assumptions enable a limited form of co-induction. This co-induction is useful when establishing the invariants of cyclic data structures, such as doubly linked lists expressed using ownership: each node points to two others, both owned by a common owner.

A few kinds of facts can never be known to be false: (recursive) predicates, existentials and nesting facts. We do not permit existentials to be false because we wish to have an open semantics. Nesting facts cannot ever be known to be false because the nesting situation may grow during execution. Predicates[3] cannot be false because if we permitted true and false assumptions then by co-induction a predicate could have inconsistent value.

Figure 5 describes the semantics of a permission Π in a given nesting situation N as a relation between these and a (fractional) heap h. The "obligation" (Ψ)

---

[3] In our Twelf formalization, this restriction applies only to recursive predicates.

S-Implication
$$\frac{h; \Psi + \Psi' \models_N^C \Pi}{h; \Psi \models_N^C \Psi' \rightarrow\!\!\!\!- \Pi}$$

S-Obligation
$$\hat{\varnothing}; \Psi \models_N^C \Psi$$

S-Formula
$$\frac{\varnothing; N \vdash \Gamma \Downarrow \text{true}}{\hat{\varnothing}; \varnothing \models_N^C \Gamma}$$

S-Cond
$$\frac{\varnothing; N \vdash \Gamma \Downarrow b \qquad h; \Psi \models_N^C \Pi_b}{h; \Psi \models_N^C \Gamma ? \Pi_{\text{true}} : \Pi_{\text{false}}}$$

S-Exist
$$\frac{h; \Psi \models_N^C [x \mapsto X]\Pi}{h; \Psi \models_N^C \exists x \cdot \Pi}$$

S-Fraction
$$\frac{h; \Psi \models_N^C \Pi}{qh; q\Psi \models_N^C q\Pi}$$

S-Combine
$$\frac{h_1; \Psi_1 \models_N^C \Pi_1 \qquad h_2; \Psi_2 \models_N^C \Pi_2}{h_1 \hat{+} h_2; \Psi_1 + \Psi_2 \models_N^C \Pi_1 + \Pi_2}$$

S-Equiv
$$\frac{\Psi \equiv \Psi' \qquad \Pi \equiv \Pi' \qquad h; \Psi' \models_N^C \Pi'}{h; \Psi \models_N^C \Pi}$$

S-Field
$$\frac{h; \Psi \models_N^{C \cup \{(h;\Psi) \prec o.f\}} N(o, f)}{u = [(o, f) \mapsto (1, o')]}$$
$$\overline{h \hat{+} u; \Psi \models_N^C o.f \rightarrow o'}$$

S-Field-Co
$$\frac{((h; \Psi) \prec o.f) \in C}{u = [(o, f) \mapsto (1, o')]}$$
$$\overline{h \hat{+} u; \Psi \models_N^C o.f \rightarrow o'}$$

Fig. 5. Semantics of Fractional Permissions with Nesting: $h; \Psi \models_N^C \Pi$

and "cycle" (C) arise while computing the semantics of implication and nesting respectively. The left-hand-side of an implication becomes an *obligation* that must be discharged syntactically while investigating the right-hand-side. This semantics of $\rightarrow\!\!\!\!-$ ensures that implications are "sufficiently precise." The *cycle* is used to implement co-induction so that if a field indirectly nests itself, we still have the ability to form the semantics.

A permission is valid for a memory if it is modeled by a fractional heap with no fractions larger than 1 and which agrees with the memory for all fields on which it is defined. We have proved that the system described here satisfies important properties (such as that an implication can indeed be combined with its antecedent, or that an existential can be unpacked) in earlier work with fully mechanized proofs [17].

5   Nesting

Nesting, a generalization of "adoption" [18] serves several purposes: it enables (linear) permissions to be transmitted through a type system non-linearly; it gives a semantics to object invariants; and it provides encapsulation. The nesting operation places an arbitrary permission inside an arbitrary field. The nested permission is yielded in the process. Nesting is irreversible, and thus the *fact* of nesting can be treated non-linearly (can be duplicated arbitrarily).

The picture here shows the composition of two permissions being put together ($\rightsquigarrow$) by nesting the darker permission Π in the lighter one k ($k \equiv \rho.f$ refers to a field of some object),

$$\Pi \quad + \quad k \to \rho' \qquad\qquad \begin{array}{c} k \to \rho' \\ \Pi \prec k \end{array} \qquad\qquad \begin{array}{c} \frac{3}{4}(k \to \rho') + \frac{1}{4}(k \to \rho') \\ \Pi \prec k \end{array}$$

after which case the darker permission is no longer (directly) accessible, but a new nesting fact $\Pi \prec k$ is known. Then this nester permission can be split into two pieces, thus implicitly splitting the nested permission. The $\Leftrightarrow$ notation (as opposed to $\rightsquigarrow$) indicates that the process can be reversed; the pieces can be put back together again. The nesting fact $\Pi \prec k$ is immutable (nonlinear) and thus can be duplicated whenever needed.

The nested permission can be accessed only if one has access to the field it is nested in (hence encapsulation); with a fraction of the field, one can get the corresponding fraction of the permission. As a result, if one has nesting, then one needs to be able to scale (apply fractions to) arbitrary permissions.

Access to the nested permission requires *carving* it out of the nester permission (Fähndrich and DeLine use the term "focus" [18]). The carve operation leaves a hole in the nester permission. The hole is represented by linear implication (*nested* ⊸ *nester*). The nester permission will not be considered complete until the nested permission is "replaced."

$$\begin{array}{c} \frac{3}{4}(k \to \rho') \\ \Pi \prec k \end{array} \qquad\qquad \frac{3}{4}\Pi \multimap \frac{3}{4}(k \to \rho') + \begin{array}{c} \frac{3}{4}\Pi \\ \Pi \prec k \end{array}$$

As seen in the picture, permission carving handles fractions transitively: if one has only a fraction of the nesting permission, one can only get a fraction of the nested permission.

Nesting permits permissions to be transmitted asynchronously (since nesting has immediate and global effect) but does not lead to race conditions since the nested permission cannot be accessed until the *knowledge* of nesting is transmitted, for example through a "volatile" field [19].

5.1 Invariants

Object invariants are an important tool for the modular reasoning of programs [20]. One difficult aspect in providing invariants with a precise semantics is knowing when they are supposed to hold. Typically, an invariant is required to hold at the start and end of public methods, but issues such as "protected" methods, call-backs and inheritance can make the rules tricky [21].

Our system of fractional permissions provides a useful foundation for "effective invariants": the invariant holds whenever one has an effect (read or write) on the state of the object. By convention the permission $o.\mathrm{All} \rightarrow 0$ refers not just to a null field "All" but to the whole state of the object. This convention is expressed by nesting the state of the fields along with the object invariant in the "All" field.

For example, assuming that we had a formula $i > j$ that was true precisely when i is greater than j, then we could express an object invariant for r, that field x is "always" greater than field y:

$$(\exists i \cdot (r.\mathrm{x} \rightarrow i) + \exists j \cdot (r.\mathrm{y} \rightarrow j) + (i > j)) < r.\mathrm{All}$$

Because nesting facts are nonlinear, this invariant fact is true always and everywhere (once established). But the fact cannot be used unless one has permission to access (read or write) $r.\mathrm{All}$. If one has fraction ξ of $r.\mathrm{All}$, one can read the fields and depend on the invariant being true. The following series of (semantics preserving) transformations (written $\rightsquigarrow$) shows how this is done. We use the shorthand $\Psi(r) = \exists i \cdot (r.\mathrm{x} \rightarrow i) + \exists j \cdot (r.\mathrm{y} \rightarrow j) + (i > j)$.

$$\xi r.\mathrm{All} \rightarrow 0 + (\Psi(r) < r.\mathrm{All}) \rightsquigarrow \xi\Psi(r) + (\xi\Psi(r) \multimap \xi r.\mathrm{All} \rightarrow 0) + (\Psi(r) < r.\mathrm{All})$$
$$\rightsquigarrow \xi r.\mathrm{x} \rightarrow r_x + \xi r.\mathrm{y} \rightarrow r_y + (r_x > r_y) +$$
$$(\xi\Psi(r) \multimap \xi r.\mathrm{All} \rightarrow 0) + (\Psi(r) < r.\mathrm{All})$$

(Formulae such as $r_x > r_y$ are unaffected by scaling: $\xi\Gamma \rightsquigarrow \Gamma$.)

If one has write access to the state ($\xi = 1$), then after the last step, one would be free to assign the fields, even if the assignment breaks the invariant. The fact $r_x > r_y$ remains true since it concerns the original value of the fields, not the value after assignment. However, not until one has established the fact that the *current* value of the x field is greater than the current value of the y field, could one reform the existential permission $\Psi(r)$ and then apply linear *modus ponens* ($\Psi(r) + (\Psi(r) \multimap r.\mathrm{All} \rightarrow 0)$ can be transformed into $r.\mathrm{All} \rightarrow 0$) and recover the permission to write the state of the object.

On the other hand, if one has no permission to access the state of the object, one cannot assume the invariant is true. Although the nesting fact is still true, we cannot use it to examine the object. We avoid the "glass wall" abstraction problem [22].

Following Wrigstad [23] (who uses the term "effective uniqueness" to describe alias burying [24]), we call this semantics of invariants "effective invariants," because the invariant is true whenever we have access to the object, for example, if the method has a read or write effect on (that is, temporary permission to access) the object in question.

How do effective invariants handle the various difficulties in nailing down the semantics of invariants? By uniting effects and invariants. Call-backs are handled by making sure that the invariant is re-established before calling any procedure (function/method) that requires access the object. Since the effects (required permissions) are part of the procedure type, we know which ones may (indirectly) access the object. The only way to give access to $r.\mathrm{All}$ is to establish the invariant.

What about inheritance? Nesting permits "monotonically increasing invariants" [17, page 13]. A subclass can nest new permissions in r.All, thus enabling this permission to give access both to the new and to the old invariants, without superclass code needing to know what the invariants are. The new invariants normallty involve the new state, not the inherited state. If every subclass invariant implies the superclass invariant, then we can assume a conventional predicate "Inv" defined as follows:

$$\text{Inv}(r) = \text{Class}(r) < C_1 \implies C_1(r) \wedge$$
$$\ldots \wedge$$
$$\text{Class}(r) < C_n \implies C_n(r)$$

Here $G_1 \implies G_2$ is short for $\neg(G_1 \wedge \neg G_2)$ and $\text{Class}(r) < C$ means that the object's class is C or a subclass. This technique simulates a version of Parkinson and Bierman's abstract predicate system [25]. A closer simulation would substitute $=$ for $<$, allowing a subclass to define an invariant that "breaks" the superclass invariant. Of course simulating a true abstract predicate system with conventions can be clumsy, but in principle the details can be hidden from the user.

So far, we have considered invariants that only address the state of a single object. More complex situations are possible. For example, if we have an object s whose f field points to an object with the previous invariant Ψ (the x field is greater than the y field) and a z field that should be less than the y field of the f sub-object. The new invariant can be expressed with the invariant of the sub-object in an open state:

$$(\exists r \cdot \ s.f \rightarrow r +$$
$$\exists r_z \cdot \ s.z \rightarrow r_z +$$
$$(\Psi(r) \multimap r.\text{All} \rightarrow 0) +$$
$$\exists r_x \cdot \ r.x \rightarrow r_x +$$
$$\exists r_y \cdot r.y \rightarrow r_y +$$
$$(r_x > r_y) + (r_y > r_z)$$
$$) < s.\text{All}$$

Suppose a procedure has an effect of s.All and wishes to call one that requires r.All. Then the invariant can be reconstituted using the implication $\Psi(r) \multimap r$.All $\rightarrow 0$ along with the information about the fields x and y. If only read access is needed, then once the second procedure is done, the existential can be unpacked into its previous state. If the second procedure needs write access, then we will need to ensure that y is still greater than z before we can re-establish our own invariant.

Incidentally, this example demonstrates the utility of permitting implication ($\multimap$) terms inside invariants. Some definitions of concurrent separation logic forbid non-precise terms in (resource) invariants [26], although it has been shown [27,28] that as long as one doesn't use the rule of conjunction, there is no problem with imprecise resource invariants. It is not clear whether the proofs carry over to dynamically allocatable resources. This issue is explored further in the following section.

6   Discussion

This sections discusses some of the features and design decisions in our model compared with those of related work.

6.1   Disjointness

Bornat *et al* [2] pose an interesting problem if one permits scaling of arbitrary predicates: a tree predicate no longer guarantees disjointness of its children if scaled by a fraction $\frac{1}{2}$ or smaller. Retert [29] gives an example of this situation obtaining when a read-only reference to a structure with two "unique" pointers can be constructed using our fractional permission system even if the two pointers are the same. Parkinson [14] and Dockins *et al* [13] solve this problem by proposing a "disjointness" requirement on permissions so that it is not possible to split a permission into two identical permissions.

We take a more pragmatic view: disjointness is not needed on read-only trees. Indeed in pure functional languages, "trees" routinely share structure without controversy. As a result, we simply ignore the "problem" that immutable trees can share structure.. Permission are use to give access and to provide "effective" properties. Uniqueness is only effective if one has write access; with read access only, one can only assume the state is (temporarily) immutable.

6.2   Recursive Permissions

In contrast with most related systems (esp. separation logic), the system described in Section 4 permits only nonlinear recursive definitions, not general permissions. Recursive predicates would be useful for describing cyclic structures in such as way as to permit unhindered transfer of nodes between uses:

$$\text{Cyclic}(r) = \exists h \cdot r.\text{head} \to h + \text{List}(h, h)$$
$$\text{List}(r, h) = \exists n \cdot r.\text{next} \to n + (n = h ? \emptyset : \text{List}(n, h))$$

The equivalent attempt using only recursive formulae has the serious flaw that then $\text{List}(r, h)$ would then be nonlinear, that is permanent. In other words, the address of the particular header node h used for the list starting at node r would be fixed.

Recursive permissions cannot be soundly given a co-inductive semantics (such as in Parkinson and Bierman's abstract predicates [25]) in which a named predicate is assigned a (fractional) heap which is then verified against a definition. The problem is that such a semantics would not necessarily be suffiently precise to permit sound fractional scaling.

However, it seems possible to use a semantics that simply expands the named predicate at every use encountered while determining a (fractional) heap. Such a system would not reject all recursive predicates, merely those not well-founded. In particular, the example above should work fine. It remains further work to check and possibly prove this conjecture.

The main motivation for our fractional permission system was to give a foundational semantics to aliasing annotations. This use doesn't require the adition of recursive permissions, and indeed recursive permissions interfere with our conventions for ownership and inheritance. But if it were established that (inductive, not co-inductive) recursive predicates were a sound addition, the system as a whole may prove more attractive for further work by us and others.

6.3 Nonlinearity

At the risk of gross simplification, nonlinear reasoning is simpler (easier to understand and to automate) but less powerful than full linear reasoning. Thus at one level the nonlinear aspects of our system of fractional permissions with nesting add no new power to a verification system, over against separation logic.

In one aspect, however, it seems there is genuinely new expressive power, and that is the monotonically increasing invariants. In particular, these make it easy to add new lockable or "volatile" [19] resources. The ability to dynamically allocate new resources and threads can be done in separation logic by fixing the invariant of these new resources and threads to be drawn from a finite predetermined set [26]. (Additionally Gotsman *et al* use fractions to distribute the ability to synchronize on the resources, not to differentiate reads and writes.) The fact that in our system new nestings can be performed dynamically allows us to avoid fixing the set of invariants statically.

6.4 Precision

A permission Π is *precise* [16], if given any memory μ and any two modelings $h_1 \models \Pi$ and $h_2 \models \Pi$ where $h_i \leqslant \mu$, then $h_1 = h_2$. As mentioned in the previous section, precision is required in certain situations with separation logic, notably for invariants when the conjunction rule is in effect.

The fractional permission system described here, while including restrictions on existentials and conditionals, does not guarantee precision [17, page 22]. Neither does the system include conjunctive permissions $\Pi \wedge \Pi'$, but such a permission combinator could be easily added with the following obvious semantics:

$$\text{S-Conjunction} \quad \frac{h;\Psi \models_N^C \Pi \qquad h;\Psi \models_N^C \Pi'}{h;\Psi \models_N^C \Pi \wedge \Pi'}$$

Using the cited example of imprecision and a permission type system (e.g., that of Boyland and Sun [30]), one can form typings of the null pointer (0):

$$\Pi \vdash 0 \Downarrow 0 \dashv \varnothing \qquad\qquad \Pi \vdash 0 \Downarrow 0 \dashv \Pi$$

where Π is the write permission to a single cyclic cell. Were the system to have a Hoare-style conjunction rule

$$\text{Conjunction} \quad \frac{\Pi_1 \vdash e \Downarrow \rho \dashv \Pi_1' \qquad \Pi_2 \vdash e \Downarrow \rho \dashv \Pi_2'}{\Pi_1 \wedge \Pi_2 \vdash e \Downarrow \rho \dashv \Pi_1' \wedge \Pi_2'}$$

these could be combined into the following nonsensical typing:

$$\Pi \vdash 0 \Downarrow 0 \dashv \emptyset \wedge \Pi$$

which (since Π cannot be modeled by the empty heap, and thus $\emptyset \wedge \Pi$ is unsatisfiable) says that evaluating the null pointer fails to terminate. Hence the conjunction rule cannot be used in our permission type system.

7   Conclusion

Fractional permissions are an intuitive concept that has been picked up and used in many systems of concurrency verification as an elegant way to permit read-read parallelism. Reference counting can be seen a special model of fractions. Scaling (and its use in nesting) restricts the variety of allowable models, still including a rational fraction model and a model including both counting and splitting (polynomials over the infinitessimal).

Nesting provides a way to incorporate simpler nonlinear reasoning within a linear framework useful for describing invariants, especially since these invariants are allowed to grow. On the whole, however, nesting and fractional scaling has seen less widespread adoption, although they make it easier to analyze dynamic allocation of resources and threads.

References

1. Boyland, J.: Checking Interference with Fractional Permissions. In: Cousot, R. (ed.) SAS 2003. LNCS, vol. 2694, pp. 55–72. Springer, Heidelberg (2003)
2. Bornat, R., Calcagno, C., O'Hearn, P., Parkinson, M.: Permission accounting in separation logic. In: Conference Record of POPL 2005: the 32nd ACM SIGACT-SIGPLAN Symposium on Principles of Programming Languages, pp. 259–270. ACM Press, New York (2005)
3. Brookes, S.: Variables as resource for shared-memory programs: Semantics and soundness. In: Twenty-Second Conference on the Mathematical Foundations of Programming Semantics, pp. 123–150. North-Holland, Elsevier (2006)
4. Bierhoff, K., Aldrich, J.: Modular typestate verification of aliased objects. Technical Report CMUISRI-07-105, School of Computer Science, Carnegie Mellon University (2007)
5. Terauchi, T., Aiken, A.: A capability calculus for concurrency and determinism. ACM Transactions on Programming Languages and Systems 30(5), 1–30 (2008)
6. Turon, A., Wand, M.: A resource analysis of the π-calculus. In: Twenty-Seventh Conference on the Mathematical Foundations of Programming Semantics (2011)
7. Dodds, M., Feng, X., Parkinson, M., Vafeiadis, V.: Deny-Guarantee Reasoning. In: Castagna, G. (ed.) ESOP 2009. LNCS, vol. 5502, pp. 363–377. Springer, Heidelberg (2009)
8. Hurlin, C.: Specification and Verification of Multithreaded Object-Oriented Programs with Separation Logic. PhD thesis, Université Nice—Sophia Antipolis (September 2009)

9. Leino, K.R.M., Müller, P.: A Basis for Verifying Multi-threaded Programs. In: Castagna, G. (ed.) ESOP 2009. LNCS, vol. 5502, pp. 378–393. Springer, Heidelberg (2009)
10. O'Hearn, P.W., Takeyama, M., Power, A.J., Tennent, R.D.: Syntactic control of interference revisited. In: Eleventh Conference on the Mathematical Foundations of Programming Semantics, vol. 1. North-Holland, Elsevier (1995)
11. Walker, D., Crary, K., Morrisett, G.: Typed memory management via static capabilities. ACM Transactions on Programming Languages and Systems 22(4), 701–771 (2000)
12. Wadler, P.: Linear types can change the world! In: Broy, M., Jones, C.B. (eds.) Programming Concepts and Methods. Elsevier, North-Holland (1990)
13. Dockins, R., Hobor, A., Appel, A.W.: A Fresh Look at Separation Algebras and Share Accounting. In: Hu, Z. (ed.) APLAS 2009. LNCS, vol. 5904, pp. 161–177. Springer, Heidelberg (2009)
14. Parkinson, M.J.: Local reasoning for Java. PhD thesis, University of Cambridge (November 2005)
15. Bierhoff, K., Aldrich, J.: Modular typestate verification of aliased objects. In: OOPSLA 2007 Conference Proceedings—Object-Oriented Programming Systems, Languages and Applications, pp. 301–320. ACM Press, New York (2007), Companion technical report:
    http://reports-archive.adm.cs.cmu.edu/anon/isri2007/CMUISRI-07-105.pdf
16. O'Hearn, P.W., Yang, H., Reynolds, J.C.: Separation and information hiding. In: Conference Record of POPL 2004: the 31st ACM SIGACT-SIGPLAN Symposium on Principles of Programming Languages, pp. 268–280. ACM Press, New York (2004)
17. Boyland, J.: Semantics of fractional permissions with nesting. ACM Transactions on Programming Languages and Systems 32(6), Article 22 (August 2010)
18. Fähndrich, M., DeLine, R.: Adoption and focus: Practical linear types for imperative programming. In: Proceedings of the ACM SIGPLAN 2002 Conference on Programming Language Design and Implementation, pp. 13–24. ACM Press, New York (2002)
19. Boyland, J.: The non-linearity of volatile in Java. In: Wrigstad, T. (ed.) International Workshop on Aliasing, Confinement and Ownership in object-oriented programming, IWACO (2007)
20. Müller, P.: Modular Specification and Verification of Object-Oriented Programs. PhD thesis, Fernuniversität Hagen (2001)
21. Ruby, C., Leavens, G.T.: Safely creating correct subclasses without seeing superclass code. In: OOPSLA 2000 Conference Proceedings—Object-Oriented Programming Systems, Languages and Applications, pp. 208–228. ACM Press, New York (2000)
22. Boyland, J.: Why we should not add readonly to Java, yet. In: 7th ECOOP Workshop on Formal Techniques for Java-like Programs (2005)
23. Wrigstad, T.: External Uniqueness: A Theory of Aggregate Uniqueness for Object-Oriented Programming. PhD thesis, Stockholm University (2004)
24. Boyland, J.: Alias burying: Unique variables without destructive reads. Software Practice and Experience 31(6), 533–553 (2001)
25. Parkinson, M., Bierman, G.: Separation Logic for Object-Oriented Programming. In: Clarke, D., Noble, J., Wrigstad, T. (eds.) Aliasing in Object-Oriented Programming. LNCS, vol. 7850, pp. 366–406. Springer, Heidelberg (2013)

26. Gotsman, A., Berdine, J., Cook, B., Rinetzky, N., Sagiv, M.: Local Reasoning for Storable Locks and Threads. In: Shao, Z. (ed.) APLAS 2007. LNCS, vol. 4807, pp. 19–37. Springer, Heidelberg (2007)
27. Gotsman, A., Berdine, J., Cook, B.: Precision and the conjunction rule in concurrent separation logic. Electronic Notes in Theoretical Computer Science 276, 171–190 (2011); Presented at Twenty-seventh Conference on the Mathematical Foundations of Programming Semantics
28. Vafeiadis, V.: Concurrent separation logic and operational semantics. Electronic Notes in Theoretical Computer Science 276, 335–351 (2011); Presented at Twenty-seventh Conference on the Mathematical Foundations of Programming Semantics
29. Retert, W.S.: Implementing Permission Analysis. PhD thesis, University of Wisconsin–Milwaukee, Department of EE & CS (2009)
30. Boyland, J., Sun, C.: Proving the correctness of fractional permissions for a Java-like kernel language. In: Zucca, E. (ed.) Informal Proceedings of 18th International Workshop on Foundations of Object-Oriented Languages, FOOL 2011 (October 2011)

Object Ownership in Program Verification

Werner Dietl[1] and Peter Müller[2]

[1] University of Washington
wmdietl@cs.washington.edu
[2] ETH Zurich
peter.mueller@inf.ethz.ch

Abstract. Dealing with aliasing is one of the key challenges for the verification of imperative programs. For instance, aliases make it difficult to determine which abstractions are potentially affected by a heap update and to determine which locks need to be acquired to avoid data races. Object ownership was one of the first approaches that allowed programmers to control aliasing and to restrict the operations that can be applied to a reference. It thus enabled sound, modular, and automatic verification of heap-manipulating programs. In this paper, we present two ownership systems that have been designed specifically to support program verification—Universe Types and Spec#'s Dynamic Ownership—and explain their applications in program verification, illustrated through a series of Spec# examples.

1 Introduction

Dealing with aliasing is one of the key challenges for the verification of imperative programs. To understand some of the difficulties caused by aliasing, consider an implementation of a list consisting of a list head and a linked node structure, and two list instances l1 and l2. Typical verification tasks include:

1. *Framing*: Does a call to l1.Add affect properties of l2 such as l2's length?
2. *Invariants*: Does a call to l1.Add possibly break the invariant of l2?
3. *Locking*: If each list method acquires the list head's lock before performing a list operation, can there be data races on the list structure?

The answers to these questions depend on aliasing. If l1 and l2 have disjoint node structures then the answer to all three questions is "no". However, if they possibly share the nodes then the answer might be "yes":

1. Appending a new node to the shared node structure affects l2's length if the length is computed by traversing the nodes until a null reference is reached.
2. Appending a node might also break l2's invariant, for instance if l2 contains a last field and the invariant last.next==null.
3. When two threads acquire the locks of l1 and l2, respectively, then they might update the shared node structure concurrently, leading to a data race.

D. Clarke et al. (Eds.): Aliasing in Object-Oriented Programming, LNCS 7850, pp. 289–318, 2013.
© Springer-Verlag Berlin Heidelberg 2013

This example shows that program verifiers need information about aliasing to decide when properties are preserved, which invariants to check, or which locks to require for a heap access, to mention just some of the most common verification tasks.

Early work on verifying heap-manipulating programs provided only partial solutions to the problems caused by aliasing. Some techniques use an explicit heap representation and require the user to reason about the consequences of each heap update explicitly [59,28], which compromises abstraction and information hiding. Moreover, the resulting proof obligations are non-modular and difficult to prove automatically. Leino and Nelson [34,43] addressed the abstraction problem by allowing a specification to provide information about the footprint of a heap property without revealing the property itself; however, the resulting proof obligations make heavy use of reachability predicates and are, thus, difficult to discharge automatically. Yet another approach is to make unsound assumptions about the effects of heap updates and to optimize the proof obligation to strike a good balance between the errors that can be detected on one side and the annotation overhead, modularity, and automation on the other side [24]. So towards the end of the last millennium, there was no verification technique for heap-manipulating programs that was sound, modular, and amenable to automation.

This situation changed with the invention of object ownership and ownership types [11]. Ownership provides two important benefits for program verification. First, it allows programmers to describe the *topology* of heap data structures in a simple and natural way, at least for hierarchical data structures. For instance, ownership can express that two lists have disjoint node structures, without resorting to reachability predicates. Ownership types provide an automatic way of checking that an implementation conforms to the intended topology. Hierarchical topologies help for instance with proving data race freedom. Second, ownership can be used to define and enforce *encapsulation disciplines*, which describe what references may exist in a program execution and which operations may be performed on these references. For instance, an encapsulation discipline may allow arbitrary objects (such as iterators) to read the nodes of a list, but only allow the list header and its nodes to modify the node structure. Restricting write accesses helps for instance with verifying object invariants.

In this paper, we summarize the topology and encapsulation disciplines that are used in ownership-based program verification (Sec. 2) and present two ways of enforcing them—a type system called Universe Types [49,22,18,20] and a verification methodology called Dynamic Ownership [37] (Sec. 3). The main part of the paper surveys applications of object ownership in program verification. We discuss how the ownership topology is used for effect specifications, framing, proving termination, and for defining the semantics of object invariants (Sec. 4). Then we show how encapsulation disciplines on top of ownership systems are used to verify object invariants, to define and check object immutability, and to prove the absence of data races (Sec. 5). For each of these verification tasks, we describe the problem, explain the ownership solution, and briefly summarize alternative solutions. We illustrate the ownership solutions using examples

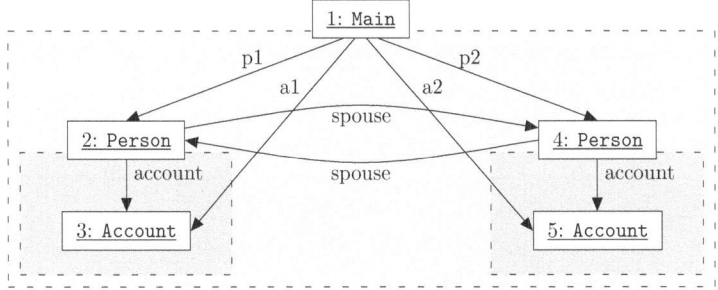

Fig. 1. Example of an ownership structure. Boxes and arrows depict objects and references, respectively. Dashed boxes enclose the objects of an ownership context; the owner of these objects sits atop the dashed box.

written and verified in the Spec# system [3,42]. The Spec# examples as well as a translation to Java with JML [29] and Universe annotations are available from www.pm.inf.ethz.ch/publications/OwnershipInVerification/.

2   Ownership Topology and Encapsulation

This section gives a brief overview of the ownership topology and the encapsulation disciplines that have been used to support program verification.

Topology. The *ownership topology* provides a hierarchical structure of the objects in the heap. Each object is *owned* by at most one other object, its *owner*. The ownership relation is acyclic, that is, the ownership topology is a forest of ownership trees, and objects without owner are roots. The set of objects with the same owner is called an *ownership context*.

Fig. 1 illustrates an ownership topology, where object 1 of class Main owns the Person objects 2 and 4. Each of the Person objects owns an Account object. Since Person objects own their Account objects, the ownership topology guarantees that Account objects are never shared among Person objects.

Some ownership systems allow the ownership topology to change during the execution of a program by supporting ownership transfer [12,37,53]. For simplicity, we ignore ownership transfer in this paper; once an object has been assigned an owner, the owner does not change for the remaining lifetime of the object.

Encapsulation. The ownership topology can be used to define various encapsulation disciplines that restrict references or interactions between objects. For the verification of imperative programs, reasoning about side effects is one of the key challenges. Therefore, the most widely used encapsulation discipline in ownership-based verification is the owner-as-modifier discipline, which restricts the heap modifications that a method may perform. An alternative encapsulation discipline is the owner-as-dominator discipline, which restricts the existence of references.

The *owner-as-modifier* discipline [22,18] enforces that all modifications of an object are initiated by the object's owner. More precisely, when a method modifies an object o then for each (transitive) owner o' of o, the call stack contains a method execution with o' as receiver. For instance, whenever a method modifies the Account object 3 in Fig. 1 then there must be method executions in progress with objects 2 and 1 as receivers.

The owner-as-modifier discipline allows an object to control modifications of the objects it (transitively) owns. In particular, the owner can prevent certain modifications or maintain properties of the objects it owns. For instance, the only way for Person object 4 to modify Account object 3 is to invoke a method on object 3's owner (object 2), which can then impose appropriate checks, for instance, to maintain its own invariant.

In order to enforce the owner-as-modifier discipline modularly, a checker needs to know which methods potentially modify the heap and which methods do not: calls to methods with side effects (*impure* methods) must be restricted, whereas side-effect free (*pure*) methods may be called on any object. For this purpose, we assume that side-effect free methods are labelled as pure. How to check method purity is beyond the scope of this paper [54,63].

The *owner-as-dominator* discipline [11] enforces that the owner o' of an object o is a dominator for every access path from a root of the ownership forest to o. For instance, all access paths from object 1 to object 3 must pass through object 3's owner, object 2. The references a1 and a2 that bypass the owning Person objects are not permitted in this discipline.

The owner-as-dominator discipline allows an object to control the existence of access paths to the objects it (transitively) owns. Therefore, the owner controls read and write access to these objects, which is for instance useful to enforce locking strategies.

3   Enforcing Topology and Encapsulation

This section describes two alternative approaches to enforce the ownership topology and encapsulation discipline: a type system called Universe Types and a verification methodology called Dynamic Ownership.

3.1   Universe Types

Universe Types [20,21,19,22] is a static type system that enforces the ownership topology and the owner-as-modifier encapsulation discipline as described in the previous section.

Ownership Qualifiers. The type system equips each occurrence of a reference type with one of five type qualifiers[1]. These *ownership qualifiers* describe the position of an object in the ownership hierarchy relatively to the current object this:

- peer indicates that an object has the same owner as the current object.
- rep (short for "representation") indicates that an object is owned by the current object.
- any indicates that no static knowledge about an object's owner is available, and the owner is arbitrary.
- lost indicates that no static knowledge about an object's owner is available, but there are constraints on the owner.
- self indicates that an object is the current object.

The example in Fig. 2 (left column) illustrates the use of ownership qualifiers. A Person object has a reference to an Account, which is owned by the Person object; therefore, the account field has a rep qualifier. A Person object and its spouse share the same owner; therefore, the spouse field has a peer qualifier. Instances of class Main own two Person objects as indicated by the rep qualifier for the fields p1 and p2.

In Universe Types, the owner of an object is determined when the object is created. The owner is indicated by a rep or peer qualifier in the new expression, as illustrated by method Demo.

Viewpoint Adaptation. The ownership qualifier of a type depends on the current object this. Therefore, when the current object changes, the ownership qualifiers need to change as well. We call this process *viewpoint adaptation*. As a simple example, consider class Person from Fig. 2. Field spouse has declared type peer Person, expressing that the current Person instance and the referenced person share the same owner. However, for any Person reference p, the type of p.spouse is not necessarily the declared type peer Person. For instance, when p is of type rep Person then p is owned by the current object this. Since p and p.spouse have the same owner, p.spouse is also owned by this and, therefore, has type rep Person. That is, the declared type of spouse was adapted to the new viewpoint, this.

More formally, we define viewpoint adaptation of declared qualifier u' from the viewpoint given by qualifier u to the current object this using function $\triangleright$, which is defined as follows:

$$
\begin{aligned}
\text{self} \triangleright u' &= u' \\
\text{peer} \triangleright \text{peer} &= \text{peer} \\
\text{rep} \ \triangleright \text{peer} &= \text{rep} \\
u \quad \triangleright \text{any} &= \text{any} \\
u \quad \triangleright u' &= \text{lost} \qquad \text{otherwise}
\end{aligned}
$$

---

[1] Arrays and instantiations of generic types may have more than one qualifier.

Universe Types:

```
class Account {
  int value;
}

class Person {
  rep Account account;
  peer Person spouse;

  Person() {
    account = new rep Account();
    spouse = null;
  }
}

class Main {
  rep Person p1;
  rep Person p2;

  void Demo() {
    p1 = new rep Person();
    p2 = new rep Person();


    p1.spouse = p2;
    p2.spouse = p1;


    any Account a1 = p1.account;
    any Account a2 = p2.account;
    int total = a1.value + a2.value;

    // forbidden by Topology
    p1.account = p2.account;
    // forbidden by Encapsulation
    a1.value += 10000;
  }
}
```

Dynamic Ownership:

```
class Account {
  int value;
}

class Person {
  [Rep] Account account;
  [Peer] Person spouse;

  Person() {
    account = new Account();
    spouse = null;
  }
}

class Main {
  [Rep] Person p1;
  [Rep] Person p2;

  void Demo() {
    p1 = new Person();
    p2 = new Person();

    expose(this) {
      p1.spouse = p2;
      p2.spouse = p1;
    }

    Account a1 = p1.account;
    Account a2 = p2.account;
    int total = a1.value + a2.value;

    // forbidden by Topology
    p1.account = p2.account;
    // forbidden by Encapsulation
    a1.value += 10000;
  }
}
```

Fig. 2. Illustration of the ownership topology and encapsulation. The code on the left uses Universe Types; the code on the right uses Spec#'s Dynamic Ownership. We omit accessibility qualifiers and non-null annotations for brevity. Execution of method Main.Demo results in the ownership structure from Fig. 1.

Let us again consider class Person from Fig. 2 where field spouse has the declared type peer Person. For a reference p of type rep Person, to determine the type of a field access p.spouse, one adapts the declared qualifier (peer) from the qualifier of the receiver (rep) to this; that is, we determine that rep ▷ peer is rep and the resulting type is therefore rep Person. This corresponds to the intuition that the field access first goes into the representation and then stays within the current representation—resulting in a reference that points into the current representation.

Viewpoint adaptation is applied whenever a declared type needs to be adapted to the current object, that is, for field accesses and updates (adapting the declared field type), method calls (adapting the declared method parameter and return types), and object instantiations (adapting the declared constructor parameter types). For generic types, it is also applied to the upper bounds of type parameters.

There is an important distinction between the ownership qualifiers any and lost. Qualifier any expresses that there is no static constraint on the ownership of the referenced object. In our example, local variable a1 can be used to reference an arbitrary account. On the other hand, lost expresses that there exists an ownership constraint, but this constraint is not expressible in the type system. In method Demo, the access p1.account first follows the rep reference p1 and then another rep reference account. There is no static qualifier to express the resulting ownership relationship. Viewpoint adaptation yields the lost qualifier for the type of p1.account. Such a reference can be used for reading, but an update of p1.account is forbidden, as the type system cannot statically ensure that the assigned value satisfies the ownership constraint expressed by the rep qualifier in the declaration of account. For the same reason, method invocations and object instantiations are forbidden if the parameter types after viewpoint adaptation contain lost. In that case, the method implementation expects a specific owner, but the type system cannot guarantee that the caller passes an argument with the expected owner because the ownership information has been lost during viewpoint adaptation.

Subtyping. The ownership qualifiers are in a simple ordered relationship. The self qualifier is used only for the current object this, which is evidently a peer of itself; therefore self is a subtype of peer. Both peer and rep are subtypes of lost as the former are more precise than the latter. Finally, all ownership qualifiers are subtypes of any, because the latter does not express any ownership information.

In method Demo, we can assign p1.account to local variable a1 because the qualifier of the right-hand side, lost, is a subtype of a1's qualifier, any.

Encapsulation. Universe Types optionally enforce the owner-as-modifier encapsulation discipline. Field updates and calls to impure methods require that the ownership qualifier of the receiver is neither any nor lost. Field reads and calls to pure methods are permitted for arbitrary receivers.

Consider the last assignment a1.value += 10000 in method Demo. This assignment does not violate the ownership topology, because field value is of a primitive type. However, it does violate the owner-as-modifier discipline. Since the receiver a1 is of type any Account, we have no static knowledge of its owner. Therefore, the type system cannot ensure that the owner controls this modification and, thus, it is forbidden.

3.2   Dynamic Ownership

Dynamic Ownership [37] enforces the ownership topology and an encapsulation discipline similar to owner-as-modifier through program verification. To support inheritance, Dynamic Ownership uses object-class pairs as owners. Here, we present a simplified version without the class-component. Dynamic Ownership has been implemented in the Spec# language, and we will be using Spec# in the rest of the paper.

Ownership Attributes. To encode the ownership relation, Dynamic Owner-ship adds a ghost field owner to each object. The ownership topology is then expressed through specifications over this ghost field. In particular, Spec# offers two attributes (annotations in Java terminology) [Peer] and [Rep] that can be added to field declarations[2]. Declaring a field f with a [Peer] attribute is similar to the following object invariant, but is enforced differently as we explain below:

invariant f **!= null ==>** f.owner **== this**.owner;

Analogously, a [Rep] attribute is similar to the following object invariant:

invariant f **!= null ==>** f.owner **== this**;

The example in Fig. 2 (right column) illustrates the use of ownership attributes. The fields account, spouse, p1, and p2 are declared with attributes analogous to the ownership qualifiers in Universe Types. In contrast to Universe Types, the declarations of methods and local variables do not include ownership in-formation. For methods, ownership information can be expressed via pre- and postconditions; for locals, the verifier keeps track of any information about the owner field.

In contrast to Universe Types, Spec# does not determine the owner of an object when it is created. Fresh objects start out as un-owned. The owner is set when an un-owned object is assigned to a rep or peer field of another object. More precisely, for a peer field f and the assignment $o.f = e$ the verifier imposes a proof obligation that either e is null, that o and e have the same owner, or that e is un-owned. In the latter case, it sets e's owner to o's owner. If both o and e are un-owned, they stay un-owned, but the verifier records that the objects are peers (we say they form a *peer group*). When one object of a peer group gets its owner assigned then the owner of all objects of the peer group is set to ensure that they stay peers of each other. The treatment of assignments to rep fields is analogous, but does not create peer groups.

Method Demo in Fig. 2 illustrates this process. After creating the first Person object, it is initially un-owned. Its owner is set to this when it gets assigned to field p1, because p1 is a rep field. The assignment p1.account = p2.account towards the end of the method fails to verify since reference p2.account is not known to be null and the owner of the object p2.account is p2, because field account is a rep field. That is, the right-hand side is neither un-owned nor owned by p1, making the assignment to a rep field of p1 invalid.

Spec#'s semantics of field updates guarantees that rep and peer fields satisfy the corresponding ownership invariants in all execution states, similar to a type system. However, Dynamic Ownership permits a more flexible initialization of an object's owner than most ownership type systems, because an object's owner need not be fixed when the object is created. Like Universe Types, Spec# does

---

[2] Additional attributes allow one to handle arrays and instantiations of generic types.

not allow the owner of an object to change after it has been set, but supporting ownership transfer is possible [37].

Encapsulation. Spec# enforces an encapsulation discipline that controls modifications of objects, similar to the owner-as-modifier discipline. In Spec#, each object is either in the *valid* or in the *mutable* state. We say that an object is *consistent* if it is valid and its owner (if any) is mutable; it is *peer consistent* if the object and all of its peers are consistent.

Valid objects must satisfy their object invariants, whereas mutable objects may violate their object invariants (but not the ownership invariants mentioned above). A proof obligation for field updates enforces that the receiver is mutable or—in case the update is known not to violate the receiver's object invariant— consistent.

Fresh objects are initially mutable and become valid when the new expression terminates. Before a valid object can be modified, it has to be *exposed*. For this purpose, Spec# provides a block statement expose(o) { ... } with the following semantics: The statement first asserts that o is consistent. Then o becomes mutable and the body of the block statement is executed. Finally, the expose statement asserts that o's object invariant holds (see Sec. 5.1) and that all objects owned by o are valid, and then makes o valid.

The Spec# methodology guarantees that in each execution state all objects (transitively) owned by a valid object are also valid. Consequently, before updating an object o, all of o's transitive owners need to be exposed. Similarly to the owner-as-modifier discipline, this gives the owners the possibility to control modifications, for instance, to maintain invariants over the owned objects.

By default, impure methods (and constructors) in Spec# require their receiver and arguments to be peer consistent and ensure that their result is also peer consistent. This allows the method to expose the receiver and the arguments and modify their state. Pure methods by default require the receiver and arguments (and their peers) to be valid, and ensure peer validity of the result.

In method Demo (Fig. 2, right column), these defaults imply that the receiver this is consistent at the beginning of the method. The newly created Person objects are consistent when their new-expressions terminate; after assigning them to the fields p1 and p2, they remain valid but are no longer consistent because they now have a valid owner, this. Therefore, before updating their spouse fields, the method has to expose this to make the Person objects consistent, which is sufficient to permit the update since class Person does not declare an object invariant. (If it did, we would also have to expose p1 and p2.) The fact that we can read the account fields as well as the value fields of the Account objects without exposing any objects illustrates that Spec#'s encapsulation discipline controls modifications, but not read access. The last statement fails to verify because the object a1 is neither mutable nor consistent. In order to verify the assignment, the method would have to ensure that all of a1's transitive owners are mutable. By the default precondition of method Demo, the verifier knows that the transitive owners of this are mutable. So it suffices to expose this and p1:

```
expose(this) {
  expose(p1) {
    a1.value += 10000;
  }
}
```

This example illustrates that Spec#'s encapsulation discipline is slightly more flexible than owner-as-modifier. For the update of a1.value, the owner-as-modifier discipline requires that on each of a1's transitive owners, a method execution is currently on the stack. By contrast, Spec# requires only that these owners are mutable, that is, that an expose block is currently being executed. However, these expose blocks may occur in any method execution, not necessarily in methods whose receiver is the owner. Here, we do not have to call a method on p1 in order to update a1.value.

4   Using Ownership Topologies in Verification

Ownership has numerous applications in program verification. In this section, we present four ways to use the hierarchical heap topology of ownership systems. Applications that in addition rely on encapsulation are presented in Sec. 5. We illustrate each application by an implementation of an array list, written and verified in Spec# [3,42]. The Spec# examples as well as a translation to Java with JML [29] and Universe annotations are available from the companion website. Fig. 3 shows a simple list interface; class ArrayList in Fig. 4 implements this interface.

```
interface List {
  void Add(object! e);
    ensures Contains(e);
    ensures Length() == old(Length()) + 1;

  void Remove(object! e);
    ensures old(Contains(e)) ==> Length() == old(Length())-1;

  [Pure] bool Contains(object! e);

  [Pure] int Length();
}
```

Fig. 3. A simple list interface. In Spec#, an exclamation point after a reference type indicates a non-null type. Method pre- and postconditions are written as requires and ensures clauses, respectively. The old keyword in postconditions is used to refer to the prestate value of an expression. The attribute Pure indicates that a method does not modify any objects that are allocated in its prestate; pure methods may be used in specifications because they are side-effect free.

4.1   Effect Specifications

Verification of imperative programs relies heavily on effect specifications to characterize the parts of the heap that a method may read, modify, de-allocate, lock, etc. [26]. For example, List's Add method may modify the internal representation of the list (for instance, an underlying array), but nothing else.

Problem. A naive approach to specifying effects is to enumerate the affected heap locations in the effect specification. For instance, one could specify the write effect of method Add in class ArrayList using the following specification clause:

```
modifies elems, next, elems[*];
```

which gives permission to modify the list's elems and next fields as well as all elements of the elems array. The problem with this approach is that it violates information hiding, which has several negative consequences: (1) Changes of the internals of a data structure become visible to clients and, thus, might require re-verification of client code. (2) Enumerating locations is not possible for interfaces, which do not have a concrete implementation. (3) It is difficult to allow overriding methods in subclasses to modify the additional fields declared in subclasses (this is sometimes called the extended state problem [36]).

When the effect of a method includes only fields of its parameters then these problems can be solved by using wildcards or static data groups [36]. For instance, Spec# provides the wildcard syntax $o.*$ to denote all fields of an object o. However, this solution does not apply to effects that include objects reachable from the method parameters such as the array object in this.elems. In this case, one needs to specify a path to the affected objects (here, elems), which reveals implementation details. This is particularly problematic when a method affects an unbounded number of locations, for instance, modifies fields of all nodes in a linked list; it is then not possible to enumerate all of these locations statically. So the problem is:

How to express implementation-independent effect specifications?

Ownership Solution. Clarke and Drossopoulou [10] showed that the hierarchical heap topology of ownership systems provides a natural abstraction mechanism for effects by using a reference to an object o to represent o and all objects (transitively) owned by o (that is, the ownership tree rooted in o).

This idea is adopted by Spec# to specify read and write effects. Unless indicated otherwise, every non-pure method in Spec# has the default write effect

```
modifies this.*;
```

which allows the method to modify all fields of the receiver object (by the wildcard) as well as all fields of all objects (transitively) owned by the receiver (by the abstraction mechanism mentioned above). This effect specification does not reveal any implementation details. In our example, it applies to the Add method

```
public class ArrayList : List {
  [Rep][SpecPublic] object[]! elems = new object[32];
  int next;

  invariant 0 <= next && next <= elems.Length;
  invariant elems.GetType() == typeof(object[]);
  invariant forall{int i in (0: next); elems[i] != null};

  public ArrayList()
    ensures Length() == 0;
  { }

  public void Add(object! e)
  {
    expose(this)
    {
      if(next == elems.Length) // resize the array
      {
        object[] tmp = new object[elems.Length * 2 + 1];
        Array.Copy(elems, tmp, next);
        elems = tmp;
      }
      elems[next] = e;
      next++;
    }
    assert elems[next-1] == e;
  }

  [Pure] public bool Contains(object! e)
    ensures result==exists{int i in (0: next); elems[i]==e};
  {
    for(int i = 0; i < next; i++)
      invariant forall{int j in (0: i); elems[j] != e};
    {
      if(elems[i] == e)
        return true;
    }
    return false;
  }
  // other methods omitted
}
```

Fig. 4. An array list implementation of the List interface. The methods inherit the contracts defined in List. The invariant clauses after the field declarations declare object invariants, whereas the invariant clause in method Contains declares a loop invariant. The forall and exists expressions quantify over half-open integer intervals. The SpecPublic attribute on elems allows the field to appear in specifications of public methods.

of interface List and of class ArrayList. Note that the latter satisfies the effect specification because it modifies at most the following locations: (1) fields of the receiver, which is permitted by the wildcard in the effect specification, (2) the array object in this.elems, which is permitted because the array is owned by the receiver, and (3) elements of the new array it allocates; the initialization of fresh objects is generally not considered a write effect and, thus, does not have to be included in the effect specification. Note that in the implementation of Fig. 4, this write effect does not allow the Add method to modify the states of the objects stored in the elems array because they are not owned by the receiver. Spec# provides an [ElementsRep] attribute for arrays to declare such an ownership relation if desired.

Similarly, the default read effect of pure methods in Spec# contains all fields of the receiver as well as all fields of all objects (transitively) owned by the receiver. Other read effects can be specified using attributes on the method declaration. The default allows methods Contains and Length of class ArrayList to read next, elems, and the elements of elems.

Spec# checks write effects by generating appropriate proof obligations [2]. A crucial property of these proof obligations is that they avoid reachability predicates (such as transitive ownership) because these are not handled well by automatic theorem provers. Read effects are checked syntactically, but a more precise checking through verification is also possible [40].

Other Solutions. Leino proposed a formalism based on explicit dependencies between model fields and concrete fields to provide implementation-independent specifications of effects [34]. When an effect includes a model field then it also includes all fields the model field (transitively) depends on. Drawbacks of this approach are that it uses reachability predicates (transitive dependencies) and that its soundness argument is complicated [43]. A similar approach is used in dynamic data groups [44], but with a simpler formalism. The second author's thesis [49] combined explicit dependencies with ownership.

Kassios developed a powerful technique to specify effects called Dynamic Frames [31]. A dynamic frame is a set of objects or locations. Effect specifications simply mention such sets; clients reason in terms of these sets and their disjointness, but do not need to know the set contents, which preserves information hiding. In Kassios' work, dynamic frames are encoded as functions of the heap. Later work, for instance on Dafny [35] and Region Logic [1] encodes dynamic frames using ghost variables to increase automation with SMT solvers.

Another approach to specifying effects is via permissions [9]. Each memory location is associated with a permission, and a method may access a location only if it has the permission to do so. Read and write effects can then be inferred from permission specifications. This approach is for instance taken in Separation Logic [5,60] and Implicit Dynamic Frames [64,41]. Abstraction is expressed via abstract predicates [58]. Both Dynamic Frames and permission systems require a higher annotation overhead than the ownership solution, but have the big advantage that they are not limited to hierarchical structures.

4.2 Framing

One of the key challenges in verifying imperative programs is to determine whether the heap modifications performed by a piece of code affect the validity of heap properties. The client class in Fig. 5 illustrates this problem. The property l1.Contains("one") is established by the call l1.Add("one"). To prove that it still holds at the end of method Frame requires framing. One has to prove that the call to l2.Remove does not invalidate the property, which could for instance happen if l1 and l2 shared the same array.

```
class Client {
  public static void Frame(List! l1, List! l2)
    requires l1 != l2;
    modifies l1.*, l2.*;
  {
    l1.Add("one");
    l2.Remove("one");
    assert l1.Contains("one");
  }
}
```

Fig. 5. A client of the List interface. Proving the assertion requires framing.

Problem. Framing is based on effect specifications. If the write effect of a piece of code is disjoint from the read effect of a heap property then executing the code does not affect the validity of the property. Framing is trivial with the naive effect specifications, where the affected locations are explicitly enumerated. However, when effect specifications use abstraction then clients must be able to determine whether two effects are disjoint without actually knowing the concrete set of affected locations. So the problem is:

How to determine whether two effects overlap?

Ownership Solution. As we discussed in Sec. 4.1, ownership-based effect specifications use the root of an ownership tree to abstract over the locations of all objects in the tree. Because each object has at most one owner, the trees rooted in objects o and p are either disjoint or one tree is a (not necessarily proper) sub-tree of the other. So to prove that the effects characterized by o and p are disjoint, it is sufficient to show that $o \neq p$ and neither o (transitively) owns p nor vice versa.

In Spec#, this property is proved as follows. As we have explained in Sec. 3.2, impure methods in Spec# require by default that the receiver and each explicit argument are consistent, that is, that they are valid and their owners (if any) are mutable. Since Spec# guarantees that all objects (transitively) owned by a valid object are also valid, this default requirement implies that it is not possible for one argument to own another. Thus, any two arguments either refer to the same object or to disjoint ownership trees. In the example from Fig. 5, the precondition guarantees that 11 and 12 point to different objects and, thus, the trees rooted in 11 and 12 are disjoint, which is sufficient to prove that 12.Remove does not affect the validity of 11.Contains("one").

Other Solutions. The three techniques for effect specifications discussed in Sec. 4.1 solve the framing problem in different ways.

Techniques that use explicit dependencies without ownership include rules that allow one to derive the absence of certain dependencies. If we know that a model field a does *not* (transitively) depend on another field b then some code with write effect a will not affect a property with read effect b. Reasoning about such specifications again involves reachability. Dynamic data groups simplify this reasoning by imposing various restrictions on dependencies. For instance in our example, the *pivot uniqueness* requirement guarantees that the lists 11 and 12 operate on different arrays.

With Dynamic Frames, specifications have to state the disjointness of frames explicitly. A common idiom is to put all locations that belong to a data structure into one frame state. Methods of the data structure then typically read or write state. With this effect specification, method Frame in Fig. 5 requires the additional precondition $11.\text{state} \cap 12.\text{state} = \emptyset$.

Permission-based systems use two ingredients for framing. First, they require every heap property (in particular, every abstract predicate) to be *self-framing*, that is, to include permissions for all heap accesses in the property. Second, they support a *separating conjunction* $*$, which holds if both conjuncts hold and their permissions are disjoint. So if formulas P and Q hold separately, and a piece of code operates using the permissions specified in P then it is guaranteed not to affect Q. In our example, let's assume an abstract predicate valid that contains all permissions for the list data structure and that is used as pre- and postcondition of methods Add, Remove, and Contains. Method Frame in Fig. 5 can then be verified using the additional precondition $11.\text{valid} * 12.\text{valid}$, which implies that 12.Remove's write effect is disjoint from 11.Contains's read effect.

4.3 Termination

Program verification often includes termination proofs for two reasons. First, termination is a desired property of many implementations. Second, many specification formalisms support recursive functions or pure methods, which are encoded for the prover as uninterpreted function symbols with appropriate axioms. To ensure the consistency of these axioms, one needs to show that the recursion is well founded [62].

Problem. The standard approach to termination proofs is to find a ranking function that maps the program state to a well-founded set such as the natural numbers, and to prove that each recursive call or loop iteration decreases the value of the ranking function [15]. Modular verifiers that check termination require a ranking function for each loop and recursive method, which is difficult to specify for loops and methods that traverse object structures. The example in Fig. 6 illustrates the problem. The recursive call in method GetHashCode should be permitted, provided that it does not eventually call GetHashCode on the list. This could for instance happen if the hash code of an array was defined in terms of the hash codes of its elements and if the list was stored in its own array.

```
[Pure] public override int GetHashCode ()
   ensures result == elems . GetHashCode ();
{ return elems . GetHashCode (); }
```

Fig. 6. GetHashCode of class ArrayList. Spec# proves that recursive specifications of pure methods are well founded. Here, the height of the receiver in the ownership hierarchy is implicitly used as ranking function.

In general, one needs to show that a recursive heap traversal does not go in cycles, which is typically done by using the distance from the end of the traversal as a ranking function. However, denoting this distance in specifications requires a reachability predicate (for instance, this list node reaches the end of the list in n steps), which are notoriously difficult to handle for automatic verifiers based on SMT solvers. A work-around is to encode the distance using ghost state; for instance, each list node stores its distance from the end of the list. However, maintaining the ghost state increases the specification overhead. Moreover, adding ghost state to library classes and arrays is not possible. So the problem is:

How to specify ranking functions for heap traversals?

Ownership Solution. Since the ownership topology is acyclic, each recursion that traverses an ownership tree only downwards or only upwards is well founded. In other words, for traversals towards the leaves, we can use the height of an object in the ownership tree as a ranking function, provided that the tree does not grow during the traversal. Analogously, we can use the depth in the tree for traversals towards the root. This approach does not lead to the annotation overhead incurred by solutions based on ghost state. Moreover, it can be checked syntactically, which avoids reasoning about reachability predicates. For downward traversals, it is sufficient to check that the receiver of each recursive call is of a rep type. One could use an analogous check for upward traversals, if the ownership system provided an "owner" type qualifier or attribute, which is not the case in Spec#.

Spec# uses a lexicographic ordering as ranking function [17]. The first component is the height of an object in the ownership tree. Since termination is proved only for pure (side-effect free) methods, the tree cannot grow during the traversal. The second component is a static ordering of all method declarations in a program; it is determined by the order in which the declarations occur in the program text and can also be specified explicitly via attributes on method declarations. The example in Fig. 6 is accepted by Spec# because the receiver of the recursive call, elems, is declared with the [Rep] attribute.

Other Solutions. Another ranking function for recursive methods is the size of their read effects [35]. If the read effect gets strictly smaller with each recursive call then the recursion will terminate eventually. For effect specifications based on dynamic frames, this property can be verified by comparing set cardinalities (if the prover supports them) or by checking set inclusion. The solution based on read effects has the advantage that it does not restrict the receivers of recursive calls, which is sometimes useful. On the other hand, the ownership-based solution works even if the read effect does not get smaller. For instance, the example in Fig. 6 would verify even if the GetHashCode method of object and of ArrayList were permitted to read the whole heap.

For effect specifications based on permissions, one can check that after passing the required permissions to the recursive call, a non-empty permission set remains with the caller. This solution works well for side-effect free methods, similar to the ownership-based solution. For methods that create new objects, it is difficult to make the checks sound and nevertheless permit calls on newly-created objects.

4.4   Multi-Object Invariants

Consistency criteria of data structures are often specified as object invariants [23,48]. Non-trivial object invariants do not hold in all execution states; for instance, the invariant of a fresh object typically does not hold until the object is initialized, and some methods violate and later re-establish an invariant when they update a data structure. Therefore, any specification language that supports object invariants must define when invariants are expected to hold.

Problem. A common semantics for object invariants is to require the invariants of all allocated objects to hold in the pre- and poststates of each method call [27,48,59]. This *visible state semantics* is suitable for object invariants that constrain the state of a single object[3], but it is too restrictive for *multi-object invariants*, which relate the states of multiple objects. The problem is illustrated by class Map in Fig. 7.

Class Map implements a map; the keys and values are stored in two lists. Consequently, Map maintains an invariant that these lists have the same length.

---

[3] Visible state semantics is also problematic in the presence of call-backs [2,23], but we ignore this issue here.

```
class Map {
  [Rep][SpecPublic] List! keys = new ArrayList ();
  [Rep] List! values = new ArrayList ();

  invariant keys.Length() == values.Length();

  public void Put(object! key, object! value)
    requires !keys.Contains(key);
    requires Owner.Different(key, this);
    requires Owner.Different(value, this);
  {
    expose(this) {
      keys.Add(key);
      values.Add(value);
    }
  }

  // other methods omitted
}
```

Fig. 7. A map implementation that stores the keys and values in two lists. The invariant relates the states of both lists. The second and third precondition of Put are necessary to show that keys and values are peer consistent after exposing this, which is required to satisfy the default precondition of List.Add (see Sec. 3.2).

This invariant is a multi-object invariant since if relates the states of a Map object and of the two List objects referenced by the Map object. Method Put adds a new key-value pair to the map by adding the key and the value to the respective lists. The call to keys.Add violates the Map invariant by increasing the length of one list. The subsequent call to values.Add re-establishes the invariant. However, note that the invariant does not hold in the poststate of the first call and in the prestate of the second call, which are visible states. This example shows that the visible state semantics is too restrictive to handle useful multi-object invariants. So the problem is:

How to define a semantics for multi-object invariants?

Ownership Solution. In ownership systems, owned objects form the internal representation of their owner, for instance, the List objects in our example form the internal representation of the Map object that owns them. Consequently, modifications of owned objects should be seen as internal operations of the owner, which may violate the owner's invariant as long as it gets re-established when the modifications are completed. This is analogous to allowing field updates to violate a single-object invariant as long as it gets re-established before the enclosing method terminates.

Based on this idea, we can use the ownership topology to refine the standard visible state semantics to the following *relevant invariant semantics* [49,52]. Consider an arbitrary execution of a method m on receiver o. In the pre- and poststate of this execution, the invariants of those allocated objects have to hold that are directly or transitively owned by the owner of o. In other words, m may assume and has to preserve the invariants of o, o's peers, and all objects (transitively) owned by o and its peers. These objects are called the *relevant objects* for o. However, m must not assume nor has to preserve the invariants of o's transitive owners. In the Map example, this semantics allows the calls to keys.Add and values.Add to break the invariant of the Map object because it owns the receivers of these calls and, thus, is not relevant for the receivers.

With the relevant invariant semantics, it is generally not possible for an object o to call methods on receivers that are not relevant for o because their invariants are not known to hold. For instance, o cannot call methods on its owner nor on objects in a different ownership tree. To address this limitation, one can allow methods to specify explicitly which invariants they require to hold [37,47]. Such a specification is similar to an effect specification, and we can employ ownership as an abstraction mechanism as discussed in Sec. 4.1. For instance, in Spec# the precondition p.IsPeerConsistent requires that all objects relevant for p satisfy their invariants. By default, a Spec# method requires that its receiver and all explicit arguments are peer consistent. In our example, the call keys.Add(key) requires implicitly that keys and key are peer consistent. The former follows from the fact that the Map object this is peer consistent (by the implicit precondition of Put) and owns keys. The latter follows from the implicit precondition of Put that key is peer consistent.

Other Solutions. VCC [14] supports two-state invariants that hold between the prestates and poststates of any action, similar to a standard visible state semantics. This semantics is enforced by checking (1) that every action of the program is legal, that is, preserves the invariants of the objects it modifies, and (2) that every invariant is admissible, that is, is reflexive and cannot be broken by any legal action. VCC would reject the invariant of class Map because it is not admissible; the action keys.Add(key) is legal (it preserves the invariant of the list), but violates the map invariant. To support interesting multi-object invariants, VCC uses ghost state to encode an ownership scheme like the one described above. The key ideas are: (1) to write an invariant I as a dented invariant of the form valid $\Rightarrow I$, where valid is a boolean ghost field, (2) to add a two-state invariant that the state of an object o does not change while o.valid is true, and (3) to relate the valid fields of o and its owner using further invariants.

Many specification formalisms do not support object invariants but instead use pre- and postconditions together with model variables [43] or abstract predicates [58] to express consistency criteria.

5   Using Ownership Encapsulation in Verification

The previous section showed that the ownership topology can be utilized in various ways to simplify verification. For some applications, however, the topology alone is not sufficient; it has to be complemented by an encapsulation discipline such as owner-as-dominator or owner-as-modifier to control which objects may be referenced and which operations can be performed on a referenced object. In this section, we present three applications of ownership-based encapsulation to program verification.

5.1   Verifying Multi-Object Invariants

In Sec. 4.4, we presented a semantics for multi-object invariants that defines when invariants are expected to hold, but we did not explain how to verify statically that the expected invariants actually hold. The textbook solution to this problem—assuming invariants to hold in each method prestate and checking at the end of each method that the receiver's invariant holds [48]—is unsound for multi-object invariants, in the presence of call-backs, and for languages that permit field updates of objects other than the current receiver.

Problem. A *sound* verification technique has to ensure that an object invariant holds in all states in which it is expected to hold. This is achieved by imposing checks (proof obligations) for code that is supposed to establish or preserve an invariant. For instance, most verification techniques impose a check that a constructor establishes the invariant of the fresh object such that later operations on this object may safely assume the invariant. A *modular* verification technique imposes checks that can be verified locally for each class, without knowing its subclasses or clients.

With multi-object invariants, a single field update potentially breaks the invariants of many objects. Consider for instance the third invariant of class ArrayList in Fig. 4, which expresses that the elements of the array elems are non-null. In general, any array update $a[j]$ = null potentially breaks this invariant for any ArrayList object o where o.elems= a. A proof obligation for the method m containing this array update would have to quantify over all (relevant) ArrayList objects o, which is non-modular because m and class ArrayList may have been developed independently, and so ArrayList is not known during the verification of m. So the problem is:

How to verify multi-object invariants modularly?

Ownership Solution. Building on the invariant semantics described in Sec. 4.4, multi-object invariants can be verified modularly as follows [37,49,52].

First, we use the ownership topology to restrict the objects an invariant may depend on. An *admissible ownership-based invariant* of an object o may depend on the fields of o and of all objects (transitively) owned by o[4]. In our example, the third invariant of `ArrayList` is admissible because the array `elems` is owned by the `ArrayList` object. Admissibility can be checked syntactically based on ownership annotations and possibly read effects of pure methods mentioned in invariants (such as method `Length` in class `Map`, see Fig. 7).

Second, we use an encapsulation discipline to restrict the modifications a method may perform. For instance with the owner-as-modifier discipline, when a method m with receiver r updates a field of an object o or an element of an array o then o is either owned by r or it is a peer of r (which subsumes the case $o = r$). In the former case, admissibility guarantees that the update affects at most the invariants of o, r (which owns o), and the (transitive) owners of r. For o and r, we can impose proof obligations that can be checked modularly. For the owners of r, no check is required according to the relevant invariant semantics because those objects are not relevant for r. In the latter case, admissibility guarantees that the update affects at most the invariants of o and the (transitive) owners of o. For o, we can impose a proof obligation that can be checked modularly. The owners of o, which are the owners of r, are not relevant for r.

When m calls an impure method n on a receiver o then again o is either owned by r or it is a peer of r. In the former case, admissibility and the verification of n ensure that all invariants potentially violated by n are checked before n terminates except for the invariants of r and r's (transitive) owners. For r, we can impose a proof obligation on m that can be checked modularly. The owners of r are not relevant for r. In the latter case, admissibility and the verification of n ensure that all invariants potentially violated by n are checked before n terminates except for the invariants of o's (transitive) owners. The owners of o, which are the owners of r, are not relevant for r.

We explained how Spec# enforces a variation of the owner-as-modifier discipline in Sec. 3.2. Using this approach, it is sufficient to check the invariant of an object o at the end of o's constructor as well as at the end of each `expose(o)` block. In class `ArrayList` (Fig. 4) the third invariant is checked at the end of the constructor (it holds because `next` is zero and, thus, the quantifier in the invariant ranges over an empty interval[5]) as well as at the end of the `expose` block in method `Add` (it holds because it held at the beginning of the `expose` block and because `e` is non-null according to its type).

Note that the `Add` method of a list l may in general violate the invariant of a `Map` object o using the list. To make o's invariant admissible, o must own l. Hence, o is not relevant for l and need not be checked in method `Add`, which would be non-modular. The check happens instead in the caller of `Add`, for instance, method `Put` (Fig. 7), where o gets exposed before calling `Add`.

The ownership solution to verifying invariants has also been adapted to model fields [38]. In this adaptation, model fields and their representation clauses are encoded as ghost fields with an appropriate invariant, respectively. Instead of

---

[4] Extra restrictions are required for a sound treatment of inheritance, which we ignore here [37].

[5] Intervals in Spec# are half-open to the right.

checking that the invariant holds, one can update the ghost field automatically such that the invariant is maintained.

Other Solutions. Not all multi-object invariants are protected by encapsulating the state the invariant depends on. *Visibility-based invariants* [49,4] may depend on fields outside the ownership tree as long as the invariant is visible wherever the field can be updated. It is thus possible to generate modular checks at each update. Visibility-based invariants relate for instance the nodes in a doubly-linked list, which do not own each other. *Monotonicity-based invariants* may depend on fields whose value changes monotonically as long as any monotonic change preserves the invariant [45]. For instance, for a counter c that only grows, a monotonicity-based invariant might express $c > 7$. When this invariant has once been established, it will not be violated by any monotonic update of c. A special case of monotonicity-based invariants is invariants over immutable state [39].

Verification methodologies based on dynamic frames [31] and permissions [41,60,64] typically do not support invariants. Consistency criteria are specified explicitly in method pre- and postconditions, with suitable abstraction mechanisms to preserve information hiding [58]. To allow implementations to hide consistency criteria altogether from clients, Region Logic introduced the concept of a dynamic boundary [55]. The *dynamic boundary* of a data structure is a set of objects (or locations) that over-approximates the read effect of the data structure's invariant. Clients of a data structure must not modify objects in the dynamic boundary, which allows the implementation of the data structure to assume the invariant whenever an operation of the data structure is invoked.

5.2   Object Immutability

Immutable data structures simplify many aspects of programming and program verification. For instance:

- Properties of immutable state are trivial to frame because they do not get invalidated by any heap update. This simplifies the specification of read effects and the framing of heap properties (see Sec. 4.2).
- Multi-object invariants may depend on the state of immutable objects without encapsulating them because no method can violate the invariant by modifying an immutable object. This reduces the need to introduce ownership (see Sec. 5.1) and, therefore, allows more sharing.
- Concurrent accesses to immutable objects do not require synchronization because all accesses are read-only. This simplifies the verification of data race freedom (see Sec. 5.3).

Problem. Immutable data structures are typically implemented as immutable classes. An immutable class such as Java's `Integer` encapsulates all its fields, initializes the fields in the constructor, and provides no methods to modify the fields. Therefore, once an object has been initialized, clients have no way of changing its state. For object structures such as string objects implemented on top of (mutable) character arrays, the class in addition has to ensure that references to mutable sub-objects are not leaked to clients. For instance, Java's String class has no method to obtain a reference to the internal character array.

While this idiom is a simple way of implementing immutable data structures, it has several shortcomings for verification. First, immutable object structures may reference mutable objects. For instance, an immutable collection may contain mutable elements. Therefore, it is necessary to delimit the portion of the data structure that is supposed to be immutable. Second, it is not entirely trivial to verify that the implementation actually guarantees immutability, for instance, that references to mutable sub-objects are not leaked and that the object does not escape from its constructor while it is still under initialization (and, thus, being modified) [65]. Third, it is often useful to have immutable instances of a class that otherwise allows mutations, for instance, an immutable instance of ArrayList. However, this is not supported by the idiom described above, which requires that a class does not offer any mutating methods. Fourth, some data structures become immutable only after a lengthy initialization phase that goes beyond the execution of the constructor. For instance, an AST might become immutable only after type checking has been completed. Again, this is not supported by immutable classes, which require that an object is fully initialized when the constructor terminates. So the problem is:

How to define and check the immutability of object structures?

Ownership Solution. Ownership provides a natural way to delimit which portion of an object structure is immutable. Ownership-based solutions to immutability [6,25,39,57] define this portion to be the ownership tree rooted in an immutable object. That is, all objects (transitively) owned by an immutable object are also immutable. This definition addresses the first problem mentioned above and supports, in particular, immutable aggregate objects. For instance, when an immutable string object owns its character array, the array also becomes immutable. In our example from Fig. 4 the elems array of an immutable ArrayList object is also immutable because it is owned by the ArrayList object, but the elements stored in the array are not.

The immutability of an ownership tree can be enforced by an encapsulation scheme that prevents modifications of the objects in the tree [6,39,57]. Spec# prevents modifications by assigning immutable objects a special owner, called the *freezer* object[6]. The freezer does not mutate any of the objects it owns and neither can other objects because they would have to expose the freezer first, which is not possible. Since Spec# does not allow an owned object to change owner, an object that is (transitively) owned by the freezer will stay owned by the freezer—and thus immutable—for the rest of its lifetime. Building on an

---

[6] The implementation of immutable objects is still experimental [46] and not part of the Spec# release yet.

existing encapsulation mechanism allows Spec# to enforce immutability without any additional checks, which addresses the second problem mentioned above. Since ownership and, thus, immutability operate on the object rather than the class level, this solution supports immutable instances of mutable classes, which addresses the third problem mentioned above.

An object is made immutable with a special statement freeze, which takes an un-owned object and sets its owner to the freezer. The freeze statement can be used anywhere in the code, which allows objects to go through a complex initialization phase before they become immutable. This addresses the fourth problem mentioned above.

```
class Cell {
  int val;

  [return: Frozen] public List SingletonList () {
    ArrayList l = new ArrayList ();
    l.Add(this);
    freeze l;
    this.val++;    // okay:   cell is mutable
    l.Add(this);   // verification error: list is immutable
    return l;
  }
}
```

Fig. 8. Method SingletonList populates a mutable list and then makes it immutable. The list elements remain mutable because they are not owned by the list. The Frozen attribute indicates that the method result is immutable.

The code snippet in Fig. 8 illustrates the ownership solution to immutability. Method SingletonList creates and initializes an ArrayList object. The subsequent freeze statement makes the object immutable. However, since the list does not own its contents, the Cell object this remains mutable as illustrated by the update of field val. Attempting to modify the list after freezing (via the second call to Add) results in a verification error because l is owned by the freezer. Since the freezer is always valid, l is not peer consistent and, thus, does not satisfy the default precondition of Add (nor any other precondition that would allow the method to modify the object).

Other Solutions. IGJ [66] uses Java's generic types to check immutability of classes, objects, and references. Objects that are reachable from an immutable object are also immutable, although fields can be explicitly excluded. IGJ provides most of the flexibility of ownership-based solutions, but requires that immutable objects are fully initialized when their constructor terminates, which prevents complex initialization schemes. Later work on OIGJ [67] combines ownership and immutability into a unified system.

5.3 Data Race Freedom

The applications of ownership we have discussed so far are relevant for the verification of both sequential and concurrent programs. However, ownership is also useful to address concurrency-specific problems, in particular, the verification of data race freedom.

Problem. A common way of preventing data races is to synchronize accesses to shared resources through locking. Verification of such programs requires one to prove that no thread accesses a shared resource without holding the lock that protects the resource. This is simple if there is a one-to-one correspondence between resources and locks, for instance, when the locations of an object are protected by the object's lock. However, many programs use more flexible locking patterns such as coarse-grained locking, where one locks protects a whole data structure consisting of many objects. A concurrent (thread-safe) version of our `ArrayList` example might use the lock associated with an `ArrayList` object to protect accesses to this object as well as to the underlying array. To handle flexible locking patterns, the specification must express which locks protect which resources, and the verification must ensure that the required locks are held whenever a thread accesses a shared resource. So the problem is:

How to verify mutual exclusion for accesses to shared resources?

Ownership Solution. A simple way of verifying mutual exclusion for coarse-grained locking is to associate exactly one lock with each ownership tree, which protects the locations of all objects in the tree. Any read or write access to an object in the ownership tree requires acquiring the tree's lock first. This requirement can be checked using an encapsulation discipline that prevents read and write accesses through non-owning references. Such a discipline is stricter than owner-as-modifier because it restricts read and write accesses, but more permissive than owner-as-dominator because it does not restrict the existence of references.

This solution has been implemented in SpecLeuven, an extension of Spec# to concurrency [32] and in VCC [13]. Both systems keep track of the set of objects a thread may safely access. A thread can get read and write access to the root of an ownership tree by locking it. Access to children is obtained by exposing their parent. This discipline is similar to Spec#, but requires exposing the receiver of both read and write accesses. VCC allows programs to implement their own locks (using volatile variables), which then own the objects they protect.

Several type systems use ownership to check data race freedom. For instance Boyapati et al. [7] employ ownership types with the owner-as-dominator discipline to check for data races. Universes for Race Safety [16] check data race freedom using the owner-as-modifier encapsulation discipline. The system associates a lock with each ownership context and therefore supports finer grained locking.

Other Solutions. There are numerous type systems, static analyses, and model checkers to detect data races [50]. In the realm of verification, permission-based systems check for each heap access that the thread has the necessary access permission. Since permissions cannot be forged, these checks ensure mutual exclusion (fractional permissions [9] can be used to allow concurrent reading). Permission-based verification is for instance supported in concurrent separation logic [56], VeriFast [33], and Chalice [41]. Locking strategies can be specified by associating permissions with locks, which requires that a thread must acquire a lock in order to obtain the associated permissions.

6 Conclusion

Program verification was one of the first applications of object ownership and ownership types. Initial work in this area focused on framing [51,49], the verification of object invariants [49], and checking data race freedom [8]. In this paper, we surveyed these and other applications of object ownership to program verification and illustrated how they are supported in the Spec# system.

Since ownership enabled the first sound, modular, and automatic verification techniques for object-oriented programs, a number of alternative approaches have been proposed. Among the most successful are separation logic [60,58] (and other permission-based logics such as Implicit Dynamic Frames [64,41]) and Dynamic Frames [30,31] (and similar logics based on explicit footprints such as Region Logic [1]). These alternatives are generally more flexible than ownership-based verification, especially for non-hierarchical data structures [4] and for data structures whose topology changes over time [61]. However, this flexibility comes at the prize of more annotation overhead, for instance, to specify access permissions or to update ghost state. So for programs that fit the ownership model, ownership-based verification is still a relatively simple and lightweight approach that scales to the verification of intricate concurrent programs as illustrated by VCC [13].

Acknowledgments. We thank the editors for inviting us to contribute to this book, and the reviewers for their helpful feedback.

References

1. Banerjee, A., Naumann, D.A., Rosenberg, S.: Regional Logic for Local Reasoning about Global Invariants. In: Vitek, J. (ed.) ECOOP 2008. LNCS, vol. 5142, pp. 387–411. Springer, Heidelberg (2008)
2. Barnett, M., DeLine, R., Fähndrich, M., Leino, K.R.M., Schulte, W.: Verification of object-oriented programs with invariants. Journal of Object Technology (JOT) 3(6), 27–56 (2004)
3. Barnett, M., Fähndrich, M., Leino, K.R.M., Müller, P., Schulte, W., Venter, H.: Specification and verification: The Spec# experience. Communications of the ACM 54(6), 81–91 (2011)

4. Barnett, M., Naumann, D.A.: Friends Need a Bit More: Maintaining Invariants Over Shared State. In: Kozen, D. (ed.) MPC 2004. LNCS, vol. 3125, pp. 54–84. Springer, Heidelberg (2004)
5. Bornat, R., Calcagno, C., O'Hearn, P., Parkinson, M.: Permission accounting in separation logic. In: Principles of Programming Languages (POPL), pp. 259–270. ACM (2005)
6. Boyapati, C.: SafeJava: A Unified Type System for Safe Programming. PhD thesis, MIT (2004)
7. Boyapati, C., Lee, R., Rinard, M.: Ownership types for safe programming: Preventing data races and deadlocks. In: Object-Oriented Programming Systems, Languages, and Applications (OOPSLA), pp. 211–230. ACM Press (2002)
8. Boyapati, C., Rinard, M.: A parameterized type system for race-free Java programs. In: Object-Oriented Programming Systems, Languages, and Applications (OOPSLA), pp. 56–69. ACM Press (2001)
9. Boyland, J.: Checking Interference with Fractional Permissions. In: Cousot, R. (ed.) SAS 2003. LNCS, vol. 2694, pp. 55–72. Springer, Heidelberg (2003)
10. Clarke, D., Drossopoulou, S.: Ownership, encapsulation and the disjointness of type and effect. In: Object-Oriented Programming Systems, Languages, and Applications (OOPSLA), pp. 292–310. ACM Press (2002)
11. Clarke, D., Potter, J., Noble, J.: Ownership types for flexible alias protection. In: Object-Oriented Programming Systems, Languages, and Applications (OOPSLA). ACM Press (1998)
12. Clarke, D., Wrigstad, T.: External Uniqueness is Unique Enough. In: Cardelli, L. (ed.) ECOOP 2003. LNCS, vol. 2743, pp. 176–201. Springer, Heidelberg (2003)
13. Cohen, E., Dahlweid, M., Hillebrand, M., Leinenbach, D., Moskal, M., Santen, T., Schulte, W., Tobies, S.: VCC: A Practical System for Verifying Concurrent C. In: Berghofer, S., Nipkow, T., Urban, C., Wenzel, M. (eds.) TPHOLs 2009. LNCS, vol. 5674, pp. 23–42. Springer, Heidelberg (2009)
14. Cohen, E., Moskal, M., Schulte, W., Tobies, S.: Local Verification of Global Invariants in Concurrent Programs. In: Touili, T., Cook, B., Jackson, P. (eds.) CAV 2010. LNCS, vol. 6174, pp. 480–494. Springer, Heidelberg (2010)
15. Cook, B., Podelski, A., Rybalchenko, A.: Proving program termination. Communications of the ACM 54, 88–98 (2011)
16. Cunningham, D., Drossopoulou, S., Eisenbach, S.: Universe Types for Race Safety. In: Verification and Analysis of Multi-threaded Java-like Programs (VAMP), pp. 20–51 (2007)
17. Darvas, Á., Leino, K.R.M.: Practical Reasoning About Invocations and Implementations of Pure Methods. In: Dwyer, M.B., Lopes, A. (eds.) FASE 2007. LNCS, vol. 4422, pp. 336–351. Springer, Heidelberg (2007)
18. Dietl, W.: Universe Types: Topology, Encapsulation, Genericity, and Tools. PhD thesis, Department of Computer Science, ETH Zurich (2009)
19. Dietl, W., Drossopoulou, S., Müller, P.: Generic Universe Types. In: Ernst, E. (ed.) ECOOP 2007. LNCS, vol. 4609, pp. 28–53. Springer, Heidelberg (2007)
20. Dietl, W., Drossopoulou, S., Müller, P.: Separating ownership topology and encapsulation with Generic Universe Types. Transactions on Programming Languages and Systems (TOPLAS) 33, 20:1–20:62 (2011)
21. Dietl, W., Ernst, M.D., Müller, P.: Tunable Static Inference for Generic Universe Types. In: Mezini, M. (ed.) ECOOP 2011. LNCS, vol. 6813, pp. 333–357. Springer, Heidelberg (2011)
22. Dietl, W., Müller, P.: Universes: Lightweight ownership for JML. Journal of Object Technology (JOT) 4(8), 5–32 (2005)

23. Drossopoulou, S., Francalanza, A., Müller, P., Summers, A.J.: A Unified Framework for Verification Techniques for Object Invariants. In: Vitek, J. (ed.) ECOOP 2008. LNCS, vol. 5142, pp. 412–437. Springer, Heidelberg (2008)

24. Flanagan, C., Leino, K.R.M., Lillibridge, M., Nelson, G., Saxe, J.B., Stata, R.: Extended static checking for Java. In: Programming Language Design and Implementation (PLDI). CM SIGPLAN Notices, vol. 37(5), pp. 234–245. ACM Press (2002)

25. Haack, C., Poll, E., Schäfer, J., Schubert, A.: Immutable Objects for a Java-Like Language. In: De Nicola, R. (ed.) ESOP 2007. LNCS, vol. 4421, pp. 347–362. Springer, Heidelberg (2007)

26. Hatcliff, J., Leavens, G.T., Leino, K.R.M., Müller, P., Parkinson, M.: Behavioral interface specification languages. Computing Surveys (2012) (to appear)

27. Hoare, C.A.R.: Proofs of correctness of data representation. Acta Informatica 1, 271–281 (1972)

28. Huisman, M.: Reasoning about Java Programs in higher order logic with PVS and Isabelle. Ipa dissertation series, 2001-03, University of Nijmegen, Holland (2001)

29. Leavens, G.T., Poll, E., Clifton, C., Cheon, Y., Ruby, C., Cok, D., Müller, P., Kiniry, J., Chalin, P., Zimmerman, D.M., Dietl, W.: JML Reference Manual (June 2008), http://www.jmlspecs.org/

30. Kassios, I.T.: Dynamic Frames: Support for Framing, Dependencies and Sharing Without Restrictions. In: Misra, J., Nipkow, T., Sekerinski, E. (eds.) FM 2006. LNCS, vol. 4085, pp. 268–283. Springer, Heidelberg (2006)

31. Kassios, I.T.: The dynamic frames theory. Formal Aspects of Computing 23(3), 267–289 (2011)

32. Jacobs, B., Piessens, F., Smans, J., Leino, K.R.M., Schulte, W.: A programming model for concurrent object-oriented programs. Transactions on Programming Languages and Systems (TOPLAS) 31(1) (2008)

33. Jacobs, B., Smans, J., Piessens, F.: A Quick Tour of the VeriFast Program Verifier. In: Ueda, K. (ed.) APLAS 2010. LNCS, vol. 6461, pp. 304–311. Springer, Heidelberg (2010)

34. Leino, K.R.M.: Toward Reliable Modular Programs. PhD thesis, California Institute of Technology, Available as Technical Report Caltech-CS-TR-95-03 (1995)

35. Leino, K.R.M.: Dafny: An Automatic Program Verifier for Functional Correctness. In: Clarke, E.M., Voronkov, A. (eds.) LPAR-16 2010. LNCS(LNAI), vol. 6355, pp. 348–370. Springer, Heidelberg (2010)

36. Leino, K.R.M.: Data groups: Specifying the modification of extended state. In: Object-Oriented Programming Systems, Languages, and Applications (OOPSLA). ACM SIGPLAN Notices, vol. 33(10), pp. 144–153. ACM Press (1998)

37. Leino, K.R.M., Müller, P.: Object Invariants in Dynamic Contexts. In: Odersky, M. (ed.) ECOOP 2004. LNCS, vol. 3086, pp. 491–515. Springer, Heidelberg (2004)

38. Leino, K.R.M., Müller, P.: A Verification Methodology for Model Fields. In: Sestoft, P. (ed.) ESOP 2006. LNCS, vol. 3924, pp. 115–130. Springer, Heidelberg (2006)

39. Leino, K.R.M., Müller, P., Wallenburg, A.: Flexible Immutability with Frozen Objects. In: Shankar, N., Woodcock, J. (eds.) VSTTE 2008. LNCS, vol. 5295, pp. 192–208. Springer, Heidelberg (2008)

40. Leino, K.R.M., Müller, P.: Verification of Equivalent-Results Methods. In: Drossopoulou, S. (ed.) ESOP 2008. LNCS, vol. 4960, pp. 307–321. Springer, Heidelberg (2008)

41. Leino, K.R.M., Müller, P.: A Basis for Verifying Multi-threaded Programs. In: Castagna, G. (ed.) ESOP 2009. LNCS, vol. 5502, pp. 378–393. Springer, Heidelberg (2009)

42. Leino, K.R.M., Müller, P.: Using the Spec# Language, Methodology, and Tools to Write Bug-Free Programs. In: Müller, P. (ed.) LASER Summer School 2007/2008. LNCS, vol. 6029, pp. 91–139. Springer, Heidelberg (2010)

43. Leino, K.R.M., Nelson, G.: Data abstraction and information hiding. Transactions on Programming Languages and Systems (TOPLAS) 24(5), 491–553 (2002)

44. Leino, K.R.M., Poetzsch-Heffter, A., Zhou, Y.: Using data groups to specify and check side effects. In: Programming Language Design and Implementation (PLDI). ACM SIGPLAN Notices, vol. 37(5), pp. 246–257. ACM Press (2002)

45. Leino, K.R.M., Schulte, W.: Using History Invariants to Verify Observers. In: De Nicola, R. (ed.) ESOP 2007. LNCS, vol. 4421, pp. 80–94. Springer, Heidelberg (2007)

46. Leu, F.: Implementation of frozen objects into Spec#. Master's thesis, ETH Zurich (2009), http://www.pm.inf.ethz.ch/education/theses/student_docs/Florian_Leu/florian_leu_MA_report

47. Lu, Y., Xue, J.: Validity Invariants and Effects. In: Ernst, E. (ed.) ECOOP 2007. LNCS, vol. 4609, pp. 202–226. Springer, Heidelberg (2007)

48. Meyer, B.: Object-Oriented Software Construction. 2nd edn. Prentice Hall (1997)

49. Müller, P.: Modular Specification and Verification of Object-Oriented Programs. LNCS, vol. 2262. Springer, Heidelberg (2002)

50. Müller, P.: Formal methods-based tools for race, deadlock and other errors. In: Padua, D. (ed.) Encyclopedia of Parallel Computing, pp. 704–710. Springer (2011)

51. Müller, P., Poetzsch-Heffter, A.: Modular specification and verification techniques for object-oriented software components. In: Leavens, G.T., Sitaraman, M. (eds.) Foundations of Component-Based Systems. Cambridge University Press (2000)

52. Müller, P., Poetzsch-Heffter, A., Leavens, G.T.: Modular invariants for layered object structures. Science of Computer Programming 62, 253–286 (2006)

53. Müller, P., Rudich, A.: Ownership transfer in Universe Types. In: Object-Oriented Programming Systems, Languages, and Applications (OOPSLA), pp. 461–478. ACM Press (2007)

54. Naumann, D.A.: Observational purity and encapsulation. Theor. Comput. Sci. 376(3), 205–224 (2007)

55. Naumann, D.A., Banerjee, A.: Dynamic Boundaries: Information Hiding by Second Order Framing with First Order Assertions. In: Gordon, A.D. (ed.) ESOP 2010. LNCS, vol. 6012, pp. 2–22. Springer, Heidelberg (2010)

56. O'Hearn, P.W.: Resources, concurrency, and local reasoning. Theor. Comput. Sci. 375, 271–307 (2007)

57. Östlund, J., Wrigstad, T., Clarke, D., Åkerblom, B.: Ownership, Uniqueness, and Immutability. In: Paige, R.F., Meyer, B. (eds.) TOOLS EUROPE 2008. LNBIP, vol. 11, pp. 178–197. Springer, Heidelberg (2008)

58. Parkinson, M., Bierman, G.: Separation logic and abstraction. In: Palsberg, J., Abadi, M. (eds.) Principles of Programming Languages (POPL), pp. 247–258. ACM Press (January 2005)

59. Poetzsch-Heffter, A.: Specification and verification of object-oriented programs. Habilitation thesis, Technical University of Munich (January 1997)

60. Reynolds, J.C.: Separation logic: A logic for shared mutable data structures. In: Logic in Computer Science (LICS). IEEE Computer Society Press (2002)

61. Rudich, A.: Automatic Verification of Heap Structures with Stereotypes. PhD thesis, ETH Zurich (2011)

62. Rudich, A., Darvas, Á., Müller, P.: Checking Well-Formedness of Pure-Method Specifications. In: Cuellar, J., Sere, K. (eds.) FM 2008. LNCS, vol. 5014, pp. 68–83. Springer, Heidelberg (2008)

63. Sǎlcianu, A., Rinard, M.: Purity and Side Effect Analysis for Java Programs. In: Cousot, R. (ed.) VMCAI 2005. LNCS, vol. 3385, pp. 199–215. Springer, Heidelberg (2005)
64. Smans, J., Jacobs, B., Piessens, F.: Implicit Dynamic Frames: Combining Dynamic Frames and Separation Logic. In: Drossopoulou, S. (ed.) ECOOP 2009. LNCS, vol. 5653, pp. 148–172. Springer, Heidelberg (2009)
65. Summers, A.J., Müller, P.: Freedom before commitment—a lightweight type system for object initialisation. In: Object-Oriented Programming Systems, Languages, and Applications (OOPSLA), pp. 1013–1032. ACM (2011)
66. Zibin, Y., Potanin, A., Ali, M., Artzi, S., Kieżun, A., Ernst, M.D.: Object and reference immutability using Java generics. In: European Software Engineering Conference/Foundations of Software Engineering (ESEC/FSE), pp. 75–84. ACM Press (2007)
67. Zibin, Y., Potanin, A., Li, P., Ali, M., Ernst, M.D.: Ownership and immutability in generic Java. In: Object-Oriented Programming Systems, Languages, and Applications (OOPSLA), pp. 598–617 (2010)

State Based Encapsulation for Modular Reasoning about Behavior-Preserving Refactorings

Anindya Banerjee[1] and David A. Naumann[2]

[1] IMDEA Software Institute, Madrid, Spain
[2] Stevens Institute of Technology, Hoboken NJ 07030 USA

Abstract. A properly encapsulated data representation can be revised for refactoring or other purposes without affecting the correctness of client programs and extensions of a class. But encapsulation is difficult to achieve in object-oriented programs owing to heap based structures and reentrant callbacks. This chapter shows that it is achieved by a discipline using assertions and auxiliary fields to manage invariants and transferrable ownership. The main result is representation independence: a rule for modular proof of equivalence of class implementations.

1 Introduction

You are responsible for a library consisting of many Java classes. While fixing a bug or refactoring some classes, you revise the implementation of a certain class in a way that is intended not to change its observable behavior, e.g., an internal data structure is changed for reasons of performance. You are in no position to check, or even be aware of, the many applications that use the class via its instances or via instances of its subclasses if any. In principle, the class could have a full functional specification. It would then suffice to prove that the new version meets the specification. In practice, full specifications are rare. Nor is there a well established logic and method for modular reasoning about the code of a class in terms of the specifications of the classes it uses, without regard to their implementations or the users of the class in question — though progress has been made, as reported in the companion chapters [1,2,3,4]. One problem is that encapsulation, crucial for modular reasoning about invariants, is difficult to achieve in programs that involve shared mutable objects and reentrant callbacks which violate simple layering of abstractions. Yet complicated heap structure and calling patterns are used, in well designed object-oriented programs, precisely for orderly composition of abstractions in terms of other abstractions.

There is an alternative to verification with respect to a specification. One can attempt to prove that the revised version is behaviorally equivalent to the original. Of course their behavior is not identical, but at the level of abstraction of source code (e.g., modulo specific memory addresses), it may be possible to show equivalence of behavior. If any specifications are available they can be taken into account using assert statements.

There is a standard technique for proving equivalence [5,6,7]: Define a *coupling relation* to connect the states of the two versions and prove that it has the *simulation property*, i.e., it holds initially and is preserved by parallel execution of the two versions of each method. In most cases, one would want to define a *local coupling* relation

D. Clarke et al. (Eds.): Aliasing in Object-Oriented Programming, LNCS 7850, pp. 319–365, 2013.
© Springer-Verlag Berlin Heidelberg 2013

for a single pair of instances of the class, as methods act primarily on a target object (self) and the *island* [8], i.e., a group of objects that comprise its internal representation. An *induced coupling* for complete states is then obtained by a general construction. A language with good encapsulation should enjoy a *representation independence* property that says a simulation for the revised class induces a simulation for any program built using the class. Suitable couplings are the identity except inside the abstraction boundary and an *identity extension lemma* says simulation implies behavioral equivalence of two programs that differ only by revision of a class. This means that from a client's point of view the behaviors of the two programs are the same. Again, such reasoning can be invalidated by heap sharing, which violates encapsulation of data, and by callbacks, which violate hierarchical control structure.

There is a close connection between the equivalence problem and verification: verification of object oriented code involves object invariants that constrain the internal state of an instance. Encapsulation involves defining the invariant in a way that protects it from outside interference so it holds globally provided it is preserved by the methods of the class of interest. Simulations are like invariants over two copies of the state space, and again modular reasoning requires that the coupling for a class be independent from outside interference. *The main contribution of this chapter is a representation independence theorem using a state-based discipline for heap encapsulation and control of callbacks.*

Extant theories of data abstraction assume, in one way or another, a hierarchy of abstractions such that control does not reenter an encapsulation boundary while already executing inside it. It is commonplace in object oriented programs for a method m acting on some object o to invoke a method on some other object which in turn leads to invocation of some method on o —possibly m itself— while the initial invocation of m is in progress. This makes it difficult to reason about when an object's invariant holds [4,9]; we give an example later.

There is an analogous problem for reasoning with simulations. The first work on representation independence for programs with shared objects [8] provides an abstraction theorem that deals with sharing and is sound for programs with reentrant callbacks — but it is not easy to apply in cases where reentrant callbacks are possible. The theorem allows the programmer to assume that all methods preserve the coupling relation when proving simulation, i.e., when reasoning about parallel execution of two versions of a method of the class of interest. This assumption is like verifying a procedure implementation under the assumption that called procedures are correct. But the assumption that called methods preserve the coupling is of no use if the call is made in an uncoupled intermediate state. For the examples in [8], we resort to ad hoc reasoning for examples involving callbacks.

In the "Boogie methodology" [10,11], reentrancy is managed using an explicit auxiliary (or *ghost*) field *inv* to designate states in which an object invariant is to hold. The ghost field is extra instrumentation added to a program for reasoning purposes but does not influence data flow or control flow in the original program in any manner; thus the behavior of the annotated program is the same as that of the original program. Encapsulation is achieved using a notion of ownership represented by an auxiliary mutable field *own*. This is more flexible than type-based static analyses because the ownership invariant need only hold in certain flagged states. Heap encapsulation is achieved not by disallowing boundary-crossing pointers but by limiting, in a state-dependent way, their use. Reasoning hinges on a global *program invariant* that holds in all states, using *inv* fields to track which object invariants are temporarily not in force because control is within their encapsulation boundary. When *inv* holds, the object is said to be *packed*; a field may only be updated when the object is unpacked.

In this chapter we adapt the *inv*/*own* discipline to proving class equivalence by simulation. The *inv* fields make it possible for an induced coupling relation to hold at some pairs of intermediate states during parallel execution of two alternative implementations. This means that the relation-preservation hypothesis of the abstraction theorem can be used at intermediate states even when the local coupling is not in force. So per-method modular reasoning is fully achieved. In large part the discipline is unchanged, as one would hope in keeping with the idea that a coupling is just an invariant over two parallel states. But we have to adapt some features in ways that make sense in terms of informal considerations of information hiding. The discipline imposes no control on field reads, only writes, but for representation independence we need to control reads as well. The discipline also allows ownership transfer quite freely, though as we will discuss later, it is not trivial to design code that correctly performs transfers. For representation independence, the transfer of previously-encapsulated data to clients (an unusual form of controlled "rep exposure" [12]) is allowed but must occur only in the code of the encapsulating class; even then, it poses a difficult technical challenge. The significance of our adaptations is discussed in Section 8.

A key insight is that, although transferring ownership and packing/unpacking involve only ghost fields that cannot affect program execution, it is useful to consider them to be observable. It is difficult to reason about two versions of a class, in a modular way, if they differ in the way objects cross the encapsulation boundary or in the points at which methods assume the invariant is in force. The requisite similarity can be expressed using assert statements, so we can develop a theory based on this insight without the need to require that the class under revision has any specifications.

The main contributions of this chapter are (a) formulation of a notion of instance-based coupling analogous to invariants in the *inv*/*own* discipline; (b) proof of a representation independence theorem for a language with inheritance and dynamic dispatch, recursive methods and callbacks, mutable objects, type casts, and recursive types; and (c) results on identity extension and use of the theorem to prove program equivalence. Together these constitute a rule by which the reasoner considers just the methods of the revised class and concludes that the two versions yield equivalent behavior for any program context.

The theorem allows ownership transfers that cross encapsulation boundaries: from client to abstraction [12], between instances of the abstraction, and even from abstraction to client [13,11,14]. The theorem supports the most important form of modularity: reasoning about one method implementation (or rather, one corresponding pair) at a time —on the assumption that all methods preserve the coupling (even the one in question, modulo termination). The theorem also supports local reasoning in the sense that a single instance (or pair of instances) is considered, together with the island comprised of its currently encapsulated representation objects.

The *inv/own* discipline can be used in any verification system that supports ghost variables and assertions in first order logic. Our formalism treats predicates in assertions semantically, avoiding ties to any particular logic or specification formalism. The original discipline is a core feature of the Spec# program verifier[1] for sequential C# programs [15] and our adaptations would not be difficult to implement. The original discipline has been adapted to concurrency and implemented as the core discipline for the VCC program verifier for multithreaded C programs [16].

This chapter is a revised version of the paper originally appearing in European Conference on Object-Oriented Programming [17]. Subsequent to the work reported in that paper, there have been further studies of representation independence using state-based notions of encapsulation. As discussed under related work (Section 7), these works include both foundational analyses and treatment of advanced language features (type polymorphism and higher order heaps —but so far not inheritance and nominal subtyping as in Java-like languages). Our work remains relevant not only for its conceptual perspective but also because it applies to a programming discipline for which there is tool support and which has been applied to substantial practical examples.

Outline. Sect. 2 sketches the *inv/own* discipline. It also sketches an example of the use of simulation to prove equivalence of two versions of a class involving reentrant callbacks, highlighting the problems and the connection between our solution and the *inv/own* discipline. Sect. 3 formalizes the language for which our result is given and Sect. 4 formalizes the discipline in our semantics. Sect. 5 gives the main definitions— proper annotation, coupling, simulation—and the abstraction theorem. Sect. 6 connects simulation with program equivalence. Sect. 7 discusses related work. Sect. 8 discusses future work and assesses our adaptation of the discipline.

2   Background and Overview

2.1   The *inv/own* Discipline

To illustrate the challenge of reentrant callbacks as well as the state based ownership discipline, we consider a class Queue that maintains a queue of tasks. Each task has an associated limit on the number of times it can be run. Method Queue.runAll runs each task that has not exceeded its limit. For simplicity we refrain from using interfaces; class Task in Fig. 1 serves as the interface for tasks. Class Qnode in the same figure is used by Queue which maintains a singly linked list of nodes that reference tasks. Field count tracks the number of times the task has been run.

In our illustrative language, all methods are dynamically dispatched and have public visibility; values of class type are references to mutable objects. For brevity we omit initialization and constructors throughout the examples. For reference to fields of self, we write f to abbreviate self.f, including the special fields *inv*, *com*, and *own*.

Fig. 2 gives class Queue; the annotations, in gray, will be discussed later. One intended invariant of Queue is that no task has been run more times than its limit. This

---
[1] Available at http://specsharp.codeplex.com/

```
class Task {    void run(){ }    }
class Qnode {
    Task tsk;    Qnode nxt;    int count, limit;
    invariant tsk ≠ null ∧ 0≤count≤limit;
    ... // constructor elided (in subsequent figures these ellipses are elided too)
    void run() { tsk.run(); count := count+1; }
    void setTsk(Task t, int lim) {
        unpack self from Qnode;

        tsk := t; limit := lim; count := 0; pack self as Qnode; }    }
    ... // other methods getNxt, getCount, getLimit, omitted
```

Fig. 1. Classes Task and Qnode. The unpack/pack statements are discussed later.

is expressed, in a decentralized way, by the invariant declared in Qnode. Some nota-tion: we write $\mathscr{I}^{Qnode}(o)$ for the predicate o.tsk≠null and o.count≤o.limit. That is, the declared invariant is considered to be a predicate parameterized on self.

Another intended invariant of Queue is that runs is the sum of the count fields of the nodes reached from tsks. This is the declared $\mathscr{I}^{Queue}$ of Fig. 2. (The reader may think of other useful invariants, e.g., that the list is null-terminated.) Note that at intermediate points in the body of Queue.runAll, $\mathscr{I}^{Queue}$ does not hold because runs is only updated after the loop. In particular, $\mathscr{I}^{Queue}$ does not hold at the point where p.run() is invoked.

For an example reentrant callback, consider tasks of the following type.

```
class RTask extends Task { Queue q;    ...
                void run(){ q.runAll(); } }
```

Consider a state in which o points to an instance of Queue and the first node in the list, o.tsks of type RTask, has count=0 and limit=1. Moreover, suppose field q of the first node's task has value o. That is, o.tsks.q = o. Invocation of o.runAll diverges: before count is incremented to reflect the first invocation, the task makes a *reentrant call* on o.runAll —in a state where $\mathscr{I}^{Queue}$ does not hold. In fact runAll again invokes run on the first task and the program fails due to nonterminating recursion.

As another example, suppose RTask.run is instead **void** run(){q.getRuns();} . This seems harmless, in that the implementation of getRuns neither depends on $\mathscr{I}^{Queue}$ nor invokes any methods. Indeed this code is useful, returning a lower bound on the actual sum of runs. It typifies methods like state readers in the observer pattern, that are intended to be invoked as reentrant callbacks.

The examples illustrate that it is sometimes but not always desirable to allow a reentrant callback when an object's invariant is violated temporarily by an "outer" invo-cation. The ubiquity of method calls makes it impractical to require an object's invari-ant to be reestablished before making *any* call —e.g., the point between n.setTsk and n.setNxt of method add in Fig. 2— although this is sound and has been proposed in the literature on object oriented verification [18,19]. A better solution is to prevent just the undesirable reentrant calls.

One could make the invariant an explicit precondition, e.g., for runAll but not getRuns. This puts responsibility on the caller, e.g., RTask.run cannot establish the precondition

```
class  Queue {
  Qnode tsks;
  int  runs := 0;
  invariant runs = (Σp ∈ tsks.nxt* | p.count);
  int  getRuns() { result := runs; }
  void  runAll() {
    assert inv = Queue && ! com ;
    unpack self from Queue ;
    Qnode p := tsks;    int  i := 0;
    while p ≠ null do  {
      if  p.getCount() < p.getLimit() then  p.run(); i := i+1; fi;
      p := p.getNxt(); }
    runs := runs + i;
    pack self as Queue;  }
  void  add(Task t, int  lim){
    assert  inv = Queue && ! com;
    unpack self from Queue;

    Qnode n := new  Qnode;  setown n to (self,Queue);
    n.setNxt(tsks); n.setTsk(t,lim); tsks := n;
    pack self as Queue;  } }
```

Fig. 2. Class Queue, with selected annotations. The assertions here serve as preconditions, as we refrain from formalizing method contracts.

and is thus prevented from invoking runAll. But an object invariant like $\mathscr{I}^{Queue}$ involves encapsulated state not suitable to be visible in a public specification.

The solution of the *inv*/*own* discipline [10,11] is to introduce a public ghost field, *inv*, that serves as a flag to explicitly indicate whether the invariant is in force[2] when *o.inv* holds we say object *o* is *packed*. Special statements **pack** and **unpack** set and unset *inv*.

A given object is an instance not only of its class but of all its superclasses, each of which may have invariants. The methodology takes this into account as follows. Instead of *inv* being a boolean, as in the simplified explanation above, it ranges over class names C such that C is a superclass of the object's allocated type. That is, it is an invariant (enforced by typing rules) that $o.inv \geq type\ o$, where *type o* is the dynamic type of *o*. Roughly, unpacking in a method of class C sets *inv* to *superC*. The discipline requires certain assertions preceding pack and unpack statements, as well as field updates, to ensure that the following is a *program invariant* (i.e., it holds in all reachable states, in the sense of small-step semantics).

$$o.inv \leq C \Rightarrow \mathscr{I}^C(o) \tag{1}$$

---

[2] Without exposing the actual invariant. This resembles abstract predicates [2]. Our condition (1) is akin to the association between an abstract predicate and its definition in their work.

for all C and all allocated objects o. That is, if o is packed at least to class C then the invariant $\mathscr{I}^C$ for C holds. Perhaps the most important stipulated assertion is that $\mathscr{I}^C(o)$ is required as precondition for packing o to level C.

Fig. 2 shows how the discipline is used for class Queue. Assertions impose preconditions on runAll and add which require that the target object is packed to Queue. In runAll, the **unpack** statement sets inv to the superclass of Queue, putting the task in a position where it cannot establish the precondition for a reentrant call to runAll, although it can still call getRuns which imposes no precondition on inv. After the update to runs, $\mathscr{I}^{Queue}$ holds again as required by the precondition (not shown) of **pack**. The ghost field com is discussed below.

In order to maintain (1) as a program invariant, it is necessary to control updates to fields on which invariants depend. The idea is that, to update field f of some object p, all objects o whose invariant depends on $p.f$ must be unpacked. Put differently, $\mathscr{I}(o)$ should depend only on state encapsulated for o. The discipline uses a form of ownership for this purpose: $\mathscr{I}(o)$ may depend only on objects transitively owned by o. For example, an instance of Queue owns the Qnodes reached from field tsks.

Ownership is embodied in an auxiliary field own, so that if $p.own = (o,C)$ then o directly owns p and an admissible invariant $\mathscr{I}^D(o)$ may depend on p for types D with type $o \leq D \leq C$. Typically, o has a field, declared or inherited in C, that points to or reaches p, by way of which there is a dependency.

The objects transitively owned by o are called its *island*. For modular reasoning, it is not feasible to require as an explicit precondition for each field update that all transitive owners are unpacked. A third ghost field, com, is used to enforce a protocol whereby packing/unpacking is dynamically nested or bracketed. They need not be lexically nested, but typically that would be the case, for which purpose Spec# and VCC provide an 'expose block'.

In addition to (1), two additional conditions are imposed as program invariants, i.e., to hold in all reachable states of all objects. The first may be read "an object is committed to its owner if its owner is packed". The second says that a committed object is fully packed. These make it possible for an assignment to $p.f$ to be subject only to the precondition $p.inv > C$ where C is the class that declares f —because owing to the additional invariants the condition $p.inv > C$ implies that all dependents of $p.f$ are unpacked.

The invariants are formalized in Def. 4 in Sect. 4. The stipulated preconditions appear in Table 1, which also describes the semantics of the pack and unpack statements in detail.[3] The diligent reader may enjoy completing the annotation of Fig. 2 according to the rules of Table 1. Consult [10,11] for more leisurely introductions to the discipline.

2.2   Representation Independence

At this point the reader may expect an alternate implementation of class Queue, perhaps using an array or doubly linked list of nodes. But recall that an invariant for a

---

[3] Preconditions like $e \neq$ **null** and "e not error" are needed for the rest of the precondition to be meaningful. Different verification systems make different choices in handling errors in assertions. Our formulation follows [20] and differs superficially from [10,11].

Table 1. Stipulated preconditions of field update and of the special commands. For brevity we leave implicit certain non-nullity conjuncts needed so the field references make sense: $x \neq$ **null** and $e \neq$ **null** above, but not for e_2.

---

assert $x.inv > C$;   /* where C is the class that declares f; i.e., $f \in dom(dfields\, C)$ */
$x.f := y$

assert $e.inv = super\, C \wedge \mathcal{I}^C(e) \wedge (\forall p \mid p.own = (e,C) \Rightarrow \neg p.com \wedge p.inv = type\, p)$;
pack e **as** C /* sets $e.inv := C$ and sets $p.com := true$ for all p with $p.own = (e,C)$ */

assert $e.inv = C \wedge \neg e.com$;
unpack e **from** C /* sets $e.inv := super\, C$ and $p.com := false$ for all p with $p.own = (e,C)$ */

assert $x.inv = \mathsf{Object} \wedge (e_2 = \mathbf{null} \vee e_2.inv > C)$;
setown x **to** (e_2,C) /* sets $x.own := (e_2,C)$ */

---

class C may depend on objects owned either at C or at some superclass of C. We aim to generalize from invariants to coupling relations, and in treating them precisely we distinguish between objects owned at C and objects owned at some superclass. For the sake of an example, we consider a somewhat contrived subclass of Queue, with two alternate implementations.

The basic setup. Consider the subclass AQueue of Queue declared in Fig. 3. It maintains an array, actsks, of tasks which is used in an overriding declaration of runAll intended as an optimization for the situation where many tasks are inactive (i.e., have reached their limit).

Method add exhibits a typical pattern: unpack to establish the condition in which a super call can be made (since the superclass unpacks from its own level); after that call, reestablish the current class invariant. In some sense, this pattern is necessary in order to match the expectations of a caller —that the object is packed to its type— with assumptions of a method implementation in some class —that the object is packed to that class. It is implemented in Spec# by re-verifying inherited code, and explained in the original paper [10] by translating inheritance into 'stub' methods consisting either of a super call or the unpack/super/pack pattern. We return to this topic in Sect. 6.

The implementation of Fig. 3 does not set actsks[i] to null immediately when the task's count reaches its limit; rather, that situation is detected on the subsequent invocation of runAll. An alternative implementation is given in Fig. 4; it uses a different data structure and handles the limit being reached as soon as it happens. Both implementations maintain an array of Qnode, but in the alternative implementation, its array artsk is accompanied by a boolean array brtsk. Instead of setting entry i null when the node's task has reached its limit, brtsk[i] is set false.

We claim that the two versions are equivalent, in the context of arbitrary client programs and subclasses. We would like to argue as follows. Let $filt1(o.\mathsf{actsks})$ be the sequence of non-null elements of $o.\mathsf{actsks}$ with count $<$ limit. Let $filt2(ts,bs)$ take an array ts of tasks and a same-length array bs of booleans and return the subsequence

```
class AQueue extends Queue {
    private Qnode[ ] actsks;
    private int  alen;
    void  add(Task t, int  lim) {
        assert inv = AQueue && ! com;
        unpack self from AQueue;
        super.add(t,lim); actsks[alen] := tsks; alen := alen+1;
        pack self as AQueue;  }
    void  runAll() {
        assert inv = AQueue && ! com;
        unpack self from AQueue;
        int  i := alen - 1;
        while i ≥ 0 do  {
            Qnode qn := actsks[i];
            if  qn ≠ null then  if  qn.getCount() < qn.getLimit()
                                then  qn.run();
                                    unpack self from Queue;  runs++;  pack self as Queue;
                                else  actsks[i] := null; fi; fi;
            i := i - 1; }
        pack self as AQueue;  } }
```

Fig. 3. First version of Class AQueue. An invariant: actsks[0..alen-1] contains any n in tsks with n.count $< n$.limit, in reverse order. (There may also be nulls and some n with n.count $= n$.limit). The elided constructor allocates actsks and we ignore the issue of the array becoming full.

of those tasks n in ts where bs is true and n.count $< n$.limit. Consider the following relation that connects a state for an instance o of the original implementation (Fig. 3) with an instance o' for the alternative: $filt1(o.\text{actsks}) = filt2(o'.\text{artsk}, o'.\text{brtsk})$. The idea is that methods of the new version behave the same as the old version, modulo this change of representation. That is, for each method of AQueue, parallel execution of the two versions from a related pair of states results in a related pair of outcomes. (For this to hold we need to conjoin to the relation the invariants associated with the two versions, e.g., the second version requires artsk.length=brtsk.length.) In brief: the coupling relation is *preserved*.

Coupling relations. In general, a *local coupling* is a binary relation on islands. It relates the state of an island for one implementation of the class of interest with an island for the alternative.

Fig. 5 depicts local coupling involving two instances of AQueue. The left side of the figure is an instance of some subclass of AQueue, sliced into the fields of Queue, AQueue, and subclasses; dashed lines show the objects encapsulated at the two levels relevant to reasoning about AQueue —namely the Qnodes reached from tsks and the array actsks. On the right is an instance for the alternate implementation of AQueue. It is the connection between these two islands that is of interest to the programmer. The

```
class AQueue extends Queue {
  private Qnode[ ] artsk;
  private boolean[ ] brtsk;
  private int len;
  void add(Task t, int lim) {
    assert inv = AQueue && ! com;
    unpack self from AQueue;
    super.add(t,lim); artsk[len] := tsks; brtsk[len] := true; len := len+1;
    pack self as AQueue; }
  void runAll() {
    assert inv = AQueue && ! com;
    unpack self from AQueue;
    int i := len - 1;
    while i ≥ 0 do {
      if brtsk[i] then
        Qnode n := artsk[i];
        int diff := n.limit - n.count;
        if diff ≠ 0 then  n.run();
                          unpack self from Queue; runs++; pack self as Queue; fi;
        if diff = 1 then  brtks[i] := false; fi; fi;
      i := i - 1; }
    pack self as AQueue; } }
```

Fig. 4. Alternative implementation of AQueue

'a'... 'd' of the figure indicate that both versions reference the same sequence of tasks, although those tasks are not part of the islands.

A local coupling lifts to an *induced coupling* relation on the complete program state: Two heaps are related by the induced coupling provided that (a) they can be partitioned into islands and (b) the islands can be put into correspondence so that each corresponding pair is related by the local coupling. Moreover, the remaining objects (not in an island) are related by equality. More precisely, equality modulo a bijection on locations, to take into account differences in allocation between the two versions. For example, 'a'... 'd' on each side of the figure might well be different references, because the two runs might allocate different references, due to different allocation by the two implementations of AQueue. But the difference will be unobservable, because the programming language does not allow comparison of references except for equality with other references. The details of lifting a coupling are not obvious and are formalized later.

Abstraction theorem. The goal is to show that the two versions of AQueue are equivalent, when used by an arbitrary client. Because the induced coupling is a kind of identity relation —on the client-visible part of the state— the two versions of a complete program have equivalent behavior provided that they preserve the induced coupling. The abstraction theorem says that for a complete program to preserve the induced coupling,

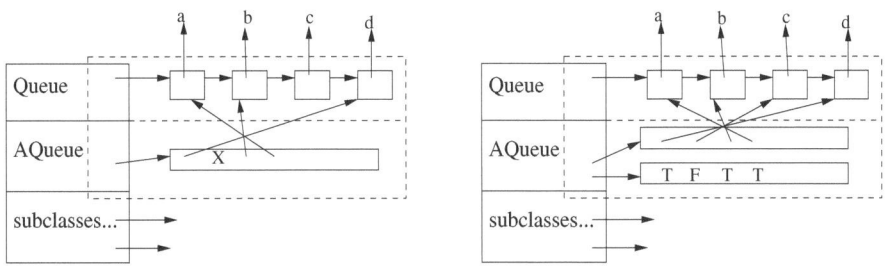

Fig. 5. Depiction of local coupling. This involves two instances of AQueue. Each is depicted as being sliced into the fields declared in class Queue, the fields declared in class AQueue, and those declared in subclasses there are down to the dynamic type of the instance.

it is sufficient that the induced coupling is preserved by methods of AQueue —provided there is sufficient encapsulation, specifically an adaptation of the *inv/own* discipline.

At first glance one might expect the proof obligation to be that each method of AQueue preserves the local coupling, and indeed this will be the focus of reasoning in practice. But in general a method may act on more than just the island for self, e.g., by invoking methods on client objects or on other instances of AQueue. As a simple example, consider the version of RTask.run that calls q.getRuns(), and an execution where o.tsks.q≠o. So in general the proof obligation is formalized in terms of the induced coupling.[4]

In fact the proof obligation is not simply that each corresponding pair of method implementations preserves the coupling, but rather that they preserve the coupling *under the assumption that any method they invoke preserves the coupling*.[5] There is also a proof obligation for initialization but it is straightforward so we do not discuss it in connection with the examples.

For example, in the case of method runAll, one must prove that the implementations given in Fig. 3 and in Fig. 4 preserve the coupling on the assumption that the invoked methods getCount, getLimit, Qnode.run, etc. preserve the coupling. The assumption is not so important for getCount or getLimit. For one thing, it is possible to fully describe their simple behavior. For another, the alternative implementation of runAll does not even invoke these methods but rather accesses the fields directly.

The assumption about Qnode.run is crucial, however. Because run invokes, in turn, Task.run, essentially nothing is known about its behavior. For this reason both implementations of runAll invoke run on the same tasks in the same order; otherwise, it is hard to imagine how equivalence of the implementations could be verified in a modular way, i.e., reasoning only about class AQueue. But here we encounter the problem with simulation based reasoning that is analogous to the problem with invariants and

---

[4] It also provides a technical simplification: we do not need to formulate a semantics of programs acting on heap fragments.

[5] The reason this is sound is similar to the justification for proof rules for recursive procedures: it is essentially the induction step for a proof by induction on the maximum depth of the method call stack.

reentrant callbacks. There is no reason for the coupling to hold at intermediate points of the methods of AQueue. If a method is invoked at such a point, the assumption that the called method preserves the coupling is of no use —just as the assumption of invariant-preservation is of no use if a method is invoked in a state where the invariant does not hold.

The inv/own discipline solves the invariant problem for an object o by replacing the declared invariant $\mathscr{I}(o)$ with an implication —see (1)— that is true in all states. As with invariants, so too with couplings: It does not make sense to ask a coupling to hold in every state, because two different implementations with nontrivial differences do not have lockstep correspondence of states. (For example, imagine that in the alternative version, the arrays are compressed every 100th invocation of runAll.) Our generalization of the inv/own idea is that the local coupling relation for a particular (pair of) island(s) is conditioned on an inv field so that the local coupling may hold in *some pairs of states* at intermediate points —in particular, at method calls that can lead to reentrant callbacks.

Proving the example. Consider corresponding instances o, o' of the two versions of AQueue. The local coupling serves to describe the corresponding pair of islands when o and o' are packed. So the induced coupling relation on all program states requires corresponding pairs of islands to satisfy the local coupling just when they are packed and the client visible states to be related by identity (modulo allocation behavior). Because inv is part of the behavior observable at the level of reasoning, we can assume both versions follow the same pattern of packing (though not necessarily of control structure) and thus include $o.inv = o'.inv$ as a conjunct of the induced coupling.

Consider the two implementations of runAll. To a first approximation, what matters is that each updates some internal state and then both reach a point where run is invoked. At that point, the *local* coupling does not hold —but the *induced* coupling relation on all states can and does hold, because the island is unpacked. In more detail it holds outside the island because the relation is the "identity" on client-visible states; note that unpacking the island does not preclude side effects outside it: however, the side effects must be the *same* for both versions. That the induced coupling holds for the island itself parallels the way $\mathscr{I}^C(o)$ can be false while $o.inv \le C \Rightarrow \mathscr{I}^C(o)$ remains true, recall (1). So we can use the assumption about called methods to conclude that the coupling holds after the corresponding calls to run.

The hardest part of the proof for runAll is at the point where the two implementations pack self to AQueue. Just as both implementations invoke run (and on the same queue nodes), both need to pack in order to preserve the coupling. And at this point we have to argue that the local coupling is reestablished. To do so, we need to know the state of the internal structures that have been modified. We would like to argue that the only modifications are only those explicit in the code of runAll, but what about the effect of run? Owing to the preconditions on add and runAll, i.e., the requirement that Queue is packed, the only possible reentrant callbacks are to getRuns and this does no updates. (In other examples, modifies specifications would be needed at this point for modular reasoning.)

This concludes the informal sketch of how our abstraction theorem handles reentrant callbacks and encapsulation using the inv/own discipline. A more formal way of establishing the relation $o.inv = o'.inv$ between two implementations of runAll would involve reasoning in a relational program logic. The development of such a logic is a topic of active research [21,22] —no such widely accepted logic exists.

To justify reasoning along the lines sketched above, several features of the discipline need to be adapted —in ways which also make sense in terms of informal considerations of information hiding. The additional restrictions are formalized in Section 5 and their significance discussed in Section 8. As a preview we make the following remarks, using "*Abs*" as the generic name for a class for which two versions are considered.

Adapting the discipline for representation independence. We first describe the adaptations needed by field access, **pack** and hierarchical ownership. We then discuss the adaptations for ownership transfer. The adaptations are summarized in Table 2.

The discipline does not constrain field access, as reading cannot falsify an invariant predicate. However, for information hiding one expects visibility —and alias confinement —to prevent reading as well as writing encapsulated state. Information hiding is exactly what is formalized by representation independence and indeed the abstraction theorem fails if a client can read fields of encapsulated objects. For the fields of the class being revised, we can rely on scope, as indicated by the 'private' modifier on the fields of class AQueue. For representation objects, we augment the discipline by making every field access $y.f$ subject to a precondition: If y is transitively owned by some instance o of the class, *Abs*, under revision, then either the field access occurs in code of *Abs* or else self is transitively owned by o.

Another problematic feature is that "**pack** e **as** C" can occur in any class, so long as its preconditions are established. This means that, unlike traditional theories, an invariant is not simply established at initialization. In our theory the local coupling must be established preceding each "**pack** e **as** *Abs*". We aim for reasoning that is modular in the sense that the proof obligations are only for the two implementations of *Abs*, so we insist that **pack** e **as** *Abs* occurs only in code of *Abs*.

Although the discipline supports hierarchical ownership, our technical treatment benefits from heap partitioning ideas from separation logic (we highlight the connections where possible, e.g., in Proposition 9). To this end, it is convenient to prevent an instance of *Abs* from transitively owning another instance of *Abs*.[6] As a result, their islands are not nested. This can be achieved by a simple syntactic restriction. It does not preclude that, say, class AQueue can hold tasks that own AQueue objects, because an instance of AQueue owns its representation objects (the Qnodes), not the tasks they contain. Nor does it preclude hierarchical ownership, in general; e.g., *Abs* could own a hashtable that in turn owns some arrays. See Sect. 8 for futher discussion on this design decision.

Ownership transfer. Finally, consider ownership transfer across the encapsulation boundary. The case of transfer from client into the encapsulated abstraction is common in practice; for example, the main routine of a compiler could construct an input stream, then hand ownership to the lexer [10]. Our example can easily be adapted to such a scenario, by making the add method take ownership of its Task argument. Transfers in and out of an abstraction occur in case the abstraction is some sort of resource manager; such

---

[6] A technical benefit is that the induced coupling does not need to be defined recursively.

Table 2. Augmented preconditions for adapting the *inv*/*own* discipline for representation independence. Compare with Table 1 and see Def. 15. The preconditions for field update, **pack**, and **unpack** are unchanged from Table 1. For clarity we omit the obvious precondition $x \neq$ **null**. An additional change is that **pack** e **as** *Abs* is disallowed outside class *Abs*.

assert $x.inv = \text{Object} \wedge (e_2 = \textbf{null} \vee e_2.inv > C)$
/* Include the following conjunct, in contexts where the static type of self is not *Abs*. */
$\wedge ((\exists o \mid o \succ_{Abs} x) \Rightarrow C = Abs \vee (\exists o \mid o \succ_{Abs} e_2));$
setown x **to** (e_2, C)

/* Use the following in contexts where the static type of self is not *Abs*. */
assert $y \neq \textbf{null} \wedge (\forall o \mid o \succ_{Abs} y \Rightarrow o \succ_{Abs} \text{self});$
$x := y.f$

examples have been considered in [13,14]. In a setting like ours where there may be many instances of the abstraction, transfers may also occur between instances; in [8] we consider the example of queues that transfer owned tasks, as might be done for load balancing. We observe in [8] that the confinement invariant used there does not depend on the ownership relation being fixed. But the formalization there does not allow ownership transfer, basically because ownership confinement is formalized as a structural property of the heap rather than being explicitly encoded in the program state.

Technically, the most challenging case is where a hitherto-encapsulated object is released to a client, e.g., when a resource manager constructs fresh instances of a resource and later transfers ownership to a client. This can be seen as a deliberate exposure of representation and thus is observable behavior that must be retained in a revised version of the abstraction. Yet encapsulated data of the two versions can be in general quite different. To support modular reasoning about the two versions, it appears essential to restrict outward transfer of objects encapsulated for *Abs* to occur only in code of *Abs*. Given that restriction, it is part of the proof obligation for simulation that such transfers preserve coupling. That is, although in general encapsulated representations can be quite different between versions, any part of the representation that is transfered outward must be observably equivalent in the two versions, at the time of transfer.

We consider in detail an example that involves transfer of owned objects between instances of our example abstraction; see Fig. 6. In accord with the discipline [10,11], method xferFirst needs to be overridden in AQueue, with the unpack/pack forcing a check that the invariant of AQueue is maintained; in this case, additional code is needed to maintain the invariant. That additional code would be different for the two versions of AQueue, and the **pack** statements trigger an obligation to show that the local coupling is preserved for both queues.

In this example, the transfer itself is in the superclass of *Abs*; indeed, the transferred node is owned at Queue. One can also imagine a variation that transfers all of the nodes from one queue to another, the latter having no tasks initially. In this variation, the overrides in the two versions of AQueue could also transfer the arrays owned at AQueue.

```
/* In Queue */
void xferFirst(Queue q) {
  assert tsks ≠ null ∧ ...
    unpack self from Queue;   unpack q from Queue;
  Qnode t := tsks;
    unpack t from Qnode;
  tsks := tsks.nxt; t.nxt := q.tsks; q.tsks := t;
  setown t to (q,Queue);
    pack t as Qnode;   pack q as Queue;   pack self as Queue;  }

/* In AQueue */
void xferFirst(Queue q) {
  assert tsks ≠ null ∧ q is AQueue ∧ ...
    unpack self from AQueue; unpack q from AQueue;
  super();
  update the arrays to maintain invariants of AQueue;
    pack q as AQueue; pack self as AQueue;
```

Fig. 6. Possible addition to class Queue in which ownership of self's first task is transferred to another queue. Possible corresponding addition to class AQueue.

Finally, consider a variation where it is code in Queue that transfers the arrays. This would be rather strange. Indeed, we are assuming the fields of AQueue are not accessed in Queue. But it would be possible for some code in AQueue to "leak" the arrays, for example by assigning to a field of Queue. Our adaptation of the discipline restricts scenarios like this: transfer of an object p owned at *Abs*, in code outside *Abs*, is only allowed if afterwards p is still owned at *Abs*. The restriction is in the form of an added precondition for **setown**, see Table 2. The precondition would hold in the variation under discussion. But it would be falsified if the code in Queue transferred ownership of the arrays to a client, or to no owner at all.

3   An Illustrative Language

Following [10,11], we formalize the *inv/own* discipline in terms of a language in which fields have public visibility, to illuminate the conditions necessary for sound reasoning about invariants and simulations. In practice, private and protected visibility and perhaps lightweight alias control would serve to automatically check most of the conditions. This section formalizes the language, adapting notations and typing rules from Featherweight Java [23] and imperative features and the special commands from our previous papers [8,20]. We choose a denotational semantics, because it enables an elegant formulation of simulations and because it was used in the latter papers.

A complete program is given as a *class table*, CT, that maps class name C to a declaration $CT(C)$ of the form **class** C **extends** D { $\bar{T}\ \bar{f}$; $\bar{M}$ }. The categories T, M are

Table 3. Grammar. The distinguished names self and result are in *VarName*.

$C \in$ *ClassName* $m \in$ *MethName* $f \in$ *FieldName* $x \in$ *VarName*	
$T ::= $ **bool** | **void** | C	data type
$M ::= T\ m(\bar{T}\ \bar{x})\ \{S\}$	method declaration
$S ::= x := e \mid x.f := y$	assign to local var. or param., update field
$\mid\quad x := $ **new** $C \mid x := e.m(\bar{e}) \mid x := y.f$	object creation, method call, field access
$\mid\quad T\ x := e$ **in** $S \mid S; S \mid$ **if** e **then** S **else** S **fi**	local variable, sequence, conditional
$\mid\quad$ **pack** e **as** $C \mid$ **unpack** e **from** C	set *inv* to C, set *inv* to $super C$
$\mid\quad$ **setown** x **to** (e, C)	set *x.own* to (e, C)
$\mid\quad$ **assert** $\mathscr{P}$	assert (semantic predicate $\mathscr{P}$)
$e ::= x \mid$ **null** | **true** | **false**	variable, constant
$\mid\quad e = e \mid e$ **is** $C \mid (C)\ e$	ptr. equality, type test, cast

given by the grammar in Table 3. Barred identifiers like $\bar{T}$ indicate finite lists, e.g., $\bar{T}\ \bar{f}$ stands for a list $\bar{f}$ of field names with corresponding types $\bar{T}$. In most respects self and result are like any other variables but self cannot be the target of assignment; the final value of result serves as the result returned by a method.

Well formed class tables are characterized using typing rules which are expressed using some auxiliary functions that in turn depend on the class table, allowing classes to make mutually recursive references to other classes, without restriction. In particular, this allows recursive methods (so without loss of generality we omit loops). For convenience, we use the some auxiliary functions on syntax. For a class C, *fields C* is defined as the inherited and declared fields of C; *dfields C* is the fields declared in C; *super C* is the direct superclass of C. We assume that a field name f uniquely determines the class, *declClass f*, that declares it; so *declClass f* $= C$ iff there is some T such that $(f : T)$ is in *dfields C*.

We use multi-letter identifiers, so one might read "*dfields C*" as a single identifier rather than, as intended, the application of a function. We use parentheses when there seems to be a risk of confusion, while avoiding them in cases where context or typography should suffice.

For a method declaration, $T\ m(\bar{T}_1\ \bar{x})\ \{S\}$ in class C, the method type *mtype*(m, C) is $\bar{T}_1 \rightarrow T$ and list of parameter names, *pars*(m, C), is $\bar{x}$. For m inherited in C, *mtype*$(m, C) =$ *mtype*(m, D) and *pars*$(m, C) = $*pars*$(m, D)$ where D is the direct superclass of C.

For use in the semantics, *xfields C* extends *fields C* by assigning "types" to the auxiliary fields: *com* : **bool**, *own* : owntyp, and *inv* : (invtyp$C$). Neither invtyp$C$ nor owntyp are types in the programming language but the slight notational abuse is convenient. These fields are present in every object, as if they were declared in class Object.

A *typing context* Γ is a finite function from variable names to types, such that self $\in$ *dom* Γ. Selected typing rules for expressions and commands are given in Table 4. A judgement of the form $\Gamma \vdash e : T$ says that expression e has type T in the context of a method of class Γ self, with parameters and local variables declared by Γ. A judgement $\Gamma \vdash S$ says that S is a command in the same context. A class table *CT* is well formed

Table 4. Typing rules for selected commands

$$\frac{\Gamma \vdash e : T \quad T \leq \Gamma x}{\Gamma \vdash x := e} \qquad\qquad \frac{\Gamma \vdash x : D_1 \quad \Gamma \vdash e_2 : D_2 \quad D_2 \leq C}{\Gamma \vdash \mathbf{setown}\ x\ \mathbf{to}\ (e_2, C)}$$

$$\frac{\Gamma \vdash e : D \quad D \leq C}{\Gamma \vdash \mathbf{pack}\ e\ \mathbf{as}\ C} \qquad\qquad \frac{\Gamma \vdash e : D \quad D \leq C}{\Gamma \vdash \mathbf{unpack}\ e\ \mathbf{from}\ C}$$

$$\frac{B \leq \Gamma x \quad x \neq \mathsf{self} \quad B \neq \mathsf{Object}}{\Gamma \vdash x := \mathbf{new}\ B} \qquad\qquad \frac{(f : T) \in \mathit{fields}(\Gamma x) \quad \Gamma y \leq T}{\Gamma \vdash x.f := y}$$

$$\frac{(f : T) \in \mathit{fields}(\Gamma y) \quad T \leq \Gamma x}{\Gamma \vdash x := y.f}$$

$$\frac{\Gamma \vdash e : D \quad \mathit{mtype}(m, D) = \bar{T} \to U \quad x \neq \mathsf{self} \quad \Gamma \vdash \bar{e} : \bar{U} \quad \bar{U} \leq \bar{T} \quad U \leq \Gamma x}{\Gamma \vdash x := e.m(\bar{e})}$$

if, for each class C, each method declaration M in $CT(C)$ is well formed in C; this is written $C \vdash M$ and defined by the following rule:

$$\frac{\bar{x} : \bar{T}, \mathsf{self} : C, \mathit{result} : T \vdash S}{C \vdash T\ m(\bar{T}\ \bar{x})\{S\}} \quad \text{if } \mathit{mtype}(m, \mathit{super}\, C) \text{ is defined then } \mathit{mtype}(m, \mathit{super}\, C) = \bar{T} \to T \text{ and } \mathit{pars}(m, \mathit{super}\, C) = \bar{x}$$

To formalize assertions, we prefer to avoid both the commitment to a particular formula language and the complication of an environment for declaring predicate names to be interpreted in the semantics. So we indulge in a mild abuse of notation: the syntax of **assert** uses a semantic predicate. We say $\Gamma \vdash \mathbf{assert}\ \mathscr{P}$ is well formed provided that $\mathscr{P}$ is a set of program states for context Γ. We return to predicates later.

In the rest of the chapter we assume types and contexts are well formed, and that typings are derivable, without explicit mention.

Semantics. We assume that a countable set Loc is given, along with a distinguished value *nil* not in Loc. We assume given a function *type* from Loc to non-primitive types distinct from Object, such that for each C there are infinitely many locations o with *type* $o = C$. This is used in a way that is equivalent to tagging object states with their type, which is immutable. It serves to slightly streamline some definitions. The syntax is desugared, in the style of separation logic, so that access and update of mutable fields occurs only in commands ($x := y.f$ and $x.f := y$). So field read $x := y.f$ is considered a primitive command rather than an instance of ordinary assignment and $y.f$ is not a stand alone expression; this choice is not essential but streamlines the formal development. In our semantics, type test and cast expressions do not depend on the heap.

Some semantic domains correspond directly to the syntax. For example, each data type T denotes a set $[\![T]\!]$ of values. The meaning of context Γ is a set $[\![\Gamma]\!]$ of stores; a *store* $s \in [\![\Gamma]\!]$ is a type-respecting assignment of locations and primitive values to the

Table 5. Semantic categories θ and domains $[\![\theta]\!]$. (Readers familiar with notation for dependent function spaces might prefer to write $[\![\text{pre-heap}]\!] = (o : Loc \nrightarrow [\![\text{state}\,(type\,o)]\!])$ and similarly for $[\![\text{state}\,C]\!]$ and $[\![\Gamma]\!]$.)

$$\theta ::= T \mid \Gamma \mid \theta_\perp$$

$$\mid \quad \text{owntyp} \mid \text{invtyp}\,C \mid \text{state}\,C \quad \textit{own and inv val., object state}$$
$$\mid \quad \text{pre-heap} \mid \text{heap} \mid \text{heap} \otimes \Gamma \quad \textit{heap fragment, closed heap, state}$$
$$\mid \quad (\Gamma \vdash T) \mid \Gamma \rightsquigarrow \Gamma' \mid \text{menv} \quad \textit{expression meaning, state transformer, method environment}$$

$$
\begin{aligned}
[\![C]\!] &= \{nil\} \cup \{o \in Loc \mid type\,o \le C\} \\
[\![\text{bool}]\!] &= \{true, false\} \\
[\![\text{void}]\!] &= \{it\} \\
[\![\text{invtyp}\,C]\!] &= \{B \mid C \le B\} \\
[\![\text{owntyp}]\!] &= \{(o,C) \mid o = nil \vee type\,o \le C\} \\
[\![\theta_\perp]\!] &= [\![\theta]\!] \cup \{\perp\} \\
[\![\Gamma]\!] &= \{s \mid dom\,s = dom\,\Gamma \wedge s\,\text{self} \ne nil \wedge \forall x \in dom\,s \mid s\,x \in [\![\Gamma x]\!]\} \\
[\![\text{state}\,C]\!] &= \{s \mid dom\,s = dom(xfields\,C) \wedge \forall (f : T) \in xfields\,C \mid s\,f \in [\![T]\!]\} \\
[\![\text{pre-heap}]\!] &= \{h \mid dom\,h \subseteq_{fin} Loc \wedge \forall o \in dom\,h \mid h\,o \in [\![\text{state}\,(type\,o)]\!]\} \\
[\![\text{heap}]\!] &= \{h \mid h \in [\![\text{pre-heap}]\!] \wedge \forall s \in rng\,h \mid rng\,s \cap Loc \subseteq dom\,h\} \\
[\![\text{heap} \otimes \Gamma]\!] &= \{(h,s) \mid h \in [\![\text{heap}]\!] \wedge s \in [\![\Gamma]\!] \wedge rng\,s \cap Loc \subseteq dom\,h\} \\
[\![\Gamma \vdash T]\!] &= \{v \mid v \in ([\![\Gamma]\!] \to [\![T]\!]_\perp) \wedge \forall s \mid vs \in Loc \Rightarrow vs \in rng\,s\} \\
[\![\Gamma \rightsquigarrow \Gamma']\!] &= [\![\text{heap} \otimes \Gamma]\!] \to [\![(\text{heap} \otimes \Gamma')_\perp]\!] \\
[\![\text{menv}]\!] &= \{\mu \mid \text{for all } C, m, \, \mu C m \text{ is defined iff } mtype(m,C) \text{ is defined,} \\
&\qquad \text{and if so then } \mu C m \in [\![\text{self} : C, \bar{x} : \bar{T} \rightsquigarrow \text{result} : T_1]\!] \\
&\qquad \text{where } pars(m,C) = \bar{x} \text{ and } mtype(m,C) = \bar{T} \to T_1\}
\end{aligned}
$$

local variables and parameters given by a typing context Γ. The semantics, and later the coupling relation, is structured in terms of category names θ given in Table 5 which also defines the semantic domains. Subtyping is embodied in a simple way: if $T \le U$ then $[\![T]\!] \subseteq [\![U]\!]$.

A *program state* for context Γ is a pair (h, s) where s is in $[\![\Gamma]\!]$ and h is a *heap*, i.e., a finite partial function from locations to object states. An *object state* is a type-respecting mapping of field names to values. A command typable in Γ denotes a function mapping each program state (h, s) either to a final state (h_0, s_0) or to the distinguished value $\perp$ which represents runtime errors, divergence, and assertion failure. An *object state* is a mapping from (extended) field names to values. A *pre-heap* is like a heap except for possibly having dangling references. If h, h' are pre-heaps with disjoint domains then we write $h * h'$ for their union; otherwise $h * h'$ is undefined. Function application associates to the left, so $h\,o\,f$ is the value of field f of the object $h\,o$ at location o. We also write $h\,o.f$. Application binds more tightly than binary operator symbols and ",".

The meaning of a derivable command typing $\Gamma \vdash S$ will be defined to be a function sending each method environment μ to an element of $[\![\Gamma \rightsquigarrow \Gamma]\!]$. That is, $[\![\Gamma \vdash S]\!]\mu$ is a state transformer $[\![\text{heap} \otimes \Gamma]\!] \to [\![(\text{heap} \otimes \Gamma)_\perp]\!]$. For a method m such that $pars(m,C) = \bar{x}$ and $mtype(m,C) = \bar{T} \to U$, the meaning $\mu\,C\,m$ will be a state transformer of type $(\text{self} : C, \bar{x} : \bar{T}) \rightsquigarrow (\text{result} : T_1)$.

Table 6. Semantics of selected commands. To streamline the treatment of $\bot$, the metalanguage expression "let $\alpha = \beta$ in ..." denotes $\bot$ if β is $\bot$. We use notation $[h \mid o \mapsto st]$ for h extended or overridden at o with value st. For brevity the nested function extension for field update is written $[h \mid o.f \mapsto v]$.

$$[\![\Gamma \vdash x := y.f]\!]\mu(h,s) \quad = \text{let } o = s\,y \text{ in if } o = nil \text{ then } \bot \text{ else } (h, [s \mid x \mapsto h\,o.f])$$

$$[\![\Gamma \vdash x := e]\!]\mu(h,s) \quad = \text{let } v = [\![\Gamma \vdash e : T]\!](s) \text{ in } (h, [s \mid x \mapsto v])$$

$$[\![\Gamma \vdash x.f := y]\!]\mu(h,s) \quad = \text{let } o = s\,x \text{ in if } o = nil \text{ then } \bot \text{ else } ([h \mid o.f \mapsto s\,y], s)$$

$$[\![\Gamma \vdash x := \mathbf{new}\ C]\!]\mu(h,s) = \text{let } o = fresh(C,h) \text{ in}$$
$$\text{let } h_0 = [h \mid o \mapsto [xfields\,C \mapsto defaults\,C]] \text{ in } (h_0, [s \mid x \mapsto o])$$

$$[\![\Gamma \vdash x := e.m(\bar{e})]\!]\mu(h,s) = \text{let } o = [\![\Gamma \vdash e : D]\!](s) \text{ in if } o = nil \text{ then } \bot \text{ else}$$
$$\text{let } \bar{v} = [\![\Gamma \vdash \bar{e} : \bar{U}]\!](s) \text{ in let } \bar{x} = pars(m,D) \text{ in}$$
$$\text{let } s_1 = [\bar{x} \mapsto \bar{v}, \mathsf{self} \mapsto o] \text{ in}$$
$$\text{let } (h_1, s_2) = \mu(type\,o)m(h,s_1) \text{ in } (h_1, [s \mid x \mapsto s_2\,\mathsf{result}])$$

$$[\![\Gamma \vdash \mathbf{assert}\ \mathscr{P}]\!]\mu(h,s) \quad = \text{if } (h,s) \in \mathscr{P} \text{ then } (h,s) \text{ else } \bot$$

$$[\![\Gamma \vdash \mathbf{pack}\ e\ \mathbf{as}\ C]\!]\mu(h,s) =$$
$$\text{let } q = [\![\Gamma \vdash e : D]\!](s) \text{ in if } q = nil \text{ then } \bot \text{ else}$$
$$\text{let } h_1 = \lambda p \in dom\,h \mid \text{if } h\,p.own = (q,C) \text{ then } [h\,p \mid com \mapsto true] \text{ else } h\,p \text{ in } ([h_1 \mid q.inv \mapsto C], s)$$

$$[\![\Gamma \vdash \mathbf{unpack}\ e\ \mathbf{from}\ C]\!]\mu(h,s) =$$
$$\text{let } q = [\![\Gamma \vdash e : D]\!](s) \text{ in if } q = nil \text{ then } \bot \text{ else}$$
$$\text{let } h_1 = \lambda p \in dom\,h \mid \text{if } h\,p.own = (q,C) \text{ then } [h\,p \mid com \mapsto false] \text{ else } h\,p \text{ in}$$
$$([h_1 \mid q.inv \mapsto super\,C], s)$$

$$[\![\Gamma \vdash \mathbf{setown}\ x\ \mathbf{to}\ (e_2,C)]\!]\mu(h,s) =$$
$$\text{let } q = s\,x \text{ in if } q = nil \text{ then } \bot \text{ else}$$
$$\text{let } p = [\![\Gamma \vdash e_2 : D_2]\!](s) \text{ in } ([h \mid q.own \mapsto (p,C)], s)$$

Meanings for expressions and commands are defined, in Table 6, by recursion on typing derivation. In some of the defining equations, the right side refers to identifiers in the typing rules. For example, T in the semantics of $x := e$ is the type of e as per the first rule in Table 4. The semantic definition for **pack** e **as** C refers to D which is the type of e in the typing rule for **pack**.

The semantics is defined for an arbitrary location-valued function *fresh* such that $type(fresh(C,h)) = C$ and $fresh(C,h) \notin dom\,h$.

Consider a method call $\Gamma \vdash x := e.m(\bar{e})$, where $\Gamma \vdash e : D$. Consider execution of the call in initial state (h,s) and let $o = [\![\Gamma \vdash e : D]\!](h,s)$; so by type soundness $type\,o \le D$. The meaning of the method body, used for the semantics of the call, is found in the method environment μ as $\mu\,(type\,o)\,m$. It is applied to state (h,s_1) with argument store s_1 that maps self to o and parameters $\bar{x}$ to their values $\bar{v}$. It returns a state (h_1,s_2) where s_2 result provides the value assigned to x.

The meaning of a well typed method declaration M in class C, of the form $M = T\,m(\bar{T}\ \bar{x})\{S\}$ is the total function in $[\![menv]\!] \to [\![self : C, \bar{x} : \bar{T} \rightsquigarrow result : T]\!]$ defined as follows: Given a method environment μ, a heap h and a store $s \in [\![\bar{x} : \bar{T}, self : C]\!]$,

$$[\![M]\!]\mu(h,s) = \text{let } s_1 = [s \mid result \mapsto default\,T] \text{ in} \\ \text{let } (h_0, s_0) = [\![\Gamma \vdash S]\!]\mu(h,s_1) \text{ in } (h_0, [result : s_0\,result]) \tag{2}$$

A method environment μ maps each C,m to a meaning obtained in this way or by inheritance. In more detail, we define for each i an environment μ_i; this is called the *approximation chain*. The basis is $\mu_0 C m$ is the everywhere-$\perp$ function, for all C,m. We define $\mu_{i+1} C m$, for m declared as M in C, to be $[\![M]\!]\mu_i$. In case m is inherited in C from B, we define $\mu_{i+1} C m$ to be $\mu_{i+1} B m$.

Note that the ith element in the chain approximates $[\![CT]\!]$ in a way such that, in operational terms, it gives the correct semantics for executions with method call stack bounded in length by i. For well formed class table CT, the semantics $[\![CT]\!]$ is defined as the least upper bound of the approximation chain. For full details see [8] or the variation that was machine checked in PVS [24].

Predicates. A *predicate* for state type Γ is just a subset $\mathcal{P} \subseteq [\![\mathsf{heap} \otimes \Gamma]\!]$. For emphasis we can write $(h,s) \models \mathcal{P}$ for $(h,s) \in \mathcal{P}$. Note that $\perp \notin \mathcal{P}$. We give no formal syntax to denote predicates but rather use informal metalanguage for which the interpretation should be clear. For example, "$\mathsf{self}.f \neq \mathbf{null}$" denotes the set of (h,s) with $h(s\,\mathsf{self}).f \neq nil$. and "$\forall o \mid \mathcal{P}(o)$" denotes the set of (h,s) such that $(h,s) \models \mathcal{P}(o)$ for all $o \in dom\, h$. Note that quantification over objects (e.g., in Table 1 and Def. 4) is interpreted to mean quantification over allocated locations; the range of quantification can include unreachable objects but this causes no problems.

To formalize encapsulation we need precise semantic formulations concerning dependence. In terms of formulas, a predicate depends on $e.f$ if it can be falsified by some update of $e.f$. Some predicates are falsifiable by creation of new objects; an example is the predicate $\forall o \mid type\, o = C \Rightarrow o = \mathsf{self}$.

Definition 1 (depends, new-closed). A predicate $\mathcal{P}$ *depends on* $o.f$ in (h,s) iff $(h,s) \in \mathcal{P}$, $o \in dom\, h$, and $([h \mid o.f \mapsto v],s) \notin \mathcal{P}$ for some v with $[h \mid o.f \mapsto v] \in [\![\mathsf{heap}]\!]$. We say $\mathcal{P}$ *depends on* $o.f$ iff there is some (h,s) such that $\mathcal{P}$ depends on $o.f$ in (h,s). We say $\mathcal{P}$ is *new-closed* iff $(h,s) \in \mathcal{P}$ implies $([h \mid o \mapsto defaults],s) \in \mathcal{P}$ for all $o \notin dom\, h$.

The condition $[h \mid o.f \mapsto v] \in [\![\mathsf{heap}]\!]$ merely ensures that v is not a dangling pointer or type-incorrect value.

4 The *inv/own* Discipline

The discipline reviewed in Sect. 2.1 is designed to make Equation (1) a program invariant for every object. This is achieved by using additional program invariants that govern ownership. We formalize this as a global predicate, *disciplined*, defined in three steps. Then we review prior results on how the discipline is enforced by proper annotation. Finally, we use ownership to partition the heap, in preparation for Sect. 5.

4.1 Ownership and Invariants

The default values for the extended fields are $inv = \mathsf{Object}$, $own = (nil, \mathsf{Object})$, and $com = false$. So initially a new object is neither packed nor owned.

Definition 2 (transitive C- and $C\uparrow$-ownership). For any heap h, the relation $o \succ^h_C p$ on $dom\ h$, read "o owns p at C in h", holds iff either $(o,C) = h\ p.own$ or there are q and D such that $(o,C) = h\ q.own$ and $q \succ^h_D p$.

The relation $o \succ^h_{C\uparrow} p$ holds iff there is some D with $C \leq D$ and $o \succ^h_D p$. This may be read "o owns p at or above C in h".

The relations are transitive in this sense: $o \succ^h_C p$ and $p \succ^h_D q$ implies $o \succ^h_C q$.

The discipline ensures that if o owns p at C and p is not packed to its type then o is unpacked at least above C. This is formalized in Corollary 6.

Definition 3 (admissible invariant). A predicate $\mathscr{P} \subseteq [\![heap \otimes (self : C)]\!]$ is *admissible as an invariant for C* provided that it is new-closed and for every h, s, o, f such that $\mathscr{P}$ depends on $o.f$ in (h,s), field f is neither *inv* nor *com*, and one of the following conditions holds: $o = s\ self$ and f is in $dom(xfields\ C)$ or $s\ self \succ^h_{C\uparrow} o$.

For dependence on fields of self, the typing condition, $f \in dom(xfields\ C)$, prevents an invariant for C from depending on fields declared in a subclass of C (which could be expressed in a formula using a cast) —while allowing dependence on fields declared or inherited in C. An invariant can depend on any fields of objects owned at C or above.

We refrain from formalizing syntax for declaring invariants. In the subsequent definitions, we assume that an admissible invariant $\mathscr{I}^C$ is given for every class C. We assume $\mathscr{I}^{Object} = \mathbf{true}$.

Definition 4 (disciplined, $\mathscr{J}$). A heap h is *disciplined* if $h \models \mathscr{J}$ where $\mathscr{J}$ is defined to be the conjunction of the following:

(D1) $\forall o, C \mid o.inv \leq C \Rightarrow \mathscr{I}^C(o)$
(D2) $\forall o, C, p \mid o.inv \leq C \wedge p.own = (o,C) \Rightarrow p.com$
(D3) $\forall o \mid o.com \Rightarrow o.inv = type\ o$

A state (h,s) is *disciplined* if h is.

Method environment μ *is disciplined* provided that every method *preserves* $\mathscr{J}$ in the following sense: For any C, m, h, s, if $h \models \mathscr{J}$ and $\mu\ C\ m\ (h,s) = (h_0, s_0)$ then $h_0 \models \mathscr{J}$.

In the sequel we refrain from reminding the reader that a hypothesis like $\mu\ C\ m\ (h,s) = (h_0, s_0)$ implies that $\mu\ C\ m\ (h,s) \neq \bot$.

Lemma 5 (transitive ownership). Suppose h is disciplined and $o \succ^h_C p$. Then

(a) $type\ o \leq C$, and
(b) $h\ o.inv \leq C$ implies $h\ p.com = true$.

Corollary 6. If h is disciplined, $o \succ^h_C p$, and $h\ p.inv > type\ p$, then $h\ o.inv > C$.

In a small-step semantics one would prove that every reachable state in a properly annotated program is disciplined. Instead, we will show that every command maps disciplined initial states to disciplined final states —just like methods in a disciplined environment. So our notion of *program invariant* is a predicate $\mathscr{P}$ that is *preserved* by commands in the sense that

$$(h,s) \models \mathscr{P} \text{ and } [\![\Gamma \vdash S]\!]\mu(h,s) = (h_0, s_0) \text{ implies } (h_0, s_0) \models \mathscr{P}$$

and similarly for predicates on the heap alone.

4.2 The Discipline

To impose the stipulated preconditions of Table 1 we consider programs with the requisite syntactic structure (similar to formal proof outlines [25]).

Definition 7 (properly annotated). The *annotated commands* are the subset of the category of commands where each **pack**, **unpack**, **setown**, and field update is immediately preceded by an **assert**. A *properly annotated command* is an annotated command such that each of these assertions implies the precondition stipulated in Table 1. A *properly annotated class table* is one such that each method body is properly annotated.

For any class table and family of invariants there exists a proper annotation: just add **assert** commands with the stipulated preconditions. For practical interest, of course, one wants assertions that can collectively be proved correct.

For a properly annotated program, $\mathscr{I}$ is a program invariant. This property is shown in terms of small-step semantics in [10,11]. For our purposes, the initial state of a complete program has an empty heap, which satisfies $\mathscr{I}$ because the quantified objects in (D1–D3) range over allocated objects. So we focus on preservation in the following formulation.

Proposition 8. If method environment μ is disciplined then any properly annotated command S preserves $\mathscr{I}$ in the sense that for all (h,s), if $h \models \mathscr{I}$ and $(h_0,s_0) = [\![\Gamma \vdash S]\!]\mu(h,s)$ then $h_0 \models \mathscr{I}$. If CT is a properly annotated class table then the method environment $[\![CT]\!]$ is disciplined, as is every method environment in the approximations of $[\![CT]\!]$.

The first statement is proved by induction on the structure of S. For the second statement, first we prove we go by induction on approximations of $[\![CT]\!]$, using the first statement. Then we show that being disciplined is preserved at the limit, so $[\![CT]\!]$ is disciplined. For details see [20]. The corollary is that S preserves $\mathscr{I}$, for any S that occurs as constituent of a method body in CT (interpreting S in $[\![CT]\!]$ or in any of the approximants).

4.3 Partitioning the Heap

Next we show how ownership is used to partition the objects in the heap in order to formalize the encapsulation boundary depicted in Sect. 2.2.

Given an object $o \in dom\,h$ and class name A with $type\,o \leq A$ we can partition h into pre-heaps Ah (the A-object), Rh (the representation of o for class A), Sh (objects owned by o at a superclass), and Fh (free from o) determined by the following conditions: Ah is the singleton $[o \mapsto h\,o]$, Rh is h restricted to the set of p with $o \succ_A^h p$, Sh is h restricted to the set of p with $o \succ_C^h p$ for some $C > A$, and Fh is the rest of h. Note that if $o \succ_B^h p$ for some proper subclass $B < A$ then $p \in dom\,Fh$. A pre-heap of the form $Ah * Rh * Sh$ is called an *island*. In these terms, dependency of admissible invariants is described in the following Proposition. As an illustration, here is the island for the left side of the situation depicted in Fig. 5 in Sect. 2.2:

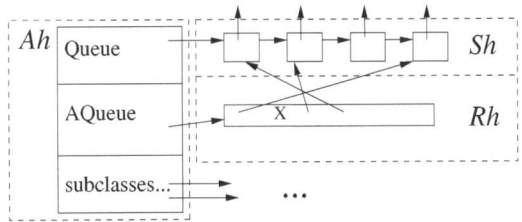

Proposition 9 (island). Suppose $\mathscr{I}^A$ is an admissible invariant for A and $o \in dom\,h$ with $type\,o \leq A$. If $h = Fh * Ah * Rh * Sh$ is the partition defined above then $Fh_0 * Ah * Rh * Sh \models \mathscr{I}^C(o)$ iff $h \models \mathscr{I}^C(o)$, for all Fh_0 such that $Fh_0 * Ah * Rh * Sh$ is a heap.

In order to work with heap partitions it is convenient to have notation to extract the one object in a singleton heap. We define *pick* by *pick h* = o where $dom\,h = \{o\}$; it is undefined if $dom\,h$ is not a singleton.

Prop. 9 considers a single object together with its owned representation; now we consider all objects of a given class.

Definition 10 (A-decomposition). For any class A and heap h, the *A-decomposition* of h is the set $Fh, Ah_1, Rh_1, Sh_1 \ldots, Ah_k, Rh_k, Sh_k$ (for some $k \geq 0$) of pre-heaps, all subsets of h, determined by the following conditions:

- $dom\,Ah_i$ contains exactly one object o and $type\,o \leq A$ (for all i, $1 \leq i \leq k$);
- every $o \in dom\,h$ with $type\,o \leq A$ occurs in $dom\,Ah_i$ for some i;
- $dom\,Rh_i = \{p \mid o \succ_A^h p\}$ where $o = pick\,Ah_i$ (for all i);
- $dom\,Sh_i = \{p \mid o \succ_{(super\,A)\uparrow}^h p\}$ where $o = pick\,Ah_i$ (for all i);
- $dom\,Fh = dom\,h \setminus (\cup i \mid dom(Ah_i * Rh_i * Sh_i))$

The conditions determine a unique decomposition. However, the numbering is not unique. Note that each Rh_i and Sh_i is transitively closed under ownership: if $p \in dom\,Rh_i$ (resp. $dom\,Sh_i$) and $p \succ_C^h q$ for some C then $q \in dom\,Rh_i$ (resp. $q \in dom\,Sh_i$).

We say that *no A-object owns an A-object in h* provided for every o, p in $dom\,h$ if $type\,o \leq A$ and $o \succ_{(type\,o)\uparrow}^h p$ then $type\,p \not\leq A$. In this case decomposition partitions the heap into separate islands of the form $Ah * Rh * Sh$. We use the term "partition" even though some blocks can be empty. Moreover, although it is the domain of the heap that is partitioned, we also use the term "partition" to refer to the corresponding factorization of the heap into a union of pre-heaps with disjoint domains.

Lemma 11 (A-partition). Suppose no A-object owns an A-object in h. Then the A-decomposition is a partition of h, that is, $h = Fh * Ah_1 * Rh_1 * Sh_1 * \ldots * Ah_k * Rh_k * Sh_k$.

We now define the function *encap* that removes from the heap the objects that are owned at *Abs*.

Definition 12 (encap). Suppose no *Abs*-object owns an *Abs*-object in h. Define the pre-heap *encap Abs h* to be $Fh * Ah_1 * Sh_1 * \ldots * Ah_k * Sh_k$ where the *Abs*-partition of h is as in Lemma 11.

Def. 16 in Sect. 5 imposes a syntactic restriction to ensure that no *Abs*-object owns an *Abs*-object, where *Abs* is the class for which two representations are compared. The restriction is expressed by means of a static approximation of ownership.

Definition 13 (may own, $\succ^{\exists}$). Given well formed CT, define $\succ^{\exists}$ to be the least transitively closed relation such that

(M1) $D_2 \succ^{\exists} D_1$ for every occurrence of **setown** x **to** (e_2, D) in a method of CT, with static types $x : D_1$ and $e_2 : D_2$
(M2) if $C \succ^{\exists} D$, $C' \leq C$ and $D' \leq D$ then $C' \succ^{\exists} D'$

Lemma 14. (a) It is a program invariant that $o \succ^h_C p$ implies $type\,o \succ^{\exists} type\,p$.
(b) If $A \not\succ^{\exists} A$ then it is a program invariant that no A-object owns an A-object.

Proof. Part (b) is a direct consequence of (a). Part (a) is proved by structural induction on commands and then induction on the approximation chain, as in the proof of Prop. 8. The only command forms that affect ownership relations are **setown** and **new**. Because **new** constructs objects with no owner, the only interesting case is **setown**.

Suppose that some method body in CT contains **setown** x **to** (e_2, C), with static types $x : D_1$ and $e_2 : D_2$. Suppose $(h_0, s_0) = [\![\text{\bf setown } x \text{ \bf to } (e_2, C)]\!](h, s)$, where the implication holds in (h, s) (for all o, p, C). We show that $o \succ^{h_0}_C p$ implies $type\,o \succ^{\exists} type\,p$, for all o, p, C, by induction on the relation $o \succ^{h_0}_C p$ in accord with Def. 2. (In essence, induction on the length of ownership chains.)

The base case is $h_0\,p.own = (o, C)$. If also $h\,p.own = (o, C)$ then we are done since the implication holds in (h, s). On the other hand, if $h\,p.own \neq (o, C)$ then we must have $o = [\![e_2]\!](h, s)$ and $p = [\![e_1]\!](h, s)$ since the command only changes the ownership of e_1. Hence by typing we have $type\,o \leq D_2$ and $type\,p \leq D_1$. By (M1) in Def. 13 we have $D_2 \succ^{\exists} D_1$ whence $type\,o \succ^{\exists} type\,p$ by (M2).

The inductive case is $(o, C) = h_0\,q.own$ and $q \succ^{h_0}_D p$ for some q, D. We have $type\,o \succ^{\exists} type\,q$ and $type\,q \succ^{\exists} type\,p$ by induction. Hence $type\,o \succ^{\exists} type\,p$ by the transitivity clause in Def. 13.

5   The Abstraction Theorem

The Abstraction Theorem generalizes Proposition 8. The Proposition considers a predicate on states and says the predicate is preserved by execution of command. The Theorem considers a relation between states and says it is preserved by a pair of executions. The Theorem builds on the use of *inv* and on ownership structure, and thus requires proper annotation. It does not directly depend on the chosen invariants, so in theory one may take $\mathscr{I}^C = \textbf{true}$ for all C.

5.1   Comparing Class Tables

We compare two implementations of a designated class *Abs*, in the context of a fixed but arbitrary collection of other classes, such that both implementations give rise to a well formed class table. The two versions can have completely different declarations, so long as methods of the same signatures are present — declared or inherited — in both. It is mainly to simplify the additional precondition needed for reading fields that we consider programs desugared into a form like that used in separation logic.

Definition 15 (properly annotated for *Abs*). The *properly annotated commands for Abs* are those that are properly annotated according to Def. 7 and moreover

(A1) fields of *Abs* have private visibility (i.e., if $f \in dfields Abs$ then accesses and updates of f only occur in code of class *Abs*)

(A2) if $\Gamma \, \mathsf{self} \neq Abs$ then $\Gamma \vdash$ **pack** e **as** Abs is not allowed

(A3) if $\Gamma \, \mathsf{self} \neq Abs$ then field access $\Gamma \vdash x := y.f$ is subject to stipulated precondition
$$y \neq \mathbf{null} \wedge (\forall o \mid o \succ_{Abs} y \Rightarrow o \succ_{Abs} \mathsf{self})$$

(A4) if $\Gamma \, \mathsf{self} \neq Abs$ then $\Gamma \vdash$ **setown** x **to** (e_2, C) is subject to an additional precondition: $x \neq \mathbf{null} \wedge ((\exists o \mid o \succ_{Abs} x) \Rightarrow C = Abs \vee (\exists o \mid o \succ_{Abs} e_2))$

(A1) merely embodies our choice to focus on change of representation for a single class and its encapsulated representations, and in particular the most common form of encapsulation, namely, private visibility. For practical purposes, other visibilities are needed and would be treated in the same manner as fields of other classes.

(A2) is needed in reasoning about simulation for **pack** e **as** Abs. This command reasserts the local coupling and we want to confine the proof obligation of simulation to code in class *Abs* as explained in Sect. 2.2.

The effect of (A3) is that a method invocation on some q not of type *Abs*, but reading an object p owned by an *Abs* object o, is only allowed if q is itself owned by o. A client should not be reading owned objects and a rep should not read objects that do not belong to its own owner. Perhaps surprisingly, (A3) does not disallow that a method invocation on one instance of *Abs* reads objects owned by another instance. The effect of (A4) is that if x is initially owned at *Abs* then after a transfer (that occurs in code outside class *Abs*) it is still owned at *Abs*.

Conditions (A3) and (A4) use transitive ownership notation, but without an explicit superscript. This is informal notation for semantic predicates. For example, "$o \succ_{Abs} e$" means $\{(h,s) \mid o \succ_{Abs}^{h} e\}$. The annotations in Table 1 use no inductively defined predicates, which is a distinct advantage for program verifiers like Spec# based on SMT provers. Direct use of transitive ownership in the program invariants (D1–D3) is no problem: these are part of the theory that justifies the discipline, not part of the verification conditions for programs. We have formulated (A3) and (A4) using transitive ownership for the sake of clarity.

Direct use of transitive ownership can be avoided by maintaining additional ghost state. For example, we can maintain an additional field, owns, of type $ClassName \rightarrow Loc$, with invariant $\forall C, o \mid (o \succ_C \mathsf{self} \Leftrightarrow o \in \mathsf{self}.owns C)$. The invariant immediately gives an alternative way to formulate (A3) and (A4). To maintain the invariant we merely augment the semantics of **setown**. For any state (h,s), we define $[\![\mathbf{setown}\ x\ \mathbf{to}\ (y,C)]\!]\mu(h,s)$ to update owns as follows. Consider the case where initially $y \neq \mathbf{null}$ and $x.own = (o,B)$ with $o \neq \mathbf{null}$. So ownership of x is being transferred from o to y. We want to remove from $o.owns B$ all p that is in $x.owns D$ for any D; and add to $y.owns C$ the union of $x.owns D$ over all D. In the cases where the old or new owner is **null**, the corresponding removal/addition is not done.[7] This treatment of transitive ownership is straightforward and would be preferable for practical use, but for clarity of presentation we do not develop it in the sequel.

Definition 16 (comparable class tables). Well formed class tables CT and CT' are *comparable* with respect to class name Abs ($\neq$ Object) provided the following hold.

- $CT(C) = CT'(C)$ for all $C \neq Abs$.
- $CT(Abs)$ and $CT'(Abs)$ have the same direct superclass and declare the same methods with the same signatures.
- CT and CT' are properly annotated for Abs.[8]
- $Abs \not\preceq^\exists Abs$ in both CT and CT'

The last condition ensures that the Abs-decomposition of any disciplined heap is a partition, by Lemmas 11 and 14. We write $\vdash, \vdash'$ for the typing relation determined by CT, CT' respectively; similarly we write $[\![-]\!], [\![-]\!]'$ for the respective semantics.

For properly annotated CT and CT', fields declared in Abs have "private scope" (see (A1)), so the two typing relations coincide except when Γ self is Abs.

In the rest of the chapter we assume CT, CT' are comparable.

5.2   Coupling Relations

The definitions are organized as follows. A *local coupling* (Def. 20) is a suitable relation on islands. This induces a family of *coupling relations* $\mathscr{R} \beta \theta$ (Def. 21), one for each category name θ and typed bijection β (Def. 17). Each relation $\mathscr{R} \beta \theta$ is from $[\![\theta]\!]$ to $[\![\theta]\!]'$. Here β is a bijection on locations, used to connect a heap in $[\![\text{heap}]\!]$ to one in $[\![\text{heap}]\!]'$. The idea is that β relates all objects except those in the Rh_i or Rh'_i blocks that have never been exposed. Finally, a *simulation* is a coupling that is preserved by all methods of Abs and holds initially.

Definition 17. A *typed bijection* is a bijective relation, β, from Loc to Loc, such that $\beta\, o\, o'$ implies $type\, o = type\, o'$ for all o, o'. A *total bijection* on h, h' is a typed bijection with $dom\, h = dom\, \beta$ and $dom\, h' = rng\, \beta$. Finally, β *fully partitions* h, h' *for Abs* if, for all p with $type\, p \leq Abs$, if $p \in dom\, h$ (resp. $p \in dom\, h'$) then $p \in dom\, \beta$ (resp. $p \in rng\, \beta$).

Lemma 18 (typed bijection and Abs-partition). Suppose β is a typed bijection with $\beta \subseteq dom\, h \times dom\, h'$ and β fully partitions h, h' for Abs. Suppose no Abs- object owns an Abs-object in h or h' (so that Lemma 11 applies). If h, h' are disciplined and partition as $h = Fh * \ldots Ah_j * Rh_j * Sh_j$ and $h' = Fh' * \ldots Ah'_k * Rh'_k * Sh'_k$ then $j = k$.

A corollary is that, under the conditions of Lemma 18, we may w.l.o.g. assume that islands in the two heaps are numbered such that $\beta\, (pick\, Ah_i)\, (pick\, Ah'_i)$, for all i.

Definition 19 (equivalence for Abs modulo bijection). For any β we define a relation $\sim_\beta$ for data values, object states, heaps, and stores, in Table 7.

---

[7] This semantics can be written as a bulk update, just like the updates to *com* in the semantics of pack/unpack, so the the axiomatic semantics used in a verifier does not need to use sets explicitly.

[8] Together with the requirement $CT(C) = CT'(C)$ for all $C \neq Abs$, this implies that the families of invariants $\mathscr{I}^C$ given for CT and CT' are the same.

Table 7. Value equivalence for the designated class Abs. The relation for heap is the same as for pre-heap. For object states, $\sim$ is independent from the declared fields of $CT(Abs)$ and $CT'(Abs)$.

$$
\begin{array}{llll}
o \sim_\beta o' & \text{in } [\![C]\!] & \Leftrightarrow & \beta\,o\,o' \vee o = nil = o' \\[4pt]
v \sim_\beta v' & \text{in } [\![T]\!] & \Leftrightarrow & v = v' \quad \text{for primitive types } T \\[4pt]
(o,C) \sim_\beta (o',C') & \text{in } [\![\text{owntyp}]\!] & \Leftrightarrow & (o = nil = o') \vee (\beta\,o\,o' \wedge C = C') \\[4pt]
B \sim_\beta B' & \text{in } [\![\text{invtyp}\,C]\!] & \Leftrightarrow & B = B' \\[4pt]
s \sim_\beta s' & \text{in } [\![\text{state}\,C]\!] & \Leftrightarrow & \forall (f:T) \in (xfields\,C \setminus (dfields\,Abs \cup dfields'\,Abs)) \mid \\
& & & \quad s f \sim_\beta s' f \\[4pt]
s \sim_\beta s' & \text{in } [\![\Gamma]\!] & \Leftrightarrow & \forall x \in dom\,\Gamma \mid s x \sim_\beta s' x \\[4pt]
h \sim_\beta h' & \text{in } [\![\text{pre-heap}]\!] & \Leftrightarrow & \forall o \in dom\,h, o' \in dom\,h' \mid \beta\,o\,o' \Rightarrow h o \sim_\beta h' o' \\[4pt]
(h,s) \sim_\beta (h',s') & \text{in } [\![\text{heap} \otimes \Gamma]\!] & \Leftrightarrow & h \sim_\beta h' \wedge s \sim_\beta s' \\[4pt]
v \sim_\beta v' & \text{in } [\![\theta_\perp]\!] & \Leftrightarrow & v = \perp = v' \vee (v \neq \perp \neq v' \wedge v \sim_\beta v' \text{ in } [\![\theta]\!])
\end{array}
$$

Equivalence hides the private fields of Abs. Later in the identity extension Lemma 31, it is used in conjunction with the *encap* function from Def. 12, to hide the objects owned at Abs.

The most important definition is of local coupling, which is analogous to an admissible object invariant but is formulated, somewhat differently, as a relation on pairs of pre-heaps. In Def. 3, we take an invariant $\mathcal{I}^C$ to be a predicate (set of states) and the program invariant $\mathcal{I}$ is based on the conjunction of these predicates for all objects and types —subject to *inv*, see Def. 4). By contrast, we define a local coupling $\mathcal{L}$ in terms of pre-heaps. And we are concerned with a single class, Abs, rather than all C. We impose the same dependency condition as in Def. 3, but in terms of pre-heaps of the form $h = Ah * Rh * Sh$. (Recall Proposition 9.)

Definition 20 (local coupling, $\mathcal{L}$). A *local coupling* is a function, $\mathcal{L}$, that assigns to each typed bijection β a binary relation $\mathcal{L}\beta$ on pre-heaps that satisfies the following. First, $\mathcal{L}\beta$ does not depend on *inv* or *com*. Second, $\beta \subseteq \beta_0$ implies $\mathcal{L}\beta \subseteq \mathcal{L}\beta_0$. Third, for any β, h, h', if $\mathcal{L}\beta\,h h'$ then there are locations o, o' with $\beta\,o o'$ and $type\,o \leq Abs$ such that the Abs partitions of h, h' are $h = Ah * Rh * Sh$ and $h' = Ah' * Rh' * Sh'$ with

- $pick\,Ah = o$ and $pick\,Ah' = o'$
- $o \succ^h_{Abs} p$ for all $p \in dom\,Rh$ and $o' \succ^{h'}_{Abs} p'$ for all $p' \in dom\,Rh'$
- $o \succ^h_{(superAbs)\uparrow} p$ for all $p \in dom\,Sh$ and $o' \succ^{h'}_{(superAbs)\uparrow} p'$ for all $p' \in dom\,Sh'$
- If $\mathcal{L}\beta$ depends on $o.f$ then f is in $xfields\,Abs$

The first three conditions ensure that $\mathcal{L}$ relates a single island, for an object of some subtype of Abs, to a single island for an object of the same type. Although $\mathcal{L}$ is unconstrained for the private fields of $CT(Abs)$ and $CT'(Abs)$, it may also depend on fields inherited from a superclass of Abs (but not on subclass fields, nor *inv* or *com*). The induced coupling relation, defined below, imposes the additional constraint that fields of proper sub- and super-classes of Abs are linked by equivalence modulo β.

The restriction against dependence on *inv* or *com* is carried over from the *inv/own* discipline. We do not have an example to show it is necessary for representation independence. For friendship based invariants it is both useful and sound to allow dependence on *inv* (see [20]), so this point may merit further investigation.

In applications, $\mathcal{L}\,\beta\,h\,h'$ would be defined as something like this: h and h' partition as islands $Ah * Rh * Sh$ and $Ah' * Rh' * Sh'$ such that $Ah * Rh * Sh \models \mathcal{I}^{Abs}$ and $Ah' * Rh' * Sh' \models \mathcal{I}'^{Abs}$ and some condition links the data structures [5]. The bijection β would not be explicit but would be induced as a property of the formula language.

For an example, note that the property defined informally in Fig. 5 relates two instances of AQueue together with objects owned at AQueue and representation objects owned at Queue.

A local coupling $\mathcal{L}$ induces a relation on arbitrary heaps by requiring that corresponding islands are related by $\mathcal{L}$. This in turn gives rise to a relation on commands. Roughly, a pair of commands or methods are related if they send a related pair of initial states to a related pair of outcomes. Howover, we cannot expect this to hold in case of methods acting on receiver objects that are owned at *Abs*. (This exclusion is similar to a type-based exclusion of "non-Rep classes" in [8].) In order to make this precise, we define for Γ-states with self in Γ an abbreviation:

$$\mathsf{nonrep}(h,s) \Leftrightarrow \neg(\exists o \mid o \succ^h_{Abs} s\,\mathsf{self})$$

Definition 21 (coupling relation, $\mathcal{R}$). Given local coupling $\mathcal{L}$, we define for each θ and β a relation $\mathcal{R}\,\beta\,\theta \subseteq [\![\theta]\!] \times [\![\theta]\!]'$ by cases on θ.

Case θ is heap: Define $\mathcal{R}\,\beta$ heap $h\,h'$ iff

- h, h' are disciplined
- $\beta \subseteq dom\,h \times dom\,h'$
- β fully partitions h, h' for *Abs*

Moreover, suppose the *Abs*-partitions are

$$h = Fh * Ah_1 * Rh_1 * Sh_1 \ldots Ah_k * Rh_k * Sh_k \text{ and}$$
$$h' = Fh' * Ah'_1 * Rh'_1 * Sh'_1 \ldots Ah'_k * Rh'_k * Sh'_k$$

where, without loss of generality we assume $\beta\,(pick\,Ah_i)\,(pick\,Ah'_i)$ for all i (in accord with the remark following Lemma 18). Then we require:

(R1) β restricts to a total bijection between *dom Fh* and *dom Fh'* (recall Def. 17);

(R2) $Fh \sim_\beta Fh'$; and

(R3) for all i,

    (i) β restricts to a total bijection between *dom Sh_i* and *dom Sh'_i*

    (ii) $(Ah_i * Sh_i) \sim_\beta (Ah'_i * Sh'_i)$

    (iii) $h(pick\,Ah_i).inv \leq Abs \Rightarrow \mathcal{L}\,\beta\,(Ah_i * Rh_i * Sh_i)\,(Ah'_i * Rh'_i * Sh'_i)$

Case θ is any other category: $\mathscr{R} \beta \theta$ is defined as follows:

$$\mathscr{R} \beta \theta \alpha \alpha' \qquad\qquad \Leftrightarrow \alpha \sim_\beta \alpha' \text{ if } \theta \text{ is } T, \text{ invtyp} C, \text{ owntyp}, \Gamma, \text{ or state} C$$

$$\mathscr{R} \beta (\text{heap} \otimes \Gamma)(h,s)(h',s') \Leftrightarrow \mathscr{R} \beta \text{ heap } h\, h' \wedge \mathscr{R} \beta \Gamma \, s\, s'$$

$$\mathscr{R} \beta (\theta_\perp) \alpha \alpha' \qquad\quad \Leftrightarrow (\alpha = \perp = \alpha') \vee (\alpha \neq \perp \neq \alpha' \wedge \mathscr{R} \beta \theta \alpha \alpha')$$

$$\mathscr{R} \beta (\Gamma \vdash T) \, v \, v' \qquad \Leftrightarrow \forall s,s' \mid \mathscr{R} \beta \Gamma \, s\, s' \Rightarrow \mathscr{R} \beta T_\perp \, (v(s))\, (v'(s'))$$

$$\mathscr{R} \beta (\Gamma \rightsquigarrow \Gamma') \, t\, t' \quad \Leftrightarrow \forall h,s,h',s' \mid$$
$$\mathscr{R} \beta (\text{heap} \otimes \Gamma)(h,s)(h',s') \wedge \text{nonrep}(h,s) \wedge \text{nonrep}(h',s')$$
$$\Rightarrow \exists \beta_0 \supseteq \beta \mid \mathscr{R} \beta_0 (\text{heap} \otimes \Gamma)_\perp \, (t(h,s))\, (t'(h',s'))$$

$$\mathscr{R} \text{ menv } \mu\, \mu' \qquad\qquad \Leftrightarrow \forall C,m,\beta \mid \mathscr{R} \beta \, (\text{self}:C,\bar{x}:\bar{T} \rightsquigarrow \text{result}:T_1)\, (\mu C m)\, (\mu' C m)$$
$$\text{where } mtype(m,C) = \bar{T} \rightarrow T \text{ and } pars(m,C) = \bar{x}$$

Condition (R3)(iii) is the key connection with the *inv/own* discipline; compare Eqn. (1). All remaining items express that the relation is observable equivalence on everything on which a client can directly depend (see Lemma 31).

Given the other conditions in the definition of $\mathscr{R} \beta$ heap, we have that $(Ah_i * Sh_i) \sim_\beta (Ah'_j * Sh'_j)$ is equivalent to the conjunction of $Ah_i \sim_\beta Ah'_j$ and $Sh_i \sim_\beta Sh'_j$. And $Ah_i \sim_\beta Ah'_j$ means that the two objects o, o' agree on superclass and subclass fields (but not the declared fields of *Abs*); in particular, $type\, o = type\, o' \leq Abs$ and $Ah_i\, o.inv = Ah'_j\, o'.inv$.

By contrast with the definition of admissible invariant (Def. 3), there is no need to separately disallow that a coupling is falsifiable by allocation. Owing to the use of partial heaps, this property follows from the form of the definition, as becomes clear in the proof of Lemma 29.

The case that θ is $\Gamma \rightsquigarrow \Gamma'$ is for state transformers t, t' denoted by commands and method declarations. It says they preserve coupling, while possibly growing the bijection β, and excluding computations where self is owned by an instance of *Abs*.

The gist of the abstraction theorem (Theorem 30) is that if methods of *Abs* are related by $\mathscr{R}$ then all methods are. In terms of the preceding definitions, we can express quite succinctly the conclusion that all methods are related: $\mathscr{R}$ menv $[\![CT]\!]\, [\![CT']\!]'$. We want the antecedent of the theorem to be that the meaning $[\![M]\!]$ is related to $[\![M']\!]'$, for any m with declaration M in $CT(Abs)$ and M' in $CT'(Abs)$. Moreover, $[\![M]\!]$ depends on a method environment. Thus the antecedent of the theorem is that $[\![M]\!]\mu$ is related to $[\![M']\!]'\mu'$ for all related μ, μ'. (It suffices for μ, μ' to be in the approximation chains defining $[\![CT]\!]$ and $[\![CT']\!]'$.)

The rest of this subsection is devoted to technical results which may be skipped.

Lemma 22. *If* $\bar{U} \leq \bar{T}$ *and* $\mathscr{R} \beta \bar{U} \, \bar{v}\, \bar{v}'$ *then* $\mathscr{R} \beta \bar{T} \, \bar{v}\, \bar{v}'$.

Lemma 23 (closure under transitive owners). *If* $Ph \sim_\beta Ph'$ *and* $\beta\, p\, p'$, *and* $o \succ_C^{Ph} p$ *then there is* o' *such that* $\beta\, o\, o'$ *and* $o' \succ_C^{Ph'} p'$.

Proof. By induction on $o \succ_C^{Ph} p$. In the base case we have $(o,C) = Ph\, p.own$. Then by $Ph \sim_\beta Ph'$ and $\beta\, p\, p'$ we have some o' with $(o',C) = Ph'\, p'.own$ and $\beta\, o\, o'$, whence $o' \succ_C^{Ph'} p'$. In the inductive case, there is q,B with $(o,C) = Ph\, q.own$ and $q \succ_B^{Ph} p$. By induction hypothesis there is q' with $\beta\, q\, q'$ and $q' \succ_B^{Ph'} p'$. By $Ph \sim_\beta Ph'$ and $(o,C) = Ph\, q.own$ there is o' such that $\beta\, o\, o'$ and $(o',C) = Ph'\, q'.own$, whence $o' \succ_C^{Ph'} p'$.

Note that there may be locations not in $dom\,Ph$ or $dom\,Ph'$ that are related by β and thus enter into whether $Ph \sim_\beta Ph'$ holds. But $o \succ^{Ph}_C p$ implies that o and p are in $dom\,Ph$ by definition of $\succ$.

Corollary 24 (splitting). Let Ph, Ph' be pre-heaps that are closed under transitive ownership, i.e., if $o \in dom\,Ph$ and $o \succ^{Ph}_{(type\,o)\uparrow} p$ then $p \in dom\,Ph$. Let β be a total bijection from Ph to Ph' and suppose $Ph \sim_\beta Ph'$. Let $o \in dom\,Ph$ and $\beta\,o\,o'$. Let Ph partition as $Ph^+ * Ph^-$ where Ph^+ contains o and the objects transitively owned by o, i.e.,

$$dom\,Ph^+ = \{p \mid p = o \vee o \succ^{Ph}_{(type\,o)\uparrow} p\}$$

Let $Ph' = Ph'^+ * Ph'^-$ where Ph'^+ and Ph'^- are determined *mutatis mutandis* for Ph' with respect to o'. Then

(a) β is a total bijection from Ph^+ to Ph'^+ and a total bijection from Ph^- to Ph'^-
(b) $Ph^+ \sim_\beta Ph'^+$ and $Ph^- \sim_\beta Ph'^-$.

Proof. By Lemma 5(a) we can restrict to $(type\,o)\uparrow$. As a consequence of Lemma 23 we get that β is a total bijection from Ph^+ to Ph'^+. The rest follows from the definitions.

Lemma 25. If $o \succ^h_C p$ and $h\,p.own = (r,B)$ then either $(r,B) = (o,C)$ or $o \succ^h_C r$.

Proof. We first prove (by induction on $o \succ^h_C p$) that if $o \succ^h_C p$ then there is a series of one or more pairs (q_i, D_i) with (omitting h for clarity) $(o,C) = q_0.own$, $(q_0,D_0) = q_1.own$, $(q_1,D_1) = q_2.own$, $\ldots (q_n, D_n) = p.own$ and thus $q_i \succ_{D_i} q_{i+1}$ for each i; also $D_0 = C$ and $(r,B) = (q_n, D_n)$. Now an induction on i shows that $o \succ^h_C q_i$ for each i.

A consequence of this result is that if $\mathscr{R}\,\beta$ (heap $\otimes \Gamma$) (h,s) (h',s') then nonrep(h,s) iff nonrep(h',s'). Hence the antecedent in the definition of $\mathscr{R}$ for $\Gamma \leadsto \Gamma'$ can be simplified.

Lemma 26 (partition and coupling). Suppose $\mathscr{R}\,\beta$ heap $h\,h'$ and $\beta\,o\,o'$. Let $h = Fh *$ $\ldots Ah_k * Rh_k * Sh_k$ and $h' = Fh' * \ldots Ah'_k * Rh'_k * Sh'_k$ be the Abs-partitions, where w.l.o.g. we assume $pick\,Ah_i \sim_\beta pick\,Ah'_i$ for all i. Then $o \in dom\,Rh_i$ iff $o' \in dom\,Rh'_i$.

Proof. Let $o \in dom\,Rh_i$, to prove $o' \in dom\,Rh'_i$ (the reverse being symmetric). Using $\mathscr{R}\,\beta$ heap $h\,h'$ and Def. 21, o' is not in any $dom\,Ah'_j$ or $dom\,Sh'_j$, nor is it in $dom\,Fh'$, as these parts of h' are connected to h bijectively. Thus by partitioning o' must be in some Rh'_j, and by Lemma 23 it must be the j such that o' is transitively owned by $pick\,Ah'_j$.

A fine point about assertions. Def. 16 of comparable class tables says $CT(C) = CT'(C)$ for all $C \neq Abs$. But recall that we have used a "shallow embedding" formulation of assertions: we embed sets of states in code. Moreover, these are well-formed states — so, if $CT(Abs)$ declares different fields from those of $CT'(Abs)$, a state for CT is not a state for CT'. So it cannot be that $CT(T) = CT'(C)$ is literally true.

The intention is that CT and CT' have "the same" assertions, which in practice would be formulas. Consider any formula F that is well formed in both CT and CT', i.e., does not refer to private fields of *Abs*. Let $\mathscr{P}$ be the interpretation of F in CT and $\mathscr{P}'$ its interpretation in CT'. We claim the following,[9] for all h, s, h', s':

$$\text{If } \mathscr{R}\, \beta \text{ (heap} \otimes \Gamma)\, (h, s)\, (h', s') \text{ then } h, s \models \mathscr{P} \text{ iff } h', s' \models \mathscr{P}'. \tag{3}$$

For ordinary assertions that may appear in code outside *Abs*, we expect that they respect scope, and so do not depend on private fields of *Abs*. For such assertions, and for the conditions in the stipulated preconditions —aside from pack— it is easy to prove the claim from usual semantics of the formulas (entirely independent from *fields Abs*). For pack, the precondition refers to $\mathscr{I}^C$ and our formulation of admissibility for invariants does not disallow dependence on private fields of *Abs*. However, the formula denoting such an invariant would not be well formed in both class tables.

In this chapter, we refrain from spelling out syntax and semantics of formulas. We simply assume that (3) holds for all corresponding assertions in classes other than *Abs*.

5.3   Simulation and the Abstraction Theorem

Definition 27   (simulation). A simulation is a coupling $\mathscr{R}$ such that the following hold.

- ($\mathscr{L}$ is initialized) For any $C \leq Abs$, and any o, o' with $\beta\, o\, o'$ and *type* $o = C$ we have
  $\mathscr{L}\, \beta\, h\, h'$ where $h = [o \mapsto [dom(xfields\, C) \mapsto defaults\, C]]$ and
  $h' = [o' \mapsto [dom(xfields'\, C) \mapsto defaults'\, C]]$.
- (methods of *Abs* preserve $\mathscr{R}$) For any disciplined μ, μ' such that $\mathscr{R}$ menv $\mu\, \mu'$ we
  have the following for every m declared in *Abs*. Let $\bar{U} \to U = mtype(m, Abs)$ and
  $\bar{x} = pars(m, Abs)$. For every β, we have

$$\mathscr{R}\, \beta\, (\text{self} : Abs, \bar{x} : \bar{U} \rightsquigarrow \text{result} : U)\, (\llbracket M \rrbracket \mu)\, (\llbracket M' \rrbracket' \mu')$$

where M (resp. M') is the declaration of m in $CT(Abs)$ (resp. $CT'(Abs)$).

Perhaps surprisingly, there is no requirement for inherited methods. Rather, for practical application of the results —and indeed for the *inv*/*own* discipline itself— it is often necessary for inheritance to be "expanded" into stubs that perform suitable unpack/pack and super calls. The stubs are then subject to the proof obligation for declared methods. We return to this topic in Sect. 6.

The main theorem is that if $\mathscr{R}$ is a simulation for comparable class tables CT, CT' then $\mathscr{R}$ menv $\llbracket CT \rrbracket\, \llbracket CT' \rrbracket'$. The theorem is proved using the following Lemmas.

Because expressions do not include field access, an expression is typable in CT just if it is typable in CT', and preservation for expressions is straightforward.

Lemma 28   (preservation by expressions). For all expressions $\Gamma \vdash e : T$ and all β, we have $\mathscr{R}\, \beta\, (\Gamma \vdash T)\, (\llbracket \Gamma \vdash e : T \rrbracket)\, (\llbracket \Gamma \vdash' e : T \rrbracket')$.

Proof. By induction on the structure of e, and by cases on e. In each case we assume $\mathscr{R}\, \beta\, \Gamma\, s\, s'$ (which amounts to $s \sim_\beta s'$) and must show

$$\mathscr{R}\, \beta\, T_\perp\, (\llbracket \Gamma \vdash e : T \rrbracket(s))\, (\llbracket \Gamma \vdash' e : T \rrbracket'(s'))$$

---

[9] Note that this does not mean there is a bijection between $\mathscr{P}$ and $\mathscr{P}'$. One or the other versions of *Abs* may have more states, owing to the type or number of fields of *Abs*.

For example, in case e is a variable x, from $\mathscr{R} \beta \Gamma s s'$ we get $\mathscr{R} \beta T (s x) (s' x)$ by definition. In case e is $(B) e$, then by induction we have $v \sim_\beta v'$ where $v = \llbracket \Gamma \vdash e \rrbracket(s)$ and *mutatis mutandis* for v'. So either $v = \bot = v'$ and by semantics both cast expressions return $\bot$, or $\beta v v'$ and thus $type\, v = type\, v'$ (because β is a typed bijection) so the casts denote the same truth value. The other cases are similar.

For commands, the preservation lemma needs to rule out code in class *Abs*, since a field access or update in $CT(Abs)$ might not even be well formed in CT'.

Lemma 29 (preservation by commands). Let μ, μ' be disciplined method environments with $\mathscr{R}$ menv μ μ'. If $\Gamma \vdash S$ is a properly annotated command for *Abs*, with Γ self $\neq Abs$, then for all β we have $\mathscr{R} \beta (\Gamma \rightsquigarrow \Gamma) (\llbracket \Gamma \vdash S \rrbracket \mu) (\llbracket \Gamma \vdash' S \rrbracket' \mu')$.

Proof. In accord with the definition of $\mathscr{R}$ for category $\Gamma \rightsquigarrow \Gamma$, we consider arbitrary β and any (h, s), (h', s') such that $\mathscr{R} \beta$ (heap $\otimes \Gamma$) (h, s) (h', s') and $\mathsf{nonrep}(h, s)$ and $\mathsf{nonrep}(h', s')$. We show, by structural induction on S, that the outcomes $\llbracket \Gamma \vdash S \rrbracket \mu (h, s)$ and $\llbracket \Gamma \vdash' S \rrbracket' \mu' (h', s')$ are related at some β_0 with $\beta_0 \supseteq \beta$. For brevity we only consider a few cases on S such as field access and update. In each case we refer to the standard partitions $h = Fh * \ldots$ and $h' = Fh' * \ldots$ where w.l.o.g. $\beta(pickAh_i)(pickAh_i')$ for each i (noting that by Def. 21 for heaps, we have that β fully partitions h, h' for *Abs*).

We never show that the result heaps are disciplined, because that follows in every case by Prop. 8.

> **Case of assignment** $x := e$ Let $v = \llbracket \Gamma \vdash e : T \rrbracket(h, s)$ and *mutatis mutandis* for v'. The outcomes are (h, s_0) and (h', s_0') where $s_0 = [s \mid x \mapsto v]$ $s_0' = [s' \mid x \mapsto v']$. We take $\beta_0 = \beta$. To show $\mathscr{R} \beta_0$ (heap $\otimes \Gamma$) (h, s_0) (h', s_0') it suffices to show $v \sim_\beta v'$ which we have by Lemma 28.

> **Case of assert** For this we rely on assumption (3), from which we get the result directly by semantics of assert.

> **Case of field access** $x := y.f$ (Recall that by typing, f is an ordinary field, not *inv*, *com*, or *own*.) In this case the output heap is the same as the input heap h. We choose $\beta_0 = \beta$ and note that $\mathscr{R} \beta$ heap h h' holds by hypothesis. Let $p = s y$ and let the updated store s_0 be $[s \mid x \mapsto h p.f]$ (and similarly for p', s_0' for s' as per our convention). To prove $\mathscr{R} \beta$ (heap $\otimes \Gamma$) (h, s_0) (h', s_0') it suffices to show $h p.f \sim_\beta h' p'.f$. By hypothesis $\mathscr{R} \beta$ (heap $\otimes \Gamma$) (h, s) (h', s') we have $p \sim_\beta p'$ i.e., either $\beta p p'$ or $p = nil = p'$. By stipulated precondition (A3) in Def. 15 neither is null, so $\beta p p'$.

Because Γ self $\neq Abs$, by the stipulated precondition for field access we get

$$\forall o \mid o \succ_{Abs}^h p \Rightarrow o \succ_{Abs}^h s\, \mathsf{self} \quad \text{and} \quad \forall o \mid o \succ_{Abs}^{h'} p' \Rightarrow o \succ_{Abs}^{h'} s'\, \mathsf{self}$$

Because $\mathscr{R} \beta$ heap h h', it suffices to consider the following cases.

- $p \in dom\, Fh$. Then $Fh \sim_\beta Fh'$ from $\mathscr{R} \beta$ (heap $\otimes \Gamma$) (h, s) (h', s'), so by definition $h p.f \sim_\beta h' p'.f$, using that f is not in *dfields Abs* or *dfields' Abs* because $type\, p \not\preceq Abs$ by definition of decomposition. (Note that $Fhp = hp$ by decomposition, so we choose to write the shorter one, hp.)
- $p = pickAh_i$ for some i. Hence $p' = pickAh_i'$. By $\mathscr{R} \beta$ heap h h' we have $Ah_i \sim_\beta Ah_i'$. By hypothesis of the Lemma, Γ self $\neq Abs$, so by proper annotation Def. 15(A1),

f is not in *dfields Abs* or *dfields' Abs*. So $Ah_i \sim_\beta Ah'_j$ implies $h p.f \sim_\beta h' p.f$ as required.

- $p \in dom Rh_i$ for some i. We show by contradiction that this case cannot happen. Suppose $p \in dom Rh_i$. Then $pickAh_i \succ^h_{Abs} p$ by definition of *Abs*-partition. By precondition we get $pickAh_i \succ^h_{Abs} s$ self, which contradicts the antecedent *nonrep(h,s)*.
- $p \in dom Sh_i$ for some i. Then by Def. 21 for heaps, item (R3), we have $\beta p p'$ and $Sh_i \sim_\beta Sh'_j$. By definition of decomposition, we have *type* $p \not\leq Abs$ so *declClass* $f \neq Abs$ and *declClass'* $f \neq Abs$, so $Sh_i \sim_\beta Sh'_j$ implies $h p.f \sim_\beta h' p.f$.

Case of field update $x.f := y$ Let $o = s\, x$ and $v = s\, y$. By typing we have $\Gamma x \leq declClass f$. The stipulated preconditions are $o \neq nil$ and $h o.inv > declClass f$. So the outcome from (h,s) is (h_0,s) where h_0 is $[h \mid o.f \mapsto v]$. *Mutatis mutandis* for o', v', h'_0. By hypothesis $\mathscr{R} \beta$ (*heap* $\otimes \Gamma$) (h,s) (h',s'), we have $v \sim_\beta v'$ and $o \sim_\beta o'$; and thus $\beta o o'$. We take β_0 to be β. To show $\mathscr{R} \beta$ *heap* $h_0 h'_0$ we have the following cases.

- $o \in dom Fh$. Then $\beta o o'$ and $Fh \sim_\beta Fh'$ from $\mathscr{R} \beta$ (*heap* $\otimes \Gamma$) (h,s) (h',s') (items (R1) and (R2) in Def. 21). It suffices to show $h_0 o.f \sim_\beta h'_0 o'.f$ which follows from $v \sim_\beta v'$.
- $o = pickAh_i$ for some i. So we have $\beta o o'$ and *type* $o \leq Abs$. We have $Ah_i \sim_\beta Ah'_i$ by (R3)(ii) in Def. 21. By hypothesis of the Lemma, Γ self $\neq Abs$, so by proper annotation Def. 15(A1), f is not in *dfields Abs* or *dfields' Abs*. Thus for (R3)(ii) to hold for the updated heaps h_0, h'_0 we need the new values to be related; indeed, we already established $v \sim_\beta v'$.

  For (R3)(iii) we rely on the discipline. We have *type* $o \leq Abs$ by decomposition. By type soundness for x, *type* $o \leq \Gamma x \leq declClass f$. By the tree property of the subtype relation, one of these two cases must apply:
  - $Abs \leq declClass f$. Then $h o.inv > Abs$ from the stipulated precondition; this falsifies the antecedent in (R3)(iii) so we are done.
  - $declClass f < Abs$: Then $\mathscr{L}$ is not allowed to depend on $o.f$ (Def. 20); this means precisely that an update of $o.f$ cannot falsify $\mathscr{L}$, so (R3)(iii) is preserved.
- $o \in dom(Rh_i * Sh_i)$ for some i. By precondition, $h o.inv > declClass f$. By type soundness for x, *type* $o \leq \Gamma x \leq declClass f$; hence $h o.inv > type\, o$.
  If $o \in dom Rh_i$, then $pickAh_i \succ^h_{Abs} o$, so by Corollary 6, $h(pickAh_i).inv > Abs$. If $o \in dom Sh_i$, $pickAh_i \succ^h_C o$ for $C > Abs$, so $h(pickAh_i).inv > C > Abs$, by Corollary 6 again. In either case, condition (R3)(iii) in Def. 21 holds in the updated heaps because its antecedent is false.
  Finally, if $o \in dom Sh_i$ we must also show condition (R3)(ii) for the updated heaps. Because $Sh_i \sim_\beta Sh'_i$ holds initially, this follows from $\beta o o'$ and $v \sim_\beta v'$ already established.

Case of allocation $x := \mathbf{new}\ B$ Let $o = fresh(B,h)$, so we have $s_0 = [s \mid x \mapsto o]$ and $h_0 = [h \mid o \mapsto [xfields B \mapsto defaults B]]$ (and *mutatis mutandis* for o', h'_0, s'_0). We choose $\beta_0 = \beta \cup \{(o,o')\}$. To show $\mathscr{R} \beta_0$ (*heap* $\otimes \Gamma$) (h_0,s_0) (h'_0,s'_0), first note that by the defaults we have $h_0 o.inv = \text{Object}$, $h_0 o.com = false$, and $h_0 o.own = (nil, \text{Object})$. By the latter default, β_0 fully partitions h_0, h'_0 for *Abs*. To complete the argument, we consider the following two cases on B.

– $B \leq Abs$. Let $Ah_{new} = [o \mapsto [xfields B \mapsto defaults B]]$, so $h_0 = Ah_{new} * h$ and the partition of h_0 has the form $h_0 = Fh * \ldots * Ah_{new} * Rh_{new} * Sh_{new}$ where the old partition is unchanged but has an added island with $Rh_{new} = Sh_{new} = \varnothing$. Similarly for o' and h'_0.

Because o and o' are fresh, they are unreachable from objects in h and h' respectively, so $Fh \sim_{\beta_0} Fh'$ follows from $Fh \sim_\beta Fh'$, and similarly for other parts of h and h'. Thus to show $\mathscr{R} \, \beta_0$ heap $h_0 \, h'_0$, we just use conditions (R1), (R2), (R3)(i), and (R3)(ii) in Def. 21 from the corresponding assumptions for β.

For condition (R3)(iii), consider any preexisting pair of corresponding islands $Ah_i *$ $Rh_i * Sh_i$ and $Ah'_i * Rh'_i * Sh'_i$. The condition (R3)(iii) pertains only to objects in these islands, and is not falsifiable by the addition of another island. For the new island, we have $Ah_{new} \sim_{\beta_0} Ah'_{new}$ in virtue of the default field values (which have no preexisting references). Moreover, we have

$$Ah_{new}(o).inv \leq Abs \Rightarrow \mathscr{L} \, \beta_0(Ah_{new} * Rh_{new} * Sh_{new})(Ah'_{new} * Rh'_{new} * Sh'_{new})$$

because the antecedent is false. The reason being that $Ah_{new}(o).inv = $ Object $= Ah'_{new}(o).inv$ and by typing $B \neq$ Object.

– $B \not\leq Abs$. Because the default owner is (nil, Object), the partition is $h_0 = Fh_0 *$ $\ldots$ where the islands are unchanged and $Fh_0 = Fh * [o \mapsto [xfields B \mapsto defaults B]]$. Because o and o' are fresh, $Fh \sim_{\beta_0} Fh'$ follows from $Fh \sim_\beta Fh'$. Moreover, we have $Fh_0 \sim_{\beta_0} Fh'_0$ because the default field values in the new objects do not refer to preexisting objects. Thus we have (R1) and (R2) in Def. 21. Condition (R3) holds for h_0, h'_0 because (R3)(iii) pertains to the unchanged part of the heap and conditions (R3)(i–ii) are preserved because o, o' are fresh.

Case of pack e as C   Owing to (A2) in Def. 15, we have $C \neq Abs$. By semantics of **pack e as C**, what is changed is the value of $e.inv$ and the *com* fields of objects owned by e at C. Let $p = [\![e]\!](s)$ and $p' = [\![e]\!](s')$ Neither p nor p' is in an Rh part of the heap, for the same reasons as in the case of field access. The objects owned by p (resp. p') at C are not owned at Abs so from $\mathscr{R} \, \beta$ (heap $\otimes \Gamma$) (h, s) (h', s') we get that the two states agree (modulo β on what is owned by p (resp. p') at C). So everything involved is related by $\sim_\beta$ and that remains true after the updates of *inv* and *com*.

Case of setown x to (e_2, C)   Let $q = sx$ and note that $q \neq nil$ by stipulated precondition. Let $p = [\![e_2 : D_2]\!](h, s)$ and for future reference let $(r, B) = hq.own$. By typing we have $type \, p \leq D_2 \leq C$. The resulting heap h_0 is $[h \mid q.own \mapsto (p, C)]$. We take β_0 to be β. As usual, q', p', r', B', h'_0 are determined *mutatis mutandis* from (h', s'). The ownership structure is changed (unless $(r, B) = (p, C)$), but what is relevant to $\mathscr{R}$ is changes in Abs-partition. To reason carefully about these cases, we give notation for the Abs-partitions of the updated heaps: $h_0 = \hat{F}h * \ldots * \hat{Ah}_n * \hat{Rh}_n * \hat{Sh}_n$ and $h'_0 = \hat{F}h' * \ldots * \hat{Ah}'_n * \hat{Rh}'_n * \hat{Sh}'_n$. Although case analysis is needed, we begin with general considerations.

By the stipulated precondition for **setown** we obtain

(a) $q \sim_\beta q'$ and $p \sim_\beta p'$ (by hypothesis and by Lemma 28 on e_2, respectively);
(b) $h \, q.inv = $ Object $= h' \, q'.inv$ (by stipulated precondition)
(c) $p = nil = p'$ or else $h \, p.inv > C$ and $h' \, p'.inv > C$ (by stipulated precondition)

(d) both h and h' satisfy $(\exists o \mid o \succ_{Abs} q) \Rightarrow C = Abs \vee (\exists o \mid o \succ_{Abs} p)$ (owing to hypothesis Γ self $\neq Abs$ and stipulated precondition (A4) in Def. 15)

(e) $r = nil = r'$ or else $h\, r.inv > B$ and $h'\, r'.inv > B'$ (from (b), Corollary 6, and hypothesis $\mathscr{R}\,\beta$ heap $h\,h'$)

We complete the proof by cases on whether q is in the domain of Fh or one of Ah_i, Rh_i, or Sh_i for some i.

Case $q \in dom\,Fh$. By $\mathscr{R}\,\beta$ heap $h\,h'$ and $q \sim_\beta q'$ we have $q' \in dom\,Fh'$. Moreover, either $r = nil = r'$ or $r \in dom\,Fh$ and also $r' \in dom\,Fh'$ by partitioning. There are the following subcases on p:

- If $p \in dom\,Fh$ or $p = nil = p'$ then the structure of the partition of h_0, h'_0 is unchanged from the initial one. We get $\mathscr{R}\,\beta$ heap $h_0\,h'_0$ because the only change is to set field *own* of q, q' to related values p, p', whence $\hat{F}h \sim_\beta \hat{F}h'$.
- If $p = pick\,Ah_i$ then by $\mathscr{R}\,\beta$ heap $h\,h'$ we have $p' = pick\,Ah'_i$. By type soundness, *type* $p \leq D_2$ and $D_2 \leq C$, and by definition of partition *type* $p \leq Abs$, so by the tree property of $\leq$ either $C < Abs$ or $Abs \leq C$.
  - If $C < Abs$ then, in the partition of h_0 we have $q \in dom\,\hat{F}h$, i.e., the partition has the same structure as initially and the same is true for $q', \hat{F}h'$. Then we get $\mathscr{R}\,\beta$ heap $h_0\,h'_0$ because the only change is to set field *own* of q, q' to related values p, p'.
  - If $Abs = C$ then q and the objects it transitively owns are being transferred into island i, i.e., the partition of h_0 has q in $dom\,\hat{R}h_i$. Similarly for q' and $\hat{R}h'_i$. By (c) we have $h\, p.inv > Abs$ and $h'\, p'.inv > Abs$, so the only condition in Def. 21 to check is (R3)(iii), which holds because the antecedent is false —"$\mathscr{L}$ is not in force".
  - If $Abs < C$ then q and the objects it transitively owns are transferred from Fh into $\hat{S}h_i$ and q' into $\hat{S}h'_i$. Again, by (c) we have $h\, p.inv > Abs$ and $h'\, p'.inv > Abs$. To show coupling for the updated islands i, j it remains to show conditions (R3)(i) and (R3)(ii) $\hat{S}h_i \sim_\beta \hat{S}h'_j$. This follows from $\mathscr{R}\,\beta$ heap $h\,h'$ and $q \sim_\beta q'$ and $p \sim_\beta p'$.
- If $p \in dom(Rh_i * Sh_i)$ for some i then p' must be in $dom(Rh'_i * Sh'_i)$ owing to Lemma 26 and $Sh_i \sim_\beta Sh'_j$. So q (resp. q') is transferred into island i (resp. j). Let $o = pick\,Ah_i$ (resp. $o' = pick\,Ah'_j$) so that there is $B \geq Abs$ (resp. $B' \geq Abs$) such that $o \succ_B^h p$ (resp. $o' \succ_{B'}^{h'} p'$). By (c) and Corollary 6 we get $h\, o.inv > B$ (resp. $h'\, o'.inv > B'$) and thus $\mathscr{L}$ is not currently in force for these islands. It remains to show that if q, q' are being transferred into Sh_i, Sh'_j (because $p \in dom\,Sh_i$ and thus $p' \in dom\,Sh_j$) then $Sh_i \sim_\beta Sh'_j$ and this follows from $\mathscr{R}\,\beta$ heap $h\,h'$ and $p \sim_\beta p'$.

Case $q = pick\,Ah_i$ for some i. So $q' = pick\,Ah'_i$. Owing to the invariant that no *Abs*-object owns an *Abs*-object, we have $r \in dom\,Fh$ and for the same reason p is also in $dom\,Fh$ *Mutatis mutandis* for r, Fh'. So again the partition structure is unchanged. We get $\mathscr{R}\,\beta$ heap $h_0\,h'_0$ because the only change is to set field *own* of q, q' to related values p, p'.

Case $q \in dom\,Rh_i$ for some i. Then $pick\,Ah_i \succ_{Abs}^h q$ by definition of *Abs*-partition. Now either $r = pick\,Ah_i$ and $B = Abs$ or $pick\,Ah_i \succ_{Abs}^h r$, by Lemma 25. By Lemma 26 we have $q' \in dom\,Rh'_i$. By (d), either $C = Abs$ or there is o such that $o \succ^h_{Abs} p$. In the case $C = Abs$, we have $type\,p \leq Abs$ (by the typing rule for **setown**) and thus $p = pick\,Ah_k$ for some k, whence $p' = pick\,Ah'_k$. In the other case, because $type\,o \leq Abs$ (by Lemma 5(a)) there is some k with $o = pick\,Ah_k$ Similarly, there is some Abs-object o' that owns p' and some l with $o' = pick\,Ah_l$. By $\beta\,p\,p'$ and Lemma 23 we have $\beta\,o\,o'$ and so $l = k$. In the rest of the argument, the two cases are treated together.

Informally, the sub-heap consisting of q and the objects it transitively owns are being transferred from island i to island k, and in particular from Rh_i into $\hat{Rh}_k$; in parallel, q' and its transitively owned objects are transferred from Rh'_i to $\hat{Rh}'_k$. So couplings for i and k are at risk. By (b) and Corollary 6 we have $h(pick\,Ah_i).inv > Abs$ and thus basic coupling $\mathscr{L}$ is not in force for i in h, nor is it in force for i in h'. By (c) and Corollary 6 we have $h\,o.inv > Abs$ (or $h\,p.inv > Abs$ in the case $C = Abs$) and thus $\mathscr{L}$ is not in force for k in either h or h'. Because the transfer of q is into $\hat{Rh}_k$ and q' into $\hat{Rh}_k$, Thus the condition (R3)(iii) holds in the final heap. The conditions (R3)(i–ii) are not affected.

Case $q \in dom\,Sh_i$ for some i. In regards to $\mathscr{L}$, this case is similar to the case for $q \in dom\,Rh_i$. By coupling of the initial states we have $q' \in dom\,Sh'_i$. The relevant islands are unpacked, by (e), so $\mathscr{L}$ is not in force and (R3)(iii) is preserved. We have to deal with the equivalence and bijection requirements (R3)(i–ii). From $\mathscr{R}\,\beta$ heap $h\,h'$ we have that β is a total bijection from Sh_i to Sh'_i and $Sh_i \sim_\beta Sh'_i$. By definition of Abs-partition, both Sh_i and Sh'_i are closed under transitive ownership. Let Sh^+_i be the sub-heap of Sh with domain consisting of q and objects transitively owned by q; *mutatis mutandis* for q' and Sh'^+_i. Let Sh^-_i and Sh'^-_i be the remainders so that $Sh_i = Sh^+_i * Sh^-_i$ and $Sh'_i = Sh'^+_i * Sh'^-_i$. Then by Corollary 24 we have that β is a total bijection from $dom\,Sh^+_i$ to $dom\,Sh'^+_i$ and from $dom\,Sh^-_i$ to $dom\,Sh'^-_i$; moreover $Sh^+_i \sim_\beta Sh'^+_i$ and $Sh^-_i \sim_\beta Sh'^-_i$. In the final heaps h_0, h'_0, $\hat{Sh}_i = Sh^-_i$ and $\hat{Sh}_i = Sh^-_i$. By the above considerations, these satisfy the bijection and equivalence conditions.

What remains is to account for Sh^+_i and Sh'^+_i which get transferred into islands k. We go by cases on p.

- If $p \in dom\,Fh$ then the partition for h_0 has $\hat{Fh} = Fh * Sh^+_i$ and similarly for h'_0. The coupling conditions hold because $Sh^+_i \sim_\beta Sh'^+_i$.
- If p is in some $dom\,Ah_k$ (resp. $dom\,Sh_k$) we have p' is the $dom\,Ah'_k$ (resp. $p' \in dom\,Sh_k$). An argument like in the case for $q \in dom\,Rh_i$ shows that $\mathscr{L}$ is not in force so (R3)(iii) is preserved. And if q is going into Sh_k (resp. q' into Sh_k) then the coupling conditions for $\hat{Sh}_k = Sh_k * Sh^+_i$ and $\hat{Sh}'_k = Sh'_k * Sh'^+_i$ hold by the earlier considerations, e.g., $Sh^+_i \sim_\beta Sh'^+_i$.
- If p is in some $dom\,Rh_k$ then the argument is similiar to the preceding case but simpler as there is no bijection or equivalence condition with which to be concerned.

Our main result says that if methods of Abs preserve the coupling then all methods do.

Theorem 30 (abstraction).
If $\mathscr{R}$ is a simulation for comparable class tables CT, CT' that are properly annotated for Abs, then $\mathscr{R}$ menv $[\![CT]\!]\,[\![CT']\!]'$.

Proof. Assume that $\mathscr{R}$ is a simulation. We show that $\mathscr{R}$ holds for each step in the approximation chain in the semantics of class tables. That is, we show by induction on i that

$$\mathscr{R} \text{ menv } \mu_i \, \mu_i' \quad \text{for every } i \in \mathbb{N}$$

The result $\mathscr{R}$ menv $[\![CT]\!]\,[\![CT']\!]'$ then follows, because $[\![CT]\!]$ and $[\![CT']\!]'$ are the least upper bounds of these ascending chains and the relation distributes over lubs of chains.

Base case, $i = 0$: We must show

$$\mathscr{R} \, \beta \, (\text{self}:C, \bar{x}:\bar{T} \rightsquigarrow T) \, (\mu_0 \, C m) \, (\mu_0' \, C m)$$

for every β, m, C, where $pars(m, C) = \bar{x}$ and $mtype(m, C) = \bar{T} \to T$. This holds by definition of μ_0, μ_0', because $\lambda(h, s) \mid \perp$ relates to itself.

Induction step: Suppose $\mathscr{R}$ menv $\mu_i \, \mu_i'$. We must show $\mathscr{R}$ menv $\mu_{i+1} \, \mu_{i+1}'$, that is, for every β, every C, and every m with $mtype(m, C)$ defined:

$$\mathscr{R} \, \beta \, (\text{self}:C, \bar{x}:\bar{T} \rightsquigarrow T) \, (\mu_{i+1} \, C m) \, (\mu_{i+1}' \, C m) \tag{†}$$

where $pars(m, C) = \bar{x}$ and $mtype(m, C) = \bar{T} \to T$.

For arbitrary m we show (†) for all C with $mtype(m, C)$ defined, using a secondary induction on inheritance chains.

The base case of the secondary induction is when class C declares m (i.e., m is declared in both $CT(C)$ and $CT'(C)$ by Def. 16). We go by cases on C.

- Case $C = Abs$. We get (†) from the assumption that $\mathscr{R}$ is a simulation. In detail: Using assumption $\mathscr{R}$ menv $\mu_i \, \mu_i'$ and Def. 27 we get

$$\mathscr{R} \, \beta \, (\text{self}:C, \bar{x}:\bar{T} \rightsquigarrow T) \, ([\![M]\!]\mu_i) \, ([\![M']\!]'\mu_i')$$

  whence (†) by definition of μ_{i+1} and μ_{i+1}'.
- Case $C \neq Abs$. Then by Def. 16 of comparable class tables we have $CT(C) = CT'(C)$ and in particular both class tables have the same declaration $T\,m(\bar{T}\,\bar{x})\,\{S\}$, which we call M for short. To show (†), observe first that by semantics we have $\mu_{i+1}\,C m = [\![M]\!]\mu_i$ and $\mu_{i+1}'\,C m = [\![M]\!]'\mu_i'$. Unfolding the definition of $[\![M]\!]\mu_i$ and $[\![M]\!]'\mu_i'$ according to (2) in Sect.3, and the definition of $\mathscr{R}\,\beta\,(\text{self}:C, \bar{x}:\bar{T} \rightsquigarrow T)$, it suffices to proceed as follows. Consider any (h, s) and (h', s') such that $\mathscr{R}\,\beta\,(\text{heap} \otimes \Gamma)\,(h, s)\,(h', s')$ where $\Gamma = (\text{self}:C, \bar{x}:\bar{T})$. Because the class tables are properly annotated and μ_i, μ_i' are in the approximation chains, we have by Prop. 8 that μ_i and μ_i' are disciplined. So we can appeal to Lemma 29, using assumption $\mathscr{R}$ menv $\mu_i \, \mu_i'$, to get that the results from S are related. That is, either $[\![\Gamma \vdash S]\!]\mu_i(h, s) = \perp = [\![\Gamma \vdash' S]\!]'\mu_i'(h', s')$ or neither is $\perp$. In the latter case, (h_0, s_0) is related to (h_0', s_0') for some $\beta_0 \supseteq \beta$, where $(h_0, s_0) = [\![\Gamma \vdash S]\!]\mu_i(h, s)$ and $(h_0', s_0') = [\![\Gamma \vdash' S]\!]'\mu_i'(h', s')$. Then, by definition of $\mathscr{R}\,\beta\,\Gamma$, we get $\mathscr{R}\,\beta_0\,(\text{result}:T)\,[\text{result} \mapsto s_0\,\text{result}]\,[\text{result} \mapsto s_0'\,\text{result}]$ from $\mathscr{R}\,\beta_0\,\Gamma\,s_0\,s_0'$. This concludes the argument that the outcomes are related by $\mathscr{R}\,\beta_0\,(\text{heap} \otimes T)$.

This concludes the base case of the secondary induction.

The induction step is for m inherited in $CT(C)$ and $CT'(C)$. By the secondary induction hypothesis we have (†) for $superC$. By semantics, $\mu_{i+1}\,C m = \mu_{i+1}\,(superC)\,m$ and $\mu_{i+1}'\,C m = \mu_{i+1}'\,(superC)\,m$ so we get (†) for C directly from the secondary induction hypothesis.

6   Using the Theorem

A complete program is a command S in the context of a class table. To show equivalence between CT, S and CT', S, one proves simulation for Abs and then appeals to the abstraction theorem to conclude that $[\![S]\!]$ is related to $[\![S]\!]'$. Finally, one appeals to an *identity extension lemma* that says the relation is the identity for programs where the encapsulated representation is not visible. We choose simple formulations that can also serve to justify more specification-oriented formulations. We say that a state (h, s) is *Abs-free* if $type\, o \nleq Abs$ for all $o \in dom\, h$.

Lemma 31 (identity extension). If $\mathscr{R}\, \beta$ (heap $\otimes \Gamma$) (h, s) (h', s')
then $encap Abs\,(h, s) \sim_{\beta} encap Abs\,(h', s')$.

Lemma 32 (inverse identity extension). Suppose (h, s) and (h', s') are *Abs*-free. If $(h, s) \sim_{\beta} (h', s')$ and β is total on h, h' then $\mathscr{R}\, \beta$ (heap $\otimes \Gamma$) (h, s) (h', s').

Definition 33 (program equivalence). Suppose programs $CT, (\Gamma \vdash S)$ and $CT', (\Gamma \vdash' S')$ are such that CT, CT' are comparable and properly annotated, and moreover S, S' are properly annotated. The programs are *equivalent* iff for all disciplined, *Abs*-free (h, s) and (h', s') in $[\![\text{heap} \otimes \Gamma]\!]$ and all β with β total on h, h' and $(h, s) \sim_{\beta} (h', s')$, there is some $\beta_0 \supseteq \beta$ with $encap Abs([\![\Gamma \vdash S]\!]\mu(h, s)) \sim_{\beta_0} encap Abs([\![\Gamma \vdash' S']\!]'\mu'(h', s'))$ where $\mu = [\![CT]\!]$ and $\mu' = [\![CT']\!]'$.

Proposition 34 (simulation and equivalence). Suppose programs $CT, (\Gamma \vdash S)$ and $CT', (\Gamma \vdash' S)$ are properly annotated and $\mathscr{R}$ is a simulation from CT to CT'. If Γ self $\neq Abs$ then the programs are equivalent.

On inheritance. The stipulated preconditions for **unpack**, **pack**, **setown** all include exact type tests on *inv*, i.e., conditions of the form self.$inv = C$. A typical pattern is for a method in class C to unpack itself from C —so, when inherited into a subclass $B < C$, the precondition of this code is bound to fail. This motivates a second pattern mentioned in Sect. 2.2: instead of simply inheriting a method, it may be better to override it with an implementation that merely unpacks, makes a super call, and repacks. In Figs. 3 and 4, method add has roughly this form, though with a little extra code.

The original paper [10] deals with programs that have explicit specifications, in which case this issue is manifest in terms of pre- and post-conditions for methods that may be inherited. That paper introduces a short-hand notation for specifications which is justified in terms of boilerplate method overrides as described just above. The Spec# tool achieves this effect, without requiring explicit method declarations, by re-verifying code inherited in subclasses.

In the present work, we are not concerned with specifications as such, but the issue is still present: in our semantics, a method of C inherited and acting on an object of dynamic type $B < C$ will return $\bot$ if it asserts $inv = C$. Our technical results are sound with no restrictions on inheritance —in particular, Def. 27 does not require inherited methods to preserve the coupling. But to be useful, an inherited method that unpacks needs to be replaced by boilerplate method implementations using the unpack/super/pack pattern as in method add. Consider a class table where inheritance has been "expanded" in this way. Methods inherited into *Abs* give rise to declarations in *Abs* that must be shown to preserve the coupling. On the other hand, a method that is inherited and does not touch state encapsulated for the subclass (e.g., getRuns in our example) necessarily preserves the coupling and is subject to no proof obligation.

7   Related Work

Representation independence. Representation independence is proved in [8] for a language with shared mutable objects on the basis of ownership confinement imposed using restrictions expressed in terms of ordinary types; but these restrictions disallow ownership transfer. The results are extended to encompass ownership transfer in [14] but at the cost of substantial technical complications and the need for reachability analysis at transfer points, which are designated by explicit annotations. Like the present chapter, our previous results are based on a semantics in which the semantics of primitive commands is given in straightforward operational terms. It is a denotational semantics in that a command denotes a state transformer function, defined by induction on program structure. To handle recursion, method calls are interpreted relative to a method environment that gives the semantics of all methods. This is constructed as the limit of approximations, each exact up to a certain maximum calling depth. This model directly matches the recursion rule of Hoare logic, of which the abstraction theorem is in some sense a generalization.

Representation independence is needed not only for modular proof of equivalence of class implementations but also for modular reasoning about improvements (called data refinement). Such reasoning is needed for correctness preserving refactoring. The refactoring rules of Borba et al. [26] were validated using the data refinement theory of Cavalcanti and Naumann [27] which does not model sharing/aliasing. A recent paper [28] achieves correctness preserving refactoring for a class based language with shared mutable objects similar to the one considered in this chapter but adapted to encompass protected visibility and ownership of instances of library classes. The ownership regime of [8] is adapted to this setting. Their abstraction theorem accounts for changes of data representation in an inheritance hierarchy of classes. The theorem entails a data refinement law (similar to our Prop. 34) and facilitates correctness proofs of several refactorings that impact entire class trees.

Filipovic et al [29] provide an elegant semantic analysis of encapsulation and simulation, also in terms of refinement rather than equivalence. By contrast with the present chapter, they consider a 'static module' that owns internal state, rather than multiple instances of an abstraction, and their programming language allows pointer arithmetic. Using an instrumented semantics, they characterize client programs that do not read/write encapsulated locations, and show that such clients are representation independent. Like the *inv*/*own* discipline, and unlike type-based approaches, it is reads and writes, rather than the existence of pointers, that is controlled. Their theory makes minimal assumptions and thus provides a fundamental account of abstraction in the presence of shared mutable objects including those that are transferred across the encapsulation boundary. By contrast, our instrumentation is more intricate and less general, but provides a practical technique whereby clients can be proved to respect encapsulation. Filipovic et al require couplings to satisfy a condition, called 'growing relations'.

Technically, it is needed due to non-determinacy of the allocator, but they argue that the semantic issue would arise even with a deterministic allocator, if specifications are taken into account, due to under-determinacy. Semantic analysis of this issue remains an open question.

In the realm of functional languages representation independence has been well studied, particularly for System F [30] and its extensions, e.g., with recursive functions [31] and general recursive types [32,33,34]. Several recent papers [35,36,37,38] consider representation independence for languages with references but do not address class based languages directly. An exception is the work of Koutavas and Wand [39] in which Kripke logical relations are used to verify the examples in our earlier work [8]. Ahmed et al. [21] achieve representation independence for a higher-order call-by-value λ-calculus with existential type abstraction as well as higher-order store (obtained by allowing general ML-style references). Their couplings are Kripke logical relations that involve 'islands' akin to ours, but which grow monotonically, disallowing ownership transfer. These semantic results are adapted by Dreyer et al [38] to a relational modal logic for the same programming language.

In a technical report [40], we generalize the results in the present chapter to a language with generic classes, but this is still first-order and quite different from ML-like languages.

Just as we show how the inv/own discipline for modular reasoning about data invariants gives rise to a form of representation indpendence, Birkedal and Yang [37] show how modular reasoning in separation logic gives rise to representation independence. They provide a relational interpretation of separation logic with higher order frame rules; such rules account for hiding of invariants on mutable state in higher order programs. The relational interpretation shows that, if a client of an abstraction is proved correct then it is independent of the hidden representation. Thamsborg et al [22] develop similar results for a version of separation logic in which 'abstract predicates' (explained towards the end of this section) serve to isolate clients from invariants/relations on internal representations.

Methodologies. Several facets of the ownership methodology and its enforcement using static analysis techniques such as ownership types are presented in this volume. Here we sample some of the existing related work. Much of the literature concerns hierarchical ownership which is imposed by arranging the heap in a manner such that there is a single dominating owner [41] of representation objects. Clients are restricted from directly accessing representation objects. Ownership confinement is maintained in all reachable program states, hence it is a program invariant.

Static analyses for confinement such as ownership type systems [42,43,44] are a means to enforce hierarchical ownership. Most ownership type systems preclude ownership transfer; where allowed, it is achieved using nonstandard constructs such as destructive reads and restrictive linearity constraints (e.g., [45,46]). The overall objective of these static analyses is to provide some means of encapsulation for the purpose of modular reasoning. However they do not formalize exactly how the confinement invariant facilitates modular reasoning.

Müller and Rudich [47] extend Universe Types which provides encapsulation and has been adopted by JML for invariants, to solve the difficult problem of ownership transfer.

Drossopoulou et al. [48] introduce a general framework to describe verification techniques for invariants. The framework is based on variations on the idea that invariants hold exactly when control crosses module boundaries, e.g., *visible state semantics* requires all invariants to hold on all public method call/return boundaries. Several ownership disciplines are studied as instances of the framework.

While ownership is widely applicable, many programs involve local object structures which do not follow the ownership discipline. For example, friends and peer dependencies [11,49,20] exhibit non-hierarchical dependencies via cooperating classes of objects. Similarly, design patterns [50] involve local object structures which do not follow the ownership discipline. In the observer pattern, neither the subject nor its observers own each other; in the composite pattern, a client can have direct access to any node (not just the root) in a composite tree.

Cameron et al. [51] addressed the need for clusters without a single dominating owner. Ownership types are adapted to a system of "boxes" (clusters) which do not ensure encapsulation. However an effect system for disjointness of boxes is provided and proven sound.

The friendship discipline [20] that augments the *inv/own* discipline, can be used for modular reasoning about dependencies involving cooperating classes of objects. For concurrent programs, the *inv/own* discipline has been generalized by Locally Checked Invariants [16] which is implemented in the VCC tool [52]. In this case, ownership is complemented by non-hierarchical dependencies which are tracked in ghost state called "claims", generalizing the friendship discipline.

A key observation about the above examples is that reasoning about hierarchical and non-hierarchical dependencies ultimately involves the preservation of global program invariants. Local reasoning [53] about global invariants allows scalability of reasoning and ease of automation. For example, in the observer pattern, although there may be global invariants that hold over all objects in a heap, at any one point of time one can reason locally about a cooperating cluster of objects comprising of a single subject and its observers. The global invariant can be factored into two parts: one part that depends on this cluster of objects and another part that is independent of the cluster. The latter cannot be falsified by operations that affect the cluster, so it is enough to establish the former to show preservation of the global invariant.

Local reasoning as described above is embodied in *frame conditions* of a procedure specification that designates what part of the state is susceptible to change, together with frame-based reasoning that "all else is unchanged". The frame condition of a command is often termed its footprint (following separation logic [53]) and can be expressed using ghost state in the form of mutable auxiliary fields and variables. Use of ghost state in frame conditions was pioneered by Kassios, who dubbed it "dynamic framing" [54]. Region logic [55,56] is a Hoare logic for object-based programs that features local reasoning with frame conditions expressed in terms of sets of references (termed *regions*). VERL [57] is a verifier based on region logic that embodies local reasoning.

We have already seen the use of ghost states such as *inv, own, com* in the *inv/own* discipline. The implicit frame condition in the discipline is that clients cannot write fields of objects they do not own. Therefore writes to owned fields do not need to appear in the frame conditions of specifications. The Spec# tool [15] automatically generates such implicit frame conditions. In these tools particular methodologies such as friendship or ownership are an integral part of the verification conditions. The goal of verifiers such as VERL or Dafny [58,59] is to decouple methodologies from verification condition generation —both for tool modularity and for methodological flexibility.

To reason about non-ownership disciplines Parkinson and Bierman [60] propose abstraction instead of hiding, via second order assertions in separation logic. The jStar [61] tool implements this idea. Client reasoning can be done by means of "abstract predicates" —predicates whose concrete implementations are unknown to the client. For example a client may use an abstract predicate whose concrete implementation might be the layout of the heap. Parkinson [62] clearly articulates the case for specifications at the level of object clusters and shows an example specification of the Observer pattern that uses abstract predicates. For more insight on these issues we refer the reader to the companion chapter [2].

8 Discussion

Adaptations of the inv/own discipline. As compared with previous work on the discipline, we have imposed some additional restrictions to achieve sufficient information hiding to justify a modular rule for equivalence of class implementations. We argue that the restrictions are not onerous for practical application, though further practical experience is needed with the discipline and with our rule.

The first restriction is on field reads. Code in a client class cannot be allowed to read a field of an encapsulated representation object, although the discipline allows the existence of the reference; otherwise the client code could be representation dependent. On the other hand, a class such as *Hashtable* might be used both by clients and in the internal representation of the class *Abs* under revision; certainly the code of *Hashtable* needs to read its own fields. A distinction can be made on the basis of whether the current target object, i.e., self, is owned by an instance o of *Abs*. If it is, then we do not need the method invocation to preserve the coupling and we can allow reading of objects owned by o. If the target object is not owned by an instance of *Abs* then it should have no need to access objects owned by *Abs*. This distinction appears in the statement of Lemma 29 and it is used to stipulate a precondition for field access (see (A3) in Def. 15).[10]

Because the coupling relation imposes the user-defined local coupling only when an *Abs*-object is packed, it appears necessary to restrict **pack** e **as** *Abs* to occur only in

---

[10] This is unattractive in that the other stipulated preconditions mention only direct ownership whereas this one uses transitive ownership. However, in practical examples code outside *Abs* rarely has references to encapsulated objects. We believe such references can be adequately restricted using visibility control and/or lightweight confinement analyses, e.g., [63,8]. Moreover, as noted following Def. 15, the transitive ownership relation can be maintained in ghost state so that the stipulated precondition can be expressed without induction.

code of *Abs* in order for simulation to be checked only for that code. In the majority of known examples, packing to a class *C* is only done in code of *C*, and this is required in Leino and Müller's extension of the discipline to handle static fields.

Similar considerations apply to **setown** *x* **to** (y, C): care must be taken to prevent arbitrary code from moving objects across the encapsulation boundary for *Abs* in ways that do not admit modular reasoning. One would expect that code outside *Abs* cannot move objects across the *Abs*-boundary at all, but it turns out that the only problematic case is transfer out from an *Abs* island. In the unusual case that **setown** *x* **to** (y, C) occurs in code outside *Abs* but *x* is initially inside the island for some *Abs*-object, *x* must end up in the island for some *Abs*-object. Our stipulated precondition says just this. In practice it seems that the obligation can be discharged by simple syntactic considerations of visibility and/or lightweight alias control.

The last restriction is that an *Abs* object cannot own other *Abs* objects. This does not preclude containers holding containers, because a container does not own its content (e.g., AQueue owns the Qnodes but not the tasks). It does preclude certain recursive situations. For example, we could allow Qnode instances to own their successors but then we could not instantiate the theory with *Abs*:=Qnode. This does not seem too important since it is Queue that is appropriate to view as an abstraction coupled by a simulation. The restriction is not needed for soundness of simulation. But absent the restriction, nested islands would require a healthiness condition on couplings (similar to the healthiness condition used by Cavalcanti and Naumann [27, Def. 5]); e.g., coupling for an instance of Qnode would need to recursively impose the same predicate on the nxt node. We disallow nested islands in the present work for simplicity and to highlight connections with separation logic.

Future work. The discipline may seem somewhat onerous in that it uses verification conditions rather than lighter weight static analysis for control of the use of aliases. (We have to say "use of", because whereas confinement disallows certain aliases, the invariant discipline merely prevents faulty exploitation of aliases.) The Spec# tool provides some support for inference of annotations [15]. For many situations, simple confinement rules and other checks are sufficient to discharge the proof obligations and this needs to be investigated for the additional obligations we have introduced. The advantage of a verification discipline over types is that, while simple cases can be checked automatically, complicated cases can be checked with additional annotations rather than simply rejected.

The generalization to a small group of related classes is important, as revisions often involve several related classes. One example would be a revision of our Queue example that involves revising Qnode as well. If nodes are used only by Queue then this is subsumed by our theory, as we can consider a renamed version of Qnode that coexists with it. The more interesting situations arise in refactoring and in design patterns with tightly related configurations of multiple objects. Naumann et al. explore this generalization in recent work [28].

We are currently working on a relational version of region logic as a basis for verification of e.g., soundness of refactorings as well as examples discussed here and in our earlier work [8]. A crucial part of this verification process is reasoning about representation independence using proof rules of the relational logic.

Acknowledgments. We thank Amal Ahmed, Mike Barnett, Lars Birkedal, Sophia Drossopoulou, Ivana Filipovic, Rustan Leino, Peter Müller, Peter O'Hearn, Uday Reddy, Wolfram Schulte, Noah Torp-Smith, and Hongseok Yang for discussions. Thanks to the anonymous ECOOP 2005 referees as well as the referees of this chapter for their detailed comments.

Banerjee was supported in part by CM Project S2009TIC-1465 Prometidos, MICINN Project TIN2009-14599-C03-02 Desafios, EU NoE Project 256980 Nessos. Naumann was supported in part by NSF grant CCF-0915611 and by Microsoft Research.

References

1. Dietl, W., Müller, P.: Object Ownership in Program Verification. In: Clarke, D., Noble, J., Wrigstad, T. (eds.) Aliasing in Object-Oriented Programming. LNCS, vol. 7850, pp. 289–318. Springer, Heidelberg (2013)
2. Parkinson, M., Bierman, G.: Separation Logic for Object-Oriented Programming. In: Clarke, D., Noble, J., Wrigstad, T. (eds.) Aliasing in Object-Oriented Programming. LNCS, vol. 7850, pp. 366–406. Springer, Heidelberg (2013)
3. Smans, J., Jacobs, B., Piessens, F.: VeriFast for Java: A Tutorial. In: Clarke, D., Noble, J., Wrigstad, T. (eds.) Aliasing in Object-Oriented Programming. LNCS, vol. 7850, pp. 407–442. Springer, Heidelberg (2013)
4. Jacobs, B., Poll, E.: Java Program Verification at Nijmegen: Developments and Perspective. In: Futatsugi, K., Mizoguchi, F., Yonezaki, N. (eds.) ISSS 2003. LNCS, vol. 3233, pp. 134–153. Springer, Heidelberg (2004)
5. Hoare, C.A.R.: Proofs of correctness of data representations. Acta Informatica 1, 271–281 (1972)
6. Mitchell, J.C.: Representation independence and data abstraction. In: ACM Symp. on Princ. of Program. Lang., pp. 263–276 (1986)
7. de Roever, W.P., Engelhardt, K.: Data Refinement: Model-Oriented Proof Methods and their Comparison. Cambridge University Press (1998)
8. Banerjee, A., Naumann, D.A.: Ownership confinement ensures representation independence for object-oriented programs. J. ACM 52(6), 894–960 (2005)
9. Müller, P., Poetzsch-Heffter, A., Leavens, G.T.: Modular invariants for layered object structures. Sci. Comput. Program. 62(3), 253–286 (2006)
10. Barnett, M., DeLine, R., Fähndrich, M., Leino, K.R.M., Schulte, W.: Verification of object-oriented programs with invariants. Journal of Object Technology 3(6), 27–56 (2004)
11. Leino, K.R.M., Müller, P.: Object Invariants in Dynamic Contexts. In: Odersky, M. (ed.) ECOOP 2004. LNCS, vol. 3086, pp. 491–515. Springer, Heidelberg (2004)
12. Detlefs, D.L., Leino, K.R.M., Nelson, G.: Wrestling with rep exposure. Research 156, DEC Systems Research Center (1998)
13. O'Hearn, P.W., Yang, H., Reynolds, J.C.: Separation and information hiding. ACM Trans. Program. Lang. Syst. 31(3) (2009)
14. Banerjee, A., Naumann, D.A.: Ownership transfer and abstraction. Technical Report TR 2004-1, Computing and Information Sciences, Kansas State University (2003)
15. Barnett, M., Leino, K.R.M., Schulte, W.: The Spec# Programming System: An Overview. In: Barthe, G., Burdy, L., Huisman, M., Lanet, J.-L., Muntean, T. (eds.) CASSIS 2004. LNCS, vol. 3362, pp. 49–69. Springer, Heidelberg (2005)
16. Cohen, E., Moskal, M., Schulte, W., Tobies, S.: Local Verification of Global Invariants in Concurrent Programs. In: Touili, T., Cook, B., Jackson, P. (eds.) CAV 2010. LNCS, vol. 6174, pp. 480–494. Springer, Heidelberg (2010)

17. Banerjee, A., Naumann, D.A.: State Based Ownership, Reentrance, and Encapsulation. In: Black, A. (ed.) ECOOP 2005. LNCS, vol. 3586, pp. 387–411. Springer, Heidelberg (2005)
18. Guttag, J.V., Horning, J.J. (eds.): Larch: Languages and Tools for Formal Specification. Texts and Monographs in Computer Science. Springer-Verlag (1993); With Garland, S.J., Jones, K.D., Modet, A., Wing, J.M.
19. Meyer, B.: Object-oriented Software Construction, 2nd edn. Prentice Hall, New York (1997)
20. Naumann, D.A., Barnett, M.: Towards imperative modules: Reasoning about invariants and sharing of mutable state. Theoretical Computer Science 365, 143–168 (2006)
21. Ahmed, A., Dreyer, D., Rossberg, A.: State-dependent representation independence. In: ACM Symp. on Princ. of Program. Lang., pp. 340–353 (2009)
22. Thamsborg, J., Birkedal, L., Yang, H.: Two for the price of one: lifting separation logic assertions. Logical Methods in Computer Science 8(3) (2012)
23. Igarashi, A., Pierce, B., Wadler, P.: Featherweight Java: A minimal core calculus for Java and GJ. ACM Transactions on Programming Languages and Systems 23(3), 396–459 (2001)
24. Naumann, D.A.: Verifying a Secure Information Flow Analyzer. In: Hurd, J., Melham, T. (eds.) TPHOLs 2005. LNCS, vol. 3603, pp. 211–226. Springer, Heidelberg (2005)
25. Apt, K.R., de Boer, F.S., Olderog, E.R.: Verification of Sequential and Concurrent Programs, 3rd edn. Springer (2009)
26. Borba, P., Sampaio, A., Cornélio, M.: A Refinement Algebra for Object-oriented Programming. In: Cardelli, L. (ed.) ECOOP 2003. LNCS, vol. 2743, pp. 457–482. Springer, Heidelberg (2003)
27. Cavalcanti, A., Naumann, D.A.: Forward Simulation for Data Refinement of Classes. In: Eriksson, L.-H., Lindsay, P.A. (eds.) FME 2002. LNCS, vol. 2391, pp. 471–490. Springer, Heidelberg (2002)
28. Naumann, D.A., Sampaio, A., Silva, L.: Refactoring and representation independence for class hierachies. Theoretical Computer Science 433, 60–97 (2012)
29. Filipovic, I., O'Hearn, P.W., Torp-Smith, N., Yang, H.: Blaming the client: on data refinement in the presence of pointers. Formal Asp. Comput. 22(5), 547–583 (2010)
30. Reynolds, J.C.: Types, abstraction, and parametric polymorphism. In: Mason, R. (ed.) Information Processing 1983, pp. 513–523. North-Holland (1984)
31. Pitts, A.M.: Typed operational reasoning. In: Pierce, B.C. (ed.) Advanced Topics in Types and Programming Languages, pp. 245–289. The MIT Press (2005)
32. Ahmed, A.: Step-Indexed Syntactic Logical Relations for Recursive and Quantified Types. In: Sestoft, P. (ed.) ESOP 2006. LNCS, vol. 3924, pp. 69–83. Springer, Heidelberg (2006)
33. Crary, K., Harper, R.: Syntactic logical relations for polymorphic and recursive types. Electr. Notes Theor. Comput. Sci. 172, 259–299 (2007)
34. Melliès, P.A., Vouillon, J.: Recursive polymorphic types and parametricity in an operational framework. In: IEEE Symp. on Logic in Computer Science, pp. 82–91 (2005)
35. Sumii, E., Pierce, B.C.: A bisimulation for type abstraction and recursion. J. ACM 54(5) (2007)
36. Koutavas, V., Wand, M.: Small bisimulations for reasoning about higher-order imperative programs. In: ACM Symp. on Princ. of Program. Lang., pp. 141–152 (2006)
37. Birkedal, L., Yang, H.: Relational parametricity and separation logic. Logical Methods in Computer Science 4(2) (2008)
38. Dreyer, D., Neis, G., Rossberg, A., Birkedal, L.: A relational modal logic for higher-order stateful adts. In: ACM Symp. on Princ. of Program. Lang., pp. 185–198 (2010)
39. Koutavas, V., Wand, M.: Reasoning about class behavior. In: Informal Proceedings of FOOL/WOOD (2007)
40. Banerjee, A., Naumann, D.A.: State based encapsulation and generics. Technical Report CS Report 2004-11, Stevens Institute of Technology (2004)

41. Clarke, D.G., Potter, J.M., Noble, J.: Ownership types for flexible alias protection. In: OOP-SLA 1998 Conference Proceedings. SIGPLAN, vol. 33(10), pp. 48–64 (October 1998)
42. Boyapati, C., Lee, R., Rinard, M.C.: Ownership types for safe programming: preventing data races and deadlocks. In: ACM Conference on Object-Oriented Programming Languages, Systems, and Applications, pp. 211–230 (2002)
43. Clarke, D., Drossopoulou, S.: Ownership, encapsulation and the disjointness of type and effect. In: ACM Conference on Object-Oriented Programming Languages, Systems, and Applications, pp. 292–310 (November 2002)
44. Boyapati, C., Liskov, B., Shrira, L.: Ownership types for object encapsulation. In: ACM Symp. on Princ. of Program. Lang., pp. 213–223 (2003) (invited paper)
45. Boyland, J., Noble, J., Retert, W.: Capabilities for Sharing: A Generalisation of Uniqueness and Read-Only. In: Lindskov Knudsen, J. (ed.) ECOOP 2001. LNCS, vol. 2072, pp. 2–7. Springer, Heidelberg (2001)
46. Smith, F., Walker, D., Morrisett, G.: Alias Types. In: Smolka, G. (ed.) ESOP 2000. LNCS, vol. 1782, pp. 366–381. Springer, Heidelberg (2000)
47. Müller, P., Rudich, A.: Ownership transfer in universe types. In: ACM Conference on Object-Oriented Programming Languages, Systems, and Applications, pp. 461–478 (2007)
48. Drossopoulou, S., Francalanza, A., Müller, P., Summers, A.J.: A Unified Framework for Verification Techniques for Object Invariants. In: Vitek, J. (ed.) ECOOP 2008. LNCS, vol. 5142, pp. 412–437. Springer, Heidelberg (2008)
49. Barnett, M., Naumann, D.A.: Friends Need a Bit More: Maintaining Invariants Over Shared State. In: Kozen, D. (ed.) MPC 2004. LNCS, vol. 3125, pp. 54–84. Springer, Heidelberg (2004)
50. Gamma, E., Helm, R., Johnson, R., Vlissides, J.: Design Patterns: Elements of Reusable Object-Oriented Software. Addison-Wesley (1995)
51. Cameron, N.R., Drossopoulou, S., Noble, J., Smith, M.J.: Multiple ownership. In: ACM Conference on Object-Oriented Programming Languages, Systems, and Applications, pp. 441–460 (2007)
52. Cohen, E., Dahlweid, M., Hillebrand, M., Leinenbach, D., Moskal, M., Santen, T., Schulte, W., Tobies, S.: VCC: A Practical System for Verifying Concurrent C. In: Berghofer, S., Nipkow, T., Urban, C., Wenzel, M. (eds.) TPHOLs 2009. LNCS, vol. 5674, pp. 23–42. Springer, Heidelberg (2009)
53. O'Hearn, P.W., Reynolds, J., Yang, H.: Local Reasoning about Programs that Alter Data Structures. In: Fribourg, L. (ed.) CSL 2001. LNCS, vol. 2142, pp. 1–19. Springer, Heidelberg (2001)
54. Kassios, I.T.: The dynamic frames theory. Formal Aspects of Computing 23(3), 267–288 (2011)
55. Banerjee, A., Naumann, D.A., Rosenberg, S.: Local reasoning for global invariants, part I: Region logic. Extended version of [64] (2011),
http://www.cs.stevens.edu/~naumann/pub/locResGloInvI.pdf
56. Banerjee, A., Naumann, D.A.: Local reasoning for global invariants, part II: Dynamic boundaries. Extended version of [65] (2011),
http://www.cs.stevens.edu/~naumann/pub/locResGloInvII.pdf
57. Verl: VErifier for Region Logic Software distribution,
http://www.cs.stevens.edu/~naumann/pub/VERL/
58. Dafny: http://boogie.codeplex.com/
59. Leino, K.R.M.: Dafny: An Automatic Program Verifier for Functional Correctness. In: Clarke, E.M., Voronkov, A. (eds.) LPAR-16 2010. LNCS (LNAI), vol. 6355, pp. 348–370. Springer, Heidelberg (2010)
60. Parkinson, M.J., Bierman, G.M.: Separation logic and abstraction. In: ACM Symp. on Princ. of Program. Lang., pp. 247–258 (2005)

61. Distefano, D., Parkinson, M.J.: jStar: Towards practical verification for Java. In: ACM Conference on Object-Oriented Programming Languages, Systems, and Applications, pp. 213–226 (2008)
62. Parkinson, M.J.: Class invariants: the end of the road? In: International Workshop on Aliasing, Confinement and Ownership in Object-oriented Programming (2007)
63. Vitek, J., Bokowski, B.: Confined types in Java. Software Practice and Experience 31(6), 507–532 (2001)
64. Banerjee, A., Naumann, D.A., Rosenberg, S.: Regional Logic for Local Reasoning about Global Invariants. In: Vitek, J. (ed.) ECOOP 2008. LNCS, vol. 5142, pp. 387–411. Springer, Heidelberg (2008)
65. Naumann, D.A., Banerjee, A.: Dynamic Boundaries: Information Hiding by Second Order Framing with First Order Assertions. In: Gordon, A.D. (ed.) ESOP 2010. LNCS, vol. 6012, pp. 2–22. Springer, Heidelberg (2010)

Separation Logic
for Object-Oriented Programming

Matthew Parkinson and Gavin Bierman

Microsoft Research
{mattpark,gmb}@microsoft.com

Abstract. In this article we propose techniques based on separation logic to reason about object-oriented programs. This leads to a modular proof system that can deal with features considered core to object-oriented programming, including object encapsulation, subclassing, inheritance, and dynamic dispatch.

1 Introduction

Encapsulation, the hiding of the internal state of an object, is one of the key principles underlying object-oriented programming. As objects combine data with operations, clients do not need to understand the internal representation that an object uses, just the operations (or *methods*) that it provides. If an object correctly encapsulates its representation, then its representation can be changed without affecting the client. This allows the programmer to think modularly about the program. Without encapsulation of state, there is no modularity.

Languages like Java and C$^\sharp$ provide some type system support for checking encapsulation. For example, fields can be marked as private, which prevents clients of the class from accessing the field, and thus provides simple encapsulation. However, the internal representation of an object often involves other objects; for instance, a set may be represented by a balanced binary tree. There is no language support in Java or C$^\sharp$ for checking the encapsulation of such more complex representations.

For example, consider implementing a connection pool for managing database connections. The class can be represented by a list of connections not currently in use (the *free list*). When a client asks for a connection, the connection pool checks if there are any free connections and, if there are, it removes a connection from the free list and returns it to the client. If there are not then it creates and returns a fresh connection. When a client returns a connection to the pool, the connection pool adds it to the free list. Importantly, no client may use a connection once it has returned it to the pool.

What is the internal state of this connection pool? We do not want the client to be able to access the free list, or any connections in the free list. To check this kind of encapsulation requires us to assume the protocol is obeyed by the client of this class. The client will still have pointers into the representation, but must guarantee not to use them. Moreover, the set of object fields, the *footprint*,

D. Clarke et al. (Eds.): Aliasing in Object-Oriented Programming, LNCS 7850, pp. 366–406, 2013.

of the representation changes over time as connections are added and removed from the pool. Ultimately, the encapsulation is challenging to check in a static type system.

Describing the shape of the representation is a task that is ideally suited to *separation logic* [1]. Separation logic has had great success in reasoning about pointer-based data structures in C-like languages; particularly in the presence of dynamic memory allocation and deallocation. In earlier work [2, 3] we proposed the addition of *abstract predicates* to separation logic to hide the representation of abstract data types.

Abstract predicates are the separation logic analogue of an abstract type. Abstract types only allow the definition of a type name to be used within the scope of a module or class. Outside that scope the name must be treated abstractly; that is, independently of the particular definition. Abstract predicates are the same; within a defined scope the predicate and its definition can be freely used. Outside of the scope it can only be treated abstractly.

For example, an abstract predicate can be defined for a set class that has a definition of a balanced binary tree. The methods of the set class are specified purely in terms of the predicate, not the representation. Thus the client can reason independently of the particular implementation choices.

Unfortunately, scaling separation logic to object-oriented languages is not just a case of adding abstract predicates; there is a second challenge, *subclassing*. Subclassing in languages like Java and $C^\sharp$ serves two purposes: it allows a class to be seen, in some sense, to behave the same as another class; and it allows a class to reuse another class's implementation. The classic pattern of subclassing is to take an existing class and extend its functionality, while preserving its previous behaviour.

In real libraries the story is not so simple. Consider the AbstractCollection class in the Java Collections API.[1] This is an abstract class that provides some of the functionality that collections typically support. It leaves some place-holders that the subclass is required to support, such as iterator and size, and some that the subclass can optionally support, such as add. Some methods are dependent on others, for example, addAll will work if the add method is supported by the subclass. In cases where a client calls an unsupported method, then the superclass throws an UnsupportedException. Statically, the type system cannot determine that an UnsupportedException will not be thrown.

To address the complications that subclassing adds to reasoning, we proposed *abstract predicate families*, which are abstract predicates that are additionally indexed by class [4]. They allow encapsulation that is dependent on the dynamic type of the object being encapsulated. Just as a method invocation selects the method definition based on the dynamic class of an object, abstract predicate families select the particular definition based on the dynamic class of the object being encapsulated.

In summary: we define a separation logic that supports encapsulation and subclassing as found in object-oriented programming languages such as Java

---

[1] A similar example can be found in the .NET collections framework.

and $C^\sharp$. This article both combines and simplifies our earlier works [2–4]. The simplifications are sufficient to enable the complete set of proof rules to fit onto a single page (see Appendix B). Whilst compact, our logic is highly expressive and can support a wide-range of inheritance patterns, beyond the capabilities of any other logic that we are aware of.

2 Motivating Separation Logic

In this section, we present the motivation for separation logic. We begin by informally using a Hoare-like logic to specify a few simple examples. We show informal, real-world documentation can naturally be represented by a Hoare triple. However, to allow reasoning about these examples purely using the specification, we find the natural specification is not strong enough, and must additionally specify what is unchanged/modified by a method. We then present a separation logic for object-oriented memory, and show how it addresses the complexities of specifying what a method changes, and more closely matches the informal documentation.

Consider the following (typical) method from the Java API documentation:

---

java.awt.Rectangle.translate(int x,int y)

Translates this Rectangle the indicated distance, to the right along the x coordinate axis, and downward along the y coordinate axis.

http://download.oracle.com/javase/1.4.2/docs/api/java/awt/Rectangle.html

---

We can reflect this informal documentation into a Hoare triple:

$$\left\{\, \mathbf{this}.\mathsf{x} = x \wedge \mathbf{this}.\mathsf{y} = y \,\right\} \mathsf{Rect::translate(x,y)} \left\{\, \mathbf{this}.\mathsf{x} = x + \mathsf{x} \wedge \mathbf{this}.\mathsf{y} = y + \mathsf{y} \,\right\}$$

The formula in brackets before the method descriptor, the *pre-condition*, specifies what should be true before executing the method; and the formula after the method descriptor, the *post-condition*, specifies what is guaranteed if the method terminates. Thus, this specification says, if before executing the method the x field of **this** has some value x and the y field has some value y then, if it returns, the x field of **this** has the value $x + \mathsf{x}$ and the y field has $y + \mathsf{y}$.

The natural reading of the informal documentation would preclude modifying other properties of the Rectangle like its height, or any other object: if the method changed them, it would be explicitly documented. However, this is not true of the Hoare logic specification; anything not mentioned can be changed. In fact, the following three method bodies satisfy the specification.

---

this.x += x;
this.y += y;
	this.x += x;
	this.y += y;
	this.h = 0;
		this.x += x;
		this.y += y;
		if(this.parent != this)
		    this.parent.x += x;

The first column represents the obvious implementation of the specification, it updates the x and y fields by adding the values supplied. The second additionally updates the h field to be 0. The post-condition of the specification does not constrain the value of the h field so updating it is, in fact, allowed by the specification. The third column potentially updates another object through a parent field. Again, the post-condition does not preclude updates to any other objects—it only requires the x and y fields of **this** to have the specified values. Thus, if a client is to reason solely using the specification it has to consider anything changing arbitrarily except the x and y fields of **this**.

To remove this burden on clients we need to add (somewhat tediously) to the method specification details about what it does *not* modify:

$$\{((z \neq \textbf{this}) \vee f \notin \{x, y\}) \wedge z.f = v\} \textsf{Rect::translate(x,y)} \{z.f = v\}$$

This specifies that any field of an object that is either different from **this**, or the field name is not x or y, will have the same value after the call. That is, the translate method at most modifies the x and y fields of **this**. This specification is often written more compactly as a *modifies clause*.

Rect::translate(x,y) modifies **this**.x, **this**.y

Using both specifications, a client can now reason about the method without having to know the precise implementation details. It can use the second specification to preserve information it has about other parts of memory, and the first to reason about the changes it makes.

Modifies clauses work well when it is easy to statically determine the fields and objects modified. However, when you have complex shapes in memory it quickly becomes much harder to specify what a method changes. Consider a class that represents a collection using a sorted list:

System.Collection.SortedList.Clear()
Removes all elements from a SortedList object.
        http://msdn.microsoft.com/en-us/library/system.collections.sortedlist.aspx

The documentation does not specify which objects and fields are modified. If we know the implementation uses a next field, then perhaps we could specify it as potentially modifying any object's next field; for example:

SortedList::Clear() modifies *.next

However, the precise set of modified fields is dependent on the state of the list. A sensible implementation would only modify the next fields reachable from the SortedList. Keeping track of these sets of fields and knowing when these two sets are disjoint can be burdensome.

This modifies clause also breaks abstraction: it reveals that the class uses a next field; a fact the client should not know. Whilst perhaps one could argue this is simply poor taste, this technique breaks down completely when considering interfaces. An interface does not know about the specific implementation details. Consider, for example:

System.Collection.IDictionary.Clear()
... removes all elements from the IDictionary.
        http://msdn.microsoft.com/en-us/library/system.collections.idictionary.aspx

There are multiple subtypes of this interface implemented in the standard library, and any programmer is free to make their own implementation of the interface. So the interface cannot actually specify the fields that are modified, because the interface writer cannot know about all possible subtypes.

To address this problem of providing a more accurate and abstract modifies clause others [5–7] have introduced some notion of *ownership*. Ownership specifies that each object is *owned* by a particular object. An object's methods can modify any objects that it owns. In the list example, the nodes of the list would be owned by the SortedList class. Thus, the list class can modify the nodes of the list as it owns the nodes. Ownership can be enforced through a type system [5, 6], or by adding extra conditions to the verification [7].

Ownership imposes a discipline of accessing objects in a certain order, which can be challenging for common design patterns [8] like Iterators, Composites, and Subject/Observer, where there are multiple objects accessing some structure. For example, it is quite common to have multiple iterators over a common list; in this case, no iterator can uniquely own the list. Rather than follow the ownership approach, we will consider an alternative starting point: *separation logic*.[2]

2.1   Separation Logic

Separation logic presents a different approach: rather than requiring explicit specification of what can be modified, it makes the modification implicit in the specification. It captures the intuitive, real-world specifications that we saw earlier in the API documentation, where anything not mentioned in the specification is not changed. Separation logic supports assertions that describe only part of the memory: the part that can be modified. To do so, separation logic models a simple heap as a partial function [1]. In our setting of objects, the modelling of heaps and state is a little more complicated.

Definition 1 (Heap). *A heap, H, is a pair of finite partial functions: the first stores the fields, H_v, and the second stores the types of objects, H_t. We constrain heaps such that every object that has a field in the heap must also have a type.*

$$H : \textit{Heaps} \stackrel{\text{def}}{=} \left\{ (H_v, H_t) \,\middle|\, \begin{array}{l} H_v \in \textsf{ObjectIDs} \times \textsf{FieldNames} \rightharpoonup_{fin} \textsf{Values} \\ \wedge\, H_t \in \textsf{ObjectIDs} \rightharpoonup_{fin} \textsf{ClassNames} \\ \wedge\, \forall(o, \_) \in dom(H_v).\, o \in dom(H_t) \end{array} \right\}$$

We use shorthands for accessing the first and second components of the heap: $(H_v, H_t).t = H_t$ and $(H_v, H_t).v = H_v$. A value $v \in \textsf{Values}$ is either an $o \in$ ObjectIDs or a constant, c.

Definition 2 (State). *A logical state, (S, H, I), is a triple consisting of a stack, S, a heap, H, and an interpretation, I, where a stack is a map from program*

---

[2] A further alternative approach has been proposed by Kassios [9]: Dynamic Frames. This approach uses a predicate that specifies the set of locations an assertion, or expression, depends upon and integrates this with a form of modifies clause.

variable names to values, and an interpretation is a map from logical variables[3] *to values.*

To describe the shape of heaps, we provide two primitive assertions. The first is written $se_1.f \mapsto se_2$ and is read as "se_1's f field points to se_2", where se_1 and se_2 are simple expressions that do not access any fields or methods. It is true in any state where the heap, H, consists of at least the single mapping from the location given by the evaluation of se_1 in the current stack and interpretation along with the field f to the value given by the evaluation of se_2. The second primitive assertion is a dynamic type assertion, written $class(se, C)$, and is read "se has dynamic type C." It is true in any state where se evaluates to an object that has dynamic type C in the heap. We use the phrase dynamic type to mean the class an object was created with, and the phrase static type to mean the type of an expression denoting that object. For example, in the assignment C x = **new** D; the static type of x is C but the dynamic type is D.

We need to be able to combine these primitive assertions to describe more complex properties of the state. We can use classical conjunction to compose assertions to specify heaps that contain multiple fields. However, as states only describe part of the heap, a second form of natural composition exists, namely disjoint heap composition. We define *separating conjunction*, written $P * Q$, to mean the heap can be split into two disjoint pieces, one satisfying P and the other Q. Thus, $x_1.f \mapsto y * x_2.f \mapsto y$ means the heap contains the field f of the object x_1 and the field f of the object x_2, and moreover $x_1 \neq x_2$. This is in contrast to the assertion $x_1.f \mapsto y \wedge x_2.f \mapsto y$ which does not ensure $x_1 \neq x_2$.

Formally, the separating conjunction, $*$, comes from the following definition of composing heaps.

Definition 3 (Heap composition). *We write $H_1 \circ H_2$ for the composition of two heaps:*

$$H_1 \circ H_2 \stackrel{\text{def}}{=} \begin{cases} (H_1.v \cup H_2.v, H_1.t) & \text{if } H_1 \perp H_2 \\ \text{undefined} & \text{otherwise} \end{cases}$$

where $H_1 \perp H_2 \stackrel{\text{def}}{=} (dom(H_1.v) \cap dom(H_2.v) = \emptyset$ and $H_1.t = H_2.t)$

We give the complete formal definition of our assertion language and its semantics in Figure 1. We write $S, H, I \models P$ to mean the formula P holds in the state (S, H, I). We write $\models P$ to mean the formula holds in all states. The standard predicate $(=)$, connectives $(\vee, \wedge, \Rightarrow)$ and quantifiers $(\forall, \exists)$ are interpreted in the usual way [1]. In addition to the standard connectives, we have the new spatial connectives $*$ and $-\!*$. As discussed earlier, the separating conjunction $P * Q$ means the heap can be split into two disjoint parts in which P and Q

---

[3] Logical variables are sometimes called *auxiliary* or *ghost* variables. They are used to express protocols of method calls, so they require a global scope. We cannot simply use the program stack as this cannot define a variable across method calls; it only contains local variables. So we define a logical interpretation that maps logical variables, e.g. x, y, etc. to values.

$P, Q ::=$ Assertions $S, H, I \models P$

true $\overset{\text{def}}{=}$ always

false $\overset{\text{def}}{=}$ never

$P \vee Q$ Disjunction $\overset{\text{def}}{=} S, H, I \models P$ or $S, H, I \models Q$

$P \wedge Q$ Conjunction $\overset{\text{def}}{=} S, H, I \models P$ and $S, H, I \models Q$

$P \Rightarrow Q$ Implication $\overset{\text{def}}{=} \forall H' \perp H.$ if $S, H \circ H', I \models P$ then $S, H \circ H', I \models Q$

$\forall x.P$ Forall $\overset{\text{def}}{=} \forall v \in \mathsf{Values}.\ S, H, I[x \mapsto v] \models P$

$\exists x.P$ Exists $\overset{\text{def}}{=} \exists v \in \mathsf{Values}.\ S, H, I[x \mapsto v] \models P$

$\mathsf{se}_1.\mathsf{f} \mapsto \mathsf{se}_2$ Field points to $\overset{\text{def}}{=} H.v(\llbracket \mathsf{se}_1 \rrbracket_{S,I}, \mathsf{f}) = \llbracket \mathsf{se}_2 \rrbracket_{S,I}$

$class(\mathsf{se}, \mathsf{C})$ Dynamic type $\overset{\text{def}}{=} H.t(\llbracket \mathsf{se} \rrbracket_{S,I}) = \mathsf{C}$

$\mathsf{se}_1 = \mathsf{se}_2$ Equality $\overset{\text{def}}{=} \llbracket \mathsf{se} \rrbracket_{S,I} = \llbracket \mathsf{se}' \rrbracket_{S,I}$

$P * Q$ Separating $\overset{\text{def}}{=} \exists H_1, H_2.\ H_1 \circ H_2 = H,\quad S, H_1, I \models P$
         conjunction   and $S, H_2, I \models Q$

$P \mathbin{-\!\!*} Q$ Separating $\overset{\text{def}}{=} \forall H_1.$ if $H_1 \perp H$ and $S, H_1, I \models P$
         implication   then $S, H_1 \circ H, I \models Q$

$\mathsf{se} ::=$ Simple Expressions

x   Program Variable $\llbracket \mathsf{x} \rrbracket_{S,I} = S(\mathsf{x})$

x Logical Variable $\llbracket x \rrbracket_{S,I} = I(x)$

c   Constant $\llbracket \mathsf{c} \rrbracket_{S,I} = \mathsf{c}$

$\mathsf{se}_1 \oplus \mathsf{se}_2$ operations $\llbracket \mathsf{se}_1 \oplus \mathsf{se}_2 \rrbracket_{S,I} = \llbracket \mathsf{se}_1 \rrbracket_{S,I} \oplus \llbracket \mathsf{se}_2 \rrbracket_{S,I}$

Fig. 1. Syntax and semantics of separation logic formulae and expressions. We use C and D as metavariables over class names; x, y and z for program variables; and f for field names. Simple expressions, se, only use stack variables, constants (including a distinguished constant, **null**) and primitive operations (such as addition), that is, they do not access fields.

hold respectively. Note that the separating conjunction, $*$, does not split the stack or the dynamic type information. We use standard Hoare-style reasoning for the program variables, so we do not need to split the stack. The dynamic type information of an object in Java or $\mathsf{C}^\sharp$ does not change, so it does not need to be considered partial as it cannot be invalidated. Finally, the adjoint to $*$, written $P \mathbin{-\!\!*} Q$, means that if the heap can be extended with any disjoint heap satisfying P then the resultant heap will satisfy Q. In the rest of this article, we do not use the adjoint and only include it here for completeness.

We provide judgements for specifying what the program does:

$$\vdash_m \{P\}\, \bar{\mathsf{s}}\, \{Q\}$$

This is read: the list of statements, $\bar{\mathsf{s}}$, satisfies the specification $\{P\}\{Q\}$ and modifies at most the local variables contained in the set m. In later sections, judgements will be considered involving contexts; these will be written to the left of the turnstile.

For a judgement to hold, the pre-condition, P, must describe all the memory required to execute the code, $\bar{\mathsf{s}}$. This is called the "tight interpretation" [1].

Importantly, if the pre-condition describes all the memory the code uses, then implicitly anything separate from the pre-condition will be unchanged.

This observation leads to the core rule of separation logic, the *frame rule*:

$$\frac{\vdash_m \{P\}\, \mathsf{s}\, \{Q\}}{\vdash_m \{P * R\}\, \mathsf{s}\, \{Q * R\}} \qquad \text{provided } m \cap fv(R) = \emptyset.$$

Returning to our **translate** method for the **Rect** class, we can specify this in separation logic as:

$$\left\{ \mathbf{this}.\mathsf{x} \mapsto X * \mathbf{this}.\mathsf{y} \mapsto Y \right\} \mathsf{Rect::translate(x,y)} \left\{ \mathbf{this}.\mathsf{x} \mapsto X + \mathsf{x} * \mathbf{this}.\mathsf{y} \mapsto Y + \mathsf{y} \right\}$$

Using the frame rule we can preserve any facts about other objects or fields that are disjoint. Since we consider a language without global variables, methods do not modify any variables visible to the caller of the method. Thus, method specifications do not require modifies clauses.

Furthermore, we can define abstract predicates to represent the internal structure of an object. These predicates can describe the fields that the object uses and other objects it depends upon. By carefully hiding the details of these predicates we can cleanly abstract specifications. For instance, returning to our **IDictionary** example, we can specify the **clear** method as

$$\left\{ \mathsf{Dictionary}(\mathbf{this}, m) \right\} \mathsf{IDictionary::clear()} \left\{ \mathsf{Dictionary}(\mathbf{this}, [\,]) \right\}$$

where the second argument to **Dictionary** is a finite map representing the contents of the dictionary. We write $[\,]$ for the empty map. The **SortedList** class that implements this interface can then specify the meaning of the **Dictionary** predicate for its class. This allows the class to satisfy the abstract specification, without revealing its implementation details to either the client or the interface.

In the rest of the article, we develop a logic for reasoning in this way about object-oriented programs.

3   Fields and Allocation

We begin by building a separation logic for a very simple Java/$C^\sharp$-like language with field manipulation, local variables and object allocation. We postpone the use and definition of methods to later sections. This enables us to first explain how separation logic can be used to describe and reason about the state associated to objects without the complexities of method dispatch.

In the rest of this section, we present the language, the verification rules to reason about this language, and some examples of using the verification rules.

3.1   Language

The core of our object-oriented language is given below.

L ::= **class** C : D{ $\overline{T}$ $\overline{f}$; ... }	Class definition
s, t ::=	Statement
x.f = y;	Field write
x = e;	Assignment
if(x == y){$\overline{s}$} **else** {$\overline{t}$}	Conditional
...	
e ::=	Expression
se	Simple expression (given in Fig. 1)
y.f	Field read
new C	Object creation
...	
T ::=	Type
C	Class
int	Integer
...	

We use ... to represent underspecified parts of the syntax, which are expanded in later sections. We also make use of the Featherweight Java [10] overbar notation, writing $\overline{x}$ for a possibly empty sequence $x_1, \ldots, x_n$, $\overline{T}\ \overline{x}$ for the sequence $T_1 x_1, \ldots, T_n x$, and similarly $\overline{T}\ \overline{x}$; for the sequence $T_1 x_1; \ldots T_n x_i$. For programs, we restrict se to not contain logical variables.

We give the operational semantics for this language (and for the various extensions defined in later sections) in Appendix A.

3.2 Verification Rules

First, we present the rule for writing to a field. We give small axioms in the style of Ishtiaq and O'hearn [11]. Field write requires the heap to contain at least the single field being written to, and the post-condition specifies it has the updated value. Implicitly the rule specifies no other fields are modified, and hence it can be extended by the frame rule to talk about additional state.

L-FWRITE $\vdash_{\emptyset} \{x.f \mapsto \_\} x.f = y; \{x.f \mapsto y\}$

This rule justifies our choice to have field assertions as the primitive assertion about the heap. The rule is given in terms of just the fields it uses, and the frame rule dictates what happens to the other values. If the primitive assertions described entire objects, we would need to give the rules in terms of the whole object and say how the other fields were affected by this assignment.

The judgement form for expressions is also written $\vdash \{P\} e \{Q\}$ and asserts that executing the expression, e, in a starting state satisfying P results in a state satisfying Q, where the post-condition, Q can contain occurrences of a distinguished variable, **ret**. This variable represents the result of evaluating e. We refer to **ret** as the return variable. The rules for assignment and simple expressions are as follows.

L-ASSIGN	$\dfrac{\vdash \{P\}\,\mathsf{e}\,\{Q\} \qquad x \notin fv(P,Q)}{\vdash_{\{x\}} \{P * \mathsf{x} = x\}\,\mathsf{x} = \mathsf{e};\,\{Q[x/\mathsf{x},\mathsf{x}/\mathbf{ret}]\}}$
L-SEXPR	$\vdash \{\mathsf{true}\}\,\mathsf{se}\,\{\mathbf{ret} = \mathsf{se}\}$

The L-ASSIGN rule for assignment saves the old value in the pre-condition $\mathsf{x} = x$ and then in the post-condition it first removes references to the old value of x by replacing it with the saved old value, x, and then replaces the return variable with x. Simple expressions do not access the heap, so the pre-condition in the L-SEXPR rule is simply true and the post-condition sets the return variable equal to the expression. It is important to note that we have only one rule for all simple expression forms.

The rules for reasoning about field access and object creation[4] are as follows.

L-FREAD	$\vdash \{\mathsf{x.f} \mapsto y\}\,\mathsf{x.f}\,\{\mathsf{x.f} \mapsto y * \mathbf{ret} = y\}$
L-NEW	$\vdash \{\mathsf{true}\}\,\mathbf{new}\ \mathsf{C}\,\{\mathit{fields}_\mathsf{C}(\mathbf{ret}) \wedge \mathit{class}(\mathbf{ret}, \mathsf{C})\}$

The field access rule, L-FREAD, simply requires the state to be known and sets the return variable equal to the contents. The L-NEW rule ensures that the appropriate fields are associated with the newly allocated object. We define the shorthand $\mathit{fields}_\mathsf{C}(x)$ to mean $x.\mathsf{f}_1 \mapsto v_1 * \ldots * x.\mathsf{f}_n \mapsto v_n * \mathit{fields}_\mathsf{D}(x)$ where $\mathsf{f}_1, \ldots, \mathsf{f}_n$ are the fields defined by the class C whose direct superclass is D, and $v_1 \ldots v_n$ are the default constants of the appropriate type, and the special case $\mathit{fields}_{\mathsf{Object}}(x)$ which is defined as true.[5]

The rules for reasoning about conditional statements and sequencing of statements are standard and as follows.

L-IF	$\dfrac{\vdash_m \{P \wedge \mathsf{x} = \mathsf{y}\}\,\bar{\mathsf{s}}\,\{Q\} \qquad \vdash_m \{P \wedge \mathsf{x} \neq \mathsf{y}\}\,\bar{\mathsf{t}}\,\{Q\}}{\vdash_m \{P\}\,\mathbf{if}(\mathsf{x} == \mathsf{y})\{\bar{\mathsf{s}}\}\ \mathbf{else}\ \{\bar{\mathsf{t}}\}\,\{Q\}}$
L-SEQ	$\dfrac{\vdash_m \{P\}\,\mathsf{s}\,\{R\} \qquad \vdash_m \{R\}\,\bar{\mathsf{s}}\,\{Q\}}{\vdash_m \{P\}\,\mathsf{s}\,\bar{\mathsf{s}}\,\{Q\}}$

Finally, we present the rules for refining specifications. We define a new judgement as follows.

$$\vdash_m \{P_1\}\{Q_1\} \implies \{P_2\}\{Q_2\}$$

We say that a specification $\{P_2\}\{Q_2\}$ refines another specification $\{P_1\}\{Q_1\}$ if, for all programs $\bar{\mathsf{s}}$ that only modifies local variables contained in the set m,

---

[4] We omit specific constructor methods. We consider construction to be done in two phases, allocation then initialisation, e.g. $\mathsf{x} = \mathbf{new}\ \mathsf{C}(\bar{\mathsf{y}});$ is expanded to $\mathsf{x} = \mathbf{new}\ \mathsf{C}; \mathsf{x}.{<}\mathsf{initC}{>}(\bar{\mathsf{y}});$. Similarly, constructor definitions $\mathsf{C}(\overline{\mathsf{T}}\ \bar{\mathsf{x}})\{\mathbf{super}(\bar{\mathsf{y}});\ \bar{\mathsf{s}}\}$ are expanded to $\mathbf{void}{<}\mathsf{initC}{>}(\bar{\mathsf{x}})\{\mathbf{this}.\mathsf{D}{::}{<}\mathsf{initD}{>}(\bar{\mathsf{y}});\bar{\mathsf{s}}\}$ where D is the direct superclass of class C. This is how bytecode represents object construction, and how tools such as jStar [12] perform verification. We illustrate how to encode reasoning about constructors in §7.4.

[5] Actually, *fields* is an abstract predicate family. This concept is defined in §6, and the specific abstract predicate family is defined in §7.4. However, at this point it suffices to consider it as a collection of shorthands.

if $\bar{s}$ satisfies the specification $\{P_1\}\{Q_1\}$ then it also satisfies the specification $\{P_2\}\{Q_2\}$. The four rules for refining specifications are as follows.

R-VARELIM	$\vdash_m \{P\}\{Q\} \Longrightarrow \{\exists x.\ P\}\{\exists x.\ Q\}$
R-CONSEQ	$\dfrac{\models P \Rightarrow P' \qquad \models Q' \Rightarrow Q}{\vdash_m \{P'\}\{Q'\} \Longrightarrow \{P\}\{Q\}}$
R-FRAME	$\vdash_m \{P\}\{Q\} \Longrightarrow \{P * R\}\{Q * R\} \qquad$ where $fv(R) \cap m = \emptyset$
R-TRANS	$\dfrac{\vdash_m \{P_1\}\{Q_1\} \Longrightarrow \{P_2\}\{Q_2\} \qquad \vdash_m \{P_2\}\{Q_2\} \Longrightarrow \{P_3\}\{Q_3\}}{\vdash_m \{P_1\}\{Q_1\} \Longrightarrow \{P_3\}\{Q_3\}}$

The first rule, R-VARELIM, allows logical variables to be removed from a specification by existentially quantifying them. The second rule, R-CONSEQ, allows logical implications to be used to weaken the pre-condition and strengthen the post-condition of a command. The third rule, R-FRAME, allows the footprint of a specification to be extended as long as the extending state does not mention any modified variable in the original specification. The fourth and final rule, R-TRANS allows specifications to be transitively refined.

These refinements can then be applied to any judgement on a statement, or expression, using the L-REFINE, or L-REFINEE rule, respectively. The L-REFINE rule also allows the modifies set to be enlarged.

L-REFINE	$\dfrac{m_1 \subseteq m_2 \qquad \vdash_{m_1} \{P\}\,\mathsf{s}\,\{Q\} \qquad \vdash_{m_1} \{P\}\{Q\} \Longrightarrow \{P'\}\{Q'\}}{\vdash_{m_2} \{P'\}\,\mathsf{s}\,\{Q'\}}$
L-REFINEE	$\dfrac{\vdash \{P\}\,\mathsf{e}\,\{Q\} \qquad \vdash_{\emptyset} \{P\}\{Q\} \Longrightarrow \{P'\}\{Q'\}}{\vdash \{P'\}\,\mathsf{e}\,\{Q'\}}$

Note that the L-REFINE rule subsumes the standard structural rules such as the rule of consequence and the frame rule.

Derived Assignment Rule. Before continuing, we find it useful in subsequent examples to use a simplified version of the assignment rule, L-ASSIGN, that applies when the post-condition does not mention the modified variable. This rule is as follows.

L-ASSIGN$'$	$\dfrac{\vdash \{P\}\,\mathsf{e}\,\{Q\}}{\vdash_{\{x\}} \{P\}\,\mathsf{x} = \mathsf{e};\,\{Q[x/\mathbf{ret}]\}} \qquad$ where $\mathsf{x} \notin fv(Q)$

This rule is derivable as follows.

$$\dfrac{\dfrac{\vdash \{P\}\,\mathsf{e}\,\{Q\}}{\vdash_{\{x\}} \{P * \mathsf{x} = x\}\,\mathsf{x} = \mathsf{e};\,\{Q[x/\mathsf{x}, \mathsf{x}/\mathbf{ret}]\}}\ \text{L-ASSIGN}}{\vdash_{\{x\}} \{P\}\,\mathsf{x} = \mathsf{e};\,\{Q[\mathsf{x}/\mathbf{ret}]\}}\ \text{L-REFINE} \qquad (1)$$

We observe that as x is not free in Q then $Q[x/\mathsf{x}, \mathsf{x}/\mathbf{ret}] \equiv Q[\mathsf{x}/\mathbf{ret}]$. The refinement can be derived as follows.

$$\{P * \mathsf{x} = x\}\{Q[\mathsf{x}/\textbf{ret}]\}$$
$$\implies \{\exists x.\ P * \mathsf{x} = x\}\{\exists x.\ Q[\mathsf{x}/\textbf{ret}]\} \qquad \text{(R-VarElim)} \qquad (1)$$
$$\implies \{P\}\{Q[\mathsf{x}/\textbf{ret}]\} \qquad\qquad\qquad \text{(R-Conseq)}$$

3.3   Examples

In this section we illustrate our verification system with two examples.

Simple Example. First, we consider the following simple statement that might typically be found in a linked list class: x = x.next;. We can verify this code as follows.

$$\left. \begin{array}{l} \{\mathsf{x.next} \mapsto \_ * \mathsf{x} = \mathsf{y}\} \\ \quad \left. \begin{array}{l} \{\mathsf{x.next} \mapsto n * \mathsf{x} = x\} \\ \quad \mathsf{x} = \{\mathsf{x.next} \mapsto n\}\mathsf{x.next}\{\mathsf{x.next} \mapsto n * \textbf{ret} = n\}; \\ \{x.\mathsf{next} \mapsto n * \mathsf{x} = n\} \end{array} \right\} \begin{array}{l} \text{L-FRead} \\ \text{L-Assign} \end{array} \\ \{\mathsf{y.next} \mapsto \mathsf{x}\} \end{array} \right\} \begin{array}{l} \text{L-Refine} \\ (2) \end{array}$$

If we did not have the x = x, and associated substitution we would lose the association of the field with the correct object, and thus would not be able to know that y still allows access to the field. We can justify the refinement step as follows.

$$\{\mathsf{x.next} \mapsto n * \mathsf{x} = x\}\{x.\mathsf{next} \mapsto n * \mathsf{x} = n\}$$
$$\implies \{\mathsf{x.next} \mapsto n * \mathsf{x} = x * \mathsf{y} = x\}\{x.\mathsf{next} \mapsto n * \mathsf{x} = n * \mathsf{y} = x\} \qquad \text{(R-Frame)}$$
$$\implies \{\exists x, n.\ \mathsf{x.next} \mapsto n * \mathsf{x} = x * \mathsf{y} = x\}\{\exists x, n.\ x.\mathsf{next} \mapsto n * \mathsf{x} = n * \mathsf{y} = x\}$$
$$\qquad\qquad\qquad\qquad\qquad\qquad\qquad\qquad\qquad \text{(R-VarElim)}$$
$$\implies \{\mathsf{x.next} \mapsto \_ * \mathsf{x} = \mathsf{y}\}\{\mathsf{y.next} \mapsto \mathsf{x}\} \qquad\qquad \text{(R-Conseq)}$$
$$(2)$$

Cell Class. Now we consider a slightly more complicated example involving a single class Cell and a simple program fragment containing three statements. We assume a variable, x, of type Cell in the fragment, given in Figure 2. We will verify each statement in turn before finally composing the three proofs. The first statement deals with the creation of a new

```
class Cell extends Object {
    int val;
}
...
y = new Cell;
temp = x.val;
y.val = temp;
```

Fig. 2. Example class and client

Cell object; its verification is as follows.

$$
\left.
\begin{array}{l}
\{\text{x.val} \mapsto x\} \\
\quad \{\text{x.val} \mapsto x * \text{true}\} \\
\qquad \left.\begin{array}{l}
\{\text{true}\} \\
\quad \text{y} = \textbf{new Cell}; \\
\{\text{y.val} \mapsto \_ * class(\text{y}, \text{Cell})\}
\end{array}\right\} \begin{array}{l}\text{L-New} \\ \text{L-Assign}'\end{array} \\
\quad \{\text{x.val} \mapsto x * \text{y.val} \mapsto \_ * class(\text{y}, \text{Cell})\} \\
\{\text{x.val} \mapsto x * \text{y.val} \mapsto \_\}
\end{array}\right\}
\begin{array}{l}\text{L-Refine} \\ \text{R-Frame}: \\ \text{x.val} \mapsto x\end{array}
\;\Bigg|\;
\begin{array}{l}\text{L-Refine} \\ \text{R-Conseq}\end{array}
\qquad (3)
$$

The rule R-Conseq is used to get the pre-condition into the correct form and the R-Frame rule is used to preserve the already existing field, x.val. The only variable modified is y, which is not contained in the framed assertion as required by the rule.

The second statement reads the value of the field x.val into the variable temp. It is verified as follows.

$$
\left.
\begin{array}{l}
\{\text{x.val} \mapsto x * \text{y.val} \mapsto \_\} \\
\qquad \left.\begin{array}{l}
\{\text{x.val} \mapsto x\} \\
\quad \text{temp} = \text{x.val}; \\
\{\text{x.val} \mapsto x * \text{temp} = x\}
\end{array}\right\} \begin{array}{l}\text{L-FRead} \\ \text{L-Assign}'\end{array} \\
\{\text{x.val} \mapsto x * \text{temp} = x * \text{y.val} \mapsto \_\}
\end{array}\right\}
\begin{array}{l}\text{L-Refine} \\ \text{R-Frame}: \\ \text{y.val} \mapsto \_\end{array}
\qquad (4)
$$

The L-Refine rule is used to frame the newly created field, y.val $\mapsto$ _.

The third statement can be verified as follows.

$$
\left.
\begin{array}{l}
\{\text{x.val} \mapsto x * \text{temp} = x * \text{y.val} \mapsto \_\} \\
\qquad \left.\begin{array}{l}
\{\text{y.val} \mapsto \_\} \\
\quad \text{y.val} = \text{temp}; \\
\{\text{y.val} \mapsto \text{temp}\}
\end{array}\right\} \text{L-FWrite} \\
\{\text{x.val} \mapsto x * \text{y.val} \mapsto x\}
\end{array}\right\}
\begin{array}{l}\text{L-Refine} \\ \text{R-Frame}: \\ \quad \text{temp} = x * \text{x.val} \mapsto x \\ \text{R-Conseq}\end{array}
\qquad (5)
$$

This proof uses the field update rule, L-FWrite, and L-Refine with R-Frame and R-Conseq. The R-Conseq rule is used to remove temp from the post-condition.

We can now combines these proofs using the sequencing rule to conclude as shown in Figure 3. In later examples, to reduce the redundancy in the proofs we will give only the intermediate assertions. For example, the derivation above would be presented as follows.

$\{\text{x.val} \mapsto x\}$
    y = **new** Cell;
$\{\text{x.val} \mapsto x * \text{y.val} \mapsto \_\}$
    temp = x.val;
$\{\text{x.val} \mapsto x * \text{temp} = x * \text{y.val} \mapsto \_\}$
    y.val = temp;
$\{\text{x.val} \mapsto x * \text{y.val} \mapsto x\}$

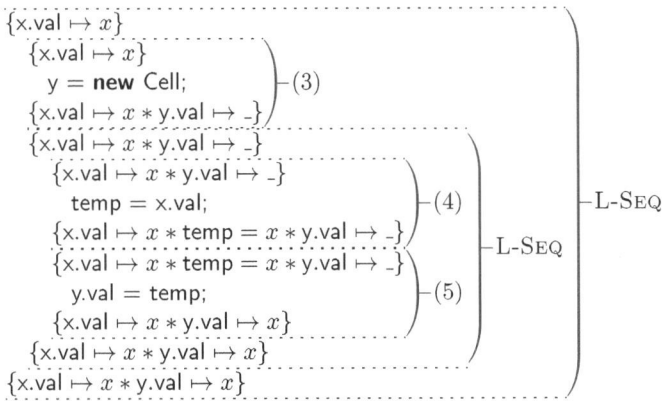

Fig. 3. Example of sequencing rule

4   Methods: Static Dispatch

Now we extend our logic to reason about methods. We split this into two sections. In this first section, we cover statically dispatched methods and illustrate the specification and verification of methods, including the handling of parameters and return values. In the following section, we address the complications of dynamically dispatched methods.

First, we need to extend our language with (statically dispatched) methods. These extensions are given below.

$L ::= \textbf{class } C: D\{\ \overline{T}\ \overline{f};\ \dots\ \overline{M}\ \}$	Class definition
$M ::=$	Method definition
$\quad T\ m(\overline{T}\ \overline{x})\ \text{Spec}\ \{B\}$	
$\quad \dots$	
$\text{Spec} ::= \textbf{static } S\ \dots$	Method specification
$S ::= \{P\}\{Q\}$	
$B ::= \overline{T}\ \overline{x};\ \overline{s}\ \textbf{return}\ e;$	Method body
$e ::=$	Expression
$\quad \dots$	
$\quad y.C::m(\overline{z})$	Direct method invocation
$\quad \dots$	

Class definitions can now contain method definitions. We make the simplifying assumption that all methods return values, i.e. we do not support void methods. This can be easily simulated using a distinguished class void and returning the null object.

All methods are annotated with a specification, written **static** $\{P\}\{Q\}$. The specification may contain occurrences of the distinguished variable, **this**, which is used to denote the receiving object. The post-condition, Q, may contain occurrences of the distinguished variable, **ret**, which is used to denote the returned value. Again, to simplify the presentation (but with no loss of expressive power) we assume that all method bodies are written in a stylized manner, where all local variables are declared before the statements, and all method bodies end with a return statement (the only occurrence of a return in the method body). We require static invocations of methods to give both the class name and the method name, e.g. y.C::m(z). We shall refer to C::m as a *static method descriptor* or, more simply, method descriptor when it is clear from context that we are referring to a statically dispatched method.

Clearly we need the method specifications to hand when verifying statements. Thus we need to extend our judgements to include an environment containing method specifications. A judgement is written as follows.

$$\Gamma \vdash_m \{P\}\bar{s}\{Q\}$$

This can be read: given a method environment, Γ, the program, $\bar{s}$, satisfies the specification $\{P\}\{Q\}$ and modifies local variables contained in the set m.

Whilst a method environment can informally be thought of as a map from a method descriptor to a specification, it is actually a little more complicated as we need to deal with instances of the this variable in the specification and also the substitution of actual arguments for formal parameters. For example, consider the following class definition fragment.

class C {

...

T m (T1 x1, ..., Tn xn) **static** $\{P\}\{Q\}$ {

...

}
}

In the specification of m there are occurrences of the variable this and of the formal parameters x1, ..., xn. However, in any invocation of m we know both the receiver and all the arguments. Indeed, because of the syntactic simplifications in our core language these will all be variables. In other words, any static invocation is of the form y.C::m(z1, ..., zn). Thus we are interested in the specification $\{P[y/\text{this}, \bar{z}/\bar{x}]\}\{Q[y/\text{this}, \bar{z}/\bar{x}]\}$.

Rather than having these substitutions explicit in several verification rules, we deal with them once and for all in the definition of a method environment. More precisely, we treat a method environment as a curried function; a map from method descriptor to a map from a pair $(y, \bar{w})$ where y is the receiver and $\bar{w}$ are the actual arguments, to a specification.

Thus a method environment, Γ, representing the code fragment above would satisfy the following.

$$\Gamma(\text{C::m})(y, \bar{z}) = \{P[y/\text{this}, \bar{z}/\bar{x}]\}\{Q[y/\text{this}, \bar{z}/\bar{x}]\}$$

Now we can give the rule for verifying statically dispatched method invocation. As expected, it is essentially the same as the standard function call rule of Reynolds [13] and is as follows.

L-CALL $\qquad\qquad$ $\Gamma \vdash \{P * y \neq \mathbf{null}\} y.\mathsf{C}::\mathsf{m}(\overline{w})\{Q\}$
$$\text{where } \Gamma(\mathsf{C}::\mathsf{m})(y, \overline{w}) = \{P\}\{Q\}$$

The method call rule states that if the pre-condition of C::m holds, then the post-condition will hold after the call. Implicitly, Γ updates the specification to use the receiver and the actual arguments. We assume the language is well-typed and thus the type system will ensure that the value of y is a subtype of C.

Let us consider a use of this rule. We assume that the Cell's get method has the following specification:

$$\Gamma(\mathsf{Cell}::\mathsf{get})(y) = \{y.\mathsf{val} \mapsto x\}\{y.\mathsf{val} \mapsto x * \mathbf{ret} = x\}$$

We can verify a call to this method as follows:

$$\left.\begin{array}{l} \{y.\mathsf{val} \mapsto x\} \\ \quad \mathsf{t} = \{y.\mathsf{val} \mapsto x\} y.\mathsf{Cell}::\mathsf{get}()\{y.\mathsf{val} \mapsto x * \mathbf{ret} = x\}; \\ \{y.\mathsf{val} \mapsto x * \mathsf{t} = x\} \end{array}\right\} \begin{array}{l} \text{L-CALL} \\ \text{L-ASSIGN}' \end{array} \qquad (6)$$

Finally, we consider verifying that a method meets its static specification. We define a new judgement, written $\Gamma \vdash_C \mathsf{M}$, where Γ is a method environment, M is the method definition and C is the class in which the method is defined. The rule for verifying a method is as follows.

$$\frac{\Gamma \vdash \{R\}\mathsf{e}\,[\overline{y}/\overline{x}]\{Q\} \qquad \overline{y} \notin fv(P, Q, \overline{s})}{\Gamma \vdash_{\{\overline{y}, \overline{w}\}} \{P * \overline{x} = \overline{y} * \overline{w} = default(\overline{\mathsf{T}}_2)\}\overline{s}\,[\overline{y}/\overline{x}]\{R\}}{\Gamma \vdash_C \mathsf{T}\,\mathsf{m}(\overline{\mathsf{T}}_1\,\overline{x})\,\mathbf{static}\,\{P\}\{Q\}\,\{\overline{\mathsf{T}}_2\,\overline{w};\,\overline{s}\,\mathbf{return}\,\mathsf{e};\}}$$

To verify the method body we must replace the formal parameters with fresh variables. This is because in Java/C$^\sharp$-like languages the method body can modify the formal parameters but these changes are not visible outside the method body. We also assume that the local variables $\overline{w}$ have been initialised with a default constant (we use an auxiliary function, *default*, that returns a default constant for a given type. For our simple core language, it simply maps type int to the value 0, and all other types to the **null** constant.)

Let us consider a very simple example that shows this rule in action. Let M be the following method definition:

int m(Cell x) **static** $\{\mathsf{x.val} \mapsto x\}$ $\{\mathsf{x.val} \mapsto x * \mathbf{ret} = x\}$
$\{$ **int** t; t = x.Cell::get(); **return** t; $\}$

We can verify this method definition as follows.

$$\frac{\Gamma \vdash_{\{\mathsf{t},\mathsf{y}\}} \{\mathsf{x.val} \mapsto x * y = x * \mathsf{t} = 0\}\mathsf{t} = y.\mathsf{Cell}::\mathsf{get}();\{\mathsf{x.val} \mapsto x * \mathsf{t} = x\}}{\Gamma \vdash \{\mathsf{x.val} \mapsto x * \mathsf{t} = x\}\mathsf{t}\{\mathsf{x.val} \mapsto x * \mathbf{ret} = x\}}{\Gamma \vdash_C \mathsf{M}}$$

The verification of the method body is as follows

$$
\left.
\begin{array}{l}
\{\mathsf{x.val} \mapsto x * \mathsf{y} = \mathsf{x} * \mathsf{t} = 0\} \\
\quad \{\mathsf{y.val} \mapsto x\} \\
\qquad \mathsf{t} = \mathsf{y.Cell{::}get()}; \\
\quad \{\mathsf{y.val} \mapsto x * \mathsf{t} = x\} \\
\{\mathsf{x.val} \mapsto x * \mathsf{t} = x\}
\end{array}
\right\} \text{--(6)} \;\; \text{--L-Refine}
$$

The L-REFINE step uses both R-FRAME and R-CONSEQ.

5   Methods: Dynamic Dispatch

In this section we consider adding what one might consider to be the essence of object-oriented programming: the dynamic dispatch of (overridden) methods.

e ::=	Expression
. . .	
$\mathsf{y.m}(\overline{\mathsf{z}})$	Dynamic method invocation
M ::=	Method definition
. . .	
override T m($\overline{\mathsf{T}}$ $\overline{\mathsf{x}}$) Spec {B}	Overridden method
Spec ::= **static** S **dynamic** S	Method specification

We extend expressions to include invocations of methods that are resolved at runtime. We refer to this as dynamic method invocation and write it using the familiar dot notation, e.g. $\mathsf{y.m}(\overline{\mathsf{z}})$. Method specifications are extended to include both a static and a 'dynamic' specification. We will elaborate on the role of these two specifications in program verification further on.

To elucidate the presentation, we make two simplifying assumptions: (1) all methods that override another method must use a $C^\sharp$-style modifier **override**; and (2) a subclass must override all its superclass's methods. In practice the first is trivial to achieve. For the second, it is easy to give a default method body is that simply calls the superclass's method. Neither of these simplifications are essential but simply make the presentation of the logic more compact.

Let us return to verifying a (dynamic) method invocation, e.g. $\mathsf{y.m}(\overline{\mathsf{z}})$. The problem is that whilst we know the static type of y, C say, all we know about the method body that will be invoked is that it is either defined in class C, inherited from a superclass of C or, more problematically, defined in some subclass of C. So how do we verify the method call? One possibility would be to consider all possible subclasses at every such method call site but this would imply that every time we extend the program with a new class, we would have to redo every proof that involves a superclass of that new class. This would render our verification non-modular. Instead we use behavioural subtyping [14], and impose semantic constraints on subclasses to ensure a modular proof system.

One novel aspect of our treatment of behavioural subtyping is that we require *two* specifications for each method. A method now has the following form.

```
class C {
...
T m (T1 x1, ..., Tn xn)
static {Ps}{Qs} dynamic {Pd}{Qd} {
...
}
}
```

The first specification, $\{P_s\}\{Q_s\}$, is intended to describe the static behaviour of the method. The second, $\{P_d\}\{Q_d\}$, is intended to specify the behaviour that it and all its subclasses must obey.

We write η to range over method descriptors, which is either a dynamic method descriptor, written C.m, or a static method descriptor, written C::m. Method environments are now extended to map both dynamic and static method descriptors to specifications. Thus, a method environment, Γ, representing the code fragment above would satisfy the following.

$$\Gamma(\mathsf{C::m})(\mathsf{y}, \bar{\mathsf{z}}) = \{P_s[\mathsf{y}/\mathsf{this}, \bar{\mathsf{z}}/\bar{\mathsf{x}}]\}\{Q_s[\mathsf{y}/\mathsf{this}, \bar{\mathsf{z}}/\bar{\mathsf{x}}]\}$$
$$\Gamma(\mathsf{C.m})(\mathsf{y}, \bar{\mathsf{z}}) = \{P_d[\mathsf{y}/\mathsf{this}, \bar{\mathsf{z}}/\bar{\mathsf{x}}]\}\{Q_d[\mathsf{y}/\mathsf{this}, \bar{\mathsf{z}}/\bar{\mathsf{x}}]\}$$

Our rule for verifying a dynamically dispatched method call is as follows.

L-DYNCALL	$\Gamma \vdash \{P * \mathsf{y} \neq \mathbf{null}\}\mathsf{y.m}(\overline{\mathsf{w}})\{Q\}$
	where y has static type C and $\Gamma(\mathsf{C.m})(\mathsf{y}, \overline{\mathsf{w}}) = \{P\}\{Q\}$.

The rule is very similar to the statically dispatched rule. The only difference is it uses the dynamic specification rather than the static specification (albeit using the static type of the receiver).

To ensure behavioural subtyping, we must clearly require that every subclass satisfies the superclass's specifications. Rather than checking a method body against the specifications of all its superclasses, we use refinement between the specifications. We often need to introduce some type information in specification refinement. To do so, we define a convenient shorthand extending the refinement judgement given earlier.

$$\vdash_m \{P_1\}\{Q_1\} \overset{R}{\Longrightarrow} \{P_2\}\{Q_2\} \quad \overset{\text{def}}{=} \quad \vdash_m \{P_1\}\{Q_1\} \Longrightarrow \{P_2 * R\}\{Q_2\}$$

We define the rules for verifying a method body. We give two rules, one for new methods, and one for overridden methods.

L-NewMethod

$$\dfrac{\vdash_{\overline{\emptyset}} \{P\}\{Q\} \overset{class(\mathbf{this},C)}{\Longrightarrow} S_C \qquad \overline{y} \notin fv(P,Q,\overline{s})}{\Gamma \vdash_{\overline{y}\cup\overline{w}} \{P * \overline{x}=\overline{y} * \overline{w}=default(\overline{T}_2)\}\overline{s}\,[\overline{y}/\overline{x}]\{R\} \qquad \Gamma \vdash \{R\}\mathbf{e}\,[\overline{y}/\overline{x}]\{Q\}}{\Gamma \vdash_C T\ m(\overline{T}_1\ \overline{x})\ \mathbf{static}\ \{P\}\{Q\}\ \mathbf{dynamic}\ S_C\ \{\overline{T}_2\,\overline{w};\,\overline{s}\ \mathbf{return}\ \mathbf{e};\}}$$

L-OverrideMethod

$$\dfrac{\vdash_{\overline{\emptyset}} \{P\}\{Q\} \overset{class(\mathbf{this},C)}{\Longrightarrow} S_C \qquad \vdash_{\overline{\emptyset}} S_C \Longrightarrow S_D \qquad \overline{y} \notin fv(P,Q,\overline{s})}{\Gamma \vdash_{\overline{y}\cup\overline{w}} \{P * \overline{x}=\overline{y} * \overline{w}=default(\overline{T}_2)\}\overline{s}\,[\overline{y}/\overline{x}]\{R\} \qquad \Gamma \vdash \{R\}\mathbf{e}\,[\overline{y}/\overline{x}]\{Q\}}{\Gamma \vdash_C \mathbf{override}\ T\ m(\overline{T}_1\ \overline{x})\ \mathbf{static}\ \{P\}\{Q\}\ \mathbf{dynamic}\ S_C\ \{\overline{T}_2\,\overline{w};\,\overline{s}\ \mathbf{return}\ \mathbf{e};\}}$$

provided the direct superclass of C is D, and $\Gamma(D.m)(\mathbf{this},\overline{x}) = S_D$.

The rule for a new method, L-NewMethod, checks two things: (1) the body and the return expression satisfy the static specification, and (2) that the static specification, assuming the type of the class, implies the dynamic specification. The second obligation shows that the method body correctly implements the dynamic specification, when dispatched on this class. The rule for an overridden method, L-OverrideMethod, is the same as the new method rule, with an additional premise that checks the superclass's method's dynamic specification refines the method's dynamic specification.

We are now in a position to give the verification rules for a class definition and a whole program. These rules embody the mutually recursive nature of the verification.

L-Class

$$\dfrac{\Gamma \vdash_C M_1 \quad \ldots \quad \Gamma \vdash_C M_n}{\Gamma \vdash \mathbf{class}\ C: D\{\ \overline{T}\ \overline{f};\ M_1 \ldots M_n\ \}}$$

L-Program

$$\dfrac{\mathsf{specs}(L_1 \ldots L_n) \vdash L_1 \quad \ldots \quad \mathsf{specs}(L_1 \ldots L_n) \vdash L_n}{\vdash L_1 \ldots L_n}$$

To verify a class definition, $\Gamma \vdash L$, we assume the method calls satisfy Γ, and we verify that each method body in the class definition satisfies its specification. To verify a program, we assume method calls for all the classes satisfy their specification, and show that under these assumptions all the method bodies satisfy their specifications. We extract all the method specifications from a program as follows.

$$\mathsf{specs}(\mathbf{class}\ C: D\{\ \overline{T}\ \overline{f};\ M_1 \ldots M_n\ \}) \overset{def}{=} \mathsf{specs}_C(M_1), \ldots, \mathsf{specs}_C(M_n)$$

$$\mathsf{specs}(L_1 \ldots L_n) \overset{def}{=} \mathsf{specs}(L_1), \ldots, \mathsf{specs}(L_n)$$

$$\mathsf{specs}_C(T\ m(\overline{T}_1\ \overline{x})\ \mathbf{static}\ S_s\ \mathbf{dynamic}\ S_d\ \{B\})$$
$$\overset{def}{=} \mathsf{spec}_{C::m(\overline{x})}(S_s), \mathsf{spec}_{C.m(\overline{x})}(S_d)$$

$$\mathsf{spec}_{\eta(\overline{x})}(S) \overset{def}{=} \lambda\eta'. \begin{cases} \lambda(y,\overline{z}).\ S[y/\mathbf{this},\overline{z}/\overline{x}] & \text{if } \eta = \eta' \\ \text{undefined} & \text{otherwise} \end{cases}$$

We write Γ_1, Γ_2 to denote partial function composition, defined as follows.

$$(\Gamma_1, \Gamma_2) \overset{def}{=} \lambda\eta. \begin{cases} \Gamma_1(\eta) & \text{if } \Gamma_1(\eta) \text{ defined} \\ \Gamma_2(\eta) & \text{otherwise} \end{cases}$$

```
class Cell {                                    class Recell : Cell {
  int val;                                        int bak;

    void set(int x)                                 override void set(int x)
      static { this.val ↦_ }                          static { this.val ↦o * this.bak ↦_ }
        { this.val ↦x }                                 { this.val ↦x * this.bak ↦o }
      dynamic S_c                                     dynamic S_r
    { this.val = x; }                               {
                                                      int tmp;
    int get()                                         tmp = this.Cell::get();
      static { this.val ↦v }                          this.bak = tmp;
        { this.val ↦v * ret=v }                       this.Cell::set(x);
      dynamic ...                                    }
    { return this.val; }                            ...
}                                               }
```

Fig. 4. Example of subclassing and the challenge of finding the right dynamic specifications

5.1   The Need for Abstraction

In the rest of this section, we show that we cannot write suitable dynamic specifications without some mechanism for abstraction.

Consider the example in Figure 4 of two classes, Cell and Recell, taken from Abadi and Cardelli [15]. The first class, Cell has a value field, which can be updated by the set and retrieved by the get method. The second class, Recell, extends this class by adding a backup field, which stores the previous value that the class was set with. This is one of the simplest examples of inheritance.

We can give static specifications that precisely describe both classes' behaviour. However, giving dynamic specifications is more challenging as they must satisfy behavioural subtyping:

$$\vdash_\emptyset S_c \Longrightarrow S_r. \tag{7}$$

Next we consider some possible dynamic specifications for the set methods.

Attempt 1. First let us simply reuse the Cell's static specification for the dynamic one:

$S_c = \{ \text{this.val} \mapsto_- \} \{\text{this.val} \mapsto x\}$

This does not work: the Recell class requires the bak field to exist in the heap, but the pre-condition of S_c does not imply this. We cannot find a specification S_r such that it is satisfied by the method body and, in addition, satisfies (7).

To prove such a specification cannot exist we can do a proof by contradiction. Assume we can find a solution to S_r. Now the following proof outline will be sound in our logic:

Cell c;

...
$\{\ class(\mathsf{c}, \mathsf{Recell}) * \mathsf{c}.\mathsf{val} \mapsto 2 * \mathsf{c}.\mathsf{bak} \mapsto 1\ \}$
  $\{\ \mathsf{c}.\mathsf{val} \mapsto 2\ \}$
    $\mathsf{c}.\mathsf{set}(3);$
  $\{\ \mathsf{c}.\mathsf{val} \mapsto 3\ \}$
$\{\ class(\mathsf{c}, \mathsf{Recell}) * \mathsf{c}.\mathsf{val} \mapsto 3 * \mathsf{c}.\mathsf{bak} \mapsto 1\ \}$ ✗

Here we use the frame rule to infer the **bak** field is unchanged. If we consider the execution of the program, it will end in a state where $\mathsf{c}.\mathsf{bak} \mapsto 2$. Thus, we have a contradiction. The only assumption we have made is that there exists a solution to S_r, so this cannot be true. Thus, we need a better dynamic specification, S_c, for **Cell**.

Attempt 2. We can restrict the dynamic specification to only apply to the **Cell** class:

$S_c = \{\ class(\textbf{this}, \mathsf{Cell}) * \textbf{this}.\mathsf{val} \mapsto \_\ \}\ \{\ class(\textbf{this}, \mathsf{Cell}) * \textbf{this}.\mathsf{val} \mapsto \mathsf{x}\ \}$

This specification only describes what happens for the **Cell** class. Thus the previous problem of implicitly specifying that the **bak** field in the **Recell** class is unmodified by the **set** method does not occur.

We can then give **Recell** a specification that is satisfied by its method body and also satisfies (7):

$S_r = \{(class(\textbf{this}, \mathsf{Cell}) * \textbf{this}.\mathsf{val} \mapsto \_) \lor (class(\textbf{this}, \mathsf{Recell}) * \textbf{this}.\mathsf{val} \mapsto v * \textbf{this}.\mathsf{bak} \mapsto \_)\}$
$\quad \{(class(\textbf{this}, \mathsf{Cell}) * \textbf{this}.\mathsf{val} \mapsto \mathsf{x}) \lor (class(\textbf{this}, \mathsf{Recell}) * \textbf{this}.\mathsf{val} \mapsto \mathsf{x} * \textbf{this}.\mathsf{bak} \mapsto v)\}$

The specification behaves like the **Cell**'s static specification if it is a **Cell** and like **Recell**'s static specification if it is a **Recell**. We can prove it is a valid behavioural subtype as follows:

$$\left\{ \begin{array}{l} (class(\textbf{this}, \mathsf{Cell}) * \textbf{this}.\mathsf{val} \mapsto \_) \lor \\ \left(\begin{array}{l} class(\textbf{this}, \mathsf{Recell}) * \textbf{this}.\mathsf{val} \mapsto v \\ * \textbf{this}.\mathsf{bak} \mapsto \_ \end{array} \right) \end{array} \right\} \left\{ \begin{array}{l} (class(\textbf{this}, \mathsf{Cell}) * \textbf{this}.\mathsf{val} \mapsto x) \lor \\ \left(\begin{array}{l} class(\textbf{this}, \mathsf{Recell}) * \textbf{this}.\mathsf{val} \mapsto x \\ * \textbf{this}.\mathsf{bak} \mapsto v \end{array} \right) \end{array} \right\}$$
$$\Longrightarrow \qquad\qquad\qquad\qquad\qquad\qquad\qquad\qquad\qquad\qquad (\text{R-Frame})$$
$$\left\{ \begin{array}{l} (class(\textbf{this}, \mathsf{Cell}) * \textbf{this}.\mathsf{val} \mapsto \_) \lor \\ \left(\begin{array}{l} class(\textbf{this}, \mathsf{Recell}) * \textbf{this}.\mathsf{val} \mapsto v \\ * \textbf{this}.\mathsf{bak} \mapsto \_ \end{array} \right) \\ * class(\textbf{this}, \mathsf{Cell}) \end{array} \right\} \left\{ \begin{array}{l} (class(\textbf{this}, \mathsf{Cell}) * \textbf{this}.\mathsf{val} \mapsto x) \lor \\ \left(\begin{array}{l} class(\textbf{this}, \mathsf{Recell}) * \textbf{this}.\mathsf{val} \mapsto x \\ * \textbf{this}.\mathsf{bak} \mapsto v \end{array} \right) \\ * class(\textbf{this}, \mathsf{Cell}) \end{array} \right\}$$
$$\Longrightarrow \qquad\qquad\qquad\qquad\qquad\qquad\qquad\qquad\qquad\qquad (\text{R-Conseq})$$
$$\{(class(\textbf{this}, \mathsf{Cell}) * \textbf{this}.\mathsf{val} \mapsto \_)\} \{(class(\textbf{this}, \mathsf{Cell}) * \textbf{this}.\mathsf{val} \mapsto x)\}$$

We take the specification for **Recell** and add $class(\textbf{this}, \mathsf{Cell})$ using the frame rule, we can then simplify the disjunctions using the rule of consequence: only one disjunction is compatible with $class(\textbf{this}, \mathsf{Cell})$, which gives the dynamic specification for **Cell**.

The problem is the **Cell** specification is too strong: it does not allow the following client verification:

{**true**}
Cell c = **new** Recell;
{ $class(\mathsf{c}, \mathsf{Recell})$ * **this**.val $\mapsto 0$ * **this**.bak $\mapsto 0$ }
$\not\Rightarrow$
{ $class(\mathsf{c}, \mathsf{Cell})$ * **this**.val $\mapsto_-$ }
c.set(3);

We require c to be of type Cell at this dynamic dispatch call site. This defeats the point of dynamic dispatch, as we cannot treat a subclass like its superclass.

Attempt 3. By using Recell's dynamic specification from above for both classes, we can verify this client:

$\mathsf{S}_c = \{(class(\mathbf{this}, \mathsf{Cell}) * \mathbf{this}.\mathsf{val}{\mapsto}_-) \vee (class(\mathbf{this}, \mathsf{Recell}) * \mathbf{this}.\mathsf{val}{\mapsto}v * \mathbf{this}.\mathsf{bak}{\mapsto}_-)\}$
$\quad \{(class(\mathbf{this}, \mathsf{Cell}) * \mathbf{this}.\mathsf{val}{\mapsto}\mathsf{x}) \vee (class(\mathbf{this}, \mathsf{Recell}) * \mathbf{this}.\mathsf{val}{\mapsto}\mathsf{x} * \mathbf{this}.\mathsf{bak}{\mapsto}v)\}$

This kind of specification is problematic as it requires the superclass to anticipate all of its subclasses' specifications, defeating modular verification. We need to introduce an abstraction to hide the varying concrete footprints and behaviours for the different classes.

6   Abstraction

In this section, we introduce *abstract predicate families*: an abstraction that reflects dynamic dispatch directly into the assertion language of the logic. The method call x.m() does not specify precisely which method definition will be used; the receiver's dynamic type combined with the method name determine which definition will be used at runtime. We are going to reflect this into the logic with predicates. Each predicate has a family of definitions indexed by the dynamic type of the first argument.

For example, we might want the following to verify the Cell/Recell inheritance example from the previous section.

$$\forall x.\ class(x, \mathsf{Cell}) \Longrightarrow \forall v.\ (\mathsf{Val}(x, v) \Leftrightarrow x.\mathsf{val} \mapsto v)$$

This is partially specifying a Val predicate; defining it just for the Cell class. We can add further axioms later to define it for other classes, such as Recell.

We extend the syntax and semantics of the assertion language to allow these predicates. We use predicate environments, δ, as environments that map the predicate to its semantic definition. It is of type $\mathsf{PredName} \rightarrow (\mathsf{Value}^* \rightarrow \mathcal{P}(\mathsf{Heaps}))$, and at the end of the section we restrict it to a simple axiom that enables relating different arities of the predicate: this is not required for soundness, but it makes the reasoning simpler.

$$P, Q, \Delta ::= \ldots \mid \alpha(\overline{\mathsf{se}}) \qquad S, H, I \models_\delta \alpha(\overline{\mathsf{se}}) \iff H \in (\delta(\alpha)(\llbracket \overline{\mathsf{se}} \rrbracket_{S,I}))$$

The rest of the semantics from earlier is unaltered except for the addition of δ.

We extend our programming language syntax to allow a predicate family's members to be defined in a class.

L ::= **class** C: D{ $\overline{\mathsf{T}}$ $\overline{\mathsf{f}}$; $\overline{\mathsf{A}}$ $\overline{\mathsf{M}}$ }   Class definition

A ::= **define** $\alpha(x, \overline{x})$ **as** P Predicate Family Member Definition

We define a predicate family member definition as well-formed iff the body only mentions predicates under an even number of negations, the free variables of the definition P are contained in the arguments $\overline{x}$, and there are not multiple entries for a predicate family within each class. This ensures that an interpretation of the predicate definitions exists; see Lemmas 2 and 3 in Appendix A for details.

Each predicate family member definition is translated into a pair of axioms. The first axiom introduces an intermediate name for the definition (this allows classes to abstractly refer to the particular entry for that class); and the second conditionally defines the predicate family for that particular class. We refer to α as the *predicate family*, and α_C as the *predicate member*. We define the translation as follows:

$[\![$**define** $\alpha(x, \overline{x})$ **as** $P]\!]_C$
$\stackrel{\text{def}}{=} (\forall x, \overline{x} \cdot \alpha_C(x, \overline{x}) \Leftrightarrow P) \wedge (\forall x, \overline{x}.class(x, C) \Rightarrow (\alpha(x, \overline{x}) \Leftrightarrow \alpha_C(x, \overline{x})))$

preds(**class** C: D{ $\overline{\mathsf{T}}$ $\overline{\mathsf{f}}$; $A_1 \ldots A_n$ $\overline{\mathsf{M}}$ })
$\stackrel{\text{def}}{=} [\![A_1]\!]_C \wedge \ldots \wedge [\![A_n]\!]_C$

To accommodate these axioms, we extend our judgements with an additional context of assumptions about predicates, Δ:

$$\Delta; \Gamma \vdash_m \{P\}\overline{\mathsf{s}}\{Q\}$$

This can be read: given the predicate assumptions, Δ, and the method environment, Γ, the program, $\overline{\mathsf{s}}$, satisfies the specification $\{P\}\{Q\}$ and modifies local variables contained in the set m. The predicate assumptions restrict the set of predicate environments for which the judgement must hold.

There are two key rules that must be amended given this change in judgement form. The new rule of consequence should check the entailments using the axioms about the abstract predicates. This allows us to use the definitions of the predicates whilst verifying the program.

R-CONSEQ $\dfrac{\Delta \models P \Rightarrow P' \qquad \Delta \models Q' \Rightarrow Q}{\Delta \vdash_m \{P'\}\{Q'\} \Longrightarrow \{P\}\{Q\}}$

We define $\Delta \models P$ as for all δ, if $\models_\delta \Delta$ then $\models_\delta P$, where $\models_\delta P$ is defined as $\forall S, H, I.\ S, H, I \models_\delta P$.

When we verify each class we introduce all the axioms for that class. However, we have no axioms about the other classes, so we must treat the other definitions abstractly, i.e. we must consider all possible definitions. All the other rules simply pass the context around unmodified (see Appendix B for details).

L-PROGRAM
$\dfrac{\mathsf{preds}(L_1); \mathsf{specs}(L_1 \ldots L_n) \vdash L_1 \quad \ldots \quad \mathsf{preds}(L_n); \mathsf{specs}(L_1 \ldots L_n) \vdash L_n}{\vdash L_1 \ldots L_n}$

```
class Cell {
    int val;
    define Val(x,v) as
        x.val↦v
    ...
}
```

```
class Recell : Cell {
    int bak;
    define Val(x,v) as
        Val_Cell(x,v) * x.bak↦_
    ...
}
```

```
class Recell : Cell {
    int bak;
    define Val(x,v,o) as
        Val_Cell(x,v) * x.bak ↦o
    ...
}
```

Fig. 5. Val definition for Cell

Fig. 6. Val definition for Recell

Fig. 7. Val definition for Recell with increased arity

Returning to our Cell/Recell example, we could define predicates to abstract the contents as in Figure 5 and 6. Note, that the Recell's predicate definition is independent of the particular fields used in the Cell class.

This definition is a little deficient as it does not allow the subclass's backup field to be specified. We would like to be able to expose more properties with the Val predicate for Recell. For example, we might want a definition with an additional parameter for the old value as shown in Figure 7. Hence, we allow a predicate's arity to be changed in subclasses. For simplicity we assume all predicates are defined for all arities, and that they satisfy the following axiom:[6]

$$\forall \overline{x} \cdot \ \alpha(\overline{x}) \Leftrightarrow \exists y \cdot \alpha(\overline{x}, y)$$

7   Complete Example

We now have all the logic in place to properly verify the Cell/Recell example. We will introduce a few shorthands in this section that embody some common verification idioms.

7.1   New Methods

We can now specify the Cell class's set method as in Figure 8. This is a common pattern of specification, where the static specification uses the predicate member, and the dynamic specification uses the predicate family. So we allow a notational shorthand of using $\alpha\$$ to represent the predicate member in the static specification, and the predicate family in the dynamic specification. We only allow \$ to occur on predicates where the first argument is **this**. We can then respecify the Cell's set method with a single specification given in Figure 9. The specification expands to the original pair of specifications given in Figure 8.

---

[6] In practice, more complex strategies are taken here. For instance, in jStar [12], abstract predicate families are defined on records and it allows width subtyping. Alternatively, van Staden and Calcagno [16] propose that axioms are exposed to allow casting between different predicate families.

class Cell {
   ...
   void set(int x)
     static { $\mathsf{Val}_{\mathsf{Cell}}(\textbf{this},\_)$ }
         { $\mathsf{Val}_{\mathsf{Cell}}(\textbf{this},x)$ }
     dynamic { $\mathsf{Val}(\textbf{this},\_)$ }
         { $\mathsf{Val}(\textbf{this},x)$ }
   { this.val = x; }
}

class Cell {
   ...
   void set(int x)
     both { $\mathsf{Val}\$(\textbf{this},\_)$ }
         { $\mathsf{Val}\$(\textbf{this},x)$ }
     { this.val = x; }
}

{ $\mathsf{Val}_{\mathsf{Cell}}(\textbf{this},\_)$ }
{ this.val $\mapsto \_$ }
  this.val = x;
{ this.val $\mapsto x$ }
{ $\mathsf{Val}_{\mathsf{Cell}}(\textbf{this},x)$ }

Fig. 8. Cell's static and dynamic set specifications

Fig. 9. Cell's combined set specification

Fig. 10. Cell's set method verification

Spec$^\sharp$ [7] uses a similar technique to allow specification to be used in different ways depending on context. It uses a single "polymorphic" specification for each method that is interpreted in one of two ways, one for static/direct dispatch, and one for the dynamic dispatch. A polymorphic specification is one containing a distinguished symbol, typically written "1", that is replaced with the expression $type(\textbf{this})$ for dynamic dispatch, and with the expression C for the static dispatch, where C is the defining class.

In general, a combined specification for a method in class C is translated as follows.

$$\textbf{both} \{\ P\ \}\ \{\ Q\ \} \quad \rightsquigarrow \quad \begin{array}{l} \textbf{static} \{\ P\ [_C/\$]\ \}\ \{\ Q[_C/\$]\ \} \\ \textbf{dynamic} \{\ P[\ /\$]\ \}\ \{\ Q[\ /\$]\ \} \end{array}$$

To verify the set method, we must first verify that the method body meets the static specification, and secondly verify the static specification implies the dynamic specification. The verification of the method body is shown in Figure 10. This uses the rule of consequence and the assumptions about the Val member for the Cell class.

We must also show that the static specification implies the dynamic specification; this holds as follows.

$$\begin{array}{l} \{\mathsf{Val}_{\mathsf{Cell}}(\textbf{this}, \_)\}\{\mathsf{Val}_{\mathsf{Cell}}(\textbf{this}, x)\} \\ \Longrightarrow \{\mathsf{Val}_{\mathsf{Cell}}(\textbf{this}, \_) * class(\textbf{this}, \mathsf{Cell})\}\{\mathsf{Val}_{\mathsf{Cell}}(\textbf{this}, x) * class(\textbf{this}, \mathsf{Cell})\}(\text{R-Frame}) \\ \Longrightarrow \{\mathsf{Val}(\textbf{this}, \_) * class(\textbf{this}, \mathsf{Cell})\}\{\mathsf{Val}(\textbf{this}, x)\} \hspace{2cm} (\text{R-Conseq}) \end{array}$$

We use the R-Frame rule to preserve the type assumption, $class(\textbf{this}, \mathsf{Cell})$. This enables us to freely move between the abstract predicate family and the abstract predicate member. Note that this verification can be generalised to all specifications that are created by the **both** construct.

7.2 Overriding

Next we turn our attention to the set method for Recell; the specification is given in Figure 11. This is basically the same specification as for Cell, but with the

class Recell : Cell {

   ...

   override void set(**int** x)
   both { Val\$(**this**,v,_) }
      { Val\$(**this**,x,v) }
    { ... }

   ...

}

$\{\mathsf{Val}_{\mathsf{Recell}}(\mathbf{this}, v, \_)\}$
$\{\mathsf{Val}_{\mathsf{Cell}}(\mathbf{this}, v) * \mathbf{this}.\mathsf{bak} \mapsto \_\}$
  $\mathsf{tmp} = \mathbf{this}.\mathsf{Cell::get}();$
$\{\mathsf{Val}_{\mathsf{Cell}}(\mathbf{this}, v) * \mathbf{this}.\mathsf{bak} \mapsto \_ * \mathsf{tmp} = v\}$
  $\mathbf{this}.\mathsf{bak} = \mathsf{tmp};$
$\{\mathsf{Val}_{\mathsf{Cell}}(\mathbf{this}, v) * \mathbf{this}.\mathsf{bak} \mapsto v\}$
  $\mathbf{this}.\mathsf{Cell::set}(x);$
$\{\mathsf{Val}_{\mathsf{Cell}}(\mathbf{this}, x) * \mathbf{this}.\mathsf{bak} \mapsto v\}$
$\{\mathsf{Val}_{\mathsf{Recell}}(\mathbf{this}, x, v)\}$

Fig. 11. Recell's set method   **Fig. 12.** Verification of Recell's set method

arity of the predicate increased to account for the previous value that this class maintains.

First, we must verify that the method body meets its specification. This is shown in Figure 12. The verification uses the static specification of the Cell's two methods, set and get. The verification does not need to know how the superclass has represented the $\mathsf{Val}_{\mathsf{Cell}}$ predicate; it is entirely abstract, just as the method body is itself independent of the field the Cell class has used.

We must also show the method's dynamic specification of the Cell is implied by the specification of Recell. This follows by using the variable elimination rule to hide the additional logical variable, and the consequence rule to decrease the arity of the predicate family:

$$
\begin{array}{ll}
\{\mathsf{Val}(\mathbf{this}, v, \_)\}\{\mathsf{Val}(\mathbf{this}, x, v)\} & \\
\implies \{\exists v.\ \mathsf{Val}(\mathbf{this}, v, \_)\}\{\exists v.\ \mathsf{Val}(\mathbf{this}, x, v)\} & (\text{R-VarElim}) \\
\implies \{\mathsf{Val}(\mathbf{this}, \_)\}\{\mathsf{Val}(\mathbf{this}, x)\} & (\text{R-Conseq})
\end{array}
$$

Technically, we must also show the static specification implies the dynamic specification. However, this holds by definition as we have used the **both** construct.

7.3 Inherited Methods

Next, we consider the inherited get method for Recell. Recall from earlier that to simplify the presentation, we require all methods to be overridden. We implement the overridden method by simply calling the superclass's method and returning the result. The problem facing us is the specification of get. Given that the method body clearly does not change the bak field, it seems reasonable to reflect this in the specification, yielding a stronger specification than the one in the Cell class.

class Recell : Cell {

   ...

   override int get()
   both {Val\$(**this**,v,o)} {Val\$(**this**,v,o) * **ret**=v}
   {

Cell c; **int** i;	Cell c; **int** i;	Recell r; **int** i;	Recell r; **int** i;
...	...	...	...
$\{\mathsf{Val}(c,v)\}$	$\{\mathsf{Val}(c,v)\}$	$\{\mathsf{Val}(r,v_1,v_2)\}$	$\{\mathsf{Val}(r,v_1,v_2)\}$
i = c.get();	i = c.get();	i = r.get();	i = r.get();
c.set(i);	$\{\mathsf{Val}(c,v) * \mathsf{i}{=}v\}$	r.set(i);	$\{\mathsf{Val}(r,v_1,v_2) * \mathsf{i}{=}v_1\}$
$\{\mathsf{Val}(c,v) * \mathsf{i}{=}v\}$		$\{\mathsf{Val}(r,v_1,v_1) * \mathsf{i}{=}v_1\}$	

Fig. 13. Example of difference in strength of Cell's specification with Recell's

```
        return this.Cell::get();
    }
    ...
}
```

But was this strengthening of the specification necessary? Could we not have used the specification from Cell? Unfortunately, whilst simpler, this would not work. Clients of Recell objects require a stronger specification than those for Cell objects. A simple example will illustrate the difference.

Consider the following code fragment.

```
Cell c;
int i;
...
i = c.get();
c.set(i);
```

As c is a Cell object, it is clear that the call to the set method is superfluous. We can verify this using the Cell specification. However, if c was instead a Recell object, the call is clearly not superfluous. The dynamic specification in Cell for the set method is not strong enough for us to show this different behaviour for Recell objects. Thus we need to define a stronger specification for the set method in the Recell class. Figure 13 shows these different cases side-by-side which highlights the difference.

Now we are happy with the specification for the get method for Recell, let us check that it is actually correct! First, we verify that the dynamic specification satisfies our behavioural subtyping requirement. This follows in an almost identical manner to the set method.

$$\{\mathsf{Val}(\mathbf{this}, v, o)\}\{\mathsf{Val}(\mathbf{this}, v, o) * \mathbf{ret}{=}v\}$$
$$\implies \{\exists o.\, \mathsf{Val}(\mathbf{this}, v, o)\}\{\exists o.\, \mathsf{Val}(\mathbf{this}, v, o) * \mathbf{ret}{=}v\} \qquad \text{(R-VarElim)}$$
$$\implies \{\mathsf{Val}(\mathbf{this}, v)\}\{\mathsf{Val}(\mathbf{this}, v) * \mathbf{ret}{=}o\} \qquad \text{(R-Conseq)}$$

We must also verify the method body meets the static specification. Importantly, the frame rule is used to preserve the bak field. As the body is just the super call, this verification is simply a specification refinement: the superclass's static specification should imply the subclass's static specification:

$$\{\mathsf{Val}_{\mathsf{Cell}}(\mathbf{this}, v)\}\{\mathsf{Val}_{\mathsf{Cell}}(\mathbf{this}, v) * \mathbf{ret}{=}v\}$$
$$\implies \{\mathsf{Val}_{\mathsf{Cell}}(\mathbf{this}, v) * \mathbf{this}.\mathsf{bak}{\mapsto}o\}\{\mathsf{Val}_{\mathsf{Cell}}(\mathbf{this}, v) * \mathbf{ret}{=}v * \mathbf{this}.\mathsf{bak}{\mapsto}o\}(\text{R-Frame})$$
$$\implies \{\mathsf{Val}_{\mathsf{Recell}}(\mathbf{this}, v, o)\}\{\mathsf{Val}_{\mathsf{Recell}}(\mathbf{this}, v, o) * \mathbf{ret}{=}v\}\qquad\qquad(\text{R-Conseq})$$

It is convenient to use a shorthand for methods whose body consists only of a direct call to the superclass method. We introduce a new modifier and simply write **inherit int** get() along with the specifications and drop the **override** modifier and method body.

7.4   Constructors

Earlier we claimed that constructors can be encoded using two operations: object creation and object initialisation. In this section we shall show how our logic is sufficiently powerful to support this encoding. For example, a call to the constructor method of the Cell class can be encoded as follows:

$$x = \mathbf{new}\ \mathsf{Cell}(v); \qquad \rightsquigarrow \qquad \begin{array}{l} x = \mathbf{new}\ \mathsf{Cell};\\ x.{<}\mathsf{initCell}{>}(v); \end{array}$$

The constructor body can be translated into an initialisation method as follows:

```
Cell(int x)                    <initCell>(int x)
both { true }                  static {fieldsCell(this)} { ValCell(this,x) }
  { Val$(this,x) }             dynamic {fieldsCell(this) * class(this, Cell) } { Val(this,x) }
{                        ⤳    {
  super();                       this.Object::<initObject>();
  this.val = x;                  this.val = x;
}                              }
```

Here we use the $ notation to allow the call to be specified differently from the point of view of a subclass calling its parent's constructor during its own construction, and when the object is created externally. The static specification is used for the recursive construction, and the dynamic specification for creating a new object. Note we use *class*(**this**, Cell) in the dynamic specification to prevent this being called on any subtype of the object.[7]

We can verify each call site meets the dynamic specification given to the constructor. We can see this by verifying a translated call, given in Figure 14. The client proof is independent of the definition of the fields$_{\mathsf{Cell}}$, and thus does not need to know it.

Implicitly in each class we define a predicate to represent the fields that class defines, and abstractly inherits the superclass's fields. For the Cell class this is given in Figure 15. Note that the fields predicate member recursively contains the parent object's fields. In this case, the fields of Object, fields$_{\mathsf{Object}}(x)$.

---

[7] We have perhaps abused the static/dynamic distinction here. We need to view the initialiser being called in two different ways, and use the static for super calls, and the dynamic for other calls. The dynamic specification is not involved in behavioural subtyping as it can never be called on subclasses.

{ **true** }   **class** Cell {   { fields$_{Cell}$(**this**)}
  x = **new** Cell;   ...   { fields$_{Object}$(**this**) ∗ **this**.val ↦_ }
{ fields$_{Cell}$(**this**)   **define** fields(x) **as**   **this**.Object::<initObject>();
  ∗ *class*(**this**, Cell)}   x.val ↦ 0 ∗   { **this**.val ↦_ }
  x.<initCell>(v);   fields$_{Object}$(x)   **this**.val = x;
{ Val(**this**,x)   ...   { **this**.val ↦x }
  ∗ *class*(**this**, Cell) }   }   { Val$_{Cell}$(**this**,x) }

Fig. 14. Cell construc- **Fig. 15.** Cell implicit **Fig. 16.**   Cell   constructor
tor call   fields definition   verification

By using an abstract predicate family to represent the fields a class defines, it enables the class's representation to be confined to that class. For example, we can verify the body of the Cell's initialiser without needing to know which fields the Object class defines. The verification is given in Figure 16.

Above we showed a specific instance of the translation of a constructor and definition of the fields abstract predicate family. For a class C with superclass D its constructor can be translated to an initialiser as follows.

$C(\overline{T}\ \overline{x})$
both { P } { Q }
{
  super($\overline{e}$);
  $\overline{s}$;
}

⤳

<initC>($\overline{T}\ \overline{x}$)
static {fields$_C$(**this**) ∗ P } { Q[$_C$/$] }
dynamic {fields$_C$(**this**) ∗ *class*(**this**, C) ∗ P } { Q[/$] }
{
  this.D::<initD>($\overline{e}$);
  $\overline{s}$;
}

The translation adds the fields to the pre-conditions of both specifications, and the type restriction to the dynamic specification. In the post-conditions it replaces the $ with the appropriate predicates. The implicit definition for the fields predicate member for this class would be:

class C : D {
  $T_1\ f_1$; ... $T_n\ f_n$;
  define fields(x) **as** x.f_1 ↦ $default(T_1)$ ∗ ... ∗ x.f_n ↦ $default(T_n)$ ∗ fields$_D$(x)
  ...
}

7.5   Further Examples

The complete, fully specified Cell/Recell example is given in Figure 17. This relatively simple example was chosen deliberately to illuminate the precise details of our techniques, but they are by no means limited to such simple cases. More complex examples of inheritance patterns have been given by Parkinson and Bierman [4] and examples of design patterns by Distefano and Parkinson[12]. We

```
class Cell {                                  class Recell : Cell {
  int val;                                      int bak;

  define Val(x,v) as x.val↦v                    define Val(x,v,o) as Val_Cell(x,v) * x.bak↦o

  Cell(int x) both {}{Val$(this,x)}             Recell(int x) both {}{Val$(this,x,_)}
  { super(); this.val=x; }                      { super(x); }

  int get()                                     inherit int get()
  both {Val$(this,v)}                           both {Val$(this,v,o)}
    {Val$(this,v) * ret=v}                        {Val$(this,v,o) * ret=v}
  { return this.val; }
                                                override void set(int x)
  void set(int x)                               both {Val$(this,v,_)}{Val$(this,x,v)}
  both {Val$(this,_)}{Val$(this,x)}             {
  { this.val = x; }                               int tmp;
}                                                 tmp = this.Cell::get();
                                                  this.bak = tmp;
                                                  this.Cell:set(x);
                                                }
                                              }
```

Fig. 17. Example of Cell/Recell using abstract predicate families

conclude this section presenting three short examples to illustrate more complex subclassing issues: IList, an example of optional methods; DCell, an example of a breaking change; and HCell, an example of abstracting multiple objects.

Optional Interfaces. Our first tricky example is one we dub 'optional interfaces.' This is very common; for example, in the collection class libraries in Java and .NET there is frequent use of the exceptions UnsupportedOperationException (Java) and NotSupportedException (.NET) to allow collections to only partially implement an interface.

Let us consider a simple example of an interface IList representing lists and containing two methods, contains and add. Now, consider two subtypes of IList; List and ReadOnlyList. Clearly the first class should support both methods, but we do not expect the latter to support the add method (and, if invoked, it would raise an exception). Whilst this style of partial implementation programming runs contrary to the basic approach of behavioural subtyping; the power of abstract predicate families means that it is, perhaps, surprisingly easy to support this style of programming. In this case, we define a predicate, iadd, specifically to indicate if a class supports the add method or not. The IList interface is specified as follows (as it is an interface we can only give a dynamic specification):

```
interface IList {
    bool contains (object x) dynamic {ilist(this,vs)}{ilist(this,vs) ∧ ret = x ∈ vs};
    void add(object x) dynamic {ilist(this,vs) ∗ iadd(this)}{ilist(this,x::vs) ∗ iadd(this)};
    ...
}
```

In implementations of IList we simple define the predicate iadd as true or false depending on whether the class supports addition:

```
class List : IList { ... define iadd(this) as true ... }
class ReadOnlyList : IList { ... define iadd(this) as false ... }
```

The constructor of the List class has the iadd(this) predicate in its post-condition, whilst ReadOnlyList does not. Thus a client will not be able to verify any call to add on an instance of ReadOnlyList.

This also illustrates why simply separating subclassing from subtyping is insufficient. The read only list partially implements the IList specification. Saying it is not a subtype would be too restrictive—it could not be used in place of the interface—and saying it is a subtype is too permissive—clients would then expect it to support an add method, which it does not. By allowing the specifications to represent which aspects are optional, we can maintain behavioural subtyping.

It is also important to note that we have not had to use exceptions in our specifications at all. Moreover, we can write code at the IList level without having to know which subtypes are involved. Consider writing an addAll method, which uses some form of iterator:

```
void addAll(IList l1, IList l2)
dynamic { ilist(l1, vs1) ∗ ilist(l2, vs2) ∗ iadd(l1) }
    { ilist(l1,rev(vs2) @ vs1) ∗ ilist(l2, vs2) ∗ iadd(l1) }
{ foreach(object x : l2) { l1.add(x); } }
```

This code works as long as the first list supports addition. It can be verified solely in terms of the IList interface.

Breaking Changes. The next difficult example of inheritance [4] can be seen as an extension of the first. Rather than where an instance of a class only partially behaves like an instance of its superclass, it covers the case where an instance behaves in a completely different way to an instance of its superclass. For example, consider the following class definition.

```
class DCell : Cell {
    override void set(int x) {
        this.Cell::set(x ∗ 2);
    }
}
```

Here we are declaring DCell as a subclass of Cell solely to inherit the get method. In other words, we are using inheritance as a means of reusing code.

It is clear that instances of DCell behave quite differently from instances of Cell, which is at odds with our assumption of behavioural subtyping. Nevertheless, we have observed this pattern of programming; in particular, in code arising from multiple upgrades [17].

As far as we are aware, no other approach to verifying object-oriented code can deal with such examples without breaking modularity. However, the flexibility of abstract predicate families mean that the subclass can define the Val predicate any way it chooses. In particular, it can define it as false, and thus this class vacuously satisfies the parent class's specification.

define Val(x,v) **as false**;
define DVal(x,v) **as** Val$_{Cell}$(x,v*2);

```
class HCell : Cell {
  HCell prev;

    define Val(x,v,os) as ∃p. x.prev ↦p * ListHCell(p,v::os)
    define List(x,vs) as
        ValCell(x,hd(vs)) * ∃p. x.prev ↦p *(tl(vs)=[] ? p=null : ListHCell(p,tl(vs)))

    //Constructor used internally for building lists
    private HCell(int v, HCell p)
    both {p=null ? vs=[] : ListHCell(p,vs)} {ListHCell(this,v::vs)}
    {
      super(v);
      this.prev = p;
    }

    HCell(int v) both {true}{Val$(this,v,[])}
    {
      super(0); //Super call required, but the value used is irrelevant
      this.prev = new HCell(v,null);
    }

    override int get() both{Val$(this,v,os)} {Val$(this,v,os) * ret=v}
    { return this.prev.Cell::get(); }

    override void set(int v) both {Val$(this,o,os)}{Val$(this,v,o::os)}
    { this.prev = new HCell(v,this.prev); }

    void undo() both {Val$(this,v,o::os)}{Val$(this,o,os)}
    { this.prev = this.prev.prev; }
}
```

Fig. 18. Example of abstracting multiple objects with a single predicate. Full Java/C$^{\sharp}$ expressions are used to aid readability. In the specifications, we write [] for the empty list, hd for the first element of a list, and tl for the list without the first element; and $P?Q : R$ to mean $(P * Q) \vee ((\neg P) * R)$.

Multiple Objects. For our final example of complex subtyping, we give a class HCell, a subclass of Cell, that remembers all the previous values it was set to. The code and specification are given in Figure 18.

The class represents the history by building a list with the HCell class that contains all the previously set values. The implementation treats the outermost HCell differently, to enable in-place update. The inner HCells form a non-empty list where the head is the current value, and the tail contains the previous values.

The class uses the Val predicate family from earlier, and also a new one, List, to represent abstractly the list of previous values. The two predicates represent the implementation strategy; the first node is distinguished and does not contain any data just a pointer to the list, the remaining nodes then contain the current and previous values of the cell. We give a pictorial representation in Figure 19.

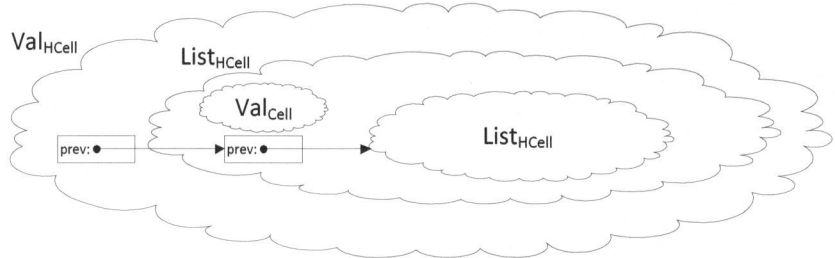

Fig. 19. Illustration of predicates used in HCell specification

This illustrates two strengths of the proof system outlined in this article: (1) we do not require the subclass to preserve the parent's representation; and (2) we can encapsulate multiple objects in a single predicate. This implementation does not use the val field to store the value returned by get() method. However, we do use the val field to store the values in the List through the Val$_{Cell}$ predicate member. The Val$_{HCell}$ predicate member contains multiple objects. By implicitly describing footprints using separation logic, we do not need to add further concepts such as ownership to provide encapsulation of multiple objects.

8   Conclusions and Related Work

In this article we have presented a simple, compact and elegant logic to reason about object-oriented programs including direct and dynamically dispatched method calls. The logic is based on separation logic, and provides a novel abstraction mechanism, abstract predicate families, that directly represents the object-oriented abstraction of dynamic dispatch in the logic. Our logic requires two forms of specification for each method: one for direct calls, and one for dynamically dispatched calls. This enables the separation of the precise specification of the details of a specific method for a particular class, from the details that all subclasses are expected to preserve due to behavioural subtyping. This combination yields a highly expressive logic that can reason about challenging inheritance patterns.

Separation logic [1, 13] was initially presented for a low-level C-like language. In this setting, pointer arithmetic makes detecting aliasing challenging. Separation logic's view of partial memories elegantly deals with the potential for aliasing and dangling pointers. This showed great promise for the low-level programming model.

The initial presentation of separation logic did not deal with programming abstractions such as modules or objects. The first work on abstraction added static modularity to separation logic [18] using a novel rule called the hypothetical frame rule. This allowed a module specification to hide some internal implementation details. This is epitomized by a memory manager that uses a free list. The module preserves the invariant that there is a free list, whilst the client of the module does not need to know the free list exists. Due to the underlying isolation provided by separation logic this state could be safely hidden from the client without complex checks for modification.

The hypothetical frame rule could only hide a single structure for a module. This did not allow for multiple structures to be encapsulated from a single module, as is required by abstract data types or object-oriented programs. Addressing this issue for abstract data types lead to the development of abstract predicates [2, 3]. Specifications are given with respect to an abstract predicate. A client can only treat the predicate abstractly, and cannot use the underlying definition of the predicate. This can then be extended to abstract predicate families to enable verification in the presence of dynamic dispatch as presented in this article.

The underlying semantics for abstract predicates can be seen as existentially quantified predicates in higher-order separation logic [19], mirroring the 'abstract types have existential types' mantra into the program logic. Many of the simplifications of our earlier work presented in this article draw on ideas from the higher-order functional setting as explored in both an ML-like language [20] and in Hoare Type Theory [21, 22].

We require two specifications for each method. This idea has occurred in several other works. Poetzsch-Heffter and Müller [23] present a logic with rules with both virtual (dynamic) and implementation (static) specifications. However, they do not explore the inter-relationship between the virtual and implementation specifications, and they do not consider how this distinction enables the inheritance of methods without reverification. The Java Modelling Language, JML [24], also has similar notions to static (known as code contracts) and dynamic specifications (known as non-code behaviour specifications). However the treatment of these specifications is different. Code contracts can be used to verify method invocations where the exact method can be statically determined. It is not used in dealing with inheritance as we have done here.

Spec[sharp] [7] only uses a single specification for each method, but it allows its specifications to be interpreted in one of two ways: one for static/direct dispatch, and one for the dynamic dispatch. The specification can contain a distinguished symbol, typically written "1", that is replaced with the expression $type(\textbf{this})$ for dynamic dispatch, and with the expression C for the static dispatch, where C is the defining class.

For separation logic, the use of two specifications for methods was independently introduced by Parkinson and Bierman [4] and Chin et al. [25]. The motivation of Chin et al. [25] was to enable more accurate verification, when the precise class is known. The logic used by Chin et al. [25] is different from the one presented here. It takes the object as the primitive unit of the heap and builds object invariants into the system. This leads to a less flexible solution than the logic we present here.

The simplicity of the ideas presented here suggest their application in *automated* verification. First steps have been taken in this direction in the jStar [12] and VeriFast [26] systems which build on the work presented in this article. Tools based on Implicit Dynamic Frames such as VeriCool [27, 28] and Chalice [29] have also used ideas from this work.

Building on our techniques, several authors have considered extensions to deal with more advanced object-oriented language features including multiple inheritance [16, 30], delegates and generics [31], and some concurrency extensions [32].

A   Soundness

Due to a lack of space, we only sketch the key details of soundness for our system. The interested reader can consult the first author's PhD thesis [3] for more details.

Before we define the operational semantics, we first define an auxiliary function, mbody, to access the (default constants for the) locals and body of a given method. If the class C contains the method definition $\textsf{T } \textsf{m}(\overline{\textsf{T}}_1 \ \overline{\textsf{x}}) \ \textsf{Spec } \{\overline{\textsf{T}}_2 \ \overline{\textsf{w}}; \ \overline{\textsf{s}}$ **return** $\textsf{e};\}$, then

$$\textsf{mbody}(\textsf{C::m}) = \lambda(x, \overline{y}; \overline{w}).\langle default(\overline{\textsf{T}}_2), (\overline{\textsf{s}} \ \textbf{return} \ \textsf{e};)[x/\textbf{this}, \overline{y}/\overline{\textsf{x}}, \overline{w}/\overline{\textsf{w}}]\rangle$$

We define a configuration as a triple containing a stack, a heap and a statement list, and include a distinguished configuration to denote erroneous configurations, which we write simply **fault**. We define the operational semantics as an evaluation relation between two configurations. First, we present the straightforward non-faulting rules:

$$(S, H, \mathsf{y.f} = \mathsf{x}; \ \bar{\mathsf{s}}) \to (S, (H.v[(S(\mathsf{y}), \mathsf{f}) := S(\mathsf{x})], H.t), \bar{\mathsf{s}})$$

$$(S, H, \mathsf{x} = \mathsf{se}; \ \bar{\mathsf{s}}) \to (S[\mathsf{x} := [\![\mathsf{se}]\!]_S], H, \bar{\mathsf{s}})$$

$$(S, H, \mathsf{x} = \mathsf{y.f}; \ \bar{\mathsf{s}}) \to (S[\mathsf{x} := H.v(S(\mathsf{y}), \mathsf{f})], H, \bar{\mathsf{s}})$$

$$(S, H, \mathsf{x} = \mathbf{new}\ \mathsf{C}; \ \bar{\mathsf{s}}) \to (S, (H.v[(o, \bar{\mathsf{f}}) := \bar{v}], H.t[o := \mathsf{C}]), \bar{\mathsf{s}})$$
$$\text{where } o \notin dom(H.t), \ \bar{\mathsf{f}} \text{ are the fields of } \mathsf{C}$$
$$\text{and } \bar{v} \text{ are their default constants}$$

$$(S, H, \mathbf{if}(\mathsf{x} == \mathsf{y})\{\bar{\mathsf{s}}_1\}\ \mathbf{else}\ \{\bar{\mathsf{s}}_2\}\ \bar{\mathsf{s}}) \to (S, H, \bar{\mathsf{s}}_1\ \bar{\mathsf{s}}) \quad \text{if } S(\mathsf{x}) = S(\mathsf{y}).$$
$$(S, H, \mathbf{if}(\mathsf{x} == \mathsf{y})\{\bar{\mathsf{s}}_1\}\ \mathbf{else}\ \{\bar{\mathsf{s}}_2\}\ \bar{\mathsf{s}}) \to (S, H, \bar{\mathsf{s}}_2\ \bar{\mathsf{s}}) \quad \text{if } S(\mathsf{x}) \neq S(\mathsf{y}).$$

$$(S, H, \mathsf{x} = \mathsf{y}_1.\mathsf{C::m}(\bar{\mathsf{z}}_1); \ \bar{\mathsf{s}}) \to (S[\bar{\mathsf{z}}_2 := S(\bar{\mathsf{z}}_1), \overline{\mathsf{w}_2} := \bar{v}], H, \bar{\mathsf{s}}_1\ \mathsf{x} = \mathsf{e}; \ \bar{\mathsf{s}})$$
$$\text{where } \mathsf{mbody}(\mathsf{C::m})(\mathsf{y}_1, \bar{\mathsf{z}}_2; \overline{\mathsf{w}}_2) = \langle \bar{v}, \bar{\mathsf{s}}_1\ \mathbf{return}\ \mathsf{e}; \rangle$$
$$\text{and } \bar{\mathsf{z}}_2 \overline{\mathsf{w}}_2 \text{ are all distinct, and } S(\mathsf{y}_1) \neq \mathbf{null}, \text{ and } \bar{\mathsf{z}}_2 \overline{\mathsf{w}}_2 \cap dom(S) = \emptyset$$

For the operational semantics of dynamic dispatch, we assume that the static type of the receiver of a method is provided as an annotation: $\mathsf{x} = \mathsf{y_C.m}(\bar{\mathsf{z}});$. (This simplifies our presentation in that we do not need to formulate a type system for our language, prove type soundness for the type system, and restrict our arguments to well-typed programs.) The reduction of a method assumes the static type is respected:

$$(S, H, \mathsf{x} = \mathsf{y_C.m}(\bar{\mathsf{z}}); \ \bar{\mathsf{s}}) \to (S, H, \mathsf{x} = \mathsf{y.D::m}(\bar{\mathsf{z}}); \bar{\mathsf{s}})$$
$$\text{where } H.t(S(\mathsf{y})) = \mathsf{D} \text{ and } \mathsf{D} \text{ is a subtype of } \mathsf{C}.$$

This is used to encode the type system information that is required for the dynamic dispatch rule. If the program executes in a way that does not respect this static type information, we consider the reduction stuck. There are many other configurations that are stuck, for instance if a program variable is not in the stack. The program logic does not prevent the program getting stuck, a type system should be used to rule out these types of errors. Note that, we do not consider issues of varying sized fields, and thus do not add constraints on the field assignment rule to check the value fits in the field.

Finally, we give the operational rules for the errors that the program logic can prevent; accessing a field that is not in the heap, and calling a method on the null constant.

$$(S, H, \mathsf{y.f} = \mathsf{x}) \to \mathsf{fault} \qquad \text{if } (S(\mathsf{y}), \mathsf{f}) \notin dom(H.v)$$
$$(S, H, \mathsf{x} = \mathsf{y.f}) \to \mathsf{fault} \qquad \text{if } (S(\mathsf{y}), \mathsf{f}) \notin dom(H.v)$$
$$(S, H, \mathsf{x} = \mathsf{y_C.m}(\bar{\mathsf{z}})) \to \mathsf{fault} \qquad \text{if } S(\mathsf{y}) = \mathbf{null}$$
$$(S, H, \mathsf{x} = \mathsf{y.C::m}(\bar{\mathsf{z}})) \to \mathsf{fault} \qquad \text{if } S(\mathsf{y}) = \mathbf{null}$$

We write $\to^j$ to mean j steps of the $\to$ relation, and $(S_1, H_1, \bar{\mathsf{s}}_1) \not\to$ to mean that there does not exist a configuration, $(S_2, H_2, \bar{\mathsf{s}}_2)$, such that $(S_1, H_1, \bar{\mathsf{s}}_1) \to (S_2, H_2, \bar{\mathsf{s}}_2)$. The following properties of the operational semantics are needed to show the soundness of the frame rule.

Lemma 1 (Locality).

- If $(S_1, H_1 \circ H_2, \bar{s}_1) \to^i$ *fault then there exists* $j \leq i$ *such that* $(S_1, H_1, \bar{s}_1) \to^j$ *fault*
- If $\forall j \leq i. \neg((S_1, H_1, \bar{s}_1) \to^j$ *fault) and* $(S_1, H_1 \circ H_3, \bar{s}_1) \to^i (S_2, H, \bar{s}_2)$ *then there exists* H_2 *such that* $H_2 \circ H_3 = H$ *and* $(S_1, H_1, \bar{s}_1) \to^i (S_2, H_2, \bar{s}_2)$
- If $(S_1, H_1, \bar{s}) \nrightarrow$, *then* $(S_1, H_1 \circ H_2, \bar{s}) \nrightarrow$.

Note that the final part shows that expanding the partial heap does not remove stuck states (type errors).

The key to the soundness of the system is the precise axiomatisation of the abstract predicate families. First, we require that the axioms for a single class are satisfiable. This holds fairly straightforwardly as the definitions can only mention other predicates in positive positions, i.e. under an even number of negations. This means a fixedpoint of the axioms can be found and thus they are satisfiable.

Lemma 2. *If* $\overline{A}$ *is well-formed, then* $[\![\overline{A}]\!]_C$ *is satisfiable.*

We can extend this result to the definitions for multiple classes. It is clear from the definition of $[\![-]\!]_C$ that the entries in one class cannot affect the satisfiability of the other classes. This means the independent verification of each class can be combined assuming the definitions for abstract predicate families for all of the classes.

Lemma 3. *If* $\overline{A}_1 \dots \overline{A}_n$ *are well-formed and* $C_1 \dots C_n$ *are distinct, then* $[\![\overline{A}_1]\!]_{C_1} \wedge \dots \wedge [\![\overline{A}_n]\!]_{C_n}$ *is satisfiable*

Second, we need a global constraint on methods to ensure the soundness of dynamic dispatch. We require that a method's static specification also refines all its superclasses' dynamic specifications. If a method environment, Γ, satisfies this constraint we call it *well-behaved*.

Definition 4. Γ *is well-behaved iff*

- C.m $\in \Gamma$ *iff* C::m $\in \Gamma$;
- *if* C.m $\in \Gamma$, *then* $\Delta \vdash_{\emptyset} \Gamma(C::m)(x, \overline{x}) \overset{class(x, C)}{\Longrightarrow} \Gamma(C.m)(x, \overline{x})$; *and*
- *if* C.m $\in \Gamma$ *and* D *is a subtype of* C, *then* $\Delta \vdash_{\emptyset} \Gamma(D.m)(x, \overline{x}) \Longrightarrow \Gamma(C.m)(x, \overline{x})$

If we have proved a program is correct then we know that its method environment is well-behaved.

Lemma 4. *If* $\vdash L_1 \dots L_n$, *then* $specs(L_1 \dots L_n)$ *is well-behaved.*

Finally, we can give the precise details of the semantics of triples, method environments and judgements. These judgements are bounded by the number of steps for which they are valid. As we are only considering partial correctness (safety) we do not need to consider infinite executions.

Definition 5 (Semantics of a triple). *We define* $\delta \models^i_m \{P\}\bar{s}\{Q\}$ *as*

$$\forall S_1, H_1, I.$$
$$S_1, H_1, I \models_\delta P \Rightarrow$$
$$\begin{pmatrix} \forall j \le i. \ \neg((S_1, H_1, \bar{s}) \to^j \textit{fault}) \\ \wedge \ \forall j \le i, S_2, H_2. \ (S_1, H_1, \bar{s}) \to^j (S_2, H_2, \ ) \Rightarrow \begin{pmatrix} S_2, H_2, I \models_\delta Q \\ \wedge \forall x \notin m.S_1(x) = S_2(x) \end{pmatrix} \end{pmatrix}$$

that is, for any state satisfying the pre-condition P, then the program will not fault in i steps or fewer, and moreover, if it terminates in i steps or fewer, then it terminates in a state satisfying the post-condition Q, and the variables not mentioned in m are unmodified.

Definition 6 (Semantics of single method specification). *We define a method as meeting a specification for i steps, written $\delta \models^i \{P\}C::m(\bar{x})\{Q\}$, as for distinct $\bar{x}, \bar{y}, \bar{w}, r$, if $mbody(C::m)(\textbf{this}, \bar{y}; \bar{w}) = \langle \bar{v}, \bar{s}; \textbf{return } e; \rangle$, then*

$$\delta \models^i_{\{r\} \cup \bar{y} \cup \bar{w}} \{P * \bar{x} = \bar{y} * \bar{w} = \bar{v} * r = r\}\bar{s}; \ r = e; \{Q[r/r, r/\textbf{ret}]\}$$

Definition 7 (Semantics of method environments). *We define the semantics of method environment, $\delta \models^i \Gamma$, for i steps as*

$$\forall P, Q, C.$$
$$\begin{pmatrix} \Gamma(C::m)(\bar{x}) = \{P\}\{Q\} \\ \vee \ \exists D. \ \Gamma(D.m)(\bar{x}) = \{P\}\{Q\} \wedge C <: D \end{pmatrix} \Rightarrow \delta \models^i \{P\}C::m(\bar{x})\{Q\}$$

that is, for each static method specification in the environment, the method must satisfy the specification for at least i steps; and, for each dynamic method specification in the environment, the method body from every subtype C of that class D must also satisfy the dynamic specification.

Definition 8 (Semantics of judgements). *We define the semantics of a judgement, written $\Delta; \Gamma \models_m \{P\}\bar{s}\{Q\}$, as*

$$\forall \delta, i. \ \models_\delta \Delta \ \wedge \ \delta \models^i \Gamma \quad \Rightarrow \quad \delta \models^{i+1}_m \{P\}\bar{s}\{Q\}$$

that is, for every semantic definition that satisfies the predicate assumptions Δ, if the method environment Γ is correct for i steps, then the program $\bar{s}$ satisfies its specification for $i+1$ steps.

Given these definitions we can then prove by induction on the verification rules that they are sound with respect to the semantics.

Lemma 5. *If $\Delta; \Gamma \vdash_m \{P\}\bar{s}\{Q\}$ and Γ well-behaved, then $\Delta; \Gamma \models_m \{P\}\bar{s}\{Q\}$*

Finally we can prove that the whole program meets its specification.

Theorem 1 (Soundness). *If $\vdash L_1 \ldots L_n$ then there exists δ such that $\forall i. \ \delta \models^i$ specs$(L_1 \ldots L_n)$ and $\models_\delta$ preds$(L_1 \ldots L_n)$*

B Complete Rules

L-SEXPR	$\Delta; \Gamma \vdash \{\text{true}\}\text{se}\{\text{ret} = \text{se}\}$
L-FREAD	$\Delta; \Gamma \vdash \{\text{x.f} \mapsto y\}\text{x.f}\{\text{x.f} \mapsto y * \text{ret} = y\}$
L-NEW	$\Delta; \Gamma \vdash \{\text{true}\}\textbf{new } \mathsf{C}\{\mathit{fields}_\mathsf{C}(\textbf{ret}) \wedge \mathit{class}(\textbf{ret}, \mathsf{C})\}$

L-REFINEE
$$\frac{\Delta; \Gamma \vdash \{P\}\text{e}\{Q\} \qquad \Delta \vdash_{\overline{\emptyset}} \{P\}\{Q\} \Longrightarrow \{P'\}\{Q'\}}{\Delta; \Gamma \vdash \{P'\}\text{e}\{Q'\}}$$

L-CALL	$\Delta; \Gamma \vdash \{P * y \neq \textbf{null}\}\text{y.C::m}(\overline{w})\{Q\}$
	$\qquad\qquad\qquad$ where $\Gamma(\mathsf{C}{::}\text{m})(\text{y}, \overline{w}) = \{P\}\{Q\}$
L-DYNCALL	$\Delta; \Gamma \vdash \{P * y \neq \textbf{null}\}\text{y.m}(\overline{w})\{Q\}$
	$\qquad\qquad\qquad$ where y has static type C and $\Gamma(\mathsf{C}.\text{m})(\text{y}, \overline{w}) = \{P\}\{Q\}.$
L-FWRITE	$\Delta; \Gamma \vdash_{\overline{\emptyset}} \{\text{x.f} \mapsto \_\}\text{x.f} = \text{y}; \{\text{x.f} \mapsto \text{y}\}$

L-ASSIGN
$$\frac{\Delta; \Gamma \vdash \{P\}\text{e}\{Q\} \qquad x \notin \mathit{fv}(P, Q)}{\Delta; \Gamma \vdash_{\{x\}} \{P * \text{x} = x\}\text{x} = \text{e};\{Q[x/\text{x}, \text{x}/\textbf{ret}]\}}$$

L-IF
$$\frac{\Delta; \Gamma \vdash_m \{P \wedge \text{x} = \text{y}\}\overline{s}\{Q\} \qquad \Delta; \Gamma \vdash_m \{P \wedge \text{x} \neq \text{y}\}\overline{t}\{Q\}}{\Delta; \Gamma \vdash_m \{P\}\textbf{if}(\text{x} == \text{y})\{\overline{s}\} \textbf{ else } \{\overline{t}\}\{Q\}}$$

L-SEQ
$$\frac{\Delta; \Gamma \vdash_m \{P\}\text{s}\{R\} \qquad \Delta; \Gamma \vdash_m \{R\}\overline{s}\{Q\}}{\Delta; \Gamma \vdash_m \{P\}\text{s } \overline{s}\{Q\}}$$

L-REFINE
$$\frac{m_1 \subseteq m_2 \quad \Delta; \Gamma \vdash_{m_1} \{P\}\text{s}\{Q\} \quad \Delta \vdash_{m_1} \{P\}\{Q\} \Longrightarrow \{P'\}\{Q'\}}{\Delta; \Gamma \vdash_{m_2} \{P'\}\text{s}\{Q'\}}$$

R-VARELIM	$\Delta \vdash_m \{P\}\{Q\} \Longrightarrow \{\exists x.\ P\}\{\exists x.\ Q\}$

R-CONSEQ
$$\frac{\Delta \models P \Rightarrow P' \qquad \Delta \models Q' \Rightarrow Q}{\Delta \vdash_m \{P'\}\{Q'\} \Longrightarrow \{P\}\{Q\}}$$

R-FRAME	$\Delta \vdash_m \{P\}\{Q\} \Longrightarrow \{P * R\}\{Q * R\} \quad$ where $\mathit{fv}(R) \cap m = \emptyset$

R-TRANS
$$\frac{\Delta \vdash_m \mathsf{S}_1 \Longrightarrow \mathsf{S}_2 \quad \Delta \vdash_m \mathsf{S}_2 \Longrightarrow \mathsf{S}_3}{\Delta \vdash_m \mathsf{S}_1 \Longrightarrow \mathsf{S}_3}$$

L-NEWMETHOD
$$\frac{\Delta \vdash_{\overline{\emptyset}} \{P\}\{Q\} \overset{\mathit{class}(\textbf{this}, \mathsf{C})}{\Longrightarrow} \mathsf{S}_\mathsf{C} \qquad\qquad \overline{y} \notin \mathit{fv}(P, Q, \overline{s})}{\Delta; \Gamma \vdash_{\overline{y} \cup \overline{w}} \{P * \overline{x} = \overline{y} * \overline{w} = \mathit{default}(\overline{T}_2)\}\overline{s}\,[\overline{y}/\overline{x}]\{R\} \quad \Delta; \Gamma \vdash \{R\}\text{e}\,[\overline{y}/\overline{x}]\{Q\}}{\Delta; \Gamma \vdash_\mathsf{C} \mathsf{T}\ \text{m}(\overline{T}_1\ \overline{x})\ \textbf{static } \{P\}\{Q\}\ \textbf{dynamic } \mathsf{S}_\mathsf{C}\ \{\overline{T}_2\ \overline{w}; \overline{s}\ \textbf{return } \text{e};\}}$$

L-OVERRIDEMETHOD
$$\frac{\Delta \vdash_{\overline{\emptyset}} \{P\}\{Q\} \overset{\mathit{class}(\textbf{this}, \mathsf{C})}{\Longrightarrow} \mathsf{S}_\mathsf{C} \quad \Delta \vdash_{\overline{\emptyset}} \mathsf{S}_\mathsf{C} \Longrightarrow \mathsf{S}_\mathsf{D} \quad \overline{y} \notin \mathit{fv}(P, Q, \overline{s})}{\Delta; \Gamma \vdash_{\overline{y} \cup \overline{w}} \{P * \overline{x} = \overline{y} * \overline{w} = \mathit{default}(\overline{T}_2)\}\overline{s}\,[\overline{y}/\overline{x}]\{R\} \quad \Delta; \Gamma \vdash \{R\}\text{e}\,[\overline{y}/\overline{x}]\{Q\}}{\Delta; \Gamma \vdash_\mathsf{C} \textbf{override } \mathsf{T}\ \text{m}(\overline{T}_1\ \overline{x})\ \textbf{static } \{P\}\{Q\}\ \textbf{dynamic } \mathsf{S}_\mathsf{C}\ \{\overline{T}_2\ \overline{w}; \overline{s}\ \textbf{return } \text{e};\}}$$
$$\text{provided the direct superclass of C is D, and } \Gamma(\mathsf{D}.\text{m})(\textbf{this}, \overline{x}) = \mathsf{S}_\mathsf{D}.$$

L-CLASS
$$\frac{\Delta; \Gamma \vdash_\mathsf{C} \mathsf{M}_1 \quad \ldots \quad \Delta; \Gamma \vdash_\mathsf{C} \mathsf{M}_n}{\Delta; \Gamma \vdash \textbf{class } \mathsf{C}: \mathsf{D}\{\ \overline{\mathsf{T}}\ \overline{\text{f}};\ \overline{\mathsf{A}}\ \mathsf{M}_1 \ldots \mathsf{M}_n\ \}}$$

L-PROGRAM
$$\frac{\text{preds}(\mathsf{L}_1); \text{specs}(\mathsf{L}_1 \ldots \mathsf{L}_n) \vdash \mathsf{L}_1 \quad \ldots \quad \text{preds}(\mathsf{L}_n); \text{specs}(\mathsf{L}_1 \ldots \mathsf{L}_n) \vdash \mathsf{L}_n}{\vdash \mathsf{L}_1 \ldots \mathsf{L}_n}$$

References

1. Ishtiaq, S., O'Hearn, P.W.: BI as an assertion language for mutable data structures. In: Proceedings of POPL, pp. 14–26 (2001)
2. Parkinson, M.J., Bierman, G.M.: Separation logic and abstraction. In: Proceedings of POPL, pp. 247–258 (2005)
3. Parkinson, M.J.: Local Reasoning for Java. PhD thesis, Computer Laboratory, University of Cambridge, UCAM-CL-TR-654 (2005)
4. Parkinson, M.J., Bierman, G.M.: Separation logic, abstraction and inheritance. In: Proceedings of POPL, pp. 75–86 (2008)
5. Clarke, D.G., Potter, J.M., Noble, J.: Ownership types for flexible alias protection. In: Proceedings of OOPSLA, pp. 48–64 (1998)
6. Dietl, W., Müller, P.: Universes: Lightweight ownership for JML. Journal of Object Technology 4(8), 5–32 (2005)
7. Barnett, M., Leino, K.R.M., Schulte, W.: The Spec# Programming System: An Overview. In: Barthe, G., Burdy, L., Huisman, M., Lanet, J.-L., Muntean, T. (eds.) CASSIS 2004. LNCS, vol. 3362, pp. 49–69. Springer, Heidelberg (2005)
8. Gamma, E., Helm, R., Johnson, R., Vlissides, J.: Design Patterns: Elements of Reusable Object-Oriented Software. Addison Wesley (1994)
9. Kassios, I.: The dynamic frames theory. Formal Aspects of Computing 23, 267–288 (2011)
10. Igarashi, A., Pierce, B.C., Wadler, P.: Featherweight Java: A minimal core calculus for Java and GJ. ACM TOPLAS 23(3), 396–450 (2001)
11. O'Hearn, P.W., Reynolds, J., Yang, H.: Local Reasoning about Programs that Alter Data Structures. In: Fribourg, L. (ed.) CSL 2001. LNCS, vol. 2142, pp. 1–19. Springer, Heidelberg (2001)
12. Distefano, D., Parkinson, M.J.: jStar: towards practical verification for Java. In: Proceedings of OOPSLA, pp. 213–226 (2008)
13. Reynolds, J.C.: Separation logic: A logic for shared mutable data structures. In: Proceedings of LICS, pp. 55–74 (2002)
14. Liskov, B.H., Wing, J.M.: A behavioral notion of subtyping. ACM TOPLAS 16(6), 1811–1841 (1994)
15. Abadi, M., Cardelli, L.: A theory of objects. Springer (1996)
16. van Staden, S., Calcagno, C.: Reasoning about multiple related abstractions with MultiStar. In: Proceedings of OOPSLA, pp. 504–519 (2010)
17. Bierman, G., Parkinson, M., Noble, J.: UpgradeJ: Incremental Typechecking for Class Upgrades. In: Vitek, J. (ed.) ECOOP 2008. LNCS, vol. 5142, pp. 235–259. Springer, Heidelberg (2008)
18. O'Hearn, P.W., Yang, H., Reynolds, J.C.: Separation and information hiding. In: Proceedings of POPL, pp. 268–280 (2004)
19. Biering, B., Birkedal, L., Torp-Smith, N.: BI hyperdoctrines, higher-order separation logic and abstraction. ACM TOPLAS 29(5) (2007)
20. Krishnaswami, N.R., Aldrich, J., Birkedal, L., Svendsen, K., Buisse, A.: Design patterns in separation logic. In: Proceedings of TLDI, pp. 105–116 (2009)
21. Nanevski, A., Ahmed, A., Morrisett, G., Birkedal, L.: Abstract Predicates and Mutable ADTs in Hoare Type Theory. In: De Nicola, R. (ed.) ESOP 2007. LNCS, vol. 4421, pp. 189–204. Springer, Heidelberg (2007)
22. Petersen, R.L., Birkedal, L., Nanevski, A., Morrisett, G.: A Realizability Model for Impredicative Hoare Type Theory. In: Drossopoulou, S. (ed.) ESOP 2008. LNCS, vol. 4960, pp. 337–352. Springer, Heidelberg (2008)

23. Poetzsch-Heffter, A., Müller, P.O.: A Programming Logic for Sequential Java. In: Swierstra, S.D. (ed.) ESOP 1999. LNCS, vol. 1576, pp. 162–176. Springer, Heidelberg (1999)
24. Leavens, G.T., Baker, A.L., Ruby, C.: Preliminary design of JML: a behavioral interface specification language for Java. SIGSOFT Software Engineering Notes 31(3), 1–38 (2006)
25. Chin, W.N., David, C., Nguyen, H.H., Qin, S.: Enhancing modular OO verification with separation logic. In: Proceedings of POPL, pp. 87–99 (2008)
26. Jacobs, B., Piessens, F.: The VeriFast program verifier. Technical report, Katholieke Universiteit Leuven (August 2008)
27. Smans, J., Jacobs, B., Piessens, F.: Implicit Dynamic Frames: Combining Dynamic Frames and Separation Logic. In: Drossopoulou, S. (ed.) ECOOP 2009. LNCS, vol. 5653, pp. 148–172. Springer, Heidelberg (2009)
28. Smans, J.: Specification and Automatic Verification of Frame Properties for Java-like Programs. PhD thesis, FWO-Vlaanderen (May 2009)
29. Leino, K.R.M., Müller, P.: A Basis for Verifying Multi-threaded Programs. In: Castagna, G. (ed.) ESOP 2009. LNCS, vol. 5502, pp. 378–393. Springer, Heidelberg (2009)
30. Luo, C., Qin, S.: Separation logic for multiple inheritance. ENTCS 212, 27–40 (2008)
31. Svendsen, K., Birkedal, L., Parkinson, M.: Verifying Generics and Delegates. In: D'Hondt, T. (ed.) ECOOP 2010. LNCS, vol. 6183, pp. 175–199. Springer, Heidelberg (2010)
32. Hurlin, C.: Specification and Verification of Multithreaded Object-Oriented Programs with Separation Logic. PhD thesis, Universite de Nice Sophia Antipolis (2009)

VeriFast for Java: A Tutorial

Jan Smans, Bart Jacobs, and Frank Piessens

iMinds-DistriNet, KU Leuven, Belgium

Abstract. VeriFast is a separation logic-based program verifier for Java. This tutorial introduces the verifier's features step by step.

1 Introduction

When writing programs, developers make design decisions that allow them to argue — at least informally — why their program does what it is supposed to do. For example, a developer may design a certain sequence of statements to compute the average of an integer array and may implicitly decide that this sequence should never be applied to `null` or to an empty array. A violation of a design decision then corresponds to a bug in the program. However, keeping track of all such implicit decisions and ensuring that the code satisfies those decisions is hard. This is particularly true for concurrent programs where the effect of concurrently executing threads must be taken into account to avoid data races.

To help developers manage their design decisions, certain programming languages provide a type system where developers can express decisions regarding the kind of data memory locations can hold. For example, consider the signature of the method `Arrays.copyOf` in the standard Java library:

```
public static int[] copyOf(int[] original, int newLength)
```

The types in the method signature make explicit the decision that `newLength` is an integer and that both `original` and the return value are integer arrays. The Java compiler statically checks that the code and the decisions described by the types are consistent. For example, the statement

```
int[] copy = Arrays.copyOf(true, 10);
```

is rejected as ill-typed by the compiler, as `true` is not an integer array. By checking consistency of the code and the types at compile-time, the compiler rules out certain run-time errors. In particular, if a Java program typechecks, then that program does not contain field- and method-not-found errors.

The expressive power of traditional type systems is limited. For example, while the signature of `Arrays.copyOf` expresses that the list of actual parameters must consist of an array and an integer, the requirements that the array must be non-null and that the integer must be non-negative lies beyond the expressive power of the Java type system. Instead, these requirements are included only in the informal documentation and an unchecked exception is thrown when they

D. Clarke et al. (Eds.): Aliasing in Object-Oriented Programming, LNCS 7850, pp. 407–442, 2013.
© Springer-Verlag Berlin Heidelberg 2013

are violated. Similarly, the implicit guarantee that the return value is non-null
and that it is a proper copy of `original` is documented informally, but it is
not expressed in `copyOf`'s return type. However, contrary to the requirement
described above violations of the guarantee do not give rise to an exception,
allowing erroneous results caused by a bug in the implementation to spread to
other components potentially causing these components to malfunction.

Formal verification is a program analysis technique where developers can insert assertions to formally specify detailed design decisions that lie beyond the
expressive power of traditional type systems and where consistency of these decisions and the code can be checked at compile-time by a program verifier. In
general, if a program verifier deems a program to be correct, then that program's
executions do not perform assertion violations.

In this tutorial, we describe a particular separation-logic based[1] program verifier for Java named VeriFast[2]. VeriFast takes a number of Java source files annotated with preconditions, postconditions and other specifications describing
assumptions made by the developer as input, and checks whether the assumptions hold in each execution of the program for arbitrary input. If VeriFast deems
a Java program to be correct, then that program does not contain assertion violations, data races, divisions by zero, null dereferences, array indexing errors
and the program makes correct use of the Java API. This tutorial is targeted
at users of VeriFast. We refer the reader to a technical report [4] for a formal
description of the inner workings of the tool for a small imperative language. We
compare VeriFast with related tools and approaches in Section 8.

We proceed by introducing VeriFast's features step by step. To try the examples and exercises in the paper yourself, download the VeriFast distribution from
the following website:

http://distrinet.cs.kuleuven.be/software/VeriFast

The distribution includes a command-line tool (`verifast`) and a graphical user
interface (`vfide`). The Java programs mentioned in this paper can be downloaded
from the website as well.

2   Verification

2.1   Assert Statements

A Java assert statement [5, section 10.14] consists of the keyword `assert` followed
by a boolean expression. By inserting an assert statement in the code, a developer
indicates that he or she expects the corresponding boolean expression to evaluate
to `true` whenever the statement is reached during the program's execution. If the
expression evaluates to `false`, an `AssertionError` is thrown (provided assertion
checking is enabled). As an example, consider the method `max` shown below:

---

[1] Separation logic is an extension of Hoare logic oriented to reasoning about imperative
programs with aliasing. The theory behind separation logic for Java is explained by
Parkinson and Bierman in a different chapter of this book [1].

[2] In addition to Java, VeriFast supports C [2,3].

```
class Max {
  public static int max(int x, int y)
    //@ requires true;
    //@ ensures true;
  {
    int max;
    if(x <= y)
      max = 0;
    else
      max = x;
    assert x <= max && y <= max;
    return max;
  }
}
```

The goal of this method is to compute the maximum of x and y. The assert statement expresses the developer's assumption that the variable max should be larger than or equal to both x and y. The program is well-typed, and is therefore accepted by the Java compiler. The assert statement holds when x is larger than y, but fails for example when x equals 5 and y equals 10.

VeriFast is a Java source code analysis tool. Contrary to standard Java compilers, VeriFast detects potential assertion violations (and other problems) at compile-time. To apply the tool to our example program, start the VeriFast integrated development environment (vfide), open Max.java and press the Verify button (▷). You should now see the following window:

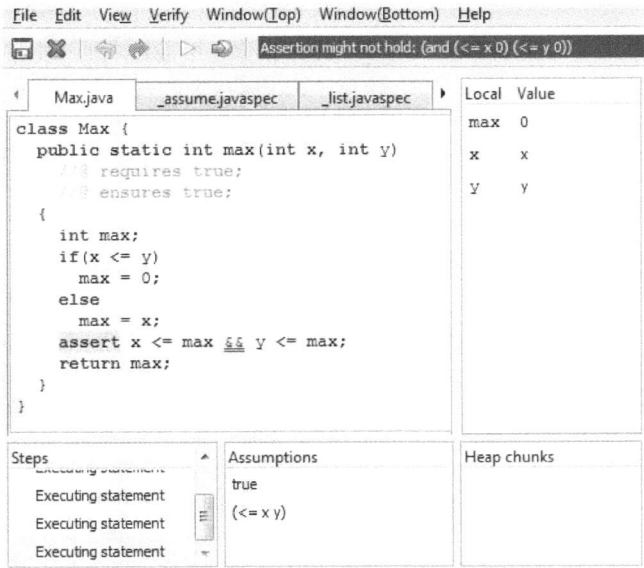

The large text box displays the source code of Max.java, the program being analysed. The body of the assert statement is highlighted in red indicating that the tool has located a potential bug in the statement. A description of the error is shown in red at the top of the window: `Assertion might not hold`. This error message indicates that VeriFast was unable to prove that the assert statement holds in each possible execution of the method. In other words, there might exist a context where execution of the assert statement fails. The other parts of the user interface contain information that can be used to diagnose verification errors as explained in Section 2.3.

To fix the bug, modify the then branch of the if statement and assign the correct value to `max`. Reverify the program. VeriFast now displays `0 errors found` in green at the top of the window, meaning that for all possible values for `x` and `y` the assert statement succeeds.

2.2   Method Contracts

The types in a method signature describe the kind of data expected and returned by a method. Each method call is then typechecked with respect to the callee's signature, not with respect to the callee's body. Therefore, typechecking is *modular*.

Performing modular analysis has a number of advantages. First of all, it is possible to analyse a method body with respect to the signature of a callee even if the callee is an interface method, the callee's body is not visible to the caller or the callee has simply not been implemented yet. Secondly, modular analysis scales to larger programs as each method body needs to be analysed only once instead of once per call. Finally, modifying the implementation of a method never breaks the correctness (e.g. type correctness in case of a type system) of its callers.

For the reasons outlined above, VeriFast performs modular verification: each method call is verified with respect to the callee's signature. However, as explained in Section 1, method signatures in traditional type systems can only express simple assumptions. Therefore, VeriFast mandates that each method signature is extended with a precondition and a postcondition. The precondition (keyword `requires`) refines the signature by defining additional constraints on the method parameters, while the postcondition (keyword `ensures`) defines additional constraints on the method's return value.

The pre- and postcondition of a method can be viewed as a contract between developers that call the method and those implementing the method body [6]. Implementers may assume that the precondition holds on entry to the method, and in return they are obliged to provide a method body that establishes the postcondition when the method returns[3]. Callers must ensure the precondition holds when they call the method, and in return they may assume that the postcondition holds when the method returns. VeriFast enforces method contracts.

As method contracts are mandatory in VeriFast, we have already annotated the method `max` in our running example with a default contract. More specifically, `max`'s current precondition is `true`, indicating that callers can pass any

---

[3] For now, we consider only normal, non-exceptional termination.

two integers for x and y. Similarly, the method's postcondition is true, indicating that the method body is allowed to return any integer. Note that method contracts — and all other VeriFast annotations — are written inside special comments (/*@ ... @*/). These comments are ignored by the Java compiler, but recognized by VeriFast.

To see that VeriFast only uses the callee's method contract to reason about a call, extend the class Max with a new method max3 that computes the maximum of three integers by calling max twice as shown below.

```
class Max {
  ...
  public static int max3(int x, int y, int z)
  {
    int max;
    max = max(x, y);
    max = max(max, z);
    assert x <= max && y <= max && z <= max;
    return max;
  }
}
```

When verifying this program, VeriFast asks us to provide a method contract for max3 (Method must have contract). To resolve this problem, annotate max3 with the same contract as max and reverify the program. The verifier now reports that the assertion in max3 might not hold. VeriFast is unable to prove this assertion because max's postcondition provides no information about its return value. According to the contract, max could potentially be implemented as return 0;, which would clearly violate the assertion if either x, y or z is larger than zero. Resolve the problem by strengthening max's postcondition to x <= result && y <= result. The variable result in the postcondition denotes max's return value. After updating the postcondition, verification succeeds.

2.3 Symbolic Execution

How does VeriFast check that a program is correct (i.e. does not contain assertion violations, null dereferences, ...)? When the developer presses the Verify button, VeriFast checks that each method in the program satisfies its method contract via symbolic execution. A method body *satisfies a method contract* if for each program state s that satisfies the precondition, execution of the method body starting in s does not trigger illegal operations (such as assertion violations and divisions by zero) and the postcondition holds when the method terminates. VeriFast only checks partial correctness so a method is not required to terminate.

The number of program states that satisfy the precondition is typically infinite. For example, consider a method with a parameter of type String. The length of the String object passed to this method is only bounded by the available memory. Moreover, execution of the method body may not terminate for certain inputs. Therefore, it is generally not feasible to enumerate all initial states satisfying the precondition and to check for each of these states that the body satisfies the contract by simply executing the body.

To verify that a method body satisfies a method contract, VeriFast uses *symbolic* instead of concrete execution. More specifically, the tool constructs a symbolic state that represents an arbitrary concrete pre-state which satisfies the precondition and checks that the body satisfies the contract for this symbolic state[4]. The verifier symbolically executes the body starting in the initial symbolic state. At each statement encountered during symbolic execution, the tool checks that the statement cannot go wrong and it updates the symbolic state to reflect execution of that statement. Finally, when the method returns, VeriFast checks that the postcondition holds for all resulting symbolic states.

A symbolic state in VeriFast is a triple (γ, Σ, h), consisting of a symbolic store γ, a path condition Σ and a symbolic heap h. The symbolic store is a mapping from local variables to symbolic values. Each symbolic value is a first-order term, i.e. a symbol, or a literal number, or an operator $(+, -, <, =, ...)$ or a function applied to first-order terms. A single symbolic value can represent a large, potentially infinite number of concrete values. For example, during verification of the method max the initial symbolic value of the parameter x is the symbol x. This symbol represents all 2^{32} possible values of x. The path condition is a set of first-order formulas describing the conditions that hold on the path being verified. For example, when verifying the then branch of an if statement, the path condition contains an assumption expressing that the condition of the if statement was true when entering the branch. Finally, the symbolic heap is a multi-set of heap chunks. The symbolic heap is the key to reasoning about aliasing and preventing data races. Its purpose will be explained in Section 3. A single symbolic state can represent a large, potentially infinite number of concrete states. For example, the symbolic pre-state of the method max represents all 2^{64} possible valuations of the parameters x and y.

When VeriFast reports an error, the symbolic states on the path leading to the error can be examined in the IDE to diagnose the problem. That is, the box in the bottom left of the IDE contains the list of symbolic states on the path to the error. When a particular symbolic state is selected, the corresponding statement or assertion is highlighted in yellow in the program. Moreover, the three components of that symbolic state are displayed: the path condition is shown in the bottom center, the symbolic heap in the bottom right and the symbolic store in the top right box. The symbolic store is a table where the left side contains the names of the local variables in scope, while the right side shows their symbolic values. One can inspect the symbolic states on a path leading to a particular statement by placing the cursor at that statement and by pressing the Run to cursor button (🔎). Similarly, the symbolic states leading to the end of the method can be examined by placing the cursor on the closing brace of the

---

[4] This is similar to universal generalization where one proves $\forall x \bullet P(x)$ by using a symbolic value x to represent an arbitrary concrete value and by showing that P holds for x.

method body and by pressing Run to cursor. Place your cursor at the closing brace of max and examine the intermediate symbolic states.

The body of each pre- and postcondition consists of an *assertion*. For now, an assertion is a side-effect free, heap-independent Java boolean expression, but we will introduce additional types of assertions in the next sections. A key part of VeriFast's symbolic execution algorithm is checking whether a symbolic state satisfies an assertion and recording the assumption that an assertion is true in a symbolic state. We call the former operation *consuming an assertion* and the latter *producing an assertion*. Consuming a Java boolean expression means symbolically evaluating the expression yielding a first-order formula and checking that this formula is derivable from the path condition. VeriFast relies on an SMT solver[7], a kind of automatic theorem prover, to discharge such proof obligations. Producing a Java boolean expression corresponds to evaluating that expression yielding a first-order formula and adding it to the path condition.

Symbolic execution of each method starts by initializing the symbolic store by assigning a fresh first-order symbol to each parameter. VeriFast selects the symbol x as the fresh term representing the symbolic value of a parameter x. Initially, the path condition and the heap are both empty. The resulting symbolic state thus represents an arbitrary concrete pre-state. To consider only states that satisfy the precondition, VeriFast first produces the precondition. The verifier then proceeds by symbolically executing the method body. At each return in the method body, VeriFast checks that the symbolic post-state satisfies the postcondition by consuming it. In the remainder of this section, we explain symbolic execution for various statements in more detail.

Assignment. Symbolic execution of an assignment to a local variable x consists of two steps. First, the right hand side is symbolically evaluated yielding a first-order term. Afterwards, the value of x in the symbolic store is changed to this first-order term. As an example, consider the method bar[5] shown below:

```
public static int bar(int x)
  //@ requires 0 < x;
  //@ ensures 10 < result;
{ x = x + 10; return x; }
```

The contract of bar states that the method's return value is larger than 10, provided x is non-negative. Symbolic execution of bar starts by constructing a symbolic pre-state that represents an arbitrary concrete pre-state by assigning a fresh symbol to each method parameter: the initial symbolic value of x is a fresh symbol x. To consider only program states that satisfy the precondition, VeriFast produces the precondition: the assumption that the symbolic value of the parameter x is non-negative is added to the path condition. Verification proceeds by symbolic execution of the method body. The assignment x = x + 10;

---

[5] To verify Bar.java, disable overflow warnings by unchecking Check arithmetic overflow in the Verify menu. In the remainder of this paper, we assume overflow checking is disabled.

updates the symbolic value of x to x + 10, encoding the fact that x's new value is equal to its original value plus ten. The return statement sets the ghost[6] variable result, which represents bar's return value, to the symbolic value of x and ends execution of the method body. VeriFast finally checks that the postcondition holds in the symbolic post-state by consuming the postcondition. The postcondition holds as the corresponding first-order formula, $10 < x + 10$, is derivable from the path condition, $0 < x$ by the SMT solver.

Assert. VeriFast checks that assert statements do not fail by consuming their bodies. That is, VeriFast checks for each such statement that its boolean expression evaluates to true by proving that the corresponding formula follows from the path condition. For example, consider the assert statement in the body of max3. The path condition of the symbolic state right before execution of this statement contains three assumptions: $true$, $x \leq max0 \wedge y \leq max0$ and $max0 \leq max1 \wedge z \leq max1$. The first assumption represents the precondition of max3 itself, while the second and third assumption respectively correspond to the postcondition of the first and second call to max. Here, the symbols max0 and max1 respectively represent the return value of the first and second invocation of max. VeriFast concludes that the assert statement succeeds for all possible values for x, y and z as the SMT solver can prove that the corresponding formula, $x \leq max1 \wedge y \leq max1 \wedge z \leq max1$, follows from the path condition.

If. In a concrete execution, the condition of an if statement evaluates to either true or false. If the condition evaluates to true, then the then branch is executed; otherwise, the else branch is taken. However, symbolic evaluation of the condition of an if statement results in a first-order formula. Based on this formula, it is generally not possible to decide which branch must be taken. For example, consider the method foo shown below.

```
public static int foo(int x)
  //@ requires 5 <= x;
  //@ ensures 10 <= result;
{
  int res = 0;
  if (10 <= x)
    res = x;
  else if (x < 5)
    assert false;
  else
    res = x + 4;
  return res;
}
```

---

[6] A ghost variable is a variable introduced only to facilitate verification but which does not exist during concrete execution of the program.

During symbolic execution of the body it is not known whether the condition of the outermost if statement, 10 <= x, holds. For that reason, VeriFast examines both branches of the if statement: the then branch (and all subsequent statements after the if statement) are verified under the assumption that $10 \leq x$, while the else branch (and again all subsequent statements) are verified assuming the negation of the condition $10 > x$. The same strategy applies to the if statement in the else branch. This tactic for dealing with branches leads to the following symbolic execution tree:

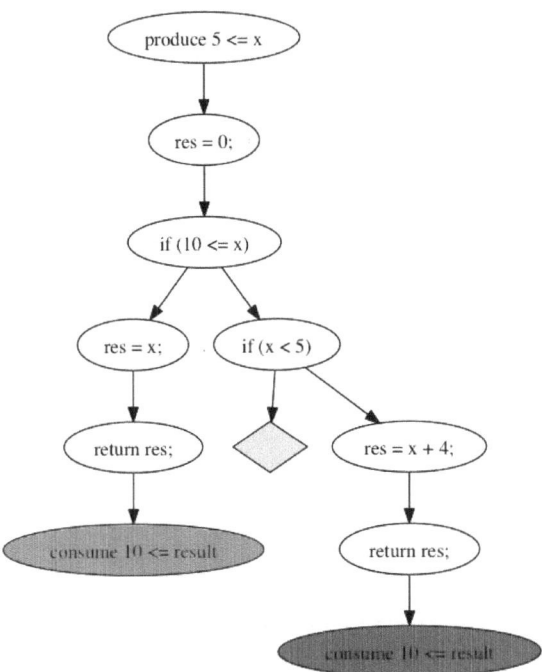

The leftmost branch of the tree corresponds to a path where the method terminates and the resulting symbolic state satisfies the postcondition. More specifically, the formula corresponding to the postcondition, $10 \leq x$, is derivable from the final path condition ($5 \leq x$ and $10 \leq x$). The diamond node represents a symbolic state with an inconsistent path condition. Such states are not reachable during concrete executions of the program. Indeed, the assert statement can never be reached as x cannot be both larger than or equal to 5 and at the same time less than 5. VeriFast does not examine infeasible paths any further. Finally, the rightmost branch of the tree ends in a verification error: a postcondition violation was detected by VeriFast. The formula representing the postcondition, $10 \leq x + 4$, is not derivable from the path condition ($5 \leq x$, $10 > x$ and $x \geq 5$). Indeed, the postcondition does not hold if x equals 5.

VeriFast traverses execution trees in a depth-first manner. Furthermore, the tool does not report all problems on all paths but stops when it finds the first error or when all paths successfully verify. The symbolic states that can be examined in the IDE are those on the path leading to the error. For our example, the IDE only displays the path from the root to the bottom right node.

Call. As explained in Section 2.2, VeriFast uses the callee's method contract to reason about a method call. More specifically, symbolic execution of a call consists of two steps: (1) consumption of the callee's precondition and (2) production of its postcondition. Both steps are executed under the callee's symbolic store. During production of the postcondition, the callee's return value is represented by the ghost variable `result`. This variable is initialized to a fresh symbol that represents an arbitrary concrete return value in the callee's symbolic store just before production of the postcondition. As an example, consider the symbolic execution tree of the method `max3`:

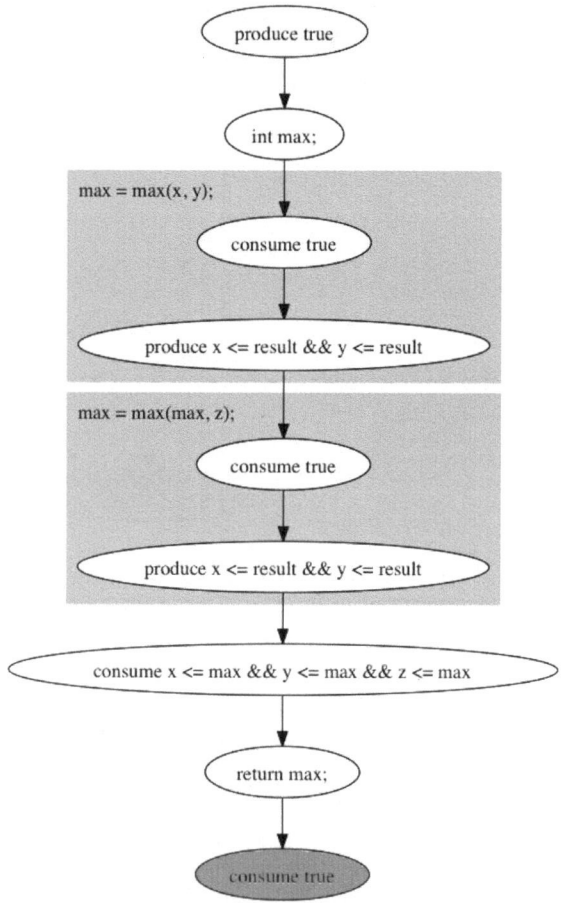

Each call to `max` is symbolically executed by consuming `max`'s precondition and afterwards producing its postcondition. To aid developers in understanding verification of method calls, the VeriFast IDE displays the signature of the callee and the callee's symbolic store in addition to the call site itself as shown below. For example, the callee's symbolic store (shown in the top right) for the second call to max maps the variable x to max0, the symbolic value returned by the first call to max.

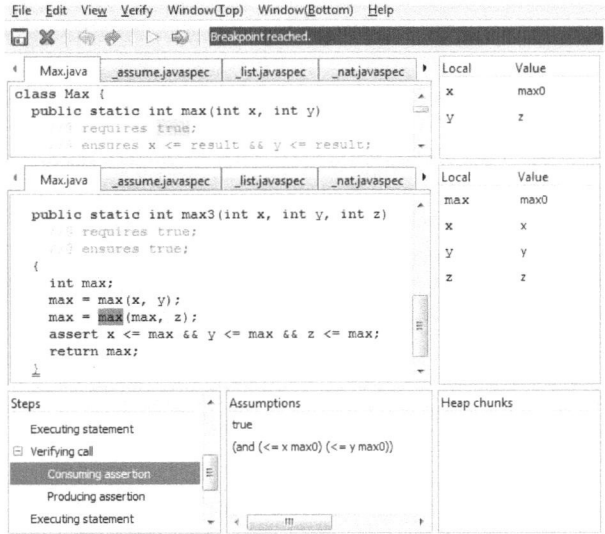

3   Classes and Objects

In a Java program without objects and without static fields, the only program state visible to a method are the values of its local variables. Local variables are not shared among activation records, meaning that a local variable can only be read and written by the method itself. In particular, it is impossible for a callee to modify the local variables of its caller. As local variables are not shared, reasoning about such variables during verification is easy: one does not need to worry that a method call will unexpectedly modify the caller's local variables or that multiple threads concurrently access the same local variable.

In Java programs with objects, the program state visible to a method consists not only of its local variables but also includes all objects in the heap transitively reachable from those variables. The set of objects reachable from distinct activation records can overlap because of aliasing. Two expressions are *aliases* if they refer to the same object. This means that one activation record can directly access state visible to another activation record. In particular, if a caller and a callee share a reference to the same object, then the callee can modify the state of that object. Moreover, if activation records in different threads concurrently access the same memory location, a data race may arise. Thus, the state visible to a method can change even though the method itself does not explicitly perform an assignment.

Modular verification in the presence of aliasing is challenging. Suppose that at a particular point in the analysis of a method the verifier knows that property P

holds for part of the heap. For example, P might state that calling a particular method of a certain object will return 5 or that some object is in a consistent state. Whenever the method performs a call, P can potentially be invalidated by the callee. Even if the method itself does not perform any calls, P could be invalidated under its feet by a different thread. To perform modular verification, VeriFast applies an ownership regime. That is, the tool tracks during symbolic execution what part of the program state is *owned* by the method, meaning that properties about that part are *stable* under actions performed by callees and by other threads.

Aliasing also complicates reasoning because it can introduce *hidden* dependencies. Suppose that at a particular point in the analysis the verifier knows that the properties P and Q hold. If P and Q involve classes that hide their internal state, the verifier does not know exactly which heap locations P and Q depend on. However, they might depend on the same heap location because of aliasing. As such whenever the method performs an operation that affects P, Q also may no longer hold. To perform modular verification, the verifier must somehow be able to deduce which properties are independent of each other. Note that a property that does not contain any direct or indirect dereferences cannot contain hidden dependencies. The set of memory locations that such a property depends on are the local variables it mentions. This set can be determined syntactically. We will refer to such properties as pure assertions.

To support modular verification in the presence of aliasing, VeriFast explicitly tracks the set of heap locations owned by the method being analysed during symbolic execution. That is, the symbolic heap is a multiset of heap chunks. Each heap chunk represents a memory region that is owned by the method. In addition to indicating ownership, the chunk can contain information on the state of that memory region. For example, the heap chunk $C\_f(o, v)$ represents exclusive ownership of the field $C.f$ of object o. The chunk additionally describes the property that the field's current value is v. Here, both o and v are symbolic values.

All heap chunks in the symbolic heap represent mutually disjoint memory regions. In particular, if the heap contains two field chunks $C\_f(o_1, v)$ and $C\_f(o_2, w)$, then o_1 and o_2 are distinct. As chunks on the symbolic heap do not share hidden dependencies, the verifier can safely assume that an operation that only affects a particular chunk does not invalidate the information in the remaining chunks.

VeriFast enforces the program-wide invariant that at any time each heap location is exclusively owned by at most one activation record[7]. Moreover, a method is only allowed to access a heap location if it owns that location. By enforcing these rules, the verifier guarantees that information about a memory region cannot be invalidated by callees or other threads, as long as the method retains ownership of that region. For example, as long as a method owns the heap chunk

---

[7] VeriFast also supports non-exclusive, partial ownership via fractions [8]. Partial ownership allows the owning method to read but not write the memory region. The program-wide invariant then states that for each heap location the total sum of fractions over all activation records is at most one.

C_f(o, v), the property that o.f equals v cannot be invalidated by other activation records, as these activation records lack the permission to assign to o.f. Conversely, if a method does not own a particular memory location o.f, then that method has no direct information on the value of that field (as that information is attached to the heap chunk). In addition, the ownership methodology ensures the absence of data races. A data race occurs if two threads concurrently access the same heap location at the same time, and at least one of these accesses is a write operation. As no two activation records can own the same memory location at the same time and hence cannot concurrently access the same memory location, such races cannot occur.

A method is only allowed to access a memory region if it owns that region. How can a method acquire ownership of a memory region? First of all, a constructor in a class C gains ownership of the fields of the new object declared in C right after calling the superclass constructor. For this reason, the constructor of the class Account shown below is allowed to initialize balance to zero. Secondly, a method can indicate in its precondition that it requires ownership of a particular memory region in order to execute successfully. Ownership of the field f of an object e1 with value e2 is denoted in assertions as e1.f |-> e2. Here, e1 and e2 are side-effect free, heap-independent Java expressions. This assertion is read as e1.f *points to* e2. For example, the precondition of deposit specifies that the method requires ownership of this.balance. Because of this precondition, the method body is allowed to read and write this.balance. The question mark (?) before the variable b indicates that the precondition does not impose any restrictions on the field's pre-state value, but binds this value to b. By naming the pre-state value, the postcondition can relate the field's post-state value to the pre-state value. Thirdly, a method can acquire ownership of a memory region by calling another method. As an example, consider the method clone. This method creates a new Account object named copy and then assigns to copy.balance. This assignment is allowed because the constructor's postcondition includes this.balance |-> 0. This postcondition specifies that ownership of the field balance of the new object is transferred from the constructor to its caller when the constructor terminates.

The set of memory locations owned by a method can not only grow as the method (symbolically) executes, but also shrink. First of all, at each method call ownership of the memory locations described by the callee's precondition is conceptually transferred from the caller to the callee. Secondly, when a method returns, the method loses ownership of all memory locations enumerated in its postcondition. Ownership of those locations is conceptually transferred from the method to its caller when it returns. For example, deposit's postcondition returns ownership of this.balance to its caller. In both cases, if the method does not own the required memory location, symbolic execution terminates with a verification error.

```
class Account {
  int balance;

  public Account()
    //@ requires true;
    //@ ensures this.balance |-> 0;
  {
    super();
    this.balance = 0;
  }

  public void deposit(int amount)
    //@ requires this.balance |-> ?b;
    //@ ensures this.balance |-> b + amount;
  {
    this.balance += amount;
  }

  public int getBalance()
    //@ requires this.balance |-> ?b;
    //@ ensures this.balance |-> b &*& result == b;
  {
    return this.balance;
  }

  public Account clone()
    //@ requires this.balance |-> ?b;
    /*@ ensures this.balance |-> b &*& result != null &*&
             result.balance |-> b; @*/
  {
    Account copy = new Account();
    copy.balance = balance;
    return copy;
  }

  public void transfer(Account other, int amount)
    /*@ requires this.balance |-> ?b1 &*& other != null &*&
             other.balance |-> ?b2; @*/
    /*@ ensures this.balance |-> b1 - amount &*&
             other.balance |-> b2 + amount; @*/
  {
    balance -= amount;
    other.deposit(amount);
  }
}
```

Assertions can be subdivided into two categories: *pure* and *spatial* assertions. Pure assertions such as 0 <= x specify constraints on local variables. Spatial assertions such as o.f |-> v on the other hand denote ownership of a heap subregion and information about that region. As explained in Section 2.3, producing and consuming a pure assertion involves respectively extending and checking the path condition. Consumption and production of a spatial assertion however affects the symbolic heap. That is, production of a spatial assertion corresponds to the acquisition of ownership by the current activation record of the memory regions described by the assertion. Therefore, producing such an assertion is implemented by adding the corresponding heap chunk to the heap. Consumption of a spatial assertion corresponds to the current activation record relinquishing ownership of the memory regions described by the assertion. It is hence implemented by searching the heap for a chunk that matches the assertion and by removing this chunk from the symbolic heap. An assertion `e1.f |-> e2` matches a chunk $C\_g(v, w)$ if f equals g, f is declared in class C and it follows from the path condition that the symbolic values of `e1` and `e2` are respectively equal to v and w. If no matching chunk is found, VeriFast reports a verification error: `No matching heap chunk`. For example, weakening the precondition of getBalance to `true` causes VeriFast to report an error at the field access `this.balance` (as the method does not have permission to read the field).

Multiple atomic assertions can be conjoined via the separating conjunction, denoted `&*&`. For example, `clone`'s postcondition specifies that the method returns ownership of `this.balance` and `result.balance` to its caller and that `result` is non-null. Semantically, `A &*& B` holds if both A and B hold and A's footprint is disjoint from B's footprint. The *footprint* of an assertion is the set of memory locations for which that assertion claims ownership. Consuming (respectively producing) `A &*& B` is implemented by first consuming (respectively producing) A and afterwards B. Note that if A is a pure assertion, then `A &*& A` is equivalent to A. However, this property does not necessarily hold for spatial assertions. In particular, as a method can only own a field once, it cannot give up ownership of that field twice. For that reason, the assertion `e1.f |-> _ &*& e1.f |-> _` is equivalent to `false`.

To gain a better understanding of ownership and ownership transfer, it is instructive to inspect the symbolic states encountered during verification of the method `transfer`. Open `Account.java`, place the cursor after the closing brace of the method `transfer` and press `Run to cursor`. As before, VeriFast starts symbolic execution of the method by constructing a symbolic pre-state that represents an arbitrary concrete pre-state. The symbolic store of this initial state contains fresh symbols for the parameters `this` and `other`, its path condition contains the assumption that `this` is non-null, and its symbolic heap is empty. To consider only program states that satisfy the precondition, VeriFast produces the three subassertions in the precondition from left to right. The pure assertion `other != null` is added to the path condition, while the symbolic heap is extended with two heap chunks, one for each spatial assertion. As the precondition does not constrain the values of the `balance` fields, VeriFast initializes both fields with fresh symbolic values. These values are respectively bound to `b1` and `b2`. Note that the first arguments of both heap chunks are equal to the symbolic values of respectively `this` and `other`. After producing the precondition, Verifast proceeds by executing the method body. To symbolically execute the assignment to this.balance, the verifier first checks that the method is allowed to read and write the field by checking that the heap contains a matching heap chunk. The heap contains the required chunk: Account_balance(this, b1). The effect of the assignment is reflected in the symbolic state by replacing this chunk with Account_balance(this, b1 − amount). To verify the subsequent method call, VeriFast first symbolically evaluates all method arguments. As explained in Section 2.3 symbolic execution of the method call itself consists of two steps: consumption of the precondition and afterwards production of the postcondition. Consumption of the precondition removes Account_balance(other, b2) from the symbolic heap. As transfer loses ownership of other.balance during the call, the verifier cannot (wrongly) assume that other.balance's value is preserved by deposit. Moreover, transfer retains ownership of this.balance during the call. Therefore, VeriFast can deduce that the callee will not modify this.balance. Production of deposit's postcondition adds the heap chunk Account_balance(other, b2 + amount) to the symbolic heap. setBalance has effectively *borrowed* ownership of other.balance from transfer in order to update its value. Finally, VeriFast checks that the postcondition of transfer holds by consuming it. Consumption of transfer's postcondition removes the two heap chunks from the symbolic heap.

Account.java successfully verifies. It is useful though to consider how VeriFast responds to incorrect variations of the program:

- If we weaken the precondition of deposit to true, then VeriFast reports an error (No matching heap chunks) which indicates that the method might not own the field this.balance when it reads the field. A method is only allowed to read a field when it owns the permission to do so.
- If we strengthen the precondition of deposit by adding the requirement that amount must be non-negative, then verification of transfer fails (Cannot prove condition) with a precondition violation. Indeed, transfer's precondition does not impose any constraint on amount and therefore the value passed to deposit might be negative.
- If we insert a bug in deposit's body, e.g. we replace += with =, then a postcondition violation (Cannot prove amount == (b + amount)) is reported by VeriFast. Although the method owns the correct memory location after execution of the method body (this.balance), the value of that location is not the one expected by the postcondition.
- If we weaken the postcondition of deposit to true, then verification of transfer fails with a postcondition violation (No matching heap chunks). The method call other.deposit(amount) then consumes ownership of the field other.balance, but does not return ownership of this field when it terminates.

Note that the ownership methodology described in this section does not impose any restrictions on aliasing. For example, an object is allowed to leak internal references to helper objects to client code. However, the methodology does impose restrictions on the use of aliases. In particular, a method can only dereference a reference (i.e. access a field) if it owns that reference.

4   Data Abstraction

Data abstraction is one of the pillars of object-oriented programming. That is, an object typically does not permit client code to directly access its internal state. Instead, the object provides methods that allow clients to query and update its state in a safe way. If an object hides its internals and forces clients to use a well-defined interface, then those clients cannot depend on internal implementation choices. This means that the object's implementation can be changed without having to worry about breaking clients, as long the observable behaviour remains the same. Moreover, clients cannot inadvertently break the object's internal invariants.

As an example of client code, consider the `main` method shown below:

```
class AccountClient {
  public static void main(String[] args)
    //@ requires true;
    //@ ensures true;
  {
    Account a = new Account(); a.deposit(100);
    Account b = new Account(); b.deposit(50);
    a.transfer(b, 20);

    int tmp = a.getBalance();
    assert tmp == 80;
  }
}
```

This client program creates and interacts with `Account` objects by calling the class' public methods. VeriFast can prove correctness of this program with respect to `Account`'s method contracts. Unfortunately, those method contracts are not implementation-independent as they mention the internal field `balance`. The correctness proof of `main` constructed by VeriFast therefore also indirectly depends on `Account`'s internal representation. If we would make internal modifications to the class, for example we could store the balance as a linked list of transactions instead of in a single field, we would have to update the method contracts and consequently have to reconsider the correctness of *all* clients. Moreover, if `Account` were an interface, then it would be impossible to specify the behavior of the methods by declaring their effect on fields as interfaces do not have fields.

Performing internal modifications to a class that do not change its observable behaviour should only require reverification of the class itself but should not endanger the correctness of its clients. To achieve this goal, we must answer the following question: How can we specify the observable behaviour of a class or interface without exposing its internal representation?

VeriFast's answer to this question is predicates [9]. More specifically, assertions describing the state associated with instances of a class can be hidden inside *predicates*. A predicate is a named, parameterized assertion. For example, consider the predicate definition shown below:

```
//@ predicate account(Account a, int b) = a.balance |-> b;
```

account is a predicate with two parameters named a and b, and with body a.balance |-> b. The assertion account(e1, e2) is a shorthand for the assertion e1.balance |-> e2. The body of the predicate is visible only inside the module defining the class Account. Outside of that module, a predicate is just an opaque container of permissions and constraints on its parameters.

The extra level of indirection provided by predicates allows us to write implementation-independent contracts: instead of directly referring to the internal fields, pre- and postconditions can be phrased in terms of a predicate. As an example, consider the new version of Account shown below. The implementation is exactly the same as before, but the contracts now specify the effect of each method with respect to the predicate account.

```
class Account {
  private int balance;

  public Account()
    //@ requires true;
    //@ ensures account(this, 0);
  {
    super();
    this.balance = 0;
    //@ close account(this, 0);
  }

  public void deposit(int amount)
    //@ requires account(this, ?b);
    //@ ensures account(this, b + amount);
  {
    //@ open account(this, b);
    this.balance += amount;
    //@ close account(this, b + amount);
  }

  public int getBalance()
    //@ requires account(this, ?b);
    //@ ensures account(this, b) &*& result == b;
  {
    //@ open account(this, b);
    return this.balance;
    //@ close account(this, b);
  }
}
```

From the client's point of view, the constructor returns an opaque bundle of permissions and constraints that relates the newly created object to 0, a value representing the balance of the account. Although the client is unaware of the exact permissions and constraints inside the bundle, he or she can deduce from the contracts of deposit and getBalance that the bundle can be passed to those methods to respectively increase and query the value representing the balance associated with the account.

VeriFast by default does not automatically fold and unfold predicates. Instead, developers must explicitly use ghost statements to switch between the external, abstract view offered by the predicate and the internal definition of the predicate. The *close* ghost statement folds a predicate: it consumes the body of the predicate, and afterwards adds a chunk representing the predicate to the symbolic heap. For example, symbolic execution of the close statement in the constructor replaces the chunk Account_balance(this, 0) by account(this, 0). Without the ghost statement, the constructor does not verify as the heap does not contain a chunk that matches the postcondition. The *open* ghost statement unfolds a predicate: it removes a heap chunk that represents the predicate from the symbolic heap and afterwards produces its body. For example, verification of deposit starts by producing the precondition: the chunk account(this, 0) is added to the symbolic heap. However, when accessing the field this.balance, the heap must explicitly contain a chunk that represents ownership of the field. As the necessary chunk is nested inside account(this, 0), the predicate must opened first. If we omit the ghost statement, VeriFast would no longer find a chunk that matches the field assertion Account_balance(this, _) on the heap and report an error. The open and close statement respectively correspond to Parkinson and Bierman's OPEN and CLOSE axioms [9, Section 3.2].

Inserting open and close ghost statements in order for VeriFast to find the required chunks on the heap is tedious. To alleviate this burden, programmers can mark certain predicates as *precise*. VeriFast automatically opens and closes precise predicates (in many cases) whenever necessary during symbolic execution. A predicate can be marked as precise by using a semicolon instead of comma somewhere in the parameter list. The semicolon separates the input from the output parameters. VeriFast syntactically checks that the values of the input parameters together with the predicate body uniquely determine the values of the output parameters. In our example, account can be marked precise by placing a semicolon between the parameters a and b. All open and close statements in the class Account shown above can be omitted once account is marked as precise. Although open and close statements need not be inserted explicitly in the program text, the symbolic execution trace does contain the corresponding steps.

AccountClient.main verifies against the new, more abstract method contracts for Account. To demonstrate that internal changes can be made to Account without having to change the method contracts — and hence without having to reverify *any* client code —, consider the alternative implementation of the class shown below.

```
class Transaction {
  int amount; Transaction next;

  public Transaction(int amount, Transaction next)
    //@ requires true;
    //@ ensures this.amount |-> amount &*& this.next |-> next;
  { this.amount = amount; this.next = next; }
}

/*@
predicate transactions(Transaction t; int total) =
  t == null ?
    total == 0
  :
    t.amount |-> ?amount &*& t.next |-> ?next &*&
    transactions(next, ?ntotal) &*& total == amount + ntotal;

predicate account(Account a; int b) =
  a.transactions |-> ?ts &*& transactions(ts, b);
@*/

class Account {
  private Transaction transactions;

  public Account()
    //@ requires true;
    //@ ensures account(this, 0);
  { transactions = null; }

  public void deposit(int amount)
    //@ requires account(this, ?b);
    //@ ensures account(this, b + amount);
  { transactions = new Transaction(amount, transactions); }

  public int getBalance()
    //@ requires account(this, ?b);
    //@ ensures account(this, b) &*& result == b;
  { return getTotal(transactions); }

  private int getTotal(Transaction t)
    //@ requires transactions(t, ?total);
    //@ ensures transactions(t, total) &*& result == total;
  {
    //@ open transactions(t, total);
    return t == null ? 0 : t.amount + getTotal(t.next);
  }
}
```

The method contracts are exactly the same as before. However, the implementation now stores the balance of the account as a linked list of Transaction objects instead of in single field. The body of deposit prepends a new Transaction object to the list, while getBalance traverses the list to compute the total sum. The new body of the predicate account reflects the changes in the implementation. account(a, b) now means that a.transactions is the head of linked, null-terminated list of Transaction objects whose total sum equals b.

Note that account is defined in terms of transactions, a *recursive* predicate. Such recursive predicates are crucial for specifying data structures without a static bound on their size. The body of transactions is a conditional assertion: if t is null, then total is equal to zero; otherwise, total is the sum of t.amount and the total of the remaining Transactions at t.next. Just as in symbolic execution of an if statement, VeriFast separately examines both branches when producing and consuming a conditional assertion.

Predicates typically specify what it means for an object to be in a *consistent* state. For example, consistency of an Account object as described by the predicate account implies that the list of Transactions is non-cyclic. As such, predicates play the role of object invariants [10]. VeriFast does not impose any built-in rules that state when invariants must be hold and when they can be temporarily violated. Instead, if a certain object is supposed to satisfy a particular invariant, then the method contract must explicitly say so.

5   Inheritance

A Java interface defines a set of abstract methods. For example, the interface java.util.List defines methods for modifying and querying List objects such as add, remove, size and get. Each non-abstract class that implements the interface must provide an implementation for each interface method. For example, ArrayList implements get by returning the object stored at the given index in its internal array, while LinkedList implements the method by traversing a linked list of nodes.

In order to be able to modularly verify client code, each interface method must be annotated with a method contract. A straightforward, but naive approach to specifying interfaces is phrasing the method contracts in terms of a predicate with a fixed definition. For example, applying this approach to (part of) the interface List would look as follows:

```
//@ predicate list(List l, int size);

interface List {
  public void add(Object o);
    //@ requires list(this, ?size);
    //@ ensures list(this, size + 1);
}
```

This approach is problematic as a predicate can only have a single definition. Yet multiple classes can implement List and each such class requires a different definition of the predicate. For example, ArrayList requires the predicate to include ownership of the internal array, while LinkedList requires the predicate to contain ownership of the linked sequence of nodes.

One could solve the aforementioned problem by case splitting in the contracts on the dynamic type of this. In our example, we could check whether this is an ArrayList or a LinkedList as shown below.

```
interface List {
  public void add(Object o);
    /*@ requires this.getClass() == ArrayList.class ?
      arraylist(this, ?size)
          :
      linkedlist(this, ?size); @*/
    /*@ ensures this.getClass() == ArrayList.class ?
      arraylist(this, size + 1)
          :
      linkedlist(this, size + 1); @*/
}
```

The complete set of subclasses is typically not known when writing the interface. In particular, clients of the interface can define their own subclasses. Each time a new subclass is added, the contracts of the interface methods must be extended with another case (which means *all* clients must be reverified). Clearly, this approach is non-modular and does not scale.

VeriFast solves the conundrum described above via dynamically bound *instance predicates* [11]. An instance predicate is a predicate defined inside a class or interface. For example, the method contracts of List can be phrased in terms of the instance predicate list as follows:

```
interface List {
  //@ predicate list(int size);

  public void add(Object o);
    //@ requires list(?size);
    //@ ensures list(size + 1);
}
```

Just like an instance method, an instance predicate does not have a single, closed definition. Instead, each subclass must override the instance predicate's definition and provide its own body. For example, the body of list in ArrayList involves ownership of the internal array (i.e. array_slice denotes ownership of the array itself) and states that size lies between zero and the length of the array as shown below. Note that the variable this in the body of the instance predicate refers to the target object of the predicate.

```
class ArrayList implements List {
  /*@
  predicate list(int size) =
    this.elements |-> ?a &*& this.size |-> size &*&
    array_slice<Object>(a, 0, a.length, _) &*&
    0 <= size &*& size <= a.length;
  @*/

  private Object[] elements;
  private int size;
  ...
}
```

The body of `list` in `LinkedList` on the other hand states that `first` is the head of a valid sequence of nodes ending in `null` with `size` elements. The body is phrased in terms of the recursive, non-instance predicate `lseg`. The assertion `lseg(n1, n2, s)` denotes that `n1` is the start of a valid sequence of nodes of length `s` ending in (but not including) `n2`.

```
/*@
predicate lseg(Node first, Node last; int size) =
  first == last ?
    size == 0
  :
    first.value |-> _ &*& first.next |-> ?next &*&
    lseg(next, last, ?nsize) &*& size == nsize + 1;
@*/

class LinkedList implements List {
  /*@ predicate list(int size) =
    this.first |-> ?first &*& this.size |-> size &*&
    lseg(first, null, size); @*/

  private Node first;
  private int size;
  ...
}
```

An instance predicate has multiple definitions, one per subclass. For that reason, each heap chunk corresponding to an instance predicate has an additional parameter indicating what version of the predicate the chunk represents. For example, heap chunks corresponding to the predicate `list` are of the form List#list(target, C, size), where target and size are the symbolic values of respectively the implicit target object and the parameter size and where C is a symbolic value that represents the class containing the definition of the predicate. Hence, the chunk List#list(l, ArrayList, s) states that l refers to a valid list with s elements, where the definition of *valid list* is the one given in the class `ArrayList`.

When producing and consuming an instance predicate assertion of the form e0.p(e1, ..., en), the verifier generally selects the dynamic type of e0 as the class containing p's definition. As an example, consider the steps in the symbolic execution of the method addNull shown below:

```
public static void addNull(List l)
  //@ requires l.list(?size);
  //@ ensures l.list(size + 1);
{ l.add(null); }
```

Open Lists.java, place the cursor after the closing brace of addNull and press Run to cursor. As shown in the symbolic execution trace, production of the precondition adds the chunk List#list(l, getClass(l), size) to the symbolic heap. Here, getClass is a function that represents the dynamic type of its argument. To symbolically execute the method call l.add(null), VeriFast first consumes add's precondition, and subsequently produces its postcondition. As l.add(null) is a dynamically bound call, the version of the instance predicate denoted by its pre- and postcondition is the one defined in the dynamic type of the target object, l.

There are a number of exceptions to the rule that the dynamic type of the target object is used as the version of an instance predicate chunk. First of all, when opening or closing an instance predicate, the definition in the static type of the target object is used. For example, if the static type of l is LinkedList, then execution of the statement close l.list(5); first consumes the body of list as defined in LinkedList and afterwards adds the chunk List#list(l, LinkedList, 5) to the symbolic heap. Secondly, when verifying the body of an instance method defined in a class C or a statically bound call of a method (e.g. super and constructor calls), instance predicate assertions of the form p(e1, ..., en) in the contract where the implicit argument this has been omitted are treated as statically bound meaning that the term representing the definition of p is equal to C. For example, when verifying List.add in LinkedList, production of the precondition produces the chunk List#list(this, LinkedList, size). This is sound since VeriFast checks that all methods are overridden [12].

VeriFast can prove correctness of the method addNull with respect to List's method contracts. Correctness of addNull implies that there do not exist values for l or states of the heap that trigger an assertion violation during execution of the method body. However, consider the class BadList shown below.

Even though each method in BadList satisfies its method contract, execution of BadList.main triggers an assertion violation. The cause of the problem is the fact that the contract used for verifying the method call l.add(null) in addNull and the contract used for verifying the implementation of BadList.add (which is executed when the dynamic type of l is BadList) are not compatible. In particular, the precondition of BadList.add states that the method should never be called, while List.add's precondition does allow calls provided l is a valid list.

To avoid problems such as the one described above, VeriFast checks that the contract of each overriding method is *compatible* [11] with the contract of its overridden method. VeriFast checks that the contract of an overriding method with precondition P and postcondition Q is compatible with the contract of an overridden method with precondition P' and postcondition Q' by checking that the body of the overridden method could statically call the overriding method: the verifier first produces P', then consumes P and afterwards produces Q, and finally consumes Q'. When verifying BadList, Verifast reports that the contract of BadList.add is not compatible with the contract of List.add as false is not provable after producing the chunk List#list(this, BadList, 0).

```
class BadList implements List {
  /*@ predicate list(int size) = true; @*/

  public BadList()
    //@ requires true;
    //@ ensures list(0);
  {
    //@ close list(0);
  }

  public void add(Object o)
    //@ requires false;
    //@ ensures true;
  { assert false; }

  public static void main(String[] args)
    //@ requires true;
    //@ ensures true;
  {
    BadList bad = new BadList();
    addNull(bad);
  }
}
```

6 Inductive Data Types and Fixpoints

The contract of List.add is incomplete. More specifically, its postcondition states that add increments the number of elements in the list by one, but it does not specify that the object o should be added to the end of the list. As a consequence, an implementation that prepends o to the front of the list or even inserts a different object altogether is considered to be correct.

To rule out such implementations, we must strengthen add's postcondition. However, the current signature of the instance predicate list does not allow us to do so as it only exposes the number of elements in the list via the parameter size. The predicate does not expose the elements themselves and their positions.

To allow developers to specify rich properties, VeriFast supports inductive data types and fixpoints. For example, we can represent a sequence using the inductive data type list:

```
//@ inductive list<t> = nil | cons(t, list<t>);
```

This declaration declares a type `list` with two constructors: `nil` and `cons`. `nil` represents the empty sequence, while `cons(h, t)` represents a concatenation of a head element `h` and a tail list `t`. The definition is generic in the type of the list elements (here `t`). For example, the sequence $1, 2, 3$ can be written as `cons(1, cons(2, cons(3, nil)))`.

A fixpoint is a total, mathematical function that operates on an inductively defined data type. For example, consider the fixpoints `length`, `nth` and `append` shown below. The body of each of these functions is a switch statement over one of the inductive arguments. The function `length` for instance returns zero if the sequence is empty; otherwise, it returns the length of the tail plus one. Note that `default_value<t>` is a built-in function that returns the default value for a particular type `t`.

To ensure that fixpoints are well-defined, VeriFast syntactically checks that they terminate. In particular, VeriFast enforces that whenever a fixpoint g is called in the body of a fixpoint f that either g appears before f in the program text or that the call decreases the size of the inductive argument (i.e. the argument switched on by the fixpoint's body). For example, the call `length(xs0)` in the body of `length` itself is allowed because `xs0` is a subcomponent of `xs` (and hence smaller than `xs` itself).

```
/*@
fixpoint int length<t>(list<t> xs) {
  switch (xs) {
    case nil: return 0;
    case cons(x, xs0): return 1 + length(xs0);
  }
}

fixpoint t nth<t>(int n, list<t> xs) {
  switch (xs) {
    case nil: return default_value<t>;
    case cons(x, xs0): return n == 0 ? x : nth(n - 1, xs0);
  }
}

fixpoint list<t> append<t>(list<t> xs, list<t> ys) {
  switch (xs) {
    case nil: return ys;
    case cons(x, xs0): return cons(x, append(xs0, ys));
  }
}
@*/
```

We can now make the specification of the interface `List` complete as shown below. First of all, we modify the signature of the instance predicate `list` such that it exposes a sequence of `Object`s. Secondly, we refine the method contracts by defining the return value and the effect of each method in terms of a fixpoint function on the exposed sequence of objects. For example, the postcondition of add specifies that the method adds o to the end of the list.

```
interface List {
  //@ predicate list(list<Object> elems);

  public void add(Object o);
    //@ requires list(?elems);
    //@ ensures list(append(elems, cons(o, nil)));

  public int size();
    //@ requires list(?elems);
    //@ ensures list(elems) &*& result == length(elems);

  public Object get(int i);
    //@ requires list(?elems) &*& 0 <= i &*& i < length(elems);
    //@ ensures list(elems) &*& result == nth(i, elems);
}
```

The specification of the interface List is idiomatic in VeriFast. That is, specifying the behaviour of a class or interface typically involves the following steps:

1. Define an inductive data type T to represent the abstract state of instances of the class. In our example, we defined the inductive data type list to represent the state of List objects.
2. Define an instance predicate p with a single parameter of type T. For example, the interface List defines the instance predicate list. Its parameter elems is of type list.
3. The postcondition of each constructor guarantees that the predicate holds.
4. The contract of each instance method requires that the predicate holds on entry to the method and guarantees that the predicate holds again when the method terminates. The effect and return value of the method are related to the abstract state via fixpoint functions. For example, size's postcondition relates the return value to the sequence of elements via the function length.

Each inductive data type constructor has a corresponding first-order function. For example, the inductive data type list has two corresponding functions named nil and cons. Instances of inductive data types are encoded as applications of these functions. For example, the expression cons(o, nil) in the postcondition of add symbolic evaluates to the term cons(o, nil). The fact that all constructors are distinct is given as an axiom to the SMT solver. For the inductive data type list, the solver can hence deduce that nil $\neq$ cons(h, t), for arbitrary h and t.

Each fixpoint function also has an associated first-order function. For example, the fixpoint length has a corresponding first-order function named length. Applications of fixpoints are encoded as applications of the corresponding function. The behaviour of the fixpoint is encoded in the SMT solver via one or more axioms that relate the function to the fixpoint's body. In particular, if the body of the fixpoint is a switch over one of its arguments, then one axiom is generated for each case. For example, the behavior of length is encoded via the following axioms:

$$\text{length}(\text{nil}) = 0$$
$$\forall h, t \bullet \text{length}(\text{cons}(h, t)) = 1 + \text{length}(t)$$

The SMT solver can use these axioms to simplify terms and formulas involving fixpoint functions. For example, the aforementioned axioms allow the solver to deduce that $\text{length}(\text{cons}(1, \text{cons}(2, l)))$ and $2 + \text{length}(l)$ are equal.

7   Lemmas

To determine whether a particular formula follows from the path condition — for example when consuming a pure assertion — VeriFast relies on an SMT solver. The SMT solver however does not perform induction. For that reason, it can fail to prove properties that require proof by induction. For example, proving that the function append is associative requires induction.

Lemma functions allow developers to prove properties about their fixpoints and predicates, and allow them to use these properties when reasoning about programs. A lemma is a method without side effects marked lemma. The contract of a lemma function corresponds to a theorem, its body to the proof, and a lemma call to an application of the theorem. VeriFast has two types of lemma methods: pure lemmas and spatial lemmas.

A lemma is *pure* if its contract does not contain spatial assertions. The contract of a pure lemma corresponds to a theorem that states that the precondition implies the postcondition for all possible values of the lemma parameters. The lemma append_assoc shown below is an example of a pure lemma that states that applying the fixpoint append is associative. The lemma's body proves the theorem by induction on xs. More specifically, the case nil of the switch statement corresponds to the base case, while the case cons corresponds to the inductive step. The recursive call in the case cons is an application of the induction hypothesis.

```
/*@
lemma void append_assoc<t>(list<t> xs, list<t> ys, list<t> zs)
  requires true;
  ensures append(append(xs, ys), zs) == append(xs, append(ys, zs));
{
  switch (xs) {
    case nil:
    case cons(h, t): append_assoc(t, ys, zs);
  }
}
@*/
```

Contrary to pure lemmas, *spatial* lemmas can mention spatial assertions in their method contracts. The contract of a spatial lemma corresponds to a theorem that states that the symbolic state described by the precondition is equivalent to the one described by the postcondition. Equivalent means that the symbolic state described by the postcondition can be reached by applying a finite number of open and close statements to the state described by the precondition. A spatial lemma does not modify the values in the heap, but only rewrites the representation of the symbolic state. Spatial lemmas are crucial whenever the symbolic state is required to have a particular form but the current state cannot be rewritten to the required one by a statically known number of open and close statements. Moreover, a spatial lemma allows a class to expose properties to clients without having to reveal its internal representation. As an example, consider the spatial lemma lseg_merge shown below. This lemma states that two list segments, one from a to b and another from b to c, are equivalent to a single list segment from a to c, provided there exists an additional list segment from c to null.

```
/*@
lemma void lseg_merge(Node a, Node b, Node c)
  requires lseg(a, b, ?elems1) &*& lseg(b, c, ?elems2) &*&
    lseg(c, null, ?elems3);
  ensures lseg(a, c, append(elems1, elems2)) &*&
    lseg(c, null, elems3);
{
  open lseg(a, b, elems1);
  open lseg(c, null, elems3);
  if(a != b) lseg_merge(a.next, b, c);
}
@*/
```

VeriFast checks termination of a lemma method by allowing only direct recursion and by checking each recursive call as follows: first, if, after consuming the precondition of the recursive call, a field chunk is left in the symbolic heap, then the call is allowed. This is induction on heap size. Otherwise, if the body of the lemma method is a switch statement on a parameter whose type is an inductive data type, then the argument for this parameter in the recursive call must be a constructor argument of the caller's argument for the same parameter. This is induction on an inductive parameter. Finally, if the body of the lemma function is not such a switch statement, then the first heap chunk consumed by the precondition of the callee must have been obtained from the first heap chunk consumed by the precondition of the caller through one or more open operations. This is induction on the derivation of the first conjunct of the precondition.

The method LinkedList.add shown below adds an object o to the end of the list. If the list is empty, then the method body assigns a new node holding o to first; otherwise, the method transverses the linked list in a loop until it reaches the last node and assigns a new node holding o to the next pointer of the last node. The method calls the lemmas lseg_merge and append_assoc to prove that the loop body preserves the loop invariant and to prove that the postcondition follows from the invariant and the negation of the condition.

```
public void add(Object o)
  //@ requires list(?elems);
  //@ ensures list(append(elems, cons(o, nil)));
{
  if(first == null) {
    //@ open lseg(first, null, _);
    first = new Node(null, o);
  } else {
    Node first = this.first, curr = this.first;
    while(curr.next != null)
      /*@ invariant curr != null &*&
          lseg(first, curr, ?elems1) &*& lseg(curr, null, ?elems2) &*&
          elems == append(elems1, elems2);
      @*/
      //@ decreases length(elems2);
    {
      //@ Object v = curr.value;
      //@ Node oldcurr = curr;
      curr = curr.next;
      //@ open lseg(curr, null, _);
      //@ lseg_merge(first, oldcurr, curr);
      //@ append_assoc(elems1, cons(v, nil), tail(elems2));
    }
    //@ open lseg(null, null, _);
    Node nn = new Node(null, o); curr.next = nn;
    //@ lseg_merge(first, curr, null);
    //@ append_assoc(elems1, elems2, cons(o, nil));
  }
  this.size++;
}
```

Like many other verification tools, VeriFast requires each loop to be annotated with a *loop invariant* (keyword invariant), describing the assertion that must hold right before evaluation of the condition in each iteration. For example, the loop invariant in the method add states (1) that curr is non-null, (2) that the method owns two valid list segments, one from first to curr and another from curr to null and (3) that the concatenation of the elements of both segments is equal to the elements of the original list. VeriFast verifies a loop as follows.

1. First, the tool consumes the loop invariant. This step proves that the invariant holds on entry to the loop.
2. Then, it removes the remaining heap chunks from the heap (but it remembers them).
3. Then, it assigns a fresh logical symbol to each local variable that is modified in the loop body.
4. Then, it produces the loop invariant.
5. Then, it performs a case split on the loop condition:

– If the condition is true, it verifies the loop body and afterwards consumes the loop invariant. This step proves that the loop body preserves the invariant. After this step, this execution path is finished.
– If the condition is false, VeriFast puts the heap chunks that were removed in Step 2 back into the heap and verification continues after the loop.

Notice that this means that the loop can access only those heap chunks that are mentioned in the loop invariant.

By default, VeriFast does not check loop termination. However, developers may provide an optional *loop measure* to force the verifier to check termination of a particular loop. A loop measure (keyword `decreases`) is an integer-valued expression. If the value of the expression decreases in each loop iteration but never becomes negative, then it follows that the loop terminates. In the example, the length of the list segment from `curr` to `null` is the measure.

The VeriFast distribution includes a specification library that contains many commonly used inductive data types (such as `list`, `option` and `pair`), fixpoints (such as `append`, `take` and `drop`) and lemmas (such as `length_nonnegative` and `append_assoc`). As a consequence, developers can use existing definitions to define abstract states and the effect of methods.

8   Related Work

VeriFast is a separation logic-based program verifier. Separation logic [13,14,1] is an extension of Hoare logic [15] targeted at reasoning about imperative programs with shared mutable state. It extends Hoare logic by adding spatial assertions to describe the structure of the heap. Spatial assertions allow for *local reasoning*: the specification of a sequence of statements S only needs to mention heap locations accessed by S. The effect of S on other heap locations can be inferred via the *frame rule*:

$$\frac{\{P\} \, S \, \{Q\}}{\{P * R\} \, S \, \{Q * R\}}$$

The separating conjunction $P * R$ (written `P &*& R` in VeriFast) holds if both P and R hold and the part of the heap described by P is disjoint from the part of the heap described by R. The frame rule then states that if the separating conjunction $P * R$ holds before execution of a statement S and S's precondition does not require R, then R still holds after execution of S. VeriFast's symbolic heap represents a separating conjunction of its heap chunks. The verifier implicitly applies the frame rule for example when verifying a method call: the chunks not consumed by the callee's precondition are stable under the call and remain in the heap.

Parkinson and Bierman [9,11] extend the early work on separation logic of O'Hearn, Reynolds and Yang with abstract predicates and abstract predicate families to allow for local reasoning for object-oriented programs. VeriFast supports abstract predicate families in the form of instance predicates. Each instance predicate override in a class C corresponds to a predicate family member definition for C. Contrary to Parkinson and Bierman's work, our verifier does not support widening and narrowing to change the arity of a predicate family definition.

The specification of a method in Parkinson and Bierman's paper [11] consists of a static and a dynamic contract. Those contracts are respectively used to reason about statically and dynamically bound calls. Developers need not explicitly write both static and dynamic contracts in VeriFast. Instead, a single "polymorphic" contract suffices and the tool interprets this contract differently for statically and dynamically bound calls [12].

Berdine, Calcagno and O'Hearn [16] demonstrate that a fragment of separation logic (i.e. without implication and magic wand) is amenable to automatic static checking by building a verifier, called Smallfoot, for a small procedural language. Smallfoot checks that each procedure in the program satisfies its separation logic specification via symbolic execution. The symbolic state consists of a spatial formula and a pure formula. VeriFast extends the ideas of Berdine *et al.* to full-fledged programming languages (Java and C). The symbolic heap corresponds to Smallfoot's spatial formula and the symbolic store and the path condition to the pure formula. Smallfoot contains a small number of built-in predicates, and rules for rewriting symbolic states involving these predicates. Contrary to VeriFast, developers do not need to explicitly open and close predicates and need not provide loop invariants because of these built-in rules.

In addition to VeriFast, Smallfoot has inspired several other separation logic-based program verifiers. For example, jStar [17] is another semi-automatic program verifier for Java. Unlike VeriFast, jStar automatically infers certain loop invariants. Whether the right loop invariant can be inferred depends on the abstraction rules provided by the developer in a separate file. Heap-Hop [18] is an extension of Smallfoot targeted at proving memory safety and deadlock freedom of concurrent programs that rely on message passing. HIP [19] is a variant of Smallfoot that focuses on automatically proving size properties (e.g. that List.add increases the size of the list by one). Tuerk [20] has developed HOL-Foot, a port of Smallfoot to HOL. He has mechanically proven that HOLFoot is sound. An interesting feature of HOLFoot is that one can resort to interactive proofs in HOL4 when the tool is unable to construct a proof automatically. As it is challenging for fully automatic tools to prove full functional correctness, several researchers [21,22,23] have used separation logic within interactive proof assistants. While this approach typically requires more input from the developer, it has resulted in a number of impressive achievements. For example, Tuch *et al.* [23] report on verifying the memory allocator of the L4 microkernel.

Besides separation logic, the research literature contains many other approaches for reasoning about imperative programs with shared mutable state such as the Boogie methodology [12], dynamic frames [24], regional logic [25], data groups [26], the VCC methodology [27], universe types [28], dynamic logic [29], etc. These approaches are often implemented in a corresponding program verifier [30,31,32,33,34,29]. A strategy for dealing with aliasing common to many of these approaches is to represent the heap as a global map from addresses to values. As a method can change the heap, verification of a method call entails havocking (i.e. assigning a fresh value to) the global map. Each approach then provides a way to relate the value of the map before the call to its new value. For example, in the dynamic frames approach each method includes a modifies clause describing a set of addresses. After each call, the verifier assumes via a quantifier that the new map is equal to the old map except at addresses included in the modified set.

Before starting the development of VeriFast, we contributed to several program verifiers based on verification condition generation and automated theorem proving [35,32,36]. However, the verification experience provided by those tools left us frustrated for three reasons. First of all, verification can be slow (which we believe is caused by the quantifiers needed to encode frame properties). Secondly, it can be hard to diagnose why verification fails. Finally, automated theorem proving can be unpredictable, as small changes to the input can cause huge differences in verification time (or even whether the proof succeeds at all). For that reason, we put a very strong premium on predictable performance and diagnosability when designing VeriFast. The only quantifiers that are made available to the SMT solver are those that axiomatize the inductive data types and fixpoint functions; these behave very predictably. The VeriFast IDE allows developers to diagnose verification errors by inspecting the symbolic states on the path leading to the error.

9 Conclusion

VeriFast is a separation logic-based program verifier for Java. In this paper, we have informally explained the key features of this verifier.

Based on our experience with VeriFast, we identify three main areas of future work. First of all, in the separation logic ownership system used by VeriFast a method either exclusive owns a memory region (meaning that it has permission to read and arbitrarily modify the state of that region), partially owns a region (meaning it has permission to read but not write that region), or does not have any permission on that region at all. However, for some programs — in particular concurrent ones — more precise kinds of permissions are required. For example, it is not possible to directly express a permission that allows a memory location to be incremented but not decremented (which may be crucial for proving correctness of a ticketed lock). As shown by Owicki and Gries [37] and more recently by Jacobs and Piessens [38,39], arbitrarily "permissions" can be constructed indirectly by adding ghost state to lock invariants and by using fractional permissions. However, using ghost state does not lead to intuitive proofs. Therefore, we consider designing a more flexible ownership system where the developer can construct his own permissions to relate the current state of a memory region to earlier, observed states a key challenge for the future. Concurrent abstract predicates [40] and superficially substructural types [41] form promising directions in this area.

VeriFast sometimes requires developers to explicitly fold and unfold predicate definitions. Moreover, to prove inductive properties, lemmas must be written and called whenever the property is needed. A second important challenge to be addressed in future work is reducing the annotation overhead by automatically inferring more open and close statements and lemma calls.

Finally, VeriFast supports only a subset of Java. For example, generics are not supported yet by the tool. In order for VeriFast to be applicable to large Java programs, we must extend the supported subset of Java.

References

1. Parkinson, M., Bierman, G.: Separation Logic for Object-Oriented Programming. In: Clarke, D., Noble, J., Wrigstad, T. (eds.) Aliasing in Object-Oriented Programming. LNCS, vol. 7850, Springer, Heidelberg (2013)
2. Jacobs, B., Smans, J., Piessens, F.: A Quick Tour of the VeriFast Program Verifier. In: Ueda, K. (ed.) APLAS 2010. LNCS, vol. 6461, pp. 304–311. Springer, Heidelberg (2010)
3. Jacobs, B., Smans, J., Piessens, F.: The VeriFast Program Verifier: A Tutorial (2012)
4. Jacobs, B., Smans, J., Piessens, F.: Verification of imperative programs: The Veri-Fast approach. a draft course text. Technical Report CW578, Department of Computer Science, K.U.Leuven (2010)
5. Gosling, J., Joy, B., Steele, G., Bracha, G., Buckley, A.: The Java Language Specification (2012)
6. Meyer, B.: Applying "Design by Contract". IEEE Computer 25(10) (1992)
7. de Moura, L., Bjørner, N.S.: Z3: An Efficient SMT Solver. In: Ramakrishnan, C.R., Rehof, J. (eds.) TACAS 2008. LNCS, vol. 4963, pp. 337–340. Springer, Heidelberg (2008)
8. Boyland, J.: Checking Interference with Fractional Permissions. In: Cousot, R. (ed.) SAS 2003. LNCS, vol. 2694, pp. 55–72. Springer, Heidelberg (2003)
9. Parkinson, M., Bierman, G.: Separation logic and abstraction. In: Symposium on Principles of Programming Languages (POPL). ACM (2005)
10. Parkinson, M.: Class invariants: The end of the road? In: International Workshop on Aliasing, Confinement and Ownership in Object-oriented Programming, IWACO (2007)
11. Parkinson, M., Bierman, G.: Separation logic, abstraction and inheritance. In: Symposium on Principles of Programming Languages (POPL). ACM (2008)
12. Barnett, M., DeLine, R., Fähndrich, M., Leino, K.R.M., Schulte, W.: Verification of object-oriented programs with invariants. Journal of Object Technology 3(6) (2003)
13. O'Hearn, P., Reynolds, J., Yang, H.: Local Reasoning about Programs that Alter Data Structures. In: Fribourg, L. (ed.) CSL 2001. LNCS, vol. 2142, pp. 1–19. Springer, Heidelberg (2001)
14. Reynolds, J.: Separation logic: A logic for shared mutable data structures. In: Symposium on Logic in Computer Science, LICS (2002)
15. Hoare, C.A.R.: An axiomatic basis for computer programming. Communications of the ACM 12(10) (1969)
16. Berdine, J., Calcagno, C., O'Hearn, P.W.: Symbolic Execution with Separation Logic. In: Yi, K. (ed.) APLAS 2005. LNCS, vol. 3780, pp. 52–68. Springer, Heidelberg (2005)

17. Distefano, D., Parkinson, M.: jStar: Towards practical verification for Java. In: Object-Oriented Programming, Systems, Languages and Applications (OOPSLA). ACM (2008)

18. Villard, J., Lozes, É., Calcagno, C.: Proving Copyless Message Passing. In: Hu, Z. (ed.) APLAS 2009. LNCS, vol. 5904, pp. 194–209. Springer, Heidelberg (2009)

19. Nguyen, H.H., David, C., Qin, S.C., Chin, W.-N.: Automated Verification of Shape and Size Properties Via Separation Logic. In: Cook, B., Podelski, A. (eds.) VMCAI 2007. LNCS, vol. 4349, pp. 251–266. Springer, Heidelberg (2007)

20. Tuerk, T.: A Formalisation of Smallfoot in HOL. In: Berghofer, S., Nipkow, T., Urban, C., Wenzel, M. (eds.) TPHOLs 2009. LNCS, vol. 5674, pp. 469–484. Springer, Heidelberg (2009)

21. Nanevski, A., Morrisett, G., Shinnar, A., Govereau, P., Birkedal, L.: Ynot: Reasoning with the awkward squad. In: International Conference on Functional Programming (ICFP). ACM (2008)

22. Hobor, A., Appel, A.W., Nardelli, F.Z.: Oracle Semantics for Concurrent Separation Logic. In: Drossopoulou, S. (ed.) ESOP 2008. LNCS, vol. 4960, pp. 353–367. Springer, Heidelberg (2008)

23. Tuch, H., Klein, G., Norrish, M.: Types, bytes, and separation logic. In: Symposium on Principles of Programming Languages (POPL). ACM (2007)

24. Kassios, I.T.: Dynamic Frames: Support for Framing, Dependencies and Sharing Without Restrictions. In: Misra, J., Nipkow, T., Sekerinski, E. (eds.) FM 2006. LNCS, vol. 4085, pp. 268–283. Springer, Heidelberg (2006)

25. Banerjee, A., Naumann, D.A., Rosenberg, S.: Regional Logic for Local Reasoning about Global Invariants. In: Vitek, J. (ed.) ECOOP 2008. LNCS, vol. 5142, pp. 387–411. Springer, Heidelberg (2008)

26. Leino, K.R.M.: Data groups: Specifying the modification of extended state. In: Object-Oriented Programming, Systems, Languages and Applications (OOPSLA). ACM (1998)

27. Cohen, E., Moskal, M., Schulte, W., Tobies, S.: Local Verification of Global Invariants in Concurrent Programs. In: Touili, T., Cook, B., Jackson, P. (eds.) CAV 2010. LNCS, vol. 6174, pp. 480–494. Springer, Heidelberg (2010)

28. Dietl, W.M.: Universe Types: Topology, Encapsulation, Genericity, and Tools. PhD thesis, ETH Zurich, Switzerland (2009)

29. Beckert, B., Hähnle, R., Schmitt, P.H. (eds.): Verification of Object-Oriented Software. LNCS (LNAI), vol. 4334. Springer, Heidelberg (2007)

30. Barnett, M., Fähndrich, M., Leino, K.R.M., Müller, P., Schulte, W., Venter, H.: Specification and verification: the Spec# experience. Communications of the ACM 54(6) (2011)

31. Leino, K.R.M.: Dafny: An Automatic Program Verifier for Functional Correctness. In: Clarke, E.M., Voronkov, A. (eds.) LPAR-16 2010. LNCS, vol. 6355, pp. 348–370. Springer, Heidelberg (2010)

32. Smans, J., Jacobs, B., Piessens, F., Schulte, W.: An Automatic Verifier for Java-Like Programs Based on Dynamic Frames. In: Fiadeiro, J.L., Inverardi, P. (eds.) FASE 2008. LNCS, vol. 4961, pp. 261–275. Springer, Heidelberg (2008)

33. Flanagan, C., Leino, K.R.M., Lillibridge, M., Nelson, G., Saxe, J.B., Stata, R.: Extended static checking for Java. In: Programming Language Design and Implementation (PLDI). ACM (2002)

34. Dahlweid, M., Moskal, M., Santen, T., Tobies, S., Schulte, W.: VCC: Contract-based modular verification of concurrent C. In: International Conference on Software Engineering (ICSE). IEEE (2009)

35. Jacobs, B., Piessens, F., Smans, J., Leino, K.R.M., Schulte, W.: A programming model for concurrent object-oriented programs. ACM Transactions on Programming Languages and Systems 31(1) (2008)

36. Smans, J., Jacobs, B., Piessens, F.: Implicit dynamic frames. ACM Transactions on Programming Languages and Systems 34(1) (2012)

37. Owicki, S., Gries, D.: Verifying properties of parallel programs: an axiomatic approach. Communications of the ACM 19(5) (1976)

38. Jacobs, B., Piessens, F.: Expressive modular fine-grained concurrency specification. In: Symposium on Principles of Programming Languages (POPL). ACM (2011)

39. Jacobs, B., Piessens, F.: Dynamic owicki-gries reasoning using ghost fields and fractional permissions. Technical Report CW549, Department of Computer Science, K.U.Leuven (2009)

40. Dinsdale-Young, T., Dodds, M., Gardner, P., Parkinson, M.J., Vafeiadis, V.: Concurrent Abstract Predicates. In: D'Hondt, T. (ed.) ECOOP 2010. LNCS, vol. 6183, pp. 504–528. Springer, Heidelberg (2010)

41. Krishnaswami, N.R., Turon, A., Dreyer, D., Garg, D.: Superficially substructural types. In: International Conference on Functional Programming (ICFP). ACM (2012)

Confined Roles and Decapsulation in Object Teams — Contradiction or Synergy?

Stephan Herrmann

GK Software AG, Schöneck, Germany

1 Many Faces of Modularity

The Object Teams programming model [1] has been developed to advance our capability to write modular programs. A central concept in this programming model is the notion of teams – instantiable classes – that serve as a container for nested classes. This nesting is stronger than it is in languages like Java, because the type system applies the concept of family polymorphism [2], so all nested classes are actually dependent classes: classes that depend on the enclosing instance. As nested classes can again be teams there are no limits to nesting.

If one would strictly apply just this one concept, any software system would be a tidily hierarchical structure with optimal support for modular reasoning of all kinds. In a perfect hierarchical structure each component can only invoke procedures of its children and reports the result back to the parent. However, as early as 1974 David Parnas [3] gave words of warnings regarding the 'buzzword' *hierarchical structure*. He pointed out that strict containment structures are unlikely to be suitable for complex, real world software systems.

After research into the difficulties of finding the perfect decomposition for a system to be built, Tarr et al. [4] conclude that it is the multitude of concerns needing to be considered that makes it impossible to find a single perfect decomposition. Regarding standard decomposition mechanisms they speak of the "tyranny of the dominant decomposition" and thus motivate n-dimensional separation of concerns. These and similar challenges regarding separation of "crosscutting concerns" yielded numerous innovative approaches including Aspect Oriented Programming [5] and Hyperspaces [6].

Object Teams supports n-dimensional separation of concerns by the concept of roles. In Object Teams the relationship between a role object and a base object to which it is bound (the role player) is similar to inheritance in prototype based languages like Self [7]. By attaching multiple role objects to the same base object it is possible to create multiple independent specializations of the common base.

The containment relationship between a team and its members can be used to establish strict hierarchical structures with strong control over which communication is possible at runtime. By contrast, the role playing relationship between a role and its base is beneficial for mastering complexity in the presence of many concerns to consider and also for painless evolution of software over time. So teams provide control and roles provide flexibility.

D. Clarke et al. (Eds.): Aliasing in Object-Oriented Programming, LNCS 7850, pp. 443–470, 2013.

In order to leverage both sides together, two issues must be addressed: First both concepts must be integrated into a single coherent programming language. In Object Teams this is done by unifying team members and roles, i.e., the same class is a contained member of a team instance subjected to the strict rules of nesting, and it is also a role that can be bound to an existing base class. Secondly, a fine balance must be found, where decomposition is free to choose the most appropriate structure and still yields a structure that is strict enough for modular reasoning.

2   Confined Roles

The Object Teams approach [1] has been defined in a language independent way, and prototypes exist for mapping this to several object-oriented programming languages. This text will continue to use the term "Object Teams" to refer to those language independent concepts of the overall approach. However, the notion of "confined roles" has only been introduced in the concrete language OT/J[8][9], which maps the Object Teams model into an extension of the Java programming language.

Confined roles are introduced to support a strict form of ownership. At the core we have a containment relationship between a team instance (instance of a class marked with the modifier **team**) and any number of nested instances. These nested instances are called "roles" but for the discussion in this section "role" will just be another word for "team member".

This containment follows the rules of family polymorphism [2], which means that role *classes* are virtual classes contained in a team *instance*. This makes the role class a dependent class: it depends on the enclosing team instance. The dependency was originally introduced to support type safe specialization of a group of mutually recursive types, but it turns out that the same concept can also be used as the basis for ownership.

We denote a dependent role type using this syntax:

```
RoleClass <@teamInstance>
```

Here the type RoleClass must be declared nested within the class of the value teamInstance. Figure 1 shows the one-step instantiation from a team class T to a team instance t1 vs. the two-step instantiation from a generic role class R<T t> to the instantiated class R<@t1> to the real instance r1. Such a dependent type R<@t1> is assignment compatible to another type R<@t2> only if t1 and t2 provably refer to the same instance. For practicality the type checker requires both instance references to be immutable (final) so that a very simple flow analysis can be used during type checking.

Next, OT/J combines the type rules of family polymorphism with Java's access modifiers. We simplify the model by requesting that each role class must be declared as either **public** or **protected**, as opposed to the weakly motivated four levels supported by Java. By adding one simple rule we extend static visibility to an ownership model:

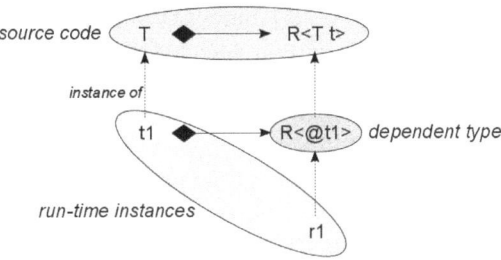

Fig. 1. Classes and instances — The generic syntax R<T t> is used to denote a class that has a parameter t which is an instance of type T. Since by definition all role classes depend on the enclosing team instance the role declaration omits the parameter T t and instead of the declared name t the syntax T.this is used for referring to a role's owner.

Rule 1 (Protected Role)
If a role class R has visibility **protected** *the only value that types from this class may depend on is* **this** *or any qualified this-reference, Enclosing Team.***this***, pointing to an enclosing team instance. For all other values t the type expression R<@t> is invalid.*

This ensures that a protected role type can only be referenced within the instance scope of the containing team instance.

A team instance owns its nested role types and thus it owns all instances of these types. By using a qualified this-reference a role may utilize the privileges of all enclosing teams at different nesting levels. Thus, ownership is actually group ownership: roles of a team can mutually refer to other protected roles, but no reference is ever allowed to a protected role of another team instance.

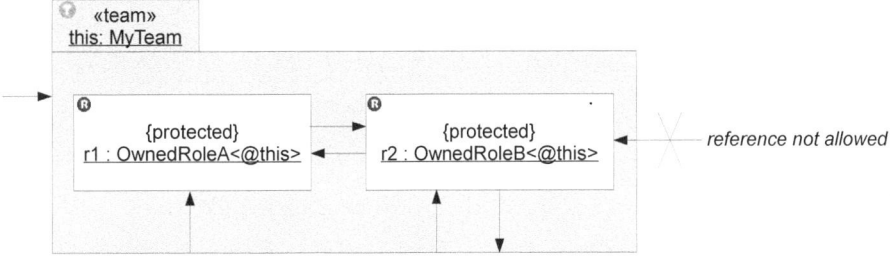

Fig. 2. Group ownership of roles contained in a team

For the types R<@this> and R<@T.this> OT/J supports the abbreviation R. Valid applications of this abbreviation coincide with valid uses of a protected role. Thus, in day-to-day programming the extra burden of explicit dependent types mildly pushes the developer towards avoiding cross-team references to roles. Similarly, the tooling (OTDT [10]) favors protected roles: when creating a new role class it is by default declared as **protected**. In both cases we work towards making confinement the normal case rather than the exception.

It should be noted that OT/J also supports role *interfaces* in addition to role *classes*. However, for the most part of this text that distinction does not add anything interesting.

2.1   Safe Polymorphism

Combining the type rules of family polymorphism with a simple visibility rule establishes a form of ownership. There is a hole which the type checker cannot detect, however: if ownership checking is based only on static typing a simple widening to an unowned type may bypass the above rule. There are good reasons for allowing that a role class may indeed inherit from a non-role class. Moreover, completely *avoiding* such inheritance is not even possible without further language rules: Since OT/J is based on Java, each role is a subclass of java.lang.Object, the latter being accessible without any checks for ownership, because it is not a dependent class. By assignment to a variable of type Object, a reference to a protected role would escape the compiler's analysis, and thus leakage to any location in the program is possible.

The solution to this hole comes in two steps: a special super-class Confined and restricted inheritance.

Confined. OT/J introduces a special super-class org.objectteams.Team.Confined, which combines two properties: (1) it is a role of class org.objectteams.Team, the implicit super-class of all teams, thus it is a dependent type, and (2) it is an inheritance root, i.e., class Confined does not inherit from Object.

Rule 2 (Role "Confined")
The predefined role class org.objectteams.Team.Confined cannot be widened to to any other type, not even to java.lang.Object.
It is illegal to override class Confined in any sub-class of org.objectteams.Team.

In order to express ownership, a role has to be declared like this:

```
public team class MyTeam {
    protected class OwnedRole extends Confined { ... }
}
```

This declaration suffices to establish the guarantee that references from outside the scope of an instance of MyTeam will never refer to an instance of OwnedRole owned by that team. The second part of the above rule enforces that Confined cannot be tampered with: while all other role classes can be overridden in sub-teams (roles are virtual classes) this is forbidden for class Confined.

This model is limited to role classes that do not inherit from any class outside the team. I will now show how cross-boundary inheritance can be made safe with respect to ownership. Additionally, roles implementing public interfaces will be discussed in section 2.3 on page 449.

Restricted Inheritance. I have not yet motivated the term "Confined Roles". This term is derived from the concept of "Confined Types" [11]. The original work defines how objects can be confined to a package by specific type rules. At the core Vitek and Bokowski give a solution to the above problem of polymorphic variables which is less restrictive than the prohibition of cross-boundary inheritance. Their solution uses two properties: *confined* (a property of a type) and *anonymous* (a property of a method). The "confined" property is similar to confined roles in OT/J with the main difference that confined types are confined to a package (static scoping) whereas confined roles are confined to a team instance (instance scope). By disallowing widening from a confined type to a non-confined type they solve part of the problem of polymorphism. Additionally, they speak of "hidden widening" to refer to situations where the this pointer is implicitly widened, as it occurs when invoking a method from a super-class. For any method that could cause such hidden widening they require the "anonymous" property, which expresses that the method in no way leaks the this pointer to third parties.

In [12] I proposed a mechanism for controlling cross-boundary inheritance similar to the rules of confined types. Instead of analyzing all calls to methods of a confined object I proposed to declare the boundary at the role class declaration.

In this approach an interface (Slicelfc below) is used to restrict inheritance to a slice of the super-class. The syntax for restricted cross-boundary inheritance is:

```
public team class MyTeam {
    protected class OwnedRole extends RegularClass
                    restrictedBy Slicelfc { ... }
}
```

Rule 3 (Restricted Inheritance)
A declaration R extends C restrictedBy I expresses an implementation inheritance between R and C with these properties:
1. R cannot be widened to C
2. R inherits from C only those methods declared also in I.
3. all methods in (2) must have the "anonymous" property.

These rules bring more flexibility to confined roles and at the same time combine the safety of the original confined types with a more explicit coding style.

2.2 From Confined Types to Confined Roles

Confined roles have similar rules and guarantees as introduced for confined types. Instances of *confined types* are confined to the static scope of a package; inside the package references to confined instances are legal but references cannot cross the confinement boundary. By contrast, *confined roles* are confined to the instance scope of a team instance, only the owning team instance and all its members may refer to a confined role, references crossing that boundary are again illegal.

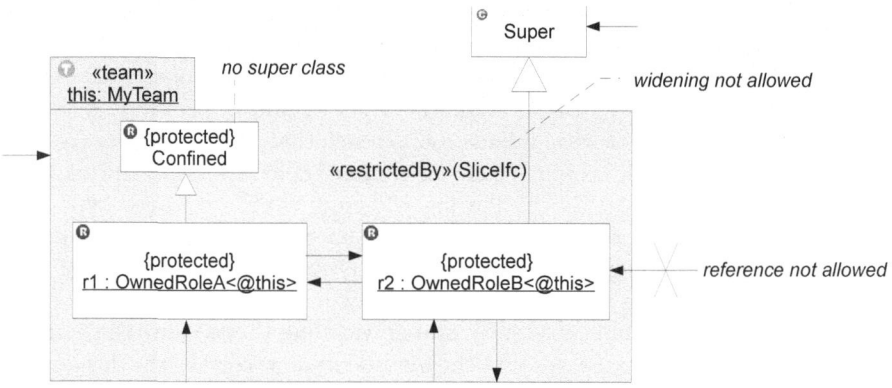

Fig. 3. Roles confined inside a team instances

The shift from package scoping to team scoping has several advantages. First, by creating multiple team instances the application can create multiple independent confinement scopes. Second, teams can be specialized using inheritance, and family polymorphism will ensure that no bad surprises happen. Third, while packages live in a flat space (qualified names are a pure convenience with no semantics) teams can be nested at will, so that nested teams can be confined within their enclosing team instance thus improving the scalability of the approach.

2.3 Adding Basic Flexibility to Confined Roles

In a perfect world, confined roles could be seen as sufficient for concerns of alias control. However, as mentioned before, much of the challenge lies in combining the strictness of an ownership model with the flexibility required in real world applications.

In this section I will discuss several concepts that gradually mitigate the burdens of ownership. A more radical discussion will follow in the next section.

Team Packages. From an organizational point of view a team can also be seen as a package: In OT/J the logical nesting of roles (and nested teams) does not require physically nesting the source code inside the team class. Roles can optionally be stored in separate role files inside a "team package" — a package of the same name as the team class. This resolves potential scalability issues: aspects like collaboration, source code control etc, don't play well with huge files. Forcing the developer to store many roles (and nested teams) in the same source file would incur a tremendous burden when nesting is extensively used in real world development. Role files are a simple but essential mechanism towards making (nested) teams a widely used grouping concept. Role files and team packages provide organizational flexibility but do not affect the semantics.

Transfer of Role Ownership? Ownership models tend to be very rigid, which makes their application in real-world development difficult. One way to make an ownership model more flexible is to allow an owned object to be transfered from one owner to another (see, e.g., [13]). OT/J has the basic mechanisms for transferring a role from one team to another. This is provided by a pre-defined interface org.objectteams.ITeamMigratable. If a role declares to implement this interface it will automatically have a method:

```
<R> R<@otherTeam> migrateToTeam(Team otherTeam)
```

This method takes care of updating implicit references (internally a role is linked to its owning team and the team has a map of its roles), and also a type change from R<@this> to R<@otherTeam> is performed. However, in its current implementation this concept is inherently unsafe as it cannot prevent the usage of existing references using the old type R<@this> after the migration. This means, when a role migrates to another team this is not a safe ownership transfer. The basic mechanics for the transfer exist, but for a safe application in the context of confined roles the role reference would need to be unique. As OT/J doesn't support a concept of uniqueness this would need to be added for safe transfer of role ownership.

On the other hand, role migration has been introduced more from an academical discussion rather than from practical needs in real-world application of OT/J. Thus, it remains to be shown whether the benefits of added flexibility balance the costs of adding uniqueness to OT/J.

Representation Encapsulation. Approaches like Universe Types [14,15] prevent external changes to the internal representation of an aggregate object, while still allowing clients to read the internal information. This is done in two steps: A **rep** keyword is introduced to mark references that should be protected against leaking to the outside, because these reference would expose internal details. Second, a **readonly** keyword is introduced for marking references that allow the invocation of only those methods that do not modify internal state.

In [12] I proposed to map this model to Object Teams in a way that qualifies the involved types rather than references: Each reference to a confined role automatically has the properties of a **rep** reference as the role type is already owned

by the enclosing team instance. readonly references can be achieved by declaring
a readonly interface and by using this interface type for references to be passed
to clients.

Consider the following structure:

```
public team class AUniverse {
    public readonly interface IReadOnlyRole {
        int pureFunction();
    }
    protected class RoleRepr extends Confined
        implements IReadOnlyRole
    { ... }
    private RoleRepr state = ...;
    public IReadOnlyRole getState() {
        return state; // applies widening to the readonly interface
    }
}
```

Here, role RoleRepr cannot be mentioned outside the enclosing instance of AU-
niverse. Its super-interface IReadOnlyRole, however, is public and thus can be
shared with external clients. Still, clients cannot break the encapsulated representation, because this interface may only include those methods that provably
do not change internal state.

This is only a sketch of how to combine the concepts of Universes and Object
Teams, but the mapping seems to be easily possible based on the fact that both
approaches use types that are interpreted relative to the current this object.

Opaque Roles. If encapsulation should protect objects not only against unwanted modification but also against leaking of (secret) information — specifically in the realm of security — OT/J provides the option to expose opaque
references. This is achieved by declaring a role class as follows:

```
protected class OwnedRole extends Confined
    implements IConfined
{ ... }
```

The predefined type org.objectteams.Team.IConfined is constructed similarly to
Confined with two differences: it is an interface rather than a class and it is
public rather than protected. The effect is that role OwnedRole can be widened
to IConfined and under this type the reference can be passed to external clients.
But this widening hides *all* properties except: identity and dependence on the
enclosing team instance.

Such a reference can be seen as a ticket that is issued by a team and can only
be further processed by the issuing team. Clients may hold on to the ticket, but
can neither access any features of the opaque role instance, nor pass it to another
team instance. The type IConfined<@issuingTeam> always keeps the connection
to the issuing team. Only inside the issuing team (where the dependent type can
be abbreviated as IConfined because it again depends on this) can the reference

be cast back to OwnedRole and processing can continue. Consider this client code:

```
1    void session (final T t1) {
2        IConfined ticket = t1.startWorkflow();
3        // ticket is almost completely useless
4        final T t2 = new T();
5        t2.process(ticket);  // compile error
6        System.out.println(ticket.toString());  // compile error
7        // but ticket can be used to trigger further processing in t1:
8        t1.process(ticket);  // OK
9    }
```

The compile error in line 5 reflects that t1 and t2 don't refer to the same team instance. The compile error in line 6 is given because IConfined has no methods, not even toString(). The only useful style of using an opaque role reference is shown in line 8: by passing the reference back to the issuing team — here t1 — the team can be asked to continue working with this role. A simple discipline, to be followed locally inside the team, will suffice to ensure safe downcasts inside method process: For each role that should be externalized as an opaque role, a specific sub-type of IConfined is created, which again has no properties, but prohibits confusing different role types:

```
public team class T {
    // externally visible opaque types:
    public interface ITicket1 extends IConfined {}
    public interface ITicket2 extends IConfined {}
    // protected implementation classes:
    protected class OwnedRole1 extends Confined
        implements ITicket1
    { ... }
    protected class OwnedRole2 extends Confined
        implements ITicket2
    { ... }
    // public methods:
    public ITicket1 startWorkflow() {
    return new OwnedRole1();  // widening to ITicket1
    }
    public void process(ITicket1 ticket) {
    OwnedRole1 r1 = (OwnedRole1) ticket;  // cast cannot fail
    }
}
```

Inside method process we have the following information regarding ticket1: It is a role of this team T; it has type ITicket1; inside T type ITicket1 has only one implementing class: OwnedRole1. Thus the cast is safe. Only through sub-classing T and violating one of these assumptions can this reasoning be invalidated. But we consider this a quite normal consequence of inheritance: inherited assumptions must be re-checked.

This concludes the discussion of hierarchical structures that support ownership either purely or some relaxed form of it.

3   Non-hierarchical Structures

With confined roles OT/J supports a strong model for hierarchical structures, where nesting is not only defined statically, but applies to runtime instances to yield a form of ownership. I have shown several extensions of the model that add specific forms of flexibility whereupon always the hierarchical structure remained the main force.

This model works great when software can be decomposed into one hierarchical structure. Unfortunately, models solely relying on hierarchical structures easily break when one tries to apply them to real world, complex problems. What if confinement boundaries cannot be drawn to yield a hierarchical structure? What if different concerns suggest different boundaries? The strength of enforcing confinement by the type checker lies in the safety that no exceptions to the intended confinement are possible. Thus a typical question in research on aliasing is how to relax constraints in exceptional cases without compromising the desired guarantees.

Object Teams adds a new relationship to object-orientation: role playing. This relationship is introduced for the purpose of better supporting modularity in complex situations. Complexity can be mastered by explicit support for multiple *perspectives* within a software design.

On the road to improved separation of concerns the role playing relationship has some properties that at first sight seem to contradict the goals of encapsulation: this relationship has the power to disregard existing encapsulation boundaries and introduces a new level of intimacy between objects. Despite all this the role playing relationship actually adds some rather interesting new options to the balancing of encapsulation and flexibility — for the benefit of both.

3.1   Role Playing

OT/J introduces a **playedBy** relationship between a role R that is a member of a team T and a base B that resides outside the team:

```
public team class T {
    protected class R playedBy B { ... }
}
```

This relationship has some properties similar to inheritance but unlike inheritance in mainstream object-oriented languages role playing is a relation between runtime instances, not just classes. Role playing is thus similar to delegation in languages like Self [7].

> **Rule 4 (PlayedBy Relationship)**
> *A playedBy declaration defines a mandatory one-way relationship such that
> each role instance at runtime will be immutably linked to an existing base
> instance of the designated type.*

In order to compare role playing to class-based inheritance four dimensions
deserve discussing: re-use, overriding, intimacy and sub-typing.

Callout Bindings for Re-use. One reason for using inheritance is the re-use
of features (fields and methods) defined in a super-class. OT/J supports this
with *callout method bindings*, which basically have the following syntax:

```
protected class MyRole playedBy MyBase {
    String getName() -> String getName();
}
```

A callout method binding connects two method signatures, one for the role (left)
and one from the base (right), so that the base method can also be invoked via
the role type. Given that role and base are two distinct instances this amounts
to simple forwarding at runtime.

Variants of callout bindings exist (a) to bind to fields of the base, (b) to adjust
signatures (names and parameters) between role and base, and (c) to abbreviate
unambiguous signatures by just using the names.

Callin Binding for Overriding. In the inverse direction *callin method bindings* enable a role to override methods from their base using this syntax:

```
protected class MyRole playedBy MyBase {
    String getPhoneNo() <- replace String getPhoneNo();
}
```

The effect of a callin binding is that method calls targeted at the base will be
intercepted and redirected to the role (again the role method is shown on the left
hand side). One of the callin modifiers **replace**, **before** or **after** must be given to
select how the role method is combined with the base method. Readers familiar
with CLOS or with any aspect language will easily recognize these combinators,
only "around" has been renamed to "replace".

A careful reader may have been surprised when callout bindings were equated
with forwarding, which seems to clash with the earlier comparison to delegation
in Self. In fact an OT/J programmer has the choice: a callout binding on its
own indeed applies the weak forwarding semantics. However, using both kinds of
method bindings in concert is equivalent to delegation. Thus it can be shown that
callout and callin method bindings suffice to implement the runtime semantics
of inheritance. How do they affect modularity, encapsulation and confinement?

Intimacy. Normally, a callout binding would have to respect the standard rules for static visibility. However, just as a sub-class may see more features of its super-class than external clients, also a role may access base features that are not normally accessible.

Rather than adding yet another visibility modifier, OT/J supports a concept called *decapsulation*:

Rule 5 (Decapsulation)
The callout and callin bindings of a role may bind to the specified base feature disregard the normal visibility rules.

The compiler signals each case of decapsulation with a warning. Severity of decapsulation warnings can be configured at two levels: Each project may define a global strategy by configuring decapsulation issues as one of error, warning or ignore. Second, in the source code each individual decapsulation warning can be suppressed using the standard annotation @SuppressWarnings with argument "decapsulation". This annotation can be applied to a role class or to individual callout bindings, where it then serves as documentation of the intimate relationship.

Decapsulation makes the relationship between a role and its base more intimate, similar to the relationship between sub- and super-classes in standard inheritance. Two differences exist: First, decapsulation is applied by individual callout bindings and each application will be reported by the compiler. Second, decapsulation is stronger than sub-classing, as it supports access even to private features.

3.2   Translation Polymorphism

The fourth dimension of comparing role playing with inheritance concerns issues of subtype polymorphism.

Consider base class Person and a team Company with a role Employee played by Person. We now, e.g., ask whether an Employee should be assignable to a variable of type Person. In order to allow this, we would have to ensure that all operations of Person can also be performed on the Employee instance. This could be achieved by forwarding all method calls that are not directly understood by Employee, but the design of OT/J decides differently: In OT/J forwarding only happens based on explicit callout bindings, e.g., a method Person.getSpouse() may intentionally be unavailable via the Employee role. So in general a role does *not* support all methods of its base. This implies that a role type is *not* a subtype of its base.

Interestingly, the assignability requested above can still be achieved by slightly extending the semantics of the assignment: OT/J automatically inserts a required translation to make the assignment type safe: instead of actually assigning a reference to the role the reference to the base instance is used. Consider the role-base pair as one object with two facets. Now the required translation is only to switch the reference from one facet (the role) to the other (the base). Because this translation serves the same purpose as subtyping does in subtype polymorphism, we say that the assignment in question is legal due to *translation polymorphism*. The translation from a role to its base is called *lowering*.

Rule 6 (Lowering)
Assignability from a role to a variable of its base type is achieved by an implicitly inserted lowering translation, which translates the given role reference to a reference to the bound base instance.

Let us extend the company example so that a company can help in arranging ride sharing among employees from the same city:

```
1   class Person {
2       City getCityOfResidence() { ... }
3   }
4   team class Company {
5       protected class Hub playedBy City {
6           void manageRides(Employee rider) { ... }
7       }
8       protected class Employee playedBy Person {
9           void call(Employee e)  -> void callOnPhone(Person p);
10          Hub getHub()           -> City getCityOfResidence();
11      }
12      void checkRideSharing(Employee emp) {
13          Hub hub = emp.getHub();
14          hub.manageRides(emp);
15      }
16  }
```

We see an application of lowering in line 9: An **Employee** inherits from the underlying **Person** the ability to call someone else on the phone. Similar to the considerations about assignments we can obviously use an **Employee** role as an argument to **callOnPhone** where actually a **Person** is expected: take the role, translate it to its base and continue with this reference.

Things get more interesting when considering the opposite direction: how can we use the result from **getCityOfResidence** within the context of a **Company** where we're not interested in a **City** but in a **Hub** (cf. line 10)?

It is a unique feature of translation polymorphism in OT/J that also this direction of translation is fully automated and supports substitutability. This translation – called *lifting* – is a bit more involved than lowering. A given base instance may not yet have a role instance of the required type or more than one role may exist which all are bound to the same base. Both problems are solved by making an enclosing team instance responsible for the lifting translation: If a required role instance does not exist the team will implicitly create one on-demand and store it in a local map for later retrieval. This map also solves the second problem: although an unlimited number of roles may be bound to the same base, only one role instance is allowed per team instance. Thus if we know the team instance, we can unambiguously look up the role in this team's internal map.

Rule 7 (Lifting)
In the context of a given team instance a base reference can be used in certain places where actually a role instance is expected, by (implicitly) inserting a lifting translation, which either retrieves an existing role for the given base from an internal map, or creates a fresh role on-demand, if no matching role was found. A role is uniquely identified by a given base instance, a given team instance, and the required role type. Language rules ensure that all three pieces of information are available wherever lifting is applied.

Using these rules, lifting and lowering are fully implicit and provide the two-way substitutability of translation polymorphism. Only in one kind of program location can lifting be explicitly requested: A team method may declare a parameter that for the client has the type of a base class but inside the method the team will see the same thing as a role instance. The syntax of declared lifting uses the keyword **as**, as shown in this example:

```
public void hire(Person as Employee novice) {
    Hub hub = novice.getHub();
    hub.manageRides();
}
```

The translation between the client view and the internal view is achieved by lifting. In the case of a hire method the intention is to create a new role, but the same syntax is frequently used for triggering an operation on an existing role, while the client — obviously — only holds a reference to the bound base instance. It is generally true that lifting and lowering occur at the team boundary: lifting base objects to roles when they enter the context of a team instance and lowering role objects to their base when leaving the team.

I started by saying that role playing is similar to inheritance both in terms of the control flows supported by callout and callin, and also in terms of the special intimacy between a role and its base. When taking translation polymorphism into the picture we will see that role playing adds very interesting options also to encapsulation and even confinement.

4   Separate Worlds, Yet Connected

The main goal pursued by the design of OT/J is to make seemingly conflicting ends meet. We want to eat the cake and have it, too. We want to create modules that strictly encapsulate what's inside, yet we need to connect these modules in ways that need to mention internal details.

The key concept here is the team: making nested modules the rule rather than the exception. From there we can create higher level designs in various dimensions, with only one kind of building blocks: teams with arbitrarily complex internal structure.

From family polymorphism OT/J inherits the capability to consistently refine a team including all its contained roles and nested teams. While this is highly valuable for larger-scale re-use it doesn't add to the options regarding encapsulation. All it does is ensure that guarantees given with respect to a super-team are preserved for its sub-teams.

With opaque roles I have shown a model where an external client may have insight regarding different types used within a team and even regarding instances of confined roles. Yet, such a client cannot cause harm by using these references, because they can only be used by passing them as arguments back into the issuing team. So, yes, the client may have references into the internal structure of a team, but, no, he cannot tamper with these references. Readonly references provide a middle road, where a bit more information is available from a role. In fact it is a design choice whether the readonly interface is placed inside the team (can only be passed back to the same team), or outside the team (role reference drops information about the owning team). In the latter case, a team receiving a role reference by the non-role super-type will need a twofold cast that checks the type *and* the instance on which the type depends. The various levels of opening up role references for external use share as their base principle the use of widening to a more visible but feature-restricted type.

4.1   Layered Designs

The picture is even more interesting when also role playing is considered. With role playing we can construct layered designs. Consider the company example above and assume that the role Employee and Hub would be confined roles. Now the team Company adds slices to existing objects of type Person and City. Each role class may define fields and methods which can be interpreted as augmentations of the base object, e.g., a field salary inside role Employee kind-of adds to the properties of a Person. These slices, however, are only visible within the enclosing instance of Company. Now the mapping between inside and outside is not based on subtype polymorphism (widening and narrowing) but on translation polymorphism (lowering and lifting).

We have seen all the program elements involved in this mapping: playedBy, callout, callin and as, and we've seen the mechanisms that translate an instance from a role to its base (lowering) or vice versa (lifting). In order to see all these working in concert consider the data flows of an invocation of method hire shown above.

The caller provides a Person instance, declared lifting translates this into the Employee being hired. Inside the method we want to check if ride sharing is available for this employee's hometown, so we invoke getHub on the Employee, but in fact that method is not executed on the **Employee** but on the underlying **Person**, i.e., to invoke base behavior the call target is first lowered. Conversely, the method result, a **City** is translated back to the company world by lifting. This example should illustrate how the two worlds of people in cities and companies are stitched together. Each world speaks its own language and translations automatically happen at the boundary.

How is the layer boundary enforced? If roles are confined they can obviously not be mentioned outside the team. A simple rule also ensures the inverse: all base classes mentioned after **playedBy** should be imported with the modifier **base** as shown here:

```
package business;
import base realworld.City;
import base realworld.Person;
public team class Company {
    protected class Hub  extends Confined playedBy City
    { ... }
    protected class Employee extends Confined playedBy Person
    { ... }
    ....
}
```

This kind of import ensures that the imported type is not used in the body of any methods of this team. Legal uses of a base-imported type are limited to the **playedBy** declaration and to all right hand sides of callout or callin method bindings plus the base side of a **Base as Role r** method argument.

This rule defines a membrane through which elements from several layers can be connected. Yet neither side *can* in its implementation refer to the respective other side.

The stitches that cross the boundaries between layers are the role playing relationships. Going back to the metaphor of role and base being different slices of the same conceptual entity, we can now see that different slices can be subject to different encapsulation. In fact, some slices can be confined roles, which could be useful, e.g., for protecting the **salary** field against access from outside the **Company**. Other slices may be publically accessible.

4.2   Improving Encapsulation by Means of Decapsulation

When creating layered designs for complex real life problems, decapsulation is an important tool that potentially cuts both ways. It is obvious that decapsulation can cause harm. That's why it should never be used unknowingly and without good reasons (remember that occurrences of decapsulation are reported by the compiler).

In order to keep confined roles sound, the language restricts decapsulation such that a confined role is immune to decapsulation. Note that for fully supporting layered designs, a team may indeed bind roles not only to plain base classes but also to roles of another team. OT/J goes so far as to allow protected roles to be used as a base class of another role in another layer, where this role playing relationship itself disregards the **protected** visibility by means of decapsulation. Only when a role is confined as declared by extending **Confined**, decapsulation is no longer allowed. This ensures that confinement can be unilaterally declared by a role, and can be relied upon without performing a global analysis.

So we know the limits of decapsulation: it cannot interfere with confinement. I hold that decapsulation actually helps to decrease the total coupling in a complex design. How? Think of an existing system where at some point in time a new feature should be added. If the implementation of the new requirement needs access to some protected detail of an existing class, standard technology offers two options: either (a) make the protected detail accessible for all, or (b) place (parts of) the new feature into the existing structure, so that access will happen from within. While (a) is obviously undesirable, it might take a closer look at (b) to see why this is not an optimal solution, either.

With decapsulation we gain a desirable third option: keep the existing design as it is without abandoning its encapsulation boundaries; develop the new feature as a new module on its own right, instead of scattering its implementation into the places where it needs access to internals; and connect the old and new worlds with a few stitches, some of which may need to apply decapsulation. Each decapsulation now defines a well-delimited exception to the general rule of encapsulation boundaries. A role that uses decapsulation has to be checked diligently for it has special privileges, but after that check it is considered a trusted proxy of an instance living in a different world.

Lastly, *gradual encapsulation* as elaborated in [16] makes allowance for the observation that some conflicts regarding encapsulation vs. decapsulation — should they arise — cannot be settled just by looking at type systems and software designs. Some of these conflicts are actually organizational or social conflicts, e.g., between a vendor of a framework protecting his code against unintended use, and a client of the framework needing access to internals in order to implement a required feature. Should such conflicts become relevant, negotiation between stakeholders should result in a *join point policy* that will be used as a parameter when checking the validity of a system that uses decapsulation. Decapsulation is the enabling concept for this shift from technology to negotiation.

While confined roles give final guarantees, decapsulation of non-confined types allows to reduce the overall coupling by allowing just a few, limited exceptions. Gradual encapsulation places the final decision into those hands that *must* be consulted, the relevant stakeholders like framework developers, application developers and end users.

4.3   Zero Reference Roles

So far, examples have assumed that behavior inside a team is triggered by invoking a team method. I played down the concept of *callin* bindings as a form of declared overriding. However, the same concept can also be used in a style that more resembles aspect-oriented programming: Method call interception can also be triggered from code that is unaware of any teams and roles. The next section will give some details on when exactly callin bindings fire, but for now let's assume they would always fire when the bound base method is invoked. Based on such use of callin bindings, OT/J is perfectly suited for unanticipated adaptation of existing code, for modularizing features that in an object-oriented implementation are notoriously cross-cutting.

For the sake of ownership we can go one step further: we can create roles to which no part of the program will ever hold a reference, yet those roles can participate in the execution. Consider the following role:

```
1   protected class Credentials extends Confined playedBy User{
2       String password;
3       installPassword <- after register;
4       checkPassword    <- replace login;
5       void installPassword() {
6           String pw1 = secureRead();
7           String pw2 = secureRead();
8           if (pw1.equals(pw2))
9               this.password = pw1;
10          else
11              reportProblem("Passwords don't match");
12      }
13      callin void checkPassword() {
14          if (this.password == null)
15              reportProblem("Not registered");
16          else if (!secureRead().equals(this.password)))
17              reportProblem("Wrong password");
18          else
19              base.checkPassword();
20      }
21  }
```

Instances of this role store the password of a given user, so these instances should never be leaked to untrusted code. Everything outside the team that defines this role can be considered untrusted. Still the role interacts with the application, because it actively takes control whenever a user registers and logs in.

The first callin binding (line 3) intercepts the control flow when a user registers. The role method uses a secure device for reading the password which the user enters twice, and upon success the password is stored locally. At any later time when the same user tries to log into the system, the same role will intercept the login() call (line 4). Within the method checkPassword the expected checks are performed. Note that the callin binding causes the call target to be lifted from User to Credentials. If no such role has been initialized we will find a role with an empty password field. An error will be reported. Another error will be reported if passwords don't match. Only if both tests are passed, will the *base-call* in line 19 invoke the original behavior, which amounts to actually executing the login method of base class User (a base-call applies the callin binding in left-to-right direction).

Because the base application cannot see the Credentials role — neither the type nor any instance — there is no way this role could be tampered with.

Analysis of whether the enclosing team, which owns the role, can do any wrong is reduced to checking that the team indeed does nothing with the role. It would be a trivial step to actually mark the role as unmentionable, so that the compiler can also check this rule.

This pattern implements the insight that the best means to avoid any risks of being compromised is to remain completely invisible.

4.4 Connecting Architecture Levels

Teams in OT/J raise modularity from individual classes to nested structures of classes and instances. For still better scalability OT/J has been integrated with the OSGi component model for Java [17]. The integration is based on the Equinox implementation of the OSGi specification, hence we speak of OT/E-quinox [18].

OSGi introduces visibility rules for specifying which classes from one component ("bundle") can be seen by which other component. These rules are checked at compile time and enforced at runtime, using Java class loaders for encapsulation boundaries. OT/Equinox adds to these rules a further constraint regulating role-base bindings: A role-base binding can only cross a component boundary if a corresponding declaration exists at component level. This declaration is called an "aspect binding" (Figure 4); it must mention the base component whose classes are to be bound as base classes and the team whose roles request binding to those base classes. Thus absence of any aspect binding declarations affecting a given component guarantees that all classes inside that component are unaffected by adaptation through roles.

```
<extension
      point=" org . eclipse . objectteams . otequinox . aspectBindings ">
   <aspectBinding>
      <basePlugin id=" org . eclipse . jdt . core " />
      <team class=" org . eclipse . objectteams . otdt . . . . SomeTeam"
            activation=" ALL_THREADS" />
   </ aspectBinding>
</ extension>
```

Fig. 4. An OT/Equinox aspect binding, defined as an Equinox extension

5 Instances and Dynamism

OT/J hasn't been designed with a primary focus on any form of alias control. Still teams and roles harmonize quite well with alias control, based on the common emphasis on instances. Protected classes don't help much if the instances of these classes can leak (e.g., using widening). OT/J's focus on instances is rooted in two fundamental concepts: Dependent types connect the worlds of types and instances. The value on which a type depends can seamlessly be used to denote the owner of a role type and all its instances. Secondly, the role playing relationship is a per-instance relationship. Where class-based inheritance would result in big instances putting all the features of all inherited classes into a single instance, roles are object slices that remain distinct even at runtime, such that different slices of an object can be owned by different owners. This combines the strength of attaching different ownership labels to individual features of a class, with the higher abstraction of assigning entire role classes (encapsulating sets of features) to teams. It could be argued that ownership tends to be a cross-cutting concern in traditional ownership models. With teams also this concern can be well localized.

With the focus on instances comes the ability to support more dynamism. Much of the dynamism in the Object Teams model comes from the last concept to be presented here: *team activation*. The question here is: how can the implicit nature of method call interception as incarnated by callin bindings be tamed so that a program has the option to control where and when and why callin bindings should fire. This question is answered by two concepts: guard predicates [19], which are beyond the scope of this text, and team activation. Team activation is again a feature of instances:

Rule 8 (Team Activation)
Each team instance can be dynamically activated and deactivated at runtime. The effect is: an inactive team will receive no calls due to callin bindings, whereas the callin bindings of an active team fire each time the bound base method is invoked.

With team activation a team instance can be used to implement a program *mode*. Simply activating/deactivating the team instance puts the program in a different mode. Team activation adds yet another option of encapsulation when we have a closer look at the supported activation scopes: a team can be activated either globally, or *per-thread*. Now consider the following design: A team has only confined roles, no team methods that would invoke any role behavior but roles do have some callin bindings. If an instance of such a team is activated for one particular thread, we immediately have the guarantee that roles inside that team will only ever act within the designated thread, so those roles are confined to that thread.

6   Practical Experience

The language OT/J and the supporting IDE, the OTDT [10] have been developed with strong focus on real world applicability — to wit: the OTDT seamlessly extends the Eclipse Java Development Tools (JDT) so as to provide the same level of convenience, which the JDT provides for Java, also for developers using OT/J. To achieve this, significant parts of the OTDT have been developed using OT/J and OT/Equinox itself. Since June 2011 the OTDT is part of the annual Simultaneous Release of Eclipse.

Based on the mature tooling, OT/J is well suitable for practical studies of various kinds. For example, in an early student project the JHotDraw framework for graphical editors was refactored to leverage OT/J for easier customization. During this project team classes with more than 80 role classes where developed, which demonstrated that team packages are indispensable for practical work.

6.1   Initial Comparative Study

During the TOPPrax project [20] a comparative study was performed where the same ERP application was developed in two versions in parallel: one in Java the other in OT/J. The design of the experiment did not yield data that stands statistic scrutiny, but still some interesting results could be extracted.

First of all, the study demonstrated the feasibility of the approach: after a modest extent of training the participants of the experiment where able to apply OT/J to develop an application according to real world requirements. The experiment was performed in the early stages of Object Teams. Thus the tooling wasn't yet mature and teaching material was still lacking essential parts, like a catalog of Object Teams specific design patterns. This situation has much improved since.

The implementation of a model-view-controller architecture exhibited much better separation of concerns in the OT/J variant than in the pure Java version. Yet, no hard data can be provided to back this observation.

One particular design choice in this study introduced an ownership-related topic "through the back door": A team class was designed as a module for all entities in the domain, entities being modeled by role classes. This team class was responsible for accessing the underlying database. Whenever other parts of the application required access to domain entities, dependent types had to be used, as enforced by the type checker.

With a simple addition this could be used to make database transactions explicit in the design: Responsibility for database transactions was given to instances of the domain team. Without further effort the type checker ensured that a domain entity obtained from one domain team instance could never be passed to a different team instance. Thus, mixing entities from different transactions was impossible.

During the design process, an attempt was made to store references to domain entities in ad-hoc objects (as part of a forecast for supply chain management). Initially, the developers complained that the type system wouldn't let them write the code they wanted. This was when a closer look revealed the transaction scenario described above. The result was to also make the ad-hoc aggregate (the forecast result) a dependent class, although not member of any team. This step allowed the developers to propagate dependency information from one module to another, without weakening the rigor of the dependent types system.

6.2 Application in Tool Smithing

Since significant parts of the OTDT are written in OT/J, more properties can be mined from the corresponding source code repository.

The main observation here emphasizes the role of OT/J for maintainability: The OTDT is a variant of the JDT, and this variant is being maintained over a period of more than five years and still counting. Never during this period did the release of a new JDT version impose a relevant disruption for the maintenance of the OTDT. For those parts, where the JDT is adapted using OT/J mechanisms, the maintenance effort was practically zero.

This implementation hasn't yet been analyzed in the light of ownership, but one advantage is already obvious: The capability to *confine role instances within a thread* is a very useful concept for this kind of architecture.

The basic scenario is like this: in order to adapt the JDT for a new requirement several locations in the base component had to be adapted. In many cases these locations have no direct connection in the base component, yet the new feature requires a data flow from one to the other. This is a typical situation, because the architecture of the base component was made without knowledge about the new feature and thus nothing could be done a-priori to keep data flows of this new feature local by any measure. The resulting conflict is an instance of the "tyranny of the dominant decomposition" [4]. An approach where the base component would be modified in-place has basically two options: Change the architecture to better accommodate the new feature (which is not a good idea if the variant should be updated from future versions of the base component) or create global variables to establish the required non-local data flows. Obviously, global variables violate locality of any modular design.

With OT/J we can do better: In the design of the OTDT such data flows are mediated by roles in a team: when the start of the behavior to adapt is observed (using a callin method binding) relevant data is stored in a role. Later, when that data is needed for further processing, the previous role instance is retrieved and the data obtained from it.

Whenever the new feature to be implemented could be associated to a specific context, and when this context could be identified as a specific behavior of the base component, the thread executing that base behavior can be used as a confinement boundary for all roles contributing to the adaptation. By only temporarily activating a fresh team instance for this particular thread it is easily guaranteed that no concurrent behavior will ever see the data stored in roles of this team instance.

Another dimension of decoupling concerns the ability to attach multiple roles to the same base class. Within the implementation of the OTDT this situation is not uncommon. These roles of the same base are unaware of each other and from an aliasing point of view it is impossible that they interact in any way. Only the very few cases where two roles intercept calls to the same base method may potentially require coordination by an independent party to ensure the expected behavior. The compiler signals these situations to alert the developer.

Role migration is not used in the implementation of the OTDT. It would, however, be wrong to conclude that teams don't share information regarding roles. When an object should be sent from one team to another, the natural solution in OT/J applies an advanced form of layered designs as shown in section 4.1. For communication between two teams, the caller team first applies lowering to send only the associated base object. Next the receiver team applies lifting to translate the base object into its own role. We call this the "ping pong" pattern, as the ball has to be dropped (lowered) to the table before it can be transfered to the other team, where it will be lifted again.

Similar results have been achieved in similar projects in the same field of tool smithing. Most prominently, OT/J was also used for prototyping a new JDT feature that a year later was merged into the JDT proper: support for annotation based null analysis. Again maintainability was drastically improved — at one point the exact same OT/Equinox plug-in could be used to add the new analysis to six distinct versions/variants of the JDT. Again the improved maintainability was achieved by much better code locality.

In most of this work, role classes are typically protected but not confined. In a few cases it is actually important to define a role class as a sub-class of a public class, even with subtyping; for these roles confinement is neither intended nor possible. It should, however, be easily possible to convert the majority of protected roles into confined roles. The main reason for not using confined roles by default is that confined roles are not the default, neither in the language OT/J, nor when creating new role classes in the IDE.

The existing code base should be perfectly suitable for analyzing the impact of turning protected roles into confined roles in bulk. If that analysis shows no significant drawback, two roads for broader adoption of confined roles are open: either just change the default behavior of the IDE so that all new role classes extend Confined, *or* change the language semantics such that not specifying a super-class makes a role confined and the opposite would need to be achieved by explicitly specifying extends Object. At that point, developers using OT/J would indeed get confinement totally for free, paying only for a few exceptions.

7   Related Work

The Object Teams model has roots in different fields of research, most prominently: virtual classes and multi-dimension separation of concerns.

7.1   Nesting, Virtual Classes, Dependent Types

The author is much indebted to Erik Ernst for his work on virtual classes in gbeta [21,2] and for many discussions on how his approach can be faithfully mapped to OT/J. Based on this close relationship, hopefully all findings from formalizing virtual classes à la gbeta (like [22]) are valid for OT/J, too.

Initially, OT/J used a path syntax for dependent types: teamInstance.RoleClass. This hints at the similarity to path dependent types in other languages, several of which were developed around the same time as OT/J like, e.g., Scala [23] and CaesarJ [24]. Also, initially OT/J had no syntax for declaring a class as dependent: team members are always dependent classes and outside of any team no dependent class could be defined. Inside a team even references to a role class do not need special syntax because the enclosing team instance is implicitly used as the type anchor. As a result the protected or confined use of roles is the natural primary usage of roles, while publically exposing roles requires more effort.

This syntax was later revised to emphasis the nature as parameterized types: references to a dependent class are now denoted as RoleClass<@teamInstance>. The new syntax not only avoids the syntactic ambiguity of qualified names, but also opens the door towards instance-dependent classes that are not team members. The latter is achieved by writing class Dependent<Owner owner>, which is to say the class depends on an instance of type Owner, which inside the class can be referred to as owner. However, non-role dependent classes are rarely used in practice and for that reason this concept has never been expanded to account also for multi-dependent types as done by Gasiunas et al. [25].

Readers interested in a comparison of different approaches using virtual classes are kindly referred to [26]. The goal of the research on Object Teams was not to advance the state-of-the-art regarding virtual classes and dependent types, but to put this concept into a larger context, asking how can dependent types be combined (a) with the concept of roles and (b) with an ownership model?

By emphasizing nesting of classes and instances, Object Teams also bears similarity with Newspeak [27]. The way in which Newspeak supports capability based programming can also be applied in Object Teams. However, Object Teams has more options of flexibility, notably by the concept of role playing, which does not exist in most of the approaches discussed in this section.

7.2   Multi-dimensional Separation of Concerns

The Object Teams model was born during discussions how multi-dimensional separation of concerns [4] can best be supported by a programming language. AspectJ [28] has become the dominant programming language in this field. The main contribution of AspectJ is the concept of "pointcuts" to denote a (possibly large) set of events that should trigger a particular piece of aspect code (advice). This concept has been de-emphasized in the design of Object Teams, to avoid new problems of maintainability arising from a new kind of implicit coupling. Conceptually, Object Teams is closer to the Hyperspaces model [6], without, however, adopting the fully symmetric approach to composition. The direct ancestor of the Object Teams approach is the idea of Aspectual Components [29], a fact that explains some similarities to other descendants of the same root like, e.g., CaesarJ [24].

Object Teams can be seen as a particularly conservative approach within the field of multi-dimensional separation of concerns, favoring existing object-oriented concepts over ad-hoc mechanisms: Pointcuts are avoided in favor of explicit bindings between methods. Teams and roles emphasize the importance of instances as modules.

In Object Teams the emphasis on instances and on connecting modules by instance relationships is supported by the concepts of lifting and lowering. CaesarJ [24] supports a similar concept called "wrapper recycling" with two decisive differences: wrapper recycling does not support the dynamism of Object Teams' smart lifting [30], where the runtime type of a base object determines the role class to use. Secondly, wrapper recycling is an explicit conversion that can be requested at any code location. Lifting, by contrast, only happens at a team boundary; only team methods may explicitly declare lifting, in callin and callout method bindings lifting even remains implicit with no special syntax.

Also Scala's implicit conversions are sometimes compared to lifting. Implicit conversion is a more general mechanism, for detailed comparison one would have to implement specific conversion functions to emulate lifting. It has not been shown that such functions can be implemented in a re-usable way, whereas Object Teams hides all infrastructure needed for lifting and lowering as implicitly provided by the language. More importantly, as with wrapper recycling, implicit conversions can occur at any program location. This opens the doors to very undisciplined use of implicit conversions that can negatively impact several aspects of quality like comprehensibility, locality etc.

All this is in contrast to lifting and lowering in Object Teams, where these translations are inherently designed for connecting otherwise separate worlds. The key is in applying lifting only at a team boundary, which is enforced by *not* providing generally applicable syntax that could be used to explicitly invoke lifting anywhere in the program (even declared lifting is bound to a team boundary). Actually, the Object Teams rules of visibility would not even allow the definition of a lifting function for a confined role, because no program location exists that is allowed to mention the input *and* output type of this function. The language provided conversions are the only possible gateway for these data flows, which is the basis for combining the role playing relationship with role confinement.

7.3 Modules for Alias Control

Work on ownership in OT/J was inspired mainly from two sources: Confined Types [11] and Universe Types [14,15]. Papers from both groups contain hints that family polymorphism would provide a significant enhancement to the respective approach. I previously elaborated how flavors of both approaches can be accommodated in OT/J [12]. While this fully subsumes Confined Types, Universe Types have been evolved to a more powerful concept than the subset discussed here. For an update see [15] in this book.

Confined Roles [12] quite likely gave inspiration to the work on Tribal Ownership [31]. Just like OT/J, Tribal Ownership combines nesting, family polymorphism and ownership into a coherent model, drawing a connection also to Confined Types [11]. Tribal Ownership assumes that all classes are either contained in a single containment hierarchy or in special "modules" allowing them to be imported in other classes. OT/J on the other hand integrates with the existing language Java paying respect to the fact that a wealth of classes exists that are unaware of ownership issues. For Tribal Ownership *all* private classes implicitly inherit from Root.PrivateObject, which corresponds to Team.Confined in OT/J. From an ownership point of view this design makes sense, but in a practical Java setting more flexibility is desirable. Consider any library function that expects an Object argument. Naturally, an owned object will not be allowed as an argument to such library function. In Tribal Ownership this will force the programmer to make the class public, because a private class is not allowed to inherit from a public class. In OT/J a compromise is possible: the programmer can revert to a regular protected role, which is a sub-type of Object. This sacrifices the confinement guarantees because widening is now possible, but the role class is still externally inaccessible.

Historically, the Confined Roles approach had no other choice than to respect library methods with arguments of type Object: at the time this approach was developed Java didn't have generics, and so type Object was abundantly used as a workaround. This situation has much improved since.

8   Conclusion

The Object Teams model has been developed for quite general purposes: advancing our capabilities towards better modularity and encapsulation in the face of complex requirements. This model has many roots in prior art ranging from multi-dimensional separation of concerns [4] — specifically work from the Demeter context [29] — up-to family polymorphism [2]. While those roots are not connected to research on alias control, it shouldn't really come as a surprise that contributions from the different strands of research on encapsulation can be synergetically merged into a combined approach.

The Object Teams model has several properties which make it specifically well suited for supporting some kind of alias control.

Object Teams focuses more on instances than mainstream object-oriented languages. If instances are to be protected against unwanted aliases, this is an essential step. More specifically, the use of dependent types can seamlessly be extended for representing ownership.

If ownership domains are found to be cross-cutting with respect to the primary software decomposition, the concepts of role playing and layered designs with teams significantly help to align ownership domains with modules.

More specifically, by decomposing a conceptual entity into a base object plus an arbitrary number of separately owned slices (role instances) fine grained ownership becomes possible while maintaining a high level of abstraction.

Elsewhere I have sketched how two existing approaches, Confined Types, and Universes, could be (partially) mapped to OT/J [12]. More work in this direction is needed to evolve OT/J into a language with full blown support for state-of-the-art alias control.

The focus on providing a mature language and tooling lays the grounds for real world studies. One potential study subject is the OTDT itself, because significant parts of it have been implemented in OT/J. It should be possible to obtain more example applications from the community.

Significant synergies should be expected when further strengthening the relationship between Object Teams and alias control. It should be fairly easy to extend the existing capabilities for expressing ownership in OT/J towards even more realistic models. On the other hand, a "normal" OT/J application, i.e., an application designed without even alias control in mind, should already exhibit a structure that is well suited for strictly enforcing encapsulation boundaries also in terms of alias control, more so than applications written in pure Java.

There are many reasons to keep pursuing better and better modularity and encapsulation. Maybe different reasons aren't necessarily in conflict with each other, maybe maintainability, evolvability, and analizability can actually leverage some of the same concepts. Teams and roles are a likely pivot for this synergy.

References

1. Herrmann, S.: Object Teams: Improving Modularity for Crosscutting Collaborations. In: Akşit, M., Mezini, M., Unland, R. (eds.) NODe 2002. LNCS, vol. 2591, pp. 248–264. Springer, Heidelberg (2003)
2. Ernst, E.: Family Polymorphism. In: Lindskov Knudsen, J. (ed.) ECOOP 2001. LNCS, vol. 2072, pp. 303–326. Springer, Heidelberg (2001)
3. Parnas, D.L.: On a 'buzzword': Hierarchical structure. In: IFIP Congress 74, pp. 336–339. North Holland Publishing Company (1974)
4. Tarr, P., Ossher, H., Harrison, W., Stan, S.J.: N degrees of separation: Multidimensional separation of concerns. In: Proc. of the 21st ICSE (1999)
5. Kiczales, G., Lamping, J., Mendhekar, A., Maeda, C., Lopes, C., Loingtier, J.M., Irwin, J.: Aspect-oriented programming. Technical Report SPL97-008 P9710042, Xerox PARC (February 1997)
6. Ossher, H., Tarr, P.: Multi-Dimensional Separation of Concerns and The Hyperspace Approach. In: Software Architecture and Component Technology: State of the Art in Research and Practice. Kluwer Academic Publishers (2001)
7. Ungar, D., Smith, R.B.: Self: The power of simplicity. In: Proc. of OOPSLA 1987 (1987)
8. Herrmann, S., Hundt, C., Mosconi, M.: ObjectTeams/Java Language Definition version 1.0 (OTJLD). Technical Report 2007/03, Technische Universität Berlin (2007)
9. Herrmann, S., Hundt, C., Mosconi, M.: ObjectTeams/Java Language Definition current version (OTJLD) (2002–2011), http://www.ObjectTeams.org/def/
10. Object Teams Development Tooling (OTDT) web site, http://www.eclipse.org/objectteams/download.php
11. Vitek, J., Bokowski, B.: Confined types in Java. Software: Practice and Experience 31(6), 507–532 (2001)
12. Herrmann, S.: Confinement and representation encapsulation in Object Teams. Technical Report 2004/06, Technical University Berlin (2004)
13. Müller, P., Rudich, A.: Ownership transfer in universe types. SIGPLAN Not. 42(10), 461–478 (2007)
14. Müller, P., Poetzsch-Heffter, A.: Universes: A type system for alias and dependency control. Technical Report 279, Fernuniversität Hagen (2001)
15. Dietl, W., Müller, P.: Object Ownership in Program Verification. In: Clarke, D., Noble, J., Wrigstad, T. (eds.) Aliasing in Object-Oriented Programming. LNCS, vol. 7850, pp. 289–318. Springer, Heidelberg (2013)

16. Herrmann, S.: Gradual encapsulation. Journal of Object Technology 7(9), 47–68 (2008)
17. OSGi: OSGi service platform, r4 core v4.3 specification. Technical report, The OSGi Alliance (April 2011),
    http://www.osgi.org/osgi_technology/download_specs.asp
18. Herrmann, S., Mosconi, M.: Integrating Object Teams and OSGi: Joint efforts for superior modularity. In: Proc. of TOOLS Europe (2007); also in: Journal of Object Technology 6(9) (2007)
19. Herrmann, S., Hundt, C., Mehner, K., Wloka, J.: Using guard predicates for generalized control of aspect instantiation and activation. In: Dynamic Aspects Workshop (DAW 2005), at AOSD 2005, Chicago (2005)
20. TOPPrax project home page (2003-2006), http://www.topprax.de
21. Ernst, E.: gbeta – a Language with Virtual Attributes, Block Structure, and Propagating, Dynamic Inheritance. PhD thesis, Department of Computer Science, University of Aarhus, Århus, Denmark (1999)
22. Ernst, E., Ostermann, K., Cook, W.R.: A virtual class calculus. In: Proc. of POPL 2006, pp. 270–282. ACM, New York (2006)
23. Odersky, M., et al.: An overview of the scala programming language. Technical Report IC/2004/64, EPFL Lausanne, Switzerland (2004)
24. Mezini, M., Ostermann, K.: Conquering aspects with caesar. In: Proc. AOSD 2003. ACM Press, Boston (2003)
25. Gasiunas, V., Mezini, M., Ostermann, K.: Dependent classes. In: Proc. Int'l Conf. Object-Oriented Programming, Systems, Languages and Applications (OOPSLA). ACM Press (2007)
26. Clarke, D., Drossopoulou, S., Noble, J., Wrigstad, T.: Tribe: a simple virtual class calculus. In: Proceedings of the 6th International Conference on Aspect-Oriented Software Development, AOSD 2007, pp. 121–134. ACM, New York (2007)
27. Bracha, G., von der Ahé, P., Bykov, V., Kashai, Y., Maddox, W., Miranda, E.: Modules as Objects in Newspeak. In: D'Hondt, T. (ed.) ECOOP 2010. LNCS, vol. 6183, pp. 405–428. Springer, Heidelberg (2010)
28. Kiczales, G., Hilsdale, E., Hugunin, J., Kersten, M., Palm, J., Griswold, W.G.: An Overview of AspectJ. In: Lindskov Knudsen, J. (ed.) ECOOP 2001. LNCS, vol. 2072, pp. 327–353. Springer, Heidelberg (2001)
29. Lieberherr, K., Lorenz, D., Mezini, M.: Programming with Aspectual Components. In: Technical Report, Northeastern University (April 1999)
30. Herrmann, S.: Translation polymorphism in Object Teams. Technical Report 2004/05, Technical University Berlin (2004)
31. Cameron, N., Noble, J., Wrigstad, T.: Tribal ownership. In: Proceedings of the ACM International Conference on Object Oriented Programming Systems Languages and Applications, OOPSLA 2010, pp. 618–633. ACM, New York (2010)

Location Types for Safe Programming with Near and Far References*

Yannick Welsch, Jan Schäfer, and Arnd Poetzsch-Heffter

University of Kaiserslautern, Germany
{welsch,jschaefer,poetzsch}@cs.uni-kl.de

Abstract. In distributed object-oriented systems, objects belong to different *locations*. For example, in Java Remote Method Invocation (RMI), objects can be distributed over different Java virtual machines. Accessing a reference in RMI has crucially different semantics depending on whether the referred object is local or remote. Nevertheless, such references are not statically distinguished by the Java type system.

This chapter presents *location types*, which statically distinguish *far* from *near* references. We present a formal type system for a minimal core language and develop a type inference system that gives maximally precise solutions satisfying further desirable properties. We prove soundness of the type system as well as soundness and correctness of the inference system. We have implemented location types as a pluggable type system for the ABS language, an object-oriented language with a concurrency and distribution model based on *concurrent object groups*. To facilitate programming with location types, we provide a tight integration of the type and inference system with an Eclipse-based integrated development environment (IDE) that presents inference results as overlays to the source code. The IDE drastically reduces the annotation overhead while providing full static type information to the programmer.

1 Introduction

In the puristic view of object-oriented programming, objects live in an *unstructured* space (or heap) and communicate via messages. This view is elegant and simple, but fails to address important software engineering principles like decomposition and encapsulation. That is why many researchers work on structuring techniques for object-oriented programming. Structuring the object space provides clear boundaries between different parts of the system. The resulting partitioning can be used to formulate and check important properties, e.g., that an object in one part does not reference an object in another part. Many ownership techniques [1,2,3] realize a hierarchical structuring of the objects into so-called ownership contexts and control access to a context from the surrounding context. The goal of our work is to support a partitioning of the object space as in distributed object-oriented programming where each object belongs to exactly one location. Thus, we can analyze whether two objects are at the same location or at different locations.

---

* This work is partially supported by the EU project FP7-231620 HATS: Highly Adaptable and Trustworthy Software using Formal Models.

D. Clarke et al. (Eds.): Aliasing in Object-Oriented Programming, LNCS 7850, pp. 471–500, 2013.

A *location* as formalized in this chapter can take many different forms; it may refer to a physical computation node, some process, or it can be a concept supported by a programming language. This versatile notion of locality is not only useful for distributed programming, but also for programs running on a single computer. For example, in object-oriented languages with concurrency models based on communicating groups of objects such as E [4], AmbientTalk/2 [5], JCoBox [6], or ABS [7], the location of an object can be considered as the group it belongs to. In these scenarios it often makes a difference whether a reference points to an object at the current location, i.e., the location of the current executing object (in the following called a *near* reference), or to an object at a different location (a *far* reference). For example, in the E programming language [4], a far reference can only be used for *asynchronous* method calls (named *eventual sends* in E), but not for *synchronous* method calls. In Java Remote Method Invocation (RMI) [8] accessing a remote reference may throw a RemoteException, where accessing a normal reference cannot throw such an exception. It is thus desirable to be able to statically distinguish these two kinds of references. In particular, this distinction is useful for documentation purposes, to reason about the code, and to statically prevent runtime errors.

We present *location types* which statically distinguish far from near references. Location types can be considered as a lightweight form of ownership types [2,3] with the following characteristics. The first is that location types only describe a *flat set* of locations instead of a *hierarchy* of ownership contexts. The second is that ownership types typically support different roles of objects. Location types only classify objects as belonging to the current location or some other location. Furthermore, location types are *not* used to enforce encapsulation, which is the main goal of many ownership type systems.

As with any type system extension, writing down the extended types can become tiresome for programmers. Furthermore, type annotations may clutter the code and reduce its readability, especially when several of such pluggable type systems [9,10] are used together. This reduces the acceptance of pluggable type systems in practice. The first issue can be solved by automatically inferring the type annotations and inserting them into the code. But this results again in cluttered code with potentially many annotations. Our solution is to leverage the power of an integrated development environment (IDE) and present the inferred types to the programmer by using visual *overlays*. The overlays give the programmer full static type information without cluttering the code with annotations nor reducing readability. Furthermore, the overlays can be turned on and off according to the programmer's need. Type annotations can still be used to make the type checking and inference modular, where the degree of modularity just depends on the interfaces where type annotations appear. This way of integrating type inference into the IDE simplifies the usage of the proposed type system and is applicable to similar type system extensions.

Notice. This chapter is a revised version of a paper that appeared at TOOLS 2011 [11]. Not having to worry about strict page limits, we present the material in more detail. In particular, we provide more depth to the setting and the examples, present additional related work, give a proof of the type soundness theorem as well as a proof of the soundness and completeness of the inference system, and provide an updated version of the case studies.

Outline. The remainder of this chapter is structured as follows. In Section 2 we give an informal introduction to location types and illustrate their usage by an example. Section 3 presents the formalization of location types for a core object-oriented language and the inference system. In Section 4 we explain how we implemented and integrated location types into an IDE, and provide a short evaluation. Section 5 discusses location types in the context of related work. Section 6 concludes.

2 Location Types at Work

In this section, we illustrate the use of location types. After a short introduction to the type system, we explain the language setting based on concurrent object groups for which we developed our implementation and show the benefits of location types using an example.

Location types. Location types statically distinguish *far* from *near* references. To do so, standard types are extended with additional type annotations, namely *location types*. There are three different location types: Near, Far, and Somewhere. Location types are always interpreted *relatively* to the current object. A variable typed as Near means that it may only refer to objects that belong to the *same* location as the current object. Accordingly, a Far typed variable may only refer to objects that belong to a *different* location than the current object. Somewhere is the super-type of Far and Near and it means that the referred object may either be Near or Far. Note that only Near precisely describes a certain location. A Far annotation only states that the location of the referred object is *not* Near. This means that a Far typed variable may over time refer to different locations which are not further defined, except that they are not the location of the current object.[1] What a location actually means is irrelevant to the type system. So whether the location of an object represents a specific Java Virtual Machine (JVM) on which the object is running or some other form of object grouping does not matter. Note, however, that the type system relies on the assumption that the location of an object does not change over time.

Concurrent object groups. We use location types to distinguish near and far references in languages with a concurrency model based on groups of objects. Concurrent object groups (COGs) follow the actor paradigm [12] and were developed to avoid data races and the complexity of multithreading and to simplify reasoning about concurrent programs. The concurrency model of COGs is used in the abstract behavioral specification language ABS [7] and in JCoBox [6], a Java-based realization of COGs. Groups are created dynamically (cf. [13]) and form the units of concurrency and distribution. Execution within a single group is sequential but groups are running concurrently with other groups. Communication between groups is

---

[1] In Section 3.2, we present a refined type system that allows to distinguish far locations.

```
interface Server {
    [Near] Session connect([Far] Client c, String name);
}
interface Session {
    Unit receive(ClientMsg m);
    Unit send(ServerMsg m);
}
interface Client {
    Unit connectTo([Far] Server s);
    Unit receive(ServerMsg m);
}
```

Fig. 1. The annotated interfaces of the chat application

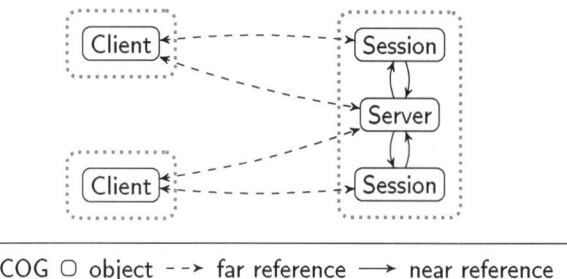

⊙ COG ○ object - -➤ far reference ⟶ near reference

Fig. 2. Runtime structure of the chat application

asynchronous. In a program using COGs, each object belongs to a group for its entire lifetime. This is similar to the Java RMI setting where objects belong to certain JVMs, which may run distributed on different machines. In the following presentation, we use ABS as the language to illustrate location types along with a detailed example. Note, however, that location types are not restricted to ABS. We selected ABS to demonstrate how location types can be used beyond traditional distributed programming.

ABS is an object-oriented language with a Java-like syntax. In ABS, the creation of COGs is related to object creation. The creation expression specifies whether the object is created in the current COG (using the standard **new** expression) or is created in a fresh COG (using the **new cog** expression). Communication in ABS between different COGs happen via *asynchronous method calls* which are indicated by an exclamation mark (!). A reference in ABS is *far* when it targets an object of a different COG, otherwise it is a *near* reference. Similar to the E programming language [4], ABS has the restriction that *synchronous method calls* (indicated by the standard dot notation) are only allowed on near references. Using a synchronous method call on a far reference results in a runtime exception. Our location type system can be used to statically guarantee the absence of these runtime exceptions.

```
1   class ClientImpl(String name) implements Client {
2       [Far] Session session;
3       Unit connectTo([Far] Server server) {
4           Fut<[Far] Session> f = server!connect(this, name);
5           session = f.get;
6       }
7   }
```

Fig. 3. Fully annotated implementation of the ClientImpl class

Using location types. As an example, we model an IRC-like chat application, which consists of a single server and multiple clients. For simplicity, there is only a single chat room, so all clients actually broadcast their messages to all other clients. The basic interfaces of the chat application in the ABS language are given in Figure 1. Note that only Server, Client, and Session are reference types, the types Unit, ClientMsg, and ServerMsg are *data types* and represent immutable data.

Figure 2 shows a possible runtime structure of the chat application. As the clients and the server run independently of each other, they live in their own COGs. This means that all references between clients and the server are far references. The Session objects that handle the different connections with the clients live in the same COG as the Server object. This means that references between Session and Server are near references. In a typical scenario, the client calls the connect method of the server and passes a reference to itself and a user name as arguments. The server then returns a reference to a Session object, which is used by the client to send messages to the server. The interfaces of Figure 1 are annotated accordingly, e.g., the connect method of the server returns a reference to a Session object that is Near to the server.

Figure 3 shows the ClientImpl class, an implementation of the Client interface. It has a field session which stores a reference to the Session object which is obtained by the client when it connects to the server. Lines 3-5 show the connectTo method. As specified in the interface, the Server parameter has type Far. On line 4, the client asynchronously (using the ! operator) calls the connect method of the server. The declared result type of the connect method is [Near] Session (see Figure 1). The crucial fact is that the type system now has to apply a *viewpoint adaptation* [14]; As the target of the call (server) has location type Far from the viewpoint of the caller ClientImpl, the return type of connect (which is Near from the viewpoint of Server) is adapted to the viewpoint of ClientImpl, namely to Far. Furthermore, as the call is an asynchronous one, a *future* is returned, i.e., a placeholder for the value to be computed. The ABS type system uses the built-in polymorphic data type Fut to type futures. The type parameter of Fut is instantiated with the type of the value that it is a placeholder for. The variable f on line 4 is thus of type Fut<[Far] Session>. On line 5, the client waits for the future to be resolved and stores the value in the session field. The built-in **get** operator is used to retrieve the value of the future, blocking if necessary until the value is ready.

Figure 4 shows the ServerImpl class, an implementation of the Server interface. It has an internal field sessions to hold the sessions of the connected clients.

```
1    class ServerImpl implements Server {
2      List<[Near] Session> sessions = Nil;
3      [Near] Session connect([Far] Client c, String name) {
4        [Near] Session s = new SessionImpl(this, c, name);
5        sessions = Cons(s,sessions);
6        this.publish(Connected(name));
7        return s;
8      }
9      Unit publish(ServerMsg m) {
10       List<[Near] Session> sess = sessions;
11       while (~isEmpty(sess)) {
12         [Near] Session s = head(sess);
13         sess = tail(sess);
14         s.send(m);
15       }
16     }
17   }
```

Fig. 4. Fully annotated implementation of the ServerImpl class

List is a polymorphic data type in ABS whose type parameter is instantiated with [Near] Session, which means that it holds a list of near references to Session objects. When a client connects to the server using the connect method, the server creates a new SessionImpl object in its current COG (using the standard **new** expression), which means that it is statically clear that this object is Near. It then stores the reference in its internal list, publishes that a new client has connected (Connected(name) yields the corresponding message), and returns a reference to the session object. In the publish method at line 14, the send method is synchronously called. Here, the location type system guarantees that s always refers to a near object so that the synchronous call does not cause a runtime exception.

3   Formalization

This section presents the formalization of the location type system in a core calculus called LocJ. We first present the abstract syntax of the language and its dynamic semantics. In Section 3.1 we introduce the basic type system for location types aswell-as its soundness properties. In Section 3.2 we improve the precision of the basic type system by introducing named Far types. In Section 3.3 we present the location type inference system.

Notation. We use the overbar notation $\overline{x}$ to denote a list. The empty list is denoted by • and the concatenation of the list $\overline{x}$ and the list $\overline{y}$ is denoted by $\overline{x} \cdot \overline{y}$. Single elements are implicitly treated as lists when needed. The notation $\mathcal{M}[x \mapsto y]$ yields the map $\mathcal{M}$ where the entry with key x is updated with the value y, or, if no such key exists, the entry is added. The empty map is denoted by [] and dom($\mathcal{M}$) and rng($\mathcal{M}$) denote the domain and range of the map $\mathcal{M}$.

$P ::= \overline{C}$

$C ::= \text{class } c \; \{ \, \overline{V} \; \overline{M} \, \}$

$V ::= T \; x$

$M ::= T \; m(\overline{V}) \; \{ \, \overline{V} \; \overline{S} \, \}$

$S ::= x \leftarrow E \mid x.f \leftarrow y$

$E ::= \text{new } c \text{ in fresh}$

$\quad \mid \text{new } c \text{ in } x \mid x$

$\quad \mid x.m(\overline{y}) \mid x.f$

$T ::= c$

Fig. 5. Abstract syntax of LocJ. c ranges over class names, m over method names and x, y, z, f over field and variable names (including this and result).

$\zeta ::= \overline{\mathcal{F}}, \mathcal{H}$ runtime config.

$\mathcal{H} ::= \iota \mapsto (l, c, \mathcal{D})$ heap

$\mathcal{F} ::= (\overline{S}, \mathcal{D})^{c,m}$ stack frame

$\mathcal{D} ::= x \mapsto v$ variable-value map

$v ::= \iota \mid \text{null}$ value

Fig. 6. Runtime entities of LocJ. ι ranges over object identifiers and l over locations.

Abstract syntax. LocJ models a core sequential object-oriented Java-like language, formalized in a similar fashion to Welterweight Java [15]. The abstract syntax is shown in Figure 5. The new aspect about LocJ is that objects in LocJ can be created at different *locations*. We do not introduce locations as first-class citizens as they can be encoded using objects. For this, the object creation expression new is augmented with an additional argument, given by the in part, that specifies the target location. The target can either be fresh to create the object in a new (fresh) location, or a variable x to create the object in the same location as the object that is referenced by x. Note that in ABS, **new cog** C() creates a new location (i.e., corresponds to "new c in fresh" in LocJ) whereas **new** C() creates a new object in the same location as the current object (i.e., corresponds to "new c in this" in LocJ). To keep the presentation short, LocJ does not include inheritance and subtyping. However, the formalization can be extended in the usual way to support these features (requiring parameter types of overriding methods to be contravariant and return types to be covariant).

Class-table. Throughout the formalization, we use a class table $\mathcal{CT}$ to look up definitions of classes, fields and methods. We assume that class names are globally unique and that field and method names are unique for each class. We then write $\mathcal{CT}(c)$ to denote the definition C of the class named c. We also write $\mathcal{CT}(c, f)$ to denote the definition V of the field named f in class c and we write $\mathcal{CT}(c, m)$ to denote the definition M of the method named m in class c.

Dynamic semantics. The dynamic semantics of our language is defined as a small-step operational semantics. The main difference with standard object-oriented languages is that we explicitly model locations to partition the heap. The runtime entities are shown in Figure 6. Runtime configurations ζ consist of a stack $\overline{\mathcal{F}}$, which is a list of stack frames, and a heap $\mathcal{H}$. A stack frame $\mathcal{F}$ consists of a list of statements $\overline{S}$ and a mapping $\mathcal{D}$ from local variable names to values. Furthermore the stack frame records with which class c and method m it is associated, which we sometimes omit for brevity. The heap maps object identifiers to object states $(l, c, \mathcal{D})$, consisting of a location l, a class name c, and a mapping $\mathcal{D}$ from field names to values.

The reduction rules are shown in Figure 7. They are of the form $\zeta \rightsquigarrow \zeta'$ and reduce runtime configurations. The rules use the helper functions initO and initF defined in Figure 8 to initialize objects and stack frames.

$$\frac{\iota \notin \mathrm{dom}(\mathcal{H}) \qquad l \text{ is fresh}}{\mathcal{H}' = \mathcal{H}[\iota \mapsto \mathrm{initO}(l,c)] \qquad \mathcal{D}' = \mathcal{D}[x \mapsto \iota]}{(x \leftarrow \text{new } c \text{ in fresh} \cdot \bar{S}, \mathcal{D}) \cdot \bar{\mathcal{F}}, \mathcal{H} \rightsquigarrow (\bar{S}, \mathcal{D}') \cdot \bar{\mathcal{F}}, \mathcal{H}'}$$

$$\frac{\mathcal{D}' = \mathcal{D}[x \mapsto \mathcal{D}(y)]}{(x \leftarrow y \cdot \bar{S}, \mathcal{D}) \cdot \bar{\mathcal{F}}, \mathcal{H} \rightsquigarrow (\bar{S}, \mathcal{D}') \cdot \bar{\mathcal{F}}, \mathcal{H}}$$

$$\frac{\iota \notin \mathrm{dom}(\mathcal{H}) \qquad (l, \_, \_) = \mathcal{H}(\mathcal{D}(y))}{\mathcal{H}' = \mathcal{H}[\iota \mapsto \mathrm{initO}(l,c)] \qquad \mathcal{D}' = \mathcal{D}[x \mapsto \iota]}{(x \leftarrow \text{new } c \text{ in } y \cdot \bar{S}, \mathcal{D}) \cdot \bar{\mathcal{F}}, \mathcal{H} \rightsquigarrow (\bar{S}, \mathcal{D}') \cdot \bar{\mathcal{F}}, \mathcal{H}'}$$

$$\frac{\mathcal{F} = (x \leftarrow y.m(\bar{z}) \cdot \bar{S}, \mathcal{D})}{(\_, c, \_) = \mathcal{H}(\mathcal{D}(y))}{\mathcal{F}' = \mathrm{initF}(c, m, \mathcal{D}(y), \mathcal{D}(\bar{z}))}{\mathcal{F} \cdot \bar{\mathcal{F}}, \mathcal{H} \rightsquigarrow \mathcal{F}' \cdot \mathcal{F} \cdot \bar{\mathcal{F}}, \mathcal{H}}$$

$$\frac{\iota = \mathcal{D}(x) \qquad (l, c, \mathcal{D}') = \mathcal{H}(\iota)}{\mathcal{D}'' = \mathcal{D}'[f \mapsto \mathcal{D}(y)] \qquad \mathcal{H}' = \mathcal{H}[\iota \mapsto (l, c, \mathcal{D}'')]}{(x.f \leftarrow y \cdot \bar{S}, \mathcal{D}) \cdot \bar{\mathcal{F}}, \mathcal{H} \rightsquigarrow (\bar{S}, \mathcal{D}) \cdot \bar{\mathcal{F}}, \mathcal{H}'}$$

$$\frac{(\_, \_, \mathcal{D}'') = \mathcal{H}(\mathcal{D}(y)) \qquad \mathcal{D}' = \mathcal{D}[x \mapsto \mathcal{D}''(f)]}{(x \leftarrow y.f \cdot \bar{S}, \mathcal{D}) \cdot \bar{\mathcal{F}}, \mathcal{H} \rightsquigarrow (\bar{S}, \mathcal{D}') \cdot \bar{\mathcal{F}}, \mathcal{H}}$$

$$\frac{\mathcal{F} = (x \leftarrow y.m(\bar{z}) \cdot \bar{S}, \mathcal{D}')}{\mathcal{D}'' = \mathcal{D}'[x \mapsto \mathcal{D}(\mathrm{result})]}{(\bullet, \mathcal{D}) \cdot \mathcal{F} \cdot \bar{\mathcal{F}}, \mathcal{H} \rightsquigarrow (\bar{S}, \mathcal{D}'') \cdot \bar{\mathcal{F}}, \mathcal{H}}$$

Fig. 7. Operational semantics of LocJ

3.1   Basic Location Types

In this subsection, we present the basic location type system and its soundness properties. To incorporate location types into LocJ programs, we extend types T with location types L (see Figure 9), where a location type can either be Near, Far, or Somewhere. We assume that a given program is already well-typed using a standard Java-like type system and we only provide the typing rules for typing the location type extension. The typing rules are shown in Figure 10. Judgments with indices i are implicitly all-quantified. For example, $c \vdash M_i$ means that for all $M_i \in \bar{M}$ the previous judgment holds. Statements and expressions are typed under a type environment $\bar{V}$, which defines the types of local variables. The typing judgment for expressions is of the form $\bar{V} \vdash e : L$ to denote that expression e has location type L. The helper functions $\mathrm{anno}(c, f)$ and $\mathrm{anno}(c, m, x)$, defined in Figure 8, return the declared location type of field f or variable x of method m in class c and $\mathrm{params}(c, m)$ returns the formal parameter variables of method m in class c.

The crucial parts of the type system are the location subtyping ($L <: L'$) and the viewpoint adaptation ($L \triangleright_K L'$) relations which are shown in Figure 11. The location types Near and Far are both subtypes of Somewhere but are unrelated otherwise. Viewpoint adaption is always applied when a type is used in a different context. There are two different directions ($K \in \{\mathsf{From}, \mathsf{To}\}$) to consider. (1) Adapting a type L *from another viewpoint* L' to the current viewpoint, written as $L \triangleright_{\mathsf{From}} L'$. (2) Adapting a type L from the current viewpoint *to another viewpoint* L', written as $L \triangleright_{\mathsf{To}} L'$.[2] In typing rule WF-FIELDGET we adapt the type of the field *from* the viewpoint of y to the current viewpoint, whereas in rule WF-FIELDSET we adapt the type of y from the current viewpoint *to* the viewpoint of x.

---

[2] Whereas in the Universe type system [14] only one direction is considered, we chose to explicitly state the direction in order to achieve a simple and intuitive encoding.

$$\text{initO}(l,c) \quad = (l,c,\mathcal{D}) \text{ if } \mathcal{D} = [][\overline{f} \mapsto \overline{\text{null}}] \text{ and } \mathcal{CT}(c) = \text{class } c \{ \overline{T\ f\ M} \}$$

$$\text{initF}(m,c,\iota,\overline{v}) = \begin{array}{l} (\overline{S},\mathcal{D})^{c,m} \text{ if } \mathcal{CT}(c,m) = T\ m(\overline{T\ x}) \{ \overline{T'\ y}\ \overline{S} \} \text{ and} \\ \mathcal{D} = [][\text{this} \mapsto \iota][\text{result} \mapsto \text{null}][\overline{x} \mapsto \overline{v}][\overline{y} \mapsto \overline{\text{null}}] \end{array}$$

$$\text{anno}(c,f) \quad = L \text{ if } \mathcal{CT}(c,f) = L\ c\ f$$

$$\text{anno}(c,m,x) \ = L \text{ if } \mathcal{CT}(c,m) = T\ m(\overline{V}) \{ \overline{V'\ S} \} \text{ and } L\ c\ x \in \overline{V} \cdot \overline{V'}$$

$$\text{params}(c,m) \ = \overline{V} \text{ if } \mathcal{CT}(c,m) = T\ m(\overline{V}) \{ \overline{V'\ S} \}$$

$$\text{loc}((l,c,\mathcal{D})) \ = l$$

$$\text{dtype}(l,l') \quad = \begin{cases} \text{Near} & \text{if } l = l' \\ \text{Far} & \text{otherwise} \end{cases}$$

$$\text{abs}(L) \quad = \begin{cases} \text{Far} & \text{if } L = \text{Far}(n) \text{ for some } n \\ L & \text{otherwise} \end{cases}$$

Fig. 8. Helper definitions

$$T ::= \cdots \mid L\ c \qquad \text{annotated type}$$
$$L ::= \text{Near} \mid \text{Far} \mid \text{Somewhere} \quad \text{location type}$$

Fig. 9. Basic location types

As an example for the viewpoint adaptation, assume a method is called on a Far target and the argument is of type Near. Then the adapted type is Far, because the parameter is Near in relation to the caller, but from the perspective of the callee, it is actually Far in that case. Important is also the case where we pass a Far typed variable x to a Far target. In that case we have to take Somewhere as the adapted type, because it is not statically clear whether the object referred to by x is in a location that is different from the location of the target object.

Type soundness. The location type system guarantees that variables of type Near only reference objects that are in the same location as the current object and that variables of type Far only reference objects that are in a different location to the current object. We formalize this under the notion of well-formed runtime configurations. We give a few helper functions in Figure 8. We define a function loc() to extract the location of a heap entry and the dynamic location type function dtype(l,l') that compares whether two locations l and l' are near or far to each other. A configuration is well-formed if heap and stack are well-formed; more precisely:

Definition 1 (Well-formed runtime configuration). *Let $\zeta = \overline{\mathcal{F}}, \mathcal{H}$ be a runtime configuration. ζ is well-formed iff all heap entries $(l,c,\mathcal{D}) \in \text{rng}(\mathcal{H})$ and all stack frames $\mathcal{F} \in \overline{\mathcal{F}}$ are well-formed under $\mathcal{H}$ and the configuration satisfies all the standard conditions of a class-based language (e.g., no dangling references, well-typed heap and stack, ...)*

A heap-entry is well-formed if its fields annotated by Near or Far only reference objects at the same or at a different location, respectively:

(WF-P)
$$\frac{P = \overline{C} \qquad \vdash C_i}{\vdash P}$$

(WF-C)
$$\frac{c \vdash M_i}{\vdash \text{class } c \{ \overline{V}\ \overline{M} \}}$$

(WF-M)
$$\frac{\text{Near } c \text{ this} \cdot T \text{ result} \cdot \overline{V} \cdot \overline{V'} \vdash S_i}{c \vdash T\ m(\overline{V}) \{ \overline{V'}\ \overline{S} \}}$$

(WF-ASSIGN)
$$\frac{\overline{V} \vdash E : L \qquad L' \_ x \in \overline{V} \qquad L <: L'}{\overline{V} \vdash x \leftarrow E}$$

(WF-FIELDGET)
$$\frac{L\ c\ y \in \overline{V} \qquad L' = \text{anno}(c, f)}{\overline{V} \vdash y.f : L' \triangleright_{\text{From}} L}$$

(WF-FIELDSET)
$$\frac{L\ c\ x \in \overline{V} \qquad L' = \text{anno}(c, f) \qquad L'' \_ y \in \overline{V} \qquad (L'' \triangleright_{\text{To}} L) <: L'}{\overline{V} \vdash x.f \leftarrow y}$$

(WF-NEWFRESH)
$$\frac{}{\overline{V} \vdash \text{new } c \text{ in fresh} : \text{Far}}$$

(WF-NEWSAME)
$$\frac{L \_ x \in \overline{V}}{\overline{V} \vdash \text{new } c \text{ in } x : L}$$

(WF-VAR)
$$\frac{L \_ x \in \overline{V}}{\overline{V} \vdash x : L}$$

(WF-CALL)
$$\frac{L\ c\ y \in \overline{V} \qquad L_i \_ z_i \in \overline{V} \qquad \overline{x} = \text{params}(c, m) \qquad (L_i \triangleright_{\text{To}} L) <: \text{anno}(c, m, x_i)}{\overline{V} \vdash y.m(\overline{z}) : \text{anno}(c, m, \text{result}) \triangleright_{\text{From}} L}$$

Fig. 10. Typing rules of LocJ. Judgments containing indices i are implicitly all-quantified.

Definition 2 (Well-formed heap entry). $(l, \_, \mathcal{D})$ *is well-formed under* $\mathcal{H}$ *iff for all* f *with* $\mathcal{D}(f) = \iota$, *we have* $\text{dtype}(l, \text{loc}(\mathcal{H}(\iota))) <: \text{anno}(c, f)$.

A stack-entry is well-formed if its local variables annotated by Near or Far only reference objects at the same location or at a different location, respectively:

Definition 3 (Well-formed stack frame). $(\overline{S}, \mathcal{D})^{c,m}$ *is well-formed under* $\mathcal{H}$ *iff for all* x *with* $\mathcal{D}(x) = \iota$, *we have* $\text{dtype}(\text{loc}(\mathcal{H}(\mathcal{D}(\text{this}))), \text{loc}(\mathcal{H}(\iota))) <: \text{anno}(c, m, x)$.

The soundness of a type system is proven by showing preservation and progress (cf. [16]).

Theorem 1 (Preservation for location types). *Let* ζ *be a well-formed runtime configuration. If* $\zeta \rightsquigarrow \zeta'$, *then* ζ' *is well-formed as well.*

As shown at the end of Appendix A, the theorem directly follows from the preservation theorem for refined location types (Theorem 2) that is presented in the next subsection.

As location annotations do not put any additional restrictions on the dynamic semantics of LocJ, the proof of progress remains the same as for Welterweight Java [15]. In ABS however, where the semantics of the synchronous call depends on location information, progress needs to be shown. For the synchronous method call $y.m(\ldots)$, ABS requires that the object ι that y refers to is in the same COG as the current object (referred to by this). In our formalization, this means that

Original	$\triangleright_K$ Viewpoint	$=$ Adapted
L	$\triangleright_K$ Near	$= L$
Near	$\triangleright_K$ Far	$=$ Far
Far	$\triangleright_K$ Far	$=$ Somewhere
Somewhere	$\triangleright_K$ Far	$=$ Somewhere
L	$\triangleright_K$ Somewhere	$=$ Somewhere

Fig. 11. Subtyping and viewpoint adaptation (where $K \in \{\text{From}, \text{To}\}$). Note that the direction K does not influence basic location types, but is important for our extension in Section 3.2.

```
1   [Far] Server server = new cog ServerImpl();
2   [Far] Client client1 = new cog ClientImpl("Alice");
3   [Far] Client client2 = new cog ClientImpl("Bob");
4   client1 ! connectTo(server); // type error
5   client2 ! connectTo(server); // type error
```

Fig. 12. The code of the main block of the chat application, annotated with basic location types

$\text{loc}(\mathcal{H}(\iota)) = \text{loc}(\mathcal{H}(\mathcal{D}(\text{this})))$. For the proof, we assume that the ABS program is well-typed; this means in particular that the location type of y is Near. The proof then follows directly from the preservation theorem. We assume that the stack frame that contains the synchronous call $y.m(\bar{z})$ is well-typed. By Definition 3, we get $\text{dtype}(\text{loc}(\mathcal{H}(\mathcal{D}(\text{this}))), \text{loc}(\mathcal{H}(\iota))) <: \text{Near}$. The claim $\text{loc}(\mathcal{H}(\iota)) = \text{loc}(\mathcal{H}(\mathcal{D}(\text{this})))$ then directly follows from the definitions of $<:$ and $\text{dtype}(,)$ in Figures 11 and 8.

3.2   Refined Location Types

The location type system presented in the last section can only distinguish near and far: Near references point to a location that is different from locations pointed to by Far references. But whether two far references point to the same location or different ones is statically not known. This makes the type system often too weak in practice. As an example, let us consider the *main block* of the ABS chat application in Figure 12, annotated with location types. Note that a main block in ABS corresponds to a main method in Java. The server and both client objects are created in their own, fresh COG, and thus they can be typed as Far, because these locations are different from the current COG (the *Main* COG). However, the method call client1!connectTo(server) does not type-check in the basic location type system. According to rule WF-CALL in Figure 10, the adaptation of the actual parameter type of the connectTo method to the caller has to be a subtype of the formal parameter type, but the adaptation Far $\triangleright_{\text{To}}$ Far yields Somewhere, which is not a subtype of the formal parameter type Far. This problem arises because the type system cannot distinguish that client1 and server point to different locations. The example shows that in its basic form, the location type system often has to

```
1  [Far(s)] Server server = new cog ServerImpl();
2  [Far(c1)] Client client1 = new cog ClientImpl("Alice");
3  [Far(c2)] Client client2 = new cog ClientImpl("Bob");
4  client1 ! connectTo(server);
5  client2 ! connectTo(server);
```

Fig. 13. The code of the main block of the chat application, annotated with refined location types

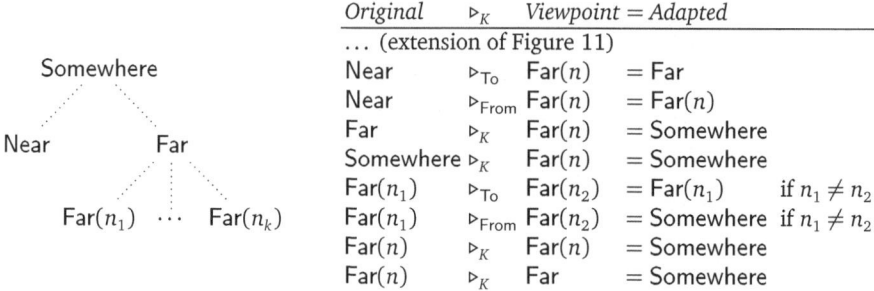

Original	$\triangleright_K$	Viewpoint	$= Adapted$	
... (extension of Figure 11)				
Near	$\triangleright_{To}$	Far(n)	= Far	
Near	$\triangleright_{From}$	Far(n)	= Far(n)	
Far	$\triangleright_K$	Far(n)	= Somewhere	
Somewhere	$\triangleright_K$	Far(n)	= Somewhere	
Far(n_1)	$\triangleright_{To}$	Far(n_2)	= Far(n_1)	if $n_1 \neq n_2$
Far(n_1)	$\triangleright_{From}$	Far(n_2)	= Somewhere	if $n_1 \neq n_2$
Far(n)	$\triangleright_K$	Far(n)	= Somewhere	
Far(n)	$\triangleright_K$	Far	= Somewhere	

Fig. 14. Subtyping and viewpoint adaptation for extended location types

conservatively use the Somewhere type to remain sound, which is often too weak to type practical programs.

To improve the precision of the location type system we introduce *named* far types:

$$L ::= \cdots \mid Far(n)$$

A named far type is a far type parametrized with an arbitrary name. We let n range over far names, a fresh syntactic category. Far types with different names represent disjoint sets of far locations and are incompatible with each other. Figure 13 illustrates the application of named far location types. The locations of server, client1, and client2 are distinguished by using different names for typing different variables. Using this technique, the programmer can distinguish finitely many Far types in a program. This is similar to static analysis techniques that use source code positions to distinguish abstract program entities [17].

The following typing rule WF-NEWFRESHP is added to the basic type system. It allows to type object creations at fresh locations by an arbitrarily named Far type:

(WF-NEWFRESHP)

$$\overline{V \vdash \text{new } c \text{ in fresh} : Far(n)}$$

The subtyping and viewpoint adaptation relations are extended accordingly in Figure 14. Adapting a Far(n_1) to a Far(n_2) for $n_1 \neq n_2$ yields a Far(n_1), as they denote different sets of locations. Adapting a Far(n) to a Far(n) does not yield Near, however, as two variables with the same Far(n) type can refer to objects of different locations. Thus, in the refined type system, the chat example in Figure 13 is type correct: The adaptation of the actual parameter type $\mathsf{Far}(s)$ of the connectTo method in Line 4 to the caller type $\mathsf{Far}(c1)$ yields $\mathsf{Far}(s)$, which is a subtype of the formal parameter type Far.

In practice, the programmer does not need to provide the names. Instead the inference system (see Sect. 3.3) automatically infers the named far types. Thus, the programmer is not confronted with more complex typing. Using the refined location type system, we were able to fully type the case studies presented in Section 4. However, other refinements or extensions to improve the expressiveness and precision of the location type system are imaginable, e.g., location type polymorphism similar to owner polymorphism in ownership type systems [2,18,19].

Type soundness. We adapt the well-formedness definitions from Section 3.1 to the refined location type system. The definitions for well-formed heap entries and stack frames are similar to the ones in the previous subsection except that we abstract away the named far types using the helper function $\mathsf{abs}(L)$ defined in Figure 8:

Definition 4 (Well-formed heap entry). $(l, \_, \mathcal{D})$ *is well-formed under* $\mathcal{H}$ *iff for all* f *with* $\mathcal{D}(f) = \iota$ *and* $(l', c, \_) = \mathcal{H}(\iota)$, *we have* $\mathsf{dtype}(l, l') <: \mathsf{abs}(\mathsf{anno}(c, f))$.

Definition 5 (Well-formed stack frame). $(\overline{S}, \mathcal{D})^{c,m}$ *is well-formed under* $\mathcal{H}$ *iff for all* x *with* $\mathcal{D}(x) = \iota$, *we have* $\mathsf{dtype}(\mathsf{loc}(\mathcal{H}(\mathcal{D}(\mathsf{this}))), \mathsf{loc}(\mathcal{H}(\iota))) <: \mathsf{abs}(\mathsf{anno}(c, m, x))$.

To formalize that far types with different names represent disjoint sets of far locations, we introduce a relation $\mathsf{reach}(\zeta)$ that denotes for a runtime configuration ζ what the types of the variables are that point to a certain location:

Definition 6 (Reachability of l under ζ). *Let* $\zeta = \overline{\mathcal{F}}, \mathcal{H}$; *We write* $\mathsf{reach}(\zeta)$ *to denote the smallest relation that satisfies the following conditions:*

- *If* $(\overline{S}, \mathcal{D})^{c,m} \in \overline{\mathcal{F}}$ *and* $\mathcal{D}(x) = \iota$ *and* $l_x = \mathsf{loc}(\mathcal{H}(\iota))$, *then* $(\mathsf{anno}(c, m, x), l_x) \in \mathsf{reach}(\zeta)$.
- *If* $(l, c, \mathcal{D}) \in \mathsf{rng}(\mathcal{H})$ *and* $\mathcal{D}(f) = \iota$ *and* $l_f = \mathsf{loc}(\mathcal{H}(\iota))$, *then* $(\mathsf{anno}(c, f), l_f) \in \mathsf{reach}(\zeta)$.

Using $\mathsf{reach}(\zeta)$, we can state that in well-formed configurations variables with different named far types refer to objects in different locations:

Definition 7 (Well-formed named Far locations). ζ *is well-formed wrt. named* Far *locations iff* $\forall (\mathsf{Far}(n_1), l_1), (\mathsf{Far}(n_2), l_2) \in \mathsf{reach}(\zeta)$ *with* $n_1 \neq n_2$, *we have* $l_1 \neq l_2$.

In summary, we get the following revised definition of well-formed runtime configurations:

Definition 8 (Well-formed runtime configuration). *Let* $\zeta = \overline{\mathcal{F}}, \mathcal{H}$ *be a runtime configuration.* ζ *is well-formed iff all heap entries* $(l, c, \mathcal{D}) \in \mathsf{rng}(\mathcal{H})$ *and all stack frames* $\mathcal{F} \in \overline{\mathcal{F}}$ *are well-formed under* $\mathcal{H}$ *and* ζ *is well-formed wrt. named* Far *locations and the configuration satisfies all the standard conditions of a class-based language.*

As explained in the last section, it suffices to show the preservation property for type soundness of the refined location type system:

Theorem 2 (Preservation for refined location types). *Let ζ be a well-formed runtime configuration. If $\zeta \rightsquigarrow \zeta'$, then ζ' is well-formed as well.*

The proof proceeds by a case analysis on the reduction rules. It is presented in Appendix A.

3.3   Location Type Inference

Without further support, the type system presented in the previous section requires the programmer to annotate all type occurrences with location types. To avoid this tedious work and make the approach practical, we developed an inference system for location types. We first present a *sound* and *complete* inference system, which makes it possible to use the location type system without writing any type annotations and only use type annotations to achieve modular type checking. A type inference system is *sound* if it yields only correct typings. It is *complete*, if every correct typing can be inferred. In the second part of this section, we improve the inference system such that it can deal with type-incorrect programs with the purpose of generating meaningful error messages. We also make the inference system configurable such that it finds not only any possible solution, but good solutions satisfying further desirable properties.

Sound and Complete Inference. The formal model for inferring location types follows the formalization of other type system extensions [20]. For a broader overview of type inference, we refer to the excellent book by Pierce [21] from which we borrow the notation. The idea is to introduce location type variables at places in the program where location types occur in our typing rules. Type inference then consists of two steps. First, generating constraints for the location type variables. Second, checking whether a substitution for the location type variables exists such that all constraints are satisfied.

To introduce location type variables into programs we extend the syntax of location types accordingly:

$$L ::= \cdots \mid \alpha \qquad \text{location type variables (also } \beta, \gamma, \text{ and } \delta)$$

In the following, P denotes programs that are fully annotated with pairwise distinct location type variables. This means that all type occurrences in P are of the form $\alpha\, c$. The constraints which are generated by the inference system are shown in Figure 15. We use the judgment $\vdash P : \overline{Q}$ to denote the generation of the constraints $\overline{Q}$ from program P and similar judgments for classes and statements. The judgment for expressions E has the form $\overline{V} \vdash E : \alpha, \overline{Q}$ with the following meaning: Assuming the bindings $\overline{V}$, the location type of E is (the solution for) α, and $\overline{Q}$ are the inferred constraints. The judgments are defined in Figure 16. Note that additional *fresh* location type variables are introduced during the constraint generation and that the constraints generated for a program are unique modulo the renaming of the fresh location type variables. Using an appropriate naming convention, we can assume without loss of generality that there is a unique constraint set for a program P, denoted by $\overline{Q}_P$.

$$Q ::= \alpha \rhd_K \beta = \gamma \qquad \text{adaptation constraint}$$
$$| \; \alpha <: \beta \qquad\qquad \text{subtype constraint}$$
$$| \; \alpha = L \qquad\qquad \text{constant constraint}$$

Fig. 15. Location type constraints

$$\frac{P = \overline{C} \qquad \vdash C_i : \overline{Q_i}}{\vdash P : \overline{Q_1} \cdot \ldots \cdot \overline{Q_k}}$$

$$\frac{\delta\; c\; \text{this} \cdot T\; \text{result} \cdot \overline{V} \cdot \overline{V'} \vdash S_i : \overline{Q_i} \qquad \delta \text{ is fresh}}{c \vdash T\; m(\overline{V})\; \{\; \overline{V'}\; \overline{S}\; \} : \delta = \text{Near} \cdot \overline{Q_1} \cdot \ldots \cdot \overline{Q_k}}$$

$$\frac{c \vdash M_i : \overline{Q_i}}{\vdash \text{class } c\; \{\; \overline{V}\; \overline{M}\; \} : \overline{Q_1} \cdot \ldots \cdot \overline{Q_k}}$$

$$\frac{\alpha\; c\; x \in \overline{V} \qquad \beta = \text{anno}(c, f) \qquad \gamma \_ y \in \overline{V} \qquad \delta \text{ is fresh}}{\overline{V} \vdash x.f \leftarrow y : \delta <: \beta \cdot \gamma \rhd_{\text{To}} \alpha = \delta}$$

$$\frac{\overline{V} \vdash E : \beta, \overline{Q} \qquad \alpha \_ x \in \overline{V}}{\overline{V} \vdash x \leftarrow E : \beta <: \alpha \cdot \overline{Q}}$$

$$\frac{\alpha\; c\; y \in \overline{V} \qquad \beta = \text{anno}(c, f) \qquad \gamma \text{ is fresh}}{\overline{V} \vdash y.f : \gamma, \beta \rhd_{\text{From}} \alpha = \gamma}$$

$$\frac{\delta \text{ is fresh} \qquad \gamma \text{ is fresh}}{\overline{V} \vdash \text{new } c \text{ in fresh} : \delta, \delta <: \gamma \cdot \gamma = \text{Far}}$$

$$\frac{\alpha \_ y \in \overline{V}}{\overline{V} \vdash \text{new } c \text{ in } y : \alpha, \bullet} \qquad \frac{\alpha \_ x \in \overline{V}}{\overline{V} \vdash x : \alpha, \bullet}$$

$$\frac{\begin{array}{c} \alpha\; c\; y \in \overline{V} \qquad \alpha_i \_ z_i \in \overline{V} \\ \overline{x} = \text{params}(c, m) \qquad \beta_i = \text{anno}(c, m, x_i) \\ \beta = \text{anno}(c, m, \text{result}) \qquad Q_i = \alpha_i \rhd_{\text{To}} \alpha = \gamma_i \cdot \gamma_i <: \beta_i \\ \gamma_i \text{ is fresh} \qquad \gamma \text{ is fresh} \end{array}}{\overline{V} \vdash y.m(\overline{z}) : \gamma, \beta \rhd_{\text{From}} \alpha = \gamma \cdot \overline{Q_1} \cdot \ldots \cdot \overline{Q_k}}$$

Fig. 16. Constraint generation rules. Judgments with indices i are implicitly all-quantified.

Let us denote the location variables of P by $\text{locv}(P)$ and those occurring in $\overline{Q}_P$ by $\text{locv}(\overline{Q}_P)$; obviously, $\text{locv}(P) \subseteq \text{locv}(\overline{Q}_P)$. Let σ be a variable substitution from $\text{locv}(P)$ (or $\text{locv}(\overline{Q}_P)$) to location types $\{\text{Near}, \text{Far}, \text{Somewhere}, \text{Far}(n_1), ..., \text{Far}(n_k)\}$. We write σP to denote the program that is obtained from P by replacing all location type variables according to σ. We call σ a *solution* of $\overline{Q}_P$, written as $\sigma \vDash \overline{Q}_P$, if the constraints $\overline{Q}_P$ are satisfied under σ. Type inference is *sound*, if every solution leads to a correct typing of P. It is *complete*, if each typing of P can be inferred.

Theorem 3 (Soundness and Completeness of the Inference). *The described inference system is sound and complete:*

- Sound: *If $\sigma \vDash \overline{Q}_P$, then $\vdash \sigma P$.*
- Complete: *If $\vdash \sigma P$ with $\text{dom}(\sigma) = \text{locv}(P)$, then there is a solution σ' of $\overline{Q}_P$ such that $\sigma'|_{\text{dom}(\sigma)} = \sigma$.*

The proof of this theorem is presented in Appendix B.

Partial and Tunable Inference. Soundness and completeness guarantee that all inferred solutions lead to correct typings and all typings can be inferred. From a practical point of view, an inference system should meet further requirements, in particular:

1. If no typable solution can be inferred, at least a partially typable solution should be provided (a message "No solution" is not really helpful to correct the program). In addition, this partially typable solution should lead to the least amount of type errors.

2. If multiple solutions exist, a "good" solution should be selected. Users do not want any solution, but a solution that satisfies further properties. For example, a "good" solution could provide more precise types than other solutions. An inference system that allows to specify such additional properties is called *tunable* [20].

To infer partial solutions that satisfy the first requirement, we extend our formal model in the following way. We introduce two constraint categories: *must-have* and *should-have*. The *must-have* constraints must always be satisfied. These are for example in Figure 16 the adaptation constraints ($\alpha \triangleright_K \beta = \gamma$) and the constant constraints ($\alpha = L$), characterizing the types of subexpressions. They also encompass the constant constraints which result from user annotations (not considered in the formalization of Figure 16, but present in the implementation). Note that there is always a solution to these constraints in our inference system as they are based on freshly allocated location type variables. The *should-have* constraints, e.g., the subtype constraints ($\alpha <: \beta$) in Figure 16, should always be satisfied in order to get a valid typing, but can be unsatisfied for partially correct solutions.

As an example for partial inference, consider the ServerImpl class in Figure 4. Assume that there are no annotations on the signature and the body of the connect method except for the return type which has been wrongly annotated by the programmer as Far. The inference system then still gives a solution where all constraints are satisfied except one *should-have* constraint, namely *typeOf*(s) <: *typeOf*(result) which is generated at the last line of the connect method (*typeOf* yields the corresponding type variable). The inference system assigns the type Near to variable s because if it were to assign Far to s, more *should-have* constraints would be unsatisfied (i.e., those resulting from lines 5 to 7).

The second requirement, namely inferring "good" solutions, can be realized by adding the additional category of *nice-to-have* constraints. The *nice-to-have* constraints are those that are used to specify further desirable properties, e.g., least amount of Somewhere annotations or Far types at the places where the precision of Far(n) types is not needed.

Inferring a partial and "good" solution consists of solving the following problem. First, all *must-have* constraints, then the most amount of *should-have* constraints, and finally the most amount of *nice-to-have* constraints should be satisfied. Prioritizing must-have and should-have constraints ensures that the inference system remains sound for the cases where a typable solution exists. The problem can be encoded as a partially weighted MaxSAT problem by assigning appropriate weights to the constraints. This means that *must-have* constraints are hard clauses (maximum weight) and *should-have* constraints correspond to soft clauses whose weight is greater than the sum of all weighted *nice-to-have* clauses. Solving such a problem can be efficiently done using specialized SAT solvers (see Section 4).

4   Implementation and IDE Integration

We have implemented the type system and the inference system for location types, including named far location types and partial inference satisfying further heuristics, as an extension of the ABS compiler suite. The type and inference system is integrated into an Eclipse-based IDE, but can also be used from the command line.

Inference System. The inference system internally uses the Max-SAT solver SAT4J [22] to solve the generated inference constraints. As the inference system may return a solution that is not fully typable, we use the type checker for location types to give user-friendly error messages.

The alias analysis based on named Far locations (cf. Section 3.2) can be configured to use scopes of different granularity: basic (no alias analysis), method-local, class-local, and global analysis. This allows the user to choose the best tradeoff between precision and modularity. For the inference, an upper bound on the number of possible named $Far(n)$ locations is needed. This is calculated based on the number of new c in fresh expressions in the current scope.

IDE integration. ABS features an Eclipse-based IDE[3] for developing ABS projects. The interesting part of the IDE for this paper is that we have incorporated visual overlays which display the location type inference results. For each location type there is a small overlay symbol, e.g., N for Near and F for Far, which are shown as superscripts of the type name. For example, a Far Client appears as $Client^F$. Whenever the user saves a changed program, the inference is triggered and the overlays are updated. They give the user complete location type information of all reference types, without cluttering the code. In addition, the overlays can easily be toggled on or off. It is also possible to write the inference results back as annotations into the source code, with user-specified levels of granularity, e.g., method signatures in interfaces.

Evaluation. We evaluated the location type system by applying it to four case studies:

CS (251 non-commented non-empty lines of code (LOC), 59 types to annotate) is an extended version of the chat application presented in Section 2.

TS (1123 LOC, 152 types to annotate) is an academic case study of a trading system for handling sales in supermarkets.

RS (3698 LOC, 104 types to annotate) models parts of an industrial case study on server-based software systems.

LS (2771 LOC, 301 types to annotate) is an academic case study of a lecture management system.

The evaluation results are presented in Figure 17. They show how precise the subject systems can be typed and how quickly the inference runs. We also restricted the alias analysis by various scopes to see its impact on performance and precision. First

---

[3] Download link for the tool:
   http://tools.hats-project.eu/eclipseplugin/installation.html

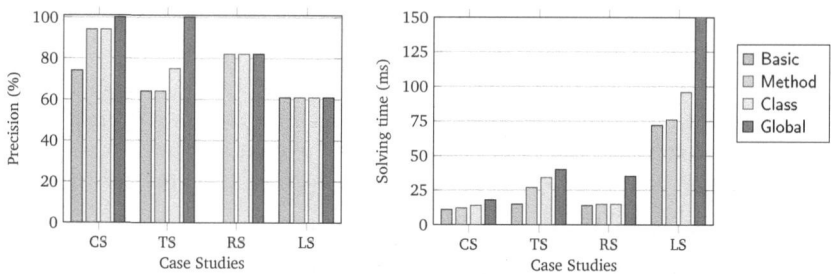

Fig. 17. Precision and solving time of the location type inference for the three case studies, using four different scopes for the alias analysis. The measurements where done on a Mac-Book Pro laptop (Intel Core 2 Duo 2.8GHz CPU, 4GB RAM, Mac OS X 10.6). We used the -Xms1024 parameter to avoid garbage collection. As working in an IDE usually consists of an edit-compile-run cycle, we provide the performance results (the mean of 20 complete runs) after warming up the JVM with 5 dry runs. We measured the time that the SAT-solver required for finding a solution using the System.nanoTime() method.

of all, all subject systems can be fully typed using our type system. The chart on the left shows the precision (percentage of near and far annotations) of the type inference. As can be seen, the basic type system already has a good precision (> 60%) in all three cases. As expected, the precision increased with a broader analysis scope. Using a global alias analysis, the inference achieved a precision of 100% for CS and TS. It is also interesting to note that, depending on the case study, extending the scope of the alias analysis can have an effect or not. RS could not be correctly typed with basic precision (but returned a partial solution in 14 ms). For CS and RS, the best precision was already achieved with a method-local scope. For LS, basic scope was sufficient.

The chart on the right shows the performance results of the inference. It shows that the performance of the inference is fast enough for the inference system to be used interactively. It also shows that the performance depends on the chosen scope for the alias analysis. In the evaluation, we used completely unannotated examples, so that all types had to be inferred. In practice, programs are often partially annotated, which additionally improves the performance of the type inference. We believe the analysis to be scalable, as it is based on a modular type system. The analysis can be applied to parts of a system, and the analysis results can then be reused to infer the types in different parts of the system.

It remains to be investigated whether other constraint encodings and backends will yield better performance. At the moment, the presented solving times strongly rely on the performance of the underlying SAT solver.

5   Discussion and Related Work

Location types are a lightweight variant of ownership types that focus on *flat* ownership contexts. This means that no nesting of locations is permitted. The object space is structured such that we can distinguish between local and non-local objects. We exploited this information in the context of distributed object-oriented programming to check whether an access or method call is local or remote. Locations can also be used for other purposes, in particular

- as scheduling units in multi-core scenarios [23],
- to raise the level of granularity of memory management and garbage collection from single objects to group of objects [24],
- for encapsulation of objects [25] or other values [13], and
- to support specification and verification techniques [26].

Ownership types [2,18,19] and similar type systems [27,28] typically describe a hierarchical heap structure. On one hand this makes these systems more general than location types, because ownership types could be used for the same purpose as location types; on the other hand this makes these systems more complex. An ownership type system which is close to location types in nature is that by Clarke et al. [29], which applies ownership types to active objects. In their system ownership contexts are also flat, but ownership is used to ensure encapsulation of objects with support for a safe object transfer using unique references and cloning. Haller and Odersky [30] use a capability-based type system to restrict aliasing in concurrent programs and achieve full encapsulation. As these systems are based on encapsulation they do not have the concept of *far* references. Places [31] also partition the heap. However, the set of places is fixed at the time the program is started. Similar in nature, but less expressive than our type system, is Loci [32], which only distinguishes references to be either thread-local or shared. Loci only uses defaults to reduce the annotation overhead. Loci is also realized as an Eclipse plug-in. Regions are also considered in region-based memory management [33], but for another purpose. They give the guarantee that objects inside a region do not refer to objects inside another region to ensure safe deallocation.

Using a Max-SAT solver with weighted constraints was also used by Flanagan and Freund [34] to infer types that prevent data-races and by Dietl, Ernst and Müller [20] to find good inference solutions for universe types. A crucial aspect of our work is the integration of type inference results into the IDE by using overlays. To the best of our knowledge there is no comparable approach. A widely used type system extension is the non-null type system [35]. For variations of this type system, there exist built-in inference mechanisms in Eclipse[4] and IntelliJ IDEA[5] as well as additional plug-ins [36]. However, none of these IDE integrations provide the option to visualize the inferred type information in all relevant places directly using overlays, but only provide specific overlays on request.

6 Conclusion and Future Work

We have presented a type system for distributed object-oriented programming languages to distinguish near from far references. We applied the type system to the

---

[4] http://wiki.eclipse.org/JDT_Core/Null_Analysis
[5] http://www.jetbrains.com/idea/webhelp/inferring-nullity.html

context of the ABS language to guarantee that far references are not used as targets for synchronous method calls. A complete type inference implementation allows the programmer to make use of the type system without making any annotations. The type inference results are visualized as overlay annotations directly in the development environment. Our evaluation of the type system to several case studies shows that the type system is expressive enough to type realistic code. The type inference implementation is fast enough to provide inference results within fractions of a second, so that interactive use of the system is possible.

We see three directions for future work. First, the type system could be applied to other settings where the location of an object is important, e.g., Java RMI [8]. Second, it would be interesting to investigate the visual overlay technique for other (pluggable) type systems, e.g., the nullness type system [36]. Third, it seems worthwhile to weaken the premise that objects stay at a location for their entire lifetime (for a motivation of object migration see Mycroft [23] and for the treatment of object transfer in relation to ownership see Müller and Rudich [37]).

References

1. Clarke, D.: Object Ownership and Containment. PhD thesis, University of New South Wales, Australia (2001)
2. Clarke, D.G., Potter, J., Noble, J.: Ownership types for flexible alias protection. In: Freeman-Benson, B.N., Chambers, C. (eds.) Proceedings of the 1998 ACM SIGPLAN Conference on Object-Oriented Programming Systems, Languages & Applications (OOPSLA 1998), Vancouver, British Columbia, Canada, October 18-22, pp. 48–64. ACM (1998)
3. Potanin, A., Noble, J., Clarke, D., Biddle, R.: Generic ownership for generic Java. In: Tarr, P.L., Cook, W.R. (eds.) Proceedings of the 21th Annual ACM SIGPLAN Conference on Object-Oriented Programming, Systems, Languages, and Applications, OOPSLA 2006, Portland, Oregon, USA, October 22-26. ACM (2006)
4. Miller, M.S., Tribble, E.D., Shapiro, J.S.: Concurrency Among Strangers. In: De Nicola, R., Sangiorgi, D. (eds.) TGC 2005. LNCS, vol. 3705, pp. 195–229. Springer, Heidelberg (2005)
5. Van Cutsem, T., Mostinckx, S., Boix, E.G., Dedecker, J., Meuter, W.D.: Ambienttalk: Object-oriented event-driven programming in mobile ad hoc networks. In: SCCC, pp. 3–12. IEEE Computer Society (2007)
6. Schäfer, J., Poetzsch-Heffter, A.: JCoBox: Generalizing Active Objects to Concurrent Components. In: D'Hondt, T. (ed.) ECOOP 2010. LNCS, vol. 6183, pp. 275–299. Springer, Heidelberg (2010)
7. Johnsen, E.B., Hähnle, R., Schäfer, J., Schlatte, R., Steffen, M.: ABS: A Core Language for Abstract Behavioral Specification. In: Aichernig, B.K., de Boer, F.S., Bonsangue, M.M. (eds.) FMCO 2010. LNCS, vol. 6957, pp. 142–164. Springer, Heidelberg (2011)
8. Oracle Corporation: Java SE 6 RMI documentation, http://download.oracle.com/javase/6/docs/technotes/guides/rmi/index.html
9. Andreae, C., Noble, J., Markstrum, S., Millstein, T.: A framework for implementing pluggable type systems. In: Tarr, P.L., Cook, W.R. (eds.) Proceedings of the 21th Annual ACM SIGPLAN Conference on Object-Oriented Programming, Systems, Languages, and Applications, OOPSLA 2006, Portland, Oregon, USA, October 22-26, pp. 57–74. ACM (2006)

10. Ernst, M.D.: Type Annotations Specification (JSR 308) and The Checker Framework: Custom pluggable types for Java, http://types.cs.washington.edu/jsr308/
11. Welsch, Y., Schäfer, J.: Location Types for Safe Distributed Object-Oriented Programming. In: Bishop, J., Vallecillo, A. (eds.) TOOLS 2011. LNCS, vol. 6705, pp. 194–210. Springer, Heidelberg (2011)
12. Hewitt, C., Bishop, P., Steiger, R.: A universal modular ACTOR formalism for artificial intelligence. In: IJCAI, pp. 235–245 (1973)
13. Cardelli, L., Ghelli, G., Gordon, A.D.: Secrecy and group creation. Inf. Comput. 196(2), 127–155 (2005)
14. Dietl, W., Drossopoulou, S., Müller, P.: Generic Universe Types. In: Ernst, E. (ed.) ECOOP 2007. LNCS, vol. 4609, pp. 28–53. Springer, Heidelberg (2007)
15. Östlund, J., Wrigstad, T.: Welterweight Java. In: Vitek, J. (ed.) TOOLS 2010. LNCS, vol. 6141, pp. 97–116. Springer, Heidelberg (2010)
16. Wright, A.K., Felleisen, M.: A syntactic approach to type soundness. Inf. Comput. 115(1), 38–94 (1994)
17. Rountev, A., Milanova, A., Ryder, B.G.: Points-to analysis for java using annotated constraints. In: Northrop, L.M., Vlissides, J.M. (eds.) Proceedings of the 2001 ACM SIGPLAN Conference on Object-Oriented Programming Systems, Languages and Applications, OOPSLA 2001, Tampa, Florida, USA, October 14-18, pp. 43–55. ACM (2001)
18. Boyapati, C., Liskov, B., Shrira, L.: Ownership types for object encapsulation. In: Aiken, A., Morrisett, G. (eds.) Conference Record of POPL 2003: The 30th SIGPLAN-SIGACT Symposium on Principles of Programming Languages, New Orleans, Louisisana, USA, January 15-17, pp. 213–223. ACM (2003)
19. Lu, Y., Potter, J.: On Ownership and Accessibility. In: Thomas, D. (ed.) ECOOP 2006. LNCS, vol. 4067, pp. 99–123. Springer, Heidelberg (2006)
20. Dietl, W., Ernst, M.D., Müller, P.: Tunable Static Inference for Generic Universe Types. In: Mezini, M. (ed.) ECOOP 2011. LNCS, vol. 6813, pp. 333–357. Springer, Heidelberg (2011)
21. Pierce, B.C. (ed.): Advanced Topics in Types and Programming Languages. MIT Press (2005)
22. Le Berre, D., Parrain, A.: The SAT4J library, release 2.2, system description. Journal on Satisfiability, Boolean Modeling and Computation 7, 59–64 (2010)
23. Mycroft, A.: Location—the other confinement form. In: Proceedings of the International Workshop on Aliasing, Confinement and Ownership in Object-oriented Programming, IWACO 2011 (2011)
24. Gay, D., Aiken, A.: Memory management with explicit regions. In: Davidson, J.W., Cooper, K.D., Berman, A.M. (eds.) Proceedings of the ACM SIGPLAN 1998 Conference on Programming Language Design and Implementation (PLDI), Montreal, Canada, June 17-19, pp. 313–323. ACM (1998)
25. Geilmann, K., Poetzsch-Heffter, A.: Modular checking of confinement for object-oriented components using abstract interpretation. In: Proceedings of the International Workshop on Aliasing, Confinement and Ownership in Object-oriented Programming, IWACO 2011 (2011)
26. Poetzsch-Heffter, A., Schäfer, J.: Modular Specification of Encapsulated Object-Oriented Components. In: de Boer, F.S., Bonsangue, M.M., Graf, S., de Roever, W.-P. (eds.) FMCO 2005. LNCS, vol. 4111, pp. 313–341. Springer, Heidelberg (2006)
27. Aldrich, J., Chambers, C.: Ownership Domains: Separating Aliasing Policy from Mechanism. In: Odersky, M. (ed.) ECOOP 2004. LNCS, vol. 3086, pp. 1–25. Springer, Heidelberg (2004)
28. Dietl, W.: Universe Types: Topology, Encapsulation, Genericity, and Tools. PhD thesis, ETH Zurich, Switzerland (2009)

29. Clarke, D., Wrigstad, T., Östlund, J., Johnsen, E.B.: Minimal Ownership for Active Objects. In: Ramalingam, G. (ed.) APLAS 2008. LNCS, vol. 5356, pp. 139–154. Springer, Heidelberg (2008)

30. Haller, P., Odersky, M.: Capabilities for Uniqueness and Borrowing. In: D'Hondt, T. (ed.) ECOOP 2010. LNCS, vol. 6183, pp. 354–378. Springer, Heidelberg (2010)

31. Grothoff, C.: Expressive Type Systems for Object-Oriented Languages. PhD thesis, University of California, Los Angeles (2006)

32. Wrigstad, T., Pizlo, F., Meawad, F., Zhao, L., Vitek, J.: Loci: Simple Thread-Locality for Java. In: Drossopoulou, S. (ed.) ECOOP 2009. LNCS, vol. 5653, pp. 445–469. Springer, Heidelberg (2009)

33. Tofte, M., Talpin, J.P.: Region-based memory management. Inf. Comput. 132(2), 109–176 (1997)

34. Flanagan, C., Freund, S.N.: Type inference against races. Sci. Comput. Program. 64, 140–165 (2007)

35. Fähndrich, M., Leino, K.R.M.: Declaring and checking non-null types in an object-oriented language. In: Crocker, R., Steele Jr., G.L. (eds.) Proceedings of the 2003 ACM SIGPLAN Conference on Object-Oriented Programming Systems, Languages and Applications, OOPSLA 2003, Anaheim, CA, USA, October 26-30, pp. 302–312. ACM (2003)

36. Hubert, L., Jensen, T., Pichardie, D.: Semantic Foundations and Inference of Non-null Annotations. In: Barthe, G., de Boer, F.S. (eds.) FMOODS 2008. LNCS, vol. 5051, pp. 132–149. Springer, Heidelberg (2008)

37. Müller, P., Rudich, A.: Ownership transfer in universe types. In: Gabriel, R.P., Bacon, D.F., Lopes, C.V., Steele Jr., G.L. (eds.) Proceedings of the 22nd Annual ACM SIGPLAN Conference on Object-Oriented Programming, Systems, Languages, and Applications, OOPSLA 2007, Montreal, Quebec, Canada, October 21-25, pp. 461–478. ACM (2007)

A   Proof of the Preservation Theorems

In the following, we present the proofs of Theorem 2 and Theorem 1. As a fist step, we state a few lemmata that relate the definitions given in Sections 3.1 and 3.2.

Lemma 1. *For all* l_1, l_2, l_3 : $\mathrm{dtype}(l_1, l_3) <: \mathrm{dtype}(l_1, l_2) \triangleright_K \mathrm{dtype}(l_2, l_3)$.

Proof. By case analyis ($l_1 = l_2 = l_3$, $l_1 = l_2 \neq l_3$, $l_1 \neq l_2 = l_3$, $l_1 = l_3 \neq l_2$, $l_1 \neq l_2 \neq l_3 \neq l_1$).

Lemma 2. *For all* l_1, l_2 : $\mathrm{dtype}(l_1, l_2) = \mathrm{dtype}(l_2, l_1)$.

Proof. Directly from definition of $\mathrm{dtype}(\_, \_)$.

Lemma 3. *If* $L_1, L_2, L_3, L_4 \in \{\mathsf{Near}, \mathsf{Far}, \mathsf{Somewhere}\}$ *and* $L_1 <: L_2$ *and* $L_3 <: L_4$, *then* $L_1 \triangleright_K L_3 <: L_2 \triangleright_K L_4$.

Proof. By case analysis.

Lemma 4. *If* $L_1 <: L_2$, *then* $\mathrm{abs}(L_1) <: \mathrm{abs}(L_2)$.

Proof. By case analysis.

Lemma 5. *If $L_1 \triangleright_{\text{From}} L_2 <: L_3$, then $\text{abs}(L_1) \triangleright_{\text{From}} \text{abs}(L_2) <: \text{abs}(L_3)$.*

Proof. By case analysis.

We introduce the predicate $\text{diffFar}(L_1, L_2)$ that determines whether L_1 and L_2 are both named far types, but with different names. Put formally, $\text{diffFar}(L_1, L_2) = \text{True}$ if $L_1 = \text{Far}(n_1)$ and $L_2 = \text{Far}(n_2)$ and $n_1 \neq n_2$, and False otherwise.

Lemma 6. *If $L_1 \triangleright_{\text{To}} L_2 <: L_3$ and $\neg\text{diffFar}(L_1, L_2)$, then $\text{abs}(L_1) \triangleright_{\text{To}} \text{abs}(L_2) <: \text{abs}(L_3)$.*

Proof. By case analysis.

Proof of Theorem 2:

Assume a well-formed configuration ζ for a program P such that $\vdash P$ and $\zeta \rightsquigarrow \zeta'$. This means that the heap entries (Definition 4) are well-formed, the stack frames (Definition 5) for ζ are well-formed and ζ is well-formed with respect to named far locations. Then prove that ζ' is well-formed as well. In the presentation of the proof we focus on the location type aspects. We assume that conditions of a standard class-based type system hold, of which we name a few:

Condition 1: We do not allow this on the left hand side of an assignment, and thus the object (and its location) referenced by this remains the same (for a certain stack frame) after reduction steps.

Condition 2: If a variable points to an object with dynamic class type c, the variable is also statically typed as c.

The proof then proceeds by a standard case analysis on the reduction rules used. We show the first rule in detail; in the presentation of the other rules, we omit uninteresting cases (e.g. transfer of null values). Throughout the proof, l_{this} is used as abbreviation of $\text{loc}(\mathcal{H}(\mathcal{D}(\text{this})))$.

Case R-ASSIGN:
$$\frac{\mathcal{D}' = \mathcal{D}[x \mapsto \mathcal{D}(y)]}{(x \leftarrow y \cdot \bar{S}, \mathcal{D})^{c,m} \cdot \bar{\mathcal{F}}, \mathcal{H} \rightsquigarrow (\bar{S}, \mathcal{D}')^{c,m} \cdot \bar{\mathcal{F}}, \mathcal{H}}$$

We distinguish two cases:

Case $x = y$: The configuration then remains unchanged and the claim follows trivially.

Case $x \neq y$:

Case $\mathcal{D}(y) = \text{null}$: Thus $\mathcal{D}'(x) = \text{null}$ and the claim follows trivially.

Case $\mathcal{D}(y) \neq \text{null}$: Let $l_y := \text{loc}(\mathcal{H}(\mathcal{D}(y)))$. We have

1. $l_{\text{this}} = \text{loc}(\mathcal{H}(\mathcal{D}'(\text{this})))$ by condition 1,
2. $l_y = \text{loc}(\mathcal{H}(\mathcal{D}'(x)))$ as $\mathcal{D}'(x) = \mathcal{D}(y)$,
3. $\text{anno}(c, m, y) <: \text{anno}(c, m, x)$ by typing rules WF-ASSIGN and WF-VAR,
4. $\text{abs}(\text{anno}(c, m, y)) <: \text{abs}(\text{anno}(c, m, x))$ by Lemma 4 from step 3,

5. $\mathrm{dtype}(l_{\mathrm{this}}, l_y) <: \mathrm{abs}(\mathrm{anno}(c, m, y))$ by well-formedness assumption of stack frame $(x \leftarrow y \cdot \overline{S}, \mathcal{D})^{c,m}$, and
6. $\mathrm{dtype}(l_{\mathrm{this}}, l_y) <: \mathrm{abs}(\mathrm{anno}(c, m, x))$ by the previous two steps using transitivity of the subtype relation.

We have two proof goals as the heap remains unchanged. We first want to prove that $(\overline{S}, \mathcal{D}')^{c,m}$ is well-formed. By Definition 5 this amounts to proving that for all z with $\mathcal{D}'(z) = \iota$, we have $\mathrm{dtype}(l_{\mathrm{this}}, \mathrm{loc}(\mathcal{H}(\iota))) <: \mathrm{anno}(c, m, z)$. As only x is modified, it is enough to prove this for x (i.e. $\mathrm{dtype}(l_{\mathrm{this}}, \mathrm{loc}(\mathcal{H}(\mathcal{D}'(x)))) <: \mathrm{abs}(\mathrm{anno}(c, m, x)))$, which follows directly from steps 2 and 6.

The second proof goal is to show that the new configuration ζ' is well-formed wrt. named Far locations. As only x is modified, we need to only consider the case $(\mathrm{anno}(c, m, x), l_x) \in \mathrm{reach}(\zeta')$ where $\mathrm{anno}(c, m, x) = \mathrm{Far}(n)$. By step 3, we then know that $\mathrm{anno}(c, m, y) = \mathrm{Far}(n)$ and consequently $(\mathrm{anno}(c, m, y), l_y) \in \mathrm{reach}(\zeta)$. As $\mathrm{anno}(c, m, x) = \mathrm{anno}(c, m, y) = \mathrm{Far}(n)$ and $l_x = l_y$ (from step 1) and by well-formedness assumption of ζ, the claim follows.

Case R-NEWSAME:

$$\frac{(l_y, \_, \_) = \mathcal{H}(\mathcal{D}(y)) \qquad \mathcal{H}' = \mathcal{H}[\iota \mapsto \mathrm{initO}(l_y, c')] \qquad \mathcal{D}' = \mathcal{D}[x \mapsto \iota]}{(x \leftarrow \mathrm{new}\ c'\ \mathrm{in}\ y \cdot \overline{S}, \mathcal{D})^{c,m} \cdot \overline{\mathcal{F}}, \mathcal{H} \rightsquigarrow (\overline{S}, \mathcal{D}')^{c,m} \cdot \overline{\mathcal{F}}, \mathcal{H}'}$$

$\iota \notin \mathrm{dom}(\mathcal{H})$

We have

1. $\mathrm{anno}(c, m, y) <: \mathrm{anno}(c, m, x)$ by typing rules WF-ASSIGN and WF-NEWSAME,
2. $\mathrm{dtype}(l_{\mathrm{this}}, l_y) <: \mathrm{abs}(\mathrm{anno}(c, m, y))$ by well-formedness assumption of stack frame $(x \leftarrow \mathrm{new}\ c'\ \mathrm{in}\ y \cdot \overline{S}, \mathcal{D})^{c,m}$,
3. $\mathrm{abs}(\mathrm{anno}(c, m, y)) <: \mathrm{abs}(\mathrm{anno}(c, m, x))$ by Lemma 4 applied to step 1,
4. $\mathrm{dtype}(l_{\mathrm{this}}, l_y) <: \mathrm{abs}(\mathrm{anno}(c, m, x))$ from steps 2 and 3 by transitivity of subtype relation, and
5. $l_y = \mathrm{loc}(\mathcal{H}'(\mathcal{D}'(x)))$ directly from the rule R-NEWSAME.

The first proof goal is to show that $(\overline{S}, \mathcal{D}')^{c,m}$ is well-formed. As only x is modified, this amounts to proving that $\mathrm{dtype}(l_{\mathrm{this}}, \mathrm{loc}(\mathcal{H}'(\mathcal{D}'(x)))) <: \mathrm{abs}(\mathrm{anno}(c, m, x))$ which follows from steps 4 and 5. The second proof goal is to show that $\mathcal{H}'$ is well-formed, which is trivially the case as all the fields of the new object contain null. The third proof goal is to show that ζ' is well-formed wrt. named Far locations, which is similar to the rule R-ASSIGN, as the newly created object is only reachable from x.

Case R-NEWFRESH:

$$\frac{\iota \notin \mathrm{dom}(\mathcal{H}) \qquad l\ \mathrm{is\ fresh} \qquad \mathcal{H}' = \mathcal{H}[\iota \mapsto \mathrm{initO}(l, c')] \qquad \mathcal{D}' = \mathcal{D}[x \mapsto \iota]}{(x \leftarrow \mathrm{new}\ c'\ \mathrm{in}\ \mathrm{fresh} \cdot \overline{S}, \mathcal{D})^{c,m} \cdot \overline{\mathcal{F}}, \mathcal{H} \rightsquigarrow (\overline{S}, \mathcal{D}')^{c,m} \cdot \overline{\mathcal{F}}, \mathcal{H}'}$$

We have

1. $\mathsf{Far}(n)$ <: $\mathsf{anno}(c, m, x)$ for some i by typing rules WF-ASSIGN and WF-NEWFRESHP,
2. Far <: $\mathsf{abs}(\mathsf{anno}(c, m, x))$ by Lemma 4 from previous step,
3. $\mathsf{dtype}(l_{\mathsf{this}}, l) = \mathsf{Far}$ as l is fresh,
4. $\mathsf{dtype}(l_{\mathsf{this}}, l)$ <: $\mathsf{abs}(\mathsf{anno}(c, m, x))$ by steps 2 and 3, and
5. $l = \mathsf{loc}(\mathcal{H}'(\mathcal{D}'(x)))$ directly from the rule R-NEWFRESH.

The proof goals are the same as for the previous rule R-NEWSAME. The claim $\mathsf{dtype}(l_{\mathsf{this}}, \mathsf{loc}(\mathcal{H}'(\mathcal{D}'(x))))$ <: $\mathsf{abs}(\mathsf{anno}(c, m, x))$ follows from steps 4 and 5. The new heap entry is trivially well-formed as all the fields contain null. The new configuration is well-formed wrt. named Far locations as l is fresh and thus l is different to all other locations.

Case R-FIELDGET:

$$\frac{(l_y, c', \mathcal{D}'') = \mathcal{H}(\mathcal{D}(y)) \qquad \mathcal{D}' = \mathcal{D}[x \mapsto \mathcal{D}''(f)]}{(x \leftarrow y.f \cdot \overline{S}, \mathcal{D})^{c,m} \cdot \overline{\mathcal{F}}, \mathcal{H} \rightsquigarrow (\overline{S}, \mathcal{D}')^{c,m} \cdot \overline{\mathcal{F}}, \mathcal{H}}$$

We only consider the case $\mathcal{D}''(f) \neq$ null. Let $l_f := \mathsf{loc}(\mathcal{H}(\mathcal{D}''(f)))$. We have

1. $\mathsf{anno}(c', f) \triangleright_{\mathsf{From}} \mathsf{anno}(c, m, y)$ <: $\mathsf{anno}(c, m, x)$ by typing rules WF-ASSIGN and WF-FIELDGET,
2. $\mathsf{dtype}(l_y, l_f)$ <: $\mathsf{abs}(\mathsf{anno}(c', f))$ by well-formedness assumption of heap entry $(l_y, c', \mathcal{D}'')$,
3. $\mathsf{dtype}(l_{\mathsf{this}}, l_y)$ <: $\mathsf{abs}(\mathsf{anno}(c, m, y))$ by well-formedness assumption of stack frame $(x \leftarrow y.f \cdot \overline{S}, \mathcal{D})^{c,m}$,
4. $\mathsf{dtype}(l_y, l_f) \triangleright_{\mathsf{From}} \mathsf{dtype}(l_{\mathsf{this}}, l_y)$ <: $\mathsf{abs}(\mathsf{anno}(c', f)) \triangleright_{\mathsf{From}} \mathsf{abs}(\mathsf{anno}(c, m, y))$ from steps 2 and 3 by Lemma 3,
5. $\mathsf{dtype}(l_{\mathsf{this}}, l_f)$ <: $\mathsf{dtype}(l_y, l_f) \triangleright_{\mathsf{From}} \mathsf{dtype}(l_{\mathsf{this}}, l_y)$ by Lemma 1 and Lemma 2,
6. $\mathsf{abs}(\mathsf{anno}(c', f)) \triangleright_{\mathsf{From}} \mathsf{abs}(\mathsf{anno}(c, m, y))$ <: $\mathsf{abs}(\mathsf{anno}(c, m, x))$ by Lemma 5 from step 1,
7. $\mathsf{dtype}(l_{\mathsf{this}}, l_f)$ <: $\mathsf{abs}(\mathsf{anno}(c, m, x))$ by steps 5, 4 and 6 using transitivity of the subtype relation, and
8. $l_f = \mathsf{loc}(\mathcal{H}(\mathcal{D}'(x)))$ as $\mathcal{D}''(f) = \mathcal{D}'(x)$.

We have two proof goals as the heap remains unchanged. The first proof goal is to show that $(\overline{S}, \mathcal{D}')^{c,m}$ is well-formed. As only x is modified, it is sufficient to show that $\mathsf{dtype}(l_{\mathsf{this}}, \mathsf{loc}(\mathcal{H}(\mathcal{D}'(x))))$ <: $\mathsf{abs}(\mathsf{anno}(c, m, x))$ which follows directly from steps 7 and 8.

The second proof goal is to show that the new configuration ζ' is well-formed wrt. named Far locations. As only x is modified, we need to only consider the case $(\mathsf{anno}(c, m, x), l_f) \in \mathsf{reach}(\zeta')$ where $\mathsf{anno}(c, m, x) = \mathsf{Far}(n)$. By step 1, we then know that either

  – $\mathsf{anno}(c, m, y) = \mathsf{Near}$ and $\mathsf{anno}(c', f) = \mathsf{Far}(n)$ or
  – $\mathsf{anno}(c, m, y) = \mathsf{Far}(n)$ and $\mathsf{anno}(c', f) = \mathsf{Near}$.

In the first case, as $(\mathsf{anno}(c', f), l_f) \in \mathsf{reach}(\zeta)$ and ζ well-formed, the claim follows directly from step 8. In the second case, $l_y = l_f$ and the claim then follows similarly to the first case.

Case R-FIELDSET:

$$\frac{\iota = \mathcal{D}(x) \qquad (l_x, c', \mathcal{D}') = \mathcal{H}(\iota) \qquad \mathcal{D}'' = \mathcal{D}'[f \mapsto \mathcal{D}(y)] \qquad \mathcal{H}' = \mathcal{H}[\iota \mapsto (l_x, c', \mathcal{D}'')]}{(x.f \leftarrow y \cdot \overline{S}, \mathcal{D})^{c,m} \cdot \overline{\mathcal{F}}, \mathcal{H} \rightsquigarrow (\overline{S}, \mathcal{D})^{c,m} \cdot \overline{\mathcal{F}}, \mathcal{H}'}$$

We only consider the case $\mathcal{D}(y) \neq$ null. Let $l_x := \mathrm{loc}(\mathcal{H}(\mathcal{D}(x)))$ and $l_y := \mathrm{loc}(\mathcal{H}(\mathcal{D}(y)))$. We have

1. $\mathrm{anno}(c, m, y) \triangleright_{\mathrm{To}} \mathrm{anno}(c, m, x) <: \mathrm{anno}(c', f)$ by typing rules WF-ASSIGN and WF-FIELDSET,
2. $\mathrm{dtype}(l_{\mathrm{this}}, l_y) <: \mathrm{abs}(\mathrm{anno}(c, m, y))$ by well-formedness assumption of stack frame $(x.f \leftarrow y \cdot \overline{S}, \mathcal{D})^{c,m}$,
3. $\mathrm{dtype}(l_{\mathrm{this}}, l_x) <: \mathrm{abs}(\mathrm{anno}(c, m, x))$ by well-formedness assumption of stack frame $(x.f \leftarrow y \cdot \overline{S}, \mathcal{D})^{c,m}$, and
4. $l_y = \mathrm{loc}(\mathcal{H}'(\mathcal{D}''(f)))$ as $\mathcal{D}''(f) = \mathcal{D}(y)$.

We distinguish two cases:

Case $\neg\mathrm{diffFar}(\mathrm{anno}(c, m, x), \mathrm{anno}(c, m, y))$: Similarly to the case R-FIELDGET we have $\mathrm{dtype}(l_x, l_y) <: \mathrm{abs}(\mathrm{anno}(c', f))$ from steps 1, 2, and 3 by Lemma 1, Lemma 2, Lemma 3, Lemma 6 and transitivity of subtyping.

One proof goal is this time to show that the heap entry $(l_x, c', \mathcal{D}'')$ is well-formed. As only f is modified, we have to prove that $\mathrm{dtype}(l_x, \mathrm{loc}(\mathcal{H}'(\mathcal{D}''(f)))) <: \mathrm{abs}(\mathrm{anno}(c', f))$. This results directly from step 4.

The other proof goal is to show that the new configuration ζ' is well-formed wrt. named Far locations. As only f is modified, we need to only consider the case $(\mathrm{anno}(c', f), l_y) \in \mathrm{reach}(\zeta')$ where $\mathrm{anno}(c', f) = \mathrm{Far}(n)$. By step 1 and case assumption, we then know that $\mathrm{anno}(c, m, x) = \mathrm{Near}$ and $\mathrm{anno}(c, m, y) = \mathrm{Far}(n)$. The claim then follows directly.

Case $\mathrm{diffFar}(\mathrm{anno}(c, m, x), \mathrm{anno}(c, m, y))$: Assume wlog that $\mathrm{anno}(c, m, x) = \mathrm{Far}(n_1)$ and $\mathrm{anno}(c, m, y) = \mathrm{Far}(n_2)$ with $n_1 \neq n_2$. We then get $\mathrm{Far}(n_2) <: \mathrm{anno}(c', f)$ from step 1. We also have $l_x \neq l_y$ by well-formedness assumption of the old configuration. Thus $\mathrm{dtype}(l_x, l_y) = \mathrm{Far}$.

One proof goal is this time to show that the heap entry $(l_x, c', \mathcal{D}'')$ is well-formed. As only f is modified, we have to prove that $\mathrm{dtype}(l_x, \mathrm{loc}(\mathcal{H}'(\mathcal{D}''(f)))) <: \mathrm{abs}(\mathrm{anno}(c', f))$. This follows directly from step 4 and the results in the previous paragraph.

The other proof goal is to show that the new configuration ζ' is well-formed wrt. named Far locations. As only f is modified, we need to only consider the case $(\mathrm{anno}(c', f), l_y) \in \mathrm{reach}(\zeta')$ where $\mathrm{anno}(c', f) = \mathrm{Far}(n_2)$. By case assumption, we know that $\mathrm{anno}(c, m, y) = \mathrm{Far}(n_2)$ from which the claim follows directly.

Case R-CALL:

$$\frac{\mathcal{F} = (x \leftarrow y.m'(\overline{z}) \cdot \overline{S}, \mathcal{D})^{c,m} \qquad (l_y, c', \_) = \mathcal{H}(\mathcal{D}(y)) \qquad \mathcal{F}' = \mathrm{initF}(c', m', \mathcal{D}(y), \mathcal{D}(\overline{z}))}{\mathcal{F} \cdot \overline{\mathcal{F}}, \mathcal{H} \rightsquigarrow \mathcal{F}' \cdot \mathcal{F} \cdot \overline{\mathcal{F}}, \mathcal{H}}$$

We consider only the case $\mathcal{D}(z_i) \neq$ null. Let $l_y := \text{loc}(\mathcal{H}(\mathcal{D}(y)))$ and $l_{z_i} := \text{loc}(\mathcal{H}(\mathcal{D}(z_i)))$. Let $\overline{x} := \text{params}(c', m')$ and $\mathcal{F}' := (\overline{S}', \mathcal{D}')^{c', m'}$. We have

1. $\text{anno}(c, m, z_i) \triangleright_{\text{To}} \text{anno}(c, m, y) <: \text{anno}(c', m', x_i)$ by typing rules WF-ASSIGN and WF-CALL,
2. $\text{dtype}(l_{\text{this}}, l_{z_i}) <: \text{abs}(\text{anno}(c, m, z_i))$ by well-formedness assumption of stack frame $\mathcal{F}$,
3. $\text{dtype}(l_{\text{this}}, l_y) <: \text{abs}(\text{anno}(c, m, y))$ by well-formedness assumption of stack frame $\mathcal{F}$,
4. $\mathcal{F}'$ is of the form $(\overline{S}', \mathcal{D}')^{c', m'}$ where $\mathcal{D}'(\text{this}) = \mathcal{D}(y)$ and $\mathcal{D}'(x_i) = \mathcal{D}(z_i)$ by definition of $\text{initF}(,,,)$, and
5. $l_{x_i} = l_{z_i}$ as $\mathcal{D}(z_i) = \mathcal{D}'(x_i)$.

We distinguish two cases:

Case $\neg\text{diffFar}(\text{anno}(c, m, y), \text{anno}(c, m, z_i))$: Similarly to the case R-FIELDGET we have $\text{dtype}(l_y, l_{z_i}) <: \text{abs}(\text{anno}(c', m', x_i))$ from steps 1, 2 and 3 by Lemma 1, Lemma 2, Lemma 3, Lemma 6 and transitivity of subtyping.
The first proof goal is to show that $\mathcal{F}'$ is well-formed. We only need to consider the parameters $\overline{x}$, as the local variables are initialized with null. We thus need to show that $\text{dtype}(l_y, l_{x_i}) <: \text{abs}(\text{anno}(c', m', x_i))$ which follows directly from step 5.
The other proof goal is to show that the new configuration ζ' is well-formed wrt. named Far locations. We need to only consider the case $(\text{anno}(c', m', x_i), l_y) \in \text{reach}(\zeta')$ where $\text{anno}(c', m', x_i) = \text{Far}(n)$. By step 1 and case assumption, we then know that $\text{anno}(c, m, y) = \text{Near}$ and $\text{anno}(c, m, z_i) = \text{Far}(n)$. The claim then follows directly.

Case $\text{diffFar}(\text{anno}(c, m, y), \text{anno}(c, m, z_i))$: Assume wlog that $\text{anno}(c, m, y) = \text{Far}(n_1)$ and $\text{anno}(c, m, z_i) = \text{Far}(n_2)$ with $n_1 \neq n_2$. By step 1, we get $\text{Far}(n_2) <: \text{anno}(c', m', x_i)$. We also have $l_y \neq l_{z_i}$ by well-formedness assumption of the old configuration. Thus $\text{dtype}(l_y, l_{z_i}) = \text{Far}$.
The first proof goal is to show that $\mathcal{F}'$ is well-formed. We only need to consider the parameters $\overline{x}$, as the local variables are initialized with null. We thus need to show that $\text{dtype}(l_y, l_{x_i}) <: \text{abs}(\text{anno}(c', m', x_i))$ which follows directly from step 5 and the results in the previous paragraph.
The other proof goal is to show that the new configuration ζ' is well-formed wrt. named Far locations. We need to consider the case $(\text{anno}(c', m', x_i), l_{x_i}) \in \text{reach}(\zeta')$ where $\text{anno}(c', m', x_i) = \text{Far}(n_2)$. By case assumption, we know that $\text{anno}(c, m, z_i) = \text{Far}(n_2)$ from which the claim follows directly.

Case R-RETURN:

$$\frac{\mathcal{F} = (x \leftarrow y.m'(\overline{z}) \cdot \overline{S}, \mathcal{D}')^{c, m} \qquad \mathcal{D}'' = \mathcal{D}'[x \mapsto \mathcal{D}(\text{result})]}{(\bullet, \mathcal{D})^{c', m'} \cdot \mathcal{F} \cdot \overline{\mathcal{F}}, \mathcal{H} \rightsquigarrow (\overline{S}, \mathcal{D}'')^{c, m} \cdot \overline{\mathcal{F}}, \mathcal{H}}$$

We only consider the case where $\mathcal{D}(\text{result}) \neq$ null. Let $l_y := \text{loc}(\mathcal{H}(\mathcal{D}'(y)))$ and $l_{\text{result}} := \text{loc}(\mathcal{H}(\mathcal{D}(\text{result})))$. We have

1. $\mathrm{anno}(c', m', \mathrm{result}) \triangleright_{\mathsf{From}} \mathrm{anno}(c, m, y) <: \mathrm{anno}(c, m, x)$ by typing rules WF-ASSIGN and WF-CALL,
2. $\mathrm{dtype}(l_{\mathrm{this}}, l_y) <: \mathrm{anno}(c, m, y)$ by well-formedness assumption of stack frame $\mathcal{F}$,
3. $\mathrm{dtype}(l_y, l_{\mathrm{result}}) <: \mathrm{anno}(c', m', \mathrm{result})$ by well-formedness assumption of stack frame $(\bullet, \mathcal{D})^{c', m'}$ and condition 1,
4. $\mathrm{dtype}(l_{\mathrm{this}}, l_{\mathrm{result}}) <: \mathrm{anno}(c, m, x)$ from steps 1, 2 and 3 similarly to the case R-FIELDGET by Lemma 1, Lemma 2, Lemma 3 and transitivity of subtyping, and
5. $l_{\mathrm{result}} = \mathrm{loc}(\mathcal{H}(\mathcal{D}''(x)))$ as $\mathcal{D}(\mathrm{result}) = \mathcal{D}''(x)$.

The first proof goal is to show that the stack frame $(\overline{S}, \mathcal{D}'')^{c, m}$ is well-formed. As only x is modified, we need to show that $\mathrm{dtype}(l_{\mathrm{this}}, \mathrm{loc}(\mathcal{H}(\mathcal{D}''(x)))) <: \mathrm{anno}(c, m, x)$ which follows directly from steps 4 and 5.

The second proof goal is to show that the new configuration ζ' is well-formed wrt. named Far locations. As only x is modified, we need to only consider the case $(\mathrm{anno}(c, m, x), l_{\mathrm{result}}) \in \mathrm{reach}(\zeta')$ where $\mathrm{anno}(c, m, x) = \mathrm{Far}(n)$.

By step 1, we then know that either

- $\mathrm{anno}(c, m, y) = \mathrm{Near}$ and $\mathrm{anno}(c', m', \mathrm{result}) = \mathrm{Far}(n)$ or
- $\mathrm{anno}(c, m, y) = \mathrm{Far}(n)$ and $\mathrm{anno}(c', m', \mathrm{result}) = \mathrm{Near}$.

In the first case, as $(\mathrm{anno}(c', m', \mathrm{result}), l_{\mathrm{result}}) \in \mathrm{reach}(\zeta)$ and ζ well-formed, the claim follows directly from step 5. In the second case, $l_y = l_{\mathrm{result}}$ and the claim then follows similarly to the first case.

Proof of Theorem 1:

Let P be a program such that $\vdash P$ and all location annotations in P are from $\{\mathrm{Near}, \mathrm{Far}, \mathrm{Somewhere}\}$. Thus, for all c, m, x, f,

$$\mathrm{abs}(\mathrm{anno}(c, m, x)) = \mathrm{anno}(c, m, x)$$
$$\mathrm{abs}(\mathrm{anno}(c, f)) = \mathrm{anno}(c, f)$$

Let ζ be a configuration for P that is well-formed according to Definition 1 and let ζ' be a successor configuration. According to Definition 6, there is no n, l with $(\mathrm{Far}(n), l) \in \mathrm{reach}(\zeta)$. Thus, ζ is also well-formed according to Definition 8. Theorem 2 guarantees that ζ' is well-formed according to Definition 8. Because of the two equations above, ζ' is also well-formed according to Definition 1. Thus, Theorem 1 holds.

B Soundness and Completeness of Type Inference

In the following, we present the proof of Theorem 3, i.e., we show that the constraint generation rules in Fig. 15 precisely collect the typing constraints defined by the typing rules in Fig. 10. P denotes programs that are fully annotated with pairwise distinct location type variables, i.e., all type occurrences in P are of the form $\alpha\, c$.

Soundness. We have to show: If $\sigma \models \overline{\mathcal{Q}_P}$, then $\vdash \sigma P$.

Let $\mathcal{T}_P^c$ be the derivation tree for P according to the constraint generation rules in Fig. 15. Each node of $\mathcal{T}_P^c$ corresponds to a rule application. Without loss of generality, we assume that each node is annotated with the conditions mentioned in the corresponding rule. Since $\sigma \models \overline{\mathcal{Q}_P}$, σ satisfies all constraints appearing in $\mathcal{T}_P^c$ and $\mathrm{locv}(P) \subseteq \mathrm{dom}(\sigma)$. To show $\vdash \sigma P$, we have to construct a derivation tree $\mathcal{T}_P$ for σP according to the typing rules in Fig. 10. Note that P uniquely determines the number of nodes and structure of $\mathcal{T}_P^c$ and of $\mathcal{T}_P$, if it exists. Consequently, there is a bijection between the nodes of the two derivation trees.

We inductively construct $\mathcal{T}_P$ starting with the leaf nodes using rules WF-NewFresh, WF-NewFreshP, WF-NewSame, WF-Var, WF-FieldGet, WF-FieldSet, WF-Call. The rule instances in $\mathcal{T}_P$ are constructed from the corresponding nodes in $\mathcal{T}_P^c$. We describe the construction here for the most interesting rules WF-NewFresh, WF-NewFreshP, and WF-Call; for the other rules, the construction works analogously.

Case WF-NewFresh, WF-NewFreshP: Let N be a leaf node of $\mathcal{T}_P^c$ annotated by $\overline{V} \vdash$ new c in fresh $: \delta, \delta <: \gamma, \gamma = $ Far. As σ is a solution, $\sigma(\delta) <: $ Far.

For the construction of $\mathcal{T}_P$, we use $\sigma(\overline{V}) \vdash$ new c in fresh $: \sigma(\delta)$ as a leaf node corresponding to N where $\sigma(\overline{V})$ denotes the substitution of the location type variables in $\overline{V}$ by σ. If $\sigma(\delta) = $ Far, this is an instance of WF-NewFresh; otherwise, it is an instance of WF-NewFreshP.

Case WF-Call Let N be a leaf node of $\mathcal{T}_P^c$ annotated by

$$\overline{V} \vdash y.m(\overline{z}) : \gamma, \beta \triangleright_{\mathsf{From}} \alpha = \gamma \cdot \overline{\mathcal{Q}_1} \cdot \ldots \cdot \overline{\mathcal{Q}_n}$$

For the construction of $\mathcal{T}_P$, we use $\sigma(\overline{V}) \vdash y.m(\overline{z}) : \mathrm{anno}(c, m, \mathrm{result}) \triangleright_{\mathsf{From}} \sigma(\alpha)$ as a leaf node corresponding to N. This is a correct instance of WF-Call, because the assumptions of the constraint generation rule yield:

- $\alpha\, c\, y \in \overline{V}$ and $\alpha_i\, \_\, z_i \in \overline{V}$; thus $\sigma(\alpha)\, c\, y \in \sigma(\overline{V})$ and $\sigma(\alpha_i)\, \_\, z_i \in \sigma(\overline{V})$.
- $\overline{x} = \mathrm{params}(c, m)$
- $\alpha_i \triangleright \alpha <: \mathrm{anno}(c, m, x_i)$ and, as σ is a solution, $\sigma(\alpha_i) \triangleright \sigma(\alpha) <: \mathrm{anno}(c, m, x_i)$

Note that for the result type L of the expression in $\mathcal{T}_P$ in a leave node we have $L = \sigma(\gamma)$ where γ is the corresponding location type variable in $\mathcal{T}_P^c$.

Induction Step. Similar to the leaf nodes, we construct the inner nodes of $\mathcal{T}_P$ by instantiating the appropriate typing rule. The only interesting case is the assignment:

Case WF-Assign: Let N be an inner node of $\mathcal{T}_P^c$ annotated by

$$\overline{V} \vdash x \leftarrow E : \beta <: \alpha \cdot \overline{\mathcal{Q}}$$

having a subtree annotated by $\overline{V} \vdash E : \beta, \overline{\mathcal{Q}}$. For the construction of $\mathcal{T}_P$, we use $\sigma(\overline{V}) \vdash x \leftarrow E$ as an inner node corresponding to N. This is a correct instance of WF-Assign, because:

- there is a subtree in $\mathcal{T}_P$ annotated by $\sigma(\overline{V}) \vdash E : \sigma(\beta)$
- $\alpha\, \_\, x \in \overline{V}$; thus $\sigma(\alpha)\, \_\, x \in \sigma(\overline{V})$.
- $\sigma(\beta) <: \sigma(\alpha)$

Completeness. We have to show: If $\vdash \sigma P$ with $\mathrm{dom}(\sigma) = \mathrm{locv}(P)$, then there is a solution σ' of $\overline{\mathcal{Q}}_p$ such that $\sigma'|_{\mathrm{dom}(\sigma)} = \sigma$.

Let $\mathcal{T}_p$ be the derivation tree for σP according to the typing rules in Fig. 10 and $\mathcal{T}_p^c$ the derivation tree for P according to the constraint generation rules in Fig. 15. As P uniquely determines the number of nodes and structure of $\mathcal{T}_p^c$ and of $\mathcal{T}_p^c$ there is a bijection between the nodes of the two derivation trees.

σ defines location types for all location type variables occurring in P at variable, parameter, field, and result type declarations. Solutions of $\overline{\mathcal{Q}}_p$ have to be also defined for the fresh variables introduced by the application of the constraint generation rules CG-M, CG-NEWFRESH, CG-FIELDSET, CG-FIELDGET, CG-CALL. Fresh variables are different in different rule applications, i.e., at different tree nodes of $\mathcal{T}_p^c$. We define a solution σ' with $\sigma'|_{\mathrm{dom}(\sigma)} = \sigma$ as follows on the fresh variables introduced by the rule applications in $\mathcal{T}_p^c$:

CG-M: $\sigma'(\delta) = \mathsf{Near}$

CG-NEWFRESH: $\sigma'(\gamma) = \mathsf{Far}$ and $\sigma'(\delta) = L$ where L is the type used in the corresponding rule application of WF-NEWFRESH or WF-NEWFRESHP in $\mathcal{T}_p$.

CG-FIELDSET: $\sigma'(\delta) = \sigma(\gamma) \triangleright_{\mathsf{To}} \sigma(\alpha)$

CG-FIELDGET: $\sigma'(\gamma) = \sigma(\mathrm{anno}(c, f)) \triangleright_{\mathsf{From}} \sigma(\alpha)$

CG-CALL: $\sigma'(\gamma) = \sigma(\mathrm{anno}(c, m, \mathrm{result})) \triangleright_{\mathsf{From}} \sigma(\alpha)$ and $\sigma'(\gamma_i) = \sigma(\alpha_i) \triangleright_{\mathsf{To}} \sigma(\alpha)$

Just as demonstrated in the soundness proof above, one can check rule by rule that the assumptions satisfied in the application of the typing rules imply that

- the assumptions in the application of the constraint generation rules are satisfied and
- σ' satisfies the constraints.

That is, we have found a solution for $\overline{\mathcal{Q}}_p$.

The Future of Aliasing in Parallel Programming

Robert L. Bocchino Jr.*

Carnegie Mellon University

In recent years, the research community has made great strides in alias annotations that support parallel programming [1]. Using these techniques, programmers no longer have to guess where aliased mutable state may cause unintended data races or nondeterminism; instead, such problems can simply be eliminated, either at compile time or at runtime. This represents a major advance in the safety and reliability of parallel code.

Unfortunately, however, there are significant barriers to the adoption of these techniques in practice. On the one hand, purely static techniques can be complex and can limit expressivity. On the other hand, dynamic techniques can impair performance, sometimes in ways that are difficult to predict. For these reasons there is still a lot of imperative parallel programming in languages like Java, C++, and C# with unrestricted side effects. I believe that to move the field forward, and to gain widespread adoption of techniques for safe parallelism, we need to do two things.

Immutable Data Structures. First, in writing parallel programs, we need to make better use of *immutable data structures* and related algorithms, as functional programmers have long advocated. The easiest solution to the problem of aliasing in parallel programs is to eliminate parallel mutation, where this is feasible.

Of course it isn't always feasible. One reason is that immutable data structures can be inefficient: they can introduce constant copying overhead (for example, in updating a single field of an object) and even asymptotic overhead (for example, in updating a single object in an array). Another reason is that the functional paradigm simply can't express some common algorithmic patterns, such as updating a shared dictionary or counter, in a straightforward way. So I think it is not realistic to eliminate mutation and aliasing entirely, and we will always need techniques like effect systems [2,3] and permissions [4,5].

However, where immutable data structures are appropriate, they provide significant benefits in program clarity and correctness. Emerging "multi-paradigm" languages such as Scala and F# provide a potential way forward, by offering robust support for both object-oriented and functional programming. Neither Scala nor F# has any particular support for managing aliasing or effects, but the techniques described in [1], as well as techniques for describing and enforcing immutable access to objects [6], can be easily integrated into these languages.

---

* Robert Bocchino is a Postdoctoral Associate at Carnegie Mellon University. He is supported by the National Science Foundation under grant #1019343 to the Computing Research Association for the CIFellows Project.

D. Clarke et al. (Eds.): Aliasing in Object-Oriented Programming, LNCS 7850, pp. 501–502, 2013.

Language Translation Tools. Second, we need *language translation tools* to help programmers take advantage of the new technologies. Such tools can help programmers describe aliasing patterns using techniques such as effects, permissions, and logical annotations [7]. The tools should let programmers declare what they think the high-level aliasing and interference patterns are or should be, and the compiler should carry out the tedious work of inserting the lower-level annotations and identifying problems.

Translation tools can also help migrate code from an imperative style based on in-place mutation to a functional style based on transformations of immutable objects. Lots of sequential code from before the multicore revolution must be parallelized, much of it making heavy use of aliasing and mutation. However, it should be possible to convert common imperative patterns to an immutable style in a straightforward way. Again, we need a compiler or analysis tool that lets the programmer identify and declare the patterns (which is the hard part requiring human insight and domain knowledge) and then carries out the transformations.

References

1. Bocchino Jr., R.L.: Alias Control for Deterministic Parallelism. In: Clarke, D., Noble, J., Wrigstad, T. (eds.) Aliasing in Object-Oriented Programming. LNCS, vol. 7850, pp. 156–195. Springer, Heidelberg (2013)
2. Bocchino Jr., R.L., Adve, V.S., Dig, D., Adve, S.V., Heumann, S., Komuravelli, R., Overbey, J., Simmons, P., Sung, H., Vakilian, M.: A type and effect system for deterministic parallel Java. In: ACM Conference on Object-Oriented Programming, Systems, Languages, and Applications, OOPSLA (2009)
3. Kawaguchi, M., Rondon, P., Bakst, A., Jhala, R.: Deterministic parallelism via liquid effects. In: ACM Conference on Programming Language Design and Implementation, PLDI (2012)
4. Stork, S., Marques, P., Aldrich, J.: Concurrency by default: Using permissions to express dataflow in stateful programs. In: Onward (2009)
5. Westbrook, E., Zhao, J., Budimlić, Z., Sarkar, V.: Practical Permissions for Race-Free Parallelism. In: Noble, J. (ed.) ECOOP 2012. LNCS, vol. 7313, pp. 614–639. Springer, Heidelberg (2012)
6. Potanin, A., Östlund, J., Zibin, Y., Ernst, M.D.: Immutability. In: Clarke, D., Noble, J., Wrigstad, T. (eds.) Aliasing in Object-Oriented Programming. LNCS, vol. 7850, pp. 233–269. Springer, Heidelberg (2013)
7. Vakilian, M., Dig, D., Bocchino, R., Overbey, J., Adve, V., Johnson, R.: Inferring method effect summaries for nested heap regions. In: International Conference on Automated Software Engineering, ASE (2009)

Aliasing Visions: Ownership and Location

Alan Mycroft

Computer Laboratory, University of Cambridge
William Gates Building, JJ Thomson Avenue,
Cambridge CB3 0FD, UK
Firstname.Lastname@cl.cam.ac.uk

Historically, concerns about aliasing and confinement in object-oriented languages arose from the *Software Engineering* or *Program Verification* viewpoint: spaghetti-data resulted in programs too delicate to modify or "... we could prove Q if only we knew that x is not aliased". By and large, these issues arose in the context of sequential systems. Nowadays, exploiting multi-core architectures generally requires concurrent programming. The issues above become magnified: in software engineering terms updates to aliased objects can now lead to unpredictable data races rather than resulting in hard-to-modify but deterministic code. Program reasoning also became harder as there are more ways to break encapsulation. For example 'x+=2;' and 'x+=1;x+=1;' are no longer equivalent.

Moreover, modern multi-core systems have *distributed memory*: each object has a physical *location* and can move between physical locations. Some cache structures preserve the single-global-memory illusion by preserving both the object's identity and its memory address as it moves from one cache to another, but objects *do* move. In other architectures memory is non-uniform (NUMA) and accessing an object may not be possible from all processing cores. More insidious problems arise both in reasoning due to *memory-model* effects (failure of sequential consistency means that executions can occur which are not an interleaving of those of the individual cores), and also in efficiency since writes by one processor in general flushes the corresponding cache line of all other processors—at significant execution cost if data is repeatedly written to by different cores.

I identify this third motivation as the *Distributed Storage* problem and the big challenge as designing languages which encourage programmers to write programs sympathetic to such distributed architectures. Mycroft [1] argues that such architectural problems can be avoided using *memory isolation* (at any given moment at most one core may be attempting to access an object); enforcing this statically requires some form of ownership.

Wrigstad and Clarke [2] note various challenges in practical use of Ownership Types [3], for example difficulties in refactoring programs. Artem Glebov [personal communication] notes that one of the problems in encouraging use of Ownership Types is that they are effectively optional: programmers could merely annotate everything as '*world*', especially when Ownership Types add a significant additional maintenance cost.

The *Distributed Storage* problem then links these two issues: for effective multi-core and many-core programming we need a language which enforces

D. Clarke et al. (Eds.): Aliasing in Object-Oriented Programming, LNCS 7850, pp. 503–504, 2013.

memory isolation (whether statically by Ownership Types or dynamically by locks) and which makes ownership transfer visible in the source as an execution cost. Such a language would then require programmers to use ownership in design and coding (the hardware already does this, but the penalties are obscure bugs and bad performance). Ownership is then longer optional—a program which annotated all objects as located in a single memory would then execute on a single core thus encouraging programmers to use stronger ownership.

The challenge then is to design a language which enforces memory isolation but renders program refactoring convenient for designers and maintainers—and optimisation convenient for compilers.

References

1. Mycroft, A.: Isolation Types and Multi-core Architectures. In: Beckert, B., Damiani, F., Gurov, D. (eds.) FoVeOOS 2011. LNCS, vol. 7421, pp. 33–48. Springer, Heidelberg (2012)
2. Wrigstad, T., Clarke, D.: Is the world ready for ownership types? Are ownership types ready for the world? In: IWACO 2011: International Workshop on Aliasing, Confinement and Ownership in Object-oriented Programming (2011)
3. Clarke, D., Östlund, J., Sergey, I., Wrigstad, T.: Ownership Types: A Survey. In: Clarke, D., Noble, J., Wrigstad, T. (eds.) Aliasing in Object-Oriented Programming. LNCS, vol. 7850, pp. 15–58. Springer, Heidelberg (2013)

Alias Analysis: Beyond the Code

Manu Sridharan

IBM T.J. Watson Research Center
msridhar@us.ibm.com

Though impressive advances have been made in the precision and scalabilty of alias analyses over the last 20 years, their applicability to real-world object-oriented programs has actually *decreased*. The growth in size of standard libraries and application frameworks has far exceeded scalability improvements in alias analysis—even analyzing a "Hello world" program in Java has become non-trivial due to enormous standard libraries. Precision gains from greater flow and context sensitivity have been countered by greater usage of reflective constructs in programs, leading analyses to either unsoundly ignore reflection or compute very coarse results. Similar complications are emerging for large JavaScript applications, and the lack of static types in such programs can make computing even a basic call graph difficult [7]. Given these trends, it seems unlikely that further incremental improvements to traditional alias analysis algorithms will be sufficient to address the challenges of analyzing current and future real-world codes.

The most exciting future advances in alias analysis will instead come from going beyond pure static code analysis to leverage other sources of useful information about aliasing. Such sources could include:

Configuration Files. For framework-based applications, key behaviors are often specified in configuration files separate from the code, and analyzing such non-code artifacts directly could yield more useful results than analyzing the reflective code that interprets the files. While there has been some initial work on this approach [5], increased automation could significantly broaden its applicability.

Dynamic Information. Aliasing patterns observed in dynamic program executions could be used to guide and improve static alias analysis. For example, the YOGI system [1] has made impressive progress analyzing device drivers by combining dynamic symbolic execution with static analysis that only considers the aliasing observed in actual runs. Extending such techniques to large object-oriented programs will require further advances.

The User. Effectively soliciting and integrating feedback from users regarding possible aliasing could dramatically improve analysis effectiveness. Recent work has shown success in posing simple questions to users to help triage error reports from a verifier [2], and perhaps a similar approach could be used to help resolve tricky aliasing. Techniques from refinement-based or staged analyses [4,6,3] may be useful for incorporating user feedback.

It remains unclear whether automatic alias analysis will ever scale to large object-oriented programs while maintaining sufficient precision for clients. Nevertheless,

D. Clarke et al. (Eds.): Aliasing in Object-Oriented Programming, LNCS 7850, pp. 505–506, 2013.
© Springer-Verlag Berlin Heidelberg 2013

novel techniques in alias analysis, particularly techniques that step outside traditional analysis boundaries, remain worth pursuing. Nearly all code continues to be written in languages with little to no restriction of aliasing, so alias analysis improvements will have a potentially large impact for the foreseeable future.

References

1. Beckman, N.E., Nori, A.V., Rajamani, S.K., Simmons, R.J., Tetali, S.D., Thakur, A.V.: Proofs from tests. In: IEEE Transactions on Software Engineering (2010)
2. Dillig, I., Dillig, T., Aiken, A.: Automated error diagnosis using abductive inference. In: Proceedings of the 33rd ACM SIGPLAN Conference on Programming Language Design and Implementation, PLDI 2012, pp. 181–192. ACM, New York (2012)
3. Fink, S.J., Yahav, E., Dor, N., Ramalingam, G., Geay, E.: Effective typestate verification in the presence of aliasing. ACM Transactions on Software Engineering and Methodology 17(2), 1–34 (2008)
4. Guyer, S.Z., Lin, C.: Client-Driven Pointer Analysis. In: Cousot, R. (ed.) SAS 2003. LNCS, vol. 2694, pp. 214–236. Springer, Heidelberg (2003)
5. Sridharan, M., Artzi, S., Pistoia, M., Guarnieri, S., Tripp, O., Berg, R.: F4F: Taint analysis of framework-based web applications. In: Proceedings of the 2011 ACM International Conference on Object Oriented Programming Systems Languages and Applications, OOPSLA 2011, pp. 1053–1068. ACM, New York (2011)
6. Sridharan, M., Bodík, R.: Refinement-based context-sensitive points-to analysis for Java. In: Conference on Programming Language Design and Implementation, PLDI (2006)
7. Sridharan, M., Dolby, J., Chandra, S., Schäfer, M., Tip, F.: Correlation Tracking for Points-To Analysis of JavaScript. In: Noble, J. (ed.) ECOOP 2012. LNCS, vol. 7313, pp. 435–458. Springer, Heidelberg (2012)

How, Then, Should We Program?

James Noble

School of Engineering and Computer Science,
Victoria University of Wellington,
New Zealand
kjx@ecs.vuw.ac.nz

*19. A language that doesn't affect the way you think about programming,
is not worth knowing.*

Epigrams on Programming, Alan Perlis

Since the first papers on "Aliasing in Object-Oriented Programming" appeared, since the Geneva Convention on Aliasing, since the developments in Ownership Types, in Separation Logic, and all the other developments related in this volume, two competing dynamics can be seen underlying the research in this area. These dynamics are not unique to aliasing: indeed given sufficiently broad definitions, most computer science or software engineering research can be ascribed to one of these approaches, or perhaps lying somewhere between the two.

The first dynamic is the *prescriptive* approach: imposing restrictions or disciplines upon programs that are thought to contribute to "good" design. An Island is an exemplar of the prescriptive approach *par excellence:* an Island both dominates and co-dominates its contents, encapsulating and co-encapsulating, forbidding any references crossing its boundary either inwards or outwards [1,2]. Flexible Alias Protection was explicitly designed as and described to be more "flexible" than Islands [3]; and a long series of subsequent work has weakened, strengthened, or modified various restrictions, but the general principle remains: we should place limitations on our programming languages in order to improve the programs that may be written therein.

The second dynamic is the *descriptive* approach: seeking to understand, to describe how programs are written or actually work in practice. Clearly understanding the "Natural Science of Programs" — the static structures and dynamic topologies of real programs in real programming languages is important for a range of reasons: to support optimisations; to underpin static or dynamic analyses; to support development environments and refactoring tools. Object-orientation in particular raises the issue of the aliasing topology of objects in the heap. Although the first "large-scale" study was in Lisp [4], topologies of mutable heap objects are critical to the semantics of object-oriented programs and much recent work has focused there [5].

How can these two dynamics be reconciled? The simple answer is: first conduct descriptive studies to determine what programs actually do, and then implement prescriptive language constructs to match those descriptions. The problem with this answer is that it admits no progress: all advances — structured programming, garbage collection, higher-level languages, objects, functional programming, aspects, — are predicated by introducing new language features and removing old ones: Scheme is a testament to

D. Clarke et al. (Eds.): Aliasing in Object-Oriented Programming, LNCS 7850, pp. 507–508, 2013.
ⓒ Springer-Verlag Berlin Heidelberg 2013

Syme's "beautiful thing, the destruction of words" [6]. This is the dialectic captured by Hume's *is-ought* problem: *descriptions* of a current state, of current programming practice are not necessarily *prescriptions* the way we should do things in the future.

In the final analysis: the question with which we are faced can only be answered by a choice: *how, then, should we program?* Underlying Islands, Alias Protection, and Ownership Types is the simple proposition that objects should encapsulate their representations behind their interfaces, that their state should be changed only via those interfaces, and that this encapsulation should be supported, statically and dynamically, by programming languages. Written down plainly, this proposition does not seem radical — but in spite of its simplicity, we still have some way to go to reach that goal.

> *The reasonable man adapts himself to the world;*
> *the unreasonable one persists in trying to adapt the world to himself.*
> *Therefore all progress depends on the unreasonable man.*

George Bernard Shaw, Man and Superman (1903)
"Maxims for Revolutionists"

References

1. Hogg, J.: Islands: Aliasing protection in object-oriented languages. In: OOPSLA Proceedings (November 1991)
2. Clarke, D., Drossopoulou, S., Noble, J.: The roles of owners. In: International Workshop on Aliasing, Confinement and Ownership (IWACO) (2011)
3. Noble, J., Vitek, J., Potter, J.: Flexible Alias Protection. In: Jul, E. (ed.) ECOOP 1998. LNCS, vol. 1445, pp. 158–185. Springer, Heidelberg (1998)
4. Clark, D.W., Green, C.C.: An empirical study of list structures in Lisp. Commun. ACM 20(2), 78–87 (1977)
5. Potanin, A., Noble, J., Frean, M.R., Biddle, R.: Scale-free geometry in Object-Oriented programs. Commun. ACM 48(5), 99–103 (2005)
6. Orwell, G.: 1984. Secker and Warburg (1949)

A Retrospective on Aliasing Type Systems: 2012-2022

Jonathan Aldrich

School of Computer Science, Carnegie Mellon University
jonathan.aldrich@cs.cmu.edu

Introduction. Over the last ten years, type systems for reasoning about aliasing have begun to be adopted into mainstream languages and tools. The most obvious benefits came in the area of concurrency, expanding on pioneering work that applied ownership [8], regions [6], and permissions [9,4] to ensure the safety of concurrent programs. However, concurrency alone was insufficient to drive adoption. Aliasing type systems really caught on when researchers found common abstractions that were also useful for other purposes: providing encapsulation [17], enhancing security [7,2], and assisting verification [16,10]–though verification remains a niche application due to the engineering time required to specify and verify code.

Beyond compelling applications, what made the widespread adoption of aliasing type systems possible? The purpose of this short article is to examine the principal research advances and factors that enabled adoption. With the benefit of hindsight, it appears that the key factors included flexibility, simple and natural abstractions, and deep language integration.

Flexibility: Description, Not Restriction. Early type systems [14] focused on enforcing restrictions that were thought to embody good design techniques or were useful for purposes such as verification. But researchers soon identified the need for flexibility [17,3], and found that less restrictive type systems were still useful for reasoning [16,10]. Once the community realized that the proper role of alias type systems is not to *restrict* aliasing but rather to *describe* intended aliasing patterns, it became possible to apply alias type systems at semi-industrial scales [13,1,12].

Simple, Natural Abstractions. While alias type systems provide many benefits, they also compete with many other language and type system features for developers' attention. Anecdotally, the author found that some of the more esoteric features of the type systems his team developed were not well-understood by students. Successful deployment of aliasing type systems required trimming features that, while useful, did not pay for their conceptual complexity. The result was the small, tightly-integrated set of aliasing abstractions we see in industrial languages today.

A related factor was identifying abstractions that were natural to programmers. While early systems were designed mostly based on the intuitions of the type system developers, approaches such as Fluid [12] gathered considerable industrial experience and were able to iteratively refine their abstractions to the

D. Clarke et al. (Eds.): Aliasing in Object-Oriented Programming, LNCS 7850, pp. 509–511, 2013.

point at which some users said the type annotations were worth using independently of the tool[1]. Later researchers applied more rigorous methodologies, improving the usability of their systems through user studies.

Deep Language Integration. While the earliest alias type system proposals were framed as native language type systems, later approaches used the annotation facilities of existing languages to express alias information. This facilitated useful experimentation, including some large scale case studies [1,5,15]. However, the resulting systems were somewhat syntactically clunky, and were limited to purely static checks. Deeper language integration not only resulted in cleaner and more appealing systems, but enabled flexible tradeoffs between static and dynamic checking. Early work in this area investigated dynamic checking of ownership constraints [11], while others looked at combining static and dynamic checks in a gradual permission system [18]. In retrospect the trend is unsurprising: essentially all industrially relevant type systems have always included some form of cast or other dynamic check to supplement static checking.

Conclusion. After two decades of exploratory research and a decade of technology transition, alias type systems have finally hit the mainstream. Factors in their success included both compelling applications in concurrency, design, and security, as well as advances in developing natural, flexible aliasing abstractions that were deeply integrated into recent programming languages and runtime systems.

Author's Note. I regret the vision described above was not clear enough to provide citations beyond the date of this writing, in 2012. However, I am certain that members of the research community will crystalize, through their work, what I hope is a bright future for reasoning about aliasing in programming languages.

References

1. Abi-Antoun, M., Aldrich, J.: Ownership Domains in the Real World. In: International Workshop on Aliasing, Confinement, and Ownership (2007)
2. Abi-Antoun, M., Barnes, J.M.: Analyzing Security Architectures. In: Automated Software Engineering (2010)
3. Aldrich, J., Chambers, C.: Ownership Domains: Separating Aliasing Policy from Mechanism. In: Odersky, M. (ed.) ECOOP 2004. LNCS, vol. 3086, pp. 1–25. Springer, Heidelberg (2004)
4. Beckman, N.E., Bierhoff, K., Aldrich, J.: Verifying Correct Usage of Atomic Blocks and Typestate. In: Object-Oriented Programming, Systems, Languages, and Applications (2008)
5. Bierhoff, K., Beckman, N.E., Aldrich, J.: Practical API Protocol Checking with Access Permissions. In: Drossopoulou, S. (ed.) ECOOP 2009. LNCS, vol. 5653, pp. 195–219. Springer, Heidelberg (2009)

---

[1] Personal communication with William Scherlis.

6. Bocchino Jr., R.L., Adve, V.S., Dig, D., Adve, S.V., Heumann, S., Komuravelli, R., Overbey, J., Simmons, P., Sung, H., Vakilian, M.: A Type and Effect System for Deterministic Parallel Java. In: Object-Oriented Programming, Systems, Languages, and Applications (2009)
7. Bokowski, B., Vitek, J.: Confined Types. In: Object-Oriented Programming, Systems, Languages, and Applications (1999)
8. Boyapati, C., Lee, R., Rinard, M.: Ownership Types for Safe Programming: Preventing Data Races and Deadlocks. In: Object-Oriented Programming, Systems, Languages, and Applications (2002)
9. Boyland, J.: Checking Interference with Fractional Permissions. In: Cousot, R. (ed.) SAS 2003. LNCS, vol. 2694, pp. 55–72. Springer, Heidelberg (2003)
10. Dietl, W., Müller, P.: Object Ownership in Program Verification. In: Clarke, D., Noble, J., Wrigstad, T. (eds.) Aliasing in Object-Oriented Programming. LNCS, vol. 7850, pp. 289–318. Springer, Heidelberg (2013)
11. Gordon, D., Noble, J.: Dynamic Ownership in a Dynamic Language. In: Dynamic Languages Symposium (2007)
12. Greenhouse, A., Halloran, T.J., Scherlis, W.L.: Observations on the Assured Evolution of Concurrent Java Programs. Science of Computer Programming 58(3), 384–411 (2005)
13. Hächler, T.: Applying the Universe Type System to an Industrial Application: Case Study. Master's thesis, Department of Computer Science, Federal Institute of Technology Zurich (2005)
14. Islands, J.H.: Aliasing Protection in Object-Oriented Languages. In: Object-Oriented Programming, Systems, Languages, and Applications (October 1991)
15. Huang, W., Milanova, A., Dietl, W., Ernst, M.D.: ReIm & ReImInfer: Checking and Inference of Reference Immutability and Method Purity. In: Object-Oriented Programming Systems, Languages, and Applications (2012)
16. Müller, P.: Modular Specification and Verification of Object-Oriented Programs. LNCS, vol. 2262. Springer, Heidelberg (2002)
17. Noble, J., Vitek, J., Potter, J.: Flexible Alias Protection. In: Jul, E. (ed.) ECOOP 1998. LNCS, vol. 1445, pp. 158–185. Springer, Heidelberg (1998)
18. Wolff, R., Garcia, R., Tanter, É., Aldrich, J.: Gradual Typestate. In: Mezini, M. (ed.) ECOOP 2011. LNCS, vol. 6813, pp. 459–483. Springer, Heidelberg (2011)

Structured Aliasing

Tobias Wrigstad

Uppsala University

Abstract. This volume describes a great number of techniques for confining, defining, analysing, etc. aliases in object-oriented programming, each with their own strengths and weaknesses. The missing chapter is the underlying theory that is able to explain them all. In this vision statement, we state the need for a theory of structured aliasing, and claim that the problem with aliasing lies not in the aliases themselves, but the low-level language constructs used to create them.

Aliasing, mutable state and stable object identities are inherent in object-oriented programming. It is a well-known fact that this combination of features causes problems for programmers, tool developers and formalists alike.

Creating and managing aliases and the resulting object structures are among the most common operations in object-oriented programming. However, even though object structures have exploded in size and complexity since the dawn of object-oriented programming in the 60's, the cutting-edge languages of today provide only the same crude, low-level support for managing them, such as reading and writing references into variables or object fields.

References are a low-level construct on which higher-level semantics is grafted. Not only are they used to allow messages to be sent to a certain object, to build graphs and enable simple dynamic structures that grow and shrink over time. References are also used as identities, as relations, and as capabilities. To understand the role of a reference in a piece of source code, one must inspect all of its uses.

Many patterns for the treatment of object references exist, with well-known properties, such as thread-local references, read-only references, borrowing, uniqueness, scope-limited references, etc. With few exceptions however, languages of today offer no help for a programmer to capture her intentions as to how a reference should be used, enforce them, or keep them invariant over change. After 50 years of aliased objects—all bookkeeping, the preservation of structural invariants, deletion of temporary aliases, etc. is still left to the programmer.

There is a need for a theory and practise of "structured aliasing" that establishes a new foundation for creating and maintaining object structures. What are the recurring patterns, what are their properties, and how do they combine? What are the prevalent object structures, and how do they change? What are the common violations of these structures—and for what purpose? Developing a theory of structured aliasing will require continued careful study of existing patterns of aliasing, static as well as dynamic, and a keen eye on the problems caused

D. Clarke et al. (Eds.): Aliasing in Object-Oriented Programming, LNCS 7850, pp. 512–513, 2013.

by aliasing—for optimisation, verification, etc.—so that they can be avoided or made clearly visible.

The problem with aliasing lies not in the aliasing (nor in mutability) per se, but in the low-level operations that we use to construct and maintain object graphs. A possible way forward is a step in the direction of declarative programs, but the underlying logic is missing for everything but the simplest data structures. Temporarily breaking structure—*e.g.*, making a binary tree a graph briefly during a delete operation—must be supported, but this be an exception (rather than the rule) which necessitates control to limit its effects. The existence of a reference, a low-level pointer into the internals of a data structure, might be considered such an exception. As such, it must be scope-wise constrained and sufficiently protected in its interaction with the structure, especially with respect to concurrent or re-entrant operations.

We need to rethink one of the most basic and ubiquitous constructs of object-oriented programming—the object reference—and how it is being used. The alias management principles and patterns described in this volume are highly relevant for this work, but the most promising way forward, we argue, is not to invent ways of analysing, controlling or restricting reference uses, but to question their given existence, and re-imagine the way objects are strung together and communicate. The replacing language constructs should not only simplify reasoning, but *prescribe and guide* object structuring and communication based on a set of well-understood principles derived from existing programs.

While safety and reasoning power have been the main drivers for much of the work on alias management, it may be the need for speed that finally pushes it into the mainstream. In the inherently parallel world of tomorrow, being able to reason about aliasing for performance or even power efficiency is crucial, if object-oriented programming is to stay relevant.

Author Index